ENCYCLOPEDIA OF NATIVE AMERICAN WARS AND WARFARE

ENCYCLOPEDIA OF NATIVE AMERICAN WARS AND WARFARE

General Editors

WILLIAM B. KESSEL, PH.D.

ROBERT WOOSTER, PH.D.

Checkmark Books®

An imprint of Facts On File, Inc.

Advisers and Consultants

Encyclopedia of Native American Wars and Warfare

Written and developed by BOOK BUILDERS LLC

Copyright © 2005 by Book Builders Incorporated
Maps copyright © 2005 Facts On File, Inc.

Checkmark Books
An imprint of Facts On File, Inc.
132 West 31st Street
New York NY 10001

Library of Congress Cataloging-in-Publication Data

Encyclopedia of Native American wars and warfare / general editors, William B.
Kessel, Robert Wooster.
p. cm.
Includes bibliographical references and index.
ISBN 0-8160-3337-4 (hc.)—ISBN 0-8160-6430-X (pbk.)
1. Indians of North America—Wars—Encyclopedias. 2. Indians of North
America—Warfare—Encyclopedias. I. Kessel, William B. II. Wooster, Robert,
1956 –
E81 .E98 2005
973—dc21   00-056200

Checkmark Books are available at special discounts when purchased in bulk quantities for businesses, associations, institutions, or sales promotions.
Please call our Special Sales Department in New York at
212/967-8800 or 800/322-8755.

You can find Facts On File on the World Wide Web at
http://www.factsonfile.com

Text design by Erika K. Arroyo
Cover design by Cathy Rincon
Maps by Jeremy Eagle, Patricia Meschino, and Dale Williams

Printed in the United States of America

VB Hermitage 10   9   8   7   6   5   4   3   2   1

This book is printed on acid-free paper.

Contents

A to Z Entries
15

List of Entries

Preface

Native American wars and warfare have been part of life in North America for thousands of years. *Encyclopedia of Native American Wars and Warfare,* however, concentrates on the conflicts that arose after Christopher Columbus set foot in the New World in 1492. From then until the late 1800s, the number of armed conflicts among Native American groups and between Indians and their non-Indian opponents reached significant proportions. Many of the names of wars and battles fought during those years, as well as the names of combatants, have become household words. The encyclopedia constitutes an attempt to sort through the plethora of historical data and identify the key people, places, and events of that period, as well as more recent times. The book itself is arranged in encyclopedia form, with more than 600 entries arranged from A to Z. The entries themselves cover a variety of topics, including wars, battles, treaties, tribes, individuals, places, ceremonies, weaponry and other paraphernalia, and concepts. It is, of course, impossible to include lengthy discussions of each topic in a one-volume encyclopedia. Therefore, the articles vary in length depending on the importance of the subject and the data available. In all cases, care has been taken to ensure that relevant, pertinent, and factual information has been included. Additionally, the volume's photographs, illustrations, and maps provide for a richer understanding of the people and places discussed.

There are several ways of using *Encyclopedia of Native American Wars and Warfare.* The most obvious procedure is simply to turn to the entry of interest. Thus, the reader interested in learning more about the battle of Little Bighorn will find an article entitled LITTLE BIGHORN. The encyclopedia, however, also can be used for more in-depth research by utilizing the extensive network of cross-references that is included. Cross-references are indicated by small capital letters. For example, perhaps the reader is interested in reading about Apache Indian raiding and warfare. The most obvious place to begin would be the entry entitled APACHE WARS, which contains an overview of the subject beginning with the raids of the early 1800s and ending with the surrender of Geronimo in 1886. Within this entry, the reader also will find many names, terms, and battles identified in small upper-case letters (for example, COCHISE). Each of these are cross-references that refer to another entry in the encyclopedia. Thus, the reader is directed to entries about the APACHE, including key Apache leaders such as GERONIMO, COCHISE, MANGAS COLORADAS, JUH, and VICTORIO, as well as white leaders who played a prominent role in the Apache Wars, such as Generals GEORGE CROOK and NELSON A. MILES. Other cross-references in the entry on Apache Wars will direct readers to specific battles, such as those at APACHE PASS, CAMP GRANT, SKELETON

CAVE, CIBECUE CREEK, and BIG DRY WASH. Each of these entries, in turn, also contains its own cross-references. By utilizing the network of entries and interlocking cross-references, a fuller picture of the subject matter unfolds before the reader.

Encyclopedia of Native American Wars and Warfare is meant to be a basic reference, a starting point for research and for topics often not covered in other basic reference works. To expand its usefulness, many of the entries also refer the reader to additional sources of information. The book also includes a bibliography that cites many standard works in the field that are not only authoritative but also accessible to the serious student.

Finally, an important challenge in preparing this encyclopedia was to ensure that it presents accurate historical material in an unbiased fashion. The coeditors were selected for this task because of their complementary backgrounds. While Dr. Robert Wooster is an expert on U.S. military history of the Indian wars, Dr. William Kessel is a cultural anthropologist and ethnohistorian who has conducted extensive fieldwork among various Native American peoples. Together they helped select the entries to be included in the encyclopedia. By scrutinizing each article they have attempted to ensure that each one reflects all perspectives in an unbiased manner. While Drs. Kessel and Wooster have authored many of the articles, they would like to thank the many researchers and writers for their contributions. While contributions of all writers have been significant, the following authored the longer articles: Philip Weeks, Grace Many Gouveia, and Roy Parker. Additionally, an advisory board, consisting of David Hallas, Darlis A. Miller, Lotsee Patterson, Philip Weeks, and Ernestine Berry, has provided guidance for the project and has reviewed most entries. Finally, the yeoman task of managing the entire project has been admirably accomplished by Lauren Fedorko and Elizabeth Dooher of Book Builders Incorporated, with the help of their project editor, Charles Roebuck.

General Editors' Note on Indian Tribal Names

The use of Indian tribal names in this encyclopedia reflects the usage most commonly found in the historical literature rather than the names that tribes used/use for themselves or that may be currently preferred. Thus, for example, the reader will find reference to the Crow Indians rather than the Absaroke or to the Navajo rather than the Diné or Dineh. The historical names, in most instances, are names that were given to the tribes by Europeans or by their Native American enemies and then adopted by Europeans. Where possible, the most common alternate name is given in parentheses at first mention in an entry.

— William B. Kessel
Bethany Lutheran College

— Robert Wooster
Texas A & M University–Corpus Christi

Traditional Tribal Locations

Arctic Ocean

INUIT   KOYUKON
ATHABASCAN   TANANA   INUIT
INGALIK
TANAINA   HARE
                    KUTCHIN
HAN
AHTENA
ALEUT   TUTCHONE   YELLOWKNIFE
          MOUNTAIN
                    DOGRIB
TLINGIT   NAHANE
          (KASKA,
          TAGISH, TAHLTAN)
                    SLAVE   INUIT
                                   Hudson
HAIDA   SEKANI   CHIPEWYAN   Bay
          TSIMSHIAN   BEAVER
BELLA BELLA   CARRIER   NASKAPI
     BELLA COOLA   SARCEE   CREE
NOOTKA   KWAKIUTL   SHUSWAP   MONTAGNAIS
COWICHAN   LILLOOET   BEOTHUK
          STALO
     CLALLAM   SONGISH
PUYALLUP   COLUMBIA   BLACKFOOT   OJIBWAY   ALGONKIN   MICMAC
          SPOKANE   ASSINIBOINE   MÉTIS   NIPISSING   MALECITE
          PEND D'OREILLE   ANISHINABE   PASSAMAQUODDY
     YAKIMA   FLATHEAD   GROS VENTRE   (CHIPPEWA)   OTTAWA   PENOBSCOT
          COEUR D'ALENE   BLOOD   MENOMINEE   HURON   ABENAKI
CHINOOK   PUYALLUP   NEZ PERCE   CROW   HIDATSA   MASSACHUSET
TILLAMOOK CAYUSE   MANDAN   WINNEBAGO   NEUTRAL   IROQUOIS MAHICAN WAMPANOAG
     KLAMATH   FOX   POTAWATOMI   NARRAGANSETT
YUROK   MODOC BANNOCK   ARIKARA   SIOUX (DAKOTA,   SAUK   LENNI SEPPINGER MONTAUK
     POMO   WINTUN   SHOSHONE   LAKOTA, NAKOTA)   MANHATTAN
          MAIDU   NORTHERN   CHEYENNE   PONCA   OMAHA   SUSQUEHANNOCK
     MIWOK   PAIUTE   KICKAPOO
               (NUMU)   ARAPAHO   IOWA   MIAMI   POWHATAN
CASTANO   UTE   PAWNEE   MISSOURI   ILLINOIS   NAHYSSAN
     YOKUT   WASHOE   OTO   SHAWNEE   MEHERRIN   SANTEE
          PAIUTE   KANSA   YUCHI   CHEROKEE   SEWEE
CHUMASH   HAVASUPAI   CUITOA   OSAGE   LUMBEE   CUSABO
LUISEÑO   CAHUILLA   QUAPAW   CHICKASAW   CATAWBA
          HUALAPAI   HOPI   NAPOCHI   CREEK   GUALE
     MOJAVE   TIWA   ALABAMA   HITCHITI   TACATACURA
HALCHIDHOMA NAVAJO   TEWA   WICHITA   TIOU   CHOCTAW TUNICA SATONWA
     YAVAPAI   ZUNI KERES   KADOHADACHO   TAHOME   FRESHWATER
YUMA   PIRO   KIOWA   CADDO   NATCHEZ   MOBILE   AIS
KOHUANA   MARICOPA   COMANCHE   HASANAI ATAKAPA   ACOLAPISSA   GUACATA
          COCAPA   APACHE   TIMUCUA   JEAGA
     TOHONO O'ODHAM   SEMINOLE
          PIMA   CALUSA
     SERI   KARANKAWA   Gulf of   Atlantic Ocean
                    JUMANO   Mexico
                    YAQUI
                         COAHUILTEC
Pacific Ocean
                                                            ARAWAK
                    TOTONAC
                    TARASCAN   MAYA   CARIB
                    AZTEC
                                                  Caribbean Sea

N
                                             CUNA

Introduction

In the spring of 1607, three small ships carrying just over 100 English colonists arrived off the Virginia coast. Sailing 40 miles up the James River to escape the notice of their Spanish rivals, the English discovered a deep anchorage near a defensible site at what they later called Jamestown. Even before the main party of colonists landed, two of their advance scouts were wounded by the area's indigenous peoples. But the warning failed to deter the English, who constructed a small fort after debarking. The English colonists faced the future confidently. Armed with muskets and steel, buoyed by their nation's recent triumphs over Spain, and secure in their belief of their cultural superiority, they assumed that a bright future lay ahead.

The English had landed in the territory of the POWHATAN CONFEDERACY, which included about 30 Algonquian-speaking tribes. The confederacy's leader, POWHATAN, was completing his conquest of a major rival, the Chesapeake Indians. To the members of the confederacy it probably seemed certain that Powhatan's 3,000 warriors could crush the new arrivals should they prove troublesome. Meanwhile, they thought that perhaps the Europeans might be useful allies against Powhatan's remaining Indian enemies. To hedge his bets, Powhatan pursued a two-pronged approach. On the one hand, Powhatan had one of his sons befriend and begin trading with English exploring parties. At the same time, however, he had 200 of his warriors raid Jamestown, killing two colonists and wounding a dozen others. Stung by the assault, the Jamestown colonists bombarded several Indian villages with their shipborne cannon.

Little did the English know that both the welcoming party and their attackers had come from the same Indian group. A series of uneasy truces, broken intermittently by acute conflicts, marked the next three decades. Finally, nearly exhausted by the outbreak of full-scale conflict in the 1640s, the English colonists captured and executed the new Powhatan leader, Powhatan's brother OPECHANCANOUGH, who had taken over when Powhatan died in 1618. This forever broke the power of the Powhatan Confederacy.

The Powhatan-English relationship illustrates the complexities of Native American warfare. Both sides took steps to advance their own interests. The English initially needed Powhatan and his people to help them produce enough food to survive; the Indians hoped to use the English to help them defeat their own Indian enemies and secure lucrative trade goods. But when an alliance no longer seemed in their best interest, both sides considered the use of violence a legitimate means of achieving their goals. Likewise, convinced of their own moral and cultural superiority, both the Powhatan Confederacy and English colonists took the war to the homes and villages of their enemies, killing or impoverishing women and children on both sides. Raids by one group sparked devastating reprisals from the other. Finally, these conflicts left the Indians destitute, overrun by the growing power of the colonists. Similar confrontations and results would mark the history of Indian and non-Indian relations for the next 300 years.

Objective analysis of these tragic conflicts is extremely difficult. In a few cases, available information is so consistent as to make judgments obvious. For example, it is quite clear that, in late 1864, several hundred army volunteers massacred about 200 inhabitants of a Cheyenne-Arapaho village at Sand Creek in the Colorado Territory during an unprovoked attack against the peaceful village. More often, however, contradictory evidence blurs the interpretation of events.

The battle at CIBECUE CREEK illustrates this point. In 1880, a growing number of APACHE started following the teachings of a prominent medicine man. As the movement grew, non-Indians became more and more concerned until they sent soldiers to arrest the prophet. While the medicine man was arrested without incident, a battle later broke out. Non-Indian sources lay the blame on militant Apache. Apache eyewitnesses, however, claim that the arresting officer broke several rules of etiquette and this precipitated the matter.

Encyclopedia of Native American Wars and Warfare seeks to present a balanced view of such conflicts. By surveying, explaining, and assessing the significance of armed conflicts between Indians and non-Indians, the work provides basic information that will enable readers to better understand and draw their own conclusions about the events. The encyclopedia emphasizes the conflicts between non-Indian inhabitants and the Indians of North America (excluding Mexico and much of Canada) rather than the conflicts between or among Indian tribes. In so doing, this volume seeks to be reasonably inclusive; thus, the wars covered are not only those involving the United States but also those with the Spanish, Dutch, Russians, British, Canadians, and French. Finally, the entries also recognize the important role played by women, blacks, Latinos, and people of mixed race in these long struggles.

Native American wars and warfare have played an important role in shaping the lives of all Americans for the past five centuries. For the frontier peoples of earlier generations, the effects are quite obvious. But those far from the immediate action also were influenced by events such as the ebb and flow of changing land claims, which were prime factors in many conflicts. Land gained from the Indians for settlement or exploita-

tion made available new resources, serving as what some American historians have called a "safety valve" for the victors. As land was taken from the losers, however, resources diminished and internal tensions increased accordingly. Even during the past century, when direct violent confrontations have been more limited, discussion about the causes, events, and results of earlier conflicts has profoundly affected relations between Indians and non-Indians. These events have also sparked, on both sides, enduring cultural legacies in the forms of oral traditions, best-selling books, and provocative films.

Only by understanding the past can we hope to understand our own times. By providing information about an important part of that past, *Encyclopedia of Native American Wars and Warfare* helps us understand something about ourselves.

— William B. Kessel
Bethany Lutheran College

— Robert Wooster
Texas A&M University–Corpus Christi

American Indians Prior to 1492

By William B. Kessel

Every schoolchild knows that "in 1492, Columbus sailed the ocean blue" and "discovered" America. It was a discovery only from the perspective of European colonial empires. For millennia the North American continent had been inhabited by people Christopher Columbus mistakenly called *Indios.* According to archaeologists, more than 12,000 years before Columbus was born (perhaps quite a bit more than 12,000), a group of hunters crossed a land bridge across the Bering Strait that connected Siberia and Alaska. It was these hunters who rightfully were the discoverers of the New World.

The Columbus discovery myth is but one misconception about Native Americans that has become entrenched in American history and popular culture. Another erroneous yet commonly held notion is that soon after discovery, Europeans landed on the east coast of North America and immediately spread west across the continent. In fact, the European exploration and exploitation of America came from different directions. In the opening decades of the 16th century, the Spanish moved from south to north—from the Caribbean islands into Florida, from Mexico into the southwestern part of what is now the United States. The French penetrated into the New World by following the St. Lawrence to the Great Lake and later proceeding south along the Mississippi to its delta. In the early 1600s, the English, Swedish, and Dutch became established on the East Coast. Two centuries later, the Russians explored the west coast of North America, including Alaska, Canada, Washington, Oregon, and northern California.

Because of their selective penetration along coastlines and rivers, the Europeans approached different tribes at different times. While some Native American tribes were trading or warring with the Europeans, other Indian groups were oblivious to the foreigners' presence. In 1519, the Spanish conquistador HERNÁN CORTÉS confronted and soon destroyed the Aztec. As early as 1513, Juan Ponce de León landed on a peninsula he named Florida, and there, in 1539, HERNANDO DE SOTO encountered the Calusa and Timucuan. On the other hand, it was not until the mid-1700s that the western UTE first saw Euro-

peans. Even later, in 1805, Meriwether Lewis and William Clark "discovered" the Northern PAIUTE (Numu).

Another prevalent misconception is that the Indians encountered by the Europeans were basically the same. Nothing could be further from the truth. In 1492, there were millions of people on the North American continent. In what is now the United States, there were more than 850,000 Native people divided into hundreds of distinct nations speaking 250 to 300 different languages.

Physically the various Native American peoples shared black hair, dark eyes, and brown skin. Beyond that, however, they displayed significant observable differences. For example, when compared to other tribes, the CROW were tall, the Ute more squat, the WINNEBAGO (Ho-Chunk) had large heads, and the MOJAVE had darker skin. Because North America has significant environmental diversity, it is not surprising that the early inhabitants satisfied their basic human needs in different ways. The PUEBLO Indians lived in stone or adobe apartment-style villages and raised corn, beans, and squash. Not far away, the AKIMEL O'ODHAM (Pima) and TOHONO O'ODHAM (Papago) lived in individual mud-covered, wood frame houses and ate cactus fruit and mesquite beans that grew wild along the rivers. Meanwhile the Chinook of the Pacific Northwest built plank houses of cedar and fished the Columbia River. Some of the tribes like the SHOSHONE of the Great Basin were divided into small nomadic bands of hunters and gatherers. Their population density was very low and their material culture limited. On the other end of the spectrum, the NATCHEZ of the lower Mississippi numbered in the thousands and lived in large villages ruled by a supreme chief.

A fourth myth of the American Indians is that at the time of Columbus the various tribes were located where they always had been. In reality, Native Americans adapted to changing environmental and social conditions; hence their societies were dynamic, not static. Centuries before Columbus, more than 5,000 Indians lived in Chaco Canyon, New Mexico. According to archaeologists, the Chaco culture peaked and declined after

A.D. 1130 because of drought and economic failure, and the ancestral Pueblo people spread out along the Rio Grande and onto mesas. Nearby, on the Colorado Plateau, the Anasazi people abandoned their villages in about A.D. 1300 because of overexploitation of natural resources, environmental changes, and warfare. They merged with the other Pueblo peoples. Hohokam cities, such as Snaketown near modern Phoenix, Arizona, were abandoned about A.D. 1450 possibly because of drought and nomadic raiders, and the ancestral Pima dispersed throughout the Arizona desert. In A.D. 1250, near modern St. Louis, Missouri, more than 40,000 Indians lived in the city of Cahokia. It also declined after that as a result of unsustainable population increases coupled with environmental degradation and possibly tuberculosis. The population spread out along the Mississippi valley, where the Natchez were found in historic times.

In a fifth misconception, some people today picture the Native Americans prior to Columbus as "noble savages," a concept popularized by the French philosopher Jean-Jacques Rousseau. As such, they are viewed as living healthy, happy, and innocent lives in harmony with the land and at peace with one another. This is not a true picture. As previously suggested, nations waxed and waned in response to environmental change. Warfare and intertribal feuds were prevalent among some native groups as well (see Wars and Warfare by William B. Kessel). For example, in A.D. 1325, the Crow Creek village site on the Missouri River in South Dakota was attacked by other Native Americans. More than 500 men, women, and children were killed and the village was overrun and burned. Likewise, when the early Spanish explorer Hernando de Alarcón visited the lower Colorado River area in the 1500s, he found armed conflicts among Native American groups. Meanwhile, in the Midwest, the MIAMI warfare against the SIOUX (Dakota, Lakota, Nakota) and the CHICKASAW was witnessed by other early European explorers.

Finally, many Americans mistakenly assume that the Indians were unable to adapt to the earliest European onslaughts.

Yet as early white explorers, traders, and colonists contacted first one Indian group and then another, the Native people responded. Some groups, such as the Iroquois negotiated with the newcomers (see IROQUOIS CONFEDERACY). Others, such as the people of Acoma Pueblo, stood and fought (see ACOMA PUEBLO). Many tribes in the Northeast took advantage of the situation and became involved in the European fur trade. With superior weapons exchanged for furs, some tribes, such as the CHIPPEWA, were able to gain the upper hand over their traditional enemies, in this case the Sioux. The Indians of the Great Plains rapidly adapted to the horse, first introduced by the Spanish in the early 1500s and widely available by the mid-1600s. They became buffalo hunters and mounted warriors.

Whether initial contacts between Native Americans and whites were friendly or hostile, there was one arrival to which the Native Americans could not adapt—contagious disease from Europe. Smallpox, cholera, diphtheria, bubonic plague, influenza, typhus, typhoid, measles, and other communicable diseases quickly decimated Indian populations. These so-called virgin-soil epidemics were unknown in the pre-Columbian New World. It is clear that the traditional medical remedies available often failed to provide relief. In addition, Native American medicine had no conception of contagion. When individuals became ill, they were not quarantined. Instead, relatives and friends often gathered around to comfort the ill, thereby spreading the disease. Thus, when a smallpox epidemic swept through the MANDAN villages in 1837, only 125 of the estimated 1,600 Indians survived. Likewise, between 1780 and 1851 the Sioux were ravaged by no fewer than nine epidemics, including smallpox, whooping cough, measles, and cholera.

In 1992, the United States rather gingerly acknowledged the 500th anniversary of Christopher Columbus's voyage. Interestingly, instead of focusing on the explorer or his discovery of America, books, newspaper and magazine articles, and television programs emphasized the people discovered. This is a sign that, perhaps today, a clearer picture is emerging of the Native Americans prior to 1492.

Warfare Terminology

By William B. Kessel

The vast literature on Native American wars and warfare contains descriptions and analyses of wars, battles, fights, engagements, actions, defeats, and massacres but generally fails to define these terms. Through common English usage of such terms, the readers are expected to know the difference.

In some writings, *war* and *warfare* are used interchangeably as convenient synonyms. A study of precise meanings, however, does indicate subtle yet significant differences in the information conveyed. Warfare is the action of waging war.

According to most dictionaries, a *war* is a state of open, declared, armed hostile conflict between political units such as tribes, states, or nations. Wars can exist only when each political unit has its own government. A manual written for the U.S. Military Academy at West Point, *Definitions and Doctrine of the Military Art Past and Present,* adds, "War is the condition in the life of a political group … in which violence and destruction of considerable duration or magnitude are directed against a rival political group that is powerful enough to make the outcome of the conflict uncertain for a time. The object of war is to impose the will of one group upon a rival." According to this definition, wars are protracted conflicts among sovereign nations where the victory is not assured from the beginning.

From the perspective of the 20th century, it is difficult to see how Indians had a chance of winning armed conflicts with the white invaders. However, the facts remain. Until the 18th century, there were more Native Americans than white people in what is now the United States. The Indians, furthermore, rapidly acquired European weapons, formed alliances, and knew the terrain. For a time, wars were waged with uncertain outcomes. The annals of Native American armed conflicts contain many wars. Some the Indians won, as in the case of RED CLOUD'S WAR (1866–68). In others, such as the MODOC WAR (1872–73), the whites emerged as victors.

Conflicts fought as parts of wars can be defined according to the length of the engagement and the damage inflicted. Again the West Point manual provides definitions:

A *battle* is a violent and prolonged confrontation of opposing military organizations. Significant casualties generally accrue to one or both sides in a battle. Violent confrontations of lesser magnitude are called *engagements,* a term that connotes an accidental meeting when information about the enemy is being sought, or *actions,* which generally are sharp, but brief, encounters.

Meanwhile a *fight* is simply a hostile encounter between opposing individuals or forces.

The conflicts between the SIOUX (Dakota, Lakota, Nakota) and soldiers at FORT RIDGELY in 1862 illustrate such battles. On August 20 of that year, about 400 warriors attacked the post defended by 180 soldiers. Two days later the Indians, this time numbering about 800, repeated their attack. The Indians were repelled by artillery, and an estimated 100 warriors lost their lives.

Armed conflicts inevitably produce winners and losers. Consider the terms *defeat* and *massacre.* In simplest terms *defeat* is used to describe the situation when an individual or group is overcome or overthrown by an opponent. A *massacre* includes the wanton, cruel, and often wholesale killing or murder of people. The West Point manual explains: "A *massacre* occurs when a considerable number of combatants or noncombatants are killed under circumstances of cruelty or atrocity."

In the annals of Native American wars and warfare, many battles were fought and many defeats suffered. In the battle of BIG DRY WASH (1882), soldiers and APACHE clashed in a fierce engagement that lasted about six hours. When the fighting was done, the Indians suffered a defeat, having lost 22 men, including their leader, and inflicting only two casualties on their opponents. Sioux warriors suffered defeats in the HAYFIELD FIGHT (1867) and WAGON BOX FIGHT (1867). Meanwhile, in 1854 Second Lieutenant JOHN L. GRATTAN unwisely attacked a group of Sioux over the loss of a cow. The Indians responded and eventually defeated the soldiers, killing all but one of them. Soldiers also were defeated in various battles for the BOZEMAN TRAIL as well as in dozens of other cases.

The list of massacres is much smaller, yet much more publicized. A few examples will suffice. Many modern historians feel comfortable labeling the FETTERMAN FIGHT (1866) a massacre. They do so, perhaps, because all 80 of Captain WILLIAM J. FETTERMAN's command were killed in the battle, but more likely because their bodies were mutilated thereafter. The Seventh Cavalry under General GEORGE ARMSTRONG CUSTER met with a similar fate in the battle of the LITTLE BIGHORN (1876), where all 200 soldiers were killed and many of the bodies mutilated. At SAND CREEK (1864), soldiers under the command of JOHN M. CHIVINGTON launched an unprovoked attack on a peaceful encampment of CHEYENNE and ARAPAHO. Ordered to take no prisoners, soldiers slaughtered 200 Indians, more than half of whom were women and children. A similar atrocity took place at CAMP GRANT (1871).

As renowned standing Rock Sioux activist and author Vine Deloria, Jr., points out in *Definitions and Doctrine of the Military Art Past and Present,* the difference between a defeat and massacre is often a matter of political interpretation and perspective:

> Many times over the years my father would point out survivors of the [WOUNDED KNEE] massacre, and people on the reservation always went out of their way to help them. For a long time there was a bill in Congress to pay indemnities to the survivors, but the War Department always insisted that it had been a "battle" to stamp out the Ghost Dance religion among the Sioux. This does not, however, explain bayoneted Indian women and children found miles from the scene of the incident.

In the final analysis, what a person calls a military action and its outcome is less important than an understanding of what took place and why. Warfare terminology often involves the use of subjective labels given to objective reality.

Armies of Empire

Colonial, State, Federal, and Imperial Forces in the Indian Wars
By Robert Wooster

Spurred by a variety of hopes and dreams—discovering mineral wealth, forging new trade relationships, seeking religious freedom, or Christianizing native peoples—many of the Europeans who came to the New World believed that the use of force against the Indians was justified. Thus, early European encounters with Native Americans often resulted in violence. Likewise, the creation and expansion of the United States were in many respects the products of war. Organizing and recruiting for conflicts against the Indians varied widely over time and place but generally involved some combination of professionals and amateurs.

Before the 18th century, the Spanish, French, Dutch, Russian, and English in North America met their military needs through a variety of sources. Each nation deployed regular professional soldiers, hired mercenaries, concluded military alliances with Indians, employed Native American auxiliaries, organized colonial militias, and called up volunteers in times of emergencies. The Spanish tended to use professional soldiers and Indian auxiliaries more often than European rivals did. By exploiting intertribal animosities, France forged alliances with various Indian tribes and confederacies against their mutual enemies. The Dutch turned more frequently to hired mercenaries. The British colonists, on the other hand, generally distrusted professional armies and placed heavier reliance on their colonial militias. Sometimes the volunteers and militiamen were expected to arm and equip themselves. In other instances, they received government assistance.

As wars against the Indians continued during the late 17th and 18th centuries, the key European powers in North America—France, Spain, and England—also engaged in a series of global struggles for dominance. As such, their wars in the Americas (KING WILLIAM'S WAR (1689–97), QUEEN ANNE'S WAR (1702–13), and KING GEORGE'S WAR (1744–48)) often pitted them against one or more of their European rivals as well. With larger imperial concerns at stake, they increased their commitments of professional soldiers from hundreds to thousands. Many of these troops looked with scorn on the colonial militias, whom they deemed ill-disciplined and poorly led.

In the FRENCH AND INDIAN WAR (1754–63), the British finally drove their European rivals from most of North America. The British success was largely due to a huge infusion of regulars onto the continent (although in some cases, such as BRADDOCK'S DEFEAT (1755), they more than met their match against the French and their Indian allies). To control its hard-won gains, England kept some 10,000 regular troops among its American colonies.

This decision antagonized many Americans and was one of the causes of the AMERICAN REVOLUTION (1775–81). The conflict focused largely on the struggle for independence, but it also featured bitter confrontations along the colonies' western frontiers. In these latter engagements—such as those in the Old Northwest under GEORGE ROGERS CLARK and the battles of WYOMING VALLEY (1778) and CHERRY VALLEY (1779)—the Americans relied heavily on traditional militias and short-term volunteer forces. JOHN SULLIVAN's campaign, which culminated in the battle of NEWTOWN (1779) and featured sizable numbers of regular Continental army forces, was a notable exception to this pattern.

It was largely due to concerns over frontier conditions that the Second Continental Congress, or the Confederation Congress, though still worried that a standing professional military posed a threat to democracy, authorized an army of 700 men to be raised in 1784. Initially this force busied itself largely with attempting to remove squatters from public lands in the Ohio River valley. Adaptation of the Constitution by the 13 states reflected a continued distrust of a large standing military establishment. As tensions with the Indians intensified, however, much of the army took the field in LITTLE TURTLE'S WAR (1790). Both the regulars and the state militiamen were humiliated in HARMAR'S DEFEAT (1790) and ST. CLAIR'S DEFEAT (1791). Only after three years of training under the disciplined leadership of General ANTHONY WAYNE did the army, temporarily know as the "Legion" and expanded to some 3,000 strong, gain its revenge in the battle of FALLEN TIMBERS (1794).

The "Legion," in somewhat reduced form, was reorganized and formed the basis for the United States Army in 1796. Growing tensions with Britain and the Indians of the Old Northwest saw an increase in the army's size as well as its frontier assignments leading up to the WAR OF 1812 (1812–14). Following that war, Congress immediately began reducing the army, and by 1821 its maximum strength had been cut to 6,183. Much of this tiny regular force patrolled the frontiers and built western roads. For administrative and organizational purposes, the nation was divided into eastern and western military divisions, each commanded by a major general. These divisions were in turn subdivided into numbered departments.

As Americans continued to push west in the 1830s, they found that both the terrain and the Native Americans they encountered had changed. Up to this point, their fights against Indians had been conducted largely on foot. But as the Spanish had found two centuries before, the prairies, plains, and deserts of the vast American West placed a greater emphasis on mobility. Many of the more powerful Indian societies of the region, such as the Lakota (see SIOUX [Dakota, Lakota, Nakota]), CHEYENNE, COMANCHE, and KIOWA, had seized on Spanish horses to become some of the finest light horsemen in the world. Although reluctant to pay the extra costs mounted units entailed, Congress in 1832 created what eventually became a regiment of dragoons. A second dragoon regiment was added four years later, and a regiment of mounted riflemen was created on the eve of the Mexican War. By this time the regular army stood at just under 9,000 men.

The regular army's responsibilities increased dramatically during the 1840s with the acquisition of Texas and the territories of California, New Mexico, and Oregon. To help meet the new challenges, Congress had raised the army's maximum authorized strength to 16,000 by 1855. Organizationally the regiment, commanded by a colonel, remained the army's basic building block. The U.S. Army now numbered five mounted regiments, 10 infantry regiments, and four artillery regiments. Artillery regiments, which often served as infantry when on frontier duty, boasted 12 companies, each led by a captain. Infantry and cavalry regiments each had 10 companies. Although authorized to have nearly 90 men when on frontier assignment, inefficient recruitment practices, desertion, detached service, extra duty assignments, and sickness commonly left units with fewer than 50 men ready for duty. Only rarely, such as in the First SEMINOLE WAR (1818–19), Second SEMINOLE WAR (1835–42), and Third SEMINOLE WAR (1855–58), did army columns in the field number more than 200 men.

Volunteers and militia continued to supplement the nation's regular army, especially in the case of the BLACK HAWK WAR (1832). But bitter rivalries made for an uneasy relationship. Critics charged that the regulars were poorly suited for warfare against the mounted Plains Indians, who usually avoided battles when the odds seemed poor. "How can they protect us against Indians," argued Senator Sam Houston, "when the cavalry have not horses which can trot faster than active oxen, and the infantry dare not go out in any hostile manner for fear of being shot and scalped!" Defenders of the army, citing an 1857 War Department report estimating that the country could have saved $30 million over 20 years by replacing volunteers with regulars, countered by arguing that volunteer forces were too expensive. Others charged that the poorly disciplined volunteers actually started many conflicts with Indians. In the Pacific Northwest, for example, Brevet Major General JOHN E. WOOL reported, "I do not apprehend any further difficulties with the Indians in Oregon and Washington Territories … if the [volunteers] can be kept out of the field" (see also YAKIMA WAR (1855–57) and ROGUE RIVER WAR (1855–56)).

With the outbreak of the CIVIL WAR (1861–65), many of the frontier regulars were transferred east to fight the Confederates. In the absence of the regulars, states and territories turned to volunteer and militia units to deal with the Indians. Thus, many of the major engagements against the Indians during the Civil War years—including the battles of WOOD LAKE (1862), BEAVER RIVER (1863), WHITESTONE HILL (1863), and SAND CREEK (1864), and the concluding phases of the NAVAJO WAR—were dominated by volunteer rather than regular units.

The Civil War also saw the regular army undergo its traditional expansion and contraction. Following the surrender of Confederate forces in 1865, congressional actions in 1866, 1869, 1870, and 1874 reduced the regular army to a maximum strength of just over 27,000 men, organized into 10 cavalry, 25 infantry, and five artillery regiments. Between 10 and 50 percent of these soldiers, however, were assigned duties in the South during Reconstruction, guarding federal arsenals or garrisoning coastal defenses and were thus unavailable for duty fighting Indians. In a marked break from the past, Congress decreed that four regiments in the reconstituted army be composed entirely of African-American enlisted personnel; these units became known as BUFFALO SOLDIERS.

Sweeping organizational changes also took place. For most of the years between the end of the Civil War and the turn of the century, the army divided the nation into the Divisions of the Atlantic, the Missouri, and the Pacific. A major general usually commanded each division. Each division then had two or more departments, which were overseen by the brigadier generals. The military Division of the Missouri, which included most of the states and territories between the Mississippi River and the Continental Divide, was the scene of many postbellum conflicts against the Indians. Most frequently, this division was broken up into the Departments of Dakota, the Platte, the

Missouri, and Texas. Of slightly less importance during the Indian Wars was the Division of the Pacific, which included the Departments of the Columbia, California, and Arizona.

Historian Francis Paul Prucha has accurately labeled the U.S. Army a "child of the frontier." Always a key force in the nation's wars against the Indians, the army played a particularly dominant role following the Civil War. Usually guided by small teams of frontier scouts or Indian auxiliaries, the U.S. Army largely fought the period's major conflicts—the SIOUX WARS (1854–90), the SOUTHERN PLAINS WAR (1868–69), the RED RIVER WAR (1874–75), the NEZ PERCE WAR (1877), the BANNOCK WAR (1878), and the APACHE WARS (1860–86). Exceptions, in which volunteer or militia units composed a significant number of those engaged, included the battle of BEECHER'S ISLAND (1868) and the CAMP GRANT MASSACRE (1871).

Wars and Warfare

By William B. Kessel

During the past 500 years, white authors have provided contradictory views of the original Americans. On the one hand, Indians have been described as savages, heathens, barbarians, and infidels. Characteristically, they have been pictured with a tomahawk in one hand and a scalp in the other. Other writers, however, have described Indians as noble savages who, prior to white contact, lived peacefully in the forests, enjoying a pristine golden age. Both descriptions of the American Indian reflect only European perceptions and ideals.

This analysis of Indian armed combat avoids both extremes. It examines conflict from the perspective of the various Native American peoples under these topics: the prevalence of combat, the motivation for combat, the types and strategies of armed conflicts, and weaponry.

When Europeans first ventured onto the North American continent, they found not one people but many tribes and nations. Some of these groups were at war with one another. In the northeastern portion of what is now the United States, Native American burial grounds reveal that warfare was prevalent in the late prehistoric period. Fighting reached its height in that region between A.D. 1400 and 1600. For protection, Iroquois (see IROQUOIS CONFEDERACY) built defenses around their villages. Likewise, in the 1500s when the Spanish first began to explore Florida, they found the Timucua living in fortified villages with guards and defensive walls. Other southeastern Indians dug ditches, made embankments, filled moats, and erected palisades or walls to protect their important villages from outside attacks.

The arrival of the Europeans did not create armed conflict but rather stimulated further conflicts among Native Americans themselves as well as with the white people. Some tribes utilized the foreigners as a means of tipping the balance of power in their favor. Thus, when the WAMPANOAG under King Philip began fighting against the colonists, the latter were joined by

MOHEGAN, PEQUOT, Niantic, Sakonnet and MASSACHUSET, who served as spies, scouts, and fighting men (see KING PHILIP'S WAR, 1675–76). The introduction of the horse onto the Great Plains in the 1500s–1600s (a result of Spanish importation of horses from Europe) also led to increased competition and friction among Indians because it allowed them to move into the territories of other tribes. Meanwhile, a variety of factors led to conflicts between the Indians and the Europeans. These included the territorial expansion of white colonists, which resulted in Indians losing their subsistence base; the fur and pelt trade, which stimulated intensive hunting and depletion of animal populations; rapid population losses among Native Americans as a result of new diseases; and the increased dependence of the Native Americans on European trade goods, firearms, and liquor.

Between A.D. 1500 and 1900, many Indians conducted raids and wars against other Indians (see Warfare Terminology). Harold E. Driver, an expert in American Indian studies, reached the conclusion, which is noted in his book *Indians of North America* that "probably as many Indians were killed fighting each other after White contact as were killed in wars with the Whites." Examples of such Native American rivalries include the Iroquois and HURON; PAWNEE and OSAGE; Pawnee and KIOWA, WICHITA against the Plains APACHE, Osage, and Tonkawa; CADDO and Tankawa; BLACKFOOT Confederacy and Sarsi against the Plains CREE and Plains Ojibwa (see CHIPPEWA); Santee SIOUX and Plains Ojibwa; Klamath, MODOC and Pit River Indians against the PAIUTE; Tlingit against the Chumash and Aleut; SHOSHONE against Northern Paiute, Southern Paiutes, UTES, and MOJAVES; Cree and Blackfoot versus Shoshone; PUEBLO against NAVAJO (Dineh) and Apache; MARICOPA and PIMA versus the YUMA and Mojave.

American Indians engaged in armed combat with one another for a variety of reasons. Wars were waged to protect, consolidate, or enlarge territories; to secure supplies, livestock, slaves, and other economic goods and commodities; for revenge; and for honor. Armed conflicts were not entered into lightly but were most often considered a sacred activity.

Some Indians fought against other Indians to maintain or expand tribal territories. Anthropologist James A. Tuck notes in *Handbook of North American Indians* that endemic warfare characterized New York State in the period beginning in A.D. 1300. He then offers a plausible explanation: The introduction of a horticultural subsistence base led to population increases. This, in turn, led to competition among the various peoples for valued resources such as local game supplies, which subsequently led to chronic warfare.

While wars between Native American groups were only rarely waged for territorial gain, they were often fought to protect a homeland from the incursion of other groups. According to one theory, the Iroquois were driven north and east out of their homeland by other Indians. When they arrived in Upstate New York and the Lake Ontario region of Canada, they found the region already occupied by Siouan- and Algonquian-speaking peoples. Warfare developed, and the Siouan groups were driven out of the area entirely. The Iroquois then formed a confederacy (see IROQUOIS CONFEDERACY)—as did the Huron, Neutral, and Susquehanna—and the Mohawk Valley became a bloody battleground. In the Pacific Northwest, a drought caused the Bella Coola to move into Kwakiutl territory, sparking warfare. Meanwhile, along the Mississippi and Missouri Rivers, competition for fertile river lowland areas led to warfare among the local Indians. Warriors finally went to war with Europeans in order to resist white expansionism.

Not infrequently, Native Americans engaged in raiding and warfare for economic gain. The Tlingit of the Pacific Northwest coast, for example, had established important trade routes into the interior. They attacked intruders or those who otherwise interfered with those routes. In the Southwest, the Apache and Navajo raided the Pueblo groups and Mexicans in order to obtain livestock as well as easily transportable goods. Plains Indians raided one another for horses. The Blackfoot Indians alone may have launched as many as 50 horse raids a year. The Indians living along the Northeast and Northwest coasts added CAPTIVES or slaves to the list of items gained in raids.

Other motivations for warfare among American Indian groups included avenging deaths and intertribal feuds. Retaliatory killings by small war parties were not uncommon among the Algonquian. The Osage often organized war parties against their traditional enemies, the Pawnee, in order to take scalps and secure goods. The hair would then be given to women in mourning to dry their tears, and the commodities would replace those material possessions destroyed as part of funeral ceremonies.

Finally, armed conflicts among American Indians were often means whereby individual warriors could gain honor and status through acts of personal bravery. CROW warriors adorned their clothes, robes, and tipis with scalps, which served as evidence of their prowess in battle. A Menominee man was given the honor of wearing an eagle feather in his hair for killing an enemy. If it was his first kill, he was given a wampum belt. The successful warrior was awarded special respect and prestige in his tribe. For the rest of his life, he would be allowed to recount his heroic deeds in certain public ceremonies. Many of the Plains Indians gained great honor in battle, not by killing but by other acts of heroism. Thus, a Crow warrior was highly esteemed for touching an enemy with something he held in the hand (see COUNTING COUP), for cutting a tethered horse from the entrance of an enemy's tipi, taking a gun away from an enemy, or leading a war party. Bravery for the Kiowa was demonstrated by touching an enemy, rescuing a fallen comrade, or charging the man leading an enemy attack. Special honor went to a Blackfoot man for jerking a gun away from an enemy without producing an injury to either party. Finally, prestige through deeds of daring in battle was encouraged in some societies through membership in warrior societies like the Catchers, Bulls, and Horns of the Blackfoot; Kit Fox of the Oglala; or DOG SOLDIERS of the CHEYENNE (see MILITARY SOCIETIES).

The nature of the armed combat and strategies employed by Native Americans was consistent with the motivation for fighting. Groups such as the Apache often formed small raiding parties to steal livestock or other commodities. They relied on stealth to take their enemies' possessions and flee, while avoiding conflict. If the enemy took an Apache life, the Indians would launch a larger retaliatory expedition designed specifically to take enemy life. In response to raids and reprisals, groups such as the Pawnee and Osage often attacked one another. In some cases, a large war party would deliberately attack an enemy village, knowing that most of the occupants were absent. The defenders would be killed, the village destroyed, and booty taken. Likewise, Tlingit raiders chose to attack an enemy village at dawn in order to quickly kill the unsuspecting Indians. Besides raids and skirmishes, some American Indian groups engaged in formal wars. The Timucua and Saturioua of Florida could amass armies of up to 2,000 warriors. Occasionally, they would shoot lighted arrows tipped with moss into the fortified villages of their enemies, thus igniting the roofs made of dried palm branches. Finally, the Pima, Maricopa, Yuma, and Mojave occasionally staged formal pitched battles where combatants lined up in rows and marched toward each other armed with poles and clubs.

The inventory of weapons employed by various Native Americans in raids and wars included BOWS AND ARROWS, KNIVES and daggers, clubs and poles, blowguns, sharpened fingernails, LANCES and SPEARS, and bolas. Some groups, such as the Klamath and Modoc, wore BODY ARMOR made of wooden slats or hide and visored helmets. Many warriors who fought out in the open ranges of the Great Plains and Southwest defended themselves with hide shields. The introduction of the breech loading rifle, however, changed the face of Indian warfare forever (see FIREARMS).

Native Americans who engaged in armed conflict were not so different from other peoples of the world. Fighting was not capricious but was well-considered and based on cause. The pain of loss and death was felt acutely by the Indians—just as it is felt by all people. (See also Wars and Warfare by Robert Wooster)

Wars and Warfare: Another View

By Robert Wooster

European impressions about the peoples whom Christopher Columbus called Indians were largely inspired by the writings of early explorers of the New World. Widely publicized by virtue of the newly developed printing press and illustrated by fanciful drawings, these images suggested basic themes that would influence the conduct of wars against the Indians for centuries to come. Although some Europeans, such as the Dominican friar Bartolomé de Las Casas, vigorously defended Native peoples, most observers found the Indians wanting. Compared with the technologies, cultures, and societies with which the Europeans were familiar, Indian practices seemed strangely primitive. The French, for example, generally labeled the peoples of the New World as *sauvages* (savages) well into the 19th century.

Blending Christian doctrine, the notion that the American "wilderness" needed to be conquered, and a seemingly insatiable appetite for wealth, many Europeans concluded that violence was a legitimate means of achieving their ends. Many claimed that this would benefit the tribes, for after crushing them in battle, they would then confer on the pacified peoples the presumed virtues of European "civilization." Others pointed out that various tribes had fought against one another long before the arrival of Europeans. Military means were not necessarily the first option in dealing with the Indians; when profitable, convenient, or demanded by conditions, even those who had little interest in Christianizing the tribes used diplomacy or economic incentives to achieve their goals. But because force had long been used, when necessary, to resolve diplomatic quarrels in Europe, it seemed natural to direct it against Indians as well.

In general, Europeans applied their own familiar concepts and beliefs to situations in the New World. Traditional approaches—diplomacy, alliances, trade, as well as warfare—would be employed in dealing with the tribes. But certain major differences between Old and New World practices were also evident. Because Europeans generally perceived Indians as less than equal to themselves, normal rules did not always apply. Differences in beliefs regarding appropriate actions toward CAPTIVES (see also PRISONERS) reinforced notions of racial superiority. Thus, warfare between Indians and non-Indians often became much more violent than either side generally practiced in different circumstances. The bloody Thirty Years' War (1618–48) in Europe clearly demonstrated that, in some cases, non-combatants would be given no mercy during conflicts between the European powers. But such ferocity was the exception rather than the general rule. European wars, especially during the late 17th and 18th centuries, were usually fought between monarchs' armies rather than between fully mobilized nations. Similarly, conflicts between warring tribes, while serious, had often emphasized acts of personal bravery rather than the complete destruction of one's enemies. In the Americas, however, when fighting erupted between groups with dissimilar beliefs and ways, wars often escalated to include not only soldiers and warriors but entire societies. Thus, during BACON'S REBELLION (1676). Virginians engaged in what amounted to a race war against all Indians. In New England, KING PHILIP'S war (1675–76) featured brutal attacks by both sides against enemy villages; the Massachusetts, Connecticut, and Plymouth colonists forcibly dispersed their enemies and greatly expanded their landholdings at the expense of the Indians.

Similar patterns were evident during the great wars for empire of the 18th century, which pitted England against France (and sometimes Spain) in a series of contests culminating in the FRENCH AND INDIAN WAR (1754–63). When fighting against other Europeans, combatants generally honored evolving customs, which banned the wholesale murder or captivity of noncombatants. But such considerations were rarely maintained when the conflicts pitted Indian against European. During the TUSCARORA WAR (1711–13), for example, North Carolina colonists retaliated for the slaughter of some 200 settlers (including 80 children) by roasting at least one Tuscarora leader alive and selling 400 prisoners into slavery. Likewise, the French sold their Indian prisoners and seized their lands during the NATCHEZ REVOLT (1729–31).

The AMERICAN REVOLUTION (1775–81) reinforced the extraordinarily brutal nature of the wars against the Indians. Along the frontiers, the revolutionary conflicts, which usually pitted American colonists against the British and Indians, were especially fierce. Both sides routinely carried the war to non-combatants. For example, at GNADENHUTTON (1782), a group of Christianized LENNI LENAPE (Delaware) Indians were slaughtered indiscriminately. In a series of raids in CHERRY VALLEY (1779), New York, hundreds of white colonists were killed with equal ferocity. These and other conflicts left a legacy of mutual distrust and fear and helped to spark continuing conflicts between Americans and Indians in the Old Northwest over the next 20 years.

A gradually emerging consensus within the United States about the broad goals of the nation's Indian policy also contributed to a climate that embraced warfare as a legitimate policy option. Although Americans disagreed about many of the specifics related to Indian policy, they generally agreed that the nation needed more land and that tribal lifestyles should be transformed to make Indians more "American." Widespread property ownership in a Euro-American sense was seen to be essential if democracy was to succeed; moreover, theorists such as Thomas Jefferson championed agriculture as the preferred means of exploiting this land. The fact that many tribes used the land differently merely reinforced notions of their inferiority.

Thus, the United States needed to find some means of securing territory from the Indians, while at the same time encouraging the tribes to become more "civilized." The federal government, not the individual states, took charge of these complex goals. Initially Congress outlined Indian policy in a series of trade and intercourse acts (1793–1834), which attempted to regulate the flow of goods and people in and out of Indian territories. However, as demands for land intensified during the 1820s and 1830s, the government more frequently insisted that Indians be relocated to areas not desired by whites. In some cases, such as the Second SEMINOLE WAR (1835–42), tribes resisted these white encroachments with force. Tragically, those who attempted to cooperate with the government's demand that they be removed to lands west of the Mississippi River often suffered enormous hardships, as exemplified in the TRAIL OF TEARS.

Territories acquired as a result of the annexation of Texas (1845), the Buchanan-Pakenham Treaty (1846), and the Treaty of GUADALUPE-HIDALGO (1848) brought enormous potential for national growth as well as conflict with resident Indians. No longer could U.S. leaders hope to establish a permanent frontier line that would conveniently divide Indian from non-Indian. Instead, under the direction of the newly formed DEPARTMENT OF THE INTERIOR, the BUREAU OF INDIAN AFFAIRS (BIA) would attempt to negotiate treaties that would place tribes on specific reservations. While on reservations, at least according to official policy, the federal government would provide teachers, tools, livestock, and food as the Indians adopted white ways. Many tribes, however, resisted efforts to move them from their traditional homelands. Thus, a series of conflicts—including the COMANCHE WARS (1840–75), the ROGUE RIVER WARS (1855–56), the Third SEMINOLE WAR (1855–58), the YAKAMA WARS (1855–57), and the COEUR D'ALENE WAR (1858)—marked Indian/non-Indian relations during the 1850s.

The outbreak of the CIVIL WAR (1861–65) stimulated even more ferocious fighting between Indians and non-Indians in the American West. In a series of incidents from New Mexico to Minnesota—including the SIOUX UPRISING (1862), the CHEYENNE-ARAPAHO WAR (1864–65), and the continuation of the NAVAJO WAR (1863–64)—combatants and non-combatants among all sides bore the brunt of the intense distrust that many from each group had for the other. Real and alleged ill-treatment of prisoners and indiscriminate atrocities antagonized both sides. With the transfer of most regular army units to the eastern fronts during the Civil War, state volunteer and militia units took a more active role in these confrontations. Disasters such as the massacre at SAND CREEK (1864) sometimes resulted out of the new freedom from federal authority.

The wars against the Indians continued for nearly three decades following the conclusion of the American Civil War. Once again, whites contended that they must be allowed to claim the continent for "civilization," and they were determined to continue placing Indians on reservations where they might learn white customs and become assimilated. Many tribes resisted these efforts, and the late 19th century was marked by another series of fierce conflicts, such as the APACHE WARS (1861–86), the SOUTHERN PLAINS WAR (1868–69), the RED RIVER WAR (1874–75), the SIOUX WARS (1854–90), and the NEZ PERCE WAR (1877).

Contrary to the charges made by some critics, the United States never saw military force as the ideal means of achieving its Indian policies (see GENOCIDE). The regular army's small size (see Armies of Empire) constrained the scope of military action. Likewise, there were limits to what the nation would accept in terms of army conduct. For example, public outcry following the battle of the MARIAS RIVER (1870) and the CAMP GRANT MASSACRE (1871) helped convince Congress to reduce military spending and place additional restrictions on the army's freedom of action. Resort to force essentially meant that diplomatic methods—offers of annuities, bribes to influential leaders, and threats—had failed. But when these more peaceful means did not work within acceptable time frames, U.S. officials believed that force represented an expedient means of achieving their goals. When Americans did go to war, they did so convinced that their need for land and the "uncivilized" manners of their Indian enemies justified the use of violence at levels that would have been unacceptable against other foes. (See also Wars and Warfare by William B. Kessel)

A to Z
Entries

Abenaki (Abnaki, Wabanaki, "easterners," "dawn land people") *confederation of Algonquian tribes and bands, including the Passamaquoddy, Kennebec, Penobscot, Pennacook, Sokoki, Pigwacket, Malecite, and Etchimin, from the Maine–New Hampshire–Vermont area*

The members of the Abenaki confederacy were closely associated with French colonists in New France, and the two groups often assisted each other against their enemies, the British and the IROQUOIS CONFEDERACY. The French first made contact with the Abenaki between 1603 and 1605, when the explorer Samuel de Champlain visited the New England area. The French also persuaded the Abenaki to trade furs with them. Around the same time, the Englishman George Waymouth led an expedition to the area but alienated the Abenaki by kidnapping five men. Perhaps because of this, the Abenaki allied themselves with the French by the middle of the 17th century. By 1670, French missionaries were spreading Catholicism among the Abenaki, raising old English religious hatreds.

After the outbreak of KING PHILIP'S WAR (1675–76), the Abenaki found themselves caught between the warring French and British. The Iroquois tribes to the south and west in New York, who were then allied with the British, raided Abenaki territory, and the Abenaki raided them in turn. The Abenaki were finally drawn into the war against the British after the young child of a *sagamore,* or chief, named Squando was murdered. The Abenaki emerged from the war victorious; the British were forced to abandon their coastal settlements in Abenaki territory.

In later conflicts, the tribes were not as fortunate. The conflict known as DUMMER'S WAR (1722–25) involved raids by British settlers on the Abenaki villages of Old Town and NOR-RIDGEWOCK (1724). The war ended with an ABENAKI TREATY (1725) negotiated by the Penobscot. Faced with the prospect of British neighbors seeking land, many Abenaki tribes chose to move to the territory of New France (Quebec and New Brunswick), while others traveled farther west and settled near Lake Michigan. Still others, including the Penobscot, made peace with the British and remained in their native territory. Many of the Abenaki who remained in the New England area fought for the patriot side in the AMERICAN REVOLUTION (1775–81). Some representatives of the tribal confederation remain on ancestral lands to the present day.

Abenaki Treaty (1725) *last of a series of three treaties that ended Dummer's War (1722–1725)*

The ABENAKI, a confederation of tribes and bands occupying what is now Maine, New Hampshire, and Vermont, found themselves in a difficult position at the beginning of the 18th century. Although their sympathies were with the traders of New France (modern Quebec), their economic ties were with the British colonies of New England. The Abenaki recognized that they could only resist pressures from both sides by maintaining a delicate balance between the two.

That balance was threatened by the outbreak in 1722 of DUMMER'S WAR, or Grey Lock's War as it was known among the western Abenaki. Feeling threatened by the British settlement of Brunswick on the coast of Maine, Abenaki canoed down the Kennebec River, burned the town, and made PRISONERS of some of the citizens. The beginning of hostilities between the British settlers and the Abenaki led to a split between the groups of the confederation. Some supported the French position; others wished to accommodate the British. Members of the Pigwacket, Arosaguntacook, and Kennebec left their native territories to live in refugee camps in Quebec. Others, including most of the PENOBSCOT, remained in New England area and negotiated with the British.

In 1725, the Penobscot, claiming to speak for all the Abenaki, negotiated a treaty with the British. The British asked for and received agreements to cease all hostilities and to return all hostages. They also asked for recognition of their land claims and the sovereignty of the king of England over Abenaki lands. Because of the terms of the treaty, the Penobscot were able to maintain their central position between the French and the British until 1763 and the end of the FRENCH AND INDIAN WAR (1754–63). The key western Abenaki leader, Grey Lock, did not attend the talks, however, and fighting continued for two more years before gradually ending, with his people still holding their traditional lands.

Abraham (1789–ca. 1870) *black Seminole who served as an interpreter for the Seminole*

Under the Treaty of PAYNE'S LANDING (1832), the U.S. government sent a SEMINOLE delegation, including Abraham, to Indian Territory (present-day Oklahoma). The delegation was to look at a possible relocation site for the Seminole among the CREEK, who had already been removed from the Southeast. The government pressured the delegates to sign the Treaty of FORT GIBSON (1833). Most Seminole, however, rejected the treaty and fiercely fought both militia and federal troops.

In 1836, Abraham served as the interpreter for Seminole peace talks with the U.S. military. The talks failed, but in 1837 Seminole chiefs favoring peace once again used Abraham as interpreter in meetings with General THOMAS SIDNEY JESUP. Jesup promised the Seminole a general amnesty. Abraham played a central role in the parley with Jesup and used his influence to promote a peace treaty that included removal to Indian Territory. All the Seminole warriors, however, would not agree and began a struggle of resistance during the Second SEMINOLE WAR (1835–39). Following this conflict, the army forcibly removed many of the Seminole to Indian Territory. There, Abraham ably helped the resettlement of new Seminole villages. He returned briefly to Florida in 1852, helping to induce BILLY BOWLEGS to surrender.

Acoma Pueblo (1599) *attack on Acoma Pueblo by Spaniards*

From 1540 to 1595, the relations between the Spanish, newly arrived in the New World, and the residents of Acoma Pueblo, a multistory adobe city built high atop a mesa in eastern New Mexico, were sporadic and, for the most part, peaceful. By 1598 Spanish explorer Juan de Oñate had been given a contract to colonize New Mexico. Zutacapan, a warrior from Acoma, heard that Oñate planned to force the PUEBLO into submission and obedience. Initially the Acoma Indians prepared to

fight but, fearing the rumor that the Spanish were immortal and known to commit atrocities during warfare, they decided to seek peace. In December 1598 Juan de Zaldívar, a nephew of Oñate, arrived at Acoma, with 20 to 30 men. He took 16 of them up the mesa into Acoma, where the villagers had promised them food. Zaldívar's men allegedly attacked some of the women, and fighting broke out. Zaldívar and 11 of his men were killed.

Oñate was outraged and immediately ordered that the residents of Acoma should be punished. He gave the task to Vincenti de Zaldívar, brother of the fallen Juan. Meanwhile, the Keres Indians of Acoma prepared for war. On January 21, 1599, Zaldívar's army of 70 men arrived. The next day the battle of Acoma Pueblo began. On the third day, 12 of Zaldívar's men ascended the mesa. Soon the Spanish took the village and blasted the homes with cannon fire. The timber roofs of the houses were then burned. Of the estimated 6,000 residents of Acoma, 500 men and 300 women and children were killed. Meanwhile, 500 prisoners were taken and subsequently sentenced to various punishments. Acoma males over 25 years of age each had a foot cut off and were held as slaves for a period of 20 years. Twenty-four men received this punishment. Males between ages 12 and 25 and females above age 12 were enslaved for 20 years. These Keres were divided among the government officials and Catholic missions. Finally, 60 of the youngest Indian girls were ruled free of guilt; nevertheless, they were sent to Mexico City, where they were parceled out among Catholic convents. While this group never saw home again, most of the Keres from Acoma did manage to escape from servitude, and by 1601 they had reestablished a community, which survives to this day.

Adobe Walls (1874) *battle between warriors of several southern plains tribes and white buffalo hunters*

In the spring of 1874, the COMANCHE invited their KIOWA friends to a SUN DANCE ceremony. Kiowa chiefs SATANTA and LONE WOLF attended and met with the half-blood Comanche chief QUANAH PARKER. This dance and meeting had been set up to provide an opportunity for the leaders to discuss a pressing situation.

Until 1870 white hunters had only killed buffalo during winter, when their fur was long. A new tanning process had been developed, however, making short-haired summer hides useful as well. That, in addition to new, more accurate rifles, had greatly increased the number of buffalo being killed by whites. This was endangering the livelihood and way of life of the Plains tribes.

Parker advocated war as necessary to halt the white buffalo hunter's slaughter of the buffalo. His allies agreed. The leaders massed a force of 700 CHEYENNE, Kiowa, and ARAPAHO warriors and set out for Adobe Walls, a buffalo hunters' settlement near the Canadian River in the upper Texas panhandle.

Before sunrise on June 27, 1874, Quanah Parker led an attack on the settlement. When two white men attempted to escape by wagon, Indians caught, killed, and scalped them. The Indians then turned their attention to the hunters' encampment and attacked with lances and knives. Within the confines at Adobe Walls were 28 buffalo hunters determined to hold their position. The defenders were armed with heavy Sharps and Remington buffalo guns capable of firing high-caliber projectiles with deadly accuracy, and they were protected by buildings. Although outnumbered 25 to 1, the hunters fought off the Indians.

During the attack, Quanah Parker's horse was shot from under him; as he scrambled for cover, a bullet creased his shoulder. Another warrior was knocked off his horse by a bullet supposedly fired by Billy Dixon (a scout for Indian Agent John D. Miles) at a range of one mile. The Indian did not die, but the remaining warriors broke off the attack.

Three buffalo hunters died along with 15 Indians in the battle of Adobe Walls. This encounter severely shook the confidence of Parker's followers in their ability to stop the slaughter of the buffalo herds. It also provided further impetus to calls for a major government counter-offensive, culminating in the RED RIVER WAR (1874–75).

Akimel O'odham (Pima) *Indian tribe in southern Arizona*

The Pima traditionally occupied the Gila and Salt River valleys of south-central Arizona and portion of northern Mexico. In the 1600s Spanish settlers moved north into Akimel O'odham territory. As they did so, they established communities and missions and forced the Indians to provide food. In 1695 some of the Akimel O'odham to the south began burning Spanish property and harassing missionaries. The revolt was quickly squashed. In 1751, the northern band under the leadership of Luis Oacpicagigua initiated a second revolt by killing 18 Spaniards and then attacking others throughout Akimel O'odham territory. It took the Spanish several months to regain control.

In the century that followed, APACHE from the north began raiding Akimel O'odham settlements with increased frequency. Meanwhile, YUMA and MOJAVE Indians to the east fought pitched battles with the Akimel O'odham and their allies the MARICOPA. Hostilities reached a head in the battle at MARICOPA WELLS (1857), in which the Akimel O'odham and Maricopa resoundingly defeated their eastern enemies, and in 1871, when Akimel O'odham relatives, the TOHONO O'ODHAM (formerly Papagos), joined Tucson settlers in the CAMP GRANT MASSACRE (1871) of the Apache.

Present-day Akimel O'odham live on the Gila River and Salt River Reservations, which they share with the Maricopa.

Algonkin (Algonquian, Algonquin) *Native American tribe that lived in eastern Canada*

During the 17th century, the Algonkin tribe lived in what is now Quebec, along the St. Lawrence and Ottawa Rivers. The Algonkin were hunter-gatherers. For most of the year they divided into small individual bands. The Algonkin encountered the French—including extensive contact with explorer Samuel de Champlain—early in the 17th century and became valued French allies against the English and IROQUOIS CONFEDERACY in what is now New York (see ALLIANCES WITH COLONISTS).

The French and the Algonkin got along well because of their mutual interest in blocking Iroquois domination of the fur trade in the Ohio Valley and southern Ontario. However, the Iroquois Confederacy forced the Algonkin out of their hunting and trapping lands. The tribe broke up and scattered to the west and north. Some Algonkin joined other ALGONQUIAN-speaking tribes, such as the OTTAWA. Some may have gone as far west as Lake Huron. Others later returned to French territory during the 18th century and aided their European allies in the conflict known as the FRENCH AND INDIAN WAR (1754–63). Today their descendants compose nine Algonkin bands who live on reservations in Quebec and one in Ontario.

Algonquian (Algonquin) *Native American language family; those tribes who speak languages in this family*

Algonquian is a language composed of related dialects spoken by American Indian groups mainly in the Northeast. The term is also commonly used to refer to those tribes speaking these dialects.

See also ALGONKIN.

alliances among Native peoples *confederations of Indians formed to control territory, wage warfare, or repulse the incursions of settlers*

When the first English settlers arrived in the area that is now Virginia in 1607, they encountered a powerful alliance of Indians in the region. Under the leadership of Chief POWHATAN, father of Pocahontas, this POWHATAN CONFEDERACY controlled territory that extended from the Potomac River in the north to Albemarle Sound in the south. The 30 or so tribes of the confederacy, which comprised some 15,000 people and 200 villages, all owed allegiance to Powhatan. He was given tribute in corn, skins, and valuables such as pearls. In waging war, Powhatan selected war chiefs from the various villages, and they recruited warriors. In 1607, the same year the English landed at what is now Jamestown, Powhatan's warriors attacked and decimated the Chesapeake tribes to the south.

Relations between the Powhatan Confederacy and the English were at first friendly. But the English discovered that the tobacco grown by the Indians could be a profitable crop. Soon they were encroaching on Indian farming and hunting lands. Rebellions broke out, resulting in the POWHATAN WARS (1622–32, 1644–46) between the Indians and the settlers. The Powhatan were finally overwhelmed by English weapons and the growing numbers of colonists. By 1646 the confederacy was smashed.

The IROQUOIS CONFEDERACY, originally an alliance of five tribes—the MOHAWK, ONEIDA, CAYUGA, ONONDAGA, and SENECA—was formed sometime in the 1500s to bring peace among those five Iroquois-speaking peoples. A sixth tribe, the TUSCARORA of North Carolina, joined the Confederacy in the early 1700s after they were forced from their lands by white settlers. Although organized to bring peace among its members, the Confederacy was almost always engaged in wars of conquest against other tribes. During the 1600s and early 1700s, the Iroquois Confederacy dominated tribes to the north and west, controlling lands from the Hudson River to Lake Erie in the west and from the Ottawa River in Canada to the Cumberland River in Kentucky.

From 1689 to 1763, colonial wars for control of North America raged on and off between the British and the French. Although the Iroquois decided to remain officially neutral, member tribes did from time to time side with the British, who encouraged Iroquois attacks on tribes in the Ohio Valley to disrupt their fur trade with the French. In 1755, during the FRENCH AND INDIAN WAR (1754–63), Mohawk warriors directly aided the British by helping to repel a French invasion force at Fort William Henry in northern New York State. The loose alliance between the Confederacy and the British was based on their extensive fur trade and the fact that the Iroquois controlled territory of strategic value to the British in their conflict with France.

Although the Iroquois attempted to remain neutral at the start of the AMERICAN REVOLUTION (1775–83), member tribes were drawn into the conflict and their loyalties became divided. The Tuscarora and Oneida supported the colonists. Led by the Mohawk chief JOSEPH BRANT, the Mohawk, Seneca, Onondaga, and Cayuga remained loyal to the British. During 1777, Iroquois warriors attacked colonial settlements along the frontiers in western New York and Pennsylvania and with British soldiers fought in the battle of ORISKANY CREEK (1777). In retaliation, a colonial force of some 2,500 troops swept through Iroquois lands in 1779. The colonials defeated an Iroquois and British force at Elmira, New York, and moved on to burn Iroquois towns and crops, destroy livestock and food supplies, and plunder the countryside. Survivors took refuge with the British in Canada. Those loyal to the colonies remained in New York, where the chiefs negotiated a treaty with the Americans in 1784 in which they were forced to cede most of their lands in Ohio, Pennsylvania, and Western New York. The power of the Iroquios Confederacy was thus broken.

In the Ohio River Valley, another confederacy was taking form following the American Revolution. A SHAWNEE chief, TECUMSEH, traveled among the tribes of the area, preaching union to resist the white settlers who were entering Indian lands in vast numbers. By 1808 Tecumseh had established a town in present-day Indiana, where warriors from the Shawnee, OTTAWA, HURON, WINNEBAGO, POTAWATOMI, and other tribes gathered to hear the chief's message of a united Indian force to drive back the whites. Tecumseh also traveled as far north as Wisconsin and as far south as Florida to enlist other tribes. Alarmed Americans defeated one of Tecumseh's forces in 1811 at the battle of TIPPECANOE (1811). Hoping for British help against the American settlers, Tecumseh joined the British during the WAR OF 1812. With his death at the battle of the THAMES (1813), the confederacy was ended.

Among the Plains tribes in the West, alliances also developed, sometimes based on shared hunting grounds and sometimes on language and culture. The ASSINIBOINE and the Plains CREE formed an early alliance to fight their traditional enemies the SIOUX and the BLACKFOOT CONFEDERACY. The Blackfeet (as members of the Confederacy were known) were a powerful alliance of five tribes—the Piegan (or Pikuni), the Blood (or Kainah), the Blackfoot (or Siksika), the Sarcee, and the Gros Ventre (Atsina).

An even more powerful alliance was the Sioux. The Sioux originally lived along the upper Mississippi, but by the mid-1700s were migrating west. These Siouxan-speaking tribes composed a loose alliance joined together to fight their enemies. Four groups made up the eastern Sioux, called the Dakota or Santee—the Mdewkanton, Sisseton, Wahpekute, and Wahpeton. They settled in what is now Minnesota. Farther west—along the Missouri in what is now South Dakota—were the Yankton (Nakota). To their north, in what is now North and South Dakota, were the Yanktonai—composed of two bands, the Yanktonai and Hunkpatina. The westernmost group were the Teton, or Lakota. The Teton were composed of seven bands: Oglala, Brulé (Sicangu), Hunkpapa, Miniconjou, Oohenonpa, Itazipco (Sans Arcs), and Sihasapa.

In the 1790s, the alliance numbered about 25,000 people. The Sioux fiercely resisted white settlement of their homelands, fighting the SIOUX WARS (1854–90). During several phases of this, they made alliances with other tribes, often the CHEYENNE and the ARAPAHO. During the war for the Bozeman Trail—or RED CLOUD'S WAR—in the mid-1860s, the three groups fought together, as they did again during the war for the Black Hills (1876–77). It was during this war that a force of Sioux, Cheyenne, and Arapaho inflicted a crushing defeat on General GEORGE ARMSTRONG CUSTER at LITTLE BIGHORN (1876) in Montana. Little Bighorn was the last great Indian victory in the Plains wars. Defeats through the summer of 1876 and into 1877, and the deaths of great war leaders CRAZY HORSE and SITTING BULL, weakened the tribes. In 1890 the massacre at WOUNDED KNEE signalled the end of the Plains Indian Wars.

Formed for conquest or protection, Indian military alliances could not, in the end, withstand the overwhelming numbers of whites and their superior weapons. However, as social and quasi-political units, some—such as the Iroquois Confederacy and the Sioux—still exist today.

Further Reading

Axtell, James. *Beyond 1492: Encounters in Colonial North America.* New York: Oxford University Press, 1992.

Utley, Robert M., and Wilcomb E. Washburn. *Indian Wars.* Boston: Houghton Mifflin, 1977.

alliances with colonists *unions between Indians and Europeans for mutual benefit through war and trade*

Native Americans and colonists—British, French, and Spanish—were allies almost as often as they were adversaries. In what is now Mexico, Indians such as the Totonac, Tlaxcalan, and Cholulan, unhappy with their Aztec overlords, joined HERNÁN CORTÉS'S 1519 expedition against Tenochtitlán and helped end Aztec power. POWHATAN, leader of the POWHATAN CONFEDERACY in Virginia, supported the British settlement at Jamestown during its most difficult years. American Indians and colonists had important financial relationships through the fur trade from the early 17th century on. Both groups made and broke treaties and informal agreements with each other in order to gain advantages over their rivals. Indians allied with colonists to defeat neighboring tribes, while the colonists used Native Americans as irregular troops in frontier conflicts that echoed wider European wars.

One early example of this in North America is the 1565 alliance of the Spanish with the Timucua of northern Florida against the local French settlers. For many years French Protestant Huguenots, a dissident religious group, had searched for a place to settle in the Americas. In June 1564 the Huguenots settled among the Timucua near present-day Jacksonville and built Fort Caroline. The colonists' main political objective, besides their desire for religious freedom, was to interfere with Spanish ships carrying gold and silver in the Caribbean. The Timucua for their part wanted the French, with their weapons and armor, as allies in their local tribal wars. The Timucua soon grew disillusioned with their French neighbors, who relied on the Indians for food and refused to fight the Timucua's Indian rivals. They welcomed the appearance of a Spanish expedition as a means to be rid of them. In 1565 the Spanish landed, fortified a local Timucua village, and, with the help of Timucua informers, stormed the French stronghold late that year. Once the French had been driven out, the Spanish built missions. By 1656, however, the Timucua had had enough of the Spanish and joined with the Apalachee to try to drive the missionaries out. They were defeated and many were killed.

Many of these Native-European alliances were based both on mutual protection and economic necessity. The French, through negotiation with the tribes of the St. Lawrence River Valley, established close relations with the confederations of the Micmac, the ABENAKI, and the ALGONQUIAN, as well as the Montagnais and the HURON. Throughout the 17th century, these tribes served the French as trading intermediaries, buying furs from tribes farther west and reselling them to the French in Quebec and Montreal. They also called on French support against their traditional rivals, the nations of the IROQUOIS CONFEDERACY, in what is now New York State. In 1609, for instance, a band of 300 Huron and Montagnais launched an ambush against about 200 MOHAWK on Lake Champlain, supported by about 10 French musketeers under Samuel de Champlain. The successful action helped cement the friendship between the French and the Canadian Indian tribes.

The close ties between Micmac, Abenaki, and ALGONKIN and French Canadian traders helped alienate tribes who were members of the Iroquois League. The Iroquois wanted a monopoly on the traffic in furs with the Europeans. They often launched expeditions against trading tribes into what is now southern Ontario and into the valleys of the Ohio River and the Upper Mississippi. The French, who wanted to reduce costs by eliminating as many Indian intermediaries as possible, resisted these incursions. During the mid-17th century, the Iroquois formed alliances with the Dutch, who supplied them with the guns and powder they needed. French training and firepower, however, forced the Iroquois into a negotiated agreement, known as the GRAND SETTLEMENT OF 1701.

However, the Iroquois found European allies in the British, traditional enemies of the French. The major contact point for the Dutch and the Iroquois had been the trading post of New Orange (Albany) in the upper Hudson Valley. When the British took the colony from the Dutch, they assumed the role of trading partner with the Iroquois. In 1677, at the conclusion of KING PHILIP'S WAR (1675–76), the British created the series of treaties and agreements known as the COVENANT CHAIN (1600s) with the Iroquois and other tribes. During the colonial wars of the 18th century between the French and the British, the British retained close ties with their Iroquois allies, providing them with arms and supplies.

When the French were driven from Canada at the close of the FRENCH AND INDIAN WAR (1754–63), their ties with the native tribes were cut abruptly. Many of their Abenaki and Algonquian allies sought refuge with other tribes farther west in the Great Lakes area. For such Iroquois and British allies as the CHEROKEE, the AMERICAN REVOLUTION (1775–81) permanently changed their relationship with the Europeans. The colonists, having removed the French threat to their peace, began moving into Iroquois hunting territory, dispossessing the native inhabitants. Iroquois warriors fought alongside Canadians and Tories during the Revolution, but after the American victory their long alliance with the British ended. The Revolution, marked an end to colonial warfare in North America, but a pattern of mutual cooperation and mistrust had been established that would color later dealings between Indians and whites.

Further Reading

Axelrod, Alan. *Chronicle of the Indian Wars.* New York: Prentice Hall, 1994.

Josephy, Alvin M., Jr. *500 Nations: An Illustrated History of North American Indians.* New York: Alfred A. Knopf, 1994.

Steele, Ian K. *Warpaths: Invasions of North America.* New York: Oxford University Press, 1994.

American Horse (Iron Shield) (ca. 1801–1876)
prominent Oglala Lakota war chief

Following the CIVIL WAR (1861–65), increasing numbers of non-Indian miners and settlers began moving westward onto Indian lands. American Horse and his cousin RED CLOUD were among the Indian leaders in the battle for the BOZEMAN TRAIL (1866–68), which ensued as a result of white encroachment.

The FORT LARAMIE TREATY (1868) officially ended the conflict, although many—including American Horse—did not accept this treaty. American Horse did accompany Red Cloud's 1870 delegation to Washington, D.C. to pursue peace, but encroachment and warfare continued. American Horse fought in the War for the Black Hills (see SIOUX WARS) and in the battle of the LITTLE BIGHORN (June 1876). That fall he headed his followers south for the winter. On September 9, 1876, a detachment of soldiers located and trapped American Horse, four warriors, and 15 women and children in a ravine in present-day South Dakota. In the battle of SLIM BUTTES (1876) that followed, the chief was seriously wounded, and he stumbled out of the ravine holding his intestines, which had been ripped open by a bullet. American Horse was taken by the soldiers to a makeshift hospital tent. He refused the chloroform offered by the surgeons, and chose instead to bite down on a piece of wood while suffering excruciating pain. His wounds proved to be fatal. After he died, the soldiers scalped him.

See also SIOUX (Dakota, Lakota, Nakota).

American Indian Movement (AIM) *modern-day Indian activist movement whose goal is the improvement of conditions for Native Americans*

The American Indian Movement (AIM) has members in the United States and Canada. Founded in 1968 in Minneapolis, Minnesota, by DENNIS BANKS, Clyde Bellecourt, and George Mitchell, AIM became one of the most militant of the activist groups. AIM founders drew inspiration from two well-known books: Dee Brown's *Bury My Heart at Wounded Knee* and Vine Deloria Jr.'s *Custer Died for Your Sins*. The organization, initiated by city and non-reservation Indians, was first concerned with aiding those who were moving from midwestern reservations to the cities. They were especially concerned with police brutality.

Joined by other Indian activists including RUSSELL MEANS, AIM began protesting the policies of the BUREAU OF INDIAN AFFAIRS (BIA). AIM vividly demonstrated its slogan of "Red Power" in 1968 when the group filed claim to various pieces of federal land. In November 1969 AIM members played a big role in the occupation of Alcatraz (a 12-acre island in San Francisco Bay and the former site of a federal prison) by "Indians of All Tribes," initially a group of about 100; 80 of these were UCLA students. The group claimed homestead rights under the FORT LARAMIE TREATY (1868). Numbers dwindled as the months wore on, but the last occupier did not leave Alcatraz until June 11, 1971.

In 1972, AIM organized a caravan that crossed the United States. Its goal was to focus attention on all the treaties the federal government had broken. Russell Means, angry over the beating death of Raymond Yellow Thunder in South Dakota, led the group from Seattle to Washington, D.C. Once there Means and other AIM members seized and for eight days occupied the building that housed the Washington Bureau of Indian Affairs. Dennis Banks arranged for files of evidence showing illegal BIA activity to be taken and later published. AIM members ended the occupation when they were allowed to present their Twenty Points to President Richard Nixon and were granted $66,000 to travel home.

In 1973, armed AIM members occupied a church at Wounded Knee in South Dakota (see WOUNDED KNEE (1973)).

An AIM member stands guard at Wounded Knee, South Dakota, 1973. *(AP/Wide World Photos)*

This was near the site where the U.S. Seventh Cavalry had massacred Sioux (Lakota) men, women, and children over 80 years earlier at WOUNDED KNEE (1890). AIM's seizure of the church was the most visible event in a struggle between traditional Lakota and tribal president Richard Wilson, the BIA, and the FBI on the Pine Ridge Reservation. During the occupation, AIM members were joined by, at times, hundreds of supporters from other tribes and non-Indians. The standoff ended after 71 days, on May 8, 1973, when the federal officials agreed to talks. By this time two Indians—Frank Clearwater and Buddy Lamont—had been killed and a federal marshal wounded.

AIM also came to the aid of Lakota at Ogalala, South Dakota, in 1975, when two federal officials were killed after an exchange of fire. AIM members led a movement for the release of Leonard Peltier, one of those accused (and later convicted) in that incident.

The loss of many of its leaders—some went underground, some went to prison, some were killed—weakened AIM. However, the group continues to be active, even though membership has greatly declined because of dissension among the leadership.

American Revolution (1775–1781) *American war for independence against Great Britain*

Participation of American Indians in the Revolutionary War differed from that of previous colonial conflicts. In earlier wars—KING WILLIAM'S WAR (1689–97), QUEEN ANNE'S WAR (1702–13), KING GEORGE'S WAR (1744–48), and the FRENCH AND INDIAN WAR (1754–63)—the Indians often outnumbered the Europeans on whose side they were fighting. In the Revolutionary War, however, Indian warriors serving with American, British, and Canadian troops were a minority. Their battles were more often directed against frontier settlements rather than the enemy's conventional armies.

In the north, Indian-white conflicts centered on New York and Pennsylvania. This was the homeland of the Iroquois (see IROQUOIS CONFEDERACY), longtime allies of the British. The Revolutionary War, however, split the Six Nations. The ONEIDA and the TUSCARORA sided with the American rebels, thanks to the influence of Samuel Kirkland, a Presbyterian minister and teacher, and James Dean, agent to the Tuscarora. On June 12, 1775, the MOHAWK, SENECA, CAYUGA, and ONONDAGA all decided to join the British cause. In turn, traditional rivalries with the Mohawk drove the Mahican into the American camp.

In part this adherence to the British resulted from that nation's promise to enforce the PROCLAMATION OF 1763, which banned further white expansion into Indian lands west of the Appalachian Mountains. The efforts of the Mohawk chief JOSEPH BRANT, brother-in-law of the British Indian agent Sir WILLIAM JOHNSON, also proved crucial. In the fall of 1775, Brant and his Mohawk warriors helped check two American assaults on Montreal. In 1776 General Burgoyne arrived in Quebec, Canada. His command included 9,000 soldiers, which included an Indian auxiliary force composed mainly of Algonquin-speaking men from Canada. The next year the force moved southward to Lake Champlain in an attempt to isolate New England from the other colonies. In 1777 Brant gathered Indian forces to serve as auxiliaries in Major General John Burgoyne's Hudson valley campaign. (see FORT STANWIX and CHERRY VALLEY). Burgoyne used the Indians's ferocious reputation to terrorize the Americans, threatening to unleash the Indians on them if they resisted. Unfortunately for Burgoyne, the Indians proved just as uncontrollable as he had advertised, and in the end they helped unify his colonial enemies by killing several Loyalist settlers, including Jane McCrea, a woman engaged to one of Burgoyne's soldiers. Burgoyne reprimanded the Indians and many of them deserted in response.

Most of the action on the northern frontier after Burgoyne's defeat at Saratoga in September 1777 took the form of the hit-and-run raids in which the Indians excelled. From 1777 through 1779, Brant and Loyalist militia leaders led raids on Patriot settlements in New York's Mohawk River valley, in Pennsylvania's Wyoming valley, and in Cherry Valley (1778). One of the major battles was at ORISKANY CREEK (1777), where an American force that had tried to lift the siege of Fort Stanwix (1777) lost more than half their number in an ambush led by Brant. The Wyoming valley came under assault in late June 1778, when a force of 1,200 Canadian militia and DELAWARE and Seneca Indians killed and mutilated 300 of the 450 American defenders. The assault on Cherry Valley in November 1778 destroyed the entire settlement and brought retaliation from the American forces. In 1779 General George Washington sent a force of 2,500 men under John Sullivan in a raid through Iroquois territory that destroyed about 50 of their villages. This was a particularly brutal campaign—some claim planned as extermination—in which villages of sleeping women and children were burned in the middle of the night, prisoners were tortured, and bodies mutilated. The campaign ended in September, leaving many survivors to starve over the winter because their stores of grain and fruit trees had intentionally been destroyed.

General Sullivan's brutal campaign left the Indians of New York desperate and looking for vengeance. General raiding continued throughout spring and summer 1780. On May 21, 1780, Sir John Johnson organized 400 Tories and 200 Indians to attack Johnstown and then Caughnawaga. Joseph Brant led 500 Indians and Tories in the attack on Canajoharie on August 1 and 2. Johnson, Brant, and Seneca chief Cornplanter joined to descend on the Scoharie Valley on October 15, then continued up the Mohawk Valley, burning everything in their path.

Things turned around that month, however, when Colonel Marius Willett's small force of American militia held out fiercely against a Tory-Indian force under Captain Walter N. Butler. Willett followed Butler's forces as winter began to fall. Low on provisions, a week from Oswego, with winter weather worsening, Willett claimed victory. The defeat of Butler meant the end of major assaults in this area. By the winter of 1781, the Iroquois and Loyalist threat in upstate New York had been largely quelled.

In the west, the SHAWNEE, Wyandot, Mingo, and some CHEROKEE launched raids on white settlements in Kentucky as early as July of 1775. By 1777 the Shawnee chiefs Black Fish and CORNSTALK had unofficially allied themselves with the British and had driven many settlers out of the territory. In the spring of that year they attacked the outposts of Harrodsburg, Boonesboro, and Saint Asaph. GEORGE ROGERS

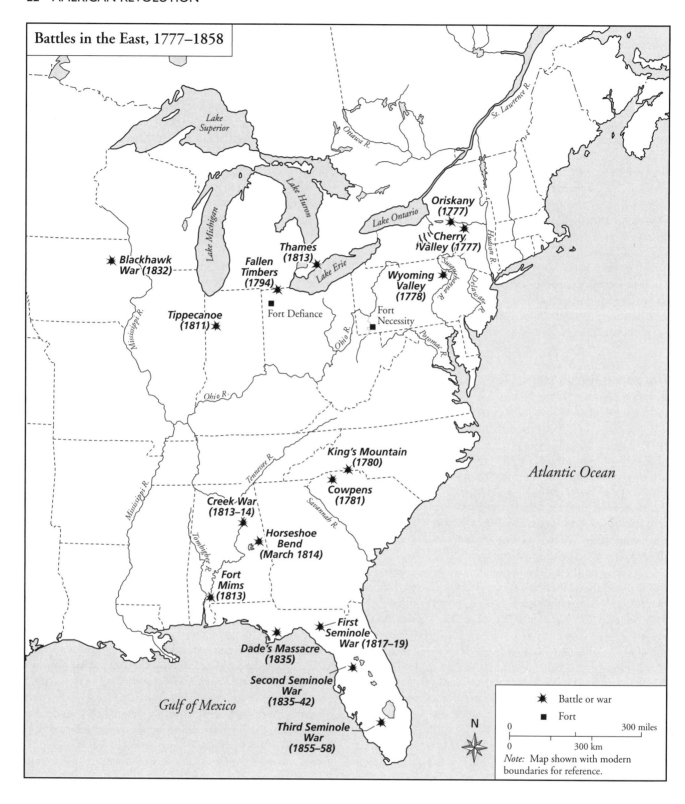

Battles in the East, 1777–1858

CLARK organized the remaining settlers' resistance. He planned a series of attacks on British forts that would relieve Indian pressure on the white frontier settlements. Cornstalk, learning of the plans, traveled to Fort Randolph on the Ohio River to warn the Americans that any invasion of the Ohio Country would lead to massive retaliation by the Shawnee and their allies. The American commander imprisoned Cornstalk, his son Silverheels, and a companion in violation of the flag of truce. The three Indians were later murdered by angry settlers.

Clark assembled a force by the spring of 1778, and during that summer he moved against the British frontier forts of Kaskaskia, Cahokia, and Vincennes. Both Kaskaskia and Cahokia fell to Clark's 175-man militia without a shot. Clark took Vincennes in the early months of 1779 through a trick, or *ruse de guerre*—he convinced the British commander Henry Hamilton that his force was much greater than it really was. So convincing was Clark's acting that some of Hamilton's KICKAPOO and Piankashaw Indian allies deserted him and helped the Americans. The capture of the British frontier forts crippled the Indians' capacity to raid in Kentucky and Ohio. Some members of the LENNI LENAPE (Delaware) tribe left the Ohio Country for good, moving to Canada and to lands west of the Mississippi. Other Indians were spurred to fight more desperately.

By the spring of 1780, the Ohio Country Indians were again attacking American settlements. On June 22, 1780, a combined force of 1,200 Indians, British regulars, and Canadian militia raided the settlement of RUDDELL'S STATION (1780) on the South Licking River. Although John Ruddell surrendered on the promise that his people would be spared, the British were unable to control their Indian allies. The settlers were massacred. In retaliation, Clark launched a campaign against the Shawnee, Mingo, Wyandot, and Lenni Lenape. He cornered them at Piqua Town and inflicted significant casualties. However, the Indians quickly recovered their strength and began raiding the Kentucky settlements again by 1781.

Although Indians in the South outnumbered colonists by a large margin—one contemporary estimated that Cherokees, CREEK, CHOCTAW, and CHICKASAW could have brought 10,000 warriors to help the British—they were never a significant factor in the American Revolution because the British did not use them effectively. When the war broke out, some Cherokee, encouraged by the Shawnee, launched a series of raids on the southern frontier. In August and September 1776, southerners fielded 6,300 militia and drove the Cherokee almost to Florida. Overwhelmed, the Cherokee traded land concessions for peace, signing away most of their territory east of the Blue Ridge Mountains. The Creek and some Cherokee continued to raid frontier settlements until October 7, 1780, when southern soldiers under JOHN SEVIER and Isaac Shelby defeated a strong Tory contingent at Kings Mountain and burned the Indian villages.

Hostilities in the west continued even as the British scaled down the war effort. The Virginia and Kentucky militia, exhausted by the demands of the war, proved unable to cope with the pressure of constant raiding. When the Lenni Lenape launched a particularly brutal series of raids in western Pennsylvania, Colonel David Williamson was dispatched to deal with the situation. Early in 1782, Williamson and 100 troops surrounded a band of peaceful Christian (Moravian) Lenni Lenape Indians at the Ohio mission town of Gnaddenhutten. He took all 90 men, women, and children prisoner and had them executed. The GNADDENHUTTEN MASSACRE (1782) was condemned by the Pennsylvania legislature, but no one took any action against Williamson. When other Lenni Lenape renewed their raids, Colonel William Crawford was dispatched on a second punitive expedition. On June 4, 1782, near the modern town of Sandusky, Ohio, a large band of Shawnee and Lenni Lenape surrounded Crawford's force. Most of the soldiers ran away, but between 40 and 50, including Crawford, were killed or captured. The Indians avenged Gnaddenhutten by torturing Crawford to death. There were several more conflicts in Kentucky, including an American defeat at BLUE LICKS (1782).

Thus the Indians were less of a decisive factor during the American Revolution than they had been during the earlier colonial wars. The British and the Americans were largely unable to organize their Native American allies into effective irregular forces. Also, the frontier had shifted westward, and most of the major American settlements were out of reach of Indian raids. Despite the signing of the TREATY OF PARIS (1783), which officially ended the Revolutionary War, fighting on the western borders continued for years. In the Ohio Valley, for example, conflicts continued through the signing of the TREATY OF GREENVILLE (1795), and, due to the efforts of the Shawnee leader TECUMSEH in the WAR OF 1812 (1812–15), into the early 19th century.

Further Reading

Axelrod, Alan. *Chronicle of the Indian Wars.* New York: Prentice Hall, 1993.
Josephy, Alvin M., Jr. *500 Nations: An Illustrated History of North American Indians.* New York: Alfred A. Knopf, 1994.

Andros, Sir Edmund (1637–1714) *British colonial governor*

Edmund Andros was the first British governor of the colony of New York. He had a significant effect on relations between Native Americans and the English through his intervention in KING PHILIP'S WAR (1675–76) and his role in the creation of the COVENANT CHAIN (1600s). He helped reverse the unfriendly relationship that the Dutch colonists of New Amsterdam had created with the Iroquois (see IROQUOIS CONFEDERACY) and created an alliance with them that kept the French-Canadians out of the New York colony in the late 17th century.

As the representative of the duke of York (later James II), Andros accepted the surrender of the colony from the Dutch in 1674. He exploited the chaos King Philip's War brought to New England in 1675 to advance New York's land claims on territory that belonged to the colony of Connecticut. However, he intervened with the MOHAWK on behalf of the New Englanders, persuading them to attack Philip while he was soliciting their help. He also intervened on behalf of the SUSQUEHANNOCK in the early months of BACON'S REBELLION (1676), offering them shelter from persecution in Maryland and Virginia. During the colonial wars of the late 17th century, he fortified New York's eastern frontier against the French-backed ABENAKI Indians.

Andros was recalled from New York in 1688, when his employer, James II, was driven from the throne.

Antelope Hills (1858) *battle between Comanche on one side and the Texas Rangers along with Native American allies*
The battle of Antelope Hills arose out of an effort by the Texas state government and United States authorities to end the influence of the COMANCHE in Texas. On April 22, 1858, Texas Ranger captain JOHN SALMON FORD, with a force of 102 Rangers and 113 Indians, headed north from Texas into Indian Territory (now Oklahoma). On the evening of May 10, two of Ford's scouts found two Comanche arrowheads. A second scouting mission spotted Comanche hunting buffalo and determined the direction in which the Indians were headed. Ford guessed that a Comanche camp was in the vicinity and determined to attack.

At dawn on May 11, Ford and his men set out to attack the Comanche. They soon found and captured a small Indian encampment near the Canadian River Valley near the Antelope Hills. From that site, near the Antelope Hills, Ford and his men could see a much larger camp across the river. This was Chief Iron Jacket's village. After crossing the river, Ford quickly organized his troops and attacked. Taken by surprise, the approximately 300 Comanche warriors in the camp were not able to mount a successful resistance, and they suffered a major defeat with 76 warriors dead. A second Ranger attack on warriors from another large encampment nearby ended in a Ranger repulse, but without many casualties. Learning of a strong third force of Comanches led by BUFFALO HUMP, Ford ordered his men to withdraw.

See also RUSH SPRINGS.

Apache *linguistically related groups in the Southwest*
The ZUNI Indians of New Mexico called them *Apache* meaning "enemy." Among themselves, however, they were "the people."

The Apache were made up of numerous separate family bands who identified themselves with larger groups who spoke related dialects such as Chiricahua, Mescalero, Jicarilla, Mimbreno, Tonto, White Mountain, and Aravaipa. While these groups shared numerous beliefs, practices, and customs, they were also different in many respects. Groups changed over time and are sometimes known by other names. For example, the San Carlos and White Mountain groups are sometimes together called the Western Apache. Furthermore, the Apache were never united as one people, and suspicion, tension, and even hostilities were known to occur among the groups.

None of the Apachean groups were united under a single chief or political rule. Rather, individual Apache identified themselves with their families, extended families, local groups, bands, or clans. Meanwhile non-Apache often gave names to various Apache groups that they encountered. In order to simplify matters, the following classification by language dialect can be employed (note each of these groups was made up of various bands):

Region	Group
in Arizona	San Carlos
	Aravaipa
	White Mountain
	Northern Tonto
	Southern Tonto
	Cibecue
in Arizona and New Mexico	Chiricahua
	Mimbreno
in New Mexico and Mexico	Mescalero
in Texas and Mexico	Lipan
in New Mexico and Colorado	Jicarilla
in Oklahoma	Kiowa-Apache

During the 1700s and first half of the 1800s the Western and Chiricahua Apache frequently raided neighboring Indian tribes and Mexicans. With the signing of the Treaty of GUADALUPE HIDALGO (1848), the U. S. government tried to stop such activities. This, coupled with an influx of miners, travelers, and settlers into Apache territory, led to the APACHE WARS (1861–86). While the Western Apache did fight their share of battles, it was the Chiricahua who bore the brunt of the action. In the end, Western Apache scouts helped capture the war leader GERONIMO and end the conflict.

To the east the Mescalero frequently fought with the COMANCHE on the Plains and raided the PUEBLO Indians along the Rio Grande and Mexicans to the south. In 1788–89 the Spanish tried to subdue the Mescalero and Lipan. This was followed by a time of peace. During the 1850s the Mescalero raided the white Americans moving into New Mexico. In 1862 General JAMES CARLETON defeated them, and about 400 were moved to BOSQUE REDONDO (a virtual prison camp set up on the Banks of the Rio Grande for Apache and Navajo) where they, in turn, were raided by Navajo.

At one time the Mescalero and Jicarilla had hunted buffalo on the Plains until they were driven west by the Comanche. The Jicarilla alternated between trading with the local Pueblo Indians and raiding them, and they allied themselves with the UTE against the NAVAJO. Meanwhile, the Jicarilla routinely raided Mexican settlements and later the American settlements. The U.S. military finally subdued them when they built a series of forts across Apache land. Between 1853 and 1887 the Jicarilla were relocated eight times as the government tried to decide what to do with them.

The traditional enemies of the Lipan Apache were the Comanche and WICHITA. In 1839 the Lipan allied themselves with the Texans against the Comanche. It was the whites, however, who turned against the Lipan between 1845 and 1856, and consequently drove them into Coahuila, Mexico.

While the group that became known as the Kiowa-Apache spoke an Apachean language, they are remarkable in that they merged with the KIOWA, who spoke a different language entirely. For the most part Kiowa-Apache history coincides with that of the Kiowa.

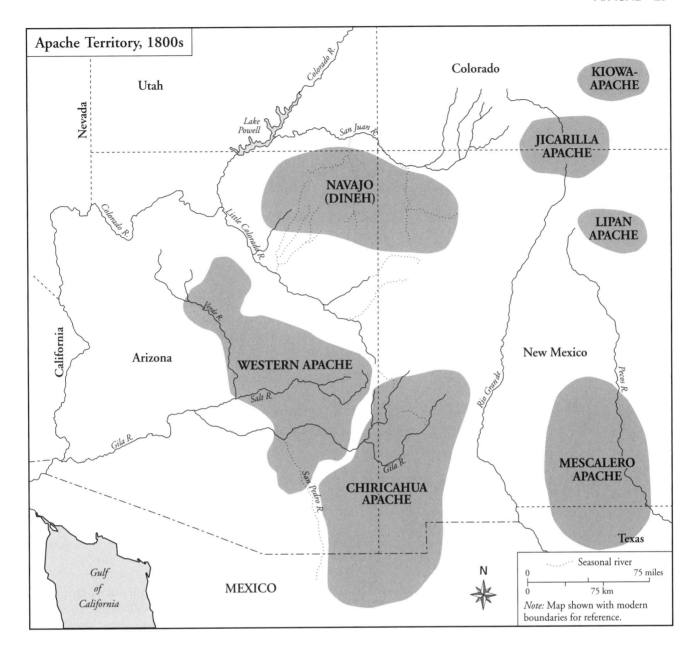

Apache Territory, 1800s

The Apache made a distinction between raiding and warfare. Raiding expeditions were organized for the purpose of stealing goods, especially livestock. When it became obvious that the meat supply was running low, often an older woman would publicly draw attention to that fact. Within a few days an experienced man would agree to lead five to 15 volunteers in a raid. Raiding parties tried to avoid detection and conflict. (Of course, raiding was not the only way the Apache got food; they also hunted, gathered, and grew crops.)

Warfare, or revenge raids, on the other hand, often had as its goal the taking of human life. If an Apache was killed, that deceased person's maternal kinsmen felt obligated to avenge the death. A war leader would recruit up to 200 men from the local group and broad-ranging clan. After dances and speeches they would set out for the enemy. The warriors preferred to attack the settlement where their relative was killed. If this was not possible they would attack people with the same racial and ethnic background as the killer.

When possible, simple tactics were followed. The war leader sent out scouts who located a target. During the night the entire force surrounded the enemy. At dawn they attacked, killing as many of the enemy as possible, capturing livestock, and retreating hastily back home.

During the 1800s, the Apache often found themselves numerically outnumbered by Mexican and U.S. forces, and yet they managed to survive. There are several reasons for this. The Apache were a seminomadic people who raided far and wide. As such they knew the Southwest—the basins and ranges, rivers and water holes—and used this knowledge to their advantage. Next, Apache youth were well trained for the rigors of raiding and warfare. As adults they could travel up to 40 miles a day on foot; easily camouflage themselves; and get by on little food, water, and sleep. Apache employed guerrilla tactics rather than open combat. They would surprise or ambush their enemies, strike hard and fast, and then withdraw. Finally, they usually had a well-thought-out plan of retreat. When withdrawing from a skirmish, the warriors would scatter in different directions, making pursuit nearly impossible. Then they would reassemble and regroup at a prearranged spot.

Historians have often portrayed the Apache as among the most warlike of American Indians. For the Apache, however, warfare was an unpleasant yet necessary task. They fought tenaciously to retain their land and their established way of life.

Further Reading

Aleshire, Peter. *Reaping the Whirlwind. The Apache Wars.* New York: Facts On File, 1998.

Goodwin, Grenville, and Basso, Keith H. *Western Apache Raiding and Warfare: From the Notes of Grenville Goodwin.* Tucson: University of Arizona Press, 1971.

Sturtevant, William C., ed. *Handbook of North American Indians,* Vol. 10, Southwest. Washington, D.C.: Smithsonian Institution, 1983.

— William B. Kessel

Apache war tools like this blade-tipped lance, rawhide sling, and bow served the Apache effectively long after firearms had been introduced by the settlers. *(Courtesy New York Public Library)*

Apache Pass (1862) *Apache ambush in southeastern Arizona of the First California Infantry, a state volunteer regiment*

When the CIVIL WAR (1861–65) erupted, Union soldiers had been manning various posts and forts throughout the Southwest. Soon, many of the soldiers were ordered east to fight, and various posts were abandoned. The APACHE, probably unaware of the Civil War and believing that they were driving the white men out of their territory, stepped up their raids into Mexico and their attacks on white settlements in Arizona and New Mexico. Meanwhile, Confederate troops moved into the Southwest and soon declared a war of extermination against the Indians.

In response to the presence of Confederates in Arizona and New Mexico, and in order to keep the Union transportation lines open to California, a column of Union soldiers led by Colonel JAMES HENRY CARLETON set out westward across southern Arizona. Lieutenant Colonel Edward E. Eyre and 140 men of the First California Cavalry went ahead to reconnoiter. On June 25, 1862, the Union forces encountered Apache near Apache Pass. The Apache, under the protection of a white flag, expressed a desire for friendly relationships. Carleton, hoping to form an alliance with the Apache against the Confederates, sent 122 men from the First California Infantry east from Tucson. Four days later, on July 14, 1862, the soldiers entered Apache Pass. There they were ambushed by the Apache, who attacked the rear of the column and fired from the rocks high above the route. The soldiers, who had marched 40 miles that day without water and were only a half mile from a spring, fought back. The soldiers raised their howitzers and fired into the rocks. The fighting continued for several hours. Before the Indians withdrew, two soldiers were killed and two wounded. Most accounts estimate that the Apache lost about 10 warriors.

The Battle at Apache Pass had a dual significance. First, it brought together various Apache leaders in an alliance against the white soldiers. Present at the battle were COCHISE and MANGAS COLORADAS, who mastermined the affair, as well as VICTORIO and the young GERONIMO. Second, as a result of the battle, Carleton argued that a post had to be built to guard the Apache Pass and to protect the spring. Fort Bowie was built, and it became one of the most important forts during the APACHE WARS (1861–86).

Apache Wars (1861–1886) *series of conflicts fought in the Southwest between Apache and U.S. forces*

For centuries the APACHE have been stereotyped as the most fierce and warlike of all American Indian groups. The very name of one of their leaders, GERONIMO, has become synonymous with daring and almost reckless abandon. As is the case with most stereotypes, however, there is a kernel of truth and much fiction. The Apache were calculating warriors, but they had definite reasons for fighting and raiding, and they felt the sting of battle as acutely as did their opponents.

During the first half of the 1800s various Apache groups raided their Mexican neighbors. Their purpose was strictly economic, to gain livestock and other commodities. In the 1830s the Mexican states of Sonora and Chihuahua sought to stem the tide of raiding by offering pesos for Apache scalps. With the signing of the Treaty of GUADALUPE HIDALGO (1848), the Mexicans turned the "Apache problem" over to the United States. The United States was slow in enforcing the treaty, and for more than a dozen years the Apache continued to raid the Mexicans with virtual impunity. War, however, lay just over the horizon.

In October 1860, a party of Apache raided the John Ward ranch in Arizona territory. They made off with some livestock and a part-Apache, part-Mexican, part-Irish boy named Felix Ward (later known as Mickey Free). The boy's adoptive father John Ward and the army mistakenly blamed the Chiricahua, led by COCHISE. The following February a brash lieutenant named George Bascom and 54 men arranged to parley with Cochise. The unsuspecting Cochise brought his brother, two nephews, a woman, and two children with him. When questioned about the boy, Cochise said he had no idea who had taken him but would try to find out. Bascom seized all seven Apache. Cochise escaped and sent his warriors out to take hostages who would be exchanged for those held by Bascom. Bascom refused the exchange. Finally, Cochise gave up negotiating and killed his hostages; the army retaliated by killing six of their hostages—including Cochise's brother. This led to all-out war.

For a while the advent of the CIVIL WAR (1861–65) limited reprisals. In 1862, however, General JAMES HENRY CARLETON marched troops into the Southwest, prepared to conduct a war of extermination against the Apache. His opponents at this time were MANGAS COLORADAS and Cochise. He met them, along with VICTORIO and young Geronimo in the battle of APACHE PASS (1862), which produced no clear winner.

A year later, gold was discovered near present-day Prescott, Arizona. Soon miners and soldiers began killing the local Western Apache. Not far to the south some settlers poisoned 24 Apache whom they had invited to a meal. Meanwhile General Carleton ordered CHRISTOPHER "KIT" CARSON to subdue the Mescalero Apache who were raiding in southern New Mexico near El Paso. After relentless pursuit they yielded and were moved to BOSQUE REDONDO, where they were joined by the NAVAJO who had come there on what is known as the LONG WALK.

As hostilities in Arizona increased, the military built a string of forts near and in Apache territory to prevent raids into Mexico and to protect white settlers. Thought was not given,

however, to protecting the Apache. In 1871 Chief Eskiminizin and 300 Apache settled peacefully near CAMP GRANT (1871). There, in an unprovoked attack, 117 of their number, mostly women and children, were massacred by a group of vigilantes from Tucson. In response to the atrocity, the U.S. government established a peace policy. In order to promote peace and "civilization," the roving bands of Apache were located on reservations where they were promised subsistence, supplies, and protection as long as they remained friendly. Meanwhile, General GEORGE CROOK assumed command of the military in Arizona and with cavalry and scouts set out after the Chiricahua. When Tonto Apache and YAVAPAI began raiding near Prescott, Crook turned his attention to them and subdued them by April 1873 (see also SKELETON CAVE).

In time the Camp Grant reservation was closed and the Indians living there were moved to San Carlos. In 1874 the other three reservations were closed and the government called for the concentration of all Western Apache, Chiricahua Apache, and Yavapai on the single reservation at San Carlos. By 1877 more than 5,000 Indians were confined at San Carlos. The one-reservation system was fraught with problems. Various Apache groups as well as Indians from other tribes were forced together. Some of these groups previously had been hostile to one another. Mistrust, disease, hunger, boredom, loss of reservation land, and the military presence made reservation life unbearable for some. Consequently Victorio, JUH, Geronimo, and others bolted from the reservation with their followers, all looking for food or freedom.

By the end of the 1870s, some of the Apache were relocated to a reservation near Camp Apache, later FORT APACHE. In 1881 a respected medicine man named Noche-del-klinne began attracting adherents to his new religion, which promised the return of dead chiefs and the removal of white people from Apache territory. A detachment of soldiers was sent to arrest him, and the battle of CIBECUE CREEK (1881) ensued, resulting in eight white and 18 Apache deaths. A month later, Geronimo, Juh, Naiche (Nachez, Nachise), Chato, and about 74 followers escaped from the San Carlos Reservation and headed for Mexico. Thus began GERONIMO'S REBELLION (1881–86).

Meanwhile on July 6, 1882, a group of White Mountain Apache under the leadership of Natiotish struck at San Carlos and then throughout central Arizona. They were finally located by AL SIEBER and defeated in the battle of BIG DRY WASH (1882).

Between 1881 and 1886, Geronimo led small groups of Apache throughout Arizona, New Mexico, and Mexico. He was pursued by and twice surrendered to General George Crook. On September 4, 1886, Geronimo surrendered for the last time, to General NELSON A. MILES. With that, the Apache Wars came to a close.

In retrospect it is clear why the Apache Wars were fought. Over the centuries the Apache had established a particular way of life that included hunting, gathering, farming, and raiding. Their numbers were few, yet they required large expanses of land. Then, in less than four decades, this lifestyle was totally disrupted by encroaching armies of miners, travelers, and settlers looking for a new starts and prosperity. Both the Apache and the newcomers required the same land. Conflict was inevitable.

Further Reading

Thrapp, Dan L. *The Conquest of Apacheria.* Norman: University of Oklahoma Press, 1967.

Adams, Alexander B. *Geronimo: A Biography.* New York: Da Capo Press, 1971.

— William B. Kessel

Arapaho (*Inuna-ina,* "Our People"; *Kananavich,* "Buffalo Path People") *Algonquian-speaking people who arrived on the northern plains from the northeastern woodlands during prehistory*

The Arapaho and their CHEYENNE allies regularly fought territorial battles with the UTE, PAWNEE, and SHOSHONE. By 1804

This group of young Indians were members of the Arapaho, a prominent Plains Indian tribe often allied with the Cheyenne. *(By permission of the Colorado Historical Society)*

the Cheyenne and Arapaho controlled much of Colorado and southern Wyoming.

In 1835, the Arapaho separated into northern and southern divisions yet remained one closely associated people. The military expeditions of Generals ALFRED SULLY and HENRY SIBLEY cemented an Arapaho-Cheyenne-LAKOTA (see SIOUX [Dakota, Lakota, Nakota]) alliance and brought war to the northern plains. At this time, the southern Arapaho were peaceful. Encroaching white settlements, however, were pushing the Arapaho off their land. Colorado citizens sought the removal of the Indians from their territory. Colorado governor JOHN EVANS favored war and, with Colonel JOHN M. CHIVINGTON, sought justification for entering battle. In 1864 a report of cattle-rustling Indians led to the massacre SAND CREEK (1864) and the CHEYENNE ARAPAHO WAR (1864–65). With the MEDICINE LODGE TREATIES (1867) and the FORT LARAMIE TREATY (1868), those who signed from both Arapaho divisions agreed to accept reservations. Many bands, however, refused reservation life and continued to resist white domination as during the RED RIVER WAR (1874–75). The southern Arapaho declared peace. The northern Arapaho also despairingly resigned themselves to reservation life. The southern Arapaho were located on a reservation along with Southern Cheyenne by virtue of the Medicine Lodge Treaty of 1867. The northern Arapaho resisted confinement on a reservation until 1878. Their last faint hope for resurgence appeared suddenly with the GHOST DANCE in 1890, but it quickly disappeared and the Arapaho began to adopt white customs and ways of living.

Arikara (Arikaree, Ree) *linguistically, the northernmost Caddoan-speaking tribe*

The Arikara separated from the PAWNEE and migrated to the upper Missouri River in Dakota Territory. Eventually, they merged culturally with their Siouan-speaking neighbors, the Hidatsa and MANDAN. The three tribes (known subsequently as the Three Affiliated Tribes) formed a military alliance against the Lakota (see SIOUX) and other enemies.

Jean-Baptiste Truteau, a trader who wintered with the Arikara in 1795–96, observed that they were "of a rather gentle nature" and exhibited no animosity toward whites. They are also mentioned in the journals of the 1803–04 Lewis and Clark expedition. As settlers moved west, conflict rose. In 1823, 13 people in a trading party were killed by Arikara. Until mid-century, the Arikara killed numerous non-Indians and became known among traders and trappers as the "Horrid Tribe." Exposure to diseases brought by non-Indians caused great suffering during this period.

After the Arikara signed the FORT LARAMIE TREATY (1851), they maintained peace with non-Indians. The Arikara played an important role as scouts for the U.S. Army during the Indian campaigns of the late 1800s.

artillery, use of *application of technology to tactics in Indian warfare*

The best way to summarize the use of artillery in Indian warfare is that non-Indians had artillery and Indians did not. Many European and U.S. military posts boasted cannons, which proved particularly useful in defense. These weapons—especially the U.S. Army's twelve-pound "mountain howitzers," and lightweight Hotchkiss "mountain guns"—often accompanied offensive operations as well. Their long range and accurate firing occasionally proved an important advantage, such as at LAKE GEORGE (1755), in the siege of the NEZ PERCE (1877), and at WOUNDED KNEE (1890). Artillery was the most dramatic example of the non-Indian technological advantage in warfare over the Indian.

Ash Hollow   See BLUEWATER CREEK.

Assiniboine *tribes originally concentrated near the Lake of the Woods in present-day southern Ontario*

By 1640, the Assiniboine had separated from their relatives the Yanktonai Lakota (see SIOUX [Dakota, Lakota, Nakota]), and formed a lasting alliance with the CREE, who armed them. By 1837 the Assiniboine were established on the northern plains as nomadic hunters. Their territory stretched from the upper Missouri to the Saskatchewan River and from James Bay to the Rocky Mountains. Edwin Denig, trader and Indian agent, estimated their population at 1,200 lodges. A smallpox epidemic on the upper Missouri in 1837–38 decimated the tribe to one-third its former size.

The Assiniboine fought with a great many of the tribes of the upper Missouri River region. The vast horse herds of the BLACKFOOT and Lakota were primary enemies of the Assiniboine. The FORT LARAMIE TREATY (1851) did not end warfare among the tribes. During the NEZ PERCE WAR (1877), NEZ PERCE messengers seeking asylum for their people with SITTING BULL's band in Canada were murdered by the Assiniboine before reaching Canada. Some Assiniboine worked as army scouts, including those in 1885 who helped the Canadian North West Field Force track down renegade Cree during the Second RIEL REBELLION. The Assiniboine were noted for their friendliness toward non-Indians and never fought the U.S. Army.

Atkinson, Henry (1782–1842) *army officer and explorer involved in the Black Hawk War (1832)*

Born in North Carolina to a prominent local politician and farmer, Atkinson was commissioned a captain in the regular army in 1808. He participated in the WAR OF 1812 in campaigns against the British, emerging from that conflict a colonel. In 1825, Atkinson, fellow commissioner Benjamin O'Fallon, and 450 soldiers proceeded up the Missouri River as the Yellowstone Expedition, negotiating 12 treaties with 16 different Indian groups. These agreements, however, had little lasting impact upon U.S.-Indian relations.

In August 1831, Atkinson was ordered to head off the continuing intertribal warfare between the Lakota (see SIOUX [Dakota, Lakota, Nakota]) and Menominee and the Sac and

Fox. The previous month a group of Sac and Fox warriors led by BLACK HAWK had surprised an unarmed camp of Menominee in Illinois and killed 28. This massacre had been carried out in revenge for the killing of Fox chiefs by the Lakota and Menominee in the prior year. Whites in Illinois were convinced that they would be next and demanded the federal government stop the intertribal warfare. General Atkinson was ordered to prevent the Lakota and Menominee from exacting revenge on the Sac and Fox. Fearing that his small force would be unable to handle the situation, Atkinson asked the governor of Illinois to supply a mounted militia. This proved to be a mistake. Traveling faster than Atkinson's soldiers, the undisciplined volunteers reached Black Hawk's group first and killed an Indian party carrying a white flag. Black Hawk consequently attacked, thus beginning the BLACK HAWK WAR. Atkinson slowly pursued Black Hawk and his band of around 2,000, catching up with them at the mouth of the Bad Axe River, where most of the band was killed. Black Hawk escaped but was later captured.

Contemporaries criticized Atkinson for not having secured Black Hawk's defeat much sooner, but Atkinson's performance in this conflict was not indicative of most of the rest of his military career. Troops under his command built several of the army's most important western forts during the first half of the century—Atkinson (Council Bluffs, Iowa), Leavenworth (Kansas), and Jefferson Barracks (Missouri). A competent bureaucrat and policeman who usually managed to secure the government's goals through negotiations, he went on to oversee the removal of several tribes, including the Potawatomi and the Winnebago, to Iowa. He died at Jefferson Barracks.

Augusta Treaty (1783) *treaty between the state of Georgia and the Creek Indians*

The Augusta Treaty was one of a series of three treaties ratified between representatives of the CREEK Nation and the state of Georgia at the conclusion of the AMERICAN REVOLUTION (1775–83). The Creek had nominally supported the British during the Revolution, but as a whole they had taken little part in the hostilities, unlike other southern tribes such as the CHOCTAW and the CHEROKEE. Nonetheless, in 1783 the Creek had to negotiate with the victorious Americans. Since the Creek had been allies of the British, the Americans demanded large land concessions—amounting to most of the Creek lands in what is now Georgia. The treaty was opposed by the Creek leader ALEXANDER McGILLIVRAY, who was part Scottish, part French, and part Creek. McGillivray repudiated the treaty, and

the following year—in an effort to prevent further losses of land to the Americans—he signed a treaty placing his people under the protection of Spain.

Autossee (1813) *attack on Creek Indian village during the Creek War (1813–1814)*

In November 1813, a force of 940 men of the Georgia militia, led by General John Floyd, launched an attack into CREEK territory in present-day Alabama. The assault was part of a U.S. campaign to put down an uprising by the Upper Creek or RED STICKS, an anti-American faction of Creek determined to fight the incursions of settlers into their territory. Included in General Floyd's force were several hundred Lower Creek or White Sticks, the pro-American faction of the Creek nation that favored accommodation with non-Indians in order to survive. Crossing the Chattahoochee River into the Mississippi Territory, Floyd's force came upon the Upper Creek village of Autossee on the Tallapoosa River. On November 29, the militia and pro-American Creek attacked the village. The village was burned, the people driven out, and 200 Upper Creek were killed.

See also CREEK WAR.

Awashonks (Squaw Sachem of the Sakonnet) (17th century) *colonial ally in King Philip's War*

Awashonks was one of at least three women chieftains in New England at the time of KING PHILIP'S WAR (1675–76). She succeeded her husband as sachem of the Sakonnet (Saconnet) Indians of Rhode Island after he was killed by neighboring NARRAGANSETT Indians. In 1671, Awashonks, along with as many warriors as she could persuade, agreed to cease the Sakonnet's long-standing war against the English and entered into a nonaggression pact with colonial authorities. Four years later, however, she succumbed to the initial successes of Philip (METACOM)—sachem of the WAMPANOAG, who attempted to drive the English from New England during King Philip's War—and allowed some of her warriors to join him in his war against the English. This alliance, however, lasted only about one year. By 1676, Awashonks met with Captain BENJAMIN CHURCH and agreed to return to peace. She allied her tribe with the English, even contributing warriors to English expeditions against Philip. In return, the English agreed that she and all her people would be spared retribution.

See also WOMAN WARRIORS.

B

Bacon, Nathaniel (1647–1676) *British dissident and Indian fighter during Bacon's Rebellion*

Nathaniel Bacon came from a wealthy family and had attended Cambridge University in England. After he lost most of his money, his family sent him to Virginia in 1673 in the hope that he could recoup his fortunes. Because of his social standing, Bacon received a position on the Virginia governing council. However, the Virginian governor WILLIAM BERKELEY (whose wife was Bacon's cousin) opposed Bacon's rough treatment of the local Indians. In the fall of 1675, Berkeley reprimanded Bacon for his treatment of some Appomattox Indians whom Bacon believed had been stealing corn. In the spring of 1676, after disagreements with Berkeley over the opening of Indian lands to settlers, Bacon helped launch the struggle that became known as BACON'S REBELLION.

The rebellion had its roots in most frontier families' belief that they were being oppressed by a rich tidewater aristocracy. Virginia's major cash crop was tobacco, and tobacco prices had recently fallen, forcing many small farmers to sell their lands. These dispossessed small farmers also resented Berkeley's program of fort-building on the Virginia frontier—a program that was paid for with their taxes and, they felt, intended to keep them from moving into new lands farther west. Bacon and his followers felt that by killing Indians—whether friendly or unfriendly—they opened more land for poor frontier families.

After Governor Berkeley denied his request of a commission in the local militia, Bacon had himself named general of a group of volunteer Indian fighters who began attacking local Indians to drive them out of the region. Declaring Bacon a rebel, Berkeley promised lenient treatment to him and his men if they gave up their vigilantism. Bacon was pacified long enough to attend the June session of the Virginia governing council, but when the council again refused Bacon's demands his armed band seized the statehouse. Having effectively stripped Berkeley of power, Bacon and his supporters made war on the Indians and menaced Jamestown for the next 15 months, eventually burning the town. The rebellion continued until Bacon's death from dysentery in October 1676. Bacon's attitudes toward Native Americans prefigured those of many later frontiersmen: any Indian was a potential threat and should be killed at the earliest opportunity.

Bacon's Rebellion (1676) *first major conflict between settlers and Native Americans in Virginia since the second Powhatan War (1644–1646)*

In many ways, Bacon's Rebellion reflected the fears raised by the contemporary KING PHILIP'S WAR (1675–76) in New England. Virginia's Governor WILLIAM BERKELEY followed a policy of separating settlers from Indians, each keeping to their own lands. However, as more people crowded into Virginia, the policy became harder to enforce. In response to violence against settlers on the Virginia frontier, NATHANIEL BACON and his followers launched an all-out campaign, rioting against the established landowners who controlled the colonial government and killing Indians in Virginia indiscriminately.

After the 1646 treaty that ended the second POWHATAN WAR, the British agreed to reserve all lands north of the York River and south of the Rappahannock River for displaced tribes. As more settlers came to the colony, however, land became scarcer. Virginia's major cash crop, tobacco, quickly exhausted the soil. Plantation owners looked for new lands in order to maintain their production. In addition, the IROQUOIS CONFEDERACY, which maintained a monopoly on the fur trade in Pennsylvania and New York, began pushing tribes people out of their own territories. These tribes sought refuge farther south, which led to further conflicts between settlers and the Native Americans in Virginia.

In July 1675, members of the NANTICOKE, or Doeg, tribe killed a white man, Robert Hen, in a dispute over money. They then fled north of the Potomac to Maryland. Vigilantes pursued them over the river and killed several of them, as well as some uninvolved SUSQUEHANNOCK tribespeople. The following month, in response to a complaint by the Maryland government, Governor Berkeley ordered a commission to investigate the incident. Instead, the commission called out the local militia, surrounded the Susquehannock in one of their forts, and killed several of them out of hand. The remaining Indians took revenge on settlers in the area the following January.

At that point, Nathaniel Bacon emerged as the leader of the militant settlers. Bacon came to Virginia in 1673 in hopes of rebuilding his fortune. His cousin's husband, Governor Berkeley, appointed Bacon to a position on the colonial council but refused him a license to trade with the Indians. After the January incident, Bacon demanded reprisals against the Susquehannock on behalf of the settlers living on the western frontier. Berkeley refused, declaring that such a war would only add to Virginia's tax burden. Bacon, in turn, accused Berkeley of being more interested in protecting his monopoly on trade with the Indians than in saving settlers' lives.

Bacon next formed a vigilante group of more than 1,000 men and began terrorizing the local Indians. He drove the PAMUNKEY out of their own territory and occupied their land. In May 1676 he encouraged the Occoneechee tribe to kill some local Susquehannock, then turned on the Occoneechee themselves and massacred them. Because Bacon's actions had destabilized the situation, the governor declared him to be in rebellion. Berkeley sent militiamen out to capture the rebels and summoned a new assembly to meet at Jamestown in June 1676. Although Berkeley tried to win favor with the backwoodsmen by extending the vote to all free men, the assembly supported Bacon's anti-Indian policy to the extent of requiring the disarmament of the local Native peoples and allowing them to be enslaved.

Bacon moved quickly against Governor Berkeley. During the summer of 1676, he seized Jamestown, burned the major buildings, and chased Berkeley across Chesapeake Bay. After that the rebellion lost momentum. With no Indians to kill, Bacon's vigilantes began to return home to bring in their harvests. In addition, the British government responded to Berkeley's reports by sending 1,100 troops to help put down the rebellion. The most decisive event, however, was Bacon's death from dysentery in October 1676.

The royal investigators who arrived with the troops denounced the behavior of Bacon's followers and agreed that the Indians had been defrauded of their land rights. They ordered that all prisoners should be returned to their own tribes. However, they were more interested in maintaining King Charles II's tax revenues on tobacco than with securing justice for the Indians. They removed Berkeley from office, stating that his policies had helped spark the rebellion. Finally, they negotiated a treaty that brought peace between the scattered remnants of the POWHATAN CONFEDERACY and the Virginians.

Further Reading

Rountree, Helen C. *Pocohontas's People: The Powhatan Indians of Virginia through Four Centuries.* Norman: University of Oklahoma Press, 1990.

Bad Axe (1832) *bloody encounter between Chief Black Hawk, leader of the Sac and Fox Indians, and U.S. troops during the Black Hawk War (1831)*

In 1829, non-Indian squatters invaded Sac leader BLACK HAWK's village, Saukenuk, while he and his followers were away on their winter hunt. When he returned, the squatters refused to leave. The two groups shared the village until spring 1831, when tensions became too high.

State militia were called in and began shelling the town, only to find that Black Hawk and his people had escaped during the night. The fleeing Indians spent the spring and early summer hiding from militia and gathering followers, among the WINNEBAGO (including their prophet White Cloud), and POTAWATOMI, and KICKAPOO.

In late July, a combined military force under Colonel Henry Dodge and General James Henry engaged Black Hawk's warriors at WISCONSIN HEIGHTS (1832). A number of Indians were killed, and the rest fled across the Mississippi.

Black Hawk decided to head toward the confluence of the Mississippi and the Bad Axe Rivers. On August 1–2, 1832, the Indian leader attempted to surrender. Black Hawk sent 150 of his men under a flag of truce to speak to the U.S. soldiers. Brevet Major General WINFIELD SCOTT, commander of the U.S. troops, had at his disposal a steamboat named the *Warrior,* which he had armed with cannon. When the soldiers saw the large band of approaching Indians, they panicked and shots were fired. In response, Black Hawk ordered his warriors to attack the vessel they called the "fire canoe." During the ensuing action, Black Hawk lost 23 warriors; he thereupon broke off the fighting and persuaded only 50 followers to head north. At almost the same time, the *Warrior* broke in retreat, as it was running dangerously low on firewood for its boilers.

On August 3, General HENRY ATKINSON and 1,300 reinforcements caught up with the Indians who had remained near the Mississippi River banks, and began firing on the Indians. When the fighting was over, some 300 Indians, including many women and children had been killed. Some of the casualties had been killed by Dakota (see SIOUX [Dakota, Lokota, Nakota]) warriors as they reached the far side of the river. Black Hawk, White Cloud, and their followers sought refuge among the Winnebago, but eventually were persuaded to surrender on August 27. In 1832 certain Winnebago signed a treaty ceding a portion of their land. In partial payment for this, the tribe was granted a reservation along the west bank of the Mississippi River later under great pressure and duress. They ceded their remaining lands in Wisconsin.

Baker, Eugene M. (1837–1884) *U.S. Army officer known for his operations against Indians in the Northwest*

Born in New York State, Baker graduated from West Point and was commissioned a brevet lieutenant colonel with the Army of the Potomac. Appointed a major in the reduced post–Civil War army, Baker proved an energetic field commander in operations against Indians in Oregon, Idaho, and Montana. Ordered to punish the Piegan, in January 1870 he mistook the camp of Heavy Runner, whose followers had remained largely at peace with the whites, for that of the more hostile Mountain Chief. Baker's command slaughtered the surprised villagers in the massacre at MARIAS RIVER (1870). One scout later claimed that Baker had been drinking heavily throughout the campaign. Known thereafter as "Piegan Baker" among army circles, even the resolute support of PHILIP SHERIDAN could not protect him from blistering civilian criticism. Baker increasingly sought solace from the bottle and allowed his command to be surprised by a SIOUX war party while escorting railroad surveyors in 1872. Despite such problems he remained in the army until his death in 1884.

Baker Massacre   See MARIAS RIVER.

Banks, Dennis (1937–   ) *Anishinabe (Chippewa, Ojibwa) leader and activist*

Dennis Banks was born on April 12, 1937, on the Leech Lake Reservation in Minnesota. Educated in white boarding schools, he served in the U.S. Air Force and eventually moved to Minneapolis in the late 1950s. Banks had difficulty finding work, and in 1966 he was jailed for burglarizing a grocery store. Released in 1968, he took a new direction as cofounder of the AMERICAN INDIAN MOVEMENT (AIM) in July 1968. A year later, to draw attention to the plight of Indians, Banks and other AIM leaders occupied Alcatraz Island, in San Francisco Bay, California, claiming it as Native American territory. The occupation lasted for almost two years. In the fall of 1972, in protest against the policies of the BUREAU OF INDIAN AFFAIRS, Banks led about 500 demonstrators into the bureau's offices in Washington, D.C., and took control of the building for five days.

The actions of Banks and other Indian leaders culminated in 1973 with AIM's 71-day occupation of WOUNDED KNEE in South Dakota. Banks was tried for his part in Wounded Knee (1973) but the charges were dismissed. In August 1975, however, Banks was convicted in another trial on charges having to do with an incident at the Custer, South Dakota, courthouse that had preceded Wounded Knee. Fearing for his life in custody, Banks fled in 1975. In 1976, California governor Jerry Brown refused to extradite Banks to South Dakota; Banks lived in exile for nearly eight years. In 1984 he turned himself in and was sentenced to three years in prison. Paroled in December 1985, Banks moved to Newport, Kentucky, where he founded a group called Sacred Run. Its members are dedicated to spreading the message of the sacredness of all life.

Bannock *a division of the Northern Paiute that migrated from western Oregon into Idaho where they became close allies of the Shoshone when they acquired horses in the 1700s*

Following a path similar to that of the SHOSHONE, the Bannock left behind the difficult existence of a food-gathering economy for more plentiful life of the Plains buffalo culture. Brush- and grass-constructed wickiups gave way to buffalo skin tipis. Rabbit fur coverings were exchanged for buffalo robes. Wild produce and small game were replaced by an abundance of buffalo meat. Although they merged culturally with the Shoshone, they maintained their dialect of the Paiute language.

Throughout the 1850s and 1860s, continuous streams of white emigrants decimated wildlife and plant life along an ever broadening swath on either side of the Oregon Trail. Mushrooming non-Indian settlements brought destruction of buffalo and other wild game, as well as domestic livestock whose grazing and hooves destroyed edible vegetation and food roots eaten by the Indians. As a result, Indians living in areas exploited by non-Indians experienced virtual starvation.

During the 1850s, the Shoshone, the Bannock, and the Paiute waged guerrilla-style assaults against travelers and settlers in order to obtain food and horses. In March 1862, the Bannock, Shoshone, and other tribes launched an all-out war effort, which became known as the SHOSHONE WAR (1862–63). The Bannock-Shoshone defeat in January at BEAR RIVER (1863) was a turning point in the war. By October all the allied tribes and bands had ceased fighting. They signed treaties that allowed peaceful travel through the area, construction of railroads, and settlement on a reservation around Fort Hall, Idaho. In exchange, the United States pledged annuities in goods and food. Following the SNAKE WAR (1866–68), the Bannock signed a treaty at Fort Bridger, Utah, that guaranteed, among other things, the rights to gather their primary staple, camas roots, from the Camas Prairie.

Although the United States neglected its treaty responsibilities, the Bannock lived peacefully, even supplying the U.S. Army with scouts during the NEZ PERCE WAR (1877). The following year, however, the Bannock found themselves in circumstances similar to those faced by the NEZ PERCE and, like the Nez Perce, they fought their own conflict with the U.S. Army. The BANNOCK WAR (1878), also involving the Northern Paiute, erupted because of the continued destruction of the camas roots by white ranchers' hogs. The war began on May 30, 1878, when a Bannock warrior shot and wounded two whites during a heated argument. With the surrender of Paiute Chief Oytes on August 12 and the capture of 131 Bannock warriors, the war was over. After spending the winter as prisoners, the Bannock returned to their reservation in the summer of 1879 and lived in peace. Meanwhile some of the Bannock who did not surrender sought refuge among the Sheepeaters in the Salmon River mountains of Idaho (see SHEEPEATER WAR of 1879).

Bannock Treaty (1868) *agreement between the U.S. government and the Bannock and Shoshone Indians of Idaho*

The 1868 Bannock Treaty was the second treaty the U.S. government signed with the BANNOCK and SHOSHONE Indians of Idaho. The first treaty, signed in 1863, was never ratified. The 1868 treaty, negotiated at Fort Bridger, Wyoming, established the Wind River Reservation in Wyoming and the Fort Hall Reservation in eastern Idaho.

Bannock War (1878) *conflict over Bannock and Paiute resistance to settlement on Idaho's Camas Prairie*

The Bannock War, fought from June to August 1878, was caused by BANNOCK resistance to being moved by the U.S. government to a reservation on the Camas Prairie in Idaho. At the Camas Prairie reservation, hogs that white settlers had brought to the area were destroying camas roots, the staple diet of the Bannock, and the government had failed to supply the Indians with an alternative food source. In an already tense situation, a Bannock shot and wounded two white men on May 30, 1878. Certain they would be punished for the action of one member of their tribe, Bannock leader Chief Buffalo Horn and his followers left their reservation on June 5 to go on a large plundering raid. Soon they were joined by discontented Paiute from the Malheur Reservation, Oregon.

White settlers fled before the Bannock-Paiute coalition and sought protection at Camp Harney, home to a company from the 21st Infantry Regiment. Volunteers from nearby Silver City killed Buffalo Horn in a June 8 skirmish. As the garrison at Camp Harney could do little more than try to defend the settlers, Brigadier General OLIVER O. HOWARD began assembling reinforcements. In mid-June, SARAH WINNEMUCCA, the daughter of a Paiute chief, undertook a final peace mission in talks with the new Bannock war leader, Egan. Unfortunately, the talks failed, so warriors on both sides broke camp. On June 23, a cavalry column led by Captain Reuben F. Bernard swept through the Indian village at Silver Creek. Casualties were light, but Bernard's troopers destroyed invaluable stores of supplies. As the pursuit continued, a pitched battle at Birch Creek on July 8 drove the Bannock and Paiute farther south.

Other columns, led by Howard and Captain Evan Miles, were also converging on the fleeing Indians. Egan, who had been wounded at Silver Creek, was killed by Umatilla Indians, angry at the intrusion by the Bannock and Paiute upon their reservation. Their coalition now shattered, many of the remaining Bannock fled east, one group being cornered in the mountains east of Yellowstone National Park. The most militant Paiute, led by Oytes, surrendered on August 12. The final engagement came in Wyoming on September 12 between a small party of Bannock and their pursuing soldiers.

In all, 731 Bannock and Paiute turned themselves in. The Bannock were ultimately returned to their reservation near the agency at Fort Hall, Idaho. The Paiute were moved to the Yakima Reservation, Washington.

Barboncito (Daghaai, "the one with the mustache"; Hastin Dagha or Hastin Daagi, "the man with the mustache"; Bislahalani, "the orator"; Hozhooji Naata, "blessing speaker"; Hashke yichi Dahilwo, "he is anxious to run at warriors")

(ca. 1820–1871) *Navajo ceremonial singer and war chief who played a prominent role in the Navajo War (1863–1864)*

As an adult he was short, slight, and sported a mustache, and so he was called by the Spanish name Barboncito, "little bearded one." Born in Canyon de Chelly, his NAVAJO names reveal that he was a religious singer among his people, leader of a tribal group, and a prominent figure in war and peace negotiations with non-Indians.

By the mid-1800s, the Navajo and U.S. military were on a collision course. In 1860, an incident occurred in which soldiers at Fort Defiance, Arizona Territory, killed some Navajo horses in a dispute over grazing rights. Barboncito joined militant MANUELITO in the battle of FORT DEFIANCE (1860), where the former was wounded. However, Barboncito sought peace, and in 1862 he joined 17 prominent chiefs in a trip to Santa Fe, New Mexico, seeking an alternative to war. General JAMES H. CARLETON bluntly refused to believe their promises and peace overtures. In April 1863, he told Barboncito that the Navajo only alternative to war was to relocate the entire tribe to BOSQUE REDONDO in eastern New Mexico. Carleton ordered the Navajo to surrender by July 20, 1863, but Barboncito refused.

After the deadline came and went unheeded, Carleton sent a regiment led by CHRISTOPHER ("KIT") CARSON after the Navajo. By that winter Carleton's tactic of destroying the Indians' food supply was working. Navajo began to surrender rather than starve. The LONG WALK of the prisoners led to Bosque Redondo, where the conditions were deplorable and many Navajo died. Meanwhile, Barboncito remained at large and continued to resist.

In September 1864, Barboncito was captured in Canyon de Chelly and taken to Bosque Redondo. Within a year he escaped with 500 followers and rejoined the resistance. In November 1866 Barboncito was forced to surrender a second time. Two years later, he and other chiefs were permitted to make a trip to Washington, D.C., to inform President Andrew Johnson of the plight of the Indians at Bosque Redondo. Barboncito and the chiefs prevailed. A peace commissioner visited Bosque Redondo and was appalled at the conditions. During the treaty negotiations that ultimately permitted the Navajo to return home, Barboncito emerged as the principal spokesperson.

In 1868, the Navajo were allowed to go home to a reservation in the Chuska Mountains of present-day Arizona and New Mexico. There the Indian agent appointed Barboncito as head chief of the Navajo. He died three years later, in 1871.

See also NAVAJO WAR.

Barnwell, John ("Tuscarora John") (1671–1724)
South Carolina militia officer and colonial agent known for his victories won against the Tuscarora
Born in Ireland, John Barnwell immigrated to South Carolina, where he held a number of government posts. He also served in the military against the French in QUEEN ANNE'S WAR (1702–13).

In the fall of 1711, spurred by territorial encroachment and British traders selling Indians into slavery, the TUSCARORA began attacking white settlements in North Carolina. The following year Barnwell led 30 militiamen and 500 Indian allies— mostly YAMASEE—to help put down the rebellion. He won two quick victories, the most significant at NOHOROCA (1713), where he burned an Indian fort and killed hundreds of Tuscarora, after which the tribe sued for peace. It was during this time that he earned his nickname, "Tuscarora John." Barnwell later fought against his former allies, the Yamasee, in the YAMASEE WAR (1715–28).

battle-ax *handheld weapon wielded by Native Americans in battle*
Battle-ax is the general term used by whites for the axlike weapon that Indians wielded in close combat. It generally consisted of a wooden handle with a head of wood, stone, or metal.

Battle-axes figure prominently in this stereotyped depiction of "savage" Indians fighting terrified troops. Like most real-life troops, those depicted are better armed than their Native American adversaries. *(Courtesy New York Public Library)*

Other terms for the ax are *WAR CLUB*, *belt ax*, *squaw ax* (used by the Iroquois), and *TOMAHAWK*.

battle talismans *charms, jewelry, or personal possessions believed to contribute to success in battle*

Battle talismans—objects that were believed to give their holder good luck in warfare—were of two types: personal and group. Personal talismans were intended to protect the bearer from death in battle and to contribute to his success. These could include such items as seeds, feathers, and fur from a bird or animal (eagle, king-bird, otter, and weasel were all popular), or significant images (of stars, the sun, or animals), usually carried by a warrior or displayed on his body. The talismans were a sign of the personal devotion between the individual warrior and his guardian spirits. Apache warriors wore necklaces of shells and stones interwoven with eagle feathers to ensure success in battle. The special Ghost Shirts worn by adherents of the GHOST DANCE religion of the 1890s were covered with images of stars, buffalo, and birds and were supposed to have the power to stop bullets.

Battle talismans could also have a less spiritual significance. According to an early Spanish document about Mexico, the Codex Mendoza, Aztec war leaders carried poles that were strapped to their backs and topped with emblems of their rank and status to help their followers see them more easily in battle. The batons carried by the Red Stick Indians during the CREEK WAR (1813–14) identified them as allies of TECUMSEH in his planned resistance to U.S. invasions of Native American lands. The guidons of the U.S. Army—small flags used to rally troops in battle—were sometimes regarded as battle talismans by their Native American opponents. Warriors were known to have taken guidons in battle and then turned them into personal talismans, signs of their personal bravery.

Baylor, John R. (1822–1894) *agent for the Comanche, agitator of anti-Indian sentiments, and Confederate commander of the Texas Mounted Rifles*

In 1857, only 18 months after his appointment as an agent for the Clear Fork Reservation in Texas, John Baylor was dismissed from office following a disagreement with Indian Superintendent ROBERT NEIGHBORS. Once out of office, Baylor devoted his energies to ridding Texas of Indians. The following year Baylor and 26 others signed and sent a protest to the current Indian agent, demanding that the Indians be removed from Texas. Although northern COMANCHE continued to raid Texas settlements, by 1859, Baylor had convinced most settlers that it was the reservation Comanche who were responsible for the thefts and murders along the frontier.

Baylor's hostility toward the Comanche came to a head in May 1859, when he led a party of 250 Texas vigilantes onto the Brazos reservation to drive the Indians out of Texas. One elderly Comanche was killed before the Indians and U.S. troops drove the vigilantes away.

During the CIVIL WAR (1861–65), Baylor was named a lieutenant colonel in the Second Texas Mounted Rifles. He led the southern Confederate invasion of New Mexico and Arizona. In 1861, he and his troops moved up the Rio Grande from El Paso into the Mesilla valley almost without opposition. Forts Buchanan, Breckinridge, and Fillmore were abandoned and evacuated. On their march to Fort Stanton, the Union troops from Fort Fillmore were forced to surrender to Baylor; Fort Stanton was also abandoned. Baylor then set up a Confederate Territory of Arizona, which incorporated all of New Mexico south of the 34th parallel, and proclaimed himself governor. The Confederate push to take all of New Mexico ended when Union forces and Colorado volunteers under Major JOHN CHIVINGTON routed the Confederate army following the battle of Glorieta Pass, New Mexico, on March 28, 1862.

Baylor had in the meantime issued a controversial order calling for the extermination of hostile Apache. President Jefferson Davis promptly removed him from civil and military command. Baylor briefly fought as a private and then won election to the Second Confederate Congress. After the Civil War, he built up a large ranch near Montell, Texas, before his death in 1894.

Bear Paw (1877) *final battle of the Nez Perce War*

After a fighting retreat across more than 1,000 miles of mountains and some 12 engagements with four U.S. Army columns, CHIEF JOSEPH and his NEZ PERCE followers fought their last battle in Montana's Bear Paw Mountains. In late September 1877, Joseph's exhausted band—at this point some 700 or so men, women, and children—stopped to rest at Snake Creek at the northern edge of the mountains at a place they called the "Place of the Manure Fire." They were only 30 miles from the Canadian border and freedom. There, on September 30, a detachment of troops—who had marched north from Fort Keogh in Wyoming—about 600 men under Colonel NELSON A. MILES caught up with the Nez Perce and cut off their retreat.

The women, children, and elderly sought safety by burrowing into the sides of the hills. The warriors prepared for the attack by digging holes from which to fire their weapons. Miles's cavalry charged into the band and was repulsed by Nez Perce riflemen, who shot some 60 troopers and held Miles at bay. But two of Joseph's war chiefs, LOOKING GLASS and Joseph's brother OLLOKOT, were killed. For five days the two sides skirmished, during which time Miles captured part of the Nez Perce's pony herd. At one point, Miles sent an officer to parlay with the chiefs, but no decision was reached. As Joseph and his chiefs made preparations for surrender, Chief White Bird and about 100 Nez Perce managed to steal through Miles's lines and escape into Canada.

On October 4, General OLIVER O. HOWARD, head of the Department of the Columbia, arrived on the scene with an advance unit of his force. Surrounded, with his people freezing and starving, Chief Joseph surrendered the remnants of his band on October 5, 1877. About 350 of the original 600 to

700 of Joseph's followers remained, most of them women and children, the elderly, and the sick and wounded. Although promised that they could return to their homelands in Oregon's Wallowa Valley, Joseph and most his people were instead assigned to the Colville Reservation in the Washington territory—but only after being sent to Fort Leavenworth, Kansas, and then the Indian Territory, where many died. In 1992, the battleground at Bear Paw was declared part of the Nez Perce National Historic Park and National Historic Trail.

Bear River (1863) *Civil War (1861–1865) engagement between U.S. volunteers and the Shoshone*
With the outset of the SHOSHONE WAR (1862–63), Colonel PATRICK E. CONNOR determined to crush the militant northwestern Shoshone band led by Bear Hunter. On January 22, 1863, Connor set out from Fort Douglas, Utah Territory, with a mixed command of some 300 infantry and cavalry. Defying winter blizzards and pushing into the Idaho Territory, on January 29 Connor's command, about 200 strong, located the Indians' fortified camp along the Bear River. Bear Hunter's people drove back an initial cavalry assault with heavy losses, but Connor's soldiers subsequently encircled the village and, after furious hand-to-hand fighting, managed to overrun the village.

What had to that point been a battle between combatants then turned into a massacre, with Connor's men indiscriminately slaughtering men, women, and children as organized resistance collapsed. Bear Hunter and others were tortured before being executed. Wounded were bludgeoned to death. Estimates of the dead Shoshone range from 250 to nearly 400. About 160 women and children were taken prisoner. Connor, who admitted losing 23 killed and 41 wounded, was promoted to brigadier general for his grisly victory.

Beaver Wars **(Iroquoian Beaver Wars)**
(1635–1684) *intermittent intertribal conflict for control of territory and domination of the fur trade with European colonists*
In the 1600s the Five Nations of the powerful IROQUOIS CONFEDERACY fought wars of conquest against more than a score of tribes north and west of their territory, including the Iroquois' traditional enemies the HURON, as well as other tribes. Dominating the territory from New York's Hudson Valley in the east to Lake Ontario in the west, the Iroquois competed with the Huron and other tribes for the lucrative beaver fur trade with Europeans.

The rivalry among the French, Dutch, and English for control of the fur trade in North America encouraged intertribal warfare among the Indians. In the early 1600s the supply of beavers in the East was dwindling, and Iroquois trade with the Dutch and English was diminishing. The Iroquois looked to western lands around the Great Lakes, where beavers still flourished. In that region the French were allied with the Huron in the fur trade, while Jesuit priests established missions and worked to Christianize the Huron.

As early as 1635, the Iroquois and Huron came into conflict as war parties met and fought, and villages on both sides were raided and burned. The conflict mounted as the tribes of the Iroquois Confederacy spread out and invaded Huron lands to the north and west. Huron Jesuit towns and villages were attacked and burned, and those not killed were taken captive. In March 1649, a force of 1,000 SENECA and MOHAWK, two tribes of the Iroquois Confederacy, descended on a group of Huron towns east of Georgian Bay near present-day Toronto, Canada. The attackers burned outlying settlements and overwhelmed the towns of Saint Ignace and Saint Louis, killing or capturing their defenders and burning the towns. The Iroquois were repulsed at the town of Sainte Marie by Huron warriors and some French soldiers stationed at the town. However, the Iroquois retreated with supplies and prisoners. The Huron who survived fled. By the end of March, 15 Huron towns were empty as a result of the fighting.

This Iroquois invasion destroyed the Huron Nation. Huron survivors fled into the wilderness and scattered westward, taking refuge with tribes along the shores of Lakes Huron and Erie. Many Huron asked for adoption into the tribes of the Iroquois Confederacy and became part of the Mohawk, Seneca, and ONONDAGA peoples, as per Iroquois tradition. It was customary among the Iroquois to adopt children and young men and women into the tribes to make up for Iroquois losses in warfare.

With the destruction of the Huron Nation, the Iroquois turned to other tribes in the Great Lakes region. First to fall were the Tobacco people, who were crushed by a force of Mohawk and Seneca in December 1649. In 1659, the Neutral tribe was broken when the Iroquois destroyed two large towns north of Lake Erie. Those who escaped abandoned their villages and scattered. The Erie people suffered the same fate as the other tribes when a force of 1,800 Iroquois attacked an Erie town near present-day Erie, Pennsylvania, in 1654. Although the town fell, the Erie regrouped and fought the Iroquois for two years until they too were conquered.

The Beaver Wars continued as the Iroquois moved farther west and north, pushing into the Ohio Valley in the 1660s. People of the OTTAWA, ILLINOIS, MIAMI, and POTAWATOMI tribes in the upper Ohio Valley fled north as Iroquois warriors raided their villages. Farther south, SHAWNEE bands were driven west to the Illinois and Mississippi rivers. The Iroquois now dominated tribes and territory from the Ottawa River in Canada south to the Cumberland River in Kentucky and from Lake Erie to the east.

The Iroquois, however, did not gain a monopoly of the fur trade in the western Great Lakes region and the region east of the Mississippi River. Tribes in those areas, supported by the French, began fighting back, launching attacks and invading Iroquois lands. In the south the Iroquois lost major battles to the SUSQUEHANNOCK and the LENNI LENAPE (Delaware). Then, in 1680, the Iroquois retaliated with an all-out war against French-allied bands along the Illinois and Mississippi Rivers. However, after some initial victories, the Iroquois were driven back. In the north the CHIPPEWA took Iroquois lands north of Lake Ontario, and the Miami moved back into their lands in Indiana.

In 1684, the Iroquois attempted and failed to take the Illinois Indians' town of Fort St. Louis on the Illinois River. This defeat marked the end of the Beaver Wars and the Iroquois' military operations to gain a monopoly of the fur trade. The powerful Iroquois Confederacy remained intact, but the devastation of the wars weakened most of the tribes to the west, making them vulnerable to later white expansion westward. The wars also forged the Indian-European alliances that would continue through the FRENCH AND INDIAN WAR (1754–63) and the AMERICAN REVOLUTION (1775–83).

Further Reading

Burns, Robert. *The Jesuits and the Indian Wars of the Northwest.* New Haven, Conn.: Yale University Press, 1966.

Colden, Cadwallader. *The History of the Five Nations.* New York: Cornell University Press, 1958.

Jennings, Francis. *The Ambiguous Iroquois Empire.* New York: W. W. Norton, 1984.

Kehoe, Alice B. *North American Indians A Comprehensive Account.* Englewood Cliffs, N.J.: Prentice Hall, 1992.

Richter, Daniel K. *The Ordeal of the Longhouse: The Peoples of the Iroquois League in the Era of European Colonization.* Chapel Hill: University of North Carolina Press, 1992.

Beckwourth, James Pierson (James Beckwith)

(ca. 1798–1866) *mountain man, trader, trapper, scout, adopted member of Crow (Absaroka) tribe*

James Pierson Beckwourth was born in Fredericksburg, Virginia, to Jennings Beckwith, a plantation overseer, and "Miss Kill," a mulatto slave. In 1823 or 1824 Beckwourth joined General William Ashley's Rocky Mountain Fur Company. Sometime around 1826, Beckwourth began living among the CROW, probably while still employed by the fur company. He remained with the Crow for the next 10 years. Beckwourth alleged that he became third counselor to the Crow nation around 1833 and first counselor, or head chief, in 1834 after the death of Chief Arapooish, also known as Rotten Belly. According to more credible sources, however, Beckwourth most probably was a subchief, as only two head chiefs—Arapooish and Long Hair—were recognized during that period.

In 1835 or 1836, Beckwourth left the Crow first to join an expedition to California, then to Florida to serve as an army scout in the Second SEMINOLE WAR (1835–42). He returned to the west in 1840, trading with the CHEYENNE for Bent, St. Vrain and Company. Between 1844 and 1858, Beckwourth lived in California, where he acquired a ranch and became a partner in a saloon and gambling parlor. In about 1850, he discovered what became known as Beckwourth's Pass, or Beckwourth's Road Trail, which facilitated American movement through the Sierra Nevada to California.

In 1862, after the start of the CIVIL WAR (1861–65) Beckwourth served briefly as an army guide for the Colorado Second Infantry. Two years later, he was guide to the 3rd Regiment of Colorado Volunteer Cavalry under Colonel JOHN M. CHIVINGTON on their march to a Cheyenne encampment in the Colorado Territory. He later admitted participating in the massacre at SAND CREEK (1864) and testified before the congressional committee investigating the incident. In 1866, Beckwourth became restless once again. That spring he returned to trapping, and by summer he was in Montana Territory, where he became a scout and messenger at Fort Laramie. These duties evolved into guide and interpreter for Colonel HENRY B. CARRINGTON, the district commander associated with the Crow.

On September 29, 1866, Beckwourth made his last trip to his adopted people, the Crow. He apparently became ill during the trip to the Crow village and died while there. He was buried by his host, Iron Bull. Before he died, however, Beckwourth secured the Crow's promise to send warriors to help the soldiers fight the Lakota (see SIOUX [Dakota, Lakota, Nakota]). The village also moved close to the fort, remaining friendly with the non-Indians in the area. His memoirs, which he had begun dictating in 1852, were first published in 1856.

James P. Beckwourth *(By permission of the Colorado Historical Society)*

Beecher's Island: *Defence from the Island,* 1868, rendered by R. F. Zogbaum in 1894 *(By permission of The Denver Public Library, Western History Department)*

Beecher's Island (Beecher Island) (1868) *military engagement that was prelude to southern plains campaigns against Cheyenne, Arapaho, Kiowa, and Comanche Indians*
The battle of Beecher's Island began on September 17, 1868, when Major GEORGE FORSYTH and his elite force of 50 white scouts formed to track down fast-moving Indian warrior bands in the western plains, encamped along the bank of the Arickaree Fork of the Republican River in eastern Colorado. At dawn camp guards thought that they heard buffalo stampeding in the camp's direction. A few moments later Forsyth warned his men that Indians were coming, a force later estimated at 600 to 1,000 Oglala and Brulé Lakota SIOUX, Cheyenne DOG SOLDIERS, northern CHEYENNE, and Arapaho.

Forsyth saw that his men would not be able to outrun the attacking Indians; they would have to find cover. The scouts withdrew to a small, sandy island in the middle of the mostly dry riverbed. The retreat was hurried, with the scouts seeking the island's relative safety as best they could. Forsyth calmly positioned his men, instructing them to keep down. One of his scouts, Sigmund Schlessinger, later remembered that Forsyth "...ordered every one of us to lie flat upon the ground, while he, still directing, kept on his feet, walking around us, leading his horse."

Forsyth ordered the horses tied to bushes near the defensive circle the scouts had established, making most of the horses quick and easy targets for the attacking Indians. Entrenching as best they could, the scouts were able to withstand several Indian charges that covered the island. Forsyth was among those wounded that day. His second in command, Frederick Beecher, was killed and buried on the island with the other scouts killed in the battle. Also killed was the Indian leader ROMAN NOSE. The island was later named after Beecher.

Eight more days of siege followed in which five scouts were killed and 18 men wounded. Indian casualties were not known, but Forsyth later claimed that 31 Indians had been killed and about three times that many wounded. Some scouts finally made it off the island to ride for help. On the ninth day Forsyth and his men were rescued by a force of BUFFALO SOLDIERS, black cavalrymen from the 10th Cavalry. The Indians involved considered Beecher's Island a minor engagement. Forsyth and his men, however, became national heroes.

Bellecourt, Clyde (1939–1974) *leader and cofounder of the American Indian Movement (AIM)*
An Ojibwa (see CHIPPEWA) from Minneapolis, Clyde Bellecourt became interested in his Native American heritage while serving

time for a burglary in state prison. Upon his release in 1968, he was instrumental in the creation of the AMERICAN INDIAN MOVEMENT (AIM), and he became its national director. His brother Vernon, who had also been in prison for a variety of petty crimes, joined him in the organization soon afterward.

Clyde Bellecourt was among those responsible for the militant stance of AIM during its early years, and he took part in the occupation of a BUREAU OF INDIAN AFFAIRS building in Washington, D.C., in 1972. He also participated in the takeover of Wounded Knee in South Dakota the following year (see WOUNDED KNEE [1973]). Bellecourt was killed in 1974 during a dispute with another Indian activist.

belts, war *sashes of shells or beads fashioned with symbolic patterns*
Belts of wampum (from an Algonquian word meaning "string of white beads") were sacred objects to the Indians of the Northeast and Great Lakes regions. Wampum belts were created to keep records, as ornaments and trade items, and as messengers of war or peace. If war was to be declared, a red belt was created—by a dye or sometimes soaked in blood—and sent by a runner to the enemy. If the tribe receiving the red belt wanted peace, it could return a wampum belt of white, a sign of peace.

See also WASHINGTON COVENANT WAMPUM BELT.

Bent, George (1843–1918) *Confederate soldier of part Cheyenne ancestry who became involved in the Plains wars*
Born on July 7, 1843, at Bent's Fort on the Arkansas River, George Bent was the son of white fur trader William Bent and Owl Woman, a Southern CHEYENNE. In 1853, William Bent sent his children to Westport, Missouri, where they lived and went to school until the start of the CIVIL WAR (1861–65). At that time Bent and others from his academy enlisted in the Confederate army, fighting in the battles of Wilson's Creek and PEA RIDGE (1862). In 1862, he was captured at the siege of Corinth in Mississippi. His brother Robert used the family's influence with Union army officers to have George paroled, with the promise that he would take no further part in the war. A year later, because of the Coloradan's hostility toward Bent for serving with the Confederacy, he joined a camp of the Southern Cheyenne (his mother's people) for safety. George went north with the main Cheyenne camps while his half brother Charlie remained on the Kansas plains with another group of Cheyenne. In 1866, George married Magpie, the niece of Cheyenne chief BLACK KETTLE.

Bent was with the Cheyenne during 1863–64, when the Lakota (see SIOUX [Dakota, Lakota, Nakota]), DOG SOLDIERS, Cheyenne, and ARAPAHO began raiding the Platte Roach, blocking wagon traffic to and from the west. In 1864, Bent and his brother-in-law Edmond Guerrier wrote letters to federal authorities on behalf of Black Kettle suing for peace. This was the beginning of the sequence of events that led up to the massacre at SAND CREEK (1864), where Bent was wounded in the hip. Afterward, although he had both Indian and white blood, he became increasingly Indian in his actions and perspective. He took part in the JULESBURG RAIDS (1865) and the South

Platte River Wars and was with the Cheyenne at the battles of MUD SPRINGS (1865) and PLATTE BRIDGE (1865). Bent was also present as an interpreter at the council talks that led to the MEDICINE LODGE TREATIES (1867). In the early 1870s, he worked as interpreter for the Cheyenne and Arapaho agent, John D. Miles, at Darlington, Oklahoma. Before his death, Bent served as an important source of information for George Hyde, a noted historian of the Indian Wars.

Bent's Fort Council (1847) *attempt to initiate systematic control over the Indian tribes of the Central Plains*
In August 1847, near the conclusion of the Mexican-American War, THOMAS FITZPATRICK, newly appointed Indian agent for the tribes of the Arkansas and upper Platte Rivers, went to Bent's Fort on the Arkansas River. Unidentified Indians had launched attacks near the fort and on the SANTA FE TRAIL, even though large bodies of American troops were in the area. Fitzpatrick knew that a show of force would not be enough to frighten the Indians. He estimated that some 2,100 CHEYENNE and 2,400 ARAPAHO were in his jurisdiction. A part of the Arkansas River Cheyenne and some Arapaho greeted Fitzpatrick when he arrived at Bent's Fort on August 29, 1847.

At the ensuing Bent's Fort Council, Fitzpatrick attempted to identify the tribes that were committing the raids on the Santa Fe Trail. Yellow Wolf, a Cheyenne, claimed that the COMANCHE were the most guilty. Fitzpatrick then reprimanded the Arapaho, who admitted that they had young warriors absent and on the warpath with the Comanche.

Fitzpatrick concluded that although the Cheyenne professed friendship, they were confederated with the Arapaho and allied with some SIOUX bands. In addition, the KIOWA and Comanche were applying heavy pressure to the Cheyenne. As a result of the discussion at the Bent's Fort Council, Fitzpatrick successfully convinced the Arapaho and Cheyenne not to join in the raids on the Santa Fe Trail.

Berkeley, William (1606–1677) *governor of Virginia during the early colonial period*
In 1644, with the outbreak of the second POWHATAN WAR (1644–46), William Berkeley traveled to England to try to raise support for the colonist cause against the POWHATAN CONFEDERACY. He returned to Virginia in 1645 without the aid he sought but with a determination to pursue the Powhatan Indians and their leader OPECHANCANOUGH to the death. In March 1646, despite the colonial assembly's desire to make peace with Opechancanough, Berkeley authorized a special expedition to capture the chief and bring him to Jamestown as a prisoner. Opechancanough was shot and killed by a soldier while in Berkeley's custody; in October 1646, the colony negotiated a peace with his successor Necotowance, ending the Powhatan Wars.

Berkeley lost his office in 1652, after Parliament beheaded Charles I during the English Civil War. Berkeley acknowledged the legitimacy of Parliamentary rule, but the colonial assembly declared its allegiance to Charles's son, Charles II. The governor

Bent's Fort Council was held by Thomas Fitzpatrick to persuade the Cheyenne to cease raids on the Santa Fe Trail. *(By permission of the Colorado Historical Society)*

fled to England because of this conflict, and he remained there until long after Charles II was restored to the throne. In 1671 Berkeley was reinstated in his position, and he returned to govern Virginia once again.

Berkeley was faced with another serious Indian uprising in 1675 with the onset of BACON'S REBELLION (1676). Conflicts between Native peoples and the British settlers had become increasingly common during the 1670s, especially with the outbreak of KING PHILIP'S WAR (1675–76) in Massachusetts. The fighting drove tribes into the Virginia colony's territory, where they came into conflict with the poorer settlers living along the frontiers. Governor Berkeley tried to resolve these conflicts by building a series of forts to protect the settled areas, but they proved ineffective. High taxes and low prices for the tobacco grown in Virginia also contributed to discontent among the poorer settlers.

The settlers found a spokesman in NATHANIEL BACON, a cousin of Berkeley's wife, who resisted his relative's defensive Indian policies. Bacon, a member of the colonial assembly, accused Berkeley of deliberately not assisting the settlers in order to preserve his monopoly on trade with the Indians. With his band of frontiersmen, Bacon drove Berkeley from the colonial capital at Jamestown and burned the town in September

1676. With the help of troops dispatched from England, Berkeley cornered Bacon at Yorktown the following month, but the rebel leader died of dysentery before he could be captured. Berkeley then embarked on a campaign of retribution against the rebels. However, he was removed from office by a royal commission, which had been sent to report on conditions in the colony. Berkeley thereupon returned to England, where he died on July 9, 1677. Charles II is supposed to have said of him on his death, "The old fool has killed more people in that naked country than I have done for the murder of my father."

Bernard, Reuben F. (1834–1903) *U.S. Army officer who served during campaigns against the Apache, Modoc, Bannock, and Ute Indians after the Civil War*

Born in Tennessee, Reuben Bernard enlisted in the First Dragoon Regiment in 1855. He rose to first sergeant before the outbreak of the CIVIL WAR (1861–65), having engaged in numerous skirmishes against the APACHE. Commissioned a second lieutenant in 1862, Bernard spent most of the Civil War fighting on the eastern front. He emerged a captain in the reduced postwar army. A large-framed man sporting a heavy beard, in 1869–70 he engaged in several hard fights against the Chiricahua Apache and their noted war leader COCHISE. Captain Bernard was later involved in the MODOC WAR (1872–73), fighting against CAPTAIN JACK (Kintpuash).

Bernard fought against the BANNOCK and UTE Indians again in 1878–79. In late May 1878, he led his command into the field in search of Bannock Indians deemed hostile by the federal government. At Silver River on June 23, Bernard and three troops of cavalry attacked the hostile Indians, sweeping through their village. Bernard's troops forced the Indians into the steep bluffs, where they took up strong defensive positions. The Indians escaped during the night, leaving Bernard short of a victory again. On July 8, 1878, Bernard gained his revenge in fighting at Birch Creek. His men also played an important role in the SHEEPEATER WAR (1879).

Transferred back to Arizona, Bernard saw his last combat against Apache under JUH at Cedar Springs (October 2, 1881) and the Dragoon Mountains (October 4, 1881). His distinguished military career included service in 103 fights and skirmishes. Before his retirement in 1896, he was made brevet brigadier general for engagements against Indians at Chiricahua Pass, Silver River, and Birch Creek.

Big Bow (Zepko-eete) (ca. 1830–ca. 1900) *Kiowa war chief*

Nothing is known of the birthplace and childhood of Big Bow, but by the 1860s he had become famous as a warrior fighting the UTE and NAVAJO. He also gained a reputation as one of the most militantly antiwhite KIOWA, as he led raids on settlers in Texas, Oklahoma, and Kansas who had invaded Kiowa lands. In 1867 leaders of the Kiowa, COMANCHE, APACHE, CHEYENNE, and ARAPAHO gathered at Medicine Lodge Creek in Kansas to negotiate peace with the United States. Big Bow refused to attend and did not accept the terms of the MEDICINE LODGE TREATY (1867), which called for the removal of the Kiowa and other tribes to reservations. Big Bow stayed in the far reaches of the Great Plains, moving out with his warriors to raid, and then withdrawing before he could be caught. By the early 1870s, after the U.S. Army had mounted a massive campaign to subdue the Kiowa, Big Bow still held out. He was finally persuaded by Kiowa Chief Kicking Bird, a respected elderly chief, to surrender. In January 1875, Big Bow led his people onto a combined Kiowa-Comanche reservation in the Indian Territory. Granted a pardon by the government, he was given a post as sergeant in the Indian SCOUTS. After serving well, he died on the reservation around 1900.

Big Cypress Swamp (1855–1856) *scene of fighting between Seminole Indians and U.S. Army*

Located in southern Florida next to the Everglades, Big Cypress Swamp is today the site of a Seminole reservation. In the mid-1800s the swamp was the geographic focus of BILLY BOWLEG's War, more commonly know as the Third SEMINOLE WAR (1855–58). The war arose from issues unsettled since the end

of the Second SEMINOLE WAR (1835–42). Since that time the federal government had worked to encourage the migration of non-Indians to Florida. Indian lands had been opened to settlement, though not areas already set aside for Seminole reservations. By 1855 the army was sending patrols regularly into the Everglades and Big Cypress Swamp. Soldiers and Indians, however, had little contact with each other.

In December 1855, a U.S. Army scouting party led by Lieutenant G. L. Hartsuff left Fort Myers, Florida, to make a reconnaissance of Big Cypress Swamp and the surrounding area, taking particular note of any Indian settlements. They were specifically ordered to be courteous to Indians, who supposedly would not attack unless provoked. The patrol did not see any significance in the two burned forts and three deserted Seminole villages that they discovered during their reconnaissance. Then, before dawn on December 20, 1855, the army patrol was attacked by 30 Seminole warriors under the leadership of Billy Bowlegs, leaving four soldiers dead and four others wounded.

By spring of 1856, fighting in the area was marked by Seminole raids and skirmishes with the army. The swamp proved an excellent defensive location, making it hard for U.S. troops to win any decisive victories without the benefit of overwhelming numbers. By later in the year, the army had changed its tactics and tried to keep the Seminole in the swamp, under the assumption that conditions there would make them want to surrender. Most of their efforts, however, were devoted to luring Indians from the swamp to locations where they could be more easily captured. In late 1856, WILLIAM S. HARNEY took command of the troops. His more determined efforts turned the tide to the army. In March 1858 the Third Seminole War was declared by the army to be at an end. Most Seminole moved to reservations in the Indian Territory, having been bribed to do so. Some 300 remained in Florida.

Big Dry Wash (Chevelon Fork) (1882) *final major battle between Apache and U.S. Army troops in Arizona*

On August 30, 1881, U.S. troops from FORT APACHE arrested a prominent medicine man, Noche-del-klinne, which resulted in the battle of CIBECUE CREEK (1881). In the months following the skirmish, some of the APACHE involved turned themselves in; others resolved to live in peace. A number of Apache, however, refused to do either. They gathered around a leader named Natiotish and bided their time. Nearly a year later, on July 6, 1882, these Apache began to strike back. A band of 58 Indians first attacked and killed the chief of police of San Carlos and three of his men. They then stripped telegraph wires to disrupt military and civilian communications and proceeded north to a small mining town where they wounded a white man. From there they headed north again into the Tonto Basin, where they killed more men.

Natiotish believed that his attacks against the whites would entice other Apache to join him on the warpath. His plan failed. When news of the attacks became known, troops from five military posts were immediately dispatched to locate and destroy Natiotish and his followers. Civilians and even other Apache also took up arms against the warriors.

On July 17, the famous Indian fighter AL SIEBER and his Apache scouts located the hostiles. Natiotish underestimated the size of the opposing force. Even as he deployed his fighters to ambush the cavalry in Chevelon Canyon at a place known as the Big Dry Wash, the troops began to surround his position. The fighting, which began about noon, was intense and the number of casualties mounted. By evening a tremendous rain and hail storm had swept over the canyon and the fighting ended.

About 22 Apache died in the battle, along with two soldiers. Natiotish was among those mortally wounded. This battle was notable for two reasons. First, it was unusual in that the Apache chose to fight a conventional battle. Second, it constituted the final major battle between the Apache and U.S. military on Arizona soil.

Big Foot, Miniconjou Lakota chief, dead in the snow after the massacre at Wounded Knee, 1890 *(Courtesy Library of Congress, Negative no. LC-US61Z534)*

Big Foot (Sitanka, Spotted Elk) (ca. 1825–1890)
leader of the Indian band slaughtered at Wounded Knee in 1890
Born ca. 1825, Big Foot was the son of Long Horn, leader of a small band of Miniconjou Lakota Indians (see SIOUX [Dakota, Lakota, Nakota]). After Long Horn's death in 1874, Big Foot assumed leadership of the band. Two years later, the Lakota were involved in the War for the Black Hills, part of the SIOUX WARS (1854–90). By 1877 the beleaguered Miniconjou survivors, including Big Foot, surrendered and were placed on the Cheyenne River Reservation in South Dakota.

In the years that followed, Big Foot became widely recognized as one of the greatest of all Miniconjou chiefs—not because of his exploits in war, but rather because of his skill as an arbitrator and a peacemaker. Often he defused volatile situations within his tribe by bringing quarreling factions together. His reputation spread and, in time, other tribes sought his counsel.

Big Foot valued compromise. Within his own life he tried to balance change and continuity. On the South Dakota reservation, he was one of the first Lakota Indians to successfully plant corn. He helped build a school for the children, and he even represented his people on a trip to Washington, D.C.

The GHOST DANCE Religion was started by a Northern PAIUTE (Numu) named WOVOKA. The wars had left many of the women widows. They now danced the Ghost Dance, desperately hoping to restore their dead husbands and to return to the old ways. In 1889 Big Foot's band of Miniconjou adopted the new religion. They were joined by other Indians in the area.

The Ghost Dance tended to unite different Indian groups and thus was threatening to white Americans. Hunkpapa Lakota chief SITTING BULL was killed when Indian agent James McLaughlin ordered his arrest and sent 40 men to a Ghost Dance he was attending in 1890. After this incident, many of his followers, fearing for their own safety, immediately fled to the Cheyenne River Reservation and joined the Miniconjou. By this point, Big Foot was no longer a follower of the Ghost Dance Religion.

On learning of Sitting Bull's death, Big Foot and his band set out to join the Oglala Lakota chief RED CLOUD at Pine Ridge Reservation, hoping to find safety there. Meanwhile, General NELSON A. MILES was unaware that Big Foot no longer participated in the Ghost Dance and that Red Cloud was friendly to non-Indians. Instead, he feared that Big Foot was attempting to join Kicking Bear and Short Bull, who practiced the new religion and were hostile to whites. Thus, Miles sent out a force to arrest Big Foot.

On December 28, 1890, soldiers of James Forsyth's 7th Cavalry located Big Foot and his band of about 350 men, women, and children. Big Foot lay in a wagon, critically ill from pneumonia. The soldiers moved the Indians to Wounded Knee Creek for the night. The next day, firing broke out as small detachments of soldiers attempted to disarm the Indians. Other units then fired into the melee. Big Foot was among the 150 casualties in the massacre. Many more died later from their wounds; up to 300 may have been killed. A blizzard prevented the soldiers from tending to the bodies. Three days later, on New Year's Day, soldiers and a civilian party returned to finish the burials. Big Foot's frozen body was placed in a common grave with others of his band.

In life Big Foot was recognized for his ability to find peaceful solutions to pressing problems. In death he became a symbol of the horrors of war.

Big Hole (1877) *the third of seven battles between the U.S. Army and the five non-treaty bands of Nez Perce Indians during the Nez Perce War*
On June 17, 1877, an outnumbered group of NEZ PERCE outfought the U.S. Army at WHITE BIRD CREEK (1877). They did the same again on July 11 at CLEARWATER (1877) and then escaped near-capture on July 27 at Fort Missoula—thereafter referred to as "Fort Fizzle." On August 8, an advance patrol from Fort Shaw sighted the Nez Perce in the Big Hole Valley.

Battle of Big Hole Basin,
August 8–11, 1877

GIBBON ATTACK

RETREAT

Nez Perce
camp

Big Hole R.

Indian camp

0   .25 mile
0   .25 km

During the night, Colonel JOHN GIBBON maneuvered his soldiers to within 150 yards of the Indian encampment.

At dawn on August 9, foot soldiers attacked the Indians as they slept. Stumbling from their tipis, men, women, and children were bludgeoned with clubs or shot. At first, Indian resistance was disorganized and ineffective. But CHIEF JOSEPH, White Bird, and LOOKING GLASS rallied the people to mount a counterattack. As the soldiers advanced toward the east end of the camp, sniper fire commenced from both sides. Caught in the cross fire, many soldiers fell. Colonel Gibbon sounded retreat, and his soldiers scurried to the safety of the hills.

The Indians returned to camp, buried their dead, and collected some of their possessions. OLLIKUT, principal military strategist, and other sharpshooters pinned the soldiers for almost 24 hours to provide escape cover for their families.

The death count from the battle of Big Hole included 29 white soldiers and 77 Nez Perce women and children. Only 12 Nez Perce warriors were killed, but among them were three of the most valiant: Red Echo, Five Wounds, and Rainbow.

Big Meadows (1856) *engagement in the Rogue River War in the Oregon Territory*

Big Meadows was a battle between the U.S. Army and Indians from several Northwestern tribes, including the Rogue River, Shasta, Klamath, and Umpqua. The battle resulted from a series of incidents between these tribes and white settlers in Oregon and was part of the ROGUE RIVER WAR (1855–56). In October 1855, the governor of Oregon Territory called up two battalions of volunteers to fight Indians in the territory. Some fighting followed, but during most of the winter and early spring the army troops acted primarily to keep peace and to shield peaceful Indians from settlers and unrestrained volunteer fighters.

In May 1856, an Indian leader named Old John persuaded two other chiefs that instead of bringing their people to surrender at Big Meadows, a site in the Rogue River Valley, they should prepare an ambush for the soldiers, who were led by Brigadier General Persifor Smith. On the evening of May 26, the day scheduled for the Indians' arrival at Big Meadows, none appeared. Smith, however was warned that evening of an attack planned for the next day. On the morning of May 27, the Indians attacked. Some fired from the surrounding hills; others crept up slopes and tried to separate the army troops. The army kept the Indians at bay, but even given time to entrench, Smith had difficulty avoiding defeat. By the next day the situation seemed grim. A third of Smith's soldiers were dead or wounded, and supplies of water and ammunition were low. That afternoon, the Indians massed for a final assault. Before they could attack, however, an army infantry column led by Captain Christopher Augur arrived and rescued Smith's men. Caught between opposing fire, the Indians fled. Within five weeks all hostile Indians in the area had surrendered.

Big Mound   See DEAD BUFFALO LAKE.

Big Tree (Adoeette) (1847–1929) *one of the last Kiowa war chiefs*

Big Tree frequently led and participated in KIOWA raids against Texans, military posts, and wagon trains. He is most noted for his participation in a raid on a civilian supply wagon train crossing Salt Creek Prairie, heading for Fort Richardson, Texas, in May 1871. The Kiowa killed seven white men and plundered the wagons. SATANTA bragged to Kiowa agent Lawrie Tatum about leading the raid and named Big Tree, Satank, and others as participants; but Big Tree did not admit to any guilt. Satanta repeated the story to General WILLIAM T. SHERMAN. While BUFFALO SOLDIERS stood guard, Sherman placed Big Tree, Satanta, and Satank under arrest. Satank subsequently provoked the soldiers to kill him during his transfer from Fort Sill to Texas.

In July 1871, Big Tree and Satanta were quickly tried, convicted, and sentenced to hang by a jury of Texas cowboys. The sentences were later commuted to life in prison. Both were paroled on August 19, 1873. After his release, Big Tree participated in a raid on September 9, 1874, against Captain Wyllys Lyman's detachment delivering supplies from Camp Supply to Colonel NELSON MILES on the Sweetwater River during the RED RIVER WAR.

On October 4, 1874, Big Tree gave up fighting. He surrendered and was detained at Fort Sill for parole violations until 1875, when he was again released. He pledged to live in peace and settled with his band on Rainy Mountain Creek. He eventually became a deacon in a Baptist mission.

Billy Bowlegs War   See SEMINOLE WAR, SECOND.

Birch Coulee (1862) *surprise Indian attack on a white burial detail*

The MINNESOTA UPRISING (1862) began on August 18, 1862, when Dakota Indians (see SIOUX [Dakota, Lakota, Nakota]) attacked the federal Indian administrative center known as the Lower Sioux Agency in southern Minnesota near modern-day Redwood Falls. During the next two weeks the Dakota attacked nearby FORT RIDGELY and NEW ULM. By August 31, the main body of Dakota seemed to have left the area; a burial party of about 170 soldiers and settlers left Fort Ridgely and proceeded to the Lower Sioux Agency. The next day they located and buried 54 victims. The burial detail bivouacked at an indefensible site along Birch Coulee Creek. As the soldiers slept, about 200 Dakota warriors surrounded the encampment. Just before dawn on September 2, the Indians attacked. The soldiers took cover behind their dead horses and began firing back. By the time white reinforcements arrived two days later, the battle was over. Two Indians lost their lives in the battle of Birch Coulee. Seventeen soldiers were dead or mortally wounded, 47 were severely injured, and many were less seriously wounded. Ninety horses lay dead. The battle of Birch Coulee resulted in the highest military casualties of the entire Minnesota Uprising.

Bird Creek   See FIRST CHEROKEE REGIMENT.

Black Elk (Hehaka Sapa, Ekhaka Sapa) (1863–1950)
Oglala Lakota medicine man who helped preserve his people's religion

Black Elk was born in 1863 somewhere along the Little Powder River in Wyoming. Thirteen years later, he was at the battle of the LITTLE BIGHORN (1876), where he shot and scalped a soldier. After that he traveled with his cousin Oglala-Brute war leader CRAZY HORSE and then with Hunkpapa chief SITTING BULL.

As Black Elk's spiritual visions increased, so did his reputation among his people. He was highly regarded by non-Indians, and between 1886 and 1889 he toured with the famous Wild West Show of WILLIAM F. (BUFFALO BILL) CODY. While Cody and Black Elk were caught up in reenactments of Indian battles, a Northern PAIUTE (Numu) prophet named WOVOKA was espousing a new Indian religion, the GHOST DANCE. The massacre at WOUNDED KNEE (1890) dashed the hopes of many new converts to this religion. Black Elk realized that the hostilities had to end and the Indians and whites had to live in peace.

In the early 1930s, a poet from Nebraska, John G. Neihardt, met the aging medicine man, Black Elk, at the Pine Ridge Reservation. The author recorded Black Elk's story and information on his beliefs and religion, immortalizing the medicine man and his religion in print in *Black Elk Speaks the Life Story of a Holy Man of the Oglala Sioux.*

Black Elk was a respected medicine man; later in his life, he became a devout Roman Catholic. He had two wives and two sons. He died on August 19, 1950 in Manderson, South Dakota.

Blackfeet Treaty (Lame Bull's Treaty) (1855) *first U.S. treaty that dealt directly with the Blackfeet Indians located east of the Rocky Mountains in north-central Montana*

The Blackfeet Treaty of 1855 was one of several that ISAAC I. STEVENS, governor and ex-officio superintendent of Indian Affairs, negotiated that year with Washington Territory tribes. The treaty was concluded on October 17, 1855, at the council ground on the Upper Missouri near the mouth of the Judith River in Nebraska Territory (present-day Montana). It dealt primarily with the Blackfeet, but the Flathead, Upper Pend d'Oreille, Kootenay, and NEZ PERCE, traditional enemies of the Blackfeet, were also parties to the agreement. The treaty confirmed the Blackfeet territorial boundaries east of the Rocky Mountains in north central Montana set by the FORT LARAMIE TREATY (1851). It also designated common hunting grounds for the involved tribes between the Missouri and Yellowstone Rivers in central Montana.

For the Blackfeet, the treaty provided a 10-year $20,000 annuity of "useful goods and services" and an additional $15,000 annuity for farm equipment, agricultural and mechanical assistance, and Christian education. The tribes agreed to live in peace with area tribes. Another stipulation was that non-Indians would be allowed free travel and settlement on Blackfeet lands. Construction of roads, telegraph lines, military posts, agencies, missions, schools, farms, shops, mills, and stations were also to be permitted and free navigation of all waterways was established.

The U.S. government established a Blackfeet Indian agency at Fort Benton in order to distribute annuity goods. In 1856, agent Edwin A. C. Hatch reported distribution of treaty goods to 8,000 Indians. Many Blackfeet who came to receive annuity goods lived north of the invisible line dividing U.S. Blackfeet from Canadian Blackfeet. The United States made a distinction between the two groups, but the Blackfeet did not. Most of the goods provided were already available to the Blackfeet through the buffalo trade, and they would not use items such as coffee and rice. The Blackfeet also profited only minimally from the education that was provided. Ultimately the treaty served to foster Blackfeet dependence upon the U.S. government and initiated the reservation system among the Blackfeet.

Blackfeet Treaty (1877) *agreement between the Canadian government and several western tribes, most notably the Blackfeet and Assiniboine*

In a series of 11 treaties, the first of which was signed in 1871, the government of Canada negotiated the transfer and acquisition of lands in its Northwest Territories, which had originally been owned and administered by the private Hudson's Bay Company. The seventh treaty in the series, known as the Blackfeet Treaty, was signed on September 22, 1877, at Blackfoot Crossing on the Bow River, east of Calgary in Canada. The treaty gave the Canadian government a right of way through Indian Territory, which was necessary to complete a planned transcontinental railroad. In return, the Blackfeet, ASSINIBOINE, Blood, Piegan,

Sarcee, and Chipewyan were allowed to retain reserve lands in present Alberta province.

Blackfoot Confederacy   *western tribe inhabiting the northern plains*

The Blackfoot ranged along the eastern edge of the Rocky Mountains throughout present-day Montana and as far north as the Saskatchewan River in Alberta, Canada. In 1800, their number was estimated at 30,000 people, who were divided into three major tribes that formed the Blackfoot Confederacy. The Northern Blackfoot called themselves the Siksika, "blackfooted people," possibly from the fact that they dyed their moccasins black. They lived in the upper Plains and into Canada. To the south were the Blood (so-called because they painted their faces with red earth), and farther south were the Piegan, whose name means "poor robes." These three tribes are often called the Blackfeet.

Known as bold and fierce warriors, the Blackfoot warred with the ASSINIBOINE, SHOSHONE, CREE, and CROW for horses, to protect hunting grounds, and to safeguard Blackfoot monopoly of the fur trade. The French and English in Canada were the first to trade with the Blackfoot, exchanging guns, tools, and alcohol for valuable beaver pelts. Despite the trade, however, the Blackfoot were suspicious of whites. The exploration of the Louisiana Territory (1804–06) by Meriwether Lewis and William Clark aroused Blackfoot hostility when, in July 1806, the explorers skirmished with a Blackfoot hunting party along the Marias River in northern Montana and killed two of the band. Blackfoot enmity was especially directed toward American trappers—Mountain Men—who hunted and trapped in Blackfoot lands in growing numbers in the early 1800s.

The incursions of traders and later settlers brought disease that ravaged the Plains tribes and the Blackfoot people. Some 8,000 Blackfoot died of smallpox in the winter of 1839–40. Later epidemics in 1857 and 1869–70 further weakened the confederacy. By the middle of the 1880s, the wholesale slaughter of the buffalo had decimated the Blackfoot. During the "starvation winter" of 1883–84, 600 of the remaining 2,000 Blackfoot people froze or starved to death because there were no more buffalo left to hunt. Through treaties in 1855 and 1877, the Blackfoot ceded land to the United States and Canada, and in the 1880s, they were moved to reservations in Alberta, Canada, and northwestern Montana.

See also BLACKFEET TREATY (1855) and BLACKFEET TREATY (1877).

Black Hawk (Ma-ka-tai-me-she-kia-kiah, Makataimeshekiakiak, Black Sparrow Hawk)

(1767–1838)   *war leader of the Sac and Fox Indians during the Black Hawk War*

Black Hawk was born in the prosperous village of Saukenuk, at the site of present-day Rock Island, Illinois. Located at the junction of the Rock and Mississippi Rivers, Saukenuk was the center of SAC and FOX territory.

At a young age Black Hawk had a vision that a sparrow hawk was his guardian spirit. Thus, he got his name. By age 15 Black Hawk had wounded his first enemy in combat, and by age 30 he was a respected war chief who led warriors against OSAGE and CHEROKEE Indians.

When the United States made the LOUISIANA PURCHASE (1803), government officials contended that the Sac and Fox should yield to the federal government. On September 18, 1804, five Sac and Fox chiefs, under pressure from U.S. officials, ceded all of their land east of the Mississippi River as well as hunting grounds to the west (lands in present-day Illinois, Wisconsin, and Missouri). In order to obtain their signatures, government officials bribed the chiefs with $2,234.50 and access to liquor. The treaty was unpopular with most of the Sac and Fox, who had no intention of leaving. To allay hostilities the U.S. government established Fort Madison in the heart of Sac country. In 1811, Black Hawk, who had not been present when the treaty was signed, and a small group of WINNEBAGO attacked the fort but withdrew when they ran out of bullets.

When the WAR OF 1812 (1812–14) erupted, Black Hawk and many of his followers sided with the British. They fought with TECUMSEH against the Americans in the Battle at RAISIN RIVER (1813) and in the sieges of Forts Meigs and Stephenson. When Black Hawk returned to his home village of Saukenuk after the war, he discovered that many Sac families had sided with the Americans and had relocated. Meanwhile, the anti-American faction that stayed behind had chosen a new war chief, Keokuk. Nevertheless, in 1814 it was Black Hawk and his warriors who attacked an American unit trying to reach a fort at Prairie du Chien in Wisconsin. Thirty-four soldiers were killed or wounded in the engagement. In retaliation, Major Zachary Taylor amassed an army of 430 men in August 1814 and set out to destroy the Indian settlements along the Rock

A painting of Black Hawk (right) and his son, by John Jarvis, 1833 *(Courtesy New York Public Library)*

Black Hawk's surrender at Fort Crawford, 1832 *(Courtesy of the National Museum of the American Indian, Smithsonian Institution #12837)*

River. Black Hawk, meanwhile, gathered more than 1,000 Sac, Fox, Winnebago, SIOUX, and British combatants and drove the Americans back to St. Louis.

After the British signed the TREATY OF GHENT (1814) with the Americans, they announced that they would withdraw from the area. Black Hawk was furious and unwilling to stop fighting. In time, however, he had no recourse but to make peace with the Americans by signing a treaty affirming the one made in 1804.

Black Hawk and other Sac Indians did not abandon their villages immediately. They remained for 15 years, even as white settlers moved into the area and began to occupy Saukenuk. In 1830 General EDMUND P. GAINES, commander of the Western Department of the Army, delivered an ultimatum for the Sac to abandon their villages and relocate. Black Hawk's rival Keokuk convinced many of his people to leave, and in late June all the Indians departed their village only hours before it was attacked by militiamen. Within a week, Black Hawk signed a document promising never to return to Saukenuk.

By April 1832, Black Hawk gathered yet another army, crossed the Mississippi River, and prepared to take back the Sac villages; he hoped to form an Indian confederacy. Meanwhile, a large contingent of military and civilian militia (including a young Abraham Lincoln) prepared to stop them. Portions of the two armies finally clashed on May 14 in a skirmish called STILLMAN'S RUN (1832). For a short time afterward, Black Hawk's small victory in that battle kindled a

fighting spirit among nearby Indians. The Indian victory, however, was short lived, as the soldiers relentlessly pursued the Indians and handily won the BLACK HAWK WAR. On August 27, Black Hawk surrendered and was imprisoned at Fort Monroe, Virginia. In subsequent years Black Hawk became a celebrity and toured eastern cities, attracting huge crowds. He died on October 3, 1838. Not long thereafter his grave was robbed by whites so that his bones could be displayed in a museum in Burlington, Iowa. The museum was destroyed by fire in 1855.

Further Reading

Josephy, Alvin M., Jr. *The Patriot Chiefs: A Chronicle of American Indian Resistance.* New York: Penguin Books, 1989.

Black Hawk. *Ma-ka-tai-me-she-kai-kiak, Black Hawk: An Autobiography* [1832], Donald Jackson (ed.). Urbana: University of Illinois Press, 1955.

Hagan, William T. *The Sac and Fox Indians.* Norman: University of Oklahoma Press, 1958.

Black Hawk War (1832) *last major Indian-white conflict east of the Mississippi River and north of Florida*

In 1804, representatives of the FOX and SAC (Sauk) tribes signed a treaty that called for these tribes to surrender all claims to land in Illinois. BLACK HAWK, the leader of the Sac tribe who had risen to prominence when he fought alongside the British during the WAR OF 1812 (1812–14), bitterly opposed the treaty.

In 1828 the tribes were ordered into Iowa, where Black Hawk made an unsuccessful attempt to create an anti–United States alliance with the WINNEBAGO, POTAWATOMI, and KICKAPOO. Black Hawk's band returned annually across the Mississippi for spring planting, frightening non-Indian settlers. When Black Hawk returned in 1832, a military force of 4,100 men under the command of General HENRY ATKINSON prepared to repulse the Indian band. For 15 weeks the military pursued Black Hawk and his 400 warriors into Wisconsin and westward toward the Mississippi. The fleeing Indians received little support from other tribes, some of which even aided the whites in pursuing Black Hawk.

On August 3, 1832, soldiers caught up with Black Hawk's band at the junction of the Mississippi and Bad Axe Rivers. During the resulting battle of BAD AXE (1832), the Indians were defeated. Soon afterward, a large force of 1,300 troops under the command of General WINFIELD SCOTT caught up with Black Hawk, whose band of warriors was again soundly defeated. Black Hawk was later apprehended and imprisoned for a short time, thus bringing an end to the Black Hawk War. This effectively removed the Fox and Sac Indians' ability to make war against settlers.

Black Hills, War for the (1876–1877) *war between U.S. troops and Cheyenne and Sioux forces for control of the Black Hills of South Dakota*

In the mid-1770s, Teton Lakota SIOUX chief Standing Bull moved his followers into the Black Hills of South Dakota. Sioux (Dakota, Lakota, Nakota) groups continued to move to the region, known as Paha Sapa, until by the 1840s, it had become the heart of Sioux country. At this time, however, the first non-Indian settlers began to appear in the Black Hills on their way west to the OREGON TRAIL.

Skirmishes between Sioux warriors and settlers necessarily ensued and led to the FORT LARAMIE TREATY (1851), which officially declared some 60 million acres in the Black Hills as Sioux territory. By 1866, settlers were again crossing Sioux territory on the newly blazed BOZEMAN TRAIL. In response, Oglala Sioux leader RED CLOUD launched the War for the Bozeman Trail. His successes against U.S. military forces resulted in the FORT LARAMIE TREATY of 1868. It formally established the Great Sioux Reservation and declared the territory around the Bighorn and Powder Rivers to be Sioux land. According to the terms of the treaty, non-Indian trespass on Sioux lands was strictly prohibited.

In 1874, however, General GEORGE ARMSTRONG CUSTER began a secret military operation in the Black Hills aimed at finding gold. He did so, and the U.S. government then tried to acquire the Black Hills territory through legal means. The Sioux refused, and the United States declared war in late 1875. The Sioux were instructed to report to local agencies or reservations or become enemies of the state.

The Sioux refused again (and the difficulty of winter travel in the region would have made acceptance impossible anyway), and the War for the Black Hills was under way. By a plan formulated by Civil War hero PHILIP HENRY SHERIDAN, converging columns would drive into the Indian camps that winter. General GEORGE CROOK would accompany 883 men under the direct command of Colonel Joseph J. Reynolds, pushing east from Fort Fetterman, Wyoming. General ALFRED TERRY was to march west from Fort Abraham Lincoln, North Dakota. Heavy winter snows, however, prevented Terry from taking the field. Meanwhile, Reynolds botched an attack against a village on the Powder River containing about 200 families, including Oglala leader He Dog and Cheyenne leader Old Bear, and the Crook-Reynolds force fell back to Fetterman.

Over the winter, Sioux and Cheyenne bands gathered into a large group under Sioux chief SITTING BULL and Cheyenne war leader CRAZY HORSE. By June 1876, the Indians had reached ROSEBUD CREEK and set up camp. At the same time, three U.S. military columns, under Generals Crook and ALFRED TERRY and Colonel John Gibbon, were converging on the spot. On June 17, Crook drew near the Indian encampment and, despite an early warning from his Crow and Shoshone scouts, Crook's troops were attacked and driven back by Sitting Bull's forces.

Meanwhile, the columns under Terry and Gibbon met up at the mouth of the Rosebud and began to formulate a plan of attack, not knowing of Crook's defeat. The officers planned to attack the Indians encampment, which they believed was located along the Little Bighorn River. On June 22, the 7th Cavalry, led by Custer, set off from Terry's main command. Three days later, Custer's Crow scouts spotted the Indian encampment, which housed some 7,000 people, many more than the U.S. commanders had imagined. Rather than waiting for reinforcements, Custer divided his forces and attacked. The bloody result of the battle has come down in popular history as Custer's Last Stand (see LITTLE BIGHORN); he and his 200 men were overwhelmed by the superior Cheyenne and Sioux forces, led by Crazy Horse and Hunkpapa Sioux chief GALL.

Although the Indians scored a decisive victory at Little Bighorn, the public outcry over the incident, raised to the level of hysteria by the media, resulted in the military takeover of the Sioux agencies, a massive increase in troops in the region, and the virtual elimination of sympathy for the Indians' position in the U.S. government.

The first retaliatory strike was launched on September 9 by Captain Anson Mills, whose troops destroyed a Sioux camp and killed a vital war chief, American Horse. In November, Colonel RANALD S. MACKENZIE engaged and defeated a Cheyenne force, led by DULL KNIFE and LITTLE WOLF, in the Bighorn Mountains. In response, several Cheyenne leaders, as well as chiefs of several other tribes, attempted to broker peace with General NELSON A. MILES, but their delegation was attacked by Crow scouts before it reached the military post. The Cheyenne and Sioux responded with more attacks on military sites in the region.

On January 7, 1877, Miles's troops engaged a force of some 500 Sioux and Cheyenne warriors in the battle of Wolf Mountain. The skirmish was indecisive, but the U.S. media played it up as a major victory for Miles. In the months that followed, several major Sioux and Cheyenne chiefs, including Crazy Horse, surrendered their bands to the reservation system.

A few chiefs refused surrender. On May 7, Miniconjou Sioux leader Lame Deer engaged Miles and his soldiers in the battle of Muddy Creek. At first the Indians agreed to surrender, but tensions resulted in an outbreak of shooting. When it was over, Lame Deer and his head warrior, Iron Star, lay dead. Then in September, Crazy Horse, who had never truly accepted reservation life and remained a thorn in the U.S. government's side, was stabbed to death in a hazily reported scuffle.

Also in September, in response to unsatisfactory conditions on the Great Sioux Reservation, Red Cloud and Spotted Tail traveled to Washington, D.C., to ask for a new reservation in their traditional homeland. Many other Sioux, including bands led by Dull Knife and Little Wolf and followers of Crazy Horse, abandoned the reservation and set out to join Sitting Bull in Canada. Disagreements resulted in the bands splitting up, however.

Dull Knife surrendered to Camp Robinson, where his people were starved and humiliated. When they tried to escape, soldiers fired on them, killing about half of the Indians. The rest were granted territory on the Pine Ridge Reservation in present-day South Dakota, in traditional Sioux territory. Little Wolf evaded the pursuing U.S. troops for five years, but he, too, was finally forced to surrender. He and the other Cheyenne were granted the Tongue River Reservation in southeastern Montana in 1884.

The final chapter in the War for the Black Hills concerns Sitting Bull, who in 1877 was living in western Canada with some 4,000 Hunkpapa, Oglala, Miniconjou, Nez Perce, and others. As long as he remained free, U.S. military leaders believed that they could not consider the war over. They spent the next four years attempting to persuade him to surrender to reservation life, and finally, on July 19, 1881, after several major defections by his followers, he agreed. With his arrival at Fort Buford, South Dakota, the long and bloody War for the Black Hills had come to an end.

A drawing rendered from a photograph of Black Kettle, a Southern Cheyenne warrior who sought peace with the American government, by John Metcalf *(By permission of the Colorado Historical Society)*

Black Kettle (Moke-ta-ve-to) (ca. 1803–1868)
Cheyenne chief during the Cheyenne-Arapaho War and Southern Plains War

Born near the Black Hills in the Dakota Territory in about 1803, Black Kettle attempted to maintain peace between his band of Southern CHEYENNE and the United States in the early 1860s. With relations between non-Indians and the Plains tribes increasingly tense, Black Kettle attempted to negotiate an agreement with the Colorado territorial government in 1864. Instructed by white authorities to camp along SAND CREEK (1864) in Colorado, his people were brutally massacred by JOHN CHIVINGTON and his troops. In a vain attempt to stop the attack, Black Kettle unfurled an American flag above his lodge as Chivington's Colorado volunteers butchered nearly 200 of his people. Black Kettle escaped the massacre and, despite the debacle, signed the MEDICINE LODGE TREATY (1867).

With the outbreak of the SOUTHERN PLAINS WAR in 1868, Black Kettle again tried to make peace with the whites. But a column of U.S. Army regulars commanded by GEORGE ARMSTRONG CUSTER was unaware of Black Kettle's peaceful intentions, and failed to distinguish between his encampment and those of several other nearby groups at the battle of the WASHITA (1868). This time Black Kettle, his wife, and another hundred of his followers, mainly women and children, were slain and his village burned. Though Black Kettle had sought to maintain peace, evidence discovered by the soldiers in some of the nearby camps suggested that he had not always been able to prevent his clan members from resorting to violence.

Block Island (1636) *punitive raid by Massachusetts Bay colony against the Narragansett Indians*

By the early 1630s, relations between the British colonists in Massachusetts and their Native American neighbors, especially the PEQUOT and the NARRAGANSET, were becoming strained. In 1634 the Niantic, a client tribe of the Pequot, killed Captain John Stone, claiming that he had kidnapped several members of their tribe to use as guides. In 1636, members of the Narragansett tribe killed Captain John Oldham on Block Island, off the coast of Rhode Island. The authorities of Massachusetts Bay colony sent a 90-man expedition, led by Captains JOHN ENDECOTT, JOHN UNDERHILL, and William Turner, to Block Island. The troops were under orders to kill all the male Native residents, capture the women and children, and secure the island for Massachusetts Bay. When the British arrived, however, they discovered that the Indians had been forewarned, and most of them had fled the island. Frustrated, Endecott's men destroyed the Pequot's property on the mainlands, burning and pillaging their fields. Endecott's mission was one of the factors that led to the start of the PEQUOT WAR (1637).

Bloody Brook (1675) *battle in King Philip's War*

After the fight at HOPEWELL SWAMP (1675), the colonial settlements along the upper Connecticut River valley became the targets of Indian raids. As a result, many of the towns were evacuated during the early part of September 1675. The evacuations themselves, however, provided the Native Americans with excellent opportunities for ambushes. On September 18, 1675, evacuees from the town of Deerfield, escorted by troops under the command of Captain Thomas Lathrop, were ambushed. They were crossing a low-lying, swampy area near a small brook only six miles south of the town when the Indians attacked. Although taken completely by surprise, the colonists put up a fierce resistance, and the arrival of nearby British reinforcements under Major Robert Treat and Captain Samuel Moseley resulted in the Indians' retreat. More than 64 colonists, including Captain Lathrop, died in the ambush—one of the worst defeats the settlers suffered in KING PHILIP'S WAR (1675–76). The battle was called Bloody Brook, in memory of the colonial dead.

Bloody Run   See PONTIAC.

Blue Jacket (Weyapiersenwah) (1750–1805)
Shawnee war leader

Blue Jacket was one of the main opponents of the U.S. forces in LITTLE TURTLE'S WAR (1786–95). Little is known for certain about his parentage. He is rumored to have had at least one European parent, or to have been a white boy adopted into the SHAWNEE tribe. Although Blue Jacket is best remembered for his role as a war leader in Little Turtle's War, he also

fought settlers in Kentucky before and during LORD DUNMORE'S WAR (1773–74) and the AMERICAN REVOLUTION (1775–81).

During the summer of 1776, the Shawnee, along with members of the IROQUOIS CONFEDERACY, LENNI LENAPE (Delaware), OTTAWA, CHEROKEE, Wyandot, and Mingo, met along the shores of the Tennessee River and agreed to ally themselves with the British in the American Revolution. They did this in hopes of regaining their hunting grounds in Ohio and Kentucky, which were then occupied by American settlers. The Shawnee fought several minor battles against the settlers, including attacks on the towns of Harrodsburg and Boonesboro in 1777. However, it was not until after the death of Chief CORNSTALK that the Shawnee began moving in force against the settlers. In February 1778 Blue Jacket, leading a war party of 102 warriors, captured the frontiersman Daniel Boone at the encampment called BLUE LICKS (1778).

At the start of Little Turtle's War in 1786, Blue Jacket and the MIAMI chief LITTLE TURTLE launched a new series of raids against settlers in the Ohio Country. Operating from bases in the Maumee River valley basin, near present-day Fort Wayne, Indiana, Blue Jacket, Little Turtle, and their warriors defeated two separate expeditions mounted against them by the U.S. government. Blue Jacket and the Shawnee were primarily responsible for winning the first of these two battles, known as HARMAR'S DEFEAT (1787). By January 1791, Blue Jacket was besieging Dunlap's Station near Fort Washington (modern Cincinnati). In November of that year, he and Little Turtle ambushed a 2,300-man American force led by ARTHUR ST. CLAIR near the Wabash River. The 1,000-warrior force drove the Americans off in a complete rout. St. Clair's rout is remembered as the worst defeat of an American force at the hands of Indians.

In 1794, Blue Jacket's confederation with Little Turtle was showing signs of strain. The British had broken their promise to supply the Indians with ammunition and artillery. In addition, some of their allies from other tribes were becoming uncontrollable. At one point warriors raped some Shawnee women; at another they launched an assault on the American Fort Recovery and were driven off with heavy losses. Despite the assistance of the young Shawnee warrior TECUMSEH, Blue Jacket was unable to hold the alliance together. Little Turtle, recognizing the futility of an attack with a disintegrating force, resigned overall command in favor of Blue Jacket. In August 1794, Blue Jacket tried to ambush an invading force commanded by General ANTHONY WAYNE at the battle of FALLEN TIMBERS (1794). The Shawnee were driven off in a rout. To make matters worse, their erstwhile British allies refused to shelter the fleeing warriors at Fort Miamis.

After Fallen Timbers, Blue Jacket admitted defeat. In January 1795 he and his warriors went to meet with General Wayne at Fort Greenville in western Ohio. The resulting TREATY OF GREENVILLE (1795) secured much of the territory of Ohio for the Americans and established a boundary between the Indians and the settlers in what is now the state of Indiana. The treaty also agreed to compensate the displaced Indians for the land they vacated. The Shawnee, including Tecumseh, later moved to Indiana territory.

Blue Licks (1782) *frontier battle of the American Revolution*
Fighting on the western frontier of the American colonies remained fierce throughout the final years of the AMERICAN REVOLUTION (1775–81). One of the worst defeats for settlers occurred on August 19, 1782, at Blue Licks on the Licking River in Kentucky. Three hundred Wyandot warriors and 30 Tory Rangers led by SIMON GIRTY attempted to raid the village of Bryant's Station near Lexington, Kentucky. Learning of the approach of a heavily armed party of 180 militiamen, including frontiersman DANIEL BOONE, Girty and his Indian allies retreated. The militia followed in pursuit, catching sight of a few Indians near Blue Licks. Suspecting a trap, Boone suggested to militia Captain Hugh McGary that the Kentuckians should wait for reinforcements. McGary refused to wait and led his troops into a classic Indian ambush. Consequently, 146 of the Americans died in the struggle, while only six Indians were killed and another 10 were wounded.

Bluewater Creek (Battle of Ash Hollow) (1855) *running battle fought between the U.S. Army and factions of the Lakota*
Outraged by the GRATTAN DEFEAT (1855), Secretary of War Jefferson Davis ordered Colonel WILLIAM S. HARNEY to go to the Dakota Territory and put down the "Indian problem" there.

Harney established his headquarters at Fort Kearney, where he assembled a force of some 600 soldiers. Although the Brulé Lakota (see SIOUX [Dakota, Lakota, Nakota]) leader Little Thunder favored peace, many of his young warriors wanted to fight.

As Harney's troops advanced toward the Indian village on Bluewater Creek, Little Thunder emerged under a flag of truce. After a brief parley, the troops launched a two-pronged assault on the Indians. Caught by fire from two sides, the Indians fled. During a running battle that stretched a distance of five to eight miles, the Brulé Lakota suffered 85 killed and 5 wounded in the bloody encounter. On the U.S. side, four were killed, seven were wounded, and one was missing during what also became known as the battle of Ash Hollow. Fewer than half of the 250 Indians who were present in the village managed to escape the army's deadly wrath. When Harley's men searched the Indian village, they found mail stolen from the Salt Lake area as well as the scalps of two white women. Harney sent 70 Indian prisoners back to Fort Kearney while he and his men continued toward the Black Hills in pursuit of fleeing Lakota warriors.

body armor *protection employed by both Native Americans and Europeans in combat*
Body armor was used in combat by some Indian tribes and by Europeans. Certain Californian and Pacific Canadian tribes, especially the Nootka, fought with neighboring tribes to push them off their land and to seize slaves. These tribes made helmets carved of wood to protect their faces and armor composed of wooden slats or heavy leather shirts. Most other Indians who

U.S. soldiers defeat the Sioux at the battle of Ash Hollow, 1855. *(By permission of the Colorado Historical Society)*

A war shield with eagle feather and a turtle image *(Courtesy New York Public Library)*

wore special clothing in combat did so for its religious or mystical significance rather than for the physical protection it provided. For example, the GHOST DANCE shirts worn by the Ghost Dancers of the late 19th century were supposed to have the power to repel bullets.

Europeans wore body armor with greater frequency than did their Native American opponents. The Spanish *conquistadores* wore 16th-century European-style armor on their expeditions through southern North America. Virginian colonists called for body armor from England to help in the defense of the colony after the beginning of the POWHATAN WARS (1622–32, 1644–46). MILES STANDISH brought 16 corselets, providing protection for upper body, to the settlement at Plymouth.

The colonists continued to use body armor for approximately a quarter century but abandoned it for several reasons. Body armor was expensive—it had to be imported from Europe—and as gunpowder weapons improved it became less and less effective. It was also uncomfortable to wear, especially in the hot, humid South. Perhaps most important, body armor was ineffective against the tactics employed by most Native American warriors. For instance, it took too long to put on in the case of a surprise attack.

By the mid-17th century, body armor had deteriorated into a small metal breastplate called a *gorget,* which looked like a necklace. Gorgets were only symbolic armor given to Indian chiefs as a symbol of rank and alliance with the British and

French. Indians continued to wear symbolic body armor throughout the period of the Indian Wars.

American Indian body armor took various forms. Chest protectors were made of overlapping plates of bone or ivory; wooden slats; wooden rods, or hardened hide. While the armor was successful in deflecting arrows, were more easily penetrated by bullets.

Indians on the open plains and in the Southwest used shields for defensive purposes. The shields used by equestrian warriors averaged about 17″ in diameter. They were made of thick buffalo, elk, or deer skin. Protective symbols and feathers adorned the outside. AKIMEL O'ODHAM (Pima), NAVAJO (Dineh), and PUEBLO foot soldiers likewise carried shields on occasion.

bone pickers *funeral officials in Choctaw burial practices*
The CHOCTAW, a southeastern tribe, once practiced secondary burial. They first wrapped their dead and placed them on a high scaffold near the house of the deceased. When the flesh had decayed, a religious official—the bone picker—climbed the scaffold and ceremoniously removed any remaining flesh from the bones. Bone pickers were specially equipped for this task: they never cut the nails of their thumb, forefinger, and index finger. The nails were said to be as hard as flint, sharp, and grown to an amazing length.

After completing the cleaning ritual, the picker bound the flesh in a bundle and carefully laid it on a corner of the scaffold. He then climbed down from the scaffold, placed the bones in a box, and set fire to the scaffold. Next the bone picker led the funeral procession to a special bone house, where he deposited the box. Each Choctaw village had a bone house, and when it was full, the villagers took the boxes to a common cemetery shared with neighboring villages. The Indians stacked them together in a pyramid shape on the ground and covered them with three or four feet of earth. Over time, the Choctaw placed each successive deposit atop the others, forming the broad, high mounds that were found in 1818 by the first missionaries in that area.

Bonneville, Benjamin (1796–1878) *U.S. Army officer, trader, explorer*
Born in France near Paris, Benjamin Louis Eulalie de Bonneville immigrated to the United States with his family in 1803. He graduated from West Point in 1815 and was sent to frontier outposts in Mississippi, Arkansas, and Oklahoma. While on a leave of absence from the army from 1832 to 1835, Bonneville set up a fur-trading post on the Green River in Wyoming and explored the northern Rocky Mountains, reporting to the army on the Indians of the region. After resuming his military career, Bonneville served in the Mexican War. In 1856 he took over command of the army's Department of New Mexico.

In 1857, following the killing of an Indian agent by APACHE, Bonneville assembled a retaliatory expedition. From bases in Albuquerque and Fort Fillmore, he headed into the Mogollon Mountains in the New Mexico Territory. In May one of Bonneville's three columns, which he himself led, encountered a group of friendly Mimbreno Apache and killed the chief, Cuchillo Negro. A month later, on June 27, Bonneville's 3rd Infantry regiment attacked a band of White Apache near Mount Graham, south of the Gila River, in present-day Arizona.

Bonneville's 1857 Gila River expedition was the first U.S. Army force to encounter southern Apache bands. Bonneville later served the Union in the CIVIL WAR (1861–65), commanding garrisons in Missouri. After the war he retired to Fort Smith, Arkansas, where he died in 1878. Bonneville Lake and Bonneville Salt Flats in Utah are named for him.

Boone, Daniel (1734–1829) *noted explorer, pioneer, scout, Indian fighter*

Daniel Boone was born near Reading, Pennsylvania, in 1734. When he was 15, his family moved first to Virginia's Shenandoah Valley and then to northwestern North Carolina. During the FRENCH AND INDIAN WAR (1754–63), Boone served as a wagoner in British General EDWARD BRADDOCK's failed attack against French and SHAWNEE Indians at Fort Duquesne (present-day Pittsburgh), after which he returned to North Carolina.

In 1756, Boone began making lengthy journeys into the western wilderness, hunting deer and selling their hides for cash. He made his first trip to Kentucky in 1767. In 1771, while heading back to North Carolina, Boone and his party were robbed of their cargo of deer hides by CHEROKEE, who warned him to stay out of Cherokee lands. Despite this warning, Boone set out to establish a settlement in Kentucky two years later. During the trip there, however, the Cherokee attacked a small group of settlers. Two boys, including Boone's oldest son, James, were killed. Thereafter, most of the settlers returned to North Carolina. Nevertheless, Boone chose a site by the Kentucky River to build a fort and to settle Boonesboro (or Boonesborough) in 1773. He spent the period of the AMERICAN REVOLUTION defending the fort and the settlement from Shawnee attack. In 1776 Boone liberated three young white girls, including his daughter, from Shawnee captivity. This inspired a similar incident that appeared in James Fenimore Cooper's novel *Last of the Mohicans,* published in 1826.

In 1778, Boone was captured by the Shawnee and later adopted by Chief Blackfish, who named him *Sheltow-ee* (Big Turtle). After three months with the Shawnee, Boone escaped. He was able to reach Boonesboro in time to warn of an impending British and Indian attack, thereby enabling the town to survive a six-month siege. The incident made him a hero.

Four years later, in 1782, Boone came to the aid of settlers in Fayette Country, Kentucky, during Indian attacks inspired and led by the British. Against Boone's advice, the local militia pursued the Indians into the BLUE LICKS region, but the Kentucky fighters were ambushed. Among those killed was Boone's son Israel.

In his later years, Boone went into politics. He eventually lost his land claims in Kentucky, but they were partially restored to him in 1814 by an act of Congress. Boone eventually returned to hunting and exploring the West, despite failing eyesight. He died of natural causes on September 26, 1820, at the home of his son Nathan, in St. Charles Country, Missouri. In 1845, the people of Missouri agreed to have his remains and those of his wife returned to Kentucky.

Bosque Redondo (1864–1868) *site in New Mexico where Navajo and Apache Indians were incarcerated*

At the end of the NAVAJO WAR (1863–64), approximately 9,000 NAVAJO made the LONG WALK from their homeland to a remote and uninviting portion of southeastern New Mexico known as Bosque Redondo. There, along the Pecos River, was Fort Sumner and a camp that housed about 400 Mescalero APACHE.

At Bosque Redondo, Brigadier General JAMES H. CARLETON planned to assimilate the Indians into mainstream American culture by having them live in adobe houses, farm, experience sedentary communal living, and attend a Christian church. The Navajo resisted the forced change. Meanwhile they had to struggle just to survive. Food and fuel shortages were commonplace, and the water was alkaline. The Indians suffered from a variety of ailments, including dysentery, malaria, pneumonia, rheumatic fever, measles, and venereal disease. In 1865, a smallpox epidemic claimed the lives of 2,321 Navajo. Some of the Indians were beaten by military personnel, and some women were raped. To make matters worse, the Navajo and Apache were raided periodically by nearby COMANCHE and KIOWA Indians.

Through the efforts of BARBONCITO, MANUELITO, and other Indian leaders, the Navajo and U.S. government signed the NAVAJO TREATY (1868), which allowed them to make the Long Walk back home to northeastern Arizona and northwestern New Mexico.

Bourke, John G. (1846–1896) *U.S. Army officer and ethnologist*

Born in Philadelphia, John Bourke enlisted in the army in 1862 at the age of 16 and served throughout the CIVIL WAR (1861–65). He went to West Point after the war and upon graduation in 1869 was posted to the 3rd U.S. Cavalry.

Bourke served with GEORGE CROOK against the APACHE in Arizona in 1872–73 and against the SIOUX in 1876 at the battles of TONGUE RIVER and ROSEBUD CREEK. Attached that same year to the command of General RANALD MACKENZIE, he also took part in the campaign at DULL KNIFE.

Bourke was a careful student of Indian culture, particularly that of the southwestern tribes. He wrote a large number of reports that became useful tools for diplomats and other officers in their dealings with Native Americans. He also produced several books for a wider audience, among them *An Apache*

Campaign (1886), *On the Border with Crook* (1891), and *Scatologic Rites of All Nations* (1892).

Bowlegs, Billy (Halpatter Micco) (ca. 1810–1864)
Seminole leader during the Second and Third Seminole Wars

Billy Bowlegs was among the last of the SEMINOLE to give up their native lands in Florida for reservations in the Indian Territory (present-day Oklahoma). He waged a guerrilla war against the U.S. Army during the Second and Third SEMINOLE WARS, leading small bands of followers on raids against government survey crews and soldiers. He operated from small camps deep in the swamps of central and southern Florida, where food could be stockpiled and U.S. Army soldiers had difficulty in moving their heavy equipment. However, constant warfare, disease, and starvation, combined with pressure from Seminole who had already accepted new lands in the Indian Territory, reduced Bowlegs's force. He left for Oklahoma on May 18, 1858. Bowlegs was a skilled negotiator as well as a warrior, and he demanded and received cash compensation for the damage the U.S. government had caused to Seminole lands. In 1861, Bowlegs fought for the North in the CIVIL WAR (1861–65) under Opothleyaholo, a CREEK leader.

bows and arrows   *Indian weapons of war*

It is not known whether the Indians of North American independently developed bows and arrows or whether ancient hunters brought them from Eurasia. Based on preserved prehistoric bows, archaeologists date their presence on the North American continent at A.D. 500 and speculate that the early hunters may have used them as early as 1500 B.C.

Each Indian culture area developed its own version of bows and arrows, depending on the available resources. There were several basic types of bows: the self-bow, sinew-backed bow, sinew-wrapped bow, and the composite bow. The eastern Woodland Indians favored the self-bow, which was made from one piece of wood four feet or more in length. These Indians made their bows from ash, hickory, oak, osage orange (bois d'arc), or other hard woods.

Indians who had access only to driftwood or other brittle woods wrapped or backed their bows with sinew. This helped strengthen the wood and provide resiliency. The Alaskan peoples favored these sinew-wrapped bows.

American Indians made composite bows by gluing or lashing together several layers of various materials. The Plains tribes favored a composite bow made from flexible wood, horn, and bone. The Inuit made their composite bows from whale ribs and an added wooden grip.

Etching of Indians using bows and arrows in attack on Overland Express *(Courtesy New York Public Library)*

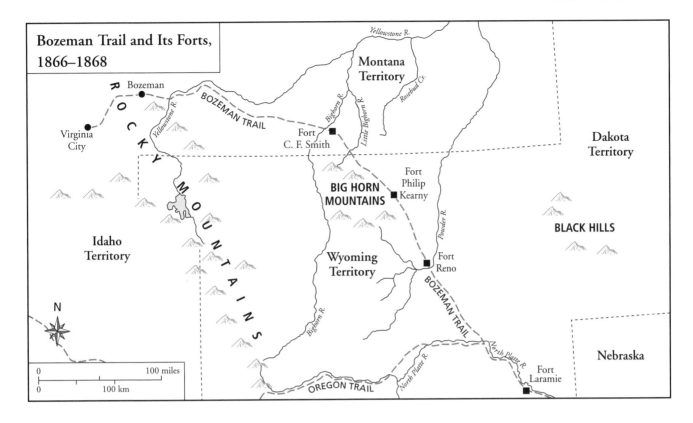

Indian arrows also varied with the different environments. Native peoples took great care when selecting canes, light tree boughs, and reeds for the arrow shafts. They first dried and then smoothed them with bone or stone tools. Then they attached arrowheads to the shafts using sinew, rawhide, or twisted fibers. They made their arrowheads from shell, stone, bone, antler, horn, wood, and later copper. The Indians sometimes loosely attached the arrowheads so they would remain in the body. Mostly, however, they were attached securely to enable the warrior or hunter to retrieve the entire arrow.

Indians such as the Inuit frequently tipped the shaft ends with split or whole feathers. The feathers gave the arrows a spin in flight. Locale also determined the types of feathers used. The most common, however, were from eagles, hawks, or turkeys. The feather ends were tied and centers attached with glue made from animal tissue, sinew, horn, hooves, gum resins, or pitch.

In the early colonial period, when Indians fought with bows and arrows, they had a distinct advantage over non-Indians who used guns. The Indians could make a hit more accurately and shoot multiple arrows more rapidly than non-Indians using single-shot muzzle loaders or early rifles, which were difficult and slow to reload. The Plains Indians shortened their bows with the advent of the horse in the late 1500s, but they suffered no loss of accuracy. They rarely used guns before 1800. The development of more accurate, longer-

ranged, and easier-loading firearms in the mid-1800s, however, eventually rendered bows and arrows obsolete.

Bozeman Trail *travel route from Fort Laramie, Kansas, to Montana gold fields*

The Bozeman Trail was mapped in the years just after the CIVIL WAR (1861–65) to provide the quickest route for settlers and gold seekers headed to Montana from Missouri. The trail, however, cut directly through Indian hunting grounds. Settlement and gold hunting in Montana were also major sources of irritation to the various Indian tribes. The Bozeman Trail became best known for provoking RED CLOUD'S WAR (see also SIOUX WARS, 1854–90). RED CLOUD, a chief of the Oglala Lakota (see SIOUX), was the most prominent leader of Lakota and CHEYENNE opposition to the Bozeman Trail.

Following bloody Indian wars in 1864 and 1865, a number of forts was built along the Bozeman and other trails. A series of treaties in the fall of 1865 had supposedly restored peace to the area. Chiefs from all the local tribes had agreed to make peace and withdraw from overland routes through their territory. However, Indian leaders who signed the treaty did not always speak for all their people. The democratic nature of Indian societies made it hard for them to compel obedience to the terms of the treaty. Leaders from the Oglala, Hunkpapa, Miniconjou, Brulé, Two Kettle, Blackfoot, Sama Arc, and Yanktonai Sioux all signed. Some of the Indian leaders who signed the treaties represented only portions of the involved nations. Their arguments were binding only on the subgroups they represented. Others felt no compulsion to comply with terms of the agreement. And several other groups, whose people had long hunted in the region, had not been represented in the peace talks.

In July 1866, Red Cloud and his followers blockaded the Bozeman Trail. Virtually every wagon train that passed along the trail lost stock to raiders. Many had to fight off attacks. The 18th Infantry Regiment under Colonel HENRY CARRINGTON did not provide much protection to travelers. That summer Red Cloud's warriors also began a siege of Fort Phil Kearny, one of three new forts built to defend the Bozeman Trail. A potential disaster was avoided on December 6, 1866, when a party of soldiers was sent to rescue a group of non-Indians gathering wood outside Fort Phil Kearny. On December 21, Captain WILLIAM J. FETTERMAN led a force totaling 81 men to rescue another wood-gathering party three miles from the Fort. Somewhere between 1,500 and 2,000 warriors waiting in ambush behind a ridge attacked Fetterman and his troops. A rescue party sent out by Carrington found the victims' bodies (see FETTERMAN FIGHT, 1866).

With the FORT LARAMIE TREATIES (1851, 1868), the U.S. government agreed to close the Bozeman Trail and abandon the forts constructed for its defense. The construction of the inter-continental railroad had made the trail obsolete and therefore no longer worth defending.

Braddock, Edward (1695–1755) *British major general following the onset of the French and Indian War*

Major General Edward Braddock was the commander of two regiments of British regulars dispatched from Ireland to assist in the capture of Fort Duquesne (modern Pittsburgh, Pennsylvania) from the French during the FRENCH AND INDIAN WAR (1754–63). Braddock was not very competent as a commander of irregulars; he proved unable to recruit or hold onto Native American allies, and he scorned the advice of American colonial militiamen, including George Washington, who assisted him in his campaign. While en route from Fort Cumberland, Maryland, to Fort Duquesne, Braddock and his troops were ambushed by the French commander Hyacinth de Beaujeu. Beaujeu had only 72 French regular troops, 146 Canadian militia, and 637 Indians of different tribes against Braddock's formidable column of 1,500 men. Nevertheless, in part because of Braddock's disdain for wilderness warfare and his reluctance to use Native scouts, Beaujeu achieved almost complete surprise and routed the British in the encounter, which became known as BRADDOCK'S DEFEAT.

Burial of General Braddock at Road Side, 1755, by J. McNevin/J. Rogers, 1868 (Courtesy New York Public Library)

Only 462 British soldiers and officers survived. French losses totalled 60. Braddock himself was fatally wounded in the encounter. Washington had him buried in the middle of the road that he and his troops had carved through the Pennsylvania forest.

Braddock's Defeat (1755) *perhaps the most embarrassing of Britain's defeats in its long wars for colonial supremacy against its French rivals*

Following the outbreak of the FRENCH AND INDIAN WAR (1754–63), the English Crown authorized the activation of two regiments of colonials, who were to be joined by two regiments of British regulars commanded by EDWARD BRADDOCK. The redcoats departed Cork, Ireland, in January 1755, charged with taking French forts in the Great Lakes and Ohio River Valley regions; the forts threatened to check British expansion into those areas. Upon learning of their enemy's move, the French likewise dispatched reinforcements to the New World.

In April 1755, Braddock arrived in Alexandria, Virginia, where he laid out his plan of attack. Assigning the Nova Scotia campaign to Brigadier General Robert Moncton, Braddock marched on Fort Duquesne (present-day Pittsburgh). The job of eliminating Fort Niagara fell to Admiral Edward Boscawen, who was instructed to intercept French troop transports heading from Brest to the colonies. Content with his plan, Braddock was confident of complete success.

While General Moncton's operation was moving along successfully, Braddock was repeatedly delayed, in part due to his inability to secure sufficient numbers of Indian auxiliaries. Believing the colonials to be almost as inept as the Indians, Braddock also mishandled attempts to raise volunteers in the New World. He had failed to notify many colonial governors of his attack plan; as such, many areas refused to pay war levies or contribute manpower. Several colonists, including Benjamin Franklin, attempted to warn the general of possible Indian ambushes. The overconfident Braddock allowed that while the Indians might do such a thing to rag-tag colonials, they could never defeat the king's well-trained and disciplined regulars.

Despite these problems, Braddock boasted a formidable strike force. In addition to his two regiments of British regulars, he had several units of colonial militia. George Washington, whose earlier actions had contributed so much to the opening of formal hostilities, served as one of Braddock's aides-de-camp. But the 2,000-strong column was overburdened with equipment and faced difficult terrain as they hacked their way west. All along the way, Indians raided British settlements and harassed the column. Following Washington's advice, Braddock detached 1,500 men to attack Fort Duquesne while the others secured his supply lines.

The French commandant of Fort Duquesne was Claude-Pierre Pecaudy de Contrecoe, Jr., whose Indian scouts kept him well informed about Braddock's movements. The French commander considered surrender, but his second-in-command encouraged an attack against Braddock's troops before they could reach the fort. A French force of approximately 900 (two-thirds of whom were Indians) set out to ambush the British column.

Hiding his men in ravines, French commander Captain Hyacinth de Beaujeu patiently awaited the arrival of Braddock's men. Meanwhile, ignorant of unconventional wilderness tactics, the British general sent no scouts forward. Consequently, his column blundered into a deadly ambush. Braddock had five horses shot from under him before he was mortally wounded; his command was shattered by the cross fire of his ambushing foe.

The British had been completely routed; only 462 of the 1,459 men who had begun the battle survived. At the height of the fighting, many British troops had fled in panic, abandoning a fortune in arms and ammunition. Also left on the battlefield were Braddock's money chest and copies of his plans for attacks against Forts Niagara and Saint Frederic. The French lost approximately 60 men. Their victory highlighted the importance of securing proper reconnaissance and forming effective alliances with the Indians along the frontiers.

Brady, Samuel (1756–1795) *frontiersman, scout*

Born in 1756 in Cumberland County, Tennessee, Samuel Brady developed a hatred for Indians after his father and brother were killed by raiding Native Americans. Commissioned a captain during the AMERICAN REVOLUTION (1775–81), he served with a company of scouts under General Daniel Brodhead against the LENNI LENAPE (Delaware) and IROQUOIS of the upper Ohio Valley. An efficient and fearless commander, Brady encouraged his men to adopt Indian dress, which allowed them to move easily through the woods and also among their enemies. On at least one occasion Brady and another scout, Lewis Wetzel, clad in breechclout, leather leggings, moccasins, and warpaint, boldly entered a Native American village to learn the tribe's strength and intentions. The scouts narrowly escaped capture when Brady's blue eyes gave him away, but the ruse contributed to his reputation as "the Daniel Boone of western Pennsylvania." He died at his home.

Brant, Joseph (Joseph Brandt; Thayendanegea, Thayandanega, "he places two bets") (1742–1807) *Mohawk warrior who fought on the side of the British in the French and Indian Wars and the American Revolution*

Thayendanegea was born in 1742, the son of MOHAWK parents. Shortly after his birth, his father died and his mother remarried. That husband was also killed. Her third husband was Nikus Brant, a Mohawk chief. The boy thus became Joseph Brant. As a youth in New York's Mohawk Valley, Joseph learned written Mohawk from Anglican missionaries. He also befriended John and GUY JOHNSON, son and nephew, respectively, of WILLIAM JOHNSON, a wealthy landowner who eventually married MOLLY BRANT, Joseph's sister.

Joseph Brant, a powerful Mohawk chief *(Courtesy New York Public Library)*

During the FRENCH AND INDIAN WAR (1754–63) William Johnson recruited Mohawk to fight for the British. Thirteen-year-old Joseph Brant subsequently participated in the battle of LAKE GEORGE (1755). In 1759 he fought in a battle against the French at Fort Niagara.

Between 1761 and 1763, Brant attended Moor's Indian Charity School in Lebanon, Connecticut (later Dartmouth College), where he learned spoken and written English and became an accomplished interpreter. Upon returning home from school, Brant again fought for the British; this time he led successful raids on two LENNI LENAPE (Delaware) Indian towns during PONTIAC'S REBELLION. Thereafter he became an interpreter and personal secretary for William Johnson, who by this time was England's northern superintendent of Indian Affairs. In 1765 Brant married an ONEIDA woman, with whom he had two children. When his wife died in 1771, Brant married her half sister, who also died two years later. When William Johnson died in 1774, his nephew Guy Johnson became the northern superintendent of Indian Affairs, and Joseph Brant went to work for his childhood friend.

In 1775, while tensions were mounting between the British Crown and the American colonists, Guy Johnson and Joseph Brant went to the British post at Niagara in western New York. They then journeyed to England, where Brant became an instant celebrity. He was befriended by writer James Boswell, had his portrait painted by artists Benjamin West and George Romney, was accepted into the Masonic Lodge, and even had an audience with King George III.

In July 1776, Johnson and Brant arrived back on American soil as the AMERICAN REVOLUTION (1775–81) was raging. Brant fought gallantly in the battle of Long Island and the siege of FORT STANWIX (1777). He also volunteered his services to General William Howe in his campaign against George Washington and the colonists in New York. As a result of his efforts, Brant received a commission as a colonel in the British army. He then tried to persuade the tribes of the IROQUOIS CONFEDERACY to join in the battle against the Americans. Many MOHAWK, SENECA, ONONDAGA, and CAYUGA heeded his advice, but the ONEIDA and TUSCARORA did not.

Between 1777 and 1778, Joseph Brant led several successful attacks on settlers and stockades throughout New York and Pennsylvania. During this time he distinguished himself not only as a warrior but also as an intelligent leader. After fighting with British and Hessian troops in the battle of ORISKANY CREEK (1777), Brant encouraged the employment of Indian battle tactics. The next year, when he found his 100 warriors outnumbered four to one by American militiamen, he chose to parley with the opposing general rather than fight a hopeless battle.

Brant continued his raids on American colonists and participated in the massacre at CHERRY VALLEY (1779). Due in part to Brant's successes, George Washington eventually decided to invade the homeland of Britain's Iroquois allies. After intense fighting, the American advance was successful, and Brant and most of the pro-British Iroquois were forced to flee north to Niagara in Canada. From there he went to Ohio, where he rallied the Indians to the British cause. In August 1781 Brant helped lead an attack on a flotilla of canoes and longboats carrying supplies for American troops commanded by GEORGE ROGERS CLARK. The Indians ambushed the Americans, killing 37 and capturing 14 boats full of provisions. This battle raised the morale of the Ohio Indians, who had suffered under Clark's forces.

From Ohio Brant traveled to Detroit, again to rally the Indians to the Loyalist cause. Britain, however, was negotiating the TREATY OF PARIS. While in Detroit, Brant heard rumors that some Iroquois were negotiating peace with the Americans. Brant opposed the separate truce but to no avail. Realizing that the Iroquoian tribes that had sided with the British would probably lose their lands, Brant used every diplomatic skill at his disposal to gain a new Mohawk homeland in Canada.

By late 1784, Mohawk families had begun filtering into the Grand River Valley in Ontario. There Brant led his people, translated the Anglican Book of Common Prayer and Gospel of Mark into Mohawk, and established a Mohawk Episcopal Chapel. As an Indian statesman, Brant, who spoke three Iroquoian languages, played a key role in the council that resulted in the FORT STANWIX TREATY (1784).

On November 24, 1807, Joseph Brant died on his estate near Brantford, Ontario, and was buried near the chapel he had built. Many years later, in 1879, a physician and medical student opened his grave and stole his bones. Eventually most of them were recovered and returned to their former resting place.

Further Reading

Kelsay, Isabel Thompson. *Joseph Brant, 1743–1807.* Syracuse, N.Y.: Syracuse University Press, 1984.

O'Donnell, James. "Joseph Brant." *American Indian Leaders, Studies in Diversity.* (R. David Edmunds, ed.) Lincoln: University of Nebraska Press, 1980, pp. 21–40.

Stone, William Leefe. *Life of Joseph Brant in Thayendanega, Including the Border Wars of the American Revolution and Sketches of the Indian Campaigns of General Harmar,* Saint Claire Shores, Mich.: Scholarly Press, 1970.

Wilson, Claire, and Jon Bolton. *Joseph Brant: Mohawk Chief.* New York: Chelsea House, 1992.

Brant, Molly (Mary Brant, Degonwadonti, Gonwatsijayenni, Konwatsi-tsianienni) (1735–1795)

Mohawk woman allied with the British during the American Revolution

Born in the Mohawk village of Canajoharie, New York, Molly Brant acquired her last name from her mother's third husband, a Mohawk chief named Nikus Brant. She was the older sister of JOSEPH BRANT, who later became a powerful Mohawk leader. Around 1753, in a Mohawk ceremony, Molly Brant married WILLIAM JOHNSON, Britain's superintendent of Indian Affairs in North America. The couple lived at Johnson Hall, Johnson's estate along the Mohawk River in present-day Johnstown, New York, and had eight children together.

Brant's influence with her people played a major role in allying the Mohawk with the British during the FRENCH AND INDIAN WAR (1754–63). After Johnson's death in 1774, Brant moved up the Mohawk Valley to the principal village of the ONONDAGA people. During the AMERICAN REVOLUTION (1775–81), she was instrumental—along with her brother Joseph Brant—in keeping the Mohawk and other Iroquois people loyal to the British (see IROQUOIS CONFEDERACY). In 1777 Molly Brant gave the British information on Patriot militia movements in the Mohawk valley. Her reports helped the British ambush a colonial relief force at the battle of ORISKANY CREEK (1777). After the American Revolution, Brant moved to what is now Kingston, Ontario, in Canada, where she received a lifetime pension from the British for her intelligence work during the war.

Bridgewater Swamp (1676) *battle that ended King Philip's War*

In the summer of 1676, the WAMPANOAG leader METACOM, known to the English as King Philip, fled to southern Massachusetts after a series of defeats in his war against the English colonists. At dawn on August 12, at a place called Bridgewater Swamp, a colonial militia commanded by Captain BENJAMIN

CHURCH surrounded Metacom's camp. Some 18 soldiers and 22 Indian auxiliaries attacked and killed the Wampanoag band. Metacom was shot and killed by a Wampanoag deserter named Alderman, who had informed the colonists of the Lord's hiding place. With the death of Metacom at Bridgewater Swamp, KINGS PHILIP'S WAR (1675–76) ended, and the confederation of New England tribes Metacom had brought together was shattered.

brown bill *favored weapon of the Virginian colonists during the Powhatan Wars*

The brown bill was a pike, or SPEAR—a broad-headed weapon mounted on a long pole—that resembled a British farming tool used to trim trees. Its brown finish helped discourage rust. The bill itself resembled an axe more than a spear. It had a long point at the end of the pole, a broad axe-like blade ending in another point at right angles, and opposite the blade another short, sharp spike. The entire blade, from haft to point, measured about $1^{1}/_{2}$ feet. The pole usually added another six to eight feet. When used by a trained soldier, the brown bill could easily overcome an enemy armed with a spear, club, or sword.

The brown bill was one of the most common weapons used by the Virginian settlers at Jamestown at the beginning of the POWHATAN WARS (1622–32, 1644–46). Because the wars began in a surprise attack, the colony was caught underarmed and unprepared. The Virginia Company, the organization that founded Jamestown colony, sought help from King James I in 1622. The Crown released 950 brown bills to be shipped to the colony the following year. (Several of these were recovered in archaeological excavations at Jamestown). With the improvement of guns in the late 17th century, the brown bill fell out of use. By the 18th century fighting in the New World had turned away from hand weapons to gunpowder weapons.

buffalo, importance of *animal upon which the Plains Indians' economy was based prior to the 1870s*

Before the arrival of Europeans in America, huge buffalo herds roamed from the Great Plains east to the Alleghenies. Estimates of their numbers at that time range from 34 to 60 million. Buffalo products sustained the Plains culture and provided a medium of exchange with agricultural tribes, such as the ARIKARA and MANDAN. Tools, weapons, combs, ornaments, and toys were fashioned from bone. Tanned hides yielded clothing, shoes, ropes, bridles, tipi coverings, and various other useful items. Fur made soft baby bunting and bedding for the family. Buffalo jerky provided winter food. The entrails were eaten raw or cooked. Milk from slain buffalo cows, mingled with the blood, made a nourishing drink. Buffalo brains softened hides in the tanning process. Buffalo chips, or dung, heated Indian lodges and cooked their food.

In addition to supplying the necessities of life, buffalo hunting provided occasions for tribal religious ceremonies and community unity. Plains Indians believed that after death the spirit ascended to a place of endless buffalo herds and hunts.

Tanned buffalo hides were too soft for commercial uses by non-Indians, making them less desirable than cattle hides. But by 1870, a tanning process that produced stiffer leather created a commercial market for buffalo hides. At about the same time, a new high-powered rifle, the Sharps (with a telescopic sight), became widely available, and buffalo hunting became a popular sport for eastern and European dignitaries. Finally, the completion of the Union Pacific Railroad made it economical to ship huge numbers of the hides east. These factors created a rush on buffalo in the 1870s similar to the gold rushes of the 1850s. Hundreds of buffalo hunters and thousands of skinners flocked to the West and littered the plains with buffalo carcasses. Forty thousand hides a day were shipped east from Dodge City, Kansas. Although the army had no official policy on the issue, it lent its implicit support to the slaughter by allowing the hunters the supplies and protection provided by its frontier forts.

General PHILIP HENRY SHERIDAN praised the hunters for their diligence in ". . . destroying the Indians' commissary. For the sake of lasting peace, let them kill, skin and sell until they have exterminated the buffalo. Then your prairies will be covered with speckled cattle and the festive cowboy."

The Indians became enraged by the thousands of skinned buffalo carcasses rotting in the sun. They deplored the waste and the wanton destruction of their livelihood and important cultural symbol. Indians on reservations mourned the loss of their freedom and the passing of their hunting traditions. They also despised the meager fare doled out by reservation agents.

In the late 1860s, the KIOWA, CHEYENNE, ARAPAHO, and COMANCHE formed an alliance to execute an all-out attack on buffalo hunters. Comanche QUANAH PARKER was chosen to lead a June 27, 1874, attack against 28 buffalo hunters stationed at ADOBE WALLS in the Texas Panhandle. However, the Indians were unable to maintain the element of surprise and were forced to retreat. Scattering out over the southern plains, the Indians attacked non-Indian settlements from Texas to Colorado. These events helped to lead to the RED RIVER WAR (1874–75).

As the southern herds were extinguished, the buffalo hunters moved north during the 1870s, continuing their slaughter. The northern herd was effectively exterminated by 1884.

To the Plains Indians, the buffalo was the source of food, shelter, clothing, and artifacts. *(By permission of the Colorado Historical Society)*

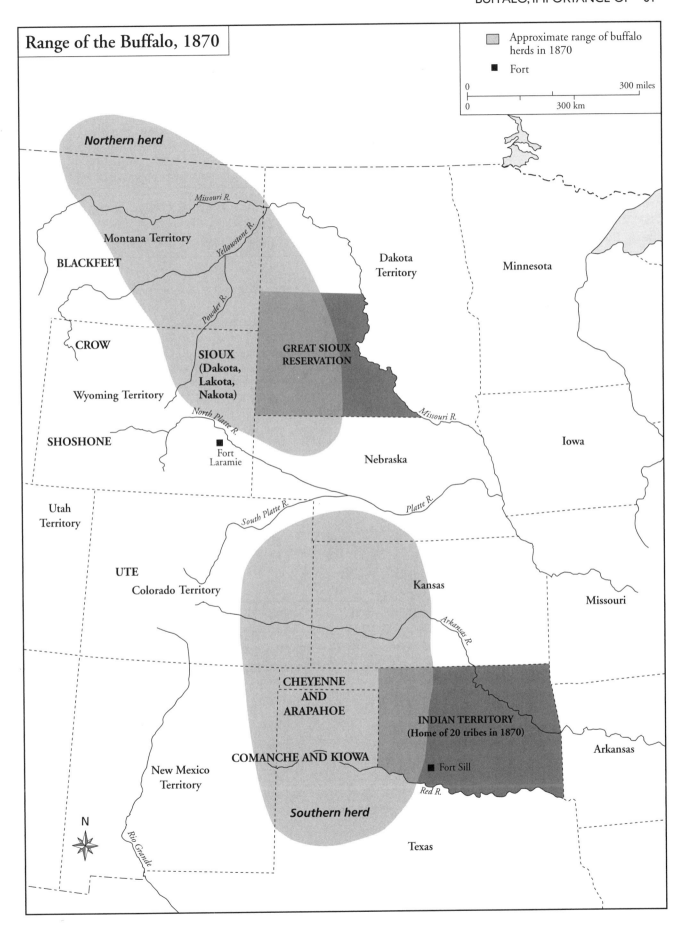

Range of the Buffalo, 1870

Approximate range of buffalo herds in 1870

■ Fort

0   300 miles
0   300 km

Northern herd

Missouri R.

Montana Territory

BLACKFEET

Yellowstone R.

Powder R.

Dakota Territory

Minnesota

CROW

SIOUX
(Dakota,
Lakota,
Nakota)

GREAT SIOUX
RESERVATION

Wyoming Territory

Missouri R.

North Platte R.

Iowa

SHOSHONE

■ Fort
Laramie

Nebraska

Utah
Territory

South Platte R.

Platte R.

UTE

Colorado Territory

Kansas

Missouri

Arkansas R.

CHEYENNE
AND
ARAPAHOE

INDIAN TERRITORY
(Home of 20 tribes in 1870)

Arkansas

COMANCHE AND KIOWA

■ Fort Sill

New Mexico
Territory

Red R.

N

Southern herd

Rio Grande

Texas

Without the buffalo to sustain them, the Plains Indians could not prolong their opposition to reservation life. Many were captured and returned to reservations, and many came straggling in of their own accord as the weather grow cold. The surrender of Quanah Parker and his Kwahadie Comanche warriors, along with 1,500 horses and 400 women and children, on June 2, 1875, brought the southern Plains Indians' buffalo culture to an end.

Buffalo Bill   See CODY, WILLIAM F.

Buffalo Hump (Pochanaw-quoip, Ko-cha-now-quoip, Bull Hump) (mid-1800s) *leader in the Comanche Wars*

Buffalo Hump emerged on the southern plains in the mid-1800s as the principal war chief of the Penateka COMANCHE. He was well known for his attacks on CHEYENNE and ARAPAHO bands and for raids into Texas and Mexico for horses. In 1838, in response to the killing of several Comanche by TEXAS RANGERS at San Antonio, Buffalo Hump led a band of warriors all the way from his homeland north of the Red River (in Oklahoma) to the Gulf of Mexico, raiding settlements along the way. On the way home, the band was attacked by TEXAS RANGERS near present-day Austin, but Buffalo Hump and most of the warriors escaped.

In the late 1850s, during the COMANCHE WARS (1840–75) the U.S. army and the Texas Rangers launched a campaign to drive the Comanche from the southern plains. An expedition under Major EARL VAN DORN attacked Buffalo Hump's band at RUSH SPRINGS (1858) on October 1, killing 56 warriors and two women. Buffalo Hump and those who escaped had to abandon most of their pony herd and other possessions. As the CIVIL WAR (1861–65) ended, and more troops were available to fight the Plains people, Buffalo Hump, along with chiefs of the KIOWA, Southern Cheyenne, and Southern Arapaho, agreed to a peace council with the U.S. government. He subsequently signed the LITTLE ARKANSAS RIVER TREATY (1865), by which the Comanche, as well as the other tribes, relinquished their lands north of the Arkansas River. Despite the treaty, hostilities continued on the southern plains. Buffalo Hump's son, also named Buffalo Hump, joined the fighting under the leadership of the Comanche war chief QUANAH PARKER.

buffalo-skin robes *animal skins used for clothing, bedding, and other purposes*

Many American Indian groups particularly the Plains tribes, made and used buffalo skin robes. Robes served as bedding, as clothing, and as canvases. Generally, women painted abstract geometric designs on the skins, and men produced realistic forms, often depicting a warrior's vision or deeds. Buffalo-skin paintings also portrayed battles or raids and detailed the number of horses stolen and the number and kinds of weapons used in battle.

Buffalo-skin robes were a part of the dress of northern Plains Indians, and they served as part of their ritual activity. For example, by wearing the buffalo head to the left, with the robe's design displayed horizontally, a man could wrap his robe in a distinctive style to signal attitude or intent. He could show anger by holding it over his head or place an end over one shoulder to show a change of attitude. The Plains Indians also used buffalo robes as a medium of trade and gave them as gifts to other tribes and to non-Indians. The eventual popularity of the buffalo robes with non-Indians and increased numbers of white hunters using newly developed guns to shoot buffalo—for food for railroad construction workers and for sport—resulted in the near-extinction of the vast herds and thus an end to the Plains hunting culture.

Buffalo Soldiers *regiments of black soldiers*

In July 1866, the U.S. Congress approved the establishment of military units composed of black soldiers commanded by white officers. The 9th and 10th Cavalry and the 24th and 25th Infantry units were thus constituted. The cavalry units, in particular, battled such formidable opponents as GERONIMO, SITTING BULL, LONE WOLF, and VICTORIO. The term *Buffalo Soldiers* was first used by Cheyenne Indians, who thought the soldiers' curly hair resembled a buffalo's mane and that the soldiers fought with the intensity of those powerful animals.

Illustration of a Buffalo Soldier, an African-American infantryman of the U.S. Army, by Frederic Remington, 1888 *(Courtesy New York Public Library)*

Colonel Edward Hatch organized the 9th Cavalry in New Orleans, and in June 1867 they were ordered to Texas. There, they were assigned to defending Texans and their communication routes from attacks by outlaws and by war parties of COMANCHE, CHEYENNE, KIOWA, and APACHE. Colonel Benjamin Henry Grierson formed the 10th Cavalry at Fort Leavenworth, Kansas. In 1867 and 1868 his unit participated in General WILLIAM TECUMSEH SHERMAN's campaign against the Cheyenne, ARAPAHO, and Comanche.

In the late 1870s, the 9th and 10th Cavalry units were transferred to the Southwest. They were given the responsibilities of guarding stagecoach and railroad crews, intervening in ranch feuds, stringing telegraph wire, defending the United States–Mexico border, battling with local tribes, and escorting defeated Native American groups to their appointed reservations.

The 10th Cavalry pursued the Apache during VICTORIO'S RESISTANCE. In 1885 and 1886, the 10th Cavalry spent 16 months on the trail of Geronimo (see GERONIMO'S RESISTANCE). Three black soldiers were awarded the congressional Medal of Honor for action in Arizona.

In 1881, the 9th Cavalry was transferred to Kansas and then to other places throughout the Midwest. In 1891 they were ordered to subdue Lakota SIOUX tribe members who had become involved in the GHOST DANCE. On December 30 of that year, they rescued a detachment of 7th Cavalry pinned down at DREXEL MISSION.

The Buffalo Soldiers later participated in the charge up San Juan Hill during the SPANISH-AMERICAN WAR (1898) and in 1916 pursued Mexican revolutionary leader Pancho Villa. Throughout their history the Buffalo Soldiers distinguished themselves for their fighting skills, bravery, and discipline.

Buffalo War   See RED RIVER WAR.

Bureau of Indian Affairs (BIA, Indian Bureau)
division of the U.S. Department of the Interior that coordinates and implements governmental policies and regulations concerning Native Americans
The duties and responsibilities of the Bureau of Indian Affairs (BIA) change according to policy goals set by Congress.

During much of the colonial period, individual colonies established and maintained their own Indian policies. In an effort to standardize Indian policy and to diminish French influence, the Albany Congress (1754), an intercolonial conference, established two Indian districts and appointed British superintendents. The American Continental Congress (1775) created a Committee on Indian Affairs based on the colonial system but added a third district. The 1781 Articles of Confederation (the original constitution of the 13 colonies) codified centralized trade with Indians and regulation of Indian affairs.

In 1786, because of conflict between Indians and Non-Indians over land boundaries, Congress established the Indian Department and placed it under the supervision of the secretary of war, Henry Knox. During the 1790s Congress enacted four trade and intercourse acts to regulate Indian trade and commerce. From 1790 until 1822, the official Indian policy was peaceful coexistence and continuing efforts toward "civilizing and Christianizing" American Indians. The Indian Department carried out this policy by managing government trading houses and dispensing appropriations to persons, usually missionaries, employed to instruct the Indians in European religion and culture.

By the 1820s, expanded treaty making vastly increased the burden of administrative duties on the Indian Department. Consequently, in 1824 Secretary of War John C. Calhoun created an unofficial Office of Indian Affairs within the WAR DEPARTMENT, which became known as the Bureau of Indian Affairs (BIA). He appointed former superintendent of Indian trade Thomas L. McKenney as its first director.

In 1830, President ANDREW JACKSON won passage of the INDIAN REMOVAL ACT, which legalized the Removal of Indian tribes east of the Mississippi to the west. Elbert Herring was appointed official COMMISSIONER OF INDIAN AFFAIRS in 1832 and was assigned the task of removal treaty negotiation and implementation. Two years later, the Department of Indian Affairs was officially organized, with a hierarchy of superintendents and agents. In 1849, after a period of relative calm in Indian-government relations, the BIA was transferred from the War Department to the newly created DEPARTMENT OF THE INTERIOR. Thereafter, the army argued continually but without result for the BIA's return to military control. The arguments became especially strident during the period of the PLAINS WARS.

In the late 1840s and early 1850s, white settlement exploded across the Mississippi, propelled by gold discoveries in the West. Trespass on Indian lands, decimation of the buffalo, and demands by non-Indians for Indian land inevitably brought conflict. By 1853 the BIA had begun negotiating treaties with Western Indian tribes to acquire Indian land and to confine the tribes within specified perimeters (reservations). From 1853 to 1856, Indian tribes (often under duress and intimidation), signed 52 treaties relinquishing 174 million acres of land to the federal government. As a result, the reservation system evolved and became a preliminary step toward individual land allotments and tribal dissolution.

The outbreak of the Plains Wars of the mid- to late 19th century (also known as the Indian Wars) prompted Congress to create a seven-man (later eight-man) peace commission in 1867 to investigate the causes of these wars, make treaties, and select reservation sites. It was led by Commissioner of Indian Affairs N. G. Taylor but became dominated by army generals WILLIAM T. SHERMAN, ALFRED TERRY, ILLIAM S. HARNEY, and C. C. Augur. The commission recommended that all superintendents' and agents' offices be vacated and reappointments be made by February 1869. The goal of President Ulysses S. GRANT'S PEACE

POLICY (1869) was reservation confinement of Indians by peaceful means. However, it did not preclude the use of force. Indian agents, appointed from among the Christian religious denominations, managed reservation Indians, coordinated education and agriculture activities, and distributed annuity goods.

The GENERAL ALLOTMENT ACT (1887), intended to assimilate Indians into the larger American society, abolished tribal governments and land ownership, enforced individual land ownership, and divested Indians of millions of acres of land. The BIA took censuses, surveyed land, sold "excess" land, assigned allotments, settled Indians on assigned tracts, and managed Indian land and money. This policy sought to separate Indians from their traditional culture and assimilate them into mainstream American culture. However, John Collier, commissioner of Indian affairs, won passage of the Indian Reorganization Act in 1934. Under this act, the BIA assisted some tribes in reversing some of the effects of allotment and attempted assimilation. Tribal governments were restored, tribal ownership of land was reinstated, constitutions were rewritten, and systems of justice were reinstituted.

During the 1950s, termination policy, as it was called, sought to extinguish certain tribes in the the government-Indian trust relationship. The BIA identified 61 tribes that it determined had developed a high degree of acculturation. These tribes were "terminated," meaning they became ineligible to participate in federal Indian programs. Termination officially ended in the 1960s and was replaced by self-determination, a policy still in effect that allows for self-governance and development of business and tribal resources and encourages renewal of Indian culture. Taking self-determination a step further in the 1990s, several tribes began "compacting" with the federal government—that is, Indian tribes contract with the federal government to administer programs, such as health and education, that were formerly administered by the BIA. The current role of the BIA is to give technical assistance and guidance during and after the transition to Self-determination.

burials of warriors   *manner of burying warriors*
Burial rites differed among the various Native American tribes, depending on their religious beliefs and customs. The NAVAJO of the Southwest would not touch the body of any deceased person because they feared its ghost. The lodge of the deceased was abandoned and could not be lived in again. Along the Northwest coast, chiefs were buried in the ground inside their canoes.

Funeral customs varied among the Plains Indians, but most groups placed the body on a platform above the ground and away from wild animals. The scaffold often was decorated with special items such as a MEDICINE WAR BUNDLE and the warrior's weapons. The deceased might also be placed in a tree and lashed to the branches. A warrior's face was painted with symbols, often those of the society, or club within the tribe, to which he belonged. If he had earned honors, eagle feathers were placed in his hair. The SIOUX (Dakota, Lakota, Nakota) and the

Above the ground burial of Sioux warriors, the Yankton Agency, Dakota Territory *(By permission of the Colorado Historical Society)*

MANDAN placed items such as a warrior's pipe and tobacco, weapons, tools to make fire, and other provisions around the corpse to help him on his journey. The warrior's body was then wrapped in two layers of buffalo hide and tightly bound. If he was a great warrior, his horse might be painted with red spots, indicating mourning. A favorite horse was sometimes killed and placed near the platform or tree.

Among other tribes, a very important person could be buried in a lodge with his personal items placed near him. The openings of the lodge were then sewn shut and the lodge was abandoned.

Burnt Corn Creek   See FORT MIMS.

Bushy Run (1763)   *battle in Pontiac's Rebellion (1763–1764)*
During PONTIAC'S REBELLION, Indians from many tribes worked together to seize the wilderness forts in the Great Lakes territory that were under British control. One of these was Fort Pitt (now Pittsburgh) in western Pennsylvania. Originally built by the French, who named it Fort Duquesne, the fort was surrendered to the British at the conclusion of the FRENCH AND INDIAN WAR (1754–63).

On June 24, 1763, a band of LENNI LENAPE (formerly Delaware) Indians surrounded Fort Pitt and demanded its surrender. In response to the threat, General Jeffrey Amherst, commander of the British forces in North America, sent orders for smallpox-infected blankets from the fort hospital to be distributed to the Indians (see SMALLPOX, EFFECTS OF). The resulting outbreak of disease helped relieve the siege of the fort. However, the infected warriors carried the disease back to their villages, causing epidemic that killed many Lenni Lenape.

Soon after, Amherst dispatched a relief expedition of 460 soldiers under Colonel Henry Bouquet to Fort Pitt. On August 5, 1763, when Bouquet's force was still 30 miles from the fort, a force of Delaware, SHAWNEE, Mingo, and HURON launched an ambush at a spot called Edge Hill. Bouquet held the Indians back until nightfall, but he was unable to keep them from surrounding his entire force and isolating them on top of Edge Hill.

The major enemy of Bouquet's force was not the Indians, but lack of water. Recognizing that his men could not survive if the Indians continued to determine the style of battle, the British commander hatched a plan. On the morning of August 6, he pretended to retreat, leaving only a thin line of defenders at the crest of the hill. The Indians, misled by the sight of the vulnerable soldiers, charged forward in a group and ran straight into two full companies that Bouquet had held in reserve. The soldiers counterattacked and drove the Indians off. Although British losses exceeded those of the Native Americans—Bouquet reported 123 men and officers killed and wounded, whereas the Indians lost about 60 warriors—the Indians retreated in dismay and allowed the British to relieve Fort Pitt.

This encounter, known as Bushy Run, that British military tactics prevailed over Indian guerrilla warfare in a European-style standup battle was a decisive battle for several reasons. First, it proved that the Indians could be beaten using conventional warfare. Second, it allowed the relief and reinforcement of Fort Pitt, an important British stronghold on the Pennsyl-vania frontier. Third, it marked the end of Shawnee and Delaware participation in Pontiac's Rebellion. On October 3, 1763, Pontiac himself admitted defeat and sought peace with the British.

Further Reading
Leach, Douglas E. *Arms for Empire: A Military History of the British Colonies in North America, 1607–1763.* New York: Macmillan, 1973.
Parkman, Francis *The Conspiracy of Pontiac.* Boston: Little, Brown, 1870.

Butler's Rangers *Loyalist regiment during the American Revolution*
In 1777, following the battle of ORISKANY CREEK in the AMERICAN REVOLUTION (1775–81), Colonel John Butler, a wealthy New York landowner who had become a deputy superintendent of Indian affairs under Superintendent WILLIAM JOHNSON, received permission to recruit an irregular regiment of British sympathizers (Tories) to serve alongside IROQUOIS allies in fighting against the American rebels. The regiment invaded Pennsylvania in the spring and summer of 1778 and took part in the battle of WYOMING VALLEY (1778). After another battle outside Forty Fort, Colonel Butler was unable to prevent his Native American allies from killing a number of white prisoners. This and other depradations earned Butler widespread fear and hatred in the region and led to General JOHN SULLIVAN's campaign against him in New York's Mohawk Valley the following year. Butler's Rangers continued their activities in the Mohawk and Schoharie valleys of New York until 1784, when they were disbanded.

Caddo *group of several Indian bands living in what is now Louisiana, Texas, Arkansas, and Oklahoma*

During the colonial period, one group of Caddo Indians lived with their kins people, the WICHITA. The two groups, known by the French as TAOVOYA, came into the French trading sphere as middlemen between the French and the powerful COMANCHE. Pressure from neighboring OSAGE forced the Taovoya and their French allies to relocate on the Red River. There they built the twin villages of San Bernardo and San Teodoro, from which they controlled the southwest fur trade. In 1759 they and the Comanche successfully defended the villages against a sustained attack spearheaded by Spanish commander DIEGO ORTIZ PARRILLA.

The Caddo in Louisiana and Texas, grouped into three confederacies, suffered tremendously as a result of imperial competition and diseases. After the United States took control in 1803, immigrants soon pushed the Caddo into Spanish Texas.

The government of the Republic of Texas failed to protect the Caddo against non-Indian aggression, and they had moved to the Brazos River region by the early 1840s. The Indian agent ROBERT S. NEIGHBORS saved them from massacre when, in the heat of July, he spirited them to safety on a 15-day forced march. The Caddo settled in Oklahoma on a reservation set aside for them on the Washita River. During the CIVIL WAR (1861–65), they remained loyal to the Union, serving as scouts for the U.S. Army.

Calumet See PEACE PIPE.

Calusa *a tribe inhabiting the gulf coast of Florida*

In the 1500s, the Calusa numbered about 10,000 people. Their fishing and trading villages stretched from their main town of Tampa south to the Florida Keys, and they extended their authority over other tribes along the Atlantic coast of Florida. A fiercely independent people, the Calusa repelled the first visit of the explorer Juan Ponce de León in 1513 with 80 war canoes in a day-long battle. Ponce de León did not return until 1521, when he was again repulsed. This time a Calusa arrow inflicted the wound from which the explorer later died.

By the 1600s, the Calusa, who had resisted every attempt by Spanish missionaries to convert them to Christianity, were trading with the Spanish at Havana, Cuba. They were also becoming prosperous from the gold and silver washed up on their shores from shipwrecked Spanish galleons. By the mid-1700s, however, European diseases and the Indian slave trade had decimated the Calusa. In 1763 the English took Florida from the Spanish, and many Calusa relocated to the West Indies. Remnants of the Calusa joined the SEMINOLE tribe, and their descendants later fought with the Seminole in the Second SEMINOLE WAR (1835–42).

Camas Creek (1877) *skirmish between the U.S. Army and Nez Perce Indians during the Nez Perce War*

Camas Creek was a skirmish that took place on August 19–20, 1877, during a time when the NEZ PERCE were attempting to reach Canada from Idaho. While pursing the Nez Perce, General OLIVER O. HOWARD and his command stopped for the night at a camp on the Meadows surrounding Camas Creek in Idaho; the camp had been abandoned by the Nez Perce that same morning. During the night, 200 Nez Perce warriors returned to the meadows and engaged in a brief battle with the soldiers when they tried to steal the soldiers' horses. The horses were heavily guarded, but the Indians managed to escape with 150 mules. Some of the mules were recovered during a subsequent chase.

The significance of this skirmish was considerable. Not only did Howard lost his pack mules, but he also lost the opportunity to overtake the Nez Perce. The warriors had time to further distance themselves from the pursuing force.

Camp Grant Massacre (Camp Grant Fight)
(1871) *major incident in the Apache Wars*
During the APACHE WARS (1860–86), early on the morning of April 30, 1871, a number of APACHE men, women, and children were killed by white vigilantes at an unimposing desert site in Arizona known as Camp Grant. The event had a long-lasting effect, not only on the Apache but also on the history of Indian/non-Indian relations.

In February 1871, five elderly Apache women appeared at Camp Grant carrying a flag of truce. They said that they were looking for a boy who had been captured by soldiers. The women were received courteously by Lieutenant Royal Emerson Whitman, the camp commander, and they were encouraged to convey to their chiefs the possibility of peace talks. A few days later, Chief Eskiminzin, weary of war, appeared in camp. By March, 300 Apache were living peacefully at Camp Grant and drawing rations. Some of them were even hired by local farmers to harvest their crops.

While these Apache were living quietly at Camp Grant, other groups of Apache continued their raiding in southern Arizona. After several deadly attacks, citizens of Tucson, appointed a prominent citizen, William Oury, head of a "Committee of Public Safety." His mission was to put a stop to the attacks. Meanwhile, the town newspaper, the *Citizen,* contended that the perpetrators were coming from the Camp Grant settlement, which was now located four miles from the camp and numbered about 500 Apache. The newspaper published this allegation unreservedly and without any apparent evidence.

Oury and the townspeople devised a plan to amass an army and attack the Apache. Most of the force came from the ranks of the local Papago (see TOHONO O'ODHAM) Indians, whose chief, Francisco Galerita, had little trouble persuading 92 of his tribe to seek revenge on the Apache, with whom they had been at war for years.

At dawn on April 30, while many of the Camp Grant Apache were still asleep, the vigilantes attacked. Less than 30 minutes later, the mob withdrew without losing a man. The Camp Grant Massacre was over, leaving 117 women and children shot or battered to death with clubs and rocks, and 27 Apache children captured. Because many of the Apache men were off hunting, only eight men were killed.

As news of the Camp Grant Massacre reached the East, popular opinion was aroused against the incident. President ULYSSES S. GRANT called it an outrage and warned Governor Safford of Arizona Territory that if the participants were not brought to trial, martial law would be declared in Arizona. Consequently, a five-day perfunctory trial was held in December for 104 of the men who had been involved. After deliberating for 19 minutes, the jury of Arizonans acquitted them all of the crime. Back in Washington, President Grant, working under the weight of popular pressure, proposed a peace policy (see GRANT'S PEACE POLICY). In order to promote "peace" and "civilization," as well as to preserve their safety, roving bands of Apache were to be located on reservations (see RESERVATION SYSTEM), where they would receive subsistence and protection for as long as they remained friendly.

Further Reading
Ogle, Ralph Hendrick. *Federal Control of the Western Apaches, 1848–1886.* Albuquerque: University of New Mexico Press, 1970.
Perry, Richard J. *Apache Reservation: Indigenous Peoples of the American State.* Austin: University of Texas Press, 1993.
Thrapp, Dan L. *The Conquest of Apacheria.* Norman: University of Oklahoma Press, 1967.
Worcester, Donald E. *The Apaches Eagles of the Southwest.* Norman: University of Oklahoma Press, 1992.

Camp Mogollon   See FORT APACHE.

Camp Ord   See FORT APACHE.

Canadian River, Battle of (1858)   See TEXAS RANGERS.

Canby, Edward R. S. (1817–1873) *U.S. Army general and veteran of the Civil War*
Edward Richard Sprigg Canby was a career soldier with extensive experience in warfare with Indians. A West Point graduate (class of 1839), Canby was commissioned as a second lieutenant and was sent to Florida to participate in the Second SEMINOLE WAR (1835–42). He also served during the Mexican War (1845–48) with General WINFIELD SCOTT. Canby drew on his experience battling the SEMINOLE after he was posted to the newly won New Mexico territory in 1855. In 1860 he fought raiding NAVAJO (Dineh) in New Mexico and Arizona.

After the CIVIL WAR (1861–65) broke out, Canby fought both Confederate forces and Native Americans. He was given command of all Union troops in New Mexico in 1861 and was primarily responsible for forcing Confederate Texas troops out of New Mexico in 1862. In association with CHRISTOPHER

Drawing of the shooting of General Canby by Modoc war leader Captain Jack, by W. Simpson, 1873 *(Library of Congress, Negative no. #40067)*

("KIT") CARSON, Canby launched a campaign against the Navajo and their chief MANUELITO in New Mexico. In 1865 he commanded a division of the Union Army that captured Mobile, Alabama.

Canby was named army commander of the Department of the Columbia, which included parts of present-day Oregon, Washington, and Idaho, in 1870. He received command of a small force and was given orders to bring some MODOC warriors and their leader, CAPTAIN JACK, under control. Canby entered negotiations with the Modoc at Tule Lake in northern California in April 1873, but after a disagreement, he was shot and killed by Captain Jack. Although many others died, Canby was the only general officer of the regular U.S. Army lost in the Indian Wars.

Canonchet (Nanuntenoo) (ca. 1630–1676) *sachem (leader) of the Narragansett in what is now Rhode Island*

The son of the great sachem MIANTONOMO, Canonchet was perceived to be a man of overbearing pride by local colonists. Nevertheless, they sought his help during KING PHILIP'S WAR (1675–76), and in 1675 they even invited him to Boston, where he was awarded a silver-laced coat as a token of friendship. These overtures failed to prevent war between the NAR-RAGANSETT and colonists in December 1675, when Canonchet refused to surrender a number of King Philip's men who had come to him for protection.

Canonchet and some of his men managed to escape the slaughter of the GREAT SWAMP FIGHT (1675) and sought refuge among the Nipmuc. The following spring he retaliated burning the settlements of Warwick and Rehoboth and ambushing a militia force that had been pursuing him. Captured by colonists in April 1676, Canonchet was offered his life in return for peace between the Narragansett and the colonists. Canonchet refused to cooperate; consequently, he was executed and beheaded.

Canyon Creek (1877) *seventh in a series of battles in the Nez Perce War*

During the NEZ PERCE WAR (1877), the chiefs of the NEZ PERCE met in council on the night of July 15, 1877, after the battle of the CLEARWATER CREEK. Chief LOOKING GLASS was the only one who had a clear plan—to take refuge with the CROW or with SITTING BULL, leader of the Hunkpapa band of the Teton branch of the Lakota (see SIOUX), in Canada. On August 9, however, the Indians were attacked by General JOHN GIBSON and lost 89 people in the battle of BIG HOLE (1877).

The Nez Perce escaped and crossed the Continental Divide to the source of the Yellowstone River. There, on September 8, Colonel Samuel D. Sturgis and his 7th Cavalry blocked the path of the retreating Indians. However, the Nez Perce outflanked Sturgis and went around him. Humiliated, the colonel pursued them and caught up with them on September 13 at a dry stream bed known as Canyon Creek. Nez Perce sharpshooters pinned the soldiers down while the rest of their people escaped. At one point, only a single Nez Perce, Teeto Hoonnad, remained behind to hold Sturgis's entire command at bay. Sturgis had committed several tactical errors, such as dismounting his forward cavalry companies. As a result he could not dislodge the warriors. The sharpshooters then blocked the soldiers' path with boulders and continued to flee toward Canada. Sturgis lost three men, and 11 were wounded; he suffered a great deal of criticism for allowing the Nez Perce to slip by him not once but twice.

Canyon de Chelly (1864) *last major engagement of the Navajo campaign led by Colonel Kit Carson*

By the end of 1863, it appeared that the miliary campaign against the NAVAJO (Dineh) was failing even though CHRISTOPHER ("KIT") CARSON's expedition (numbering 736 and supported by an additional 326 soldiers under Colonel J. Francisco Chavez at Fort Wingate) was the largest ever assembled to fight the Indians. On December 5, 1863, General JAMES H. CARLETON ordered Carson to Arizona to attack Canyon de Chelly, the Navajo's last citadel and a sacred place.

A month later, on January 6, 1864, Carson and 389 soldiers left Fort Canby for Canyon de Chelly, arriving six days later at the west end of the canyon. For three days, as Carson and a small group searched for a way to descend to the bottom of the valley, Navajo watched from the opposite rim of the canyon. Word went out among the Indians that Red Clothes (as the Navajo called Carson because of his long, red underwear) had come for them. When the colonel rejoined his main command, Sergeant André Herrera and 50 men had already engaged the Indians. Finding some Navajo families trying to escape into the canyon, Herrera's men opened fire, killing 11 and wounding five; two women and two children were taken captive. The Canyon de Chelly campaign had begun.

On January 14, Captain Albert Pfeiffer, whom Carson had previously ordered to traverse the east section of the canyon (now known as Canyon del Muerto), rejoined Major José Sena at the mouth of the gorge. Slowed by severe snowstorms, Pfeiffer reported skirmishes with warriors two days earlier. These skirmishes resulted in the capture of six Navajo and the deaths of three others, including a woman who had hurled rocks and wood down at the soldiers.

After Pfeiffer's fight, many Navajo decided to surrender, their circumstances desperate. Carson's "scorched-earth" policy of destroying everything had left them with no food stores and shelter and little clothing. Women and children were starving; yet many Navajo feared that if they surrendered, they would

be shot to death, as had happened earlier at Fort Canby. Carson finally convinced the Navajo that those who surrendered would be treated fairly; by January 16, 1864, the campaign was over. The troops headed back to Fort Canby with the Indians following. Carson later had two companies under Captain Asa B. Carey march through the canyon and destroy Navajo homes and peach orchards. Canyon de Chelly was their last stronghold, and the Navajo understood that neither they nor their property would be safe from the soldiers. Increasing numbers of them arrived at Fort Canby in the following days. By mid-January, Carson reported that there were more than 500 Navajo ready to begin their trek to BOSQUE REDONDO in New Mexico, a desolate camp used to house Indians.

General Carleton called Carson's expedition on the "crowning act" in the colonel's long career. But the Canyon de Chelly campaign was not a great military victory. No large battles had been fought nor had Carson crushed the Navajo with a superior army. The Indians, reduced to fighting with rocks, sticks, bows and arrows, and suffering from the elements and starvation, eluded the soldiers many times. The significance of the Canyon de Chelly campaign lay in Carson's success in talking to the Navajo and convincing them that the government did not intend to murder them and their families. The Navajo's choices, however, were few. The government would remove them to Bosque Redondo or they could hold fast to their hide-

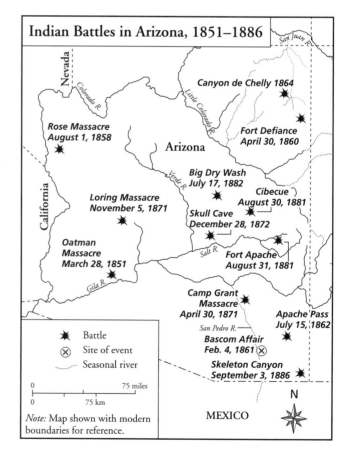

Indian Battles in Arizona, 1851–1886

outs, where they might freeze or starve to death. Untold numbers had already died, and it appeared that many more would follow. For the Navajo, removal was not an attractive alternative, but it seemed the only chance for survival. Thus, they surrendered.

Captain Jack (Kintpuash, Keintpoees, Kientpoos, Peintpres) (ca. 1837–1873) *leader in the Modoc War*

Captain Jack—so called because he often wore a blue military-style coat—is best remembered for having shot and killed General EDWARD R. S. CANBY during negotiations for the return of the MODOC to their Klamath Reservation in Oregon. (See also MODOC WAR (1872–73.) Found guilty of the general's murder, Captain Jack was hanged by the army on October 3, 1873.

In many ways Captain Jack's death was the result of rivalries between Native American tribes and factions within his own clan. During the 1860s the tribe had been resettled on the Klamath Reservation, located entirely on the land of the Klamath tribe. The Klamath, feeling no sense of brotherhood with the dispossessed Modoc, harassed them and extorted work from them in return for the "use" of Klamath territory. In 1865 Captain Jack and a small band of followers returned to traditional Modoc territory on the Lost River in northern California, near the California-Oregon border.

For four years, government agents and officers tried to convince Captain Jack to return to the reservation. Late in 1869, Captain Jack yielded. However, the rivalry between the Klamath and the Modoc quickly heated up again. Their uneasy truce finally broke in 1870, when Captain Jack killed a Klamath shaman who had accidentally killed his niece during an operation. The Klamath complained, a warrant was issued for Captain Jack's arrest, and in April 1870, he and about 370 Modoc fled to Lost River. The remainder of the tribe stayed on the reservation but removed themselves from the settlements of the Klamath and formed a new village of their own.

The nearby presence of Captain Jack and the Modoc made settlers in northern California uneasy, and they made frequent demands to the government that the Indians be removed. On November 29, 1872, a military detachment of 40 men and three officers found Captain Jack's band at their camp near Lost River and tried to remove them by force. In the fight that followed, the army suffered eight casualties, the Modoc lost only two men. To slow down pursuit, Captain Jack led his followers into rough volcanic terrain near TULE LAKE. The lava formations served as natural fortifications, sheltering the Indians from hostile gunfire.

At this time several members of Captain Jack's band slipped out from under his control. One of these, a man named Hooker Jim, was attacked by a posse of local white residents. In retaliation, Hooker Jim and his followers, along with another band under the leadership of a Modoc named Curly Headed Doctor, killed 12 settlers at a nearby ranch. The combined bands then joined Captain Jack in the lava beds, raising his

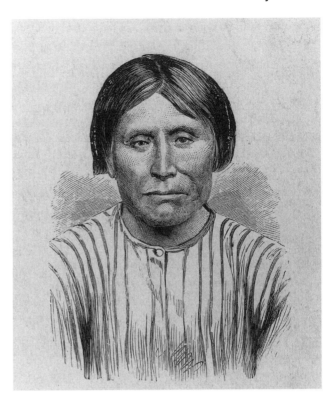

Captain Jack was hanged on October 3, 1873, for killing General Edward S. Canby. *(Courtesy New York Public Library)*

numbers to about 200, including 80 warriors. They also seized an army ammunition train, increasing their firepower. The army took action against the Modoc in January 1873, at what came to be known as the battle of the LAVA BEDS, or the Stronghold. However, the Indian position proved to be too strong to take through infantry action. The soldiers lost 37 men before retreating; the Modoc were untouched.

General Canby, an experienced Indian fighter recently appointed to the top military command in the area, recognized the seriousness of the situation. He began assembling a large army and opened peace negotiations with the tribe, with Modoc Winema (Toby Riddle) and her husband, Frank Riddle, acting as interpreters. This caused much dissention among the Modoc. A majority of the Modoc tribespeople, including some that were wanted by local officials for non-Indian deaths, challenged Captain Jack's authority and insisted that he kill the negotiators. Captain Jack protested, declaring that such an act would only strengthen the army's resolve. In the end, however, he allowed himself to be persuaded. (See also SCARFACE D. CHARLEY.) Winema learned of the threat to the negotiators, but Canby refused to believe her.

On April 11, 1873, the Modoc, General Canby, and a team of arbitrators met near the lava beds. Captain Jack demanded that the Modoc be allowed to live in peace on the barren lava beds. When Canby refused, Captain Jack and his followers attacked the arbitrators, killing Canby and a

Methodist minister named Eleaser Thomas and wounding Indian agent Alfred Meacham and a government official named L. S. Dyer.

Military control tightened on the lava beds, and the Modoc began to surrender. Hooker Jim bargained for his own life by agreeing to turn Captain Jack over to the army. Captain Jack and three of his confederates finally surrendered to U.S. authorities in May 1873. They were tried and executed in October. The remaining Modoc were shipped off to Indian Territory (present-day Oklahoma).

Further Reading

Luger, Harriett M. *The Last Stronghold: A Story of the Modoc Indian War, 1872–1873*. North Haven, Conn.: Linnet Books, 1995.

Murray, Keith A. *The Modocs and Their War*. Norman: University of Oklahoma Press, 1959.

Payne, Doris P. *Captain Jack: Modoc Renegade*. Hillsboro, Ore.: Binford & Mort, 1979.

Riddle, Jeff C. *The Indian History of the Modoc War*. San Jose, Calif.: Urion Press, 1975.

Sherron, Victoria. *Political Leaders and Peacemakers*. New York: Facts On File, 1994.

Sowneborn, Liz. "Winema." *A to Z of Native American Women*. New York: Facts On File, 1998, pp. 194–197.

captives, war *prisoners claimed by Native Americans or Europeans as spoils of war*

Warfare waged between Indian groups was generally fought for material reasons–e.g., to increase the tribe's number of warriors. Some members of the IROQUOIS CONFEDERACY, for example, adopted prisoners into their tribes or ritually killed them (see PRISONERS). For their part, the Europeans had a long tradition of holding prisoners of war as slaves, dating back to the time of the Roman Empire. Spanish *conquistadores* routinely raided the North American coast and enslaved Indians, later making slaves of APACHE and NAVAJO (Dinch) as well.

The British also followed this example; many of the prisoners seized in the PEQUOT WAR (1636–37), for instance, ended their lives as slaves on Caribbean islands or in Spanish America. Nansemond Indians taken captive by the Jamestown colonists during the Second POWHATAN WAR (1644–46) were also sold into slavery in the West Indies. One of the major factors that led to the start of the TUSCARORA WAR (1711–13) was the persistent slave-raiding by South Carolina colonists.

It was not until after the arrival of the Europeans that Native Americans also began taking prisoners as plunder, to be traded later for goods such as food, blankets, clothing, or firearms. Such exchanges were most common in New England and French Canada during KING WILLIAM'S WAR (1689–97), QUEEN ANNE'S WAR (1702–13), and KING GEORGE'S WAR (1744–48).

The idea of Indian captivity so captured the colonial imagination that during the late 17th century "captivity narratives"—stories based on real experiences of people who had been captured by the Indians—became very popular. For example, in 1682 Mary Rowlandson published *The Sovereignty & Goodness of God*, telling of her capture by Indians during KING PHILIP'S WAR (1675–76). The Reverend John Williams, seized by French-allied Indians in the DEERFIELD RAID (1704), published his story under the title *The Redeemed Captive* (1706). These works set a pattern for later captivity narratives in which the narrator was seized from his or her home by ferocious savages and witnessed the brutal deaths of friends, spouses, or children. The narrator also typically attributes the sparing of his or her life to the mercy of God or divine providence, giving the story a moral tone. The stories portrayed Indians as brutal and inhuman, and their popularity helped to spread the concept of Indians as bloodthirsty savages as well as to heighten the colonists' fear of them. While this was the standard "captivity narrative," Mary Jemison's story, published as *The Life of Mary Jemison: The White Woman of the Genesee*, tells of a woman who chose to remain with the Indians. While less common, her story was not unique. The "captivity narrative" tradition remained popular throughout the 19th century.

Carleton, James Henry (1814–1873) *U.S. Army officer who influenced the course of American policy toward the Mescalero Apache and Navajo*

James Carleton was born and raised in Maine and joined the U.S. Army in 1839. He fought alongside General Zachary Taylor during the Mexican War (1845–48). By the time the CIVIL WAR (1861–65) broke out, Carleton had become colonel of the First California Regiment. During the Civil War, Carleton led 1,800 troops into New Mexico and assumed command of the area. He was subsequently was sent to head off a Confederate invasion of New Mexico but found that Colorado Volunteers and regular units under militia leader JOHN CHIVINGTON had already driven them back. General Carleton's California and New Mexico Volunteers thus spent the rest of the war years fighting the APACHE and NAVAJO (Dineh).

A man of great ability and enthusiasm, Carleton was also arrogant and capricious. He undertook warfare with the Indians with zeal, persistence, and little compassion for his enemy. Ordered to keep the east-west communication lines open, Carleton declared a war of extermination, first on the Apache and then on the Navajo. In October 1862 Carleton ordered his men into the field against the Mescalero Apache, telling them to kill anyone they found and to take women and children as PRISONERS. Once Carleton had defeated the Mescalero and Navajo, he intended to remove the survivors to a 40-square-mile plot in southeastern New Mexico known as BOSQUE REDONDO. He had already established a post, Fort Sumner, to oversee the camp of Bosque Redondo. His plan was to have companies of cavalry and one company of infantry guard and enforce Indian residence on the camp.

Between October 1862 and January 1864, Carleton proceeded with his plans. The Apache, numbering some 400 people, were successfully relocated to Bosque Redondo by the end of March 1863. Carleton then turned his attention to the Navajo. In April 1863 Navajo chiefs BARBONCITO and Delgadito met with him in an effort to seek peace. Carleton, however, informed them that to be considered peaceful, all Navajo had to go to Bosque Redondo. The chiefs rejected the proposal. Two months later, Carleton reiterated his ultimatum: The Navajo were given until July 20, 1863, to move to the camp.

On June 15, 1863, Carleton sent Colonel CHRISTOPHER ("KIT") CARSON after the Navajo. His troops drove the Indians from their homes, burned crops and grain stores, destroyed orchards and homes, and captured or scattered cattle, sheep, and horses. By fall 1863 those Navajo brought in by troops were suffering from malnutrition and exposure to the elements. When Carson marched into the CANYON DE CHELLY in 1864, many Navajo were ready to surrender. By the end of that year, some 8,000 people, or about three-fourths of the tribe, were relocated to Bosque Redondo. The remainder fled into the deserts and mountains.

General Carleton's experiment at Bosque Redondo failed to transform the Indians into peaceful Christians as he had hoped. In October 1867, the Navajo were released; the Mescalero had already escaped in late 1865. Nine months later, the Navajo signed a treaty with the government, allowing them to return to their homeland, known as Dinétah. By then General Carleton had given up his New Mexico command for service in the Department of Texas.

Further Reading

Prucha, Francis Paul. *The Great Father: The United States Government and the American Indians.* Vol. 1. Lincoln: University of Nebraska Press, 1984.

Carr, Eugene A. (1830–1910) *major general who was part of Philip Henry Sheridan's campaign into Indian Territory in November 1868*

During the SOUTHERN PLAINS WAR, Major General Eugene A. Carr and his troops combined with those of Major William H. Penrose and pushed into the region of the upper Beaver and Wolf Creeks in Indian Territory (now Oklahoma), with the intention of driving any Indians toward the forces led by PHILIP H. SHERIDAN and GEORGE ARMSTRONG CUSTER. The trek was uneventful. Carr, however, clashed with CHEYENNE DOG SOLDIERS, a tribal war society, in April 1869. That month a number of Cheyenne chiefs, including Little Robe, Minimic, and Grey Eyes, brought their bands into Fort Sill, in present-day Oklahoma. Told to go north to Camp Supply (later Fort Supply), most simply returned to the Plains. A council held among the Cheyenne resulted in a clash between Little Robe's peace faction and the Dog Soldiers led by TALL BULL and White Horse, who preferred war. Several hundred Dog Soldiers left soon after for the Republican River in western Kansas. On May 1, 1869, Carr was

sent after the Dog Soldiers; 12 days later his 5th Cavalry attacked the village. About 500 Dog Soldiers resisted but were driven north after losing about 25 men. In retaliation the Dog Soldiers attacked settlements and transportation routes, killing 13 people and taking two women captive. Carr followed in June and after a month of minor clashes, he caught up with Tall Bull's band at SUMMIT SPRINGS near the Platte River in Colorado. Tall Bull was killed, his village destroyed and his people scattered.

Carr later fought against the various tribes historically known as the SIOUX (Dakota, Lakota, Nakota) in the War for the Black Hills (see SIOUX WARS) and led campaigns against the APACHE in Arizona and New Mexico.

Carrington, Henry B. (1824–1912) *U.S. Army officer involved in the War for the Bozeman Trail and the Fetterman Fight*

Henry B. Carrington was born in Connecticut in 1824. After graduation from Yale Law School, he moved to Columbus, Ohio, to practice law. He served as a staff officer in the CIVIL WAR (1861–65), following which he became a colonel in the regular army, commanding the 18th Infantry Regiment.

In the summer of 1866, Carrington's unit was dispatched from Fort Kearny, Nebraska, into the area along the Platte and Powder Rivers. At this time, Lakota SIOUX leaders, including Oglala leader RED CLOUD, were meeting with Indian Bureau and military officials at Fort Laramie to discuss encroachment onto their lands, primarily by way of the BOZEMAN TRAIL. Carrington's unit was assigned to construct forts along the trail to protect travelers headed to Montana's mining country. Carrington's arrival caused the Indian leaders to accuse the U.S. government representatives of deception. Red Cloud and the other Indian leaders withdrew from the conference and declared hostilities against anyone who crossed their hunting lands.

Carrington's forces then proceeded up the Powder River to establish Fort Phil Kearny in Montana, near the forks of the Little Piney and Big Piney Rivers. Construction efforts were immediately hampered by bands of Lakota, ARAPAHO, and Northern CHEYENNE. In December 1866, a wagon train returning with wood for the fort's construction was attacked by Lakota warriors a few miles from the fort. Carrington allowed Captain WILLIAM FETTERMAN to lead a relief column of some 80 men against the attackers. Fetterman exceeded his orders and chased a small band of Indians over a hill into an ambush of about 2,000 warriors. No soldiers survived the ambush, which became known as the FETTERMAN FIGHT (1866).

Though later exonerated, Carrington was deemed partly responsible for the Fetterman Fight and relieved of his command. After his retirement from the military, Carrington taught military tactics, wrote books on the AMERICAN REVOLUTION (1775–81), and helped negotiate an 1889 treaty with the Flathead Indians. In 1892, he supervised removal of northern plains Indians to Montana reservations.

Carson, Christopher ("Kit") (1809–1868) U.S.
Army officer and scout, Indian agent

Kit Carson was born in Kentucky in 1809 but was raised in Missouri until age 14. In 1825, tiring of the saddle-making trade to which he had been apprenticed, Carson joined a caravan bound for Santa Fe, New Mexico. From 1828 to 1831, he traveled throughout what is now southern Arizona and California, trapping and hunting. He won a reputation as a man of strong character and great courage and was respected by Native Americans and non-Indians alike.

While Carson was on his way to visit his family in Missouri in 1842, he met John C. Fremont, an explorer and future presidential candidate, who was organizing an expedition to the West. Fremont hired Carson as a guide, and the trapper accompanied the explorer on two expeditions. Carson also served as a scout and guide for the U.S. Army during the Mexican War (1845–48) and the California Bear Flag Rebellion that preceded it. Following the Mexican War he settled down on a ranch near Taos, New Mexico, to raise sheep. In 1853, Carson was appointed Indian agent to the NAVAJO (Dineh) of the area. His fair and honest treatment of the Native Americans won him their respect.

At the outbreak of the CIVIL WAR (1861–65), Carson resigned as Indian agent to join the First New Mexico Volunteer Cavalry. In 1862, he came under the command of General JAMES HENRY CARLETON, who ordered Carson into action against the Mescalero APACHE, the Navajo, the COMANCHE, and the KIOWA. Although Carson was sympathetic toward the tribes, he carried out his orders with vigor, harassing and pursuing the Indians onto reservations specially created for them. Many of the Indian prisoners who surrendered were held at BOSQUE REDONDO in what is now southeastern New Mexico.

Perhaps the bloodiest of the conflicts in which Carson took part involved the Navajo of southern New Mexico. In April 1863 Carleton sent an ominous message to Delgadito and BARBONCITO, the Navajo's peace chiefs, instructing them to remove their people to Bosque Redondo. The Navajo refused to move, and on July 20, 1863, Carson set out with 736 soldiers to coerce them to surrender. By the end of July he had killed 11 warriors and captured 13 women and children.

Carson not only fought Indians directly, he also waged war on their supplies, confiscating their sheep and horses and burning their crops and homes. On January 6, 1864, Carson and 389 men and officers, struck at the Navajo stronghold of CANYON DE CHELLY (1864). Within six days, 11 warriors had been killed and 60 more surrendered. Although bands of Navajo continued to surrender throughout 1864, the Canyon de Chelly campaign broke the tribe's power (see NAVAJO WAR, 1863–64). By March of that year, more than 2,100 Navajo had been sent to the Bosque Redondo Reservation, and by the end of the year three-quarters of the tribe's population had relocated there.

Carson continued in military service for a period after the end of the Civil War. He was briefly placed in charge of Fort Garland in Colorado before retiring to Boggsville in the same state with his wife and family. He died of a hemorrhage on May 23, 1868.

Further Reading

Dunlay, Tom. *Kit Carson and the Indians.* Lincoln: University of Nebraska Press, 2000.

Guild, Thelma S., and Harvey L. Carter. *Kit Carson: A Pattern for Heroes.* Lincoln: University of Nebraska Press, 1984.

Sanford, William R. *Kit Carson: Frontier Scout.* Springfield, N.J.: Enslow Publishers, 1996.

Christopher (Kit) Carson, an Indian scout and agent *(By permission of the Colorado Historical Society)*

Cayuga *one of several tribes allied in the Iroquois Confederacy*

Along with their Iroquois (Haudenosaunee) confederates, the Cayuga conquered and dominated a region that ranged from New York through Pennsylvania to Ohio and from the St. Lawrence River to the Ohio River. The other Confederacy members were the MOHAWK, the ONEIDA, the ONONDAGA, the SENECA, and, after 1722, the TUSCARORA.

During the AMERICAN REVOLUTION (1775–81), the IROQUOIS CONFEDERACY collapsed when four of the member tribes, including the Cayuga, sided with the British. The two other Iroquois tribes, the Oneida and Tuscarora, fought on the side of the Americans. During the war the opposing tribes clashed at ORISKANY CREEK (1777), each inflicting casualties on the other.

After the Revolution, the FORT STANWIX TREATY (1784) set territorial boundaries for the six Iroquois tribes. Many Cayuga, however, fled to Canada and established villages there.

Non-Indian settlers advancing west demanded land cessions, causing dispersal of the Cayuga. By 1807 the tribe had given up all of its New York land and moved onto SENECA reservations. Some joined other Iroquois groups in Ohio. During the WAR OF 1812 (1812–14), the Ohio Iroquois fought against the British for the United States. After passage of the INDIAN REMOVAL ACT (1830), they were sent to Oklahoma.

Cayuse *Native American tribe of the Pacific Northwest*

The Cayuse were known primarily as horse traders in historical times, and in fact the name of the tribe has become a word for "pony." The Cayuse made their homes along tributaries of the Columbia River. Each band was composed of several families under a single chief. They lived primarily as fishers, supplementing their diet with small game and wild berries and roots.

In 1847, angered over a recent heavy influx of settlers into the Oregon Territory (settlers who brought with them the deadly measles virus), the Cayuse raided a mission settlement near Walla Walla, Washington. The ensuing massacre led to the CAYUSE WAR (1848–50). Later, the Cayuse were among the treaty signatories at the WALLA WALLA PEACE COUNCIL (1855). Though some warriors joined the YAKAMA and NEZ PERCE in later uprisings against non-Indians, most Cayuse settled on a reservation with the Umatilla and the Walla Walla in Pendleton, Oregon.

Cayuse War (1848–1850) *conflict between Cayuse and non-Indian settlers in Oregon*

In 1836, TILOUKAIKT, a CAYUSE chief, allowed Dr. Marcus Whitman and his wife, Narcissa, to build a Protestant mission on Indian land at Waiilatpu in the Walla Walla Valley of Oregon. In 1838, after the Whitmans had established their mission, a Catholic priest arrived at Walla Walla. Competition between Catholic and Protestant missionaries among the Indians wrought a great deal of confusion. Soon after, a new wave of settlers introduced measles to the Cayuse, who watched their tribal members die as most non-Indians recovered from the disease. (Indians had no developed immunity to European diseases.) The Cayuse interpreted this as bad medicine. They traditionally held their medicine men strictly accountable for healing. Should a patient not respond to treatment, the next successful medicine man often directed the patient's family to kill the unsuccessful one. Whitman, a doctor, was unable to cure the Indians, and some claimed that he had poisoned them. The Cayuse also suspected that Dr. Whitman, with the aid of American military, planned to take the Indians' land.

In retaliation for Indian deaths, a Cayuse party, including Chief Tiloukaikt and Tomahas, killed Dr. Whitman, his wife,

Narcissa, and approximately 12 others. The Cayuse took the rest (about 50) as slaves. The murders and captures led to the Cayuse War.

The Provisional Oregon Territory authorized the raising of 500 mounted riflemen to capture Tiloukaikt and the others accused of the murders. Tiloukaikt's group cemented an alliance with their neighbors the Palouse, Umatilla, and a few Walla Walla and NEZ PERCE Indians. On February 24, 1848, while members of the Kalispel, Coeur d' Alene (Skitswish), and Flathead tribes observed them, the two belligerents fought their battle at Sand Hollow, eight miles east of Wells Springs on the Immigrant Road. The Cayuse hoped to decisively defeat the volunteer riflemen and thus bring the observing Indians into their coalition. Instead, the three-hour battle was inconclusive, destroying the chance for the expected alliance with the observers as well as most of the Nez Perce, the YAKAMA, and the Spokane. An additional bad omen was dissension within the Cayuse ranks.

The volunteer force then constructed Fort Waters with materials from the Waiilatpu buildings. They pursued the Indian forces in early March. On March 14, Colonel Cornelius Gilliam and the volunteers rode into a Cayuse and Palouse camp of 400. The Indians convinced the volunteers of their loyalty and said that the murderers were north of them. After the volunteers left, the Cayuse joined ranks with the Palouse and turned on their pursuers at the Touchet River. The battle raged for 30 hours, until the volunteers succeeded in crossing the river. Those accused of murder began to retreat into the mountains. The war was over and in response to settlers' demands, the government opened Cayuse land to settlement.

ceremonial rattles *instruments used to accompany songs and dances or to help scare away evil influences*

Ceremonial rattles were often part of the prayers, visions, and rituals that gave spiritual power to Indian warriors and helped them defeat their opponents. Warriors who shared similar dreams during their passages into adulthood banded together into warrior societies (see MILITARY SOCIETIES). Each society had its own organization, costume, and rituals. Rattles figured in many ceremonies and were used by Plains tribes such as the CHEYENNE and BLACKFOOT CONFEDERACY as part of the initiation ceremonies that welcomed new warriors to the tribe.

Most Native American rattles were of two basic types. The first and most common type consisted of a dried gourd, skin, or hide container, or a hollow piece of wood filled with small stones or seeds. The second type was simpler; it consisted of small shells or birds' beaks strung along a stick or rod so that they clacked together when shaken.

See also DANCES, WAR.

ceremonies, war *ritual activities prior to or following battle*

Native Americans prepared for war in various ways. Among most tribes, men were conditioned for toughness and trained in

Drummer at a traditional Crow Indian dance ritual *(Courtesy of the National Museum of the American Indian, Smithsonian Institution #9332)*

methods of war from the time they were very young. Young warriors also were conditioned mentally and became steeped in the desire to prove their skills and courage and to defend the tribe and their families.

Certain procedures were followed just before going into battle, with warriors usually taking the lead and others joining in to express solidarity. In many tribes men sang specific songs; in some tribes the battle songs of men who did not return were never sung again.

War ceremonies included war dances, (see DANCES, WAR) and other ritualized activities. The Ojibwa (Anishinabe) nation, for example, would erect a large pole in the center of the community. At sunset on the evening before a war party was to leave, a bonfire would be lit near this pole. Wood for the fire was collected by children and by younger warriors who had not yet been in battle. The tribe was summoned by the beat of a large drum. The main drummer then tuned the drum by the heat of the bonfire, after which several drummers began to play it at one time, starting softly and then getting louder. The drummers changed and eventually the tempo slowed. The war leader and the other warriors, dressed in full war regalia, emerged from the darkness and circled the fire four times.

The war leader then addressed the people, explaining the reason for war. He pledged to make right these wrongs and then told of past war achievements, striking the war post as he did so. Each warrior, in order of rank, told of his own deeds and struck the post. Untested warriors were also permitted to strike the post. The warriors then ate from the liver of a dog sacrificed for the ceremony. After four more circles of the fire, followed by the rest of the community, the ceremony came to an end and a feast followed.

War ceremonies similar to this one were held in most tribes to evoke passion among the warriors and to strengthen community support.

Cherokee *tribe originally inhabiting parts of the southeastern United States*

Cherokee territory prior to European contact included portions of West Virginia, Virginia, Kentucky, Tennessee, Georgia, and the Carolinas. In 1735, the Cherokee population is estimated to have been at between 17,000 and 21,000. The Cherokee are related linguistically to the Iroquoian family, being the southern most member of the group.

Cherokee families were organized according to a clan system with matrilineal descendance. Cherokee towns functioned independently except during war. When war was declared, war chiefs assumed control, and the towns functioned as a unit. Certain towns were designated cities of refuge, where bloodshed was not permitted. In the period prior to the arrival of Europeans, the Cherokee were polytheists whose religion centered on the forces of nature, the origin of disease, and other natural phenomena. Medicine men, or shamen, performed chants and divinations and applied their knowledge of pharmacology. Women and children performed agricultural duties, and men supplied deer and other wild game to the villages.

The first contact between the Cherokee and colonists occurred shortly after the settlers in Virginia defeated the POWHATAN CONFEDERACY in 1654. Close to 700 Cherokee descended from the mountains and camped at the James River falls. The Virginians immediately dispatched a force of settlers and PAMUNKEY Indians to intercept them. The ensuing battle ended in a crushing defeat for the Virginians.

Regular contact between the Cherokee and colonists began in about 1690. Although relations were generally friendly, there were some hostile incidents. In 1691, without provocation, a number of South Carolina colonists attacked and killed several Cherokee. In 1705, South Carolina governor JAMES MOORE commissioned several men to capture Cherokee and other Indians. The Indians were sold into slavery, and Moore divided the profits with his coconspirators. Between 1711 and 1713, the TUSCARORA tribe, perennial enemies of the Cherokee, were expelled from North Carolina by the colonists and their Yamasee allies. The Tuscarora fled north to Iroquois territory and were accepted into the IROQUOIS CONFEDERACY. In 1715, several tribes, including the Cherokee and the YAMASEE, vigorously attacked South Carolina settlements to avenge past grievances, including those mentioned above. Fearing total defeat, the colonists quickly and effectively responded, forcing the Cherokee to sue for peace in 1716. As part of a trade agreement, the Cherokee signed their first land-cession treaty at Charleston, South Carolina, in 1721.

The CHEROKEE WAR (1760–61) erupted when Cherokee warriors returning home from British service at Fort Duquesne were murdered by frontiersmen. To avenge the warriors, Cherokee was parties attacked white settlements, killing about 20 people. The Cherokee then requested a peace council, but South Carolina governor William Lyttleton declared war. Three subsequent Cherokee peace requests were likewise rejected. Peace came only after Colonel ARCHIBALD MONTGOMERIE destroyed the lower Cherokee towns in June 1760, and Lieutenant Colonel James Grant devastated the middle Cherokee towns in June 1761. There followed a flood of settlers to Cherokee territory and a rapid succession of Cherokee land-cession treaties.

Disagreement over land cessions prior to the AMERICAN REVOLUTION (1775–81) caused the first wartime split among the Cherokee. The peace faction, led by Chiefs Attakullakulla and Oconostota, desired to remain neutral but favored the Americans. The Cherokee CHICKAMAUGA band, led by the young chiefs DRAGGING CANOE and John Watts, accepted arms from the British and waged guerrilla warfare against non-Indian settlements until forced to surrender in 1794. Thereafter, the Cherokee enjoyed 20 years of peace and prosperity.

During the WAR OF 1812 (1812–14) and the CREEK WAR (1813–14), the Cherokee fought alongside the frontier recruits of General ANDREW JACKSON. After Jackson became president, he lobbied Congress for passage of the INDIAN REMOVAL ACT (1830), which would relocate all southeastern tribes to what is now Oklahoma. According to Cherokee law at the time, land cession was a capital crime. Nevertheless, in 1835 an unofficial Cherokee delegation, including Major Ridge, John Ridge, STAND WATIE, and Elias Boudinot, signed the NEW ECHOTA TREATY (1835), consenting to Cherokee removal to Indian Territory (Oklahoma). In August 1838 the final and largest group of Cherokee, led by Chief JOHN ROSS (who fought emigration) journeyed to Indian Territory on what became known as the TRAIL OF TEARS. After the Cherokee arrived, Major Ridge, Elias Boudinot, and John Ridge were assassinated for their endorsements of the New Echota Treaty. Stand Watie, who could not be found, escaped execution. Three distinct political groups existed in the western Cherokee Nation—the John Ross faction, the Stand Watie faction, and the Old Settlers, who had arrived from Arkansas in 1832. The assassinations served to deepen the schism between the Watie and Ross factions and persisted long after the CIVIL WAR (1861–65).

During the Civil War, the Watie faction, consisting mostly of mixed-blood slaveholders, quickly joined the Confederacy of the South. Chief Ross, supported by a majority of full-blooded KEETOOWAH SOCIETY Cherokee, sought neutrality. However, as political and monetary pressures mounted, Ross also allied with the South. Although Keetoowah Cherokee objected to slavery, preservation of Cherokee national independence was

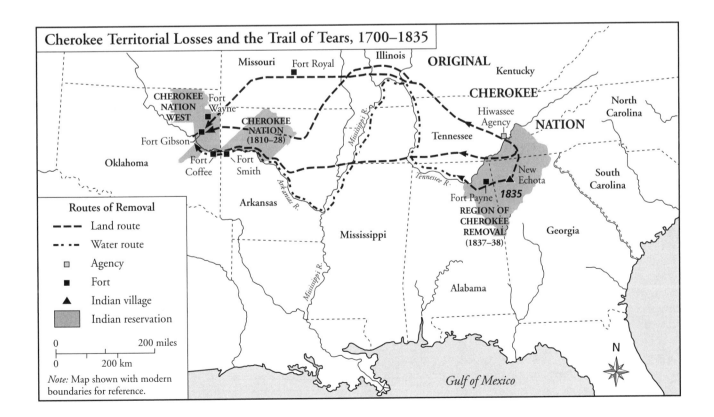

Cherokee Territorial Losses and the Trail of Tears, 1700–1835

Routes of Removal
- - - Land route
- · - · Water route
□ Agency
■ Fort
▲ Indian village
▨ Indian reservation

0   200 miles
0   200 km

Note: Map shown with modern boundaries for reference.

their primary goal. In 1862, believing a Union alliance offered the best hope of accomplishing both goals, the Keetoowah defected to serve the Union until the end of the war.

The Cherokee, Creek, CHICKASAW, CHOCTAW, and SEMINOLE were exempted from the GENERAL ALLOTMENT ACT (1887), which ended tribal land ownership. However, the Curtis Act (1889), intended to prepare Oklahoma for statehood, had essentially the same effect on the five tribes as the 1887 act. Tribal governments were dissolved, land was allotted to individual Indians, and unallotted lands were opened for settlement. Hundreds of full-blooded Keetoowah Cherokee refused to enroll and accept land allotments. Some, who fled to the hills, were hunted down, jailed, and forcibly enrolled. Others who hid did not enroll and received no share of tribal land. To many Cherokee the allotment process represented final resistance and dispossession.

Presently there are three federally recognized Cherokee governments: the Eastern Band, descendants of the Cherokee who hid in the hills of North Carolina and refused emigration to Indian Territory; the United Keetoowah Band, organized under the Indian Reorganization Act (1934) and the Oklahoma Indian Welfare Act (1936), and approved in 1950; and the Cherokee Nation of Oklahoma, organized under a new Constitution in 1976.

See also FIRST CHEROKEE MOUNTED RIFLES; FIRST CHEROKEE REGIMENT; HONEY SPRINGS, (1863); HOPEWELL TREATIES (1785–1786); LOCUST GROVE (1862); PEA RIDGE (1862); WORCESTER v. GEORGIA.

Further Reading

Leeds, Georgia Rae. The United Keetoowah Band of Cherokee Indians in Oklahoma: 1950 to the Present. Norman: University of Oklahoma Press, 1992.

McLoughlin, William G. After the Trail of Tears: The Cherokees' Struggle for Sovereignty, 1839–1880. Chapel Hill: University of North Carolina Press, 1993.

———. Cherokee Renascence in the New Republic. Princeton, N.J.: Princeton University Press, 1986.

Mooney, James. Myths of the Cherokee. Mineola, N.Y.: Dover, 1996.

Cherokee treaties *series of official agreements between the British and U.S. governments and the Cherokee Nation*
By the middle of the 18th century, the CHEROKEE had a history of cooperation and alliance with the British colonies of Georgia, North and South Carolina, and Virginia. Early in the century, South Carolina Governor Charles Craven negotiated a treaty with the tribe that promised mutual protection from other Native American groups. During the 1750s, however, British traders and settlers began moving into Cherokee territory. In 1760, while the FRENCH AND INDIAN WAR (1754–63) was going on in the North, the CHEROKEE WAR (1760–61) against the British broke out. The Cherokee proved unable to attract allies, perhaps because the British controlled access to gunpowder that other tribes needed for hunting. Thus, the Cherokee were forced to sign a peace treaty with the British in 1761 that ceded a large section of their territory in what is now North and South Carolina.

The peace that the Cherokee bought with their land lasted for approximately 60 years. During that time the Cherokee began to adopt European American culture, and they restructured their tribal government based on the American systems. The acculturalization of the Cherokee was so successful that they became known as one of the "Five Civilized Tribes," along with the SEMINOLE, CHOCTAW, CHICKASAW, and CREEK.

The success of the Cherokee, however, attracted the envy of their non-Indian neighbors. The people of Georgia, in particular, resented the rich Cherokee land over which the state government had no jurisdiction. As early as 1802, Georgia obtained a promise from the federal government that it would expel all Indians from the state. It was not until 1817, however, that ANDREW JACKSON convinced several chiefs to exchange Cherokee territory in Georgia for lands west of the Mississippi. At that time relocation was voluntary, and about 6,000 Cherokee had moved west by 1835.

Relocation of the Cherokee and the breaking of the treaties did not become an issue until after Jackson's election as president in 1828. Jackson was publicly committed to the removal of all remaining Indians from lands east of the Mississippi. In addition, gold was discovered on Cherokee territory in Georgia in 1829, and thousands of miners and settlers flooded into Cherokee territory in disregard of treaties. The Georgia legislature, with Jackson's cooperation, passed laws forbidding Indians to mine gold, testify in court, or hold political meetings. On May 28, 1830, Congress passed the INDIAN REMOVAL ACT (1830), requiring the displacement of all tribes remaining east of the Mississippi.

The Cherokee and their sympathizers tried to challenge the legislation in court in cases such as *Cherokee Nation v. Georgia* (1831) and *WORCESTER v. GEORGIA* (1832), in which their claims were upheld by the Supreme Court. President Jackson, however, chose to disregard the ruling, and in 1838, the remaining Cherokee were driven out of their ancestral lands by soldiers under the command of General WINFIELD SCOTT. Their losses and suffering on the long trip to their new home caused the Cherokee to name the journey the TRAIL OF TEARS.

Cherokee War (1759–1761) *war between the British and the Cherokee*
During the early 1750s, while the FRENCH AND INDIAN WAR (1754–63) was raging, British traders and pioneers in the colonies of Virginia and North and South Carolina restricted their trips into Indian country. As the war wound to its close, however, the traders and settlers began pressing westward again. Consequently, they came into conflict with the CHEROKEE, a strong, populous Indian nation that had often allied with the British. The pressures caused by the westward-moving settlers and dishonest traders finally broke out into open warfare between the British and the Cherokee.

Because the French held the Mississippi valley from the Great Lakes to Louisiana, the British built two forts on Cherokee land: Fort Prince George and Fort Loudoun. South Carolina governor Charles Craven had previously negotiated an agreement with the Cherokee, promising to help them protect their families against their enemies in return for their support in British colonial wars. In the eyes of the British, these forts were meant to protect the Cherokee from hostile raids by the French and their Indian allies, in accordance with the terms of the treaty. To the Cherokee, however, the forts came to represent the increasing numbers of intrusions by the British on native lands. By 1758 many Cherokee were openly hostile to the British.

A band of Cherokee warriors traveling through Virginia after helping the British in a campaign against the French at Fort Duquesne (modern Pittsburgh, Pennsylvania) captured some wild horses. Virginia frontiersmen confronted them, claiming that the horses were their property. Twelve of the Cherokee died in the fight that followed. The frontiersmen then took the horses and scalped the Indians. They later collected a bounty from the colonial authorities on the Cherokee scalps by declaring that the trophies came from enemy Indians. The Indians retaliated by raiding frontier settlements in North Carolina, killing 20 to 30 settlers and threatening Forts Loudoun and Prince George.

By the fall of 1759, the Cherokee and the British were openly at war. At that time Governor William Henry Lyttelton of South Carolina led a military expedition to Fort Prince George. He demanded that the Cherokee there hand over the members of their tribe that had killed settlers; he also ordered the seizure of Indian leaders to use as hostages. On December 26, 1759, Cherokee leaders agreed to meet his demands. However, they did not speak for all of their tribespeople. The following month, some Cherokee began raiding again, killing dozens of settlers. On February 3, the frontier settlement of Ninety-Six suffered an attack. Somewhat later a band of Cherokee shot the commandant of Fort Prince George during a parley. The fort's garrison killed all their Indian hostages in retaliation.

In response to this violence, General Jeffrey Amherst, commander of the British forces in North America, sent a detachment of about 1,300 Scottish Highlanders under Colonel ARCHIBALD MONTGOMERIE into South Carolina to punish the Cherokee. Warned of their approach, the Cherokee war chief Oconostota harassed the troops with such success that by June 1760 he had driven the entire force from his territory and laid siege to Fort Loudoun. The garrison of the fort negotiated a surrender on August 7 and received permission to leave Fort Loudoun and travel unmolested to Fort Prince George. On the way, they were ambushed by warriors seeking revenge for the hostage killings, and many of the troops were killed.

After the summer of 1760, the number of Cherokee raids slackened. However, the government of South Carolina, angry at the deaths of the Fort Loudoun garrison, demanded that General Amherst dispatch a second expedition to punish the Cherokee. In June 1761, Lieutenant Colonel James Grant led a force of about 2,500 men, including regular army soldiers, ranger auxiliaries, and allied Indians, deep into hostile territory. On June 10, 1761, near the spot where the Cherokee had ambushed the Fort Loudoun garrison the year before, Grant and his men repelled an Indian attack. Through the rest of the month, the British burned 15 Cherokee towns and destroyed crops and orchards. The Cherokee, discouraged by the devastation of their fields, the lack of support from other tribes, and the lack of trade with the British, finally sought peace. In August 1761 Chief Attakullakulla, leader of the peace faction among the Cherokee, opened negotiations with Colonel Grant. The following December, the British and the Cherokee signed a treaty ending the Cherokee War. The treaty also ceded Cherokee territory to South Carolina, reopened trade with the British, and restored Fort Loudoun to its builders. The Cherokee returned to their alliance with the British.

Further Reading
Leach, Douglas E. *Arms for Empire: A Military History of the British Colonies in North America, 1607–1763.* New York: Macmillan, 1973.
Steele, Ian K. *Warpaths: Invasions of North America.* New York: Oxford University Press, 1994.

Cherry Valley (Cherry Valley Massacre) (1778)
battle in the American Revolution
On November 11, 1778, MOHAWK war chief JOSEPH BRANT (Thayendonegea) led a raid on Cherry Valley in upstate New York. Brant, who held a commission in the British army as a colonel during the AMERICAN REVOLUTION (1775–81), had under his command a combined force of about 700 IROQUOIS CONFEDERACY warriors, Tory militia, and Canadian Rangers led by Captain Walter Butler (see BUTLER'S RANGERS). At that time, the stockade in the valley was controlled by the 7th Massachusetts Regiment, commanded by Colonel Ichabod Alden. Brant and Butler failed to capture the stockade, but they did cause many casualties among the American settlers and the Massachusetts soldiers—so many that the battle for Cherry Valley became known as the Cherry Valley Massacre.

Part of the reason for the raid's success came from the fact that Alden, not expecting trouble, failed to post guards along the trails into the valley. Settlers from outlying colonies, given no warning of the British/Indian assault, were picked off by the warriors or the British rangers. Others at work in various corners of the valley were cut off by the sudden onslaught. When the fighting ended, Brant and Butler had killed 32 Americans, including Alden himself, and captured another 40, whom they took as prisoners to Fort Niagara. Brant was reputed to have spared the lives of many of the Americans by exerting control over his warriors.

One of the results of the Cherry Valley Massacre was that General George Washington sent two columns of troops under Generals John Sullivan and James Clinton in a pincer movement against the Iroquois' home territory. The joint campaign successfully took the Iroquois out of the war by eliminating about 40 of their villages and destroying many of their fields and crops.

Chevelon Fork   See BIG DRY WASH.

Cheyenne (Tsetchestahase, Tsistsistas, Dzitsistas)
Plains Indian tribe
The Cheyenne are first recorded as living in the area of present-day Minnesota. French explorers first mentioned contact with a peaceful agricultural and trading people they called the Chaa in 1680. Not long after this, the Chaa were forced to move westward as a result of pressure from eastern tribes, themselves pushed westward by settlers. The tribe eventually migrated to the area of the Cheyenne River in present-day South Dakota, where they gained their current common name.

At first the Cheyenne formed in sedentary villages. But by 1750, two developments had come to affect the area where the Cheyenne lived. The use of guns, introduced to Indians by the English and French had spread westward and horses, introduced by the Spanish in Mexico, had moved northward. Horses, in fact, probably helped save the tribe, enabling them to ride away when European epidemic diseases swept the area.

In the early 19th century, the tribe split into two independent groups: the Northern Cheyenne and the Southern Cheyenne. The Northern Cheyenne were close allies of the SIOUX (Dakota, Lakota, Nakota). The much smaller Southern Cheyenne developed close ties with the ARAPAHO. In the 1860s, the Northern Cheyenne fought alongside Oglala Lakota leader RED CLOUD to close the BOZEMAN TRAIL to non-Indians. Peace was then kept until 1874, when GEORGE ARMSTRONG CUSTER and his expedition violated the sacred Black Hills in their search for gold. The Indians there did not own land individually, so they could not respond to offers to buy the land.

The SIOUX WARS (1876) began when the Lakota and the Cheyenne were ordered to report to reservations but not given sufficient time to comply. One outcome of this was extensive Cheyenne participation at the battle of the LITTLE BIGHORN (1876). By 1877, non-Indian retaliation for the Little Bighorn massacre had forced the Cheyenne to surrender with the Lakota and relocate to a reservation in Indian Territory (now Oklahoma). The tribe's primary leaders, LITTLE WOLF and DULL KNIFE, were told that if the Cheyenne did not like life on the reservation, they could return to the north. Conditions on the reservation proved so bad that the two leaders soon realized that the Northern Cheyenne would not survive if forced to stay there. In September 1878, they left, even though they had been denied permission to leave. The leaders eventually split up. Little Wolf and his followers made it to Montana, but Dull Knife and his group were captured when they went to the Red Cloud agency in Nebraska. Agency officials tried to starve the Cheyenne at the Red Cloud agency into submission. Substan-

tial numbers were killed in a January 1879 escape attempt. The survivors made it to the Great Sioux Reservation in South Dakota, where they were allowed to remain.

The Southern Cheyenne were victims of the massacre at SAND CREEK (1864), where sizable numbers of their peace faction, led by BLACK KETTLE, were killed. The DOG SOLDIERS, a military society that had evolved into a separate band and intermarried with the ARAPAHO, played a major role in the violent revenge for Sand Creek. They grew in influence until the battle of SUMMIT SPRINGS (1869), after which most Southern Cheyenne were forced into reservation life.

Further Reading
Bancroft-Hunt, Norman. *Warriors: Warfare and the Native American Indian.* London: Salamander Books, 1995.
Moore, John H. *The Cheyenne Nation: A Social and Demographic History.* Lincoln: University of Nebraska Press, 1987.

Cheyenne-Arapaho War (Colorado War)
(1864–1865) *conflict between the federal government and the Southern Cheyenne and Arapaho Indians*
As the CIVIL WAR (1861–65) was raging, Colorado governor JOHN EVANS failed in his efforts to secure access to mineral-rich Indian hunting grounds in exchange for reservation space. An angry Evans called upon Colonel JOHN M. CHIVINGTON, a former Methodist minister who despised all Indians. Chivington advocated the complete extinction of all Native Americans, including children, whom he believed should be killed and scalped.

Leaders of the CHEYENNE and ARAPAHO often differed in their views and goals. Some, such as BLACK KETTLE, sought peace with non-Indians. Other groups, however, including the DOG SOLDIERS, opposed any effort to live peacefully with whites. In an effort to resolve the impending crisis, Black Kettle spoke to government representatives, who demanded that the Indians surrender their weapons. After the Indians did so, they settled in peacefully at SAND CREEK (1864), thinking they would now live in peace. On the morning of November 29, 1864, with an American flag and a flag of truce flying in their camp, 200 Indians, including some 100 women and children, were slaughtered by Chivington's volunteers. The massacre at Sand Creek served as the catalyst for the beginning of the Cheyenne-Arapaho War.

Although Black Kettle continued to hold out for peace, other leaders launched a series of raids against settlers. One of the largest came on January 7, 1865, when approximately 1,000 warriors gathered just south of the settlement at Julesburg, Colorado. The village was protected by Fort Rankin, so the Indians sent out a warrior to draw the soldiers out of the fort. The ploy worked, but overeager warriors attacked too early, allowing the soldiers time to react. The troops, under the command of Captain Nicholas J. O'Brien, managed to retreat to the fort, having lost 14 soldiers and four civilians. The Indians looted the town and moved north to the Powder, Tongue,

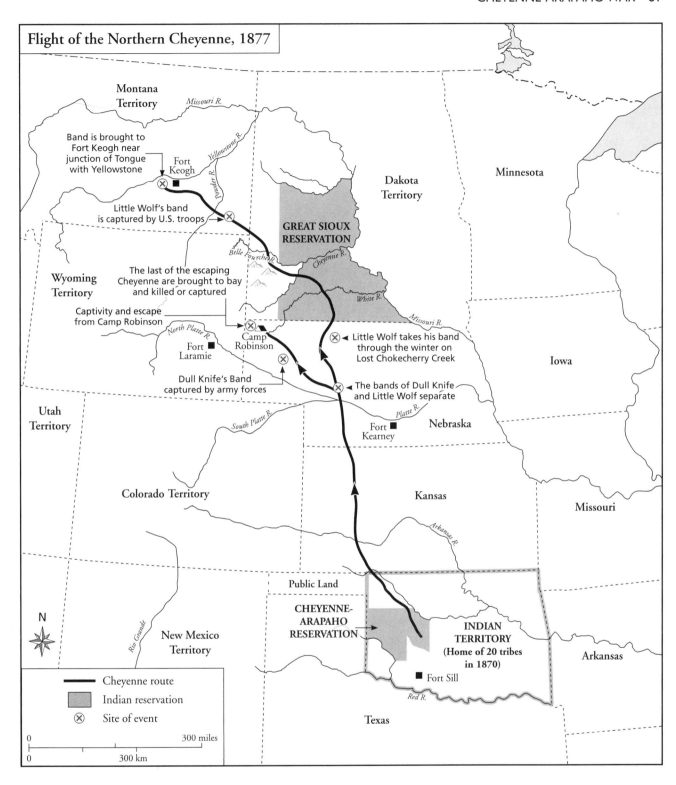

Flight of the Northern Cheyenne, 1877

and Yellowstone Rivers, hoping to join with Lakota (see SIOUX) and Northern Cheyenne warriors there.

In response to the JULESBURG RAIDS, army units pursued those Indian raiding parties still wreaking havoc along the Republican River. These chases proved ineffective, however,

and the Indians returned to Julesburg in January, where they finished their earlier work. In early February a group of between 500 and 1,000 warriors skirmished indecisively against smaller army units near Forts Mitchell and Laramie. The raids continued; during one four-day period that month, the Indians killed 50 settlers, stole 1,500 head of cattle, burned numerous buildings, and destroyed large caches of supplies.

Delayed by bad weather, Major General JOHN POPE drew up an elaborate plan for an offensive campaign using cavalry and infantry. But Pope's controversial manner antagonized Congress, which was still furious over the Sand Creek debacle. In the meantime, Jesse J. Leavenworth, Indian agent for the Upper Arkansas Agency, desperately attempted to forge peace with the Indians but ultimately was unsuccessful. Generals James H. Ford and Grenville M. Dodge then fought the Indians in minor skirmishes. This back-and-forth battling between Indians and white soldiers reached its head on July 26, 1865, when between 1,000 and 3,000 warriors assembled to attack a large cavalry unit guarding the Oregon-California Trail's North Platte River crossing.

Major Martin Anderson commanded the 11th Kansas and two elements of Ohio units from his camp at the Upper Platte Bridge. He dispatched Lieutenant Caspar W. Collins and 20 cavalrymen to escort a wagon train past suspected Indian positions. The small band of soldiers lost five men, including Lieutenant Collins, but inflicted severe casualties among the Indians in the process, claiming to have killed 60 and wounded another 130. The Indians destroyed the wagon train and then drew off to prepare for the fall buffalo hunt.

Brigadier General PATRICK E. CONNOR responded by dispatching 3,000 soldiers into the Powder River country. The troops burned an Arapaho village and fought several minor engagements, but bad weather set in again, fouling the army's efforts. With his troops near starvation and totally exhausted, Conner withdrew, thus bringing an end to the Cheyenne-Arapaho War. The conflict, which failed to achieve decisive results, had cost the federal government some $20 million.

Chickamauga *faction of the Cherokee Nation that withdrew from the main body of the tribe after 1777*

The separation of the Chickamauga from the Cherokee represented the first non-Indian–inspired factionalization of the tribe. In 1775, chief DRAGGING CANOE and other warriors refused to sign the Treaty of Sycamore Shoals, by which 27,000 square miles of Kentucky and Tennessee land were sold to private speculators. Instead, the warriors seized the opportunity offered by the AMERICAN REVOLUTION (1775–81) to fight for the land. In July 1776, using British arms, the Indians attacked white settlements and Forts Eaton's Station and Watauga in Tennessee. Frontier militias, led by James Robertson and JOHN SEVIER, struck back, burning villages and destroying crops.

In 1777, Dragging Canoe's band established towns along the Tennessee River near Chickamauga Creek. Becoming known as Chickamauga, they were eventually joined by approximately one-fourth of the Cherokee tribe. The white settlements in the Cumberland region were kept under attack until the Chickamauga towns were destroyed by frontier militias in 1782. Moving downstream, the Chickamauga built what became known as the five

lower towns. They continued their guerrilla warfare until 1794, when the lower towns were likewise destroyed. Peace and prosperity marked the 20-year period following Chickamauga surrender. Nevertheless, "Remember the Chickamaugas" became the cry of southern advocates of what eventually became the INDIAN REMOVAL ACT (1830). The Cherokee were finally dispossessed of all their traditional homelands and forced over the TRAIL OF TEARS to Indian Territory (present-day Oklahoma) in 1839.

Chickasaw *small tribe in the Muskogean linguistic family of the Southeast*

Closely related to the CHOCTAW, the Chickasaw originally lived in northern Mississippi and western Tennessee. In the late 1600s, they occupied seven principal towns; Chukafalaya, with more than 200 families, served as the capital. Although the Chickasaw were a small tribe, they boasted well-trained, competent warriors.

The Chickasaw sheltered and fed Spanish explorer HERNANDO DE SOTO and his men through the winter of 1540–41. When he insolently demanded 200 Chickasaw as slaves, they set his crude barracks afire, destroying the contents and killing 12 men.

The Chickasaw subsequently befriended the English and helped them gain dominance over the French in the Lower Mississippi region. They continued to ally themselves with the English during the AMERICAN REVOLUTION (1775–81). In 1786, they signed one of the HOPEWELL TREATIES (1785–86)—their first land-cession treaty with the United States.

In 1811, the Chickasaw refused to join SHAWNEE leader TECUMSEH's Indian Confederacy. Instead, they fought under General ANDREW JACKSON against the RED STICK faction of the CREEK (Tecumseh's allies) at the battle of HORSESHOE BEND (1813).

Many Chickasaw relocated west in the 1820s. After the INDIAN REMOVAL ACT (1830) was passed, the remaining Chickasaw signed the Treaty of Doaksville (1837) and were forced from their Mississippi homes to Indian Territory (now Oklahoma).

During the CIVIL WAR (1861–65), the Chickasaw were the first tribe to declare Confederate allegiance. As one of the "Five Civilized Tribes" (along with the CHEROKEE, Choctaw, Creek, and SEMINOLE), the Chickasaw were exempted from the GENERAL ALLOTMENT ACT (1887). However, in preparation for Oklahoma statehood, the 1889 Curtis Act ended the independent Chickasaw government.

Chickasaw Resistance (Chickasaw War)
(1720–1763) *first Chickasaw war with the French*

During the early 1700s, several factors led many of the CHICKASAW to align closely with the English, putting them at odds with the French in the region. In 1720, pro-English Chickasaw executed a Frenchman living in their nation under the protection of some pro-French Chickasaw and believed to be a spy for the governor of Louisiana. For the first time, the pro-English faction began raiding French settlements. Within three years Louisiana commerce was at a standstill.

The governor of Louisiana, Jean-Baptiste Le Moyne, sieur de Bienville, fought the Chickasaw primarily with CHOCTAW mercenaries, who were organized into companies by French officers. As an added incentive, Bienville paid the Choctaw bounties of arms and ammunition for Chickasaw scalps as well as prisoners, who were sold as slaves.

The French-Choctaw offensive only slightly affected the Chickasaw Nation as a whole, but it threatened their trade with England. The English also were interested in establishing trade with the Choctaw. English traders therefore prompted Chickasaw leaders to make peace with the Choctaw. Concerned that their own lucrative trade with the Choctaw was in danger, the French decided that the Chickasaw had been punished enough. The first Chickasaw-French conflict ended early in 1725, with the previous alliance still in place.

For the next four years a misleading quiet settled over Louisiana. During the first conflict, the English had realized the military potential of the Chickasaw Nation, which could be used to divide French settlements in Louisiana and Illinois. The Chickasaw could also serve as commercial and diplomatic agents to expand English trade among tribes allied with the French. Thus, the Chickasaw found factions within many tribes willing to listen to English promises. By 1729, some Choctaw bands and the NATCHEZ, to the south of the Chickasaw, were willing to try English trade goods. However, the calm was disrupted in November 1729, when Natchez warriors attacked the French garrisons at Fort Rosalie and Fort St. Peter.

The second Chickasaw-French war began in 1731. After the Natchez killed at least 250 Frenchmen and captured about 300 women and children, a combined French-Choctaw force decimated the Natchez in February 1730. Survivors fled and took refuge with the Chickasaw. When the French demanded the surrender of these Natchez, the Chickasaw refused. In 1731 pro-French Choctaw, urged on by the new French governor, responded by burning three captured Chickasaw agents at the stake. In retaliation, Chickasaw and Natchez raided French ships on the Mississippi, while Choctaw forces blockaded Chickasaw towns. Despite this pressure, the Chickasaw refused to bow to French demands.

For almost 30 years skirmishing between the Chickasaw and the French continued, but the French attempts to destroy Chickasaw power backfired. Rather than being intimidated into surrender, the Chickasaw intensified their efforts to defeat their enemy. Chickasaw agents, for example, used British goods to alienate the Choctaw from the French, creating serious divisions within the tribe. Then, when the French sent loyal northern tribes (POTAWATOMI, MIAMI, tribes of the IROQUOIS CONFEDERACY, and Illinois) against them, the Chickasaw reacted by extending their raiding into French Illinois.

In 1736, the Chickasaw scored two victories against the French. In late February, Major Pierre D'Artaguette assembled an army of 30 French regulars, 100 French militia, and about 400 Miami, Iroquois, and Kaskaskia (Illinois) warriors. Arriving at Chickasaw Bluffs, D'Artaguette was to rendezvous with Governor Bienville's forces, supposed to be advancing from the south. After three weeks, with most of his provisions gone, D'Artaguette had not found Bienville. His scouts located the Chickasaw town of Chocolissa, and D'Artaguette was pressured into attacking it for supplies. On March 25, when D'Artaguette attacked Chocolissa, the Chickasaw pinned the French down, and warriors from a neighboring town moved in to surround them. The Miami and Kaskaskia troops fled, and when the fighting ceased only 20 of D'Artaguette's men survived. Most of the prisoners were burned alive by the angry Chickasaw.

Bienville's army, which included 600 Choctaw, was not ready until early April. On May 26, 1736, his troops attacked the town of Akia. Flushed with the success of burning the first three compounds, the French rushed for the town's center, where they met stiff resistance as the Chickasaw caught the French in an intense crossfire. For three hours the French charged and were driven back; 53 men were seriously wounded and 24 killed. Of the Choctaw mercenaries, 22 were wounded and killed. Bienville retreated.

Between 1736 and 1763, the French intensified efforts to destroy the Chickasaw, maintaining pressure with Choctaw and allied Indians. Taking three years to assemble a 3,600-man army, in autumn 1739 Bienville landed at Chickasaw Bluffs. However, his army was almost immediately stranded by heavy rains. During a three-month period of inactivity, a plan was conceived whereby a 600-man force would attack and capture a Chickasaw town, arrange for a prisoner exchange, and invite the Indians to a council. The army did capture a town, but it was forced to retreat after a two-day siege. The Chickasaw nevertheless accepted Bienville's council invitation. In February 1740 a peace was negotiated and Bienville withdrew.

In 1743 Bienville was removed as governor of Louisiana because of this second failure to destroy the Chickasaw. From 1743 to 1752 the Chickasaw continued their raids. Bienville's successor, the marquis de Vaudreuil, once again planned their destruction. With a 700-man army of regulars and a large number of Indian allies, Vaudreuil marched against the Chickasaw. But once again the French failed to dislodge the Indians from their palisaded towns. After a brief struggle and some losses, the French set fire to the deserted village and farms, ran off Chickasaw livestock, and left.

The Treaty of Paris (1763) ended the SEVEN YEARS' WAR (1754–63) between France and Great Britain. The British triumph meant the surrender of French power in North America. As a result, the Chickasaw-French controversy also came to an end.

Further Reading

Gibson, Arrell. *The Chickasaws*. Norman: University of Oklahoma Press, 1971.

Chief Joseph (Hin-mah-too-yah-lah-ket, "Thunder Coming from Water over Land," Young Joseph)

(ca. 1840–1904) *Indian leader during the Nez Perce War*
Chief Joseph was born in 1840, the son of the chief of the Wallowa band of the NEZ PERCE, in northeastern Oregon. The local non-Indians called his father Joseph, so the boy became known as Young Joseph. He grew to be a tall man, six feet two inches, and was respected for his thoughtful ways and wise advice.

In the 1850s, growing numbers of settlers invaded Nez Perce land. In 1863, about one-third of the local chiefs signed a treaty confining the Indians to the Lapwai Reservation. Old Joseph and others nonsigners refused to go. By 1871, Young Joseph had replaced his deceased father as chief. As white settlers began filing into the Wallowa Valley, Joseph and the Nez Perce

Chief Joseph, leader of the Nez Perce, gained fame for his skill in battle and his role as a tribal spokesperson. *(By permission of the Colorado Historical Society)*

objected. In 1873 President ULYSSES S. GRANT declared the valley a reservation. By 1875, however, Grant started to bend under political pressure and allowed homesteading in the area. Joseph realized that the Nez Perce and the settlers could not easily share the valley. He also knew that his tribe could not match the firepower of the U.S. Army. Reluctantly, Joseph acquiesced to General OLIVER OTIS HOWARD's demand that the Native Americans relocate to the Lapwai Reservation. While en route, some young warriors left camp and killed more than a dozen settlers in the valley. Upon learning of the incident, Joseph, who had always pursued peace, realized that war was inevitable.

On June 17, 1877, the Nez Perce War began with the battle of WHITE BIRD CREEK (1877). In July the Nez Perce moved east across a treacherous mountain pass in the Bitterroot Mountains and circumnavigated a manned barricade hastily built to stop them. On August 8 the Indians camped along the banks of Beaver Creek in the Big Hole Valley of Montana. Unbeknownst to them, Colonel JOHN GIBBON's force of regulars and volunteers was approaching. At dawn Gibbon attacked the sleeping Indians. The battle of BIG HOLE (1877) involved ferocious hand-to-hand combat. The surprised Nez Perce rallied and fought the soldiers to a draw, but as many as 89 Indians (including women and children) and 33 soldiers died. The battle was over, but the war dragged on. By September, Joseph had decided to lead his weary people to safety in Canada. The Nez Perce were only 30 miles from the border when Colonel NELSON A. MILES surprised the group in the northern reaches of the Bear Paw Mountains. The battle of BEAR PAW (1877) lasted from September 30 through October 5. Joseph realized a continued fight was suicide. Thus, he surrendered to General Howard (who had arrived the previous day) and Colonel Miles. Miles assured Joseph that his people could go to the Lapwai Reservation. Instead the survivors were sent to Indian Territory (now Oklahoma).

Chief Joseph spent years trying to persuade the government to let his people go home. Finally, in the spring of 1885 they were allowed to return to the Pacific Northwest. Joseph spent the remainder of his days living on the Colville Reservation in Washington State. He died on September 21, 1904. The local doctor reported the cause of death as "a broken heart."

In retrospect, it appears that Nez Perce chiefs Toohoolhoolzote, White Bird, LOOKING GLASS, Poker Joe, and others were primarily responsible for the tribe's successes in war. But because Joseph was the spokesman for his people, the national newspapers mistakenly dubbed him the "Indian Napoleon" and pictured him as a fierce war leader. Chief Joseph was a leader, but he promoted restraint, clear thinking, and compassion.

In response to General Howard's surrender demand, Lieutenant C. E. S. Wood attributed a "speech" to Joseph, in which the latter reportedly vowed "to fight no more forever." Whatever the words might have been, Joseph's life stands as an eloquent, if tragic, testimonial to his desire to protect his people.

Further Reading
Beal, Merrill D. *"I Will Fight No More Forever": Chief Joseph and the Nez Perce War.* Seattle: University of Washington Press, 1963.

Josephy, Alvin M., Jr. *The Nez Perce Indians and the Opening of the Northwest.* New Haven, Conn.: Yale University Press, 1965.

Hampton, Bruce. *Children of Grace: The Nez Perce War of 1877.* New York: Henry Holt, 1994.

Scott, Robert A. *Chief Joseph and the Nez Perces.* New York: Facts On File, 1993.

Chippewa (Anishinabe, Ojibwa, Ojibway)
Algonquian tribe of the western Great Lakes region

The Chippewa were among the largest and most powerful of North American Indian tribes. With their ALGONQUIAN allies, the OTTAWA and POTAWATOMI, they dominated much of the land between Lake Huron and the Missouri River—a region that includes much of present-day Wisconsin, Minnesota, Michigan, North Dakota, and southern Ontario. Though sometimes forced to migrate when wildlife grew scarce, the Chippewa were successful farmers who stayed in one place for long periods of time. Like other Algonquian peoples, they believed in Manitou, the one all-powerful spirit from which all lesser spirits drew power.

The Chippewa were early allies of the French, from whom they received firearms. With these weapons they enjoyed an advantage in conflicts against their enemies the Dakota SIOUX (Dakota, Lakota, Nakota), KICKAPOO, and the tribes of the IROQUOIS CONFEDERACY. In their birchbark canoes they fought naval battles against the FOX (Mesquakie) to gain control of Lake Superior in the 1660s.

As allies of the French, the Chippewa fought against the British in the SEVEN YEARS' WAR (1754–63) and in PONTIAC'S REBELLION (1763–64) (see OTTAWA) following the expulsion of the French from Canada. Like most Native American tribes during the AMERICAN REVOLUTION (1775–81), the Chippewa perceived the colonists to pose the greater threat; as a result they fought on the side of the British in this conflict and also in the WAR OF 1812 (1812–14). After the War of 1812, the Chippewa signed a treaty with the United States, and they maintained friendly relations thereafter.

Though pushed southward in the 1830s to reservations in Indian Territory (present-day Oklahoma), the Chippewa continued on friendly terms with non-Indians. They also remained a people proud of their independent heritage. In 1968 three Chippewa founded the AMERICAN INDIAN MOVEMENT (AIM), a radical political group based on regaining Indian rights and improved social conditions. The group participated in the 1969 takeover of Alcatraz Island, the 1972 occupation of the Federal Bureau of Indian Affairs offices in Washington, D.C., and the seizure of the WOUNDED KNEE massacre site in 1973. These incidents raised public awareness of poverty among and political mistreatment of Native Americans.

Chivington, John M. (1821–1894) *U.S. Army officer responsible for the Sand Creek Massacre*

John M. Chivington, a Methodist minister turned soldier (and later politician), became a hero during the CIVIL WAR

Colonel John M. Chivington, known as the fighting parson, was responsible for the deaths of 200 men, women, and children at the Sand Creek massacre, 1864. *(By permission of the Colorado Historical Society)*

(1861–65). Known as the "Fighting Parson," Chivington led the Union forces that routed the Confederate army HENRY HOPKINS SIBLEY, at Glorieta Pass in the New Mexico Territory on March 28, 1862, thus forcing the Confederates to retreat from the territory. By 1863, Chivington was the military commander of the District of Colorado. Large in ego and ambition as well as stature, Chivington harbored political ambitions in Colorado's application for statehood.

In September 1863, the Colorado territorial governor, John Evans, tried to force the CHEYENNE and ARAPAHO chiefs who had signed the FORT WISE TREATY (1861) to abide by its conditions. One of those provisions had been that the peace chiefs would induce the tribal members who had not signed the treaty to accept it. These chiefs, including BLACK KETTLE and White Antelope of the Cheyenne Nation and Little Raven of the Arapaho, failed in their attempts. As a result, Governor Evans failed to hold a council to move the Indians to their new reservation and allot their lands.

Evans perceived the Indians' refusal to cooperate with his plans as a threat to Colorado's destiny. He expected war and planned for it. In this he was aided by Colonel John Chivington. Because of the burgeoning mining frontier and the gold strikes in Colorado in 1858, the Civil War did not interrupt the westward migration. Non-Indians continued to pour into the area. The movement west cut sharply into Indian hunting grounds, and they reacted by conducting sporadic raids on forts and settlements in the summer of 1864. When Colorado settlers panicked, Evans and Chivington called for military action to crush the "hostile" Indians and restore safety to the territory. During that same time, rumor held that both Evans and Chivington sought higher elected offices.

In November 1864 Chivington led the 1st and 3rd Colorado Cavalries in attacks on the camps of Black Kettle and White Antelope at SAND CREEK. The slaughter of 200 Indian men, women, and children led to greater unrest among the Plains Indians as well as calls for peace by non-Indians in the East. The U.S. government began three separate investigations into the incident, but by this time Chivington and his men had been mustered out of the military. As a result, Chivington and his lieutenants could not be held accountable for their deeds.

In his remaining years Chivington worked as a journalist, operated a freight business, and held public office in Colorado.

Choctaw *Muskogean-speaking tribe closely related to the Chickasaw and the Creek*

Although not overly active in warfare, the Choctaw were not timid and often found themselves involved in battles initiated by their allies, the French, who sought domination of the American interior. After the NATCHEZ attacked French Ft. Rosalie in 1729, killing 250 and taking 300 captive, the Choctaw joined the retaliatory French force that virtually exterminated the Natchez. Following their victory over the Natchez, the French became intent upon likewise destroying the CHICKASAW. To that end they initiated several unsuccessful campaigns with Choctaw, Illinois, and MIAMI support.

During the Revolutionary War, British strategy for involving their Choctaw allies was inept and ineffective. In the fall of 1779, British General John Campbell sent for several hundred Choctaw in anticipation of an attack on Mobile by Spanish forces allied to colonial forces. The Choctaw, poorly provisioned, could not endure the prolonged wait and returned home. Mobile subsequently fell to the Spanish on February 10, 1780. The Choctaw also assisted the British against Spain in the battle for Florida.

In spite of SHAWNEE chief TECUMSEH's urging to the contrary, the Choctaw supported the Americans in the WAR OF 1812 (1812–14). They served as scouts and messengers and fought at the Battles of HOLY GROUND (1813), HORSESHOE BEND (1813), and New Orleans.

After the INDIAN REMOVAL ACT (1830) was passed, a few Choctaw signed away tribal land in Mississippi under the DANCING RABBIT CREEK TREATY (1830), even though they were unauthorized to do so. As a result, the tribe was forced to relocate, along with the CHEROKEE, Chickasaw, CREEK, and SEMINOLE, to Indian Territory.

Church, Benjamin (1639–1718) *colonial militia officer*

Born in Plymouth, Benjamin Church grew up on the Massachusetts frontier, where he became influential among the Native Americans of the region. When KING PHILIP'S WAR (1675–76) broke out, Church persuaded many Wampanoag not to join their fellow tribespeople in battle.

During the war, Captain Church advocated aggressive pursuit of the enemy rather than reliance on static defensive measures, but his advice was largely ignored. He was twice wounded at the GREAT SWAMP FIGHT (1675). The following spring, as the colonists' fortunes rose, he began enlisting Indian prisoners to fight alongside his men. Church led the small force that killed Philip in August of that year, thus ending the war.

Church remained active throughout his life, fighting against the French and their Indian allies in KING WILLIAM'S WAR (1689–97) and QUEEN ANNE'S WAR (1702–13). Church died in 1718 after falling from his horse in a riding accident.

Cibecue Creek (Cibicu Massacre) (1881) *incident following the arrest of an Apache medicine man*

In 1880 Nakaidoklini (Noch-ay-del-klinne), a prominent White Mountain APACHE medicine man, started a new religion. He proclaimed that he had the ability to raise two important chiefs from the dead and said that the white man would be gone from the Apache's territory by the time the corn was ripe.

Nakaidoklini's prophecies and dances alarmed the military personnel at FORT APACHE because they attracted and unified various Indian factions. Thus, on August 29, 1881, a detachment of 117 men of the 6th Cavalry, including 23 Apache scouts, set out from the Fort Apache under Colonel EUGENE A. CARR to arrest the prophet. The next afternoon they arrived at Cibecue Creek, where they located, manhandled, and arrested Nakaidoklini. The troops then traveled a short distance toward Fort Apache, before stopping for the night. Soon a large number of Apache circled the encampment. A shot was fired, and a battle began. On this rare occasion the Apache army scouts mutinied and joined their fellow Indians. Meanwhile, Carr ordered the medicine man to be shot. As the fighting continued, a soldier saw Nakaidoklini, bleeding from a gunshot wound to the head, crawling toward the Apache lines. The soldier picked up an ax and dispatched the medicine man with two blows.

The death of Nakaidoklini confused the Apache, as they were now without strong leadership. Carr seized the opportunity and secretively forced his troops to march the 40 miles to Fort Apache; they arrived without incident. The number of fatalities from the battle at Cibecue Creek included eight whites and an estimated 18 Apache, including six scouts and

Nakaidoklini. Two soldiers and an undetermined number of Apache were wounded. In the days that followed, hostilities continued as Apache attacked Fort Apache.

Further Reading

Collins, Charles. *Apache Nightmare: The Battle at Cibecue Creek.* Norman: University of Oklahoma Press, 1999.

Cruse, Thomas *Apache Days and After.* Caldwell, Caxton Printers, 1941.

Kessel, William B. "The Battle of Cibecue and Its Aftermath: A White Mountain Apache's Account." In *Ethnohistory,* vol. 21, no. 2, 1994, pp. 123–134.

Civil War (1861–1865) *bloodiest war in U.S. history, in which Indians participated on both sides*

For the Indians of the Plains, in the Southwest, and in the Far West, the Civil War's most noticeable impact was the withdrawal of the regular troops who had formerly garrisoned the army's frontier posts. The resulting power vacuum pitted Indian groups, anxious to reassert their dominance, against non-Indian state and local volunteer units, just as determined that the Indians should not. Ominously, many of these volunteers had little respect for the niceties of what was then recognized as civilized warfare.

The war years were particularly violent for the Native American peoples of Minnesota and the Dakotas, Colorado and Utah, and New Mexico and Arizona. On the northern plains and prairies, the MINNESOTA UPRISING (1862) resulted in the decimation of the military power of the Santee Dakota (Eastern) SIOUX. To the south, intermittent raiding by Indians and non-Indians also led to several bitter conflicts, including the SHOSHONE WAR (1862–63) and the massacre at SAND CREEK (1864). In the far Southwest, JAMES HENRY CARLETON and CHRISTOPHER "KIT" CARSON conducted cruelly effective campaigns against the APACHE and the NAVAJO (Dineh). But in a very real sense, these conflicts between 1861 and 1865 are indicative, not of the special circumstances of the bitter war between the Union and the Confederacy, but as part of the ongoing struggle between Indians and non-Indians for domination of the American West.

More directly related to the Civil War was the brutal contest for control of the Indian Territory (present-day Oklahoma), home to the nearly 100,000 members of the so-called Five Civilized tribes—the CHEROKEE, CHOCTAW, CHICKASAW, CREEK, and SEMINOLE. Loyalties cut across ethnic, cultural, and tribal lines. Those who had become more acculturated into non-Indian society, including the majority of mixed-bloods and almost all the slaveowners, tended to support the Confederacy, while traditionalists most often sympathized with the Union. The Chickasaw and Choctaw generally favored the Confederacy, and they supplied the FIRST CHICKASAW AND CHOCTAW REGIMENT to the Southern cause. The Cherokee were bitterly divided. Factions supportive of JOHN ROSS, principal chief of the Cherokee, were sympathetic to the North. Ross's chief rival, STAND WATIE, led those who supported the Confederacy. The Creek were, if anything, even more deeply divided. Opothleyahola's faction was strongly pro-Union, but half brothers Daniel N. and Chilly McIntosh backed the South and would raise a regiment of Creek fighters. Most Seminole attempted to remain neutral, although John Jumper, an ordained minister, would help enlist a number of his people into the McIntosh's Creek regiment.

In summer 1861, the Confederate government dispatched Brigadier General Albert Pike, a lawyer who had recently won a $140,000 suit for the Creek, to drum up support for the Southern cause in the Indian Territory. Fearing a Confederate victory, the careful Ross agreed to a treaty of alliance with the Richmond government and even agreed to raise another Cherokee regiment. Unionist Creek and Seminole refugees headed north with Opothleyahola, fighting past pro-Confederate forces near the present-day town of Yale on November 19 and again near present-day Tulsa on December 9. On the 26, however, pro-Confederate Indian forces, led by Watie and supplemented by three regiments of Texans, routed the Unionists and drove them in disarray into Kansas.

With the Indian Territory seemingly cleared of the Union threat, in early 1862 Pike led the two Cherokee regiments (totaling about a thousand men) to link up with a Confederate army under EARL VAN DORN. Pike's men participated in the Confederate defeat at PEA RIDGE (1862); demoralized by their loss and by the South's failure to supply them, they then withdrew back to Indian Territory. Pike would soon resign, disgusted with the government's lack of support.

A federal counteroffensive came that summer. Some 6,000 Union troops, including two Indian regiments (one composed of Creek and Seminole and the second recruited from the refugees who had fled to Kansas), pushed into Indian Territory. The Creek distinguished themselves in the Union victory at Locust Grove (July 3); that same day, Stand Watie's Cherokees were also routed by federal troops. The other Cherokee Confederate regiment soon defected to the Union, and John Ross effectively renounced his alliance with the Richmond government. But campaign momentum shifted with the withdrawal of several federal regiments back to Missouri, and by the end of September the pro-Confederate Indian forces once again controlled the territory.

Early 1863 was marked by raids and counter-raids by the Indians of one side against those of the other. This civil war within the Civil War left much of the once-prosperous Indian Territory destitute. On July 17, Indian regiments on both sides participated in the battle of HONEY SPRINGS a Union victory. The fall of Little Rock to federal forces that September placed even more pressure on the Confederate forces in Indian Territory. In December 1863, a 1,500-man strong Union Indian Brigade, composed of the three loyalist Indian regiments struck deep into Choctaw and Chickasaw lands, inflicting serious property damage and leaving some 250 pro-Confederate Indians dead.

Watie's raids into the lands of his pro-Northern Cherokee rivals and against Union supply lines continued nonetheless, earning him a promotion to brigadier general in May 1864. And on September 19, Watie's new brigade of about 800 Cherokee, Seminole, and Creek, cooperating with a brigade of Texans, captured a 300-wagon enemy train loaded with more than $1.5 million in supplies near Cabin Creek. The spectacular affair was the biggest Confederate victory in the Indian Territory.

Guerrilla warfare along the Arkansas River valley would continue, but affairs elsewhere marked the Confederacy's death knell. On June 23, 1865, Watie finally surrendered, the last Confederate general of the war to do so. The United States, which held that the prewar treaties had been abrogated, dealt harshly with the tribes that had supported the Confederacy. New treaties agreed to in 1866 required the Five Civilized tribes to make room for several other Indian groups, who were to be removed from Kansas and other areas and relocated to Indian Territory.

Further Reading

Josephy, Alvin M., Jr. *The Civil War in the American West.* New York: Alfred A. Knopf, 1991.

Clark, George Rogers (1752–1818) *American commander of irregulars during the American Revolution*

George Rogers Clark was one of the most successful American officers of the AMERICAN REVOLUTION (1775–83). Originally a surveyor for the colony of Virginia, working in the territory of Kentucky, Clark began his military career in 1774 and participated in LORD DUNMORE'S WAR (1773–74), fighting the SHAWNEE under their chief, CORNSTALK. Clark's greatest successes, however, came during the Revolutionary War. During that time, Clark was promoted to major general and led a series of attacks on British frontier forts. He adopted Indian tactics in his battles, fighting from concealed positions and moving his troops quickly through the backwoods. In the summer of 1778, he took a small force of Virginia and Kentucky militia to the Kaskaskia River in Indiana, seized the Indian towns of Kaskaskia and Cahokia, and captured Fort Sackville at Vincennes without losing a single soldier. His greatest success occurred in early 1779 at the second fall of Vincennes, where he launched a midwinter assault, capturing both the town and British Lieutenant Henry Hamilton, who was known as "the hair buyer" because of the bounty he placed on American scalps.

From 1780 to 1782, Clark served as the chief American military officer on the Ohio frontier. He remained in Ohio country after the American victory and served as Indian Commissioner for the old Northwest Territory. He lost this position after the beginning of LITTLE TURTLE'S WAR (1786–95), when he proved unable to bring the Shawnee and their allies to battle. Clark returned to private life in 1799 and died in obscurity in Jefferson County, Kentucky, in 1818.

Clearwater (1877) *third in a series of battles in the Nez Perce War*

After routing U.S. cavalry at the battle of WHITE BIRD CREEK (1877) during the NEZ PERCE WAR (1877), the NEZ PERCE fled toward Clearwater Creek in Idaho. General OLIVER O. HOWARD prepared to follow them with more than 580 troops and scouts. Local citizens, however, convinced Howard that LOOKING GLASS, a neutral Nez Perce chief, was going to join the hostile bands. On June 29, 1877, Howard sent Captain Stephen G. Whipple with two cavalry troops and two Gatling guns after Looking Glass. When Whipple arrived at the Indian encampment on July 1, he attempted to speak to the chief, but his efforts were disrupted when his civilian guides provoked a fight and began firing into the Indian village. Wipple did nothing to stop the incident, which sent the Indians running. Angered by this hostile action, Looking Glass joined other Nez Perce in resisting the whites.

Around July 3, Looking Glass and the other Nez Perce leaders united and set up a camp of about 300 warriors and 500 women and children on the south fork of Clearwater Creek. Eight days later, Howard caught up with the tribe on a plateau above the Creek. For two days, while Howard maneuvered into position behind the Nez Perce, the Indians besieged a volunteer force at Mount Misery, a hilltop west of the Clearwater. Howard then committed a series of blunders. Because the troops had kept away from the river bluffs to escape detection by the Nez Perce, they passed by the Indian village before they realized it was there. Too far away from the village to do any damage, Howard nevertheless ordered the big guns fired, thus announcing the soldiers' presence to the Nez Perce.

While Howard reversed his march to attack the village, the Nez Perce had time to move forward and successfully block Howard on three sides. Nez Perce chief Old Toohoolhoolzote and 24 warriors were the first to arrive on the scene. Indian sharpshooters quickly stopped the troopers, many of whom were poor shots, lacked training, and were facing fire for the first time. Toohoolhoolzote's resistance was enough to save the Indian camp. Two other groups of warriors, realizing that there was a battle going on, headed for the site. Some of the tribe's best war chiefs, including Rainbow, Five Wounds, and Ollokot, led slightly less than 80 men to hold Toohoolhoolzote's position. Howard was forced to deploy his men on the open prairie. Surrounded on three sides, Howard and about 560 men were thus pinned down by fewer than 100 warriors.

Rather than escape under the cover of night, the Nez Perce fought the soldiers for two days, a type of protracted combat not usually seen in Indian warfare. On the second day of the battle, two developments saved General Howard. The first was the gradual disintegration of Nez Perce unity as warriors began questioning the chiefs' decision to continue fighting when the lives of woman and children were being endangered. The second development was the arrival of Captain James B. Jackson's 1st Cavalry, which had been sent out from Fort Klamath to find and join Howard. Howard sent Captain Marcus P. Miller and his 4th Artillery battalion to escort Jackson into the battle.

As Miller returned, he suddenly wheeled and charged, flushing the weakened line of Nez Perce from the ravine. Jackson's main body then attacked. The warriors retreated across the Clearwater to the village, which was abandoned as all fled north. Army casualties included 13 dead and 27 wounded. Howard claimed to have killed 23 Nez Perce, but the Indians later reported only four killed and six wounded.

After the battle, Howard blundered again. Instead of immediately pursuing the routed Indians, which might have ended the war, he lingered until the following morning. Thus, the Nez Perce were able to escape once again.

Clinch, Duncan Lamont (1787–1849) *U.S. Army officer*

Born in North Carolina, Duncan Clinch joined the U.S. Army in 1808 and rose steadily through the ranks. He fought with distinction against the SEMINOLE in the First SEMINOLE WAR (1818–19), most notably at the siege of Negro Fort on Florida's Apalachicola River. Clinch led the land force in the assault that destroyed this heavily armed structure, which had become a haven for runaway slaves.

Promoted to the rank of brigadier general in 1829, Clinch was put in command of federal troops in Florida during the Second SEMINOLE WAR (1835–42). During that conflict, when his troops stumbled into an ambush at the WITHLACOOCHEE RIVER (1835), Clinch's coolness under fire turned the tide of battle and allowed his army to withdraw intact. The following year, the death of his wife and son from scarlet fever forced Clinch to resign his commission so that he could tend to his family. He later settled in Georgia and represented that state in Congress in 1844–45.

club, war *weapon for close-in fighting*

War clubs varied in style among the different Native American tribes. Commonly, the weapon was carved from wood, with a handle designed to fit a warrior's hand and a heavy, thick head at the other end. One style was the round-headed club, whose end was shaped into a solid ball or bulb that delivered a deadly blow. Another widespread style was the spike war club, in which a spike of bone was embedded in the head; it could be used for clubbing or spiking an enemy.

A Sioux war club, decorated with two buffalo, a male figure, and other symbols *(Courtesy New York Public Library)*

The traditional war club began to change when metal and guns were introduced by non-Indian traders. Bone spikes were often replaced by blades of iron or steel inserted into the head. Many Indians adopted a version called the gunstock club, which was shaped like the stock of a rifle and fitted with a metal blade at the head. Whatever the style, a warrior's club was a highly prized possession. Using the club bravely in hand-to-hand combat earned a warrior battle honors.

Coahuiltec Indians *Native American group who inhabited a region in present-day Mexico and Texas near the Rio Grande*

When Spanish explorer Álvar Núñez Cabeza de Vaca first reached their territory in the late 16th century, the Coahuiltec Indians were a large group of tribes sharing a common language and some customs. In 1675 Spanish explorer Fernando del Bosque traveled through their land. He was followed in 1689 and 1690 by Juan Ponce de León, who explored the area in search of gold. In 1677 Spanish Franciscan monks and priests established a mission at Nadadores in the Coahuiltec homeland. More missions were established later on the Rio Grande and near modern San Antonio, Texas. However, the concentration of the Coahuiltec-speaking Indians in the missions encouraged the spread of diseases to which the Indians had no immunity (see SMALLPOX, EFFECTS OF).

The Coahuiltec language group is considered today to be extinct. None of the original tribes survive in Texas. A modern estimate suggests that as late as 1690 they measured around 15,000 people. Where the Coahuiltec were not killed by European diseases, they were displaced by the APACHE and the COMANCHE, who moved into the northern part of their territory during the 17th and 18th centuries. By the late 19th century, only two tribes of the whole group survived, and they could no longer speak their native language.

Cochise (Cheis) (1823–1872) *Apache chief involved in events that led to the Apache Wars*

By all accounts, Cochise was perhaps the greatest APACHE military strategist; but he was also a man of peace. When he was born in 1823, he was given the Chiricahua Apache name *Cheis* ("wood") because his young body was so firm. Forty-seven years later, near the time of his death, he stood five feet nine inches high, weighed 164 pounds, had broad shoulders and a stout frame. By then he was known as *Cocheis* or Cochise ('hard wood').

Cochise was the son of a Chiricahua Apache chief Nachi. In his early years, like many Apache warriors living in the mountains of southeastern Arizona, Cochise regularly raided Mexican ranches, stealing horses and other goods. He also fought in battles with other Indian groups. His bravery and battle tactics brought him notoriety.

By the time Cochise had succeeded his father as chief, non-Indian settlers and miners were filtering into Apache territory. Cochise attempted to pursue a peaceful coexistence with

Painting believed by many to be of Cochise, a Chiricahua Apache chief who played a significant role in the Apache Wars *(By permission of the Western History Collections, University of Oklahoma Library)*

Within the next 60 days, about 150 settlers and an unknown number of Apache were killed.

Not long thereafter, the military withdrew many of its troops from the Southwest to fight in the CIVIL WAR (1861–65). Cochise and his warriors subsequently grew bold and confident, and the chief became an implacable foe of non-Indians. Using guerrilla tactics combined with smoke-and-mirror communications among his warriors, he launched a series of devastating attacks against non-Indians in Arizona. Following the Civil War, regular troops returned in large numbers, but found it impossible to corner the skillful Cochise, who spent much of the time in Mexico until about 1870. Chiricahua raids continued unabated, however, attributed by the federal government to Cochise. In desperation, in early fall 1872 Major General OLIVER O. HOWARD, a deeply religious man known as the "Christian General," prevailed on army scout Thomas Jeffords to arrange a meeting with the chief who had returned to Arizona. Cochise, who respected and knew Jeffords, agreed. After being promised a reservation that included all Apache traditional hunting grounds (amounting to a tract approximately two-thirds the size of Connecticut), with Jeffords as the sole Indian agent, Cochise declared, "Hereafter the white man and the Indian are to drink the same water, eat the same bread and be at peace."

Almost two years later, Cochise contracted a disease (probably stomach or colon cancer); he died on June 8, 1874. For his burial, he was dressed in his finest clothing, wrapped in a blanket, and seated on his favorite horse. The funeral procession came to a deep chasm in the rocks high in the Dragoon mountains. There Cochise was buried along with his horse and dog. The exact location of the grave remains a secret.

Further Reading

Roberts, David. *Once They Moved Like the Wind: Cochise, Geronimo, and the Apache Wars.* New York: Simon and Schuster, 1993.
Sweeney, Edwin R. *Cochise: Chiricahua Apache Chief.* Norman: University of Oklahoma Press, 1996.
Thrapp, Dan L. *The Conquest of Apacheria.* Norman: University of Oklahoma Press, 1967.

Cody, William F. (Buffalo Bill Cody) (1846–1917)
producer of "Wild West" shows, U.S. military scout, Pony Express rider, buffalo hunter

William "Buffalo Bill" Cody had a varied career, from Pony Express rider to army scout during the CIVIL WAR (1861–65). He also spent a long period as a scout for the U.S. Army in the West and acted in, managed, and produced "Wild West" shows for audiences in the eastern United States and in parts of Europe.

During the Civil War, Cody joined pro-Union Kansas militias and the Ninth Kansas Volunteers, for whom he drove horse teams in the 7th Kansas Volunteer Cavalry. After the Civil War, Cody operated a hotel in Kansas. When that venture

them and had a contract to supply the Butterfield Stage Line with wood for its station. The peace was eventually shattered, however. One winter day in 1860 some Apache, probably from the Pinal band, raided the ranch of John Ward and made off with some oxen, horses, and Ward's teenage foster son, Felix (later known as Mickey Free). Ward was convinced that Cochise and the Chiricahua were responsible and insisted that military action be taken against them. In February 1861 Lieutenant George N. Bascom and 54 men set out to capture Cochise. They soon made contact with the chief, who denied knowledge of the boy. Bascom refused to believe him and decided to hold him hostage until Felix was returned. Cochise immediately produced a knife, slashed the rear wall of the tent, and escaped. Six Apache were then seized as hostages. Cochise, in turn, took hostages and proposed a prisoner exchange. The overture was refused, and PRISONERS on both sides were killed. This was the spark that ignited the APACHE WARS (1861–86).

failed, he started a shipping business, but it was ruined by Indians who captured his wagons and horses.

After speculating in land and working in railroad construction, Cody was employed as a buffalo hunter to provide food for crews laying tracks for the Kansas Pacific Railroad. His remarkable skill with a rifle earned him the now-famous nickname "Buffalo Bill." Legend holds that he killed more than 4,000 buffalo in this employ. From 1868 to 1872, Cody served as a civilian scout for military forces fighting Plains Indians. He was awarded the Medal of Honor for his role in a battle with Indians on the Platte River in 1872. The award was rescinded in 1916 because Cody had not been a member of the regular army at the time it had been given, but the award was restored to Cody by the U.S. Army Board of Correction of Records in June 1989. In 1876, Cody again engaged in skirmishes with

Indians, serving as a scout and participating in several battles, including the battle of WAR BONNET CREEK (1876) against the northern plains Indians.

Despite his numerous experiences with warfare and other hardships, Cody never stopped encouraging non-Indian settlement of the West. He even founded a town there—Cody, Wyoming. In the 1870s, Cody began his most famous career as creator, promoter, and performer in his "Wild West" shows. It began when he played the leading role in *Scouts of the Prairies,* which costarred Wild Bill Hickok. Thereafter he, formed his own traveling show in 1883, calling it "Buffalo Bill's Wild West." Hunkpapa Lakota (see SIOUX) leader SITTING BULL and markswoman Annie Oakley were among the show's stars. Cody's Wild West show, which featured a mock battle between "cowboys" and Indians, met with great success while touring the

William F. Cody (Buffalo Bill), posing with several Sioux members from his tent show *(Courtesy New York Public Library)*

United States and Europe. In 1890, General NELSON A. MILES asked Cody to attempt to bring in SITTING BULL on the eve of the GHOST DANCE conflict, but the local Indian agent vetoed this special mission. Cody continued performing until 1913, when the show was lost to creditors. He died four years later and was buried on top of Lookout Mountain in Denver, Colorado.

Coeur d'Alene War (1858) *conflict between the U.S. Army and Indian tribes living on the Idaho-Washington border*

The YAKAMA WAR (1855–56) in the Oregon Territory was followed by a brief and uneasy truce. Tensions remained high because miners by the hundreds continued to cross what were still Indian lands on their way to the gold fields on the upper Columbia River. In May 1858, a column of 164 soldiers bound for the mines was ambushed by a force of several hundred Native American warriors that included YAKAMA, Coeur d'Alene, Spokane, and Palouse. Outnumbered, the troops were routed and had to abandon their heavy artillery.

The army response to this embarrassment was swift and effective. Colonel GEORGE WRIGHT put together a force of 700 soldiers, arming them with long-range rifles and artillery. Accompanied by 30 NEZ PERCE scouts and a 400-mule pack-train, they set out for the Spokane Valley at the end of the summer. In the Battles of SPOKANE PLAINS (1858) and FOUR LAKES (1858), fought in early September, Indian forces were flushed from thick woods out onto open ground, where they sustained heavy casualties. Realizing their position, the Indians proposed a truce, but Wright refused the offer. He burned villages and food stores, slaughtered horses, and executed several chiefs. KAMIAKIN, the great Yakama leader, managed to escape to Canada. Following the war, most tribes in the area were forced to settle on reservations that had been agreed upon at the WALLA WALLA PEACE COUNCIL (1855).

Coloradas, Mangas   See MANGAS COLORADAS.

Comanche (Nermurnuh, Komantcia) *Great Plains tribe closely related to the Shoshone*

The Comanche tribe consists of several bands, including the Kewatsona, Kotsai, Kwahadie, Motsai, Nokoni, Patgusa, Penateka, Pohoi, Tanima, Wasaih, and Yanparika. The traditional culture of the Comanche is closely related to that of the northern Rocky Mountain and Great Basin SHOSHONE. Prior to the arrival of Europeans, the Comanche harvested wild roots, greens, nuts, and berries in season and hunted small game. The Comanche were one of the first tribes to acquire Spanish horses in the 17th century. They became horse suppliers to northern tribes and were early participants in the buffalo culture of the Great Plains.

The Comanche and KIOWA became close allies around 1790 and frequently conducted raids together into Mexico and Texas, taking horses and prisoners. The NAVAJO (Dineh)

were among other targets of Comanche raids, as were traders along the Arkansas River and the Santa Fe Trail. Raiding was an activity through which young Comanche men could gain notoriety and honor. It was a sport that netted many benefits, both political and social, for its participants.

The Comanche declined to attend the U.S. government's FORT LARAMIE TREATY (1851) effort in Wyoming saying their vast horse herds would not be safe among the local Lakota (see SIOUX) and CROW. Later, however, Indian agent THOMAS FITZ-PATRICK secured the presence of many Comanche leaders at the FORT ATKINSON TREATY (1853) negotiations. Although U.S. government agents and Comanche leaders agreed upon the terms of the treaty, neither side kept its agreement. The provisions promised by the government were slow to come, inferior, or nonexistent. And although the Comanche refrained from attacks along the Arkansas River and the Santa Fe Trail, they did not totally forgo their raiding. Texans and Mexicans continued to receive the brunt of Comanche assaults; one of the primary goals of the TEXAS RANGERS (1835) organization was to defend against Comanche and Kiowa raids.

On May 11, 1858, Captain JOHN "RIP" FORD, a Texas Ranger and veteran of the Indian Wars, took a 100-man and force attacked a Comanche village near ANTELOPE HILLS (1858) in northwestern Indian Territory (now Oklahoma). The Comanche courageously defended their position but eventually suffered their first serious defeat by an American force.

Although he had received annuity goods along the Arkansas River, Chief BUFFALO HUMP, of the Penateka band, at first apparently plotted against the Texans for the Antelope Hills rout. But he subsequently exchanged pledges of peace and friendship with the commander of Fort Arbuckle. Whether Buffalo Hump was sincere or was simply masking his true intentions is not known. Nevertheless, Major EARL VAN DORN, commander of the army's Wichita Expedition, received no word of Buffalo Hump's peace agreement. On October 1, 1858, Van Dorn attacked Buffalo Hump's sleeping camp at RUSH SPRINGS (1858), killing 58 Comanche, burning 120 lodges, and capturing 300 horses. The following spring Van Dorn's troops trapped a band of Comanche in a ravine at CROOKED CREEK (1859). The troops killed 49, wounded five, and took 37 PRISONERS. These disastrous defeats were but preliminary battles in the Comanche's 20-year struggle against American domination.

During the CIVIL WAR (1861–65), with most Texans away serving in the Confederate army, the Comanche increased the frequency of their raids. Colonel CHRISTOPHER "KIT" CARSON, whose forces had recently defeated the NAVAJO and APACHE, attacked the Comanche and KIOWA at ADOBE WALLS (1864) in the Texas Panhandle. The Indians escaped, but their winter provisions were destroyed. After the Civil War, General PHILIP HENRY SHERIDAN renewed the army campaign against central and southern plains tribes. The Comanche, Kiowa, ARAPAHO, and CHEYENNE were persuaded to sign the MEDICINE LODGE TREATY (1867). Two Comanche bands, the Kotsoteka and Kwahadi, representing about one-third of the tribe, refused to take part. The treaty established a reservation for the

Comanche in Indian Territory (Oklahoma). Anger and frustration soon spread throughout the reservation as hunger and other realities of daily reservation life became apparent. Hundreds of young Comanche men left the reservation to join the nontreaty bands in their raids against Texas settlements for food, horses, and guns farther west.

In 1868, General WILLIAM TECUMSEH SHERMAN responded to the raids by abrogating the hunting privileges assured by the Medicine Lodge Treaty. The Comanche became more desperate, angry, and determined to secure their freedom. On December 25, 1868, Sheridan's forces attacked a combined camp of Comanche and Kiowa at SOLDIER SPRING (1868) on the north fork of the Red River. Once again, Comanche food and shelter were destroyed. In March 1872, Colonel RANALD S. MACKENZIE attacked the Kotsoteka band on McClellan Creek in the Texas Panhandle, killing 23 warriors and taking 124 prisoners. The Kotsoteka, who usually only wintered on the reservation, returned there to stay.

By 1874, the southern plains were on the verge of full-scale war. General Sheridan, with the assistance of Generals JOHN POPE and Christopher C. Augur, planned an all-out campaign, known as the RED RIVER WAR (1874–75), against the southern plains tribes. In response, the resisting groups retreated to the Texas Panhandle. The key event of the war became the battle of PALO DURO CANYON (1874), in which the Kwahadi band, led by QUANAH PARKER, were engaged. Although the Indians suffered few casualties, the army captured their horses and destroyed their food and tipis.

With winter fast approaching, the first Indians began to surrender at Fort Sill on October 1, 1874. Throughout the winter, small parties continued to straggle in. By June 1875, the last of the southern plains tribes, including the Kwahadi Comanche warriors led by Quanah Parker, surrendered. Indian leaders determined responsible for the rebellion were arrested and imprisoned at Fort Marion in St. Augustine, Florida.

Although forced to give up their hunting culture, the Comanche nevertheless continued to assert their independence through other means. Under the leadership of Quanah Parker, who quickly learned to use politics and negotiation to the Comanche's advantage, the Comanche fared better than other tribes forced into reservation life.

Contemporary Comanche have holdings in seven counties in present-day Oklahoma.

Further Reading

Andrist, Ralph K., *Long Death: The Last Days of the Plains Indian.* New York: Macmillan, 1993.
Capps, Benjamin. *The Great Chiefs.* New York: Time-Life Books, 1975.
Carlson, Paul H. *The Plains Indians.* College Station: Texas A & M University Press, 1998.
Marshall, S. L. A. *Crimsoned Prairie: The Indian Wars.* New York: Da Capo, 1972.
Terrell, John Upton. *American Indian Almanac.* New York: Barnes & Nobles Books, 1994.
Utley, Robert M., and Wilcomb E. Washburn. *The American Heritage History of the Indian Wars.* New York: Barnes & Noble Books, 1992.
Wallace, Ernest, and E. Adamson Hoebel. *The Comanches: Lands of The South Plain.* Norman: University of Oklahoma Press, 1987.

Comanche–Republic of Texas Wars (1840–1845)
conflicts between the Comanche and the Republic of Texas
After Texas gained its independence from Mexico in 1836, the Comanche represented a major military challenge to the Texans. Their territory encroached upon by non-Indian settlers, the tribe raided frontier settlements, stole cattle, killed settlers, and took women and children captive.

In 1838, Mirabeau Lamar replaced the relatively pro-Indian Sam Houston as president of the independent Texas republic. Lamar invited the Comanche chief Muguara and other chiefs to come to San Antonio for peace talks. On March 19, 1840, Muguara, 30 warriors, and several women and children arrived in San Antonio. They brought with them one non-Indian captive, a 15-year-old girl. The Texans were incensed at the girl's condition and at her report of at least 15 other prisoners.

While the Indians were in the San Antonio council house, three companies of TEXAS RANGERS surrounded the building. Indians and Texans had both brought weapons inside. Gunfire broke out soon after the Comanche were informed that they would be held hostage for the return of the white prisoners. When the fighting ended, Muguara was one of 34 dead Comanche. One woman survivor was sent to warn the Comanche that this was the fate of any who dealt in bad faith with the Texans. The rest of the survivors were held as "servants."

The outraged Comanche first tortured to death all but two of their prisoners. One of those killed was a six-year-old girl. Several hundred warriors rode into San Antonio, but they hesitated to act without their leaders, who had been killed at the Council House affair. Muguara's nephew, BUFFALO HUMP, meditated about a more organized response. While meditating, he had a vision of Texans being driven into the sea.

Buffalo Hump assembled a force of about 400 warriors and 600 women and children. They headed toward the Gulf of Mexico. After attacking the town of Victoria, the Indians reached the tiny port of Linville. All but five of the residents escaped by fleeing into the Gulf in small boats, almost as Buffalo Hump had seen in his vision. The Indians then headed north, only to be soundly defeated by Texas Rangers at PLUM CREEK (1840). After a second defeat at the Colorado River, the surviving Comanche retreated farther north into what later became Oklahoma.

By this time Lamar's term ended, and Sam Houston was again the Texas president. Houston was determined to make peace. Buffalo Hump's band of Comanche had done such a good job of hiding, however, that it took until August 1843 for the Texas peace delegation to reach them. By 1844, at a

This highly romanticized print shows five Comanche taking a white woman prisoner, March 20, 1858. *(Courtesy New York Public Library)*

council including most Comanche chiefs, Houston had worked out a shaky peace agreement. On occasion the Texas government even gave supplies to Comanche conducting raids into Mexico. The annexation of Texas by the United States in 1845 meant the short-lived Republic's problems with the Comanche would be assumed by the federal government.

Further Reading

Chalfant, William Y. *Without Quarter.* Norman: University of Oklahoma Press, 1991.

Dawson, Joseph G., III, ed. *The Texas Military Experience.* College Station: Texas A&M University Press, 1995.

Lee, Nelson. *Three Years among the Comanches: The Narrative of Nelson Lee, The Texas Ranger.* Norman: University of Oklahoma Press, 1967.

commissioner of Indian Affairs *appointed federal administrative position within the Department of the Interior*
The post of commissioner of Indian Affairs was officially established by an act of Congress in 1832, but the need for such a position had been apparent for years before then. After the AMERICAN REVOLUTION (1775–81), Indian affairs, apart from

trade, were handled by the secretary of war. From 1806 to 1822, the superintendent of Indian Trade, an official within the WAR DEPARTMENT, handled trade with the Indians. When this position was abolished by Congress, trade was put under the direct authority of the secretary of war.

In the early 1820s, Secretary of War John C. Calhoun tried unsuccessfully to get Congress to establish an office dealing with all Indian issues. Consequently, on March 11, 1824, he created the BUREAU OF INDIAN AFFAIRS (BIA). An Office of Indian Affairs was recognized by Congress in 1832, with an act authorizing the president to appoint a commissioner of Indian Affairs; the commissioner was to direct all of the government's Indian-related matters under the direction of the secretary of war. The office, and its commissioner remained within the War Department until 1849, when it was transferred to the newly created Interior Department (see DEPARTMENT OF THE INTERIOR). During the years that followed, the influence of the commissioner fluctuated, with the military having a greater influence over Indian policy until the 20th century. In 1947, the office officially became the Bureau of Indian Affairs. Currently, the bureau seeks to work with tribal governments improve economic, educational, and social opportunities for recognized tribes within the United States.

Conestoga Massacre   See PAXTON RIOTS.

Connor, Patrick E. (1820–1891) *army officer during the Civil War*
Born in Ireland, Patrick Connor came to the United States as a child and eventually settled in Texas. He commanded a company of Texas volunteers during the Mexican War, suffering a wound before resigning in 1847. Connor later migrated to California, and with the outset of the CIVIL WAR (1861–65), he again secured a volunteer commission.

As commander of the military district of Utah and Nevada, Connor inflicted a sharp defeat on the BANNOCK and SHOSHONE in the BEAR RIVER Campaign (1863). During CHEYENNE-ARAPAHO WAR (1864–65), he led 3,000 troops into the Powder River country of Wyoming, burning an ARAPAHO village and engaging in several minor skirmishes. He failed, however, to inflict the decisive blow on the Indians that the federal government had envisioned. Mustered out of the army in 1866, Connor settled in Utah, where his anti-Mormon sentiments often inflamed public opinion.

Cooke, Philip St. George (1809–1895) *soldier and veteran of the Black Hawk War and the Civil War*
Born in Leesburg, Virginia, on June 13, 1809, Philip St. George Cooke is best remembered for his service during the CIVIL WAR (1861–65). After graduating from West Point in 1827, Cooke took part in expeditions into the West and gained considerable frontier experience. He served in the BLACK HAWK WAR (1831) and participated in the battle at BAD AXE (1832), both against the SAUK (Sac). In the 1840s, he led a number of expeditions farther west, past the Rocky Mountains.

During the 1840s and 1850s, Cooke served in campaigns against the APACHE. In the summer of 1853 the army stopped distributing rations to the Jicarilla Apache, which led to rioting. Cooke led pursuits of the Jicarilla leaders. On March 5, 1854, he defeated Lobo Blanco; later that month he began pursuing Chacón. He was ambushed at the Rio Caliente on April 8, 1854, but he surprised and defeated a Jicarilla camp in turn the following month.

After the Civil War, Cooke commanded the military departments of the Platte (1866–67), the Cumberland (1869–70), and the Lakes (1870–73) before retiring with the rank of brevet major general. He recorded memories of his service in the West in his book, *Scenes and Adventures in the Army* (1857). He died on March 20, 1895.

Cornplanter (Corn Plant, Gyantwaia, Garganwahgah, John O'Bail) (1735–1836) *Seneca war chief during the American Revolution*
Cornplanter was born to a SENECA woman and John O'Bail, a British trader front of Albany, New York. Cornplanter fought as a war chief against the British during the FRENCH AND INDIAN WAR (1754–63) and was reportedly a member of the party that defeated General EDWARD BRADDOCK's expedition to Fort Duquesne in 1755.

When the AMERICAN REVOLUTION broke out, Cornplanter allied himself with the British. During the late 1770s he served with MOHAWK irregulars led by JOSEPH BRANT and Canadian militia in raids on American frontier settlements in New York and Pennsylvania, including the CHERRY VALLEY Massacre (1779). In 1780, Cornplanter learned that Brant had captured his father; he negotiated to have him escorted to safety in Fort Plain, New York. At the war's conclusion the Seneca chief participated in various peace negotiations with the Americans, including those resulting in the treaties of FORT STANWIX (1784) and FORT HARMER (1789); he agreed to give up large sections of Seneca territory in exchange for promises of peace. When these treaties were broken, usually by American settlers, Cornplanter served as a negotiator for his people, meeting with President George Washington in 1790 and President Thomas Jefferson in 1801. He also worked as a peacemaker, along with RED JACKET and Joseph Brant, between the Americans and the Indians of the Ohio Country during LITTLE TURTLE'S WAR (1786–95).

After laying down his arms at the end of the Revolutionary War, Cornplanter never again fought against the Americans. Instead, he settled down on his Pennsylvania farm, which had been granted to him in recognition of his services. By the early 1800s he had acquired 1,300 acres and established his relatives and followers, the Cornplanter Seneca, on them. His influence with the tribe was great enough to persuade the Seneca to support the United States in the WAR OF 1812 (1812–15), and his son Henry served in the American army. Later in life, Cornplanter questioned his earlier support for the United States, which had repeatedly reneged on promises to the Indians. He destroyed all the gifts he had received from non-Indian officials, but he never again actively resisted the U.S. government.

Cornstalk (Keigh-tugh-qua) (ca. 1720–1777) *Shawnee chief*
Cornstalk was one of the major opponents of settlers moving west of the Appalachian Mountains immediately before the AMERICAN REVOLUTION (1775–81). He played an important role in LORD DUNMORE'S WAR (1773–74), the first of the colonial wars for the Ohio territory. He also led the Indian forces in the battle of POINT PLEASANT (1774), in what is now West Virginia, but was driven off in defeat. Cornstalk's SHAWNEE and their IROQUOIS CONFEDERACY allies were forced to yield much of what is now Kentucky as a result.

Cornstalk later sought to build Indian support for the British during the Revolutionary War. In 1777, in an effort to put off an American invasion of the Ohio Country, he visited Fort Randolph (Point Pleasant) under a flag of truce. The commander of the fort, Captain Matthew Arbuckle, ignored the flag, seized Cornstalk and two companions, and imprisoned them. On November 10, 1777, a group of angry settlers broke into Cornstalk's cell and killed and mutilated all three men. Cornstalk's death drove the Shawnee into open alliance with the British.

Coronado, Francisco Vázquez de (ca. 1510–1554)
Spanish explorer and conquistador

Francisco Vázquez de Coronado was Spain's governor of the northern Mexican province of Nueva Galicia in 1539, when reports of Indian cities of great wealth just north of Mexico—the fabled Seven Cities of Cíbola—began to spread in the region. Remembering the fantastic riches of the Aztec and Incan civilizations, both of which had fallen only within the preceding 20 years, Coronado and other Spanish governors decided to investigate the claims. Several expeditions, including one led by conquistador HERNÁN CORTÉS, set out to explore the area. On January 6, 1540, Coronado himself left Mexico to search for the fabled riches of Cíbola and claim them for Spain. With a force consisting of 292 European soldiers, a Franciscan friar, about 800 allied Indians, and livestock to feed them, he slowly moved north and arrived at Cíbola, or Hawikuh Pueblo (see ZUNI) in present-day western New Mexico on July 7, 1540.

Hawikuh's Zuni residents felt threatened by the Spanish presence, and met the strangers with a hail of arrows, spears, and stones. The Spanish, carrying guns, wearing armor, and mounted on horses, responded by storming the town. The Zuni, terrified by the noise and mindful of legends of heavenly messengers *(katsinas)* that would come from the west and conquer their country, quickly surrendered. Coronado's troops occupied Hawikuh from July through November of 1540, sending out exploratory expeditions to Arizona as far west as the Grand Canyon and as far east as Kansas. In each case, the Spanish found nothing to match the legends—no gold, no silver, and no fine silks, only hostile Indians, cold, and hunger.

Misunderstandings between the Spanish and the PUEBLO INDIANS frequently escalated into violence. During the winter of 1540–41, Spanish troops stationed at Alcanfor Pueblo extorted food and blankets from the neighboring Tiguex Pueblo. They also sexually abused Indian women; as a result the Pueblo leaders declared war. The Spanish, with their technological advantages, quickly overcame the Indians and punished them severely. About 100 Indian men died by burning at the stake, and hundreds of others were killed when they tried to flee.

Coronado continued his explorations throughout the spring and summer of 1541. The Indians of New Mexico had spread rumors of a large, wealthy city called Quivira located to the north and east of their land (in modern Kansas). Coronado found that these rumors were false; they had been circulated in order to get the Spanish out of the Pueblo Indians' cities and onto the Plains, where the Indians' superior numbers would give them the advantage over the invaders' weapons. Through the end of 1541 the Spanish fought almost constantly with the Native Americans, using up ammunition and suffer-

ing casualties. The constant warfare also kept them from finding adequate food and shelter.

In the spring of 1542, Coronado learned of a rebellion in the Mexican state of Sonora and decided to give up his by now hopeless quest for riches. With the remnants of his army, he retreated from New Mexico. Only six years later, silver lodes were discovered along Mexico's northern frontier. Rather than waste their resources searching for riches in the barren north, the Spanish turned their energies to mining in the south. For the next 40 years New Mexico was left to its Indian inhabitants. For his part, Coronado returned to Mexico City in some disgrace. In 1546 Coronado was found innocent at the charges that he committed cruel acts against Indians in his army. He died in 1554.

Council Grove Treaty (1870) *second treaty negotiated in 1864 with the Modoc, the Klamath, and the Yahooskin band of Shoshone of present-day southern Oregon and northern California*

On February 14, 1864, at Council Grove, California, a treaty was negotiated with the MODOC, Klamath, and Yahooskin SHOSHONE by Judge Elijah Steele, Indian agent for Northern California, whom the Indians trusted and respected. The main objectives of the Steele treaty were to end intertribal warfare and provide for peaceful, amicable relations among cultural groups throughout the region. The treaty found broad acceptance and adherence among the Indians. The U.S. government, however, found it objectionable because it lacked provisions for land cessions and reservations. Steele was subsequently relieved of his duties through the efforts of Senator John Conness of California. Nine months later, in October 1864, Superintendent J. W. Perit Huntington arrived at Fort Klamath to renegotiate the treaty. The first article of the new treaty extinguished tribal land ownership and created a reservation. It further reserved to the United States the right of allotting lands to groups or to individuals. Huntington characterized the reservation as a "high fence" that the Indians could not scale without permission.

The remainder of the treaty contained all the "proper" provisions according to U. S. treaty-making etiquette of the time: Non-Indians were forbidden to trespass; annuity goods would serve as payment for the land; and education in manual arts—agricultural and technical skills such as farming and ranches—would be provided to encourage what the U.S. government considered acceptable Indian behavior.

The Klamath apparently agreed without much argument, but the Modoc, especially their leader Kintpuash (see CAPTAIN JACK), were not so easily convinced. Nevertheless, after the application of much pressure, Kintpuash reluctantly agreed and signed.

The treaty specifically stated that removal to the reservation would occur "immediately after ratification." But the Indians were instead moved after the signing on October 14, 1864, and settlers soon began to occupy Modoc lands. Ratification, however, did not occur until December 1869. Further, the treaty was not formally proclaimed in Washington until February 17, 1870, with another year passing before President ULYSSES S. GRANT issued an executive order reserving a 768,000-acre reservation for the treaty tribes. In the 1860s and 1870s all Shoshone bands were assigned reservations.

By the time the acreage was formally set aside, Kintpuash and his followers had tried reservation life twice and twice rejected it. Settlers living on former Modoc land demanded the return of the Modoc to the reservation. Oregon Indian Superintendent Thomas B. Odeneal, new to the job, received orders to force the Modoc back to the reservation by whatever means necessary. In November 1872, a detail from Fort Klamath was sent to arrest Kintpuash and other leaders, who were now settled at Lost Valley. During the meeting of the two groups, shots were fired, signaling the start of the MODOC WAR (1872–73). After several battles, Modoc leaders, including Kintpuash, Schonchin Jack, SCARFACED CHARLEY, and Black Jim surrendered, were charged with murder, and hanged. The remainder of the Modoc, numbering about 155, were exiled to Indian Territory (Oklahoma), where many died of malaria. Longings for their old home persisted, and in 1909 those who wanted to return to the Klamath reservation were allowed to go. A small remnant remain in Oklahoma.

Council House Massacre See COMANCHE–REPUBLIC OF TEXAS WARS; PLUM CREEK.

councils, war *meetings of tribal decision makers preparatory to war*
War was a fact of life for virtually all tribes in North America. They were fought not only to protect the tribe members and secure the tribe's reputation among others, but also to enable warriors to prove their courage and skill. Raiding and fighting by individuals and small groups often took place as a means of settling personal or family matters of honor. However, for matters affecting the whole band or tribe, the highly democratic nature of most Indian societies necessitated decision making by consensus. This was particularly true of the important decision to go to full-scale war.

Those most likely to lead war councils were called *chief.* The term was used for a man or woman at the pinnacle of authority, who was highly respected. Indian tribes and bands had many chiefs who served different functions. Among the most notable distinctions were "war chiefs" and "peace chiefs," with diverging responsibilities that reflected these two titles. Some chiefs inherited their position. Custom and the power of the individual played a role, but generally chiefs had to rule by consensus, by getting everyone to agree on actions, rather than by exerting power over others.

Seldom did one person have the power to speak for the entire tribe, though some, by wisdom and deeds, earned great influence. This created problems for non-Indian negotiators, who were used to dealing with powerful individuals able to speak for many. Sometimes non-Indians tried to select a single person within a tribe and give him or her the responsibility for signing agreements for the whole tribe. But even legitimate chiefs could not do this.

Plains Indians distinguished between two kinds at councils. Civil councils saw to the day-to-day operations of the tribe including movement from place to place & settling disputes. Meanwhile the council of war chiefs chose the war leader for each military raid. A man could not be a war chief and civil chief at the same time.

The decision to go to war was made in many tribes by a formal council of the bravest and most respected warriors, usually holding the "rank" of chief. These council members in turn often sought advice from medicine men and prophets as well as from women of the tribe who were thought to be especially wise, such as elders.

The council typically reached a decision only after lengthy public debate. It rarely went against the wishes of the majority of the people. The opinion of a head chief carried a great deal of weight, yet he had no formal power. People listened to him only to the degree that his opinions made good sense. It is not surprising, then, that whatever their other qualifications, usually including great achievements in war, the chiefs tended to be good and persuasive speakers.

A major disadvantage of the war council system was that, because of the need for consensus, Indian tribes sometimes could not react as quickly to situations as non-Indians, who acted alone or on orders from superiors.

See also TACTICS, NATIVE AMERICAN; TACTICS, NON-NATIVE AMERICAN.

counting coup *act of touching a living enemy with a hand or a special coup stick without being harmed*
Among the Plains tribes, counting coup was a greater, more laudable feat than was killing an enemy. A warrior who actually touched his enemy with his hand or a COUP STICK was considered very brave. If a person upon whom coup had been counted was killed during battle, honor went to the first coup counter, not to the one who did the killing. Warriors who accumulated a high coup count and lots of captured horses could earn the title of war chief.

See also COUP STICK.

coup stick *staff used by warriors of the Plains tribes to attain glory through their acts of bravery and courage*
Among the Plains tribes, while killing an enemy during a battle or raid was important, the face-to-face confrontation was even more so. The ultimate act of bravery was to simply get close enough to touch the foe (see COUNTING COUP). To accomplish this, each warrior carried a coup stick, or wand, which was used to strike an enemy. At each warrior's home was a special pole stuck in the ground. When a raiding or

Blackfoot man holding coup stick and shield *(Courtesy of the National Museum of the American Indian, Smithsonian #20713)*

warring party returned, each warrior who had touched an enemy with a coup stick would strike the pole as a declaration of his bravery.

Courthouse Rebellion (1849) *incident involving Métis and English fur traders in Canada*

In 1821, the Hudson's Bay Company, a British fur-trading company in Canada, merged with another trading company, the North West Company. Its power greatly increased by this merger, the Hudson's Bay Company began trying to impose strict trading regulations on independent MÉTIS hunters, including a prohibition on trading with Americans. Because trade with American merchants in the western Great Lakes region was vital to their economy, the Métis—individuals of mixed Indian and non-Indian ancestry—protested these actions.

Tensions festered for years. Then, in 1849, the Hudson's Bay Company brought a Métis hunter and trader, Guillaume Sayer, to trial for trying to smuggle goods across the border from Canada into the United States. In response, 300 armed

Métis, led by LOUIS RIEL, gathered at Fort Garry in present-day Manitoba and threatened violence. In the face of this rebellion, a nervous jury found Sayer guilty but recommended his immediate release. Violence was thus averted.

For the next 20 years, Métis trade and commerce remained relatively free of restrictions, and Métis trade caravans regularly traveled between Manitoba and Minnesota and the Dakotas. Although the Courthouse Rebellion was resolved without hostilities, more violent Métis uprisings occurred later in the century. They became known as RIEL'S REBELLIONS (1869–70, 1884–85), after their leader, LOUIS RIEL Jr.

Covenant Chain (1600s) *series of treaties between the British colonies and Indian tribes of the American Northeast*

In 1677, the British colonies made peace with the tribes of the IROQUOIS CONFEDERACY at Albany in the colony of New York. The major negotiator for the British was Sir EDMUND ANDROS, the governor of the former Dutch colony of New Amsterdam (later New York). This peace was the first in a series of treaties known as the Covenant Chain, which linked the British colonies of the mid-Atlantic and New England regions to the local Indians. The agreements kept peace between the two groups for about 100 years, until the AMERICAN REVOLUTION (1775–81) permanently changed the political landscape.

The symbol used for the treaties was a silver chain, linking the British to the Indians in permanent friendship. The Covenant Chain was important for several reasons. First, the negotiations and treaties were based on mutual respect for the viewpoints of both the British and the Indians. Second, the agreement benefited both sides, maintaining peace between tribes on the New York/New England frontier and expanding the lucrative fur-trade market between the British and the Indians. Third, it pressured the French to keep the peace because the powerful Iroquois Confederacy was linked with the British, long time enemies of the French.

Crazy Horse (Tashunca-Uitco, His Horse Is Crazy; Curly; Light-Haired Boy) (ca. 1842–1877) *Oglala Lakota (Sioux) chief during the Sioux Wars (1867)*

Crazy Horse was born near present-day Rapid City, South Dakota, between 1841 and 1844, into the Oglala band of the Lakota Nation (see SIOUX). During his youth he was called Curly, but by age 16 his name was changed. He Dog, a lifelong friend of Crazy Horse, reported that in a fight against another tribe, the latter repeatedly rammed his horse into those of his enemies, knocking the riders off. He thus became known as Crazy Horse.

When Crazy Horse was still young, he undertook a vision quest in which he learned that he would be a great warrior. This turned out to be prophetic. Crazy Horse's first battles were against the CROW Indians. Later, he fought alongside Oglala chief RED CLOUD in a series of engagements with non-Indians along the BOZEMAN TRAIL. On December 21, 1866, Red Cloud's forces attacked a woodcutting detail near Fort Phil Kearny. A relief column of 80 men under the command of Captain WILLIAM FETTERMAN came to the detail's aid. Crazy Horse led a small party of warriors that decoyed Fetterman beyond a defensible position into an ambush (see FETTERMAN FIGHT). Later, on August 2, 1867, he participated in the WAGON BOX FIGHT. Because of his exploits, Crazy Horse was made an Oglala war chief in 1868.

Ten years later, the SIOUX WARS for the Black Hills erupted; Crazy Horse emerged as an important leader. He was young, five feet eight inches tall, limber, and sinewy, and on his face was a scar. He made a striking appearance in battle, easily recognizable in his colt-hide cape. Throughout the Sioux Wars, he distinguished himself as a fearless warrior and brilliant strategist, universally respected by his followers.

On June 17, 1876, Oglala and CHEYENNE warriors under the direction of Crazy Horse and SITTING BULL attacked the force led by General GEORGE CROOK in the battle of ROSEBUD CREEK (1876). Unable to cope with the Crazy Horse's military tactics, Crook was forced to withdraw. Less than two weeks later, on June 25, 1876, Crazy Horse and GALL led the fight in the battle of the LITTLE BIGHORN (1876), annihilating the 7th Cavalry under General GEORGE ARMSTRONG CUSTER.

Following Custer's defeat, troops under commanders such as Colonel NELSON A. MILES relentlessly pursued the Sioux (Dakota, Lakota, Nakota). After various taxing battles and skirmishes, most notably the battle of WOLF MOUNTAIN (1877), the Indians began to consider surrender. On May 5, 1877, Crazy Horse, with slightly fewer than 900 followers, finally surrendered at the Red Cloud Agency in northwestern Nebraska.

In August 1877, the NEZ PERCE WAR erupted in Oregon. Lieutenant William Philo Clark of the Red Cloud Agency was ordered to enlist the services of a group of Sioux scouts to help subdue the NEZ PERCE. At a meeting with the Sioux, Crazy Horse apparently said that he would fight until there were no Nez Perce left. The interpreter, however, reported the message that the chief would fight until there were no *white men* left. Not long thereafter, an Indian named Woman's Dress, who was jealous of Crazy Horse, falsely reported that the chief was planning to kill General Crook. Consequently, Crazy Horse was escorted to Camp Robinson near the Red Cloud Agency. As he was being taken to the jail on September 5, 1877, a scuffle ensued, and Crazy Horse was bayoneted in the back by an army guard while an Indian named Little Big Man grabbed the chief's arms. That night at about 11:00 P.M., Chief Crazy Horse died of his wound. His father and mother claimed their son's body and buried it in a private location. A few days after his death, his ailing wife also died.

Crazy Horse is best remembered as a key figure in the Indian victory at the Little Bighorn. For many Sioux, however, he is revered as one of their greatest leaders, a man who resisted non-Indian encroachments for most of his adult life.

Further Reading

Clark, Robert A., ed. *The Killing of Chief Crazy Horse*. Lincoln: University of Nebraska Press, 1988.

Sajna, Mike. *Crazy Horse: The Life Behind the Legend*. New York: John Wiley, 2000.

Sandoz, Mari. *Crazy Horse: The Strange Man of the Ogalas*. Lincoln: University of Nebraska Press, 1992.

Crazy Woman Fight (1866) *battle on the Bozeman Trail during Red Cloud's War*

When Lakota (see SIOUX) and CHEYENNE war leaders RED CLOUD, SPOTTED TAIL, STANDING ELK, and DULL KNIFE visited Fort Laramie (in present-day Wyoming) in spring 1866, they believed that the U.S. government would abandon the roads it had cut through their territory and leave them in peace. They discovered that they had been misled. The terms of the treaty signed the previous autumn actually stated that the Indians would withdraw from all roads the U.S. government had built or would build in the future.

On July 13, 1866, Colonel HENRY B. CARRINGTON began constructing Fort Phil Kearny between the Big Piney and Little Piney Creeks in southern Montana in hopes of protecting the BOZEMAN TRAIL from Indian attack. However, the Lakota and Northern Cheyenne had no intention of allowing the army to garrison a road that cut through the heart of their homelands. In late July a Native American force ambushed a military supply train headed for Fort Phil Kearny in the canyon formed by Crazy Woman Creek. The Indians failed to overwhelm the supply train on their first attack, and the wagon train's drivers managed to hold them off throughout the day. At dusk a relief force of soldiers arrived from Fort Phil Kearny, forcing the Indians to withdraw. The battle at Crazy Woman Creek marked the beginning of RED CLOUD'S WAR (1866–88).

Cree *Indian tribe whose traditional territory spanned much of central Canada*

Various Cree bands, numbering about 20,000 members, once inhabited an enormous stretch of land, from southeast of Hudson Bay in present-day Quebec to northwest of the Saskatchewan River in present-day Alberta. Scholars today distinguish between the East, West Main, and Western Wood Cree, but all spoke a common Algonquian language and shared common adaptation strategies for living in their subarctic environment.

French traders and missionaries first made contact with the Cree during the early 1600s. Within a few decades the Indians were serving the French as guides and fur hunters. By 1667 the British had established the Hudson's Bay Company on Hudson Bay, and a rivalry broke out between the two European groups over competition for the Indians' support and patronage in the fur trade.

The Cree enjoyed easy access to the Hudson Bay trading posts, an advantage desired by the neighboring ASSINIBOINE

Indians. Consequently, the Assiniboine formed an alliance with the Cree. Armed with guns and powder, the Assiniboine, a tribe closely related to the Yanktonai Nakota (see SIOUX), escalated their warfare against their enemies and former relatives, the Dakota (Sioux). The subsequent evacuation of the Dakota from the southern Great Lakes region allowed the Cree to migrate down into the present-day United States. There the Plains Cree and their allies, the Assiniboine, also fought against the Blackfeet (see BLACKFOOT CONFEDERACY).

In ensuing years, many Cree intermarried with French and Scottish settlers. Known as MÉTIS, or "mixed bloods," they developed their own culture and economic concerns. Tensions between the Métis and Canadian fur traders eventually led to the RIEL REBELLIONS (1869–70; 1884–85), named after the Métis LOUIS RIEL Jr., who led the rebellions. The Métis were joined during these conflicts by full-blooded Cree.

The Cree today occupy reserve land in Canada. Some Cree also share a reservation with the CHIPPEWA (Anishinabe) in Montana.

Creek *Indian tribe of the southeastern United States eventually relocated to Indian Territory (present-day Oklahoma)*

By the precolonial period, Creek villages were located in what are now the states of Georgia and Alabama, and portions of Tennessee, Florida, and Louisiana. In 1540, Spanish explorer HERNANDO DE SOTO became the first European to make contact with the various bands of what became known as the CREEK CONFEDERACY, which also included other nearby tribes and bands. Within the next two centuries the Creek established trade relationships with the British. Later, some, but not all, Creek bands sided with the British in the FRENCH AND INDIAN WAR (1754–63) and still later in the AMERICAN REVOLUTION (1775–81).

Creek hostilities against the newly established U.S. government reached a crisis point during the second decade of the 19th century. By this time the Creek were divided into war and peace factions—the RED STICKS and the White Sticks, respectively. The former were determined to wage war against settlers, while the latter favored peaceful coexistence. Peace was not to be had, however. In 1813 a Red Stick named Little Warrior led a Creek force in the battle of RAISIN RIVER (1813). Later that year, RED EAGLE lead about 1,000 of his warriors against FORT MIMS (1813) in a major battle of the CREEK WAR (1813–14). After breaching the fort's walls, the Indians killed about 400 settlers inside. General ANDREW JACKSON then led troops, including the legendary Dave Crockett, in retaliatory pursuit. Warfare between the Creek and the army continued until March 1814, when Red Eagle's warriors were defeated in the battle of HORSESHOE BEND (1814). The TREATY OF HORSESHOE BEND (1814) officially ended the Creek War and opened about 23 million acres, about two-thirds of Creek land, to white settlement.

In 1830, Andrew Jackson, now the U.S. president, signed the INDIAN REMOVAL ACT (1830). Six years later, the Creek, along with the CHOCTAW, CHICKASAW, SEMINOLE, and CHEROKEE, were forced to march to Indian territory on what came to be known as the TRAIL OF TEARS. Of approximately 15,000 Creek who set out on that journey, about 3,500 died of disease and exposure during and immediately following their removal. The majority of the Creek, are now located in Oklahoma, but some remain in Alabama, Georgia, and Florida.

Creek Confederacy *association of tribes in what is now the southeastern United States during the 17th and 18th centuries*

The Creek Confederacy was an alliance of Native American tribes living in southeastern North America, primarily in the present-day states of Florida, South Carolina, Georgia, and Alabama. The term *CREEK* itself is actually a name given to these Indians by the English; it evolved from the idea of "Indians living along the creek." Among the most prominent Creek tribes was the Muskogee Indians; other bands included the Alabama and Coushatta. The SEMINOLE Indians of Florida are an offshoot of the southern bands of the Creek Confederacy.

Oral histories of the Creek tribes indicate that they immigrated into the southeastern United States from somewhere to the west and may be related to the Mound Builder culture of prehistoric times. These Muskogean-speaking immigrants arrived about 1200, blending with local populations as they settled. The diverse tribes in the area eventually formally agreed to live in peace. Evidence of precisely how this happened does not exist, however. Most likely they saw peace with their immediate neighbors as more advantageous than fighting. Aggression was channelled into athletic competition. The alliances gradually grew stronger, eventually leading to what might be considered a common culture and the establishment of a distinct Indian nation. The chiefs of each Creek town would meet in council from time to time to discuss issues of concern. Individual villages and bands had a certain amount of autonomy, though they usually followed the same policies when dealing with outsiders.

The Creek Confederacy offered refuge to harassed tribes from other areas, either by formal invitation or by granting what can be considered asylum to refugee tribes. In some cases, bands from other tribes, such as the CHOCTAW, lived in Creek territory and were part of the confederacy.

The Creek Confederacy was divided into two geographical regions, which the Europeans called Upper and Lower towns. This division predated trade relations with British colonies, but the names came from Native American trade routes. The Upper and Lower towns had what was effectively separate governments. The two groups acknowledged kinship as well as similar cultures and world views, but they held different councils and did not necessarily follow the same foreign policy.

Among the Upper and Lower Creek, each town was classified as either "red" or "white." The color white symbolized peace, while red represented blood, the color of war. White towns were involved with peace and treaty making, and red towns, where the warriors lived, handled war. The CHEROKEE, non-Creek Confederacy members, used a similar system, though each community had two councils: white for peacetime, red for war. The Creek town arrangement also functioned as a type of sports league, as only teams from different types of towns could play each other.

Men would rise in the peace or war hierarchy according to war honors, the best way to win the respect of their fellow tribe members. Creek conflicts, often with the Cherokee, would frequently involve only a few towns, though the entire nation could act as a body if necessary. If war was imminent, the Creek War Speakers would encourage their young warriors with speeches outlining the grievances behind the declaration of war and making promises of the glory to be won in war. Village speakers would try to get allies in the conflict by sending emissaries to other villages.

The system may have been confusing to outsiders, but the Creek tended to have a strong awareness of their identities, whether they were from a red or white town or were Upper or Lower Creek. The system, however, did suffer from unrest in the late 1700s and early 1800s, under pressure from non-Indians to give up some Creek lands. The CREEK WAR (1813–14), and the rise of ANDREW JACKSON to military and political prominence, were the result. After the passage of the INDIAN REMOVAL ACT (1830), the Creek, along with other southeastern tribes were forced to leave their homelands and relocate west of the Mississippi River to Indian Territory (present-day Oklahoma).

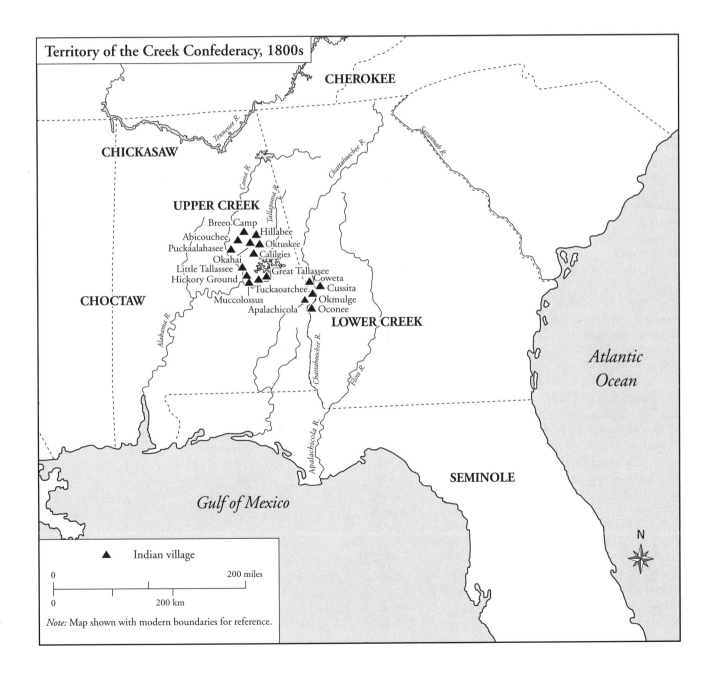

Territory of the Creek Confederacy, 1800s

CHEROKEE

CHICKASAW

Tennessee R.

Coosa R.

Tallapoosa R.

Chattahoochee R.

Savannah R.

UPPER CREEK

Breeo Camp
Abicouchee ▲ ▲ Hillabee
Puckaalahasee ▲ ▲ Oktuskee
Okahai ▲ Calilgies
Little Tallassee ▲ Great Tallassee
Hickory Ground ▲ Coweta
Tuckaoatchee ▲ Cussita
Muccolossus ▲ Okmulge
Apalachicola ▲ Oconee

CHOCTAW

LOWER CREEK

Alabama R.

Chattahoochee R.

Flint R.

Apalachicola R.

Atlantic Ocean

SEMINOLE

Gulf of Mexico

N

▲ Indian village

0   200 miles
0   200 km

Note: Map shown with modern boundaries for reference.

Further Reading

Bancroft-Hunt, Norman. *Warriors: Warfare and the Native American.* London: Salamander Books, 1995.

Grayson, G. W. *A Creek Warrior for the Confederacy: The Autobiography of Chief G. W. Grayson.* Edited by W. David Baird. Norman: University of Oklahoma Press, 1988.

Holland Braund, Kathryn E. *Deerskins and Duffels.* Lincoln: University of Nebraska Press, 1943.

Creek War (1813–1814) *bitter conflict between warring factions of Creek Indians and the U.S. Army*

In Georgia and Alabama, the CREEK Indians had for years engaged in a bloody civil struggle with non-Indian settlers. The Lower Creek, known also as the White Sticks, believed it was in their best interest to cooperate with non-Indians. The Upper Creek, known also as RED STICKS, adamantly opposed the white intruders. To fuel the fire of dissention among the factions of the Creek nation, Little Warrior of the Red Sticks, who had fought against the United States during the WAR OF 1812 (1812–14), was captured and executed by the White Sticks.

Equipped by the Spanish in Pensacola and led by mixed-blood Peter McQueen, Red Sticks attacked and defeated settlers at Burnt Corn Creek. This engagement was overshadowed on August 30, 1813, when RED EAGLE led another Red Stick assault on FORT MIMS (1813), resulting in 400 dead settlers. Furious with this attack on non-Indians, the Tennessee legislature allocated $300,000 to raise an army under General ANDREW JACKSON to put an end to the Red Stick menace. Jackson organized 5,000 Tennessee militiamen, 19 companies of CHEROKEE auxiliaries, and 200 White Sticks. In early November 1813, a detachment under Colonel John Coffee, accompanied by Davey Crockett, ambushed a large party of Red Sticks at the battle of TALLASAHATCHEE (1813). Red Stick losses were 186 dead; Coffee's losses totalled five killed and 41 wounded. Later that month, Jackson led a force to relieve the besieged White Sticks at their settlement of TALLADEGA (1813), killing 290 Red Sticks and losing only 15 of his own soldiers.

Assisted by General William Claiborne but plagued by high desertion rates among his volunteers, Jackson vainly pursued Red Eagle for the next several months. In January 1814, Jackson received 800 reinforcements, and during the month he fought two skirmishes against the Red Sticks at Emuckfaw and Enotachopco Creek. He also systematically burned every Red Stick town he came upon in an effort to force a climactic battle. In March, 600 regulars from the U.S. 39th Infantry Regiment joined Jackson's command. On March 27 his force attacked a fortified Red Stick village at HORSESHOE BEND (1814) on the Tallapoosa River. After a daylong struggle, Jackson's men finally destroyed the village. Seven hundred and fifty of the 900 Red Sticks in the village were killed in the battle. Several days later, Red Eagle, who had been absent during the battle, surrendered. Jackson allowed Red Eagle to go free, while his troops abused their Cherokee allies by stealing their horses, taking their food, and harassing their families. In the resulting

TREATY OF HORSESHOE BEND (1814), 23,000,000 acres (some of which belonged to the White Sticks), was stripped from the Creek. Most of the tribe was forced to move to Indian territory (present-day Oklahoma). Those Creek who rejected the terms fled to Florida, where they continued to resist white encroachments in the Seminole Wars (see First, Second, and Third SEMINOLE WARS).

Crook, George (1828–1890) *American general who played a prominent role in the Civil War and Plains Wars*

Born in Ohio, George Crook graduated from West Point in 1852. He served in Northern California and Washington until the start of the CIVIL WAR (1861–64). In September 1861 Crook was appointed colonel of an Ohio volunteer regiment. He was named a brigadier general in August 1862 and spent the duration of the war in the east. At the end of the war, during the 1866 reorganization of the army, Crook returned to his rank of lieutenant colonel in the 23rd Infantry.

Crook's first major assignment after the Civil War was commanding Fort Boise, Idaho, during the PAIUTE WAR (1866–68). By 1868, Crook's determination and actions had forced the PAIUTE to make peace. Crook, still a junior lieutenant colonel, then served two years as acting commander of the Department of the Columbia.

Crook's next major assignment was in Arizona, where the APACHE were conducting raids and fighting off and on with non-Indians. At dawn on April 30, 1871, a force of soldiers and Indians from other tribes attacked CAMP GRANT, a settlement of Apache who had taken no part in the raiding. After the massacre at Camp Grant (1871), the army department commander responsible was relieved of duty. President ULYSSES S. GRANT then gave the command to Crook, despite the seniority of 40 other colonels.

Crook decided that the Apache would have to be beaten militarily before peace could be arranged, but he had to suspended operations upon the arrival of a peace commissioner from Washington. The commissioner gave the Apache until February 15, 1872, to report to an assigned Indian agency; they failed to respond. A second peace commissioner, OLIVER O. HOWARD, came to the area that summer and he also failed to make peace with legendary Apache chief COCHISE.

With the failure of both these peace attempts and the continuation of Apache raids, Crook finally began military operations on November 15, 1872. His great success was credited to three factors: extensive use of Indian scouts as allies against the Apache; efficient use of mule supply trains to substantially increase his mobility; and high morale, confidence, energy, and determination among his troops. His army columns were unstoppable, and by the fall of 1873, Crook had won the Apache's surrender. His immediate and nearly unprecedented reward was to skip the grade of colonel in the regular army and be promoted directly to brigadier general.

When unrest again came to Arizona, Crook was one of the primary military commanders sent to help restore peace. In

1875, however, he was sent to the Dakotas, where the SIOUX WARS (1854–90) were intensifying.

In November 1875, the BUREAU OF INDIAN AFFAIRS informed the Northern CHEYENNE and the Lakota (see SIOUX) in the Powder River region that they had until January 1876 to move to the Great Sioux Reservation. When they failed to meet this virtually impossible deadline, the army was called in. Crook commanded one of three columns that General PHILIP HENRY SHERIDAN ordered into the area.

In June, the Northern Cheyenne and Lakota learned of Crook's approach, with 1,300 men, along ROSEBUD CREEK (1876). On June 17, perhaps a thousand attacked an advance column of soldiers, forcing it back onto Crook's main force. After a six-hour battle, the Indians, aware that other soldiers were approaching, abandoned the fight. Crook withdrew to his supply base after what most considered a clear Indian victory. Later in 1876, Crook played a role in the final campaigns against the Lakota.

By 1882, warfare again broke out in Arizona. The government, determining that a major source of trouble was the administration of Indian affairs, ordered Crook, his reputation somewhat tarnished by Rosebud Creek, to return to his former battle territory. Crook now undertook a series of campaigns against Apache leader GERONIMO, using the same methods that had worked effectively 12 years before. When negotiations with the Apache broke down, Sheridan, uneasy with Crook's growing reliance on Indian auxiliaries, accepted the latter's angry offer of resignation. Brigadier General NELSON A. MILES then oversaw Geronimo's surrender.

In 1888, Major General Crook took over the Department of the Missouri, a position he held until his death in 1890. Crook is generally recognized, along with Nelson A. Miles and perhaps RANALD S. MACKENZIE, as one of the nation's most effective military figures of the wars against the Indians.

Further Reading

Aleshire, Peter. *The Fox and the Whirlwind: General George Crook and Geronimo: A Paired Biography.* New York: John Wiley, 2000.

Bourke, John Gregory. *On the Border with Crook.* Lincoln: University of Nebraska Press, 1971.

Crook, George. *General George Crook: His Autobiography.* Norman: University of Oklahoma Press, 1986.

Hedren, Paul L. *With Crook in the Black Hills: Stanley J. Morrow's 1876 Photographic Legacy.* Boulder, Colo.: Pruett, 1985.

Utley, Robert M. *Frontier Regulars.* New York: Macmillan, 1973.

Vaughn, J. W. *With Crook at the Rosebud,* Lincoln: University of Nebraska Press, 1988.

Crooked Creek (1859) *military engagement between the Comanche and the U.S. Cavalry*

In 1859, inspired by the success of TEXAS RANGERS in fighting the COMANCHE, General David Twiggs, U.S. Army commander in Texas, ordered EARL VAN DORN to take a battalion of the 2nd Cavalry and establish a base inside Indian Territory (present-day Oklahoma) for a campaign against the Comanche. A scouting force, sent ahead to select a site for the base, chose a spot on Otter Creek, just west of the Wichita mountains. Van Dorn arrived soon after with four companies of cavalry and one of infantry and built a stockaded military post.

The WICHITA Indians, peacefully settled on Rush Creek near what is now RUSH SPRINGS, Oklahoma, had been urged by the federal government to persuade the Comanche to come to Fort Arbuckle for a peace council. While on their way to the council, the Comanche were invited to stop at the Wichita village for a feast, which they did, not expecting trouble. On October 1, 1858, Van Dorn ordered his Indian allies to stampede the Comanche ponies. One troop of cavalry attacked the lower end of the village, and Van Dorn led the other three troops against the upper end. Despite the surprise and the lack of their ponies, the Comanche put up a fierce but futile resistance in the brief battle. They were eventually forced to flee to nearby hills. More than 50 Comanche were killed, as were five soldiers.

Van Dorn later claimed that he knew nothing of federal peace efforts when he ordered his men to attack the Comanche camp. The Comanche considered the attack a betrayal on the part of the government, making them reluctant to make peace in the future.

Van Dorn led his men out on another campaign against the Comanche on April 30, 1859. Four days later, they captured a young Comanche boy. Under threat of death, he was forced to lead the troops to the Comanche camp at Crooked Creek. Before attacking, the soldiers captured the Comanche horses. Van Dorn began his assault with two patrols that approached the camp on foot to determine Indian strength. He withdrew the patrols when they ran into heavy resistance. Deprived of the ability to fight on horseback, the Comanche warriors were quickly routed by the better-armed cavalry. Out of a village of probably fewer than 100 inhabitants, Comanche losses included 41 men and 8 women killed and 36 captured. Cavalry losses were 1 killed and 13 wounded, including 2 Indian scouts.

Crow (Absaroka, or "bird people") *kin and allies of the Hidatsa, traditionally living along the upper Missouri River in Dakota Territory*

The Crow were primarily hunters and gatherers. They also cultivated two kinds of tobacco, one for smoking and the other for ceremony or "medicine." In the early 18th century, a dispute with the Hidatsa caused the closely related Crow to split and migrate to the Powder River basin in Montana. In 1837, when a smallpox epidemic (see SMALLPOX, EFFECTS OF) decimated the Upper Missouri tribes—MANDAN, ARIKARA, and Hidatsa—the Lakota (see SIOUX) drove the Crow farther southwest to the eastern slopes of the Rocky Mountains in Montana. Raids and counterraids were thereafter common between the Crow and the Lakota and their allies—the CHEYENNE, ARAPAHO, Blackfeet (see BLACKFOOT CONFEDERACY), and ASSINIBOINE.

Drawing of five Crow Indians with headdresses, shields, and weapons, by David Henderson, 1800s *(Courtesy New York Public Library)*

In signing the FORT LARAMIE TREATY (1851) with the U.S. government, the Crow and other treaty tribes agreed to vacate areas along western trails used by non-Indian travelers and to stay within defined territories. In consideration of Indian agreements and to pay for damages sustained by the tribes to their property, the government promised annuity goods at $50,000 per year for 10 years, to be divided among the seven tribes.

The Crow accepted a reservation in 1868 and were accommodating to soldiers sent to build forts and guard white migration over the BOZEMAN TRAIL. Their friendliness toward non-Indians resulted at least partially from their adversarial relationship with neighboring tribes. They very often acted as scouts during the army's conflicts with these tribes. Crow scouts ran reconnaissance on an encampment of Indians along the TONGUE RIVER near Fort Kearny prior to the FETTERMAN FIGHT (1866). They reported the presence of 4,000 Lakota, Cheyenne, and Arapaho warriors within a one-hour ride. WILLIAM FETTERMAN chose, however, to discount the report and attack with only 80 men; all were killed.

The scouting and fighting skills of 180 Crow and 86 SHOSHONE Indians enabled General GEORGE CROOK to avoid utter disaster at the battle of ROSEBUD CREEK (1876). The scouts riding out ahead of General Crook and his men reported the presence of 1,000 Lakota, Cheyenne, and Arapaho warriors. They also fought tenaciously in the forefront of the battle. Crook claimed victory, although it was a hollow one, since his troops barely hobbled back to the Goose Creek supply station after the Indians withdrew. Eight days later, on June 25, Colonel GEORGE ARMSTRONG CUSTER and his men were killed by these same warriors at the battle of the LITTLE BIGHORN (1876).

During the NEZ PERCE WAR (1877), as they were being relentlessly pursued by General OLIVER O. HOWARD, the NEZ PERCE sought help from the Crow, their allies and reservation neighbors. The Crow explained that they were at peace with the whites and that many Crow were working as army scouts. Soon after the Nez Perce left the Crow reservation, the army attempted to recruit additional Crow scouts but were met with reluctance and uncharacteristic incompetence on the parts of those few who did agree to scout. This concession by the Crow, however, was small consolation to the beleaguered Nez Perce, who surrendered about one month later on October 5.

Contemporary Crow live on or near their reservation in Montana, near the site of the battle of the Little Bighorn.

Curly (Ashishishe or Shishi'esh, "the Crow")
(ca. 1859–1923) *Crow scout for the U.S. Army during the Sioux Wars*
Born into the CROW tribe around 1859 on the Rosebud River in Montana, Curly became a U.S. Army scout as a young man. He was attached to General GEORGE ARMSTRONG CUSTER's 7th Cavalry when it confronted the combined Lakota (see SIOUX) and CHEYENNE forces in Montana at the battle of the LITTLE BIGHORN (1876). Curly and the other Indian scouts with Custer did not take part in the battle but were ordered to leave the column before the attack began. Curly watched the fighting from a distance and, seeing Custer's force over-

Curly, a Crow Indian, was a scout for the U.S. Army during the Sioux Wars. *(By permission of the Colorado Historical Society)*

whelmed, rode off. A day or so later, Curly appeared at the junction of the Little Bighorn and Bighorn Rivers, where an army supply boat was anchored. Through sign language, drawing, and an interpreter, Curly was the first to deliver the news of Custer's defeat. Because his account was quite accurate, experts believe that Curly saw the battle but did not take part in it, since at the time he did not claim to have been in the battle. But eventually a legend developed that he had actually fought and escaped the massacre. In later years, Curly stopped denying he had fought with Custer and gave out the story that he had gotten away by disguising himself as a Lakota warrior. He was often sought out by historians to give details of the battle. Curly died on May 22, 1923, and is buried in the national cemetery on the Little Bighorn battlefield.

Custer, George Armstrong (1839–1876) *American leader noted for his defeat at the battle of the Little Bighorn*
George Armstrong Custer was born in 1839 in Ohio but was raised in Michigan. He graduated from West Point in 1861, last in his class. After West Point, Custer was immediately ordered to active duty in the CIVIL WAR (1861–65). He joined the main Union army—the Army of the Potomac—in time to take part in the First Battle of Bull Run. In June 1863, a few days before the battle of Gettysburg, Custer was promoted from temporary captain to brigadier general of volunteers. Starting with the battle of Gettysburg, Custer distinguished himself as an effective but sometimes recklessly aggressive cavalry brigade and division commander. Much of this service was under General PHILIP HENRY SHERIDAN.

In 1866, Custer received the regular rank of lieutenant colonel of the new 7th Cavalry, and for the next 10 years he was the regimental field commander. Custer took part in WINFIELD SCOTT HANCOCK's 1867 expedition against the CHEYENNE and Lakota (see SIOUX). However, he was courtmartialed for being absent without leave to visit his wife during the campaign. Though the sentence of one year's suspension without pay was upheld by General ULYSSES S. GRANT, Custer was restored to duty by Sheridan a few months later.

In November 1868, Custer led the attack on the Cheyenne camp under chief BLACK KETTLE in the battle of WASHITA (1868) as part of Sheridan's winter campaign against the Indians. Black Kettle, whose followers had previously been attacked without warning at SAND CREEK (1864), was still a noted peace chief who favored accommodation with non-Indians. Some of his warriors, however, had apparently been raiding non-Indian settlements without permission, and there were large numbers of other Indians in the vicinity. As with Sand Creek, Black Kettle and his followers had camped to show their peaceful intentions. Custer's surprise dawn attack occurred on the same day that Black Kettle and his people had planned to send an emissary to General Sheridan to declare their wish to live peacefully.

In 1873, Custer took part in Colonel David Stanley's expedition to the Yellowstone region. In 1874, he led an exploratory mission into the Black Hills of South Dakota. The

Colonel George A. Custer and a force of cavalry were defeated and killed by the Sioux at Little Bighorn, 1876. *(Courtesy New York Public Library)*

mission found gold, touching off a massive gold rush into lands considered sacred by the Lakota and off limits to others. This provoked the great SIOUX WARS (1876).

Custer and the 7th Cavalry made up the leading elements of ALFRED H. TERRY's column, part of Sheridan's plan to squeeze the Lakota and Cheyenne from several directions. Custer did not wait for other units and upon learning from his scouts of a large Lakota and Cheyenne encampment along the

LITTLE BIGHORN River, determined to immediately attack, rather than risk having the Indians escape.

On June 25, 1876, Custer divided his regiment into three main groups—one led by Captain Frederick W. Benteen, whom he sent to the south to prevent the Indians from escaping in that direction; the second under Major Marcus A. Reno, whom he ordered to cross the river to attack the village; and the third under his own command. After fierce fighting in the valley, Reno's beleaguered troops retreated to the other side of the river, where they were later joined by Benteen's group. Custer and his soldiers, who had gone north and downstream, were about four miles (6.5 kilometers) away from Reno and Benteen's site when they were attacked by Indian warriors. In fighting that lasted only about an hour, Custer and all 210 of his men were killed. The Indians continued fighting Benteen and Reno's troops until June 26, after which time the warriors decamped. Terry and his soldiers arrived a day later.

A controversy soon erupted surrounding "Custer's Last Stand." Americans found it hard to believe that any group of Indians could have killed an officer as famous as Custer and wipe out so much of the 7th Cavalry. Custer's enemies, however, accused him of disobeying orders by attacking the Indian warriors without waiting for Terry's troops. Custer's supporters claimed that Reno had behaved like a coward by retreating and that he could have saved Custer. Others blamed Terry for not knowing the size of the American Indian force. Ultimately, no one really knows why Custer was defeated, and Little Bighorn remains the most famous defeat of American soldiers at the hands of Native Americans.

Further Reading

Sklenar, Larry. *To Hell with Honor: Custer and the Little Bighorn.* Lincoln: University of Nebraska Press, 2000.

Utley, Robert. *Cavalier in Buckskin.* Norman: University of Oklahoma Press, 1988.

Dade's Battle   See GREAT WAHOO SWAMP.

Dakota   See SIOUX.

Dakota Conflict   See MINNESOTA UPRISING.

dances, war   *ceremonies performed before or after going to war; ritual pleas for or celebrations of success in battle*
Many Native American groups held war dances to ensure victory in battle or on a raid and to give warriors the courage and the power to overcome their enemies. Dances performed before battle helped to bond the warriors together as a group and focus on the coming fighting. Victory dances after battle celebrated not only the defeat of an enemy but the warriors' power. In some cases they served to purify people and weapons used in war especially when they were involved in the taking of a human life. Dances were typically accompanied by singing and the playing of instruments such as drums and rattles.

War dances prior to a battle in some societies were performed by warriors of military societies, each of which had its own distinctive ritual that only its warriors could carry out. Dancers wore ceremonial regalia and special symbols of their society. If they associated themselves with an animal, they imitated the behavior of the animal to take on its attributes. For example, before going off to war, the Omaha Indians performed the wolf dance to give them the wolf's cunning; they imitated the animal's movements to symbolize such feats as

tracking a foe and attacking quickly. They also mimicked motions of combat.

Often entire villages would take part in victory dances. When a war party returned with many scalps—proof of victory in battle (see SCALPING)—many Plains tribes performed the Hair-Kill dance, led by the women, their faces painted red or black and wearing clothing decorated with beads and quill work. Both men and women danced in a circle, holding aloft poles with the scalps of the enemy. The SHOSHONE displayed enemy scalps on a pole around which important leaders danced, surrounded by the people and children of the village. In other victory dances, warriors acted out the recent battle, each demonstrating what he had done or planned to do to the enemy he was facing.

Dancing Rabbit Creek, Treaty of   (1830)   *treaty between the Choctaw and the U.S. government, the first negotiated under the Indian Removal Act*
The Treaty of Dancing Rabbit Creek provided for the exchange of CHOCTAW lands in Mississippi for lands in Indian Territory (now Oklahoma). The earlier DOAK'S STAND TREATY (1820) provided for voluntary emigration of the Choctaw to Indian Territory. The Choctaw, however, with no desire to move west, remained in Mississippi. In 1830, the state of Mississippi took jurisdiction over the Choctaw and dissolved their government. Fines and imprisonment were imposed to discourage its reestablishment. President ANDREW JACKSON, who declined to intercede, promoted Removal as the only solution. He sent Secretary of War John H. Eaton and General John Coffee to negotiate with the Choctaw at

The Discovery Dance performed by the Sauk and Fox tribes. In perfect time, the dancers mimicked the discovery of approaching game or enemies. *(Courtesy New York Public Library)*

the forks of Dancing Rabbit Creek on September 18. After 10 days of negotiating—at times accentuated by threats from Eaton and Coffee—the treaty was signed. The Choctaw were then marched, on the TRAIL OF TEARS, to their new home.

The treaty established boundaries of the new Choctaw Nation between the Arkansas, Canadian, and Red Rivers in Indian Territory. Among the other provisions of the treaty, the Choctaw were guaranteed self-government and perpetual freedom from the imposition of state or territorial law. Annuities were provided and the United States pledged to protect the Choctaw from enemies both foreign and domestic. None of these promises were kept, however.

The basic treaty held until preparation began for Oklahoma statehood. In 1898 the Curtis Act dissolved the Choctaw government and imposed state law. However, in the 1950s the Choctaw regained their right to self-government. Present-day Choctaw hold lands in and around Durant, Oklahoma, and a reservation at Pearl River, Mississippi.

Dawes Act   See GENERAL ALLOTMENT ACT.

Dead Buffalo Lake (1863) *largest of three battles fought over a two-day period between the U.S. Army and the Lakota and Dakota (see SIOUX) after the Minnesota Uprising*
In late 1862, several prominent Santee Dakota (see SIOUX) leaders were executed after the MINNESOTA UPRISING

(1862). In the aftermath, Major General John Pope (see BOZEMAN TRAIL) decided to pursue the remaining Santee participants in the uprising who had joined their Teton Lakota relatives in North Dakota. He sent two of his subordinates, Brigadier Generals ALFRED SULLY and HENRY SIBLEY, into the heart of the Lakota homeland in hopes of forcing an engagement.

The campaigns opened in the late spring of 1863. Sibley and his Minnesota Brigade, numbering some 3,000 troops, discovered the trail of Chief Standing Buffalo and on July 20 managed to overtake the Indians at Big Mound near present-day Bismarck, North Dakota. Standing Buffalo asked for a parlay, saying he did not want to fight the army. While these arrangements were being made, one of the Indian warriors shot and killed an army surgeon. Consequently, Sibley attacked the Lakota village, but warriors managed to delay the soldiers while most of the inhabitants fled.

Sibley continued the pursuit. On July 26, he encountered about 1,600 Sioux warriors massing around Dead Buffalo Lake. Sibley ordered his troops to open fire with four howitzers. The angry warriors attacked Sibley's line but met with a fierce counterattack each time. The battle then broke off and was resumed the following day at Stoney Lake.

Having lost much of their camp equipment and possessions, the Indians fled across the Missouri River to safety. Because his own horses were too exhausted to continue, Sibley broke off the campaign. During the engagements at Big Mound, Dead Buffalo Lake, and Stoney Lake, Sibley claimed to have killed 150 warriors, while losing only a dozen of his own men. The three battles effectively drove the Lakota and Dakota out of eastern North Dakota. However, as historian Alvin Josephy concluded, Sibley's campaigns, directed against many tribes not involved in the Minnesota Uprising, had "initiat[ed] a conflict with the Sioux tribes of the plains that would last for a quarter of a century."

Deerfield Raid (1704) *surprise attack on British settlers by a French troops and their Indian allies*

During QUEEN ANNE'S WAR (1702–13), the New England frontier was very vulnerable to attack from New France. Just after midnight on February 28, 1704, a combined force of about 48 French troops, led by Lieutenant Jean-Baptiste Hertel de Rouville, and their ABENAKI, HURON, and MOHAWK allies surprised the town of Deerfield, Massachusetts. According to contemporary statistics, 48 of the Deerfield residents were killed and 112 were captured. Some of the 112 died or were killed by their captors during their long trek north to Canada. French and Indian losses were placed at between 50 and 65 men.

Delaware See LENNI LENAPE.

Delaware Prophet (Neolin) (ca. 1760s) *Lenni Lenape prophet and medicine man*

Little is known of the LENNI LENAPE (Delaware) religious leader Neolin, who is often called the Delaware Prophet. The message he proclaimed, however, had a significant impact on his listeners and inspired the thinking of OTTAWA chief PONTIAC.

In 1762, the Delaware Prophet, who lived at Cayahaga, near Lake Erie, proclaimed his message throughout the countryside. He carried with him a map drawn on a piece of deerskin about 15 inches square. The map was a visual representation of the doctrine given to the Prophet by the Master of Life. It showed that the best route to the heavenly regions was traveled by those who rejected European ways and customs and returned to traditional Indian ways. The Prophet's teachings specifically renounced the white man's rum, trade goods, and firearms and called for a unification of Indian groups that previously had been at odds with one another. Furthermore, he announced that the Master of Life would return plentiful game to the area after the Indians waged war on the white people and drove them away.

The Prophet's teachings were welcomed by the Lenni Lenape, SHAWNEE, and Ottawa along with other tribes in the Ohio valley. Among those who adopted the new religion was Pontiac, who referred to Neolin's message as a justification for leading an attack on DETROIT (1763). To a great extent, PONTIAC'S REBELLION (1763–64) was a logical result of the Delaware Prophet's proclamations.

Delaware Wars (1641–1868) *long series of conflicts between the Lenni Lenape (Delaware) and their Indian and non-Indian neighbors*

The Delaware Wars typified the Native American experience with European Americans. The Delaware (now LENNI LENAPE) of the early 17th century lived along the east coast of North America at the headwaters of the Delaware River. Related tribes also lived as far east and north as modern New York. In the 1620s Dutch leader Peter Minuit bargained with one of the bands for the right to establish the colony of New Amsterdam (modern New York City). Relations between the Dutch and the Lenni Lenape deteriorated quickly, and the outbreak of KIEFT'S WAR (1641–45) marked a low point in the relationship between the two parties. Eleven local tribes laid siege to New Amsterdam for more than a year, from 1643 to 1644. In the aftermath of the PEACH WAR (1655–64), which began when a Dutch farmer shot and killed a Lenni Lenape woman who was picking green peaches from his orchard, many Lenni Lenape were adopted by other tribes or scattered to join their relatives to the south and west.

The tribespeople living around the headwaters of the Delaware River had been dominated by the larger SUSQUEHANNOCK tribe—enemies of the IROQUOIS CONFEDERACY—for much of the 17th century. They worked with the Susquehannock as allies of the French and of the Swedish colonists in New Sweden (now part of modern New Jersey) from 1638 to 1655. The Susquehannock were dispersed after BACON'S REBELLION (1676); the Lenni Lenape then enjoyed better relations with the English. In 1682, Quaker William Penn established the colony of Pennsylvania in Lenni Lenape territory. For 30 years he and his fellow Quakers lived peaceably with their Indian neighbors. After Penn's death in 1718, however, the situation changed dramatically. Penn's son Thomas produced a document claiming that Lenni Lenape chiefs had sold his father a parcel of land west of the Delaware River equal to a day and a half's walk. Thomas Penn's interpretation of this WALKING PURCHASE TREATY—which involved hiring three men to trot the distance—forced the Lenni Lenape out of their homeland.

By the 1740s, the Lenni Lenape had resettled in the Susquehanna River valley. Some of their relatives had preceded them, looking for better hunting and trapping grounds. However, this territory was controlled by the Iroquois. They agreed to allow the Lenni Lenape to settle there in return for political concessions. The Lenni Lenape, who had been a free people before the Walking Purchase Treaty, resented the restrictions placed on them by the Iroquois. During the 1750s, a group of Lenni Lenape led by Chief Shingas crossed the Allegheny Mountains and reestablished themselves along the banks of the Ohio and Allegheny Rivers. In memory of their ancestral homeland, they renamed themselves Delaware.

The Delaware were much more hostile to Europeans, and especially the British, than were the Lenni Lenape. Shingas and the Delaware allied themselves with the French during the FRENCH AND INDIAN WAR (1754–63). They raided colonial frontier settlements and participated in attacks on George Washington at Fort Necessity and at BRADDOCK'S DEFEAT

(1755). Following the war's end, the tribe expected to be left alone in their territory west of the Alleghenies. When colonial settlers established homesteads close to the Ohio, the Delaware—inspired by the DELAWARE PROPHET—joined with other tribes in PONTIAC'S REBELLION (1763–65). The Delaware suffered tremendous losses when blankets infected with smallpox were distributed to them during the siege of Fort Pitt (see SMALLPOX, EFFECTS OF).

After their defeat at BUSHY RUN (1763), the Delaware moved further west, to the Tuscarawas River valley in what is now east-central Ohio. Moravian missionaries, who had converted the Lenni Lenape who had remained in Pennsylvania, converted many Delaware and helped them establish their own towns along the river. At the outbreak of the AMERICAN REVOLUTION (1775–81), the Indians generally preferred not to choose sides between the British and the colonists. On September 17, 1778, however, the Delaware and the Colonial forces signed a treaty allowing American troops to pass through Delaware territory in return for protection against British retaliation. When the Americans broke the treaty, the Delaware began raiding frontier settlements in Kentucky and Ohio. American forces burned the Delaware town of Coshocton in retaliation.

For the next eight decades, the Lenni Lenape retreated before the oncoming tide of settlement. Treaties with the United States forced them out of their villages along the Tuscarawas River and into western Ohio. After the battle of FALLEN TIMBERS (1794), the Lenni Lenape moved again, to the White River Valley in southern Indiana. By this time a large part of the tribe advocated cooperation with the United States. They did not join TECUMSEH'S REBELLION (1807–11) or the WAR OF 1812 (1812–15). WILLIAM HENRY HARRISON, governor of Indiana Territory, praised the Lenni Lenape for their loyalty to the United States. Despite this, in 1820 the U.S. government asked the Lenni Lenape to leave Indiana for new lands west of the Mississippi River. In 1829, they resettled in Kansas. During the CIVIL WAR (1861–65), most of the Lenni Lenape of fighting age joined the Union Army—but a new treaty required them to sell their Kansas lands and relocate to Indian Territory (present-day Oklahoma). In 1868, they finally settled on land of their own, after one of the longest migrations of any Indian group.

Further Reading

The American Indians: Algonquians of the East Coast. New York: Time-Life Books, 1995.
Maynard, Jill, ed. *Through Indian Eyes: The Untold Story of Native American Peoples.* Pleasantville, N.Y.: Reader's Digest, 1995.
Steele, Ian K. *Warpaths: Invasions of North America.* New York: Oxford University Press, 1994.

Department of the Interior   *U.S. government department charged with the management of Indian lands and affairs*

The acquisition of vast new territories following the Mexican War (1846–48) led to the organization of the Department of the Interior in 1849. That same year, the BUREAU OF INDIAN AFFAIRS (BIA) was transferred to this new department from the WAR DEPARTMENT, in the belief that the government's relationship with Native Americans, especially those on reservations, should not be a military matter.

The Interior Department advocated a generally peaceful approach to the problem of relocating the Plains Indians to reservations. This policy, combined with wide-ranging corruption throughout the department, fueled army efforts to regain authority over Native American affairs. The controversy continued until the 1880s, when the growth of a professional civil service began to weed out corruption in the department. Another major development was the creation of an Indian police force in 1878, which meant that the Interior Department's Indian agents no longer had to rely on the army to patrol the reservations. The Department of the Interior continues to be responsible for Indian affairs today through the BIA.

Detroit   (1763)   *unsuccessful siege by Ottawa chief Pontiac during Pontiac's Rebellion*

In 1701, the French established Fort Detroit to assist their fur trade with western tribes and to secure contact with Indian missions on the upper Great Lakes. However, at the end of the FRENCH AND INDIAN WAR (1754–63), the French agreed to hand over the fort, along with their other fortifications in the Great Lakes area, to the British. The OTTAWA war chief PONTIAC had been a faithful ally of the French during the French and Indian War. When he received word of the terms of the TREATY OF PARIS (1763), he became worried that the British would try to punish all the Indians who had been French allies.

On April 2, 1763, Pontiac summoned a council of about 500 Ottawa, Ojibwa (see CHIPPEWA), Potawatomi, and Huron warriors in the Detroit area. They met in what is now Lincoln Park, Michigan, and agreed to launch a secret attack on the 120-man British garrison holding Fort Detroit. Pontiac planned to surprise the British by smuggling weapons into the fort under blankets during a peace parlay. On May 7, Pontiac approached the fort with 60 warriors as planned and requested admittance to the fort. When the Indians entered the fort, they found the commander, Major HENRY GLADWYN, and the entire garrison armed and ready for trouble. Local tradition relates that a young Ojibwa woman named Catharine, who was Gladwyn's mistress, had warned the commander of Pontiac's plan. Other sources suggest that another woman was responsible, or that local French Canadians or an Ottawa warrior had revealed the war plans. Faced with a heavily armed garrison, Pontiac and his warriors retreated. They returned on May 9, but Gladwyn refused to admit any Indians except the chiefs. Checked in their efforts to infiltrate the fort's defenses, Pontiac and his warriors launched a general assault, but were driven off taking only a few prisoners with them. Thus began PONTIAC'S REBELLION (1763–65).

The Indians tried to break British resistance by killing their PRISONERS—including Gladwyn's second in command—

and attacking his supply lines and reinforcements. On May 28, at Point Pelee, they attacked a supply column escorted by Lieutenant Abraham Cuyler and 96 Canadian Rangers. Half the British force and nine-tenths of the provisions were lost. In August Pontiac's warriors ambushed an assault force led by Captain James Dalyell, killing him and 19 others. For his part, Gladwyn was able to resist the Native American forces because the Indians' supply of gunpowder was limited. The Indians also were also unable to stop his two armed sloops or the 261 reinforcements who reached the fort in late July.

Pontiac ended the siege of Detroit in October 1763 for several reasons: His warriors were becoming bored with siege warfare, and many wanted to return home and hunt to secure stores of food for the winter. News had also reached the war leader that the French were maintaining the peace established with the British and would not come to his assistance. After lifting the siege, Pontiac sent messages of peace to Gladwyn and withdrew the Ottawa from the vicinity of Detroit.

Further Reading

Josephy, Alvin M., Jr. *500 Nations: An Illustrated History of North American Indians.* New York: Alfred A. Knopf, 1994.

Parkman, Francis. *The Conspiracy of Pontiac.* 2 volumes. Boston: Little, Brown, 1870.

Steele, Ian K. *Warpaths: Invasions of North America.* New York: Oxford University Press, 1994.

Dine   See NAVAJO.

diplomacy/peace treaties   *process of negotiation among tribes and between tribes and white governments, and the documents that result*

Although Indian and European negotiating practices shared many aspects, there were significant differences between the way these groups viewed treaties and agreements. The assumptions of each side colored the view of treaty making and the adherence to agreements.

First, European and colonial governments were used to an organized hierarchy of authority in which signers of treaties spoke for an entire nation. Treaties required ratification by government bodies, but the procedures required to put the treaty into effect were known in advance. European and colonial governments also considered a treaty to be a legal document that was subject to revision, just as any other law or legal document As a result, they frequently did not live up to their pledges, even though the governments pledged to enforce treaties.

Indian negotiators practiced a less hierarchical, more democratic approach to diplomacy than did non-Indian negotiators. The degree to which they spoke for their tribes or bands depended on their prestige within the tribe. However, Indians gave a treaty far more weight than non-Indians, at least until they saw how the Europeans and later, the Americans regarded treaties and agreements. It was not just an agreement between peoples, or governments, but a sacred agreement involving the spirit world. Breaking a treaty risked the displeasure of more than just a government or tribal leadership.

The U.S. government negotiated agreements with Indian tribes through treaties. The term *treaty* applies to formal written documents signed by both parties, rather than verbal agreements. When the U.S. government signed treaties they were binding on the nation. Not having the same concept of government, some Indian leaders who signed represented only a portion of their people and consequently other members of their nation did not feel obliged to keep such treaties. Nonetheless, Indians were viewed as sovereign nations and agreements with them were via treaties until 1871. By that time, some 370 had been made.

Doak's Stand Treaty   (1820)   *treaty between the U.S. government and the Choctaw Nation*

The Doak's Stand Treaty was negotiated in response to settlers' demands for CHOCTAW land following the WAR OF 1812 (1812–14) and Mississippi statehood in 1817. Under political pressure from settlers, Mississippi and federal officials attempted several times to win Choctaw land cessions prior to the treaty. Finally, ANDREW JACKSON, a strong advocate for trans-Mississippi removal of all Indians, volunteered to negotiate with the Choctaw.

The meeting with Jackson was held October 10–18, 1820, at a tavern known as Doak's Stand on the Natchez Road near Pearl River. After a week of negotiations, during which Jackson often showed his indignation by ranting and stomping, Choctaw chiefs Pushmataha and Moshulatubbee reluctantly signed Jackson's treaty.

The Doak's Stand treaty set new boundaries for Choctaw land east of the Mississippi and encouraged voluntary immigration to the new western territory. Each warrior who immigrated would receive provisions for his family for one year: a blanket, a kettle, a rifle, bullets, and corn. Part of the ceded land was to be sold in order to provide for Choctaw schools both in Mississippi and in the new territory. The treaty prohibited whiskey in the new territory except when used at "public stands" or approved by the agent or the three chiefs. A $200 annual appropriation was initiated for the establishment of a Choctaw police force called the Lighthorse.

Most of the Choctaw had no desire to immigrate to the west and remained in Mississippi. Settlers soon began to occupy the eastern portion of the new Choctaw territory in present-day Arkansas. Consequently, in 1824, a supplemental treaty was negotiated with Washington, whereby the Choctaw ceded their Arkansas land to the United States. Settlers also began encroaching on Choctaw lands in Mississippi, and disputes became common. The DANCING RABBIT CREEK TREATY (1830) ultimately settled the land disputes in Mississippi by forcing almost the entire Choctaw Nation to immigrate to Indian Territory in present-day Oklahoma.

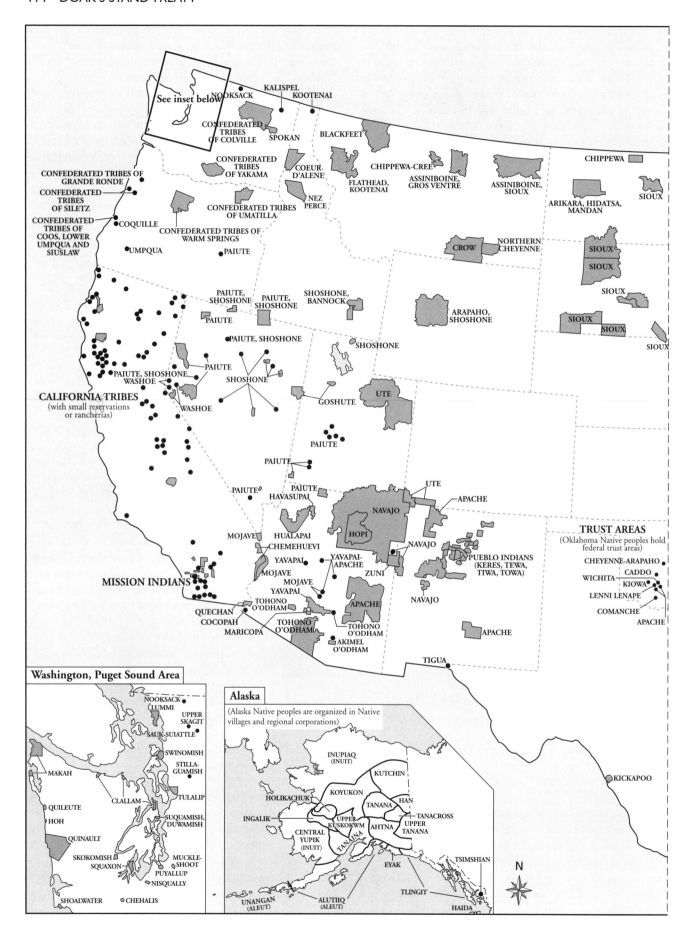

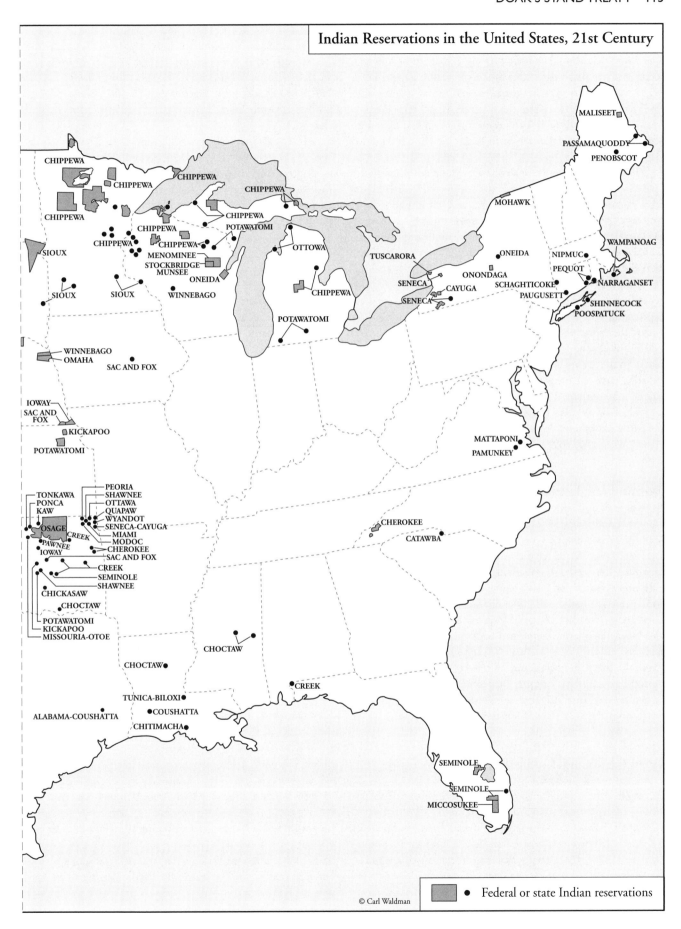

Indian Reservations in the United States, 21st Century

MALISEET

PASSAMAQUODDY
PENOBSCOT

CHIPPEWA

CHIPPEWA

CHIPPEWA

CHIPPEWA

MOHAWK

CHIPPEWA

CHIPPEWA

POTAWATOMI

CHIPPEWA

WAMPANOAG

OTTOWA

TUSCARORA

ONEIDA

NIPMUC

CHIPPEWA

PEQUOT

SIOUX

CHIPPEWA

MENOMINEE
STOCKBRIDGE
MUNSEE

ONEIDA

ONONDAGA

SCHAGHTICOKE

NARRAGANSET

SIOUX

SIOUX

WINNEBAGO

CHIPPEWA

SENECA

CAYUGA

PAUGUSETT

SENECA

SHINNECOCK
POOSPATUCK

POTAWATOMI

WINNEBAGO
OMAHA

SAC AND FOX

IOWAY
SAC AND
FOX

KICKAPOO

MATTAPONI
PAMUNKEY

POTAWATOMI

PEORIA
SHAWNEE
OTTAWA
QUAPAW
WYANDOT
SENECA-CAYUGA
MIAMI
MODOC
CHEROKEE
SAC AND FOX
CREEK
SEMINOLE
SHAWNEE

TONKAWA
PONCA
KAW

OSAGE

CREEK

PAWNEE
IOWAY

CHEROKEE

CATAWBA

CHICKASAW

CHOCTAW

POTAWATOMI
KICKAPOO
MISSOURIA-OTOE

CHOCTAW

CHOCTAW

CREEK

TUNICA-BILOXI

ALABAMA-COUSHATTA

COUSHATTA

CHITIMACHA

SEMINOLE

SEMINOLE
MICCOSUKEE

© Carl Waldman

● Federal or state Indian reservations

Dog Soldiers   *Plains Indian warrior society that rose to prominence in the mid-1800s*

The Dog Soldiers were one of a number of warrior or military societies common to the Plains Indians. Noted for their bravery, Dog Soldiers were especially prestigious among the CHEYENNE and KIOWA. With the acquisition of the horse from Spanish settlers and the Indians' resulting switch to a nomadic way of life, these societies served in much the same fashion as clans among other tribes.

The Dog Soldiers were a cohesive group who had their own chiefs and were not subject to the authority of tribal chiefs. The warrior societies went on raids and fought together. Among the Cheyenne, Dog Soldiers made up half of all warriors and controlled the entire tribe. Although other warrior societies accepted women as members, the Cheyenne Dog Soldiers did not.

The Dog Soldiers elected a chief and seven assistants according to their bravery and success in war. The chief was expected to rally the members in the face of defeat during battle and therefore could expect to die. After a member exhibited valorous deeds, he wore a buckskin coat decorated with fringe made from the enemies' hair. Brave deeds were ranked hierarchically, with the most important being a Dog Soldier who had led his comrades on to victory after apparent defeat.

The Dog Soldiers' power was essentially broken in 1869 at the battle of SUMMIT SPRINGS (1869), part of the SOUTHERN PLAINS WAR (1868–69).

Domínguez de Mendoza, Juan   (1631–post 1684)
Spanish military leader during the Pueblo Rebellion

Having been in New Mexico since age 12, Juan Domínguez de Mendoza accompanied several Spanish expeditions into Texas as a young man. With the outbreak of the PUEBLO REBELLION in 1680, Domínguez de Mendoza fell back from New Mexico with other Spanish officials after heavy fighting. He was then appointed lieutenant general in charge of the Spanish counteroffensive. Leading a mixed force of 250 Spanish soldiers and Indian auxiliaries, he pushed back into New Mexico and assaulted several Pueblo villages. His *entrada* (drive) failed to crush the revolt, however, and he was later criticized for not having conducted his campaign more ruthlessly. In 1683–84, he led an expedition into Texas, establishing a presidio and mission among the APACHE and Jumano at San Clemente.

Dove Creek   (1865)   *battle between a force of Texas Confederates and the Kickapoo Indians*

During the CIVIL WAR (1861–65), a dissatisfied group of about 700 Northern and Southern KICKAPOO, loosely allied with the Union, left Kansas to join a group of their relatives in Mexico. They were led by chiefs Nokowhat, Pecan, and Papequah. On New Year's Day, 1865, an approaching storm caused the Indians to stop and pitch camp at a sheltered spot on Dove Creek, a tributary of the South Concho River in Texas. A few days earlier, a Texas Confederate scouting party had run across their trail and alerted Texas forces. On January 8, Captains S. S. Totten and Henry Fosset arrived at the Kickapoo campsite with a combined force of 400 men. They planned to overwhelm the Indians by charging the camp from two sides. What followed, however, was the worst defeat ever inflicted on Texans by Indians.

Taking shelter in the ravines behind Dove Creek, the Kickapoo quickly recovered from the surprise attack. Equipped with long-range rifles, they took deadly aim. Close fighting continued for 30 minutes until the Confederate line broke and the Kickapoo launched a counterattack, turning the Confederate retreat into a rout. When the battle was over, 26 Texans lay dead and 60 were critically wounded. The Kickapoo, having lost only 15 men, safely hurried into Mexico.

Dragging Canoe   (Tsi'yugunsi'ny)   (1733–1792)
leader of the Chickamauga band of Cherokee

Dragging Canoe waged a 17-year war of resistance to white domination. In 1775, he opposed the sale of 27,000 square miles of CHEROKEE land in Tennessee and Kentucky to private land speculators, Richard Henderson, DANIEL BOONE, and others. During a council meeting to discuss the sale, Dragging Canoe stood up and, repudiated his father, CHICKAMAUGA peace chief Attakullakulla, for considering the sale of the land. He then vowed to make non-Indian settlement of the land "dark and bloody."

The outbreak of the AMERICAN REVOLUTION (1775–81) provided an opportunity for Dragging Canoe to carry out his threat. He led attacks on settlers in the ceded land along the Nolichucy, Holston, and Watauga Rivers. Some government officials welcomed the war; Thomas Jefferson declared, "I hope the Cherokees will now be driven beyond the Mississippi." In response to the attacks, frontier militias under Colonel Arthur Campbell and Colonel JOHN SEVIER brought devastation to upper Cherokee towns in the summer of 1776. Dragging Canoe then retreated to southwestern Cherokee territory, where he continued his guerrilla warfare until his death in 1792. In 1794, Chickamauga chiefs reluctantly signed a peace treaty with the United States.

Dreamer Religion   (Dreamer Cult)   *revivalist religion that became popular among the Indians of the Pacific Northwest in the second half of the 19th century*

Smohalla, or "The Preacher," was chief of a small band of Wanapam Indians at Priest Rapids on the Columbia River in eastern Washington. A gifted orator, proven warrior, and medicine man, Smohalla already had hostile feelings toward the incoming white settlers, the agricultural polices of U.S. government officials, and the actions of Christian missionaries. These hostile feelings intensified following a series of wars between settlers and Indians in the Pacific Northwest in 1855 and 1856.

Although Smohalla's influence was not substantial until after the CIVIL WAR (1861–65), he began his messianic career in 1850. Around that time he received spiritual visions directing him to protect his people from settlers coming into the area. Ten years later, Smohalla fought with a neighboring chief and was seriously wounded. Although left for dead, he crawled to the Columbia River and climbed into a boat. Sometime later he was rescued by a white settler and nursed back to health. Rather than return to the scene of the fight, Smohalla traveled south. He later returned to his people and told them that he had died and traveled to the spirit world, but had been directed to return and guide them to a better life.

As with the later GHOST DANCE, which originated among the Northern PAIUTE (Numu) in the 1870s, Smohalla prophesied a future time in which all Indians, both living and dead, would be restored to their rightful place and former power. Together they would make a tremendous force that would destroy their white oppressors and, when this was done, the Indian world would be restored to them. Although certain ritual details of his ideas were borrowed from the earlier Waashat religion and Catholicism, the content of Smohalla's prophecies was essentially a reworking of traditions.

Smohalla's teachings were incorporated into a new religion called the Dreamer Religion, thus called because believers spent long periods in meditation and many fell into trances in which new revelations were revealed to them. Smohalla urged his followers to abandon non-Indian ways and return to their old tribal customs, including respect for nature and Indian deities. As with many reservation-era prophets, Smohalla also emphasized abstention from alcohol. When the federal government began creating reservations in the Pacific Northwest, Smohalla added a militant aspect to his teachings, encouraging overt resistance to reservation life and assimilation policies.

From the 1870s until his death in 1895, Smohalla was the principal force opposing Christian missions, the federal government, and white settlers. He and his priests traveled from reservation to reservation throughout the Northwest, preaching resistance to white culture rather than acceptance of it. Regular jailings only increased Smohalla's determination to rescue Indians from subjugation by white culture. Many Indian leaders, such as old Joseph of the NEZ PERCE, were followers of the Dreamer Religion. Some of the Dreamer rituals continue today.

Drexel Mission (1890) *military engagement between the Lakota and the U.S. Army*

The engagement at Drexel Mission took place on December 30, 1890, the day after the massacre at WOUNDED KNEE. Lakota (see SIOUX) Indians fleeing Wounded Knee moved to a camp along White Clay Creek, roughly 15 miles north of the Pine Ridge Agency in South Dakota. Some warriors from the camp set fire to sheds near Drexel Mission church, four miles north of the agency. JAMES FORSYTH and the 7th Cavalry were sent to investigate, but Indians pinned them down in a valley, and they had to be rescued by the 9th Cavalry. The camp was broken up the next month and the Indians were forced back to the Pine Ridge Agency by General NELSON A. MILES.

Dry Lake (1873) *final battle in the Modoc War (1872–1873)*

By spring 1873, the U.S. Army were still at war with the MODOC, who continued to hold out in northern California under their leader CAPTAIN JACK (see LAVA BEDS, 1873). Following the rout of an army unit by the Modoc in April, the military became determined to capture the Modoc. In May 1873, a cavalry column under Captain H. C. Hasbrouck headed to the lava beds to dislodge the Modoc. Approaching from the east side of the lava beds, where Modoc had been last sighted, Hasbrouck's column included two companies of cavalry, some artillery, and a group of Indian scouts. The column stopped at a muddy body of water east of the lava beds called Dry Lake. The Modoc, who had seen the force approach, decided on a surprise attack to trap the column between them and the muddy lake. At dawn the Indians attacked and drove the soldiers to the shores of the lake, where they huddled in panic. Captain Hasbrouck, however, rallied his men, and they pushed forward toward the oncoming Modoc, firing as they advanced. The Modoc had not expected the troopers to rally and were also being fired upon by Indian scouts at their rear. Thus taken by surprise, they retreated from the battlefield. One Modoc was fatally wounded in the fight, and the cavalry lost three soldiers and two Indian scouts.

The soldiers captured 24 pack horses, which carried much of the Modoc's ammunition and other supplies, leaving the fleeing Indians with few resources. For 10 days Hasbrouck and some 300 men pursued Captain Jack. In the meantime, other bands of Modoc, overcome by hunger and fatigue turned themselves in. On June 1, 1873, Hasbrouck caught up with Captain Jack east of the lava beds, and the Modoc leader surrendered.

Dull Knife (Tash-me-la-pash-me) (ca. 1810–1883) *a principal chief of the Northern Cheyenne*

Dull Knife was a CHEYENNE war leader who fought alongside RED CLOUD and the Oglala Lakota (see SIOUX) in the FETTERMAN FIGHT (1866). He also fought in November 1876 against Colonel RANALD S. MACKENZIE's 4th Cavalry at the battle subsequently named after him, at Red Forks on the Powder River in Montana. He is best known, however, for his role in leading his people back from exile in Indian territory to their traditional Montana homeland.

Dull Knife had been a famous warrior in his day, but by the 1870s he was elderly and more interested in living in peace. The U.S. government, in reaction to Northern Cheyenne participation in the Fetterman Fight, insisted that the tribe settle on a reservation either in Montana, Dakota territory, or Indian territory (present-day Oklahoma). The government put more pressure on the tribe to make a decision by blocking much-needed supplies.

Finally, in 1874, the Northern Cheyenne agreed to join the Southern Cheyenne and the ARAPAHO in Indian territory.

The discovery of gold in Lakota territory (the Black Hills of South Dakota) created more tensions between the U.S. government and the Northern Cheyenne. In 1876, the U.S. Army fought several battles with the Sioux and their allies, including some Northern Cheyenne. The most famous of these was the battle of the LITTLE BIGHORN (1876) in Montana. Dull Knife did not participate in that engagement, but the 4th Cavalry under Mackenzie targeted his village for attack on November 25, 1876 (see DULL KNIFE, BATTLE OF). The following spring, in the aftermath of their defeat, Dull Knife and about 1,000 of his people began their trek to reservations in Indian Territory.

The Northern Cheyenne were quickly disillusioned with reservation life in Indian Territory. Overcrowding and unsanitary conditions bred disease, and gangs of white criminals preyed upon the Indians. The Northern Cheyenne were also unwilling to abandon their traditional way of life and learn the farming practices of their new neighbors. Early in September 1878, Dull Knife and a band of about 350 Cheyenne quietly left Indian Territory, intending to head back to their homeland in the north.

The army chased Dull Knife and his party across Oklahoma and Kansas through the month of September, skirmishing with them on at least four occasions. Although the Indians killed about 40 settlers in northeast Kansas, most of the casualties from the engagements were Northern Cheyenne. Each time, however, Dull Knife and his followers escaped the government troops and continued their journey north. In October, the army finally caught up with Dull Knife at Chadron Creek in Nebraska and captured his band. They were taken to nearby Fort Robinson.

On January 3, 1879, Captain Henry W. Wessells, Jr., commander of Fort Robinson, decided that the Northern Cheyenne would have to return to Indian Territory. Dull Knife and his followers refused and consequently were imprisoned in an army barracks at Fort Robinson. On January 9, the Cheyenne made a break for freedom, firing their guns to discourage pursuit. Soldiers responded with more gunfire. Some 30 Cheyenne were killed or wounded, including Dull Knife's daughter. The Indians escaped in the darkness, but another skirmish 12 days later resulted in 23 more casualties. Dull Knife and his family escaped capture and were hidden by friendly Lakota near Wounded Knee Creek. The Northern Cheyenne were scattered, and it was only in 1884 that a presidential executive order established a home for them in their native Montana.

Dull Knife, battle of (battle of the Powder River's Red Fork) (1876) *engagement between U.S. troops and Northern Cheyenne villagers during the Sioux Wars*

Following the defeat of Colonel GEORGE ARMSTRONG CUSTER at the battle of the LITTLE BIGHORN (1876), waves of army reinforcements streamed onto the northern plains. Despite the initial success of a large coalition of CHEYENNE and Lakota (see SIOUX), by fall 1876, unending pressures from pursuing troops and internal divisions among the various tribes had led many groups to follow their separate leaders. As General NELSON A. MILES relentlessly chased Hunkpapa Lakota leader SITTING BULL and his followers, General GEORGE CROOK organized a huge column from Fort Fetterman, Wyoming. Boasting some 2,200 men (11 troops of cavalry, 15 companies of infantry, and some 400 Indian auxiliaries), Crook's massive column, often known as the Powder River Expedition, moved out on November 14 in pursuit of Oglala-Brulé leader CRAZY HORSE. On November 23, after learning from his scouts that a large Cheyenne village headed by chiefs BULL KNIFE and Little Wolf lay to the west in the Big Horn Mountains, Crook dispatched 800 cavalry and the Indian auxiliaries under Colonel RANALD S. MACKENZIE to strike the camp quickly.

Meanwhile, the Northern Cheyenne had discovered the presence of the large army column. Mackenzie's command still had to go thorough several narrow passages en route to the Cheyenne village along the Red Fork of the Powder River. This was to the Indians' advantage. In addition, one medicine man experienced a vision in which he saw soldiers attacking from the east. But factional rivalries between followers of the KIT FOX SOCIETY and many of the other Cheyenne led the villagers to disregard suggestions that they either rejoin the Lakota or prepare an ambush of Mackenzie's approaching expedition. Instead, most of the Cheyenne celebrated a recent victory over some rival SHOSHONE Indians.

In the early hours of November 25, Mackenzie's 1,100 horsemen burst into the village. There were about 200 lodges clustered in a canyon of the Red Fork on the Powder River. Cheyenne warriors, caught by surprise, managed to get out of their lodges with only their rifles and ammunition belts. About 400 warriors hurried their families toward the safety of a nearby bluff and then took up firing positions. From their vantage point, the warriors rained effective and deadly fire on Mackenzie's troops.

The fighting became fierce and many shots were fired at point-blank range. There were also instances of hand-to-hand fighting, with Mackenzie's Indian scouts bearing the brunt of the battle. By mid-afternoon the sounds of weapon firing became sporadic at best, and Mackenzie's men set about the task of burning the village and its contents. The soldiers herded together some 700 Indian ponies and discovered military equipment with 7th Cavalry markings including a guidon (a small banner with the unit identification on it) that had been taken in the defeat of Custer at the battle of the Little Bighorn (1876).

Deprived of their possessions, the Cheyenne were forced to embark on a grueling three-week trek through the harsh winter to find comfort with Crazy Horse's people. Mackenzie later chastised himself for not having launched a full-scale pursuit of his retreating foes, but his attack on Dull Knife's village had dealt them a devastating blow. Mackenzie lost six killed and 26 wounded, the Cheyenne admitted 40 killed in the battle itself, plus countless others in their ensuing retreat.

Dummer's War (Râle's War, Lovewell's War, Grey Lock's War) (1722–1727) *New England colonial war between the Abenaki and the colonial forces of Massachusetts*

Dummer's War was unusual among late 17th- and early 18th-century colonial conflicts because it was not part of a larger European war. It did, however, have a European connection. British settlers from Massachusetts were colonizing an area around the mouth of the Kennebec River (present-day Maine) that was part of the Eastern Abenaki's territory. The French, believing that the New Englanders were threatening Quebec, incited the Abenaki to attack the British settlers. In 1722, Indians in canoes traveled down the Kennebec, burned the town of Brunswick, and took prisoners from the British population.

The government of Massachusetts responded in kind. One of the most eager proponents of war was the acting governor of the Massachusetts Bay colony, William Dummer, who believed that the French were responsible for Abenaki hostility. Dummer suspected that the Indians had been incited by a Jesuit missionary named SÉBASTIEN RÂLE, who had established his mission at NORRIDGEWOCK (1724) near the headwaters of the Kennebec River. In August 1724, a British military expedition surprised the settlement, burned it down, and killed Râle and many of the Indian inhabitants.

Dummer's War ended in 1727, for both military and economic reasons. The Abenaki tribes had received inadequate military support; no French troops accompanied the Indians on their raids. The Abenaki also discovered that French prices for trade goods were not competitive with British prices, in addition to which British goods were made better and were more plentiful. Furthermore, the British were supplying the IRO-QUOIS CONFEDERACY, the traditional enemies of the Abenaki, with these goods, and the Iroquois were expanding their power at Abenaki expense. Consequently, in an effort to preserve a neutral position between the British and the French, the Abenaki signed a series of treaties that ended the war.

Dutch-Indian hostilities (1632–1664) *bloody series of conflicts between Dutch trading colonies and local Native Americans*

The Dutch were unusual among European colonists in the New World because their primary interest was trade, rather than conquest, land, fishing rights, or religious conversion. The Indian territories of what is now New York and New England were rich in furs as early as the 17th century, and the Dutch wanted to exploit this resource. As early as 1614, a group of Dutch entrepreneurs built a fort and trading post, Fort Nassau, at the site of what is now Albany, New York. These businessmen traded primarily with the Mahican, an ALGONQUIAN tribe whose closest relatives lived in northern New England and Canada and whose trading partners were mostly French Canadians. The Dutch strengthened their presence in the area when they established Fort Orange, across the Hudson River from Fort Nassau, in 1624.

The enemies of the Mahican were the MOHAWK, members of the IROQUOIS CONFEDERACY who obtained the furs they traded by raiding other tribes. Between 1624 and 1628, the Mohawk and Mahican fought over access to Dutch goods in what became known as the Mohawk-Mahican War. The Mohawk won, driving the Mahican out of New Amsterdam (present-day New York) and into New England and Canada. They then set themselves up as the primary trading partners of the Dutch, controlling access to Fort Orange for Native Americans and Europeans alike. The Dutch tried to maintain neutrality when dealing with the tribes in the region. Indeed, the traders did not even retaliate against the LENNI LENAPE (Delaware) when they attacked the settlement at Swaanendael (1632), choosing to negotiate rather than launch a counterattack. In 1639, however, Dutch businessmen were faced with the loss of their original trade monopoly. The new French settlements of Montreal and Fort Richelieu in 1642 provided unwelcome competition.

By this time, some Dutch settlers had arrived in New Amsterdam, intending to create European-style farms. These settlers came into conflict with local Indians, who did not understand European concepts of land management and who resented the Dutch presence in their homelands. In 1641, the Raritan Indians of Staten Island retaliated when Dutch cows destroyed their cornfields. During what became known as KIEFT'S WAR (1641–45), the governor-general of the colony, Willem Kieft, imposed taxes on the tribes of Manhattan and Long Island and used the newly armed Mohawk to enforce his will. Eleven local tribes rose against the Dutch and put New Amsterdam under siege for more than a year. The siege was not lifted until British soldier JOHN UNDERHILL, a veteran of the PEQUOT WAR (1637), launched a campaign against the Indians that eventually forced them to make peace.

The coming of farmers to New Amsterdam changed the nature of the Dutch settlements. The Dutch now found themselves in the same sort of conflicts that plagued the British in Virginia and New England. Hostilities broke out again in 1655, when a Dutch farmer shot a Lenni Lenape woman who was gathering peaches from his orchard. The revolt that followed—known as the PEACH WAR (1655–64)—lasted intermittently until Governor Peter Stuyvesant finally seized Lenni Lenape hostages and enlisted the help of the Mohawk to bring this war to an end.

See also DELAWARE WARS.

Easton Treaty (1758) *treaty between colonists in Pennsylvania and the Lenni Lenape Indians*

BRADDOCK'S DEFEAT (1755) had unleashed a period of Indian violence against non-Indians on the Pennsylvania frontier, marking the low point in English fortunes during the FRENCH AND INDIAN WAR. It thus became necessary to regain the longstanding friendship of the LENNI LENAPE (Delaware), particularly those in the Ohio River area, who were still outraged over what they considered English deception in the negotiation of the WALKING PURCHASE TREATY (1737).

A series of four conferences took place between 1756 and 1758 to discuss peace and other issues. The colonists were led by Conrad Weiser, an interpreter and negotiator who was greatly respected among the Indians. Also in attendance were Benjamin Franklin, William Denny (the governor of Pennsylvania), and a number of Quakers, a sect that had always remained on friendly terms with Native Americans.

Prominent among the Native Americans at the conferences was the Lenni Lenape chief Teedyuscung, a convert to Christianity who had learned several negotiating tactics from his experience with the colonists. Though invited to Philadelphia for the peace talks, Teedyuscung preferred to have the colonial delegates meet with him on his home ground at the town of Easton on the Delaware River. At the July 1757 meeting, Teedyuscung, noting that Governor Denny had a private secretary to take the minutes, delayed the proceedings until he'd been assigned his own clerk.

The first three meetings accomplished relatively little, in part because the Pennsylvanians questioned the motives of the Indians, whom they suspected were in attendance only for the gifts customarily exchanged at such gatherings and also to drink the colonists' alcohol. A larger problem, however, was Teedyuscung, who called himself "King," but was referred to sarcastically as "Honest John" by the colonists. Teedyuscung acknowledged that he represented only the friendly Lenni Lenape of the Susquehanna, not those on the Ohio. He also hinted that he had authority to speak for the powerful IROQUOIS CONFEDERACY, a claim that greatly insulted the tribes of the much more powerful Six Nations.

A frustrated WILLIAM JOHNSON, superintendent of Indian affairs for North America, was able to use his influence to gather almost 400 Native Americans—including delegates from the Iroquois Confederacy, the SHAWNEE, and the Lenni Lenape—in Easton in September 1758. The conference ran through the month of October, most of the time taken up with drinking and infighting among the Indians.

In the end, the Iroquois chiefs, whose democratic tradition had made them good negotiators, gained the ascendancy and steered the talks in more productive directions. Governor Denny agreed to establish the Allegheny Mountains as the decisive boundary for white settlement. Settlers would be prohibited from crossing the mountains, and the Lenni Lenape could enjoy their traditional hunting grounds in peace.

Despite the agreement, westward expansion continued, particularly after the fall of Fort Duquesne in 1758. As a result, two additional conferences at Easton were needed to reaffirm the original agreement.

The Easton Treaty was significant because it brought to an end the Ohio tribes' alliance with the French and, as such, proved to be a turning point in the French and Indian War.

Emuckfaw   See CREEK WAR.

Endecott, John (1588–1665) *Massachusetts colonial official whose actions helped precipitate the Pequot War*
Born in Devonshire, England, John Endecott was one of six Puritan leaders who established a colony in the New World. Endecott helped found the settlement of Salem in 1628 and later became the first governor of the Massachusetts Bay Colony. A very devout man, he relentlessly persecuted dissenters from the Puritan faith, especially Quaker's. He brought this same zealousness to his relations with the Native Americans, who were dealt with harshly if they could not be converted to Christianity.

In 1636, to avenge the murder of an English trader, Endecott and some 90 volunteers attacked PEQUOT settlements on BLOCK ISLAND, part of present-day Rhode Island. Most of the Indians fled, but Endecott killed 14. Then, in frustration, he "destroyed some of their dogs instead of men" and burned the deserted wigwams. He proceeded to the Connecticut mainland, where the Pequots continued to refuse to engage in open battle. Endecott therefore burned several more villages before heading home. His raid on the Indian settlements led to the PEQUOT WAR between the colonists and Pequot in the spring of 1637. After the war, Endecott remained a public servant for the Bay Colony; he also became one of the first overseers of Harvard University.

Enotachopco Creek   See CREEK WAR.

Evans, John (1814–1897) *governor of Colorado Territory whose actions led to the massacre at Sand Creek*
In 1861, federal agents at Fort Lyon, Colorado, persuaded CHEYENNE peace chiefs BLACK KETTLE, White Antelope, and others, as well as Black Raven and other ARAPAHO leaders to sign a treaty accepting a significantly reduced reservation in southeast Colorado. The territory's appointed governor, John Evans, arrived shortly afterward. Evans tried unsuccessfully to get the other chiefs of the neighboring tribes to agree to the new terms for the reservation. Meanwhile, those who originally agreed changed their minds and refused to move.

Rumors of a possible Confederate invasion and the beginning of the MINNESOTA UPRISING (1862) inflamed the settlers on the Plains. Governor Evans, however, continued to try to convince more Indians to accept the Fort Lyon treaty. He first reported to authorities that the Plains Indians were quiet. Then, in November 1863, he suddenly began to send frantic reports of a conspiracy among the Plains tribes to begin total war. His claims have never been corroborated. Some historians believe that rumors rampant at the time had panicked Evans. Others, however, believe that Evans deliberately schemed to drive out the Indians through military force after he failed to negotiate their voluntary removal. Either Evans's panic or his deception led Colonel JOHN M. CHIVINGTON to launch a vicious attack on the peaceful Cheyenne and Arapaho in 1864 that is now known as the SAND CREEK massacre.

Fallen Timbers (1794) *crucial victory in the U.S. occupation of the Ohio Territory*
Following the AMERICAN REVOLUTION (1775–81), the United States became embroiled in armed conflict with several Indian tribes. Indian forces led by chiefs LITTLE TURTLE of the MIAMI tribe, and BLUE JACKET, a SHAWNEE, successfully raided non-Indian settlements and eluded capture. In response, President George Washington assigned General ANTHONY WAYNE to put a stop to the Indian raids. Wayne would lead the "Legion of the United States," a force of 5,120 men.

General Wayne wasted no time in moving against the Indians. As he proceeded into Indian territory, he built forts along the way. The forts and the sheer size of Wayne's column convinced Little Turtle that his people could not win and therefore must sue for peace. Blue Jacket, however, refused to discuss peace and thus assumed an even greater leadership role. He hoped to intercept Wayne's army opposite the rapids of the Maumee River. The area known as Fallen Timbers, was laced with deep ravines, and tree trunks littered the ground as a result of an earlier tornado. Blue Jacket chose this location because the British Fort Miami, which he assumed was empty, was nearby, and he could seek refuge there should the battle go badly for his people. What he did not know was the British had closed the fort's gates to avoid an open conflict with the United States.

Wayne was informed by his scouts of the Indians' position, but he stopped his advance to build Forts Greenville and Recovery. On August 20, 1794, he set out from Fort Recovery to engage Blue Jacket and his warriors. Whether planned or accidental, halting to build a fort worked greatly in Wayne's favor, due to the Indians' custom of fasting before a battle. Blue Jacket's warriors had expected to see action sooner and had not eaten for several days. Thus, on the day of the battle many had set out in search of food. This left Blue Jacket's position undermanned and vulnerable to an attack.

Also on August 20, Blue Jacket attempted to lure Wayne into a trap. He planned to entrap Wayne in a vast half-moon-shaped line. However, one of his Indian leaders reacted prematurely, charging his warriors into an advance guard of 150 mounted militia troops. The militia fled in panic, causing the front line of infantry to do likewise. When Wayne saw this, he rallied his troops and turned them to attack the Indians. In the face of a bayonet charge, Blue Jacket's warriors fled in retreat to Fort Miami, only to be refused assistance. Wayne remained in pursuit for a few days, then withdrew, destroying Indian towns along the way. He stopped at Kekionga, the main village of the Miami tribe, and there constructed Fort Wayne. Blue Jacket later surrendered in January 1795 at Fort Greenville (see TREATY OF GREENVILLE).

Fetterman, William J. (ca. 1833–1866) *U.S. Army officer responsible for the Fetterman Fight*
William Judd Fetterman was born to a career army officer and the daughter of a Connecticut family who lived near Fort Trumbull, where his father was stationed. Little else is known about Fetterman's life before he joined the Union army in 1861. During the CIVIL WAR (1861–65) he was promoted to the rank of brevet major for his bravery and gallantry in the battles of Murfreesboro and Jonesboro. After the war Fetterman entered the regular army with the rank of captain. In September 1866,

he was assigned to the 27th Infantry, stationed at Fort Phil Kearny, Wyoming. He arrived there in November and reported to his commanding officer, Colonel HENRY B. CARRINGTON.

The 27th Infantry was part of an expeditionary force charged with securing safe passage on the BOZEMAN TRAIL. The trail cut through Lakota (see SIOUX) territory, thus endangering miners on their way to the gold fields of Montana. The Lakota, including representatives from the Oglala, Brulé, and Miniconjou bands, and their CHEYENNE and ARAPAHO allies objected to the presence of the miners on their hunting grounds. Led by Oglala chief RED CLOUD, the warriors scouted the territory around Fort Phil Kearny, waiting for an opportunity to drive the government troops and miners off tribal lands.

According to contemporary reports, Fetterman was a congenial person, popular with his subordinates. However, he had little respect for Indian warfare or for Carrington's conservative approach. On December 6, 1866, he helped drive off an Oglala assault on the fort's supply train, which was bringing wood for fuel. This success reinforced his belief that Carrington's approach was wrong and that the Indians could be driven off by a reasonable show of force. At one point, Fetterman declared that, given 80 men, he could ride straight through the Lakota nation.

On December 21, 1866, when Indian warriors were again sighted in pursuit of the fort's supply train, Fetterman demanded that Carrington send him out to bring the supplies in safely. Carrington agreed. He stipulated, however, that Fetterman was not to go beyond the crest of Lodge Trail Ridge, which was out of sight of the fort. Fetterman disobeyed orders and chased a small party of warriors over the crest. In doing so he rode into an ambush of about 2,000 warriors led by Red Cloud and his Oglala associate chief CRAZY HORSE. Fetterman and all his soldiers died in the fighting.

For the U.S. Army, the FETTERMAN FIGHT was one of the most bitter humiliations of the Indian wars, ranking with the earlier HARMAR'S DEFEAT (1790) and ST. CLAIR'S DEFEAT (1791) and with and the defeat of GEORGE ARMSTRONG CUSTER at LITTLE BIGHORN (1876).

Fetterman Fight (Fetterman Defeat, Fetterman Massacre, Fort Phil Kearny Massacre) (1866) *battle resulting in one of the U.S. Army's greatest losses to Native Americans in the 19th century*

The Fetterman Fight was a major battle in what became known as the War for the Bozeman Trail (see BOZEMAN TRAIL). In 1865, U.S. Army troops led by General John Pope attempted to open a new route to western Montana. John Bozeman, who pioneered the trail, had made a much shorter trip to the region, but in the process he cut across the Powder

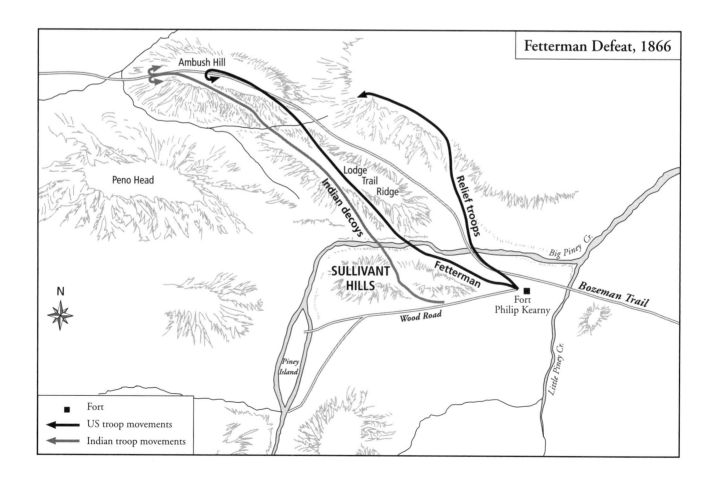

River, which was prime hunting territory for the Lakota (see SIOUX) and their ARAPAHO and CHEYENNE neighbors. Pope's expedition failed to secure the new trail against Indian attacks. The following year the federal government sent a battalion of 700 soldiers under Colonel HENRY B. CARRINGTON to the area with instructions to build a series of forts to garrison the trail.

Carrington arrived at Fort Laramie, Wyoming, at the worst possible time. He encountered a band of Oglala Lakota, Cheyenne, and Arapaho, who were there in a meeting with government negotiators. When Carrington revealed that he was under orders to build forts along the Bozeman Trail, Oglala war chief RED CLOUD protested and pulled many Oglala out of the meeting. In summer 1866, Carrington and his troops built three forts along the trail; he established his headquarters at Fort Phil Kearny near the Wyoming-Montana border. The Oglala, led by Red Cloud and CRAZY HORSE, harassed the forts throughout the rest of the summer and fall of 1866, attacking supply trains and travelers on the trail.

Carrington's overly methodical approach, his lack of combat experience, and his unwillingness to risk an attack on the Oglala irritated many of his subordinates. One of the most outspoken of these was Captain WILLIAM J. FETTERMAN, a veteran of the CIVIL WAR (1861–65) who had been promoted for his role in the battles of Murfreesboro and Jonesboro. Encouraged by the failure of an Indian assault on a wagon train at LODGE TRAIL RIDGE (1866), on December 6 Fetterman declared that he could ride through the entire Sioux nation with only 80 troopers.

On December 21 Carrington learned of a new assault on supply wagons bringing fuel from nearby wooded hills. Fetterman demanded the right to lead a relief column of troops. Carrington agreed but, fearing a trap, ordered Fetterman not to pass beyond the crest of Lodge Trail Ridge, about three and a half miles from the fort. Fetterman chose 80 men and rode off to rescue the supply wagons.

Soon afterward, Carrington heard sounds of shooting and sent a reconnaissance force of 40 troopers to investigate. They discovered the bodies of Fetterman and all 80 of his men, stripped and mutilated, lying some distance away from the road. Fetterman had disobeyed his orders, left the road, and crossed the ridge. Red Cloud and Crazy Horse had massed between 1,500 and 2,000 warriors and had lured Fetterman into a massive ambush.

In the inquiry that followed the Fetterman Fight, the army decreed that Carrington was partly responsible for the deaths of his men because of his unwillingness to deal decisively with the Indians. A civilian trial later acquitted him. Fetterman was also considered partly responsible because he had disobeyed orders.

The Fetterman Fight helped prolong the War for the Bozeman Trail because the army, wishing to recover its reputation, refused to make peace with the Indians. The Oglala and their allies were never able to repeat their success. Peace negotiators from Washington finally brought the War for the Bozeman

Monument on Massacre Hill commemorating the Fetterman Fight, 1866 (Courtesy of the National Museum of the American Indian, Smithsonian Institution #22987)

Trail to an end through the FORT LARAMIE TREATY (1868), in which the Oglala were guaranteed the right to their lands and were promised that the forts in the Powder River territory would be decommissioned.

Further Reading

Brown, Dee Alexander. *The Fetterman Massacre: Formerly Fort Phil Kearny, an American Saga.* Lincoln: University of Nebraska Press, 1984.

Goble, Paul. *Brave Eagle's Account of the Fetterman Fight, 21 December 1866.* Lincoln: University of Nebraska Press, 1992.

firearms *weapons, particularly guns, that Native Americans acquired from Europeans*

Indians began acquiring firearms from European traders in the 17th century. These early muzzle-loading flintlocks were not much good for hunting because they were not very accurate, took too long to reload, had a short range, and often were useless in wet weather. They did, however, provide an advantage in warfare. The noise, smoke, and fire from these weapons could terrify enemies and send them fleeing. Tribes such as the CREE and the CHIPPEWA, early traders with non-Indians who lived on the western edge of the Eastern woodlands, used guns in intertribal warfare, pushing the SIOUX (Dakota, Lakota, Nakota) onto the Plains.

Muskets were replaced in the 1800s by the so-called trade guns, made especially for Indians, which were more accurate and had a longer range than normal smooth-bore weapons. These guns quickly found their way west; explorers Meriwether Lewis and William Clark reported that Indians near the Columbia River were in possession of trade guns by the 1830s. Making the most of these weapons, the mounted warriors of the Plains tribes could ride at full tilt, load and reload with both hands, and shoot under or over the necks of their horses at close range.

It was not until the mid-19th century that Plains Indians began to acquire rifles and carbines, either captured from wagon trains heading west or in trade. Although Indians desired guns, they did not have the materials to repair them, and ammunition was often in short supply. The lance and bow and arrow thus remained the primary weapons in warfare until the Winchester rifle appeared in 1873 and began to replace traditional weapons. The Winchester was a lightweight, repeating rifle and was easy to repair. Highly valued among many tribes, and clearly an advantage in battle, such firearms nonetheless further increased dependency of many tribes on non-Indian suppliers.

First Cherokee Mounted Rifles   *Civil War regiment made up mostly of Keetoowah, or Cherokee, enlisted as Cherokee Home Guards by Chief John Ross*

On October 7, 1861, when JOHN ROSS, chief of the CHEROKEE, and Albert Pike, the Confederate Commissioner of Indian Tribes, signed a treaty of alliance, the 1,200 man Cherokee Home Guard became the First Cherokee Mounted Rifles. The Cherokee thus entered the CIVIL WAR (1861–65) on the side of the Confederacy. According to the agreement, the regiment was to be used only within the boundaries of the Cherokee Nation. Their commander was Colonel John Drew, who was married to Chief Ross's niece.

The regiment's first assignment was to prevent black slaves, pro-Union CREEK, and SEMINOLE, led by Opothleyaholo, from reaching Kansas. The full-blood Keetoowah band of Cherokee (see KEETOOWAH SOCIETY) were committed to protecting the Cherokee Nation, but they opposed slavery and strongly objected to fighting for the Confederacy. When Drew and Colonel Douglas Cooper caught up with Opothleyaholo at Bird Creek, 420 of 480 members of the Cherokee Mounted Rifles deserted Drew to join the ranks of the enemy. Many continued into Kansas with Opothleyaholo and joined Union forces. STAND WATIE and the FIRST CHEROKEE REGIMENT stepped up to fulfill the duties of the deserters. Some deserters later returned to the Cherokee Nation and rejoined the First Cherokee Mounted Rifles under terms of amnesty granted by Chief Ross.

First Cherokee Regiment   *Confederate Cherokee regiment, led by Brigadier General Stand Watie, that consisted of mostly Cherokee mixed-blood slaveowners*

In spring 1861, with a promise of arms from the Confederacy, STAND WATIE recruited 300 soldiers for a Confederate CHEROKEE regiment to support the South during the CIVIL WAR (1861–65). Most of these men were also members of a secret society known as the Knights of the Golden Circle, or Southern Rights Party, that had been organized to actively defend slavery.

The regiment conducted offensive raids into neutral Cherokee lands in Kansas and conducted many retaliatory raids against Cherokee who supported the Union. When the Cherokee Nation officially aligned with the South on October 7, 1861, Stand Watie's regiment became known as the Cherokee Mounted Volunteers. After Colonel John Drew's FIRST CHEROKEE MOUNTED RIFLES defected at the battle of Bird Creek, the First Brigade of the Army of the Trans-Mississippi Department was reorganized. Watie's regiment was then renamed as the First Cherokee Regiment. They subsequently fought at the battles of LOCUST GROVE (1862) and Bird Creek on Cherokee lands and PEA RIDGE (1862) in Arkansas. By 1864 General Watie commanded five Confederate Indian regiments, including the First Cherokee Regiment led by Lieutenant Colonel C. N. Vann.

First Choctaw and Chickasaw Mounted Rifles
Confederate Indian military unit during Civil War

In May 1861, the Confederate government in Richmond, Virginia, authorized the formation of three regiments from Indian Territory, (present-day Oklahoma); four were formed. One was a regiment composed of CHOCTAW and CHICKASAW, who were nearly unanimous in their support for the South. Colonel Douglas H. Cooper, former Indian agent for both tribes, commanded the regiment.

In November 1861, the regiment took part in the first CIVIL WAR battle in Indian Territory. Six thousand pro-Union Creek and Seminole trying to flee north to Union territory in Kansas were attacked at Round Mountain by a combined force of Indians and Texans under Cooper's command. After this and two other attacks, the disorganized pro-Union Indians fled into Kansas, where many died from exposure and starvation.

The regiment took part in the battle of PEA RIDGE (1862) in Arkansas. For the remainder of that year, the regiment participated in several skirmishes in Missouri, Kansas, and Indian Territory. It was also part of a combined force of Indians and Texans, again under Colonel Cooper, that was defeated by a smaller federal force at the battle of HONEY SPRINGS (1863), a result of inferior gun powder and ammunition. In 1864, the

The First Cherokee Regiment, led by Stand Watie (on the right, rear), was one of the Native American regiments to assist the Confederates against the Union army in the Civil War. *(Courtesy New York Public Library)*

regiment participated in General Sterling Price's unsuccessful raid into Missouri.

First Riel Rebellion   See RIEL'S REBELLIONS.

Fitzpatrick, Thomas (ca. 1799–1854) *U.S. Indian agent for the Upper Platte and Arkansas Agency*
Thomas Fitzpatrick, known as "Broken Hand" to the Indians because an exploding rifle had cost him three fingers, knew the

West intimately. For more than 20 years he worked as a trapper with the likes of Jedidiah Smith, CHRISTOPHER "KIT" CARSON, and Jim Bridger. He served as a guide to settlers' wagon trains and to General Stephen Kearney's army on its march to New Mexico. On November 30, 1846, he officially accepted an appointment as Indian agent.

Fitzpatrick favored a military approach to dealing with Indians, believing that Indian councils were useless until the Plains Indians had been defeated. Nevertheless, because the army could not accomplish this goal, Fitzpatrick finally resorted to peace councils. In 1851, he organized the council that led to the FORT LARAMIE TREATY (1851) and, two years later, to the FORT ATKINSON TREATY (1853). However, Fitzpatrick was opposed to the reservation system, which he branded as "the legalized murder of a whole nation." Fitzpatrick died of pneumonia in 1854 in Washington, D.C.

Flathead (Salish) *Indian people whose traditional lands lay within the Bitterroot Valley of western Montana*

The Flathead are a Salish-speaking tribe belonging to a group of Indian tribes known as the Plateau Indians. In 1805, explorers William Clark and Meriwether Lewis encountered the Flathead and called them "Ootlashoots," probably from the Indians' name for the Bitterroot River, meaning red willows. Traditional Flathead clothing was soft, tanned deerskin whitened with clay. The women wore ankle-length, loose-fitting robes tied at the waist. The men wore leggings with loose-fitting, knee-length shirts. After they began trading with Europeans, the Flathead adapted these styles to the woven trade cloth. They hunted buffalo on the Plains and gathered wild berries and roots from the hills and valleys of their homeland.

The Flathead sometimes allied with the NEZ PERCE, Umatilla, Cayuse, and Walla Walla in raids against their common enemies the BLACKFOOT CONFEDERACY, CROW, Lakota (see SIOUX), and ASSINIBOINE. The Flathead particularly hated the tribes of the Blackfoot Confederacy. After a smallpox epidemic in the 1780s, the Blackfoot recovered more quickly than neighboring tribes. Taking advantage of the weakened, vulnerable Flathead and Kootenai, the Blackfoot drove them to the western slopes of the Rocky Mountains.

The Flathead Indians were one of the few tribes that never warred against non-Indians. Instead, they cultivated a mutually beneficial relationship during the fur-trading period. The Flathead became dependent upon guns, gun powder, and metal arrowpoints—items they needed to achieve a more equal footing with the Blackfoot. During the 1840s, at the request of the Flathead, French Jesuits from St. Louis established missions among them. Although younger Flathead later rejected the Jesuits' teaching, many remained faithful.

The Hellgate Treaty (1854) was the first land cession treaty signed by the Flathead. The governor of Washington Territory, ISAAC STEVENS, arbitrarily combined the Flathead, Kalispel (Pend D'Oreilles), Spokan, and Kootenais into one "nation" called the Flathead Nation. The combined tribes relinquished 25,000 acres to the United States. Over the following 60 years, a series of land cessions, which the Flathead verbally protested, opened more Flathead land to non-Indian settlement. In 1910, the final dispossession of the Flathead was consummated without any shots fired. Each Flathead was allotted 80 acres of land and the remainder of their reservation was sold to non-Indians. However, their reservation was later reinstated and currently occupies territory south of Flathead Lake near Dixon, Montana.

Flint Creek (1789) *battle between Southern state militias and the Chickamauga Cherokee*

In the aftermath of the AMERICAN REVOLUTION (1775–83), American settlers began moving westward from Georgia and South Carolina into CREEK territory. In response to these pressures, the Creek, CHOCTAW, and CHICKASAW all negotiated treaties allying themselves with the Spanish, who supplied them with guns and ammunition, which they used to harass American settlements in Indian territory. On April 2, 1786, the Creek Nation declared war on the United States. In raids on the southern frontier during the following two years, the Creek killed, wounded, and captured some 200 people.

The raids brought retaliations from Southern state militias. In 1788 and 1789, the Americans, raided settlements of the Creek and a hostile group of CHICKAMAUGA CHEROKEE. They were led by JOHN SEVIER, an experienced Indian fighter and future governor of Tennessee. In January 1789, Sevier brought the Chickamauga Cherokee to bay at Flint Creek, near the present-day border between Alabama and Mississippi. During the course of this battle, the Indians suffered heavy casualties, losing 145 warriors, while Sevier and the militia escaped virtually unscathed. The battle at Flint Creek sobered the Cherokee to the dangers of opposing the United States and helped lead to the HOLSTON TREATY (1791).

Ford, John Salmon ("Rip" Ford) (1815–1897) *frontier soldier noted for his Indian-fighting exploits*

Born in South Carolina, John Salmon Ford moved to Texas in 1836 and served for two years in the Texas army. He then practiced medicine and edited a newspaper until the Mexican War (1845–48), in which he served as adjutant of a regiment of volunteer Texas cavalry. In that capacity his habit of beginning death notices with the phrase "Rest in Peace," later shortened during wartime conditions to "R.I.P.," earned Ford his nickname.

In 1849, Ford, along with ROBERT S. NEIGHBORS, blazed what eventually became a well-used trail across western Texas. As a member of the TEXAS RANGERS from 1849 to 1851, Ford led several skirmishes against the APACHE and COMANCHE in south Texas. Following a term in the Texas state senate and another stint editing a newspaper, he returned to the Texas Rangers in 1858. That year Ford led a column of more than 200 Rangers and allied Indians including CADDO, into present-day Oklahoma, where, in the Canadian River valley, he and his forces defeated a large group of Comanche. Ford fought for the Confederacy during the CIVIL WAR (1861–65) and later held a number of elected offices in the Lone Star State. He died in San Antonio, Texas, in 1897.

Forsyth, George Alexander (Sandy Forsyth) (1837–1915) *U.S. Army officer and aide to General Philip Sheridan, best known for his role at the battle of Beecher's Island*

Born in Pennsylvania, George Alexander Forsyth was a distinguished veteran of the CIVIL WAR (1861–65), in which he served in the federal cavalry and as staff officer for General PHILIP HENRY SHERIDAN. After the war, Forsyth remained in the army as a major in the 9th Cavalry.

In 1868, while serving with Sheridan, Forsyth was instructed to organize a 50-man scouting force for frontier duty as protection for the Kansas Pacific Railroad. On September 17, 1868, Forsyth and his unit were in pursuit of a raiding party of CHEYENNE and Lakota (see SIOUX). At the Arickaree Fork of the Republican River in Colorado, the Indians counterattacked. Forsyth and his scouts were forced to take refuge on a small, sandy island in the river where, for the next eight days, they were besieged by an estimated 600 Cheyenne DOG SOLDIERS and Oglala Lakota. Army reinforcements were summoned from Fort Wallace, Kansas, 125 miles away. Forsyth was wounded in the battle, and nearly half his troops were killed or wounded by the time a unit of BUFFALO SOLDIERS arrived. Forsyth's second in command, Lieutenant Frederick Beecher, was one of those killed in this engagement, which came to be known as the battle of BEECHER'S ISLAND (1868).

With his promotion to lieutenant colonel in 1881, Forsyth left Sheridan's staff and transferred to field duty with the 4th U.S. Cavalry. Forsyth was the regiment's field commander, nominally second to RANALD S. MACKENZIE, who was in charge of the Department of New Mexico, with headquarters in Santa Fe. Forsyth led the regiment in campaigns against APACHE leaders GERONIMO, Loco, NANA, Naische, and Chihuahua in 1882 and 1885–88. Forsyth and his regiment were in the field in July 1886, when Geronimo ended the APACHE WARS (1861–86) by surrendering to General NELSON A. MILES.

In 1888, Forsyth was suspended from the army for filing false financial claims against the government. His suspension was overturned in 1890, but he was ordered to retire on disability as a full colonel.

Forsyth, James W. (1834–1906) *U.S. Army officer most remembered for commanding troops at Wounded Knee*

Born in Ohio, James W. Forsyth graduated from West Point in 1856. After serving in the CIVIL WAR (1861–65) as a brevet brigadier general, Forsyth was returned to the rank of lieutenant colonel in the postwar army. He served on the staff of General PHILIP HENRY SHERIDAN in various roles from 1869 to 1878. He saw limited action during the BANNOCK WAR (1878), and in 1886 was promoted to colonel of the 7th Cavalry Regiment.

During the GHOST DANCE crisis among western reservation Indians, in late 1890 division commander NELSON A. MILES gave Forsyth the delicate task of leading about 500 Lakota (see SIOUX) Indians back to their reservation. Led by BIG FOOT, most of these Indians were members of the Miniconjou band who had fled what they feared to be the army's wrath. Big Foot's followers settled into the valley of a creek called WOUNDED KNEE (1890) in the Dakota Territory. During the late afternoon and evening of December 28, 1890, Forsyth's command took up positions around the Indian encampment, positioning artillery pieces and Gatling guns above the valley.

The next day he demanded that the Indians surrender their weapons. Finding themselves in a dilemma, the Miniconjou gave up many of their older FIREARMS. It soon became evident, however, that they had not revealed their new Winchester repeating rifles. Furious, Forsyth ordered his soldiers to search tipis, disregarding orders that he must not separate his troops in the face of the enemy. With emotions running high, a scuffle broke out and a fierce battle erupted. Indian women and children were among the warriors, so when the shots rang out, many were in the line of fire. The artillery then began a murderous barrage, totally leveling the Indian village. The frightened Indians broke into a run, and after the fire subsided, more than 150 Sioux lay dead, including Chief BIG FOOT, and another 50 were wounded. Army losses totaled 25 killed and 39 wounded.

The following day Forsyth was sent to investigate a fire set by angry tribespeople at nearby White Clay Creek. Once again handling his command poorly, Forsyth led his troops into a valley where they became trapped because they had failed to secure the ridges above. His command was saved only by the arrival of the 9th Cavalry's BUFFALO SOLDIERS, who had ridden some 50 miles the night before.

Outraged by the incident at Wounded Knee, Miles relieved Forsyth of his command and convened a court of inquiry to investigate why Forsyth had allowed women and children to be killed and why he had deployed his troops so close to the Indians. Miles further accused Forsyth of being guilty of incompetence, inexperience, and irresponsibility. Despite Miles's charges, Secretary of War Redfield Proctor restored Forsyth to full command status amid a more general army effort to limit the public outcry over Wounded Knee. Forsyth was promoted to brigadier general in 1894 and major general in 1897 before his retirement. He died at his home in Ohio in 1906.

Fort Apache *most famous of a line of forts constructed by the U.S. military in the 1870s to repel Apache raids*

The APACHE WARS (1860–86) began in southern Arizona in 1860. Over the next 10 years, Apache routinely raided non-Indian settlements in the United States and Mexico. They also attacked travelers throughout the territory. Meanwhile, the U.S. Army initiated a war of extermination against these Indians, with hundreds of people killed on both sides. In order to subdue the APACHE, the military constructed a line of forts across Apache territory.

The post that came to be known as Fort Apache was located four miles from Whiteriver in the mountains of east-central Arizona. It lay in the very heart of the territory occupied by White Mountain and Cibecue Apache. It was initially named Camp Ord then renamed Camp Mogollon, followed by Camp Thomas. In late 1870, however, the famous Apache chief COCHISE visited the post. In honor of his visit and to promote peace, the site was renamed Camp Apache and eventually Fort Apache.

Like most installations, Fort Apache never had a protective log wall. This was considered unnecessary because the fort was located on a high plateau bordered on its north and west sides by vertical cliffs that dropped several hundred feet to rivers below. No Indians could attack from those directions. With the trees removed from the other sides, the soldiers felt confident that they could see the enemy coming and protect themselves.

While the fort was in operation, it hosted some of the most famous names in southwestern history. In addition to Cochise, Apaches leader Chiquito visited the post, and Mangus and GERONIMO were temporarily incarcerated there. Dr. Walter Reed (later known for his work with typhoid fever) was the post medic. General GEORGE CROOK and his famous Apache Scouts, who relentlessly pursued Geronimo and other Apache throughout Arizona and Mexico, were stationed at the fort. The 10th U.S. Cavalry, an all-black unit earlier nicknamed the BUFFALO SOLDIERS, was stationed there for a time as well.

During the time of the Apache Wars, detachments of soldiers from the post were constantly engaged in pursuit of the elusive Apache. Only once was the fort itself the scene of a battle. In late August 1881, a detachment of soldiers led by General EUGENE A. CARR was sent to CIBECUE CREEK to arrest Nakaidoklini, a White Mountain Apache medicine man and prophet who had promised his followers that white people would be gone from the land by the time the corn was ripe. Not long after he was arrested, the shooting began. The fatality list from the Cibecue Creek massacre, as the battle became known, included eight soldiers and an estimated 18 Apache, including the prophet. The surviving soldiers waited until dark then marched all night and half the next day to reach Fort Apache, which was 45 miles from the battle. The following afternoon the Apache attacked the fort. With their prophet dead and a lack of leadership, the Apache were repelled with relative ease by General Carr and his troops.

Fort Atkinson Treaty (1853) *treaty between the U.S. government and the Kiowa, Comanche, and Apache*

With the expansion of U.S. territory after the TREATY OF GUADALUPE HIDALGO (1848) and the discovery of gold and other minerals in the West, settlers began trekking across the Great Plains by the thousands. The government's intention to provide unrestricted freedom of passage for white travelers made it necessary to regulate the movements and activities of the Plains tribes. The FORT LARAMIE TREATY of 1851 had been negotiated with tribes that might threaten the Oregon Trail. To protect the Santa Fe Trail, the government negotiated the Fort Atkinson Treaty in Kansas with the KIOWA, COMANCHE, and APACHE. The treaty gave the government the right to establish roads, highways, and military and other posts on Indian land. The Indians were required not only to refrain from attacks upon settlers passing through their territory, but also to aid those in need. Additionally, the tribes agreed to forgo their frequent incursions into Mexico and restore all Mexican prisoners to their homes.

In return for their acquiescence, the Kiowa, Comanche, and Apache were to receive goods, provisions, or agricultural implements in the amount of $18,000 per year for 10 years, with a possible extension of another five years. The president could, however, divert the promised annuity, without the tribes' consent, into a fund for the purpose of establishing tribal farms—an indirect reference to the imminent reservation system. In addition, the United States promised to "protect and defend" the Indians and their land from depredations by non-Indian citizens.

From the time of signing, the Fort Atkinson Treaty was fraught with non-compliance on both sides. White contractors, who delivered substandard goods and supplies, pocketed most of the appropriated funds themselves. The U.S. government seemed unable to inspire or require honesty from its contractors. Additionally, it failed to "protect and defend" Indians from intruding settlers, who continually trespassed on Indian land. Conversely, full understanding and concurrence with all treaty provisions by the Indians also proved unlikely. For centuries the tribes had taken young prisoners from Mexico; this was an accepted method of bolstering tribal populations and compensating for low birth rates. Additionally, the treaty tribes had never been farmers and could not envision themselves settling down to "scratch in the dirt." Though the Indians' comprehension of treaty terms may have been incomplete, their understanding of threats of the war and bribery imposed on them at treaty councils was very clear.

The Plains tribes received annuity goods at an appointed place along Beaver Creek. They therefore refrained from raids against traders on the Arkansas River and the Santa Fe Trail. Yet raids against targets in Texas and Mexico continued, partly because nontreaty bands felt no obligation to the agreement and partly because raiding was an established element of Plains culture. It was one of the principal ways by which young men could gain the prestige and honor necessary to elevate them in tribal society.

The Fort Atkinson Treaty exemplified the ineffectiveness of most treaties made between the United States and Indian nations—two totally divergent cultures with conflicting goals, purposes, and expectations.

Fort C. F. Smith *fort built to guard the Bozeman Trail*

The BOZEMAN TRAIL was the major immigrant road from Fort Laramie, Wyoming, to the recently discovered gold mines in Virginia City, Montana. Before dealing with the Indians in that region, the government sent a military contingent to fortify the trail and begin building Forts Reno and Phil Kearny. A contingent from Kearny then constructed the northernmost outpost, Fort C. F. Smith, in southern Montana. The principal chiefs of the Lakota (see SIOUX) and CHEYENNE, including RED CLOUD of the Oglala Lakota and Two Moon and DULL KNIFE of the Cheyenne, adamantly opposed the construction of forts without being consulted. They vowed to stop non-Indian immigrants from crossing their prime buffalo-hunting lands and began to harass the forts and travelers along the trail.

In December 1866, outside Fort Phil Kearny, the Sioux annihilated Captain WILLIAM J. FETTERMAN and his force of 80 cavalrymen (see FETTERMAN FIGHT, 1866). Several months later, in August 1867, Red Cloud, led a Sioux attack on Fort Phil Kearny, while a force of 500 to 600 Cheyenne, led by Dull Knife and Two Moon, moved to attack Fort C. F. Smith. There the Cheyenne trapped 30 soldiers and civilians in a hay field about two miles outside the fort. The resulting HAYFIELD FIGHT (1867) helped convince the government to abandon the Bozeman Trail.

Fort Defiance   site of an attack during the Navajo Wars

Established in 1851, Fort Defiance was one of a series of U.S. posts constructed in present-day Arizona. In the wake of NAVAJO (Dineh) raids against settlers in the area, Colonel BENJAMIN BONNEVILLE, commander of U.S. forces in Santa Fe, New Mexico, met with Indian leaders in an attempt to reach peace. During talks held in December 1858, the Navajo agreed to avoid non-Indian settlements along a line 25 miles east of the fort. In addition, the Indians agreed to pay for all stolen property in their possession, to release all prisoners, and to appoint a single chief as their spokesman.

Colonel Bonneville believed that the Navajo sincerely desired peace, but he took no chances, retaining 21 Indian PRISONERS as hostages to ensure that the Navajo complied with the treaty terms and strengthening the force on duty within the fort. The following summer he sent mounted troops out in a demonstration of force to ensure that the Navajo understood his determination. A year of peace followed. Then, in mid-January 1860, a strong Indian force attacked a supply train en route to Fort Defiance. On February 8 some 500 warriors attacked a herd guard about seven miles north of the post. The defenders repelled both assaults with heavy losses.

Just before dawn on April 30, about 1,000 Navajo attacked Fort Defiance itself from three different directions. Some of the buildings fell into Indian hands until Brevet Major Oliver L. Shepherd formed three companies of the 3rd Infantry to stop the penetration. The attack against Fort Defiance lasted about two hours. When there was sufficient daylight, Shepherd led a counterattack into the nearby hills. The Indians broke off their attack, and the hostilities ended for that day. The battle resulted in one soldier killed and two wounded, while Navajo losses were put at 12 killed or wounded.

Rarely in the annals of Indian-non-Indian conflict was a military post actually assaulted in such a manner. With the attack against Fort Defiance, the United States concluded that aggressive offensive campaigns against the Navajo were necessary (see NAVAJO WARS); Fort Defiance would serve as the launching point.

Fort Finney Treaty   (1786)   treaty between the U.S. government and the Shawnee

Following the AMERICAN REVOLUTION (1775–81), the United States claimed that Indian tribes who had supported the British during the war had forfeited all rights to their lands. The SHAWNEE were thus forced to sign a treaty in which they relinquished their lands north of the Ohio River.

Like most pacts signed with Native Americans immediately following the TREATY OF PARIS (1783), the Fort Finney Treaty was largely ineffective because the new republic lacked the means to enforce it. This deficiency was later addressed in the FORT HARMAR TREATIES (1789), by which the Shawnee and other tribes were compensated for surrendering their lands to the United States.

Fort Gibson Treaty   (1833)   agreement between the U.S. government and the Creek, western Cherokee and Seminole

In 1826, a small group of CREEK known as the McIntosh party signed the so-called McIntosh Treaty and immigrated to Indian Territory about two years later. Their land, which had been neither surveyed nor patented by the United States, was included with land sold to the western CHEROKEE in 1828. The Cherokee settled on this land in 1832, and boundary disputes immediately erupted. The Fort Gibson Treaty set territorial limits for the Creek Nation and established a boundary between the Creek and the Cherokee in Indian Territory (present-day Oklahoma). The treaty also provided for the merger of the SEMINOLE with the Creek in Indian Territory. U.S. negotiations were undertaken by the Stokes Commission (established to settle disputes among immigrant tribes from the east and tribes already settled in Indian Territory).

The Fort Gibson Treaty established Creek territory in a pan-shaped swath across the middle of present-day Oklahoma and restored most of the Creek land previously sold to the Cherokee. The Seminole portion of the treaty was accomplished with the clear purpose to provide for removal of the Seminole, whether or not their final consent was given. The treaty was worded in such a manner as to convey the impression of free-will consent by the Seminole with reference to the PAYNE'S LANDING TREATY (1832). Regardless of the proclamations of the Stokes Commission, many Seminole struggled to maintain their Florida homelands. Between 1835 and 1842, approximately 3,000 Seminole were force-marched west by the U.S. military. In 1842, the federal government gave up trying to force Seminole capitulation. After the Third SEMINOLE WAR (1855–58), Chief BILLY BOWLEGS'S band agreed to move to Indian Territory, but many Seminole continued to defy the United States by retreating deeper into the Florida Everglades.

Fort Harmar Treaties   (1789)   agreements between the U.S. government and several tribes in the Old Northwest Territory

Following the end of the AMERICAN REVOLUTION (1775–81), the United States signed a number of treaties with Native American tribes to open up the new lands that had been added to the country between the Allegheny Mountains and the Mississippi River for settlement by non-Indians. In the Old Northwest Territory—an area that would eventually become the states of Ohio, Indiana, Illinois, Michigan, Wisconsin, and part of Minnesota—treaties were signed at FORT STANWIX (1784), Fort McIntosh (1785), and Fort Finney (1786). These treaties were largely ineffective for a number of reasons. First, the U.S. government believed that, as former allies of the defeated British, the Indians had forfeited all rights to their lands, which meant that they could be removed from them with little negotiation and no compensation. Second, the British continued to exert their influence across the Canadian border, inciting the Indians to acts of violence against the westward-moving American settlers. Finally, the settlers could expect little protection from their own government, which had difficulty raising the money necessary to secure the frontier.

By 1789, the government had decided that it would be cheaper to pay the Native Americans for their lands than to fight them. This new policy was reflected in the Fort Harmar Treaties, signed in January of that year, which for the first time recognized Indian ownership of lands and provided compensation for transfer of Indian property to the United States. Fort Harmar was located at the month of the Muskigum in Ohio. The first agreement, signed with the Wyandot, Delaware (see LENNI LENAPE), POTAWATOMI, OTTAWA, and SAC, provided for the tribes to be reimbursed for the lands they had given up at Fort McIntosh in 1785. A similar agreement was then reached with the IROQUOIS CONFEDERACY, which confirmed the cession of lands agreed to in the Fort Stanwix Treaty.

Although perhaps motivated more by practical considerations than any humanitarian or egalitarian principles, the Fort Harmar Treaties marked a new phase in relations between settlers and Indians in the Old Northwest Territory.

fortifications *defensive structures built to protect settlements and strategic locations*

Popular images of Native American warfare often feature Indians attacking white soldiers in strong wooden forts. In reality some Indian groups used fortifications at least as often as the U.S. army. In Eastern America, for example, fortifications were a traditional part of a tribe's defensive system. Individual Indian warriors most often took the offensive in battle, but the defense of the tribe as a whole was also important. Warriors had a duty to the tribe as well as to prove themselves in battle. They could therefore take practical measures for tribe's defense.

A tribe fearing an enemy's attack might consider striking first. It would also send out scouts to learn about an impending attack. The "civilians" in the tribe could then either be scattered, or they could be gathered in fortified villages. Some eastern tribes lived permanently inside such structures, while others used them only in times of danger.

Indian fortifications generally consisted of a series of 10-foot tree trunks secured in the ground in a circle or rough square around the village. Narrow entrances were obstructed by brush and guarded by armed defenders. Few attackers would risk trying to storm the well-defended entrances. Prudent chiefs kept the fortifications, or stockades, well stocked with supplies and water.

Fortifications were sturdy enough to give defenders good odds of resisting even attacks that included the use of early FIREARMS. It was not considered acceptable war-making practice for warriors laying siege to set fire to buildings within the stockade by shooting flaming arrows. Attackers usually tried to lure defenders out by insults. If any of the defenders responded and were killed or captured, the attackers generally would end the siege.

Non-Indians also constructed a diverse array of fortifications. In the Southwest, the Spanish built adobe presidios to protect strategic sites and to serve as defensible bases for offensive operations. Along the East Coast and throughout the Great Lakes, the Dutch, French, and English constructed similar strongpoints of wood and, on occasion, stone. The strongest of such fortifications bristled with artillery. After securing its independence, the United States continued this practice in the eastern woodlands and along the Mississippi River. Farther west, privately constructed fortifications, such as that at Bent's Fort, Colorado, occasionally guarded key supply and trading centers. But in general, as the United States pushed into the Great Plains, the army eschewed such defenses as being unnecessary. Rather than walled stockades, the army's trans-Mississippi forts were typically collections of buildings grouped rather haphazardly around an open parade ground. Indeed, Native American assaults against such posts were exceedingly rare, as smaller groups of civilians or soldiers in the field were much more vulnerable to the hit-and-run tactics favored by Indians. More prevalent in the region were the temporary fieldworks—rifle pits and hastily collected rocks and timber—constructed by field commands on the eve of combat.

Fort Jackson Treaty (1814) *treaty forced upon the Creek by General Andrew Jackson after the Creek War*

In 1811 the Red Stick CREEK (tribal warriors of the Upper Creek towns) were persuaded by SHAWNEE leader TECUMSEH to join his pan-Indian struggle to expel settlers from Indian lands and to return to traditional Indian ways. At the outbreak of the CREEK WAR (1813–14), the RED STICKS, led by RED EAGLE (William Weatherford), executed their first attack on settlers and assimilated Creek at FORT MIMS (1813). The final battle at HORSESHOE BEND (1814) between Jackson's troops and about 1,000 Red Sticks led by MENEWA ended in catastrophe for the Indians. The 70 Creek survivors reluctantly submitted to peace.

General Thomas Pinckney had previously set forth peace terms, vowing that the United States would remember its allies among the Creek chiefs by making special provisions for them. Nevertheless, General ANDREW JACKSON, the sole negotiator, had his own predetermined agenda. General Jackson bullied Creek chiefs into signing the Fort Jackson Treaty, which required a 14-million-acre cession of land, the largest ever forced upon southeastern Indians. The Creek promised to abandon all communication with the British and Spanish and to allow the United States to establish forts and build roads across their remaining territory. Many embittered Creeks fled to Florida and settled among the SEMINOLE. Their anger erupted quickly in the SEMINOLE WAR (1818–19). The treaty also required the cession of 2.2 million acres of land from allied CHEROKEE.

Fort Laramie Treaty (1851) *treaty between the U.S. government and several Plains Indian tribes*

The decade of the 1840s was an ominous one for the Native Americans of the Great Plains. What had begun as a steady trickle of migrants on the Oregon Trail became a flood in 1848–49, after the discovery of gold in California. The acquisition of new lands in the Southwest following the Mexican War (1845–48) ensured that the flood of migrants would continue. Besides the threat posed by new settlements in the West, the people traveling on the wagon trains spread disease, especially cholera, among the Plains Indians while driving away the buffalo herds on which the Indians depended for their survival. In response to these threats the Indians attacked and otherwise harassed migrants and settlers at every opportunity. The U.S. government, faced with protecting its citizens, sought to buy peace from the Native Americans.

In September 1851, 10,000 Indians gathered together at Fort Laramie, at the juncture of the North Platte and Laramie Rivers (in present-day Wyoming) to meet with government representatives. THOMAS FITZPATRICK and David Mitchell, the principal U.S. negotiators, were astonished at the number of Indians, more than had ever before been assembled in one spot. The tribes represented at the fort—SIOUX (Dakota, Lakota, Nakota), CHEYENNE, CROW, ARIKARA, SHOSHONE, ARAPAHO, and others—had evidently managed to set aside old enmities and gather peacefully to sit side by side for the 18 days of the council. Most, however, had had no choice: The summer hunting season had been poor, and the government agents had promised them food, blankets, and even guns.

The treaty that was signed at Fort Laramie pledged both sides to a "lasting peace between all the nations assembled." The Native Americans promised to keep the peace among themselves and respect each tribe's boundary lines as established by the treaty, while recognizing the right of the United States to construct roads and forts on the Plains. In return the tribes would receive the collective sum of $50,000—payable in cattle, farming tools, grain, and seed—every year for 50 years, and they were promised protection from attacks by non-Indians.

Both sides left Fort Laramie happy. The tribes collected their gifts at the signing and looked forward to the annuity; the Sioux, in fact, would forever after refer to 1851 as the Year of the Great Giveaway. It is doubtful, however, that many of the Native Americans expected that they would actually abide by the terms of the treaty themselves, as the terms were incompatible with the realities of Plains life. That the annuity would be paid in farming equipment indicated the government's unrealistic desire for the Indians to give up their mobile existence. Moreover, the treaty outlawed raiding and horse stealing—activities that disturbed and angered bureaucrats in Washington, but that brought honor to Plains warriors and authority to their tribes. Finally, the Sioux were not about to return the valuable hunting grounds they had won from the KIOWA and Crow, as required under the terms of the treaty. It was not long, in fact, before the tribes resumed warring with one another.

The U.S. government also had its own problems with the terms of the treaty. Despite Mitchell's argument that $50,000—less than a dollar per tribe member—was a small price to pay "to save the country from the ruinous and useless expense of a war against the prairie tribes, which would cost many millions," the U.S. Senate was unconvinced, and the annuity was reduced from 50 years to 10.

Though flawed from the start, the Fort Laramie Treaty of 1851 did manage to establish an uneasy truce between Native Americans and wagon trains, and for a few years at least, emigrants could make the westward trek in relative peace. That did not last, however, as encroachment on Indian land continued.

Fort Laramie Treaty (1868) *treaty between the U.S. government and several northern plains tribes*

Disappointed with the military's recent failures in the campaigns of General WINFIELD SCOTT HANCOCK on the southern plains and along the BOZEMAN TRAIL to the north, in summer 1867 Congress established a Peace Commission to end the violent disputes between Native Americans and non-Indians in the trans-Mississippi West. Chaired by Commissioner of Indian Affairs Nathaniel G. Taylor, the commission included three other civilians and three generals—WILLIAM T. SHERMAN, WILLIAM S. HARNEY, and Alfred Terry. In October, the Peace Commission concluded agreements with several southern Plains groups in the MEDICINE LODGE TREATY.

Talks with northern plains tribes proved much more difficult. The draft document promised that the government would abandon its Bozeman Trail forts, a condition that the most influential chief, RED CLOUD, had insisted upon. This was a tacit acknowledgment, not only of the recent Native American victory in the FETTERMAN DEFEAT (1866) and the army's inability to protect travelers in the region, but also that the construction of the Union Pacific Railroad would ultimately render the overland trail obsolete. The agreement also established a huge reservation in Dakota west of the Missouri River, and it preserved extensive hunting rights for the northern tribes in Nebraska and Wyoming. Non-Indians could travel in the Powder River country only with tribal consent. The government also promised to provide annuities and teachers at reservation agencies. In return, the Indians were to give up their other claims and promise to end any depredations.

Through much of the winter of 1867–68, government agents tried to convince Lakota SIOUX and CHEYENNE leaders to come to Fort Laramie, Wyoming, the following April. But the Indians were very slow to respond, with only a few smaller groups appearing even as summer ended. In November, after the army actually abandoned several of its forts along the Bozeman Trail, the most important chiefs, including Red Cloud, finally assented to the agreement. The Senate ratified the document on February 24, 1869.

See also SIOUX WARS.

Fort McIntosh Treaty (1785) *treaty between the U.S. government and a number of tribes in the Old Northwest Territory*

In January 1785 delegates from the LENNI LENAPE (Delaware), CHIPPEWA, OTTAWA, and Wyandot tribes gathered at Fort McIntosh, near present-day Pittsburgh, Pennsylvania. There, as punishment for having supported the British during the AMERICAN REVOLUTION (1775–81), the tribes were ordered to give up their hunting grounds north and west of the Ohio River, lands that would later form most of present-day Ohio.

Like many such pacts signed immediately after the TREATY OF PARIS (1783), the Fort McIntosh Treaty accomplished little because the government of the newly formed United States was unable to enforce it effectively. British agents in Canada continued to incite the Native Americans, endangering the settlers moving westward to the surrendered lands. Moreover, the settlers received little protection from their own government, which found it difficult to raise enough money to provide army protection for the frontier.

Under a new policy that required the government to compensate Native Americans rather than simply order them from their lands, the cession of the Ohio lands made at Fort McIntosh was confirmed four years later, at the first of the FORT HARMAR TREATIES (1789).

Fort Mims (1813) *battle that transformed a Creek civil war into a war fight against the United States*

Traditionalist CREEK warriors known as RED STICKS, encouraged by SHAWNEE leader TECUMSEH's belief that a return to Indian ways prior to contact with settlers was possible, began a campaign in 1813 to purge the Upper Creek towns of chiefs and mixed-blood Creek who had adopted a European-style way of life. The Red Sticks were careful, however, to avoid killing non-Indians. Then, on August 27, 1813, a detachment of Red Sticks returning from a supply trip to Pensacola were attacked at Burnt Corn Creek by 180 Mississippi militiamen. The Creek were victorious, and the battle ignited their hatred for the U.S. government and set the stage for further violence.

On August 30, 1813, 400 wealthy mixed-blood farmers, blacks, and white squatters took refuge from the Red Stick attack at Fort Mims, near the Tombigbee and Alabama Rivers in Creek territory, a few miles above present-day Mobile, Alabama. Major John Beasley, leader of the 120-man Louisiana militia stationed there, neglected to secure the gate and post a sentry. At noon, Red Sticks led by RED EAGLE jumped from the tall grass outside the fort and attacked. Although taken completely by surprise, the occupants of the fort held out for six hours before fire-tipped arrows ignited the fort. Forced to escape the suffocating smoke and flames, the fort's occupants ran forward into a barrage of arrows and gunfire. Only 36 individuals escaped.

The Red Stick victory at Fort Mims cost them the lives of approximately 300 warriors. It also provided southern Americans (who desired more Creek land) with their long-sought excuse to invade Creek territory. Several thousand U.S. troops and militiamen were immediately called into action, as were friendly CHOCTAW, CHEROKEE, and Creek. ANDREW JACKSON, recovering from injuries sustained in a dual, commanded a column headed for Creek territory. Within eight months Jackson had taken the entire Creek territory and devastated its people.

Fort Ridgely (1862) *engagement between the U.S. Army and Dakota Indians during the Sioux Wars*

Fort Ridgely was probably named after Captain Randolph Ridgely, an artillery officer who died in the Mexican War. It was established in 1853 on a bluff overlooking the Minnesota River Valley in Minnesota, near the federal Indian administrative center known as the Lower Sioux Reservation. However, those who designed the fort had apparently paid little attention to defensive needs. There was no stockade, and deep ravines ran within musket range immediately to the north, east, and southwest, providing places where attackers could hide and fire. To the northwest was open prairie.

On August 18, 1862, a group of Dakota (see SIOUX) attacked the Lower Sioux Agency 13 miles away from Fort Ridgely. When the fort's commanding officer heard the news, he set out for the burning agency with 46 enlisted men. Along the way, excited settlers warned Captain Marsh that he would face an overwhelming Indian force (see MINNESOTA UPRISING), but he failed to heed their advice. The soldiers reached the Redwood Ferry, but just as they were preparing to cross the Minnesota River to the agency, the Indians attacked. Twenty-four soldiers died, including Marsh; the rest managed to make it back to the fort. Only one Indian was killed.

After this attack, raiding parties targeted settlers throughout southern Minnesota, killing hundreds. The survivors fled to sites where they thought they might be safe, including Fort Ridgely and NEW ULM (1862).

On August 20 nearly 400 Indians attacked Fort Ridgely. The Dakota, under the able leadership of LITTLE CROW, clearly had the numerical advantage. Lieutenant Timothy J. Sheehan, 26 years old, commanded only 180 defenders, but they had several cannons. Never before had these Indians encountered artillery, and they were deathly afraid of the "rotten balls" that flew into pieces when fired. Nightfall and heavy rains temporarily ended the fighting. Two days later, the Dakota launched a second attack on the fort, this time with 800 men. At first the Indians tried to set fire to the fort's buildings, but the recent rains made the task difficult. Then they laid down heavy fire. Finally, they launched an all-out attack, but again they were repelled by cannon fire. The casualties for the two attacks on Fort Ridgely numbered three dead soldiers and an estimated 100 Indians. Within a week, reinforcements reached the site, and Fort Ridgely became a haven for survivors and a staging point for punitive expeditions led by the military.

Fort Stanwix (1777) *battle in the American Revolution between colonial forces and Iroquois and British allied forces*
During the AMERICAN REVOLUTION (1775–81), settlers in the Mohawk River Valley in north-central New York faced a continual problem of raids by Indians of the IROQUOIS CONFEDERACY. On August 3, 1777, a combined force of approximately 1,600 British troops and Iroquois warriors under Lieutenant Colonel Barry St. Leger and MOHAWK leader JOSEPH BRANT moved on Fort Stanwix (near present-day Rome, New York) as part of General John Burgoyne's campaign designed to cut off New England from the rest of the rebellions colonies. American commander Colonel Peter Gansevoort refused to surrender, and on the following morning St. Leger began an artillery bombardment of the fort.

Gansevoort hoped for relief from the local patriot militia under the leadership of Nicholas Herkimer, stationed at a local Indian town called Oriskany, about 10 miles to the south. Herkimer sent about 200 men to ambush part of St. Leger's force. The expedition succeeded in its mission, but it did not relieve the siege. The ambush also alerted St. Leger to Herkimer's presence in the area. When he learned out that Herkimer was advancing toward Fort Stanwix, St. Leger laid a trap, ambushing the militia just outside of Oriskany on August 6. Half the American force was killed in the ambush, including Herkimer. Nevertheless, the remaining troops drove the British and Indian attackers back, inflicting heavy casualties.

The Americans' victory did not relieve the siege of Fort Stanwix; this was accomplished by General Benedict Arnold. Arnold captured two Loyalists, Walter Butler and Hon Yost Schuyler, on his way to relieve the siege. He struck a bargain with Schuyler: in return for having his property restored, Schuyler agreed to report that Butler—Brant's friend and influential with the Indians—would be executed. Schuyler also exaggerated the size of Arnold's force. When he made his report, many of St. Leger's Indian allies deserted. St. Leger himself dropped the siege on August 22.

Burgoyne's entire effort ended in failure. In addition to St. Leger's inability to take Fort Stanwix, Burgoyne and nearly 6,000 British, German, and Indians surrendered at Saratoga, New York, thus ending the campaign.

Fort Stanwix Treaty (1768) *treaty between the British and the Iroquois Confederacy*
To discourage frontier fighting between Indians and settlers after the FRENCH AND INDIAN WAR (1754–63), King George III of

Britain declared land west of the Appalachian Mountains off-limits to settlement in the PROCLAMATION OF 1763. In defiance of this and similar past agreements, however, settlers continued to establish themselves beyond the line of demarcation. In response, Native Americans resumed their raids on frontier settlements.

In 1768, Sir William Johnson, British superintendent of Indian affairs, organized a meeting of colonial authorities and sachems of the IROQUOIS CONFEDERACY at Fort Stanwix (the site of Rome, New York). Known as the Fort Stanwix Congress, this body established a new agreement for peace on the frontier. The Fort Stanwix Treaty established a new line of demarcation, farther west, beyond which further non-Indian settlement was prohibited. To make this possible, the Iroquois Confederacy relinquished their claims to what is now western Pennsylvania, West Virginia, and Kentucky, in exchange for payment of £10,000. Once again, however, settlers ignored the treaty and continued to settle on traditional Native American hunting grounds, prompting the negotiation of the FORT STANWIX TREATY (1784) between the U.S. government and the Iroquois Confederacy.

Fort Stanwix Treaty (1784) *treaty between the U.S. government and the Iroquois Confederacy*
After the AMERICAN REVOLUTION (1775–81), the Americans negotiated a separate peace with the Six Nations of the IROQUOIS CONFEDERACY who were not included in the TREATY OF PARIS (1783) between the United States and Great Britain. Named after Fort Stanwix in New York, where it was negotiated and signed, the treaty had four separate provisions. PRISONERS on both sides were to be released, and hostages were to be exchanged to ensure that the releases took place. The Americans acknowledged the Iroquois's right to their own lands and set forth the boundaries of these lands in the treaty. The Americans also agreed to seal the treaty by giving the Indians gifts. Most important, however, the Six Nations gave rights to their lands west of the Ohio River to the United States. This last provision was the basis for later American claims on the Ohio Country, which led to LITTLE TURTLE'S WAR (1786–95) and other conflicts in the Old Northwest Territory.

Fort Wise Treaty (1861) *treaty between the U.S. government and the Arapaho and Cheyenne Indians*
After gold was discovered at Pikes Peak in Colorado, the U.S. government in 1861 invited the CHEYENNE and ARAPAHO to Fort Wise on the Arkansas River to reach an agreement concerning the thousands of miners and settlers flooding the Indian territories on the Plains on their way to the Colorado goldfields. Under the final treaty, the Indians agreed to live in an area bounded by Sand Creek and the Arkansas River. The Indians, however, also believed that the treaty guaranteed them freedom to hunt outside this region. The legality of the treaty was somewhat doubtful, because although the signatories

included several influential Indian leaders, including Cheyenne leader BLACK KETTLE, in the end only six of the 44 Cheyenne chiefs were actually represented at the treaty talks and at the signing. The Fort Wise Treaty failed to halt western expansion of settlers and miners, though it did slow the process somewhat.

Four Lakes (1858) *one of two battles that led to the end of Indian warfare in the Pacific Northwest*

After the end of the YAKAMA WAR (1855–57), most Indian tribes in the Columbia River Basin, with the exception of the NEZ PERCE, united to resist the continuing invasion of their lands. In early August 1858, Colonel GEORGE WRIGHT sent troops and supplies to the Snake River crossing, where a fort was being built. This fort served as a supply base for Wright while he organized an attack force of 600 men. Nez Perce scouts reported to Wright that large numbers of Spokane, Coeur D'Alene, Palouse, and a few Kalispel were assembling in the area of the Four Lakes (southwest of present-day Spokane).

On August 30, as Wright and his men reached the Great Spokane Plains, Indians appeared on the surrounding hills. By September 1 there were enough Indians directly in the line of march that Wright knew a fight was imminent. Leaving behind two companies and a howitzer, Wright used the rest of the men to take a hilltop. From there he could see 400 to 500 warriors readying themselves for battle. More Indians clustered in the nearby forest. Wright sent Captain Frederick T. Dent's 9th Infantry battalion and a howitzer against the Indians gathered among the trees. The 3rd Artillery, under Captain Erasmus D. Keyes, was ordered down the slope in skirmish formation, and Brevet Major William N. Grier's First Dragoon followed.

Wright hoped to use his troops to draw the Indians out of their hiding places so Grier's troops could get to them. New long-range rifles helped win the day. Even at 600 yards, the rifles were able to find their marks, while the Indians bows and arrows and muskets could not. When Captain Dent flushed the Indians from the forest onto the open plains, Grier's forces drove their horses into the Indians and attacked with sabers and pistols. Under the soldiers' onslaught, the warriors broke rank and retreated. The troops pursued the Indians for about a mile, but their tired horses soon fell behind. By the time the infantry caught up with Grier, only a few Indians could be seen. The battle of Four Lakes ended with no casualties for the army; the Indians suffered about 60 dead and numerous wounded.

Fox (Mesquakie) *Algonquian tribe that inhabited the Fox River area of present-day eastern Wisconsin*

The Fox (now known as Mesquakie) were—traditionally farmers in the summer and hunter-gatherers during the winter. Summer dwellings were bark-covered houses and winter homes were portable wigwams. War chiefs won their positions by feats of battle, while the office of peace chief passed from father to son. In 1734, the Fox formed a permanent alliance with the

SAUK. By the late 18th century there were three principal bands of Fox and Sauk: one east of the Mississippi in Illinois, one west of the Mississippi in Iowa, and one near the Osage River in Missouri.

From the outset of European contact, the Fox were an implacable foe of colonization. The FOX WAR (1720–35) disrupted French trade on Lake Michigan and portage routes to the Mississippi, which interfered with trade to Louisiana. The Fox eventually were driven south and west to the Wisconsin River by the French and their CHIPPEWA allies. White pressure on Indian land in the Northwest Territory following the AMERICAN REVOLUTION (1775–81) and the LOUISIANA PURCHASE (1803) brought increased conflicts with non-Indians and led to Fox participation in LITTLE TURTLE'S WAR (1790–94). In 1803, encouraged by the Spanish, the Fox and Sauk of Missouri started a war with the OSAGE Indians. In 1804 WILLIAM HENRY HARRISON arrived at St. Louis to mediate peace between the tribes. Harrison tricked the Missouri Fox and Sauk chiefs into ceding the lands of the Mississippi Fox and Sauk to the United States. This deception motivated many Fox and Sauk to join TECUMSEH'S REBELLION (1809–11) and to ally with the British during the WAR OF 1812 (1812–14). In 1829, Sauk Chief Keokuk led his followers west across the Mississippi to Iowa.

The loss of Fox and Sauk land and the murder of several Fox chiefs by non-Indians in 1830 ignited the BLACK HAWK WAR (1831–32). Black Hawk surrendered to U.S. troops in July 1832, declaring, "Farewell my nation, Black Hawk tried to save you, and avenge your wrongs. . . . He can do no more. . . . Farewell to Black Hawk." Black Hawk's Fox and Sauk rejoined Keokuk's people in Iowa. The Fox later relinquished their Iowa land for a reservation in eastern Kansas. In 1867 they relinquished the Kansas reservation for one in Indian Territory (present-day Oklahoma). Sometime afterward, several Fox and a few Sauk returned to Iowa to purchase land with their own money. Their reservation in Indian Territory was ceded to the United States in 1890, and individual land allotments were made to the Indians. The remainder of Fox and Sauk land (385,000 acres) was then opened for white settlement on September 22, 1891, during the so-called Oklahoma land runs.

Currently, the two tribes, known as the Sac and Fox Tribe, hold reservation and trust lands in Kansas and Oklahoma. The descendants of the Fox and Sauk tribes people who purchased land in Iowa still live on that land and call themselves the Mesquakie Nation.

Fox War (Fox Resistance) (1712–1742) *war between the Fox nation and the French and their Native American allies*

The Fox War was a side effect of the economic struggle among the IROQUOIS CONFEDERACY, the French, and the British. As early as 1670, the FOX (Mesquakie) who traditionally lived along the western shore of Lake Michigan, had made peace with the Iroquois, who were pushing westward to take control of the fur-trapping trade in the Ohio Valley and Great Lakes area. When the French and the Iroquois made peace in the GRAND SETTLEMENT OF 1701, the Fox, who had been trading with the British at Albany were put in an awkward position. Furthermore, the French supplied the Ojibwa (see CHIPPEWA), traditional enemies of the Fox, with guns and powder.

Matters came to a head in 1711, when more than 1,000 Fox accepted an invitation from the French to relocate to Fort DETROIT (present-day Detroit, Michigan). The new French commander of the fort showed the newcomers little respect. The Fox also argued with other tribes who had settled in the area, including such traditional enemies as the MIAMI, the POTAWATOMI, the Illinois, and the Ojibwa. Relations between the garrison and the Fox camp deteriorated. On a stormy night in 1712, fearing that the Fox were planning an attack on the fort, the French surrounded the Fox camp and killed most of its inhabitants, including some 1,000 Fox warriors.

In retaliation, the Fox who had not accepted the French invitation began a systematic series of raids on French settlements in the Great Lakes area from their bases around Green Bay (in modern Wisconsin). They made life difficult and trade practically impossible for the French at their outposts at Michilimackinac (present-day Michigan) and threatened the Mississippi trade routes that linked French Canada with the port of New Orleans. In 1716 the French mustered a force of 400 Canadians and 400 Native Americans and laid siege (with cannon brought in by canoe) to the Fox fortress of Butte de Mort in present-day Wisconsin. The Fox were eventually forced to negotiate a peace.

The terms of the peace were soon violated. By 1720 the Fox were again at war, disrupting the fur trade as far west as the Rocky Mountains. In 1727 they killed eight Canadian traders heading west through Fox territory to trade with the Dakota (see SIOUX). The French, through negotiations with the Illinois and the Great Lakes tribes, isolated the Fox from their potential allies. They decided that the best solution to the recurring Fox problem was to move the remaining tribespeople to Detroit, where their activities could be monitored. By 1729, however, French opinion had shifted from displacement to extermination. Their Ojibwa allies agreed.

By this time the Fox had split over their war policy. A majority wanted to seek peace with the French or, if that was not possible, to seek safety among the SENECA, members of the allied Iroquois Confederacy. The Fox who wanted to continue fighting dispersed throughout Wisconsin. The others set out to find the Seneca along the shores of Lake Ontario. They were seen by French-allied Illinois warriors, who alerted the French to their presence. Of 1,100 Fox who began the trip from Lake Michigan to Lake Ontario, 500 were captured and sold into slavery, 400 were killed outright, and 200 managed to flee. Most of those who escaped were children who found shelter with the SAUK tribe. Only 50 adult Fox survived the French-instigated attacks.

The Fox who had not gone with the mission to the Seneca kept up hostilities against the French for several years, raiding and killing the command at Green Bay and Michilimackinac.

However, their numbers had been so reduced by the deaths in Illinois that by 1738 only a few hundred Fox remained. Most of these were being sheltered by the Sauk or other nations that had questions about French intentions. Finally, in 1742 a few Fox traveled to Montreal and made a lasting peace with the French.

Further Reading

Axelrod, Alan. *Chronicle of the Indian Wars*. Englewood Cliffs, N.J.: Prentice Hall, 1993.
Steele, Ian K. *Warpaths: Invasions of North America*. New York: Oxford University Press, 1994.

Fremont Orchard (1864) *battle between the U.S. Army and Cheyenne Dog Soldiers*

Following reports of Indian raids in eastern Colorado, Colonel JOHN M. CHIVINGTON ordered detachments of his First Colorado Cavalry to pursue the CHEYENNE relentlessly. On April 12, 1864, 40 troopers from the cavalry, in pursuit of a small Cheyenne band accused of driving off a homesteader's livestock, caught up with a band of Cheyenne DOG SOLDIERS at Fremont's Orchard, on the Platte River in Nebraska. Each side blamed the other for starting the brief fight that left three Indians and four soldiers wounded; two of the soldiers later died. The battle was one of several incidents that led to the CHEYENNE-ARAPAHO WAR (1864–65).

French and Indian War (Seven Years' War)

(1754–1763) *last of the great colonial conflicts between France and Britain in North America*

The French and Indian War marked one of the few times in the 18th century that British and French regular troops confronted each other in a colonial American setting. The Native Americans who were involved in the conflict served for the most part as auxiliaries. Those who were not attached to either the French or the British fought the settlers on the borders of Pennsylvania, Maryland, and Virginia, and in the Ohio Country. The French and Indian War was, for both the settlers and their Indian neighbors, a total war that involved civilians, including women and children, as well as soldiers and warriors.

In some ways the French and Indian War was simply a continuation of the fighting that had gone on in the frontier regions of North America for more than 100 years. Indeed, some scholars use the term *French and Indian wars* to cover a number of smaller wars from 1689 to 1763. The largest proximate cause, however, was probably the influx of British colonists across the Appalachian mountains into western Pennsylvania and New York, in some cases as far as present-day Kentucky and Ohio, to settle and exploit the lands there. As the colonists moved west they drove Native American tribes from the east before them: LENNI LENAPE (Delaware), remnants of the SUSQUEHANNOK and NANTICOKE, the SHAWNEE, and many others. These displaced tribes were under the nominal protection of the IROQUOIS CONFEDERACY, who claimed the Ohio territory by right of conquest. The lands the Indians took over were largely depleted of the game animals they relied on for food because the Ohio Valley and Great Lakes region had been thoroughly trapped and hunted by the French and their Indian trading partners. The French still valued the area, however, because the Ohio River allowed them to ship furs from their Canadian territories to the Mississippi River. A British presence in the Ohio country threatened the fur trade, and, since British trade goods were often of higher quality than those of the French, it also threatened French relations with the tribes of the area.

The major Native American objective in the French and Indian War was to keep the Ohio valley and western lands free of European settlers and FORTIFICATIONS. A secondary objective was to maintain trade with the Europeans, whether the French or the British. Many Indians had already become dependent on European muskets and ammunition for hunting, and these weapons could only be obtained through trade. Members of the Iroquois Confederacy often cast themselves as intermediaries in the trading process, trying to negotiate with both European sides. The Iroquois had built their power for the better part of a century on their ability to play French and British interests against each other.

The French and Indian War—and its European equivalent, the SEVEN YEARS' WAR—began in the backwoods of Pennsylvania. In 1749, after the end of KING GEORGE'S WAR (1744–48), a MIAMI Indian chief named Memeskia (Old Briton) broke with the French at DETROIT and moved south to Sandusky (in present-day Ohio), where he could barter with Pennsylvania traders. The Canadian governor, Jacques-Pierre de Jonquiere, retaliated by beginning a series of French forts from the Great Lakes to the Forks of the Ohio (present-day Pittsburgh, Pennsylvania). On June 21, 1753, a French Indian agent named Charles Langlade launched a raid on the major British trading center at the Miami town of Pickawillany (Piqua, Ohio). Memeskia was killed, and the trading post was destroyed. The British made no response to the destruction of Pickawillany, but they took a dim view of the new French forts rising between Lake Erie and the upper Ohio valley.

During the winter of 1753–54, the state of Virginia dispatched a young officer named George Washington to talk to the French and warn them to leave. The French refused. Washington returned to the area in April 1754 with a force of between 120 and 150 men and a mission to protect the new British fort at the Forks of the Ohio. A Mingo chief called Half King joined him with a small force of the local SENECA. By the time Washington arrived, however, the French had already taken over the fort. On May 28, Washington and Half King combined their forces and ambushed a 33-member reconnaissance force under Ensign Joseph Coulon de Villiers de Jumonville near the fort. Ten French soldiers were killed, including Jumonville.

The French Canadian government, furious at the loss, launched a punitive raid with a force of about 900 French regulars accompanied by their LENNI LENAPE, OTTAWA, ALGONKIN, ABENAKI, and Wyandot allies. On July 3, the French forces surrounded Washington at Great Meadows, Pennsylvania, at a hastily constructed barricade called Fort Necessity. Washington surrendered on July 4, 1754, having lost half his men.

The death of Jumonville and the loss of Fort Necessity marked the beginning of the French and Indian War. The Indians were divided during the course of the war. The Iroquois maintained an official neutrality, but dependent tribes and small bands from the Six Nations sometimes ended up fighting on opposite sides. Warriors from the Seneca, MOHAWK, and ONONDAGA tribes often fought alongside the French, in part because their villages were vulnerable to attacks from French Canada. For instance, a large force of French soldiers and Native American allies participated in the ambush and defeat of Major General EDWARD BRADDOCK at the battle of the Wilderness near Fort Pitt on July 9, 1755. Other Iroquois tribes sided with the British. Some Mohawk, under old Chief HENDRICK, fought as allies of British Indian agent WILLIAM JOHNSON at the battle of LAKE GEORGE (1755) in upstate New York on September 7. The Indians also warred against one another.

The early years of the French and Indian War were hard on the British. On March 27, 1756, a French-led band of soldiers, Indians, and Canadian irregulars attacked Fort Bull near Lake Oneida in New York. The official French report declared that of the British defenders only one woman and a few soldiers had emerged alive. Such incidents caused the colonial frontiers to contract so much that by midsummer of 1756 the Virginia frontier was 150 miles to the east of where it had been before the war.

Fort Oswego, in upstate New York, fell to 3,000 French and Indian troops on August 14, 1756. The French, led by the Marquis de Montcalm, proved unable to control their Indian allies, who killed about 100 soldiers after the garrison surrendered, including 30 taken from the fort's hospital and an unknown number of civilians. Some of the sick who were killed had been infected with smallpox, which the Indians spread to their tribes when they returned home. The following year Fort William Henry met a fate similar to that of Fort Oswego. Frontiersmen struck back in September 1756, when they surprised and destroyed the Ohio Delaware village of Kittanning.

The British tried to recruit their own Indian allies. They met with some initial success among the CHEROKEE in North and South Carolina and in Georgia, asking them for help in protecting the Virginia frontiers from raiding bands of Shawnee and other French allies. The Cherokee, originally friendly to the British, responded with assistance, but they were alienated by anti-Indian attacks from frontier settlers and by the prejudices of regular British army officers. In spring 1759, some British officers assaulted Cherokee women whose husbands were off hunting. As a result, by October 1759 the Cherokee were fighting their own war with the British (see CHEROKEE WAR, 1759–61).

The successes of the French from 1755 to 1757 attracted more Native American allies to their cause. The 1757 election of British Prime Minister William Pitt, who was dedicated to winning the war, changed its course. Pitt greatly increased British commitment to securing North America. He replaced top military commanders, ordered 2,000 troops to make assaults on French Canada, and increased military spending. The interest of the new British prime minister brought results. The French fortress of Louisbourg fell in the summer of 1758. On September 18 of the following year, Quebec, the capital of New France, surrendered to the army of General James Wolfe, effectively ending the French and Indian War. In July 1759, the British took Fort Niagara, Fort Ticonderosa, and Crown Point. Then in September they won the Battle of Quebec. For all intents and purposes this ended the French and Indian Wars. In 1760, Amherst took Montreal. The treaty officially came in 1763.

The cost of the war was tremendous in both money and lives. Thousands had been driven from their homes as refugees, and thousands more had died either in battle, as noncombatant victims of angry fighters, or from disease. Perhaps the greatest casualty of the war, however, was the Iroquois Confederacy itself. For nearly a hundred years it had maintained a neutral position between the French and the English, keeping its independence by playing on their mutual animosity. With the British victory the Iroquois could no longer maintain their intermediate position. In addition, the fact that many of their dependent tribes fought as French allies caused dissent among the Six Nations. The Iroquois lost their dominance in eastern North America, and the French, by the terms of the TREATY OF PARIS (1763), lost their American colonies altogether.

Further Reading

The American Heritage History of the Thirteen Colonies. New York: American Heritage Publishing, 1967.

Axelrod, Alan. *Chronicle of the Indian War.* Englewood Cliffs, N.J.: Prentice Hall, 1994.

Ferling, John. *Struggle for a Continent: The Wars of Early America.* Arlington Heights, Ill.: Harlan Davidson, 1993.

Josephy, Alvin M., Jr. *500 Nations: An Illustrated History of North American Indians.* New York: Alfred A. Knopf, 1994.

Leach, Douglas E. *Arms for Empire: A Military History of the British Colonies in North America, 1607–1763.* New York: Macmillan, 1973.

French Peace Wampum Belt *Native American historical artifact, marking the end of the Beaver Wars between the French in New France (Canada) and the Iroquois Confederacy*

Wampum—woven strings of beads made of shell or glass—was an important symbolic gift among Native Americans, especially among the tribes of the IROQUOIS CONFEDERACY and the French-allied ALGONKIN Indians of the eastern coast. For important meetings, gifts of wampum strung together and woven into belts served as ways of recording the words of the speakers. If a listener refused the wampum, it meant that he or she did not accept the speaker's words as true and refused to accept the terms of the agreement. If the listeners accepted the gift of wampum, however, the strings served as a record of the terms of the agreement. When the Iroquois made peace with the French at Montreal in the GRAND SETTLEMENT OF 1701, the terms of the peace were preserved in wampum belts that still survive in museums and private collections today.

Frenchtown, battle of   See RAISIN RIVER.

G

Gadsden Treaty (1853) *treaty and land purchase arranged between Mexico and the United States*

On December 30, 1853, the U.S. Congress ratified a treaty with Mexico that had far-reaching consequences for the federal government. The Gadsden Treaty had several provisions: it guaranteed the United States the right to build a road or a canal across the Isthmus of Tehuantepec from the Atlantic to the Pacific Ocean, and it authorized the purchase, for $15 million, of a slice of territory—about 55,000 square miles—south of the Gila River, consisting of most of southern Arizona and parts of New Mexico. This territory became known as the Gadsden Purchase in honor of James Gadsden, President Franklin Pierce's minister to Mexico, who had negotiated the treaty.

The Gadsden Purchase marked the end of American continental expansion in the lower 48 states. Jefferson Davis, the main supporter of the purchase, argued that it was valuable because the Gila River valley provided easy railroad access through the Rocky Mountains to the state of California. However, it also brought the United States into conflict with the local Indians, especially the APACHE. U.S. authorities realized that the proposed railway could not become a reality until the Indians were either pacified or defeated. Between 1854 and 1885, the United States had to keep a constant military presence in the area to protect local settlers and miners. Violence between the Apache and U.S. troops did not end until GERONIMO surrendered in September 1886.

Gaines, Edmund P. (1777–1849) *U.S. Army officer*

Born in Virginia and raised in North Carolina and Tennessee, Edmund P. Gaines was commissioned a second lieutenant in 1801. He was stationed at several army posts and was charged with arresting former vice president Aaron Burr on charges of treason in 1807. Gaines received several promotions during the WAR OF 1812 (1812–14) and emerged from that conflict a brevet major general. Along with ANDREW JACKSON, he oversaw U.S. operations during the First SEMINOLE WAR (1816–18).

While commanding the army's Western Division during the 1820s and early 1830s, Gaines set up headquarters at St. Louis in Missouri. Upon the outbreak of the Second SEMINOLE WAR (1835–42), he went to Tampa, Florida, organized a 1,000-strong expeditionary force, and marched into the Florida interior. On February 26, 1836, his troops were ambushed by SEMINOLE Indians on the WITHLACOOCHEE RIVER (1836). The Indians killed five of Gaines's men and wounded nearly 50, including their commander. Unbeknownst to Gaines, however, the government had already assigned WINFIELD SCOTT, with whom he had long feuded over matters of seniority, to take charge of operations in Florida. Conflicts over rank and personality soon paralyzed effective operations.

A court of inquiry censured both Gaines and Scott, who nonetheless continued their bitter feuding. At the outset of the war with Mexico, Gaines, by then in command of the newly reorganized Western Department, was court-martialed on claims that he had illegally called up volunteers; this case was also dismissed. Transferred to command the Eastern Department, he died of cholera at New Orleans in 1849.

Gaines long championed the importance of internal railroad construction to military preparedness along the Indian frontiers. But his vanity, jealousy, and tendency to fixate on trivial matters rendered him less effective than his talents might otherwise have suggested.

Gall (Pizi) (1840–1894) *Hunkpapa Lakota leader in the Sioux Wars*

Gall was born to Hunkpapa Lakota (see SIOUX) parents along the Moreau River in South Dakota. His father died while Gall was still a child, and his mother was very poor. Hunkpapa villagers therefore assisted in raising him. During this time he developed a close friendship with SITTING BULL.

As an adult, Gall was stocky, powerful, and brave; his name soon became synonymous with warfare. When Gall was about 25, he was involved in a skirmish with an army unit south of Fort Berthold, North Dakota. Although bayoneted three times and left for dead, he recovered. In RED CLOUD'S WAR (1866–68), Gall and others devised a strategy for luring their enemies into traps, where they fell easy prey.

By 1866, when Sitting Bull began his defense of the Black Hills, Gall was highly regarded by his fellow warriors as a brilliant tactician. Along with CRAZY HORSE, Gall led the attack against Colonel GEORGE ARMSTRONG CUSTER and his 7th Cavalry at the battle of the LITTLE BIGHORN (1876). Earlier on the day of that battle, Custer's Ree (see ARIKARA) scouts had killed Gall's two wives and three children.

Not long after the Little Bighorn battle, Gall fled to Canada. In 1881 he and about 300 of his followers voluntarily surrendered at the Poplar River Agency in Montana, where Gall lived until his death in 1894.

General Allotment Act (Dawes Act) (1887) *act of Congress by which the Indian reservation system was dissolved and land was parcelled out to individuals*

By the late 1870s, it had become clear to many that the Indian reservation system as it existed was a failure. The system had served as the cornerstone of the federal government's Indian policy for much of the 19th century. However, abuses by Indian agents and the army, as well as the government's frequent practice of moving tribes to undesirable lands, usually left the reservation Indians impoverished and demoralized. Reformers such as SARAH WINNEMUCCA, a PAIUTE who wrote *Life Among the Paiutes,* and Helen Jackson, who wrote *A Century of Dishonor,* informed the nation of the reservation injustices.

The European-American example of individual, rather than tribal land ownership, was seen as by both white Christian reformers and land-hungry settlers as a possible solution to the Indians' plight. Although some reformers were genuinely concerned about the Indians, the idea that no one should own more land than he or she could farm, whether or not the person wished to farm, was always an element in their thinking. And acquisition of more Indian land for settlement was at the forefront of U.S. policy making.

In 1886, Senator Henry Dawes of Massachusetts steered the General Allotment Act, known as the Dawes Act, into law.

The provisions of the act enabled the president to select Indian reservations that were suitable for agriculture or grazing. It also provided for a body, later known as the Dawes Commission, to supervise allotment of reservation land to individual Indians and their families. Following land surveys, the commission assigned 160 acres (based on the 1862 Homestead Act) to each Indian adult. If the lands were suitable only for grazing, the allotments were doubled. If earlier treaties designated larger allotments, the treaties were to prevail. The secretary of the Interior was to approve the allotments and issue a patent, or permit, for each.

To protect the Indians from unscrupulous land speculators, the federal government held each allotment in trust for 25 years for the allotee and his or her heirs. Thus, the Indians could not sell their lands without government approval. The president could also extend the trust period beyond 25 years. Following allotment, the secretary of the Interior was to negotiate with the tribes for the purchase of the remaining, unalloted acreage within their reservations. The Treasury Department held the money from the purchase for each tribe's use and could appropriate it for purposes of the tribe's education and other needs.

The Dawes Act also provided for Indian citizenship. It stipulated that Indians who "accepted" allotment or had voluntarily separated from their tribe and adopted "civilized" lives were U.S. citizens. Those Indians were then subject to the laws of the United States, although each Indian retained rights to tribal or other property. Tribal governments, however, were abolished, and assimilation was forced on many tribespeople.

Unlike white Americans, Indians did not share a family name. In an effort to further break up tribal organization, the commission assigned last names to allottees, as well as surnames whenever they considered Indian names "inappropriate." This process of renaming was a traumatic experience for the Indians, one refused by many even though refusal meant they would not get an allotment of land.

The effects of the General Allotment Act were disastrous. Millions of former reservation acres were lost as "surplus" land. And uneducated about U.S. law and unprepared for shady land dealers, thousands of Indians were cheated out of their allotments. Indians held more than 155 million acres in 1881; by 1900, they retained only 78 million. Following Allotment, many Christian reformers lost interest in the plight of the Indians because they wanted to work with "Native" peoples. The reformers felt that Indians with allotted lands were no longer truly Native but were like white people. These reformers abandoned them to the capriciousness of unethical whites. It was not until the 1920s that the government began to retreat from Allotment and Assimilation as official policies and move toward returning power to tribal governments, and restoring reservation lands.

genocide *deliberate, systematic destruction of political, social, or ethnic groups*

The practice of genocide was very rare among Native Americans before the coming of Europeans. Most Indian cultures

were too apolitical to conduct to completion a deliberate campaign of destruction against their neighbors. There were some exceptions. In the late 16th or early 17th century, for instance, POWHATAN, head chief of the POWHATAN CONFEDERACY, destroyed the tribes of the Kecoughtan and the Chesapeake, who had refused to acknowledge his overlordship. It is believed that Powhatan may have also participated in the destruction of Virginia's Roanoke Colony, the first English settlement in North America, in the 1580s.

Europeans, on the other hand, have been more commonly associated with the destruction, sometimes deliberate, of Native peoples. From the outset, European-style warfare had tended to be more violent than that of the Indians, and the more centralized forms of government among non-Indians made it possible to organize and direct the systematic destruction of their enemies. Colonial expeditions against the PEQUOT and the NARRAGANSETT during the PEQUOT WAR (1636–37) and KING PHILIP'S WAR (1675–76), respectively, were designed to obliterate complete tribes. During PONTIAC'S REBELLION (1763–65), British general Jeffrey Amherst introduced germ warfare against the LENNI LENAPE (Delaware) in an effort to break their siege of Fort Pitt (see SMALLPOX, EFFECTS OF).

But non-Indian governments almost invariably stopped short of officially sanctioning the genocide of an entire people. More often than not, devastating attacks against the homes and villages of Native Americans were intended to force the survivors into becoming slave laborers, giving up their lands, or acknowledging their fealty to the victors. Defeated peoples would then be moved aside, allowing non-Indians to seize their traditional homelands. In the 19th century, for example, the United States established hundreds of reservations designed to facilitate this process.

Such practices had devastating effects. Disease, broken promises, corruption, and the poor lands reserved for Indian use decimated Native American populations. Fired by racial prejudice or beliefs in their own cultural superiority, individual American and European leaders sometimes directed ruthless assaults against the homes and villages of targeted Native American homes and villages. Ironically, forcible and systematic efforts to assimilate Indian peoples into American and European cultures, although often sponsored by those who believed themselves to be "friends" of the Indians, verged on cultural genocide. Such practices took a heavy toll, further demoralizing the very people they were seeking to help.

Geronimo (Goyathlay, "One Who Yawns"; Gokhlayeh) (ca. 1829–ca. 1909) *Chiricahua Apache renowned for his guerrilla tactics and leadership in the Apache Wars*

Goyathlay was born about 1829 near the headwaters of the Gila River in eastern Arizona. By age 10 he had joined hunting expeditions, and by age 17 he had become eligible to go on raiding parties and to war. As a young adult, Goyathlay married an Apache woman, Alope, with whom he had three children.

In 1858 an event occurred that changed Goyathlay's life. That summer a group of Chiricahua Apache camped outside the Mexican town of Kashiyeh (Janos) and traded with the local residents. One day Mexican troops raided the Apache camp, killing men, women, and children, and absconding with horses, weapons, and supplies. When their chief, MANGAS COLORADAS, viewed the scene, he ordered the Apache to retreat to New Mexico and arm themselves. Goyathlay left behind his dead mother, wife, and children, swearing revenge on the Mexican troopers.

Almost exactly a year to the day after the massacre at Kashiyeh, three Apache bands went to war against the Mexicans. They included groups led by Mangas Coloradas, COCHISE, and JUH. Goyathlay served as their guide into Mexico. The Apache confronted the Mexican troops at Arizpe, and Goyathlay was given the honor of directing the battle, which ended in an Apache victory. At Arizpe the Mexicans apparently had prayed to St. Jerome for protection; from then on Goyathlay became known as Geronimo (after Jerome).

While most of the Apache believed the Kashiyeh killings had been properly avenged, Geronimo was not satisfied. He persuaded other Apache to join him in another attack on Mexicans. This became his personal mission. For more than a dozen years Geronimo recruited small numbers of Apache and led them in guerrilla-type raids into Mexico. For the most part, the Indians were after livestock and lightweight booty that they could easily transport back home and divide among their people. Geronimo was wounded on at least seven occasions, but he

From the 1860s through the 1880s, Apache war chief Geronimo was known for his fierce opposition to white settlers and Mexicans. *(Courtesy New York Public Library)*

always managed to survive. Since he also suffered a series of failed raids, he was not considered a war leader at this time.

In 1877, Geronimo was captured by Indian agent John Clum and taken to the reservation in San Carlos, Arizona. He despised the climate and terrain there, and he envied the freedom enjoyed by Loco and VICTORIO, who had recently escaped from the reservation. Although liquor was forbidden on the reservation, Geronimo managed to acquire some. While drunk, he unjustly berated his nephew, who later killed himself. Ashamed and filled with guilt, Geronimo sneaked off the reservation with his family, his ally JUH, and some other Chiricahua and fled into Mexico, where they probably operated out of strongholds deep in the Sierra Madre.

In December 1879, Geronimo and Juh again tired of fighting. They surrendered and were returned to San Carlos. Geronimo, however would never be content with reservation life. Three times during the next decade, Geronimo escaped from reservations (see GERONIMO'S REBELLION, 1881–86). His procedure in each case was the same. He and his renegades left at night, getting a head start on the cavalry. As they traveled they attacked wagon trains, ranches, and travelers unfortunate enough to be along their route. When the cavalry approached, some warriors held them off from defensible positions while the main body pushed on ahead.

Twice, General GEORGE CROOK induced Geronimo to surrender. He surrendered for the last time on September 3, 1886, to Brigadier General NELSON A. MILES. The aging leader was taken to Fort Pickens and Fort Marion in Florida. A year later, Geronimo was moved to Mount Vernon Barracks in Alabama; he was relocated to Fort Sill, Oklahoma, in 1894. At Fort Sill, Geronimo dictated his memoirs to S. M. Barrett, appeared as a celebrity in various cities, and made money by selling signed photographs of himself. He died of pneumonia in 1909 and was buried at the fort.

Much misinformation has been printed about Geronimo. Contrary to popular belief, he was not a chief. By most accounts he was a medicine man who became recognized as a war leader. He was devastated by the death of his wife Alope, but he eventually remarried. Geronimo is pictured as a solitary leader, yet he fought side by side with many of the greatest of Apache warriors, including Cochise, Mangas Coloradas, Mangus, Victorio, Eskiminizin, and Juh. For the most part, Geronimo led only small groups of dissident Apache. He is often portrayed as beloved by Apache and hated by whites. However, many Apache also considered Geronimo a threat. In his autobiography, *Geronimo's Story of His Life* (told to and edited by S. M. Barrett, New York: Garrett Press, 1969), Geronimo admitted that during the 1870s and 1880s he resorted to tricks, lies, and occasionally kidnappings to maintain a fighting force against non-Indians. In the end, it was Apache scouts who were instrumental in capturing him.

Who, then, was Geronimo? For nearly a century he has been portrayed as the most bloodthirsty murderer ever to stain the pages of history, "the worst Indian who ever lived" [Sonnichsen, C. L. "The Remodeling of Geronimo," in *Arizona Highways* 62(9):2–11]. However, the historical pendulum has swung completely. In recent decades Geronimo has been elevated to a position as one of the most formidable of all Indian military leaders of the late 19th century.

Further Reading

Adams, Alexander B. *Geronimo: A Biography.* New York: Da Capo Press, 1971.

Roberts, David. *Once They Moved Like the Wind: Cochise, Geronimo, and the Apache Wars.* New York: Simon and Schuster, 1993.

Sweeney, Edwin R., and Angie Debo. *Great Apache Chiefs: Cochise and Geronimo.* New York: Fine Communications, 1997.

Geronimo's Resistance (Geronimo's Rebellion, The Geronimo Campaign) (1881–1886) *events surrounding Geronimo's escapes from reservations and pursuit by the U.S. Army*

In 1881, Geronimo and many APACHE groups resided on the San Carlos Reservation in Arizona. On August 30 of that year, a prominent medicine man, Nakaidoklini was killed in an arrest attempt that was connected to the battle of CIBECUE CREEK (1881). The subsequent military buildup caused anxiety among the reservation Indians. On September 30, 1881, the Indian leaders JUH, Nachise, and Chato and 74 of their followers fled the reservation toward safety in Mexico. Among them was Geronimo. In April 1882 they returned to the reservation, killed a chief of police, and departed, taking more Indians with them. Soon, after General GEORGE CROOK was reassigned to Arizona and given the task of rounding up the hostile Apache. Crook, realizing that his own soldiers were unfamiliar with the Indians' hiding places, enlisted the service of ALBERT SIEBER and Apache scouts (see SCOUTS). For two years Geronimo's warriors left a trail of destruction throughout the Southwest and into Mexico. Finally, deep in the Sierra Madre of Mexico, Crook negotiated the surrender of Geronimo and nearly 400 Chiricahua Apache in March 1884.

Geronimo and a small band of Chiricahua were taken to FORT APACHE, where most of the Indians were content to live in peace. In spring 1885, however, Geronimo caused a stir regarding denial of the Apaches' right to produce and consume their native alcoholic beverage, tiswin. He also chafed under the prohibition against wife-beating. On May 17 Geronimo, Nachise, and NANA, along with 33 warriors, eight boys of fighting age, and 92 women and children, escaped from the reservation and fled toward Mexico. Again Crook pursued the Apache into the Sierra Madres. On March 25, 1886, at Cañon de los Embudos, Crook negotiated a surrender, with Geronimo agreeing to a two-year imprisonment.

While en route to Fort Bowie, Geronimo, Nachise, and 24 others made a third escape. Crook was humiliated and relieved of his command. He was replaced by General NELSON A. MILES, who pursued the two dozen renegades with an army of 5,000 soldiers. Finally, On September 4, 1886, Geronimo surrendered for the last time; the APACHE WARS (1860–86) were over.

Ghent, Treaty of (1814) *treaty that ended the War of 1812*
The Treaty of Ghent, signed on December 24, 1814, came just two weeks before ANDREW JACKSON's victory over the British at the battle of New Orleans, which signaled the end of the WAR OF 1812 (1812–14). Essentially, the treaty marked a return to the state of affairs that had existed before the war began. The major issues that had begun the war—impressment of American sailors and demands by the British for territorial concessions in Maine and Minnesota—were abandoned, and the warring parties agreed to stop hostilities, release prisoners, and submit territorial disputes to arbitration.

According to the terms of the Treaty of Ghent, the eastern Native Americans were the war's big losers. Initially the British, portraying themselves as protectors of Indian rights, demanded that a separate Indian nation be established in the Old Northwest Territory (which included the present-day states of Ohio, Indiana, Illinois, Wisconsin, and Michigan). Additionally, the British called upon the United States to restore captured Indian territory to its rightful owners. Since most Indian lands had been seized through negotiation or treaty, however, this clause had little meaning. With their principal spokesman, SHAWNEE leader TECUMSEH, dead in the battle of the THAMES (1813), and with the loss of their British allies, the Indian tribes had no one to speak in defense of their rights, although Article IX did demand that the United States come to terms with the various groups. The lack of an Indian homeland led to Andrew Jackson's eventual signing of the INDIAN REMOVAL ACT (1830).

Ghost Dance *messianic religious and social movement among reservation Indians during the late 19th century*
The Ghost Dance originated among the Northern PAIUTE (Numu) Indians of Nevada around the year 1870. Its basis lies in the visions of a Northern Paiute medicine man named Tavibo. Late in his life, Tavibo had a series of visions that he believed were sent to him by the Great Spirit. He believed that one day the earth would rise up and swallow all the whites in the world. Later visions refined Tavibo's view: the earth would swallow all people but Indians—or, in later versions, true believers in Tavibo's visions—would be resurrected into a world restored to its original pristine condition. Tavibo attracted a few believers among the BANNOCK, SHOSHONE, and UTE, but as time passed and his predictions failed to come true, his followers fell away.

Tavibo's ideas were adopted and refined by WOVOKA, another Northern Paiute medicine man commonly believed to be Tavibo's son. In late 1888 Wovoka fell ill and, during an eclipse of the sun on January 1, 1889, had a vision similar to Tavibo's. Like the earlier prophet, Wovoka foresaw the destruction of this world and the coming of a new one, which would restore the purity of life enjoyed by the Indians before the coming of the whites. However, in Wovoka's view, this new world would be inherited by all Indians, including the dead, and they would all live together forever after in harmony. The advent of the new world would also be signified by the coming of a mes-

siah, who would call Indians to repentance: to live in harmony with one another, wash often, and give up white tools and ways, especially FIREARMS and the consumption of alcohol. He called his new religion the Ghost Dance.

Many of Wovoka's adherents believed that the prophet was himself the promised messiah and gave him the title of "Red Man's Christ." Wovoka may in fact have been influenced by Christianity in his concept of the Ghost Dance; in his younger days he lived with a devout white Christian family named the Wilsons on a Nevada ranch. He also discouraged mourning for the dead, who would soon be resurrected. Instead, he recommended ritual meditation, prayer, song, and dance to hasten the day when the messiah would come and to give believers a glimpse of the paradise that they would one day inherit.

The Ghost Dance spread quickly among tribes of the Great Basin and Great Plains. It was especially popular among Indians who had been confined to reservations, including the Shoshone, ARAPAHO, Northern CHEYENNE, and Oglala Lakota (see SIOUX). Members of the Oglala from the Pine Ridge Reservation in South Dakota, including Kicking Bear and Short Bull, traveled west to Nevada to learn the Ghost Dance from Wovoka himself. However, these representatives interpreted the Ghost Dance differently than Wovoka. Seeing the religion as a means of preserving their own Native American culture, the Oglala fastened on the promise that all whites and their tools and weapons would be eliminated.

The Oglala were greatly embittered by the hunger, disease, and long warfare that the Europeans had brought and turned eagerly to the new religion, renewing their self-respect in the process. Natural disasters, including painful losses of cattle and crops, added credence to the belief that the world would soon come to an end. The Oglala Ghost Dancers began making special Ghost Dance shirts embroidered with eagle, buffalo, and morning-star patterns that would, they believed, be impervious to bullets. In addition, they gathered to celebrate the Ghost Dance in great numbers, men and women together holding hands and circling slowly, singing and chanting together without accompaniment.

The U.S. government viewed these gatherings with misgivings. They had not forgotten the role the Oglala had played in the uprisings of the 1870s, and in the battle of the LITTLE BIGHORN (1876) (see SIOUX WARS, 1864–90). Even though the Ghost Dance religion as Wovoka interpreted it discouraged violence, government agents foresaw the possibility of another bloody Indian uprising. Agents began arresting individual Ghost Dancers, charging them with anti-Christian activities. From the government's point of view the Oglala—who were holding large gatherings at which they prayed for the destruction of the white way of life—were moving toward renewed warfare.

Ghost Dancers and government forces finally came into direct conflict in December 1890. The U.S. 7th Cavalry, which had pursued certain Ghost Dancers believed to be armed for revolt, entered the Pine Ridge Reservation on December 15. They had orders to arrest Lakota Chief SITTING BULL, a veteran of the 1876 campaign, who had begun supporting the Ghost Dance religion. Rather than allow the army free run of

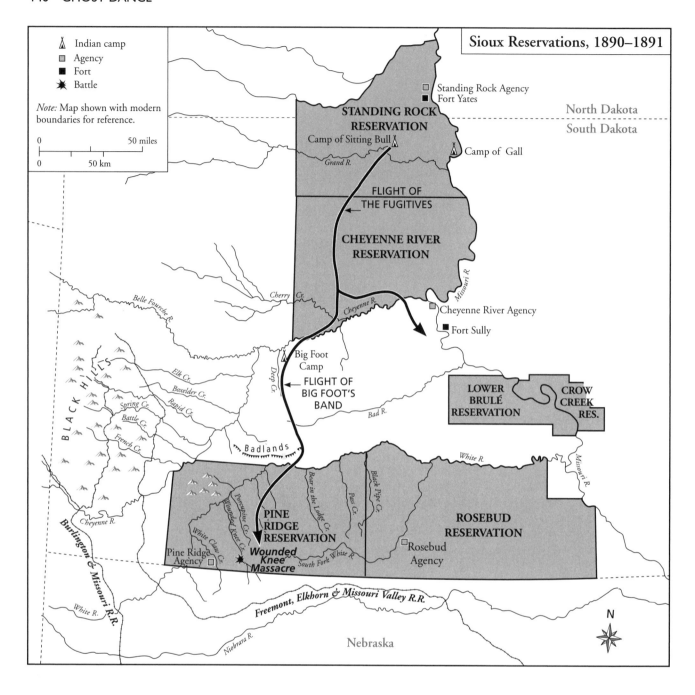

Indian camp
Agency
Fort
Battle

Note: Map shown with modern boundaries for reference.

0   50 miles
0   50 km

Sioux Reservations, 1890–1891

Standing Rock Agency
Fort Yates

North Dakota
South Dakota

STANDING ROCK RESERVATION

Camp of Sitting Bull

Camp of Gall

Grand R.

FLIGHT OF THE FUGITIVES

CHEYENNE RIVER RESERVATION

Belle Fourche R.

Cherry Cr.

Missouri R.

Cheyenne R.

Cheyenne River Agency

Fort Sully

Big Foot Camp

Elk Cr.

Boxelder Cr.

Rapid Cr.

B L A C K   H I L L S

Spring Cr.

Battle Cr.

French Cr.

Deep Cr.

FLIGHT OF BIG FOOT'S BAND

LOWER BRULÉ RESERVATION

CROW CREEK RES.

Bad R.

Badlands

White R.

Missouri R.

Cheyenne R.

Bear in the Lodge Cr.

Pass Cr.

Black Pipe Cr.

PINE RIDGE RESERVATION

ROSEBUD RESERVATION

White Clay Cr.

Porcupine Cr.

Wounded Knee Cr.

Pine Ridge Agency

Wounded Knee Massacre

South Fork White R.

Rosebud Agency

Burlington & Missouri R.R.

White R.

Freemont, Elkhorn & Missouri Valley R.R.

Niobrara R.

Nebraska

N

the reservation, Indian agent James McLaughlin sent a force of 43 reservation policemen to arrest Sitting Bull. One of the Lakota shot a policeman, and in the ensuing confusion Sitting Bull himself was killed. Later in the month, the cavalry rounded up members of Chief BIG FOOT's band near Wounded Knee Creek. On December 29 the Indians were ordered to lay down their weapons. As they did so, however, one of the guns went off. The soldiers opened fire, killing 200 men, women, and children.

The massacre at WOUNDED KNEE (1890) was the last significant armed conflict between U.S. government forces and

Native Americans. It also marked the effective end of the Ghost Dance religion. Wovoka, shocked by the bloodshed, firmly renounced violence and preached peace with non-Indians. Some tribes, including the Arapaho and the Cheyenne, continued to perform the dance or adapted it into other elements of their culture. Wovoka himself long outlived his religion, dying at his home in the Walker River Reservation in Nevada in 1932.

What forces brought about the Ghost Dance, with its mystical beliefs in an Indian paradise? Oglala leader RED CLOUD felt that the dance expressed the unhappiness of the Indians who had lost their free way of life. He said, "We felt that we were mocked in our misery. . . . We were faint with hunger and maddened by despair. We held our dying children, and felt their little bodies tremble as their souls went out and left only a dead weight in our hands. . . . Some [were] talking of the [Messiah]. . . . The people did not know; they did not care. . . . The white men were frightened, and called for soldiers. We had begged for life, and the white men thought we wanted theirs." (Johnson, p. 201)

Further Reading

Johnson, W. Fletcher. *The Red Record of the Sioux, Life of Sitting Bull and the History of the Indian War of 1890–91.* Philadelphia: Edgewood, 1891.

Labarre, Weston. *The Ghost Dance: Origins of Religion.* New York: Doubleday, 1970.

Mooney, James. *The Ghost Dance Religion and the Sioux Outbreak of 1890.* Chicago: University of Chicago Press, 1965.

Utley, Robert M. *The Last Days of the Sioux Nation.* New Haven, Conn.: Yale University Press, 1963.

Gibbon, John (1827–1896) *U.S. Army officer who fought against the Lakota in the War for the Black Hills and participated in the Nez Perce War*

Born in Philadelphia, John Gibbon grew up in North Carolina. After graduating from West Point in 1847, Gibbon served in the Mexican War, but saw no enemy action. He also served in Florida during the SEMINOLE wars. During the CIVIL WAR (1861–65), Gibbon began as an artillery commander and was promoted to brigadier general in the infantry in 1862. He took part in most major battles in the eastern theater of the Civil War, including the battle of Gettysburg, where he was wounded while commanding a division of General WINFIELD SCOTT HANCOCK's corps.

In 1866, Gibbon was assigned to command the 7th Infantry at Fort Ellis in Montana territory. Three months after leaving the fort in March 1876, he commanded one of three columns of troops pursuing SITTING BULL and CRAZY HORSE (see SIOUX WARS) Gibbon's men were part of Brigadier General ALFRED TERRY's column, which rescued the survivors of the 7th Cavalry after the battle of the LITTLE BIGHORN (1876). On August 9, 1877, Gibbon's men attacked the NEZ PERCE encampment of CHIEF JOSEPH at the Big Hole River in Montana (see BIG HOLE; NEZ PERCE WAR). The battle of Big Hole was a draw, and a Nez Perce counterattack forced Gibbon, who was wounded in the engagement, to withdraw his forces. Eventually promoted to general, Gibbon remained in the army until 1891. He died five years later.

Gila River   See MARICOPA WELLS.

Girty, Simon (1741–1818) *non-Indian, raised by Seneca Indians, who defected to the British during the American Revolution*

Simon Girty is traditionally remembered in American history for his role in leading British and Indian troops against American soldiers and civilians during the AMERICAN REVOLUTION (1775–81). However, he was as much a SENECA Indian as he was a settler, and his actions demonstrated his divided loyalties. During the FRENCH AND INDIAN WAR (1754–63), Simon and his brothers James and George were taken from their frontier home by French-allied Native Americans—probably ALGONKIN and HURON. Simon ended up in the hands of the Seneca, westernmost members of the IROQUOIS CONFEDERACY, who were allied with the British against the French. He lived with the Seneca for three years before joining settlers living Fort Pitt (modern Pittsburgh, Pennsylvania). Girty's sympathies, however, remained with the Indians.

In the years between the end of the French and Indian War and the beginning of the American Revolution, Girty worked on the Ohio frontier as a scout and interpreter with the SHAWNEE, Mingo, and other tribes. In 1778 he joined the British in their struggle against American independence, working with Indian agent Alexander McKee at DETROIT to unite the western tribes against their colonial neighbors. Two years later, he and his brothers joined a joint British and Indian assault on RUDDELL'S STATION (1780) in Kentucky. The following year he participated with the Shawnee and LENNI LENAPE (Delaware) in an act of revenge for the destruction of the Lenni Lenape mission village in the GNADDENHUTTEN MASSACRE (1782). The combined forces destroyed Colonel William Crawford's command at Sandusky, Ohio. According to tradition, Girty himself ordered Crawford—wounded and taken captive after the battle—tortured to death. He also led Indian and Pro-British forces in the battles of Bryant's Station (1782) and BLUE LICKS (1782).

After the war Girty remained on the frontier, working with the Shawnee and MIAMI. During LITTLE TURTLE'S WAR (1786–95), he participated in the attack that resulted in ST. CLAIR'S DEFEAT (1791) and served at the battle of FALLEN TIMBERS (1794). For the most part, however, he worked as a diplomat, urging the Indians to reject the terms of the TREATY OF GREENVILLE (1795). When Shawnee and Miami leaders signed the treaty, Girty—who was still wanted by the U.S. authorities for his role in the Revolution—escaped to Canada. He played no significant part in the WAR OF 1812 (1812–14), and was living quietly in Amherstburg, Ontario—across the river from Detroit, Michigan—at the time of his death in 1818. Although he often fought against the Americans, Girty did help bridge the gap between Native American and European cultures.

Gladwyn, Henry (1729–1791) *officer in command of British forces at the siege of Detroit during Pontiac's War*

Henry Gladwyn was born in Derbyshire, England, on November 19, 1729. After entering the British army, he gained wilderness fighting experience while serving in Major General EDWARD BRADDOCK's ill-fated campaign against Fort Duquesne in 1755 at the beginning of the FRENCH AND INDIAN WAR (1754–1763). During the summer of 1762, General Jeffrey Amherst, worried by rumors of unrest among the local Native American tribes, dispatched Gladwyn with reinforcements to DETROIT. He took charge of the 120-man garrison from Captain Campbell.

On May 6, 1762, Gladwyn received word—perhaps through his Ottawa mistress Catherine or from one of the local French Canadians—that Fort Detroit would be attacked in the morning by Chief PONTIAC and his OTTAWA, Ojibwa (see CHIPPEWA), POTAWATOMI, and HURON warriors. Forewarned, Gladwyn refused to admit the Indians to the fort the following morning. He continued to hold off Pontiac until October 1763, when the French informed the Indians that they would not attack the British. Thanks to his experience with Indian ways, Gladwyn was one of the few commanders during PONTIAC'S WAR (1763–65) who resisted Native American assaults and preserved the lives of his garrison. He died on June 22, 1791.

Gnadenhutten Massacre (1782) *massacre of Christian Indians in Ohio by American militia*

In 1771, Moravian missionary David Zeisberger and his LENNI LENAPE (Delaware) Indian converts journeyed westward, leaving the colony of Pennsylvania and entering the Tuscarawas Valley in eastern Ohio to establish an agrarian mission village. Zeisberger called the initial settlement Schoenbrunn, meaning "beautiful Spring" or "well." A substantial migration followed, spreading downriver into two more settlements: Gnadenhutten, or "cabins of grace," and Lichtenua, "pasture of lights." The newcomers were able to live at peace under the protection of the Lenni Lenape tribe. The missions, thanks to the help of Chief White Eyes of the Turkey clan, were a great success.

The AMERICAN REVOLUTION (1775–81) upset the peace. The Lenni Lenape lands were directly on the path from DETROIT to Fort Pitt, the former a British stronghold, the latter an American one. The Moravians, both white and Indian, had selected the difficult and dangerous course of remaining neutral in the conflict. As the revolution progressed, however, the Christian Lenni Lenape came to be viewed as enemies by all other tribes in the region: Mingo to the north, SHAWNEE to the west, and, above all, the powerful Wyandot (HURON), located some 100 miles to the northwest on the Sandusky River and supplied and reinforced by the British at Detroit.

By 1780, substantial French aid was being given to the Americans, and victory in the east was becoming a reality. However, the war in the west still raged, and the prospect of an American victory was not nearly so certain. The Moravians continued to hold to their position of neutrality and would not violate their pacifist beliefs, although with the help of the Lenni Lenape they invited retribution by warning settlers of impending British attacks. In late 1781 they were instrumental in thwarting a British and Wyandot raid on Fort Henry (now Wheeling, West Virginia). Captain Matthew Elliot, leader of the British attack, took his force to the Tuscarawas area and ordered the inhabitants of the mission towns to go with him to the Sandusky River area.

The Indians protested that their corn crop was standing in the field ready to be harvested; without it they would starve. Elliot refused permission to let them stay, but promised that he would personally make sure that they were adequately fed—a promise he never kept. David Zeisberger spent the winter as a prisoner at Detroit, and the Lenni Lenape converts experienced a terrible time in the camps along the Sandusky. By the following spring, they were so close to starvation that the Wyandot relented and allowed 150 to return to their fields in eastern Ohio to harvest and bring back last year's crops.

The Pennsylvania frontier had also gone through a miserable winter. Although the war in the east had ended in victory for the Americans, the British and their Indian allies had gained strength in the west as one tribe after another joined their side. Throughout the winter months, they had raided American settlements in western Pennsylvania. It was under this shadow that the American militia in Pennsylvania heard that the Moravian Lenni Lenape were now harvesting their fields. Forgetting that these Indians had been considered good friends and had provided much useful military intelligence, 400 militiamen made their way to Gnadenhutten to punish the Lenni Lenape for the deeds of other Indians.

Arriving at night, they waited quietly in the woods around Gnadenhutten until morning. When the sun rose, they saw an unexpected number of Indians working in the fields. There could be no possibility of mistaken identity. The Christian Indians had given up painting and decorating their faces and bodies; they dressed like settlers and wore their hair like Europeans. The militiamen carefully surrounded the town so no one could escape. Six Indians were encountered in the woods, one a woman. All were immediately killed.

As the militiamen closed in around the fields, the Indians made no attempt to resist or run away. They had been told that they were to be removed to Fort Pitt, where they would be safe for the rest of the war, and they had no reason to believe otherwise. They went to their chapel where they calmly awaited the start of the journey to Pennsylvania. Meanwhile, outside a kind of kangaroo court was convened and all but 18 of the militiamen voted for the deaths of the Lenni Lenape. The 18 argued that these Indians had been their friends during the Revolution and had been peaceful toward settlers on the frontier. But their pleas were ignored; the sentence was to be carried out promptly.

During this time, the Christian Indians still had no hint of what awaited them. After being notified of their fate, they were allowed to have the night to prepare themselves. The shocked Indians spent the time praying, singing hymns, and offering farewells. At dawn they were dragged by rope, two and three at a time, to several houses in Gnadenhutten, referred to as the "slaughter houses" by the militiamen. There they were executed by blows to the head with a cooper's mallet. In all, 90 Lenni Lenape were murdered—29 men, 27 women, and 34 children. All were scalped and the "prizes" taken home. The survivors of the Moravian mission towns fled to Canada. They settled along the Thames River in southern Ontario, where their descendants live today.

Goyathlay See GERONIMO.

Grande Ronde Valley (1856) *battle during the Yakama War*

On July 17, 1856, militia troops under Colonel Benjamin Franklin Shaw met 300 Walla Walla and CAYUSE warriors in the Grande Ronde Valley in north-central Oregon during the YAKAMA WAR (1855–57). The Indians, exposed in the valley and at the mercy of the militia's long-range artillery, lost 40 after brief fighting; Shaw's losses included five dead and four wounded. The YAKAMA had already extended peace offers, and the defeat at the Grande Ronde Valley encouraged the Walla Walla and Cayuse to do the same.

Grand Settlement of 1701 *peace agreement between the Five Nations of the Iroquois Confederacy and the French colony of New France*

Despite the IROQUOIS CONFEDERACY's agreement among the individual tribes, which dated back to the 16th century, members often disagreed over policies toward their French and British neighbors. Tribes nearer the Great Lakes, such as the SENECA, favored alliances with the French, while those in the east, such as the MOHAWK, preferred to trade with the Dutch or the British. The Iroquois Confederacy resolved the issue by establishing themselves as middlemen in the fur trade, collecting furs from tribes farther west and reselling them to European traders. Hostilities between the Five Nations, which also included the ONONDAGA, ONEIDA, and CAYUGA, and traders and colonists in New France began when French Canadians established their own connections with western tribes, cutting the Iroquois out of the competition. The struggle between the two groups lasted for most of the 17th century.

In the early years of the French occupation of New France, the Iroquois had been at peace, if not allied, with the French Canadians. In 1624, for instance, representatives of the Five Nations loaded 35 canoes filled with furs and traveled to the French settlement of Lachine to trade. However, this relationship ended in 1627, partly because of rivalry with the local Montagnais tribe. In addition, a British blockade at the mouth of the Saint Lawrence—part of a larger war against France—cut off the supply of manufactured goods. The Iroquois responded by taking their furs to Dutch trading stations in New Amsterdam, particularly Fort Orange (now Albany).

Thanks to their central position in what would later become New York State, the Iroquois enjoyed easy access to the rich fur-bearing lands of the Great Lakes, the Ohio valley, and the upper Mississippi. Their traditions of raiding and hunting, combined with their desire for European weapons and other trade goods, led the Iroquois to try to dominate all trade in skins between the Native Americans of the interior and the European settlements on the coast. The French, who preferred to establish their own contacts with the interior tribes, resisted Iroquois interference and encouraged other tribes to disrupt this trade whenever possible.

The Iroquois responded to the French resistance with violence. In 1648–49 the Five Nations directed raids in the area around Montreal against Christianized HURON Indians and their French Jesuit teachers. The Jesuits were tortured to death; the Huron were left to starve among their burned fields. Many Huron fled the region, settling among the French near Quebec or farther to the west along the shores of Lake Superior. Between 1665 and 1667 the French counterattacked, directing punitive raids against the Mohawk and building a string of forts linking New France to Mohawk territory near the Hudson valley. In 1669 the Iroquois agreed to a truce that lasted 16 years and allowed French missionaries and traders access to the Great Lakes and the Mississippi valley.

Not until the outbreak of KING WILLIAM'S WAR (1689–97) and the destruction of the village of Lachine in 1689 did the Five Nations again move against the French. For the next seven years, Iroquois tribes and French Canadians fought one another in a series of increasingly bitter raids, seizing PRISONERS, killing, looting, and burning. In 1696 Louis de Buade de Frontenac led a massive retaliatory strike into the heart of Iroquois country, devastating the territory of the Oneida and the Onondaga. With the French successes in western New York, the pro-French party gained strength. Finally, during summer 1700, the peace party among the Iroquois opened negotiations with the French and their Native American allies.

The peace, known as the Grand Settlement, was ratified in July 1701 at Montreal. About 1,300 French Indian allies, French Canadians, and Iroquois emissaries met together and declared a lasting peace. At the same time other representatives from the Five Nations were in Albany, renewing the COVENANT CHAIN agreement with the British. Thanks to skillful negotiations, the Iroquois were able to maintain a sometimes uneasy neutrality between the French and the British for a good part of the 18th century.

Grant, Ulysses S. (1822–1885) *senior Union general during the Civil War president of the United States during the Indian wars*

Ulysses S. Grant served as general-in-chief of the U.S. Army during the last year of the CIVIL WAR (1861–65). He became president of the United States in 1869, serving in this office during many of the major battles between the U.S. army and various Native American groups.

Grant was born in Ohio on April 27, 1822; his name at birth was Hiram Ulysses Grant. While attending West Point, Grant excelled only in horsemanship and graduated 21st out of the 39 members of the class of 1843. After graduation, he was assigned to the infantry. He served well in the Mexican War but developed a drinking problem while serving in quiet western posts in the peacetime army. He resigned from the army in 1854 but joined an Illinois volunteer regiment after the outbreak of the Civil War. Grant proved to be a very capable commander and rose quickly in rank. Given command of all Union armies in 1864, he played a major role in winning the war for the North.

Between the end of the Civil War and Grant's inauguration as president in 1868, most of his attention was focused on the aftereffects of the Civil War—the Reconstruction of the South. WILLIAM TECUMSEH SHERMAN, second in command of the army, became the chief architect of military policy under President Grant. Grant's administration began with what came to be called GRANT'S PEACE POLICY, an attempt to use peaceful persuasion to get the Indians to adopt mainstream American culture. However, supporters of this policy failed to note that Grant had also reserved the right to use force if peace did not work.

Grant's administration became known for the generally poor quality of his political appointments. Corruption and incompetence were rampant. This held true for employees of the Indian Bureau and other officials dealing with Indians. Poor conditions on Indian reservations, major food shortages, and problems with Indian agents during his presidency played major roles in provoking Indians to leave reservations and try to resume their old ways of life. Some groups considered that

Ulysses S. Grant, president of the United States, 1869–1877, was known for his peace policy toward Native Americans. (*Courtesy New York Public Library*)

since the army would react, and war was inevitable, they might as well start the fighting themselves.

Grant's peace policy was not successful, and his administration faced a large portion of the major post-Civil War Indian wars including the major campaigns of the SOUTHERN PLAINS WAR (1868–69), the RED RIVER WAR (1874–75), and part of the SIOUX WARS (1854–90). One of the last events of Grant's administration was the defeat of GEORGE ARMSTRONG CUSTER and most of the 7th Cavalry at the battle of the LITTLE BIGHORN (1876) by the Lakota (see SIOUX), CHEYENNE, and their allies.

Grant's Peace Policy (1869–c. 1874) *popular term for a civilian-oriented approach toward "civilizing" American Indian tribes*

Grant's Peace Policy can be said to have started in January 1869, during the four-month period between ULYSSES S. GRANT's election as president and his taking office. As president-elect, Grant was given numerous suggestions and requests for the incoming administration. On January 25, 1869, he met with a group of Quakers who had come down to Washington, D.C., from their national convention in Baltimore. The Quaker convention had passed resolutions urging an Indian policy based on peace and Christianity rather than military power. The Quakers urged the president-elect to adopt such a policy and to appoint men of religious conviction as Indian agents. Grant supposedly agreed and asked for the names of Quakers to appoint. However, he is also quoted as having said that those Indians who did not embrace the policy would find the administration ready to resort to war, if this proved necessary.

Grant was open-minded about treatment of the Indians. Since 1865, he had relied on the judgement of his friend and second-in-command, WILLIAM TECUMSEH SHERMAN, who was very anti-Indian. However, Grant also listened to his aide ELY PARKER, a mixed-blooded Seneca and supporter of a milder policy. Military measures over the several previous decades, ranging from passive fortifications to active campaigns, did not seem to have worked. They had also provoked public outrage. As a result, Grant tried a more peaceful, political approach to Indian policy.

Grant's Peace Policy was more a catch-all term than a specific policy. Most measures undertaken arose from particular circumstances and many did not work. The basic policy aims were to get the Indians to go to reservations, adopt mainstream American culture, and give up their traditional Indian ways of life. It demanded that Indians give up free-roaming hunting as well as the warrior ethic of extreme self-reliance and proving one's self in combat. In essence, the policy aimed to make Indians like white people. Many Indians resisted these goals, and the U.S. military also disliked the policy. This resulted in frequent conflicts with the idealistic but inexperienced and often naive Christian Indian agents. Growing corruption in Grant's administration, including problems with several heads of the Indian Bureau, lowered public opinion of anything connected with the administration, including support for Grant's Peace Policy. In the end, the cultural clash between non-Indians and Indians was too great for the policy to work.

Grattan, John L. (ca. 1830–1854) *U.S. Army officer instrumental in starting the Sioux Wars*

As a young second lieutenant fresh from West Point in 1853, John Grattan was assigned to Fort Laramie in Wyoming. Eager to show his prowess, Grattan spoke constantly of fighting Indians and had little respect for the Plain Indians' military ability. He boasted that given 30 men he could defeat the whole CHEYENNE nation. He also bragged about what he would do to the Lakota (see SIOUX) if given the opportunity. He got his chance in August 1854, when he provoked a confrontation with a local tribe. Facing a combined force of at least 200 from a Brulé Lakota (see SIOUX) village, Grattan and 29 of his men were killed. Angry warriors mutilated most of the bodies; Grattan's body was found with 24 arrows protruding from it and was identified only by his watch.

See also GRATTAN'S DEFEAT, 1854.

Grattan Defeat (Grattan Fight, Grattan Massacre) (1854) *event that precipitated war with the Lakota Sioux in 1855*

The Grattan fight began in August 1854, when Mormon emigrants traveling to Utah passed near camp of Brulé Lakota (see SIOUX) near Fort Laramie, Wyoming. A cow escaped from the Mormon group and was subsequently shot and butchered by a Miniconjou Lakota man. When the Mormons reached the fort, they reported the incident but said that the Indian had stolen the cow. The Brulé head-chief, Conquering Bear, also rode to the fort to give his version of the incident. Although Conquering Bear suggested waiting until the Indian agent arrived, the young officers at the fort, especially Second Lieutenant JOHN L. GRATTAN, wanted immediate action.

On August 19, MAN-AFRAID-OF-HIS-HORSES, head chief of the Oglala Lakota arrived. By then Lieutenant Grattan was preparing to arrest the Miniconjou who had killed the cow. With 29 volunteers and two howitzers, Grattan brazenly headed for the Sioux camp, which included 80 Brulé and 20 Miniconjou lodges. Man-Afraid-of-His-Horses accompanied the soldiers to help Conquering Bear prevent a fight. When Grattan reached the camp, he lined up the infantry and faced his howitzers toward the Indian lodges. Conquering Bear came from his camp and, together with Man-Afraid-of-His-Horses, talked to both parties, trying to get the Miniconjou man to surrender and Grattan to leave until the Indian agent arrived. The tribesman would not submit to arrest, saying that he would rather die. He asked the other Lakota to leave and allow the soldiers to deal with him alone. Several Lakota later reported that the post interpreter, who was drunk at the time and shouting insults, was not translating their words correctly.

Soon Grattan became impatient and ordered his men to fire some shots toward the Miniconjou lodges. As Conquering Bear leapt forward, shouting for the Lakota not to return the fire, the soldiers fired again and discharged the howitzers. Conquering Bear was mortally wounded. The Lakota returned fire, and Grattan and the men near the howitzers were killed instantly. The remaining soldiers fled, with the Brule and Miniconjou following. As these soldiers retreated, the Lakota in the rear caught up with them, and Oglala from a nearby camp charged from the front. Caught between the two groups of Indians, the remainder of Grattan's men were killed.

The Lakota looted trading posts in the area and the left for their hunting grounds. Conquering Bear's relatives, however, sought revenge for the killing of his people. When news of the incident reached the Missouri frontier in September, Conquering Bear was blamed for leading the soldiers into a trap, and it was reported incorrectly that all the Lakota were hostile. The army did not retaliate, and some Lakota returned to raiding in the spring of 1855. By the following September, however, General WILLIAM S. HARNEY marched after the Lakota, and the ensuing hostilities marked the true beginning of the SIOUX WARS (1854–90).

Great Swamp Fight (1675) *crucial battle between New England colonists and the Narragansett during King Philip's War*

In early December 1675, a colonial army had gathered at Wickford, Rhode Island, under the command of Governor Josiah Winslow of Plymouth colony. But rather than attack the local WAMPANOAG Indian, with whom the colonists were involved in KING PHILIP'S WAR (1675–76), Winslow pushed forward in a blinding snowstorm to attack a peaceful NARRAGANSETT stronghold located at a frozen swamp at Kingston, Rhode Island.

On December 18, 1675, Winslow and his army arrived to find an extremely formidable force of Indians. Prior to the arrival of the main body of troops, two colonial companies had attacked the Indian stronghold but were repelled. A second assault was launched successfully but at a terrible price for both sides. In the fierce fighting, 80 of Winslow's soldiers were killed, including 14 of his company commanders. Indian losses were placed at 600, half of whom were women and children. One of Winslow's commanders, BENJAMIN CHURCH, begged the soldiers to leave the wigwams in place because the wounded would need them for shelter during the bitter night. His plea fell on deaf ears and soldiers torched the structures, burning alive many Indians who were hiding within them.

With the loss of so many commanders and a shortage of supplies, Winslow decided not to carry the fight any farther, and he led the army in retreat to Wickford. This battle inflicted heavy losses on the Narragansett, who lost 300 warriors and 20 chiefs. More important, it deprived them of greatly needed supplies. The Great Swamp Fight rendered the Narragansett helpless against the colonists for some time.

Great Wahoo Swamp (1835) *one of many bitter exchanges between settlers and Seminole Indians*

In addition to the problem of removing the Seminole from Florida, the United States had to contend with thousands of fugitive slaves who had sought refuge with the Indians. Although many blacks served the Indians as slaves, they were allowed more freedom often living among the Seminole in their own villages. There were also intermarriages between Seminole tribes people and blacks. African Americans were therefore apt to side with Indians in a conflict, fearing they would be returned to white slave owners should the tribes be defeated. Raiding parties frequently entered Florida on Indian land to recapture fugitive slaves, resulting in great anger among the Indian people.

By the provisions of the TREATY OF TAMPA, signed in September 1823, the Seminole were required to surrender all lands in Florida. In exchange, they would be moved to a reservation located in the central part of that territory. Moving the Seminole, however, proved to be a difficult task. The United States negotiated their removal through Indian Agent Wiley Thompson and Brevet General DUNCAN L. CLINCH, commander of all regular troops in Florida. In 1835 Clinch ordered the Seminole to report for removal at specific points in Florida. With this order he added a strong warning that if the Seminole did not comply, they would be removed by force. Clinch commanded 14 companies of regulars, and when the Indians failed to report, he dispatched his troops to round them up.

On December 28, 1835, Indian Agent Wiley Thompson and an army officer were murdered by a group of Indians led by Seminole leader OSCEOLA. On the same day, a few miles north of the WITHLACOOCHEE RIVER near the Great Wahoo Swamp, a group of Seminole and blacks ambushed and nearly annihilated a company of troops commanded by Major Francis Dade. Dade and his troops were on their way from Fort Brooke to Fort King to remove the Seminole. During the encounter, all but three officers and 102 soldiers were killed; Indian losses were unknown. This act of defiance proved to be the beginning of the Second SEMINOLE WAR (1835–42)

See also INDIAN REMOVAL ACT.

Greenville, Treaty of (1795) *treaty to negotiate peace between the U.S. government and Indian tribes in the Old Northwest Territory and to obtain land cessions*

A year after the battle of FALLEN TIMBERS (1794), in which the American general ANTHONY WAYNE defeated Indian forces in Indiana, Wayne called a meeting of tribes in the Old Northwest Territory to conclude a peace treaty. Wayne was also instructed by the government to obtain the surrender of much of the Indians' lands in present-day Ohio and Indiana.

In the summer of 1795, some 1,130 chiefs and warriors assembled at Fort Greenville in western Ohio. The Indian leaders who attended represented a number of tribes, including the LENNI LENAPE (Delaware), SHAWNEE, OTTAWA, CHIPPEWA, MIAMI, KICKAPOO, and POTAWATOMI. After several days of talks and assurances of future peace on both sides, Indian leaders and Wayne signed the Treaty of Greenville on August 3, 1795. In addition to agreeing to peace, the tribes ceded an enormous part of their territory: two-thirds of modern Ohio, a large area of eastern Indiana, and other lands in Michigan. For ceding eastern and southern Ohio the tribes were to receive $20,000 in goods and were promised an annual payment of $9,500.

Part of the treaty included the establishment of a boundary between lands the Indians would retain and those open to settlement. Called the Greenville Line, the boundary ran along the Cuyahoga River to the Maumee and Wabash Rivers to a point on the Ohio River opposite the mouth of the Kentucky River. The tribes were to retain lands west and north of the Greenville Line, with the exception of DETROIT and several French settlements to the north. The United States also reserved 150,000 acres of land around the Ohio River in Kentucky, which was given as a reward to veterans of the AMERICAN REVOLUTION (1775–81) who fought with General GEORGE ROGERS CLARK in the region.

The Indians believed that the Treaty of Greenville had guaranteed their remaining lands in the Old Northwest Territory and that the established boundary between the tribes and non-Indian settlement was secured. But in fact the U.S. government was simply buying a period of peace in its efforts to expand its frontiers westward to the Mississippi River. Among Wayne's instructions was a letter from the U.S. secretary of war observing that more Indian lands could be obtained as settlers advanced onto the frontiers. The Treaty of Greenville was therefore of major significance in pushing the frontier westward. The vast territory beyond the Ohio valley was opened to settlement, with little fear of conflict with Indian tribes.

The Treaty of Greenville also set a precedent for objectives in future treaties with Indians—that is, obtaining cessions of land, advancing the frontier through white settlement, and obtaining more cessions through treaties. With the tribes' surrender of most of Ohio, settlers began entering the Northwest Territory in greater numbers. In the near future, more treaties would further diminish the Indians' territory.

Grey Lock's War   See DUMMER'S WAR.

Guadalupe Hidalgo, Treaty of (1848) *treaty in which Mexico ceded land to the United States in exchange for money and protection from raiding Indian tribes*

During the first half of the 19th century, APACHE Indians raided northern Mexico with virtual impunity. Mexicans responded by initiating an extermination policy against their foes by offering pesos in exchange for Apache scalps. This policy, however, failed to have the desired effect, and raiding continued.

Meanwhile, Mexico became embroiled in a war with the United States in 1846. When Mexico lost the war in 1848, representatives signed the Treaty of Guadalupe Hidalgo, which recognized Texas independence. It also stated that, in exchange for lands ceded to the United States (including what is now California, Nevada, Utah, and portions of Colorado, Arizona, and New Mexico), the American government would pay $15 million, assume about $3 million that Mexico owed Americans, and end the incursions of tribes (notably the Apache) into Mexican territory. The treaty stipulated that if the government was unable to stop the raids, the United States would punish the Indians with the same diligence as if the offenses were committed against its own citizens. Thus, the U.S. government had assumed the responsibility of regulating the Apache.

Anthropologist and historian Edward Spicer summarized the illogic of the situation: "It also became apparent to the Apache that the Anglos had adopted a position which was totally without reason, namely, that the Anglos, by virtue of having conquered the Mexicans, in some way became proprietors of Apache territory. The Mexicans had never conquered the Apaches and hence how could the Anglos, as a result of conquering the Mexicans, lay claim to Apache land?" The Treaty of Guadalupe Hidalgo led to increased friction between the Americans and the Apache. By 1860 the tensions had erupted into the APACHE WARS (1860–86).

Further Reading

Spicer, Edward. *Cycles of Conquest: The Impact of Spain, Mexico, and the United States on the Indians of the Southwest, 1533–1960.* Tucson: University of Arizona Press, 1962.

Guipago   See LONE WOLF.

H

Hackensack
tribe of Indians that inhabited much of northern New Jersey

An agricultural people, the Hackensack congregated in river meadows, where they grew corn, beans, and squash. As members of the Delaware Confederacy, (see LENNI LENAPE) they shared a belief in the Great Spirit, which permeated all existence.

Like most nearby tribes, the Hackensack at first coexisted peacefully with the Dutch settlers of New Amsterdam (now New York). Relations worsened, however, with the appointment of Willem Kieft as director-general of the colony in 1637. Resolved to "make the savages wipe their chops," Kieft launched a surprise attack on February 25, 1643, on a village of Hackensack on Staten Island. The ensuing massacre of 80 Native Americans, who had been asleep, led to Indian reprisals and then open warfare (see KIEFT'S WAR, 1642–45).

Like other tribes in the region, the Hackensack were pushed westward by encroaching colonial settlements, especially following the English takeover of New York in 1664. The tribe eventually ended up in Indian Territory (present-day Oklahoma).

Hallalhotsoot
See LAWYER.

Hancock, Winfield Scott
(1824–1885) *U.S. Army officer in command of troops on the Southern Plains between 1867 and 1868*

Winfield Scott Hancock was born in Montgomery County, Pennsylvania. After graduating from West Point in 1844, Hancock served in the Mexican War. Before the start of the CIVIL WAR (1861–65), he fought against the SEMINOLE in Florida, served in conflicts in Kansas during the mid-1850s, and was assigned garrison duty in southern California. During the Civil War he served in most major conflicts in the east, including the battle of Gettysburg, in which he was wounded. At the end of the war Hancock, now a major general, was given command of the Department of the Missouri, which consisted of Missouri, Kansas, Colorado, and the territory of New Mexico.

In early 1867, as a result of the FETTERMAN FIGHT (1866), Hancock was ordered to establish a strong military presence in Kansas. The army wanted to show the Indians that the federal government was willing to use force to protect travelers on the Santa Fe Trail and workers building the Kansas-Pacific Railroad. In the spring of 1867, Hancock met leaders of the Southern CHEYENNE, Southern ARAPAHO, COMANCHE, KIOWA, and Lakota (see SIOUX). The military wanted the Indians to restrict their hunting to assigned areas south of the Arkansas River, under terms of the LITTLE ARKANSAS RIVER TREATIES (1865).

When Cheyenne DOG SOLDIERS and their Lakota allies, concerned about the presence of Hancock's men, withdrew from their village near Fort Dodge, Hancock saw this as the start of an Indian offensive. He therefore ordered GEORGE ARMSTRONG CUSTER and the 7th Cavalry to destroy the village, thus provoking a war. Indian war parties retaliated by conducting raids in western Kansas and eastern Colorado—effectively cutting off transportation in the area through the summer of 1867. Custer and the 7th Cavalry tried to pursue the Indians, but were halted by a lack of supplies. Soon afterward, Hancock and General PHILIP HENRY SHERIDAN switched jobs. Hancock took command of the Fifth Military District, which was based in New Orleans but also included Texas, and Sheridan took command of the Missouri Division. Hancock later commanded the Department of Dakota, the Division of the Atlantic, and the Department of the East, where he was when he died in 1886.

Hancock's War   See WAGON BOX FIGHT.

Harmar, Josiah (1753–1813)   *U.S. Army officer best remembered for his defeat at the hands of Miami leader Little Turtle*

Born in Philadelphia, Joseph Harmar served in the Pennsylvania regiment during the AMERICAN REVOLUTION (1775–81). After the war, Harmar had the honor of carrying the ratified TREATY OF PARIS (1783) to France.

Upon his return from France, Harmar was made commander of the army and assigned to the Old Northwest Territory. He also became the U.S. government's Indian agent to the tribes of the Ohio valley. While on the Ohio frontier, Harmar took part in the negotiations of the FORT MCINTOSH TREATY (1785) and then commanded the forces responsible for driving Indians from ceded lands and evicting settlers from Indian territories as required under the terms of the treaty. In 1790, he led an expedition against a coalition of Native American tribes led by MIAMI chief LITTLE TURTLE (see also LITTLE TURTLE'S WAR). Harmar burned several villages and destroyed corn crops, but a detachment of his army was destroyed. Overall, the campaign was a failure (see HARMAR'S DEFEAT.) Although a court of inquiry following the disaster cleared him of charges, Harmar was replaced by ARTHUR ST. CLAIR. With his military command over, Harmar resigned from the army in 1792.

Harmar's Defeat (1790)   *first battle in Little Turtle's War*
JOSIAH HARMAR was a trained army officer who had learned warfare during the AMERICAN REVOLUTION (1775–81) under Generals George Washington and Henry Lee. He was also an experienced diplomat, having been present during the negotiations leading to the TREATY OF PARIS (1783) that ended the war. Under the federal government established by the Articles of Confederation, Harmar became an Indian agent in the Ohio valley country, administering treaties that had been negotiated with local tribes, evicting settlers who were squatting on Indian lands and Indians who were still residing on lands ceded to the United States. In 1789, Harmar—recently made a brigadier general—established Fort Washington on the Ohio River, at the present site of Cincinnati.

Around this time the Indians in the Ohio territory, including the SHAWNEE and the MIAMI, were growing restless (see LITTLE TURTLE'S WAR). Many of them were members of tribes who had been forced from their homes by treaties negotiated with European settlers. The Shawnee, in particular, had been

driven westward from Virginia in the aftermath of LORD DUNMORE'S WAR (1773–74). Led by competent fighters such as LITTLE TURTLE and BLUE JACKET, and supplied by the British from their bases in Canada, the Indians expressed their resentment by raiding towns and homesteads in the Northwest Territory and what is now Kentucky. President Washington ordered Harmar to assemble his few regular army soldiers, along with about 1,500 local militia, and move against the tribes in order to stop the raids. In April 1790, Harmar and his militia marched 170 miles north from Fort Washington, looking for Indian raiders. He found none and succeeded only in burning some deserted villages. He started north again in the fall, with the objective of eliminating crops, villages, and warriors.

Harmar reached the Maumee valley near what is now Fort Wayne, Indiana, without mishap. On October 18, however, he ran into an ambush planned and executed by Little Turtle. Over the next four days, Harmar and his men tried to extricate themselves from the trap. In separate fights, on October 18 and 22, the undisciplined Kentucky militia panicked when the Miami, who pretended to run away to lure the settlers closer, turned on them. In all, Harmar lost 150 men in the clash—about one-tenth of his entire force. He had to lead his disorganized troops in a retreat to Fort Washington, suffering harassing attacks from the Indians all the way.

Harmar's defeat on the banks of the Maumee River had several effects on warfare in the Ohio country. Harmar himself appeared before a military court to defend his conduct in the battle. The court acquitted him of all charges, but he was replaced as commander by another Revolutionary War veteran, ARTHUR ST. CLAIR. Little Turtle and his followers were emboldened by the army's failure, and during 1791 they increased the number and intensity of their raids on settlements in what are now Ohio, Indiana, and Kentucky.

Harney, William S. ("Mad Bear") (1800–1889)
U.S. Army officer who participated in many significant battles with Native Americans

As a colonel, Tennessee native William Harney participated in the BLACK HAWK WAR (1832) and the Second SEMINOLE WAR (1835–42). After the GRATTAN DEFEAT (1855) Secretary of War Jefferson Davis placed Colonel William Harney in command of pacifying the Lakota (see SIOUX). "By God I'm for battle—no peace," Harney insisted. Harney routed Little Thunder's Brulé and some Oglala in the Battle of Blue Water (1855) in August. The following year he met with Lakota chiefs and coerced them into signing a treaty of such harsh terms that all knew it could not be met. The treaty was never ratified by Congress. Harney's appointments of head chiefs and subchiefs as representatives of their tribes became a route through which the government ultimately dealt with the Indians.

In 1858, Harney was promoted to brigadier general and later given command of the Department of the West. Married to a wealthy Missourian and friends with many slaveowners,

Harney refused to move against pro-secessionist forces at the outset of the CIVIL WAR (1861–65). He was relieved from command in late May 1861, and he retired in August 1863 but was honored with a final promotion, to major general, in March 1865. Following the Civil War, Harney served as a member of a commission that held a peace conference at Fort Smith, Arkansas, with the Five Civilized Tribes (CHEROKEE, CREEK, CHOCTAW, CHICKASAW, and SEMINOLE), most of whom had fought on the side of the Confederacy. In 1867, Harney served on the U.S. Indian Peace Commission that was responsible for the MEDICINE LODGE TREATY (1867). A year later, Harney was among the negotiators and signers of the FORT LARAMIE TREATY (1868).

Harney lived in retirement in St. Louis, Missouri, and Pass Christian, Mississippi. In 1884, he married his housekeeper and nurse, Mary Cromwell St. Cyr. He died at Orlando, Florida.

Harrison, William Henry (1773–1841) *commander of U.S. troops and governor of Indiana Territory during Tecumseh's Rebellion and the War of 1812, and U.S. president*

The son of a wealthy Virginian family, William Henry Harrison studied medicine in Philadelphia. He embarked on an army career after the defeat of JOSIAH HARMAR by LITTLE TURTLE and his allies in 1791 (see LITTLE TURTLE'S WAR). Harrison was posted to Fort Washington (at present-day Cincinnati, Ohio) and became aide-de-camp to General ANTHONY WAYNE during the campaign that culminated in the battle of FALLEN TIMBERS (1794). He was also present during the negotiations leading to the TREATY OF GREENVILLE (1795). Harrison later resigned from the army and in 1800 was appointed governor of the Indiana Territory.

While serving as territorial governor of Indiana, Harrison came into conflict with SHAWNEE leaders and brothers TECUMSEH and TENKSWATAWA. In 1804, in violation of the terms of the Greenville treaty, he negotiated with leaders of the SAUK and FOX (Mesquakie) tribes for land deals that were highly favorable to the U.S. government. He acquired much of present-day Missouri, Illinois, and Wisconsin at a price of about one cent an acre. Another land deal, set forth in the treaty of Fort Wayne in 1809, obtained most of central Indiana for the United States. Tecumseh, who believed that Native Americans held all land in common, met with Harrison twice at Vincennes, Indiana, in 1810 and 1811, to protest the land sales. On November 7, 1811, Harrison brought a force of 1,000 men to Tecumseh's home of Prophetstown and drove his allies off in the battle of TIPPECANOE (1811). Nevertheless, Indian protests over the terms of the deals later led to the BLACK HAWK WAR (1832).

During the WAR OF 1812 (1812–14), Harrison served as a brigadier general, leading campaigns against Tecumseh and the British in the Great Lakes region. After the defeat of nearly a third of his army at the RAISIN RIVER (1813), he built Fort Meigs (near present-day Toledo, Ohio) and defended it against

Election propaganda such as this 1840 lithograph recalled General William Henry Harrison's Indian-fighting days of the 1810s. He became president of the United States in 1841. *(Courtesy Library of Congress)*

British assaults throughout the summer. In the fall that year, his troops recaptured DETROIT and, on October 5, defeated the combined British and Indian troops at the Battle of the THAMES (1813), in which Tecumseh was killed.

Harrison later served as a U.S. representative and senator from Indiana, campaigning on the basis of his victory over the Shawnee. In his successful 1840 presidential campaign, he recalled his Indian-fighting reputation in the campaign slogan "Tippecanoe and Tyler, Too." He died less than six months after his inauguration, leaving Indian policies up to his successor, John Tyler.

Hartford Treaty of 1638 See NARRAGANSETT TREATY.

Hayfield Fight (1867) *military engagement during Red Cloud's War*

On August 1, 1867, while on their way to attack FORT C. F. SMITH on the BOZEMAN TRAIL, an estimated 500 CHEYENNE warriors encountered a group of 12 civilians and 19 soldiers mowing hay in a hayfield some two miles from the fort. The civilians and soldiers took refuge in a log corral, but their commanding officer was killed almost immediately. Though outnumbered 20 to 1, the soldiers were armed with new breechloading rifles, whose rapid rate of fire allowed them to fend off four separate charges by the Indians. They were finally relieved after six hours by men from the fort. By the time the battle was over, three soldiers had been killed and two wounded; Indian casualty estimates vary wildly.

Although many soldiers magnified the importance of this victory and another the following day against the Teton Lakota (see SIOUX; WAGON BOX FIGHT; RED CLOUD'S WAR), a more realistic General WILLIAM TECUMSEH SHERMAN was alarmed by the number of warriors mustered by the Native Americans in the two engagements and the implications of this for future confrontations in the region.

Hays, John C. (1817–1883) *western scout best known for his work with the Texas Rangers*

Born in Tennessee, John Coffee Hays worked as a surveyor before going to Texas in 1836 to join in that state's fight for liberation from Mexican rule. After the struggle had ended, the TEXAS RANGERS were expanded in 1840. Hays was made a captain of one of the new companies and was quickly promoted to major.

Organized four years before, the Rangers had begun as an irregular force of lightly armed cavalry. They might have remained just that except for Hay's influence. His company achieved a level of discipline, martial skill, and effectiveness that became a model for the entire force. The Rangers became a true light cavalry force, invaluable for scouting, skirmishing, and tactical support against the COMANCHE. Hays was also one of the first to popularize the use of the new Colt six-shot revolver, which came into widespread use in the late 1840s. With this potent weapon in their holsters, and inspired by Hay's leadership, the Rangers contributed to the permanent settlement of Texas by pushing forward the frontier.

During the Mexican War (1846–48), Hays served as the colonel of a volunteer cavalry regiment and fought with distinction, particularly at the capture of Monterrey, Mexico. Following the war, Hays went to California, where he became a sheriff and then state surveyor-general. He retired from public life and became a successful businessman, in real estate and banking. In 1860, he commanded a force of 800 troops that engaged the PAIUTE at Pinnacle Mountain during the PAIUTE WAR. Afterward, he died in 1883.

headdresses *head coverings of Native Americans*

Indians wore a variety of headdresses: caps, turbans, hoods, and brimmed hats, among others. The bonnet of long, trailing feathers so often featured in pictures was only one of many kinds of headgear worn by warriors. Iroquois men often wore a round cap whose frame was made of splints and whose top was decorated with eagle feathers. Some Eastern tribes wore animal heads, such as panther and bear, and often the rest of the skin was draped over the shoulders. Warriors of various prairie tribes, such as the PAWNEE, Iowa, and SAUK, often shaved their heads, leaving only a tuft of hair in the middle. Plains warriors sometimes wore a "roach" of animal hair attached to the scalp lock. Although mostly ceremonial, Omaha warriors wore roaches of deer tails and turkey feathers dyed red to signify men who had won first honors in COUNTING COUP.

Among nearly all tribes, eagle feathers were highly prized as a symbol of courage and swiftness. Among the Plains Indians, a warrior who had distinguished himself in battle by counting coup was awarded the tail feather of a male golden eagle, which he inserted at the base of his scalp lock. When the warrior had won enough eagle feathers, he was allowed to fashion them into a WARBONNET. Wearing the bonnet into battle told the enemy how powerful the warrior was; thus, warriors with such headdresses were usually sought out by the enemy. A warrior could earn great distinction by capturing a foe who wore an eagle bonnet.

On the Great Plains the buffalo-horn bonnet was also a symbol of power and was awarded only to warriors of the highest rank. Wearers of horn bonnets believed that the headdress imparted the characteristics of the buffalo—dignity, stamina, toughness—and the warriors were expected to exhibit these qualities in defending their people in warfare.

Markomete, Menominee war chief, wearing a headdress typical of his tribe, 1831 *(Courtesy New York Public Library)*

Hendrick (Theyanoguin) (ca. 1670–1755) *Mohawk warrior, diplomat, British ally at the battle of Lake George*

Born a MOHAWK, Chief Hendrick was a leader of the IRO-QUOIS CONFEDERACY, which had maintained close relations with the British in New York from the mid-17th century. However, in the aftermath of BRADDOCK'S DEFEAT near Fort Duquesne (present-day Pittsburgh) during the FRENCH AND INDIAN WAR (1754–63), the British began to lose support among their former Indian allies. Leaders of the British colonies of New York, Massachusetts, Connecticut, Rhode Island, New Hampshire, and Pennsylvania tried to address Iroquois complaints at the Council of Albany in 1754. Hendrick, who had a close relationship with commissioner WILLIAM JOHNSON, warned the council of French activities among the Iroquois. He explained that the British had alienated many of the tribes by defrauding the Indians of their lands. He also urged the colonists to unite, forming a confederacy on the Iroquois model. Hendrick's speech inspired the commissioners to pass Benjamin Franklin's Albany Plan—the first plan for a union of the British colonies.

Hendrick proved unable to persuade the commissioners to address the Iroquois's complaints. Nonetheless, when Johnson called for help in a raid on Fort St. Frederic on Lake Champlain, Hendrick came to his assistance with a small band of Mohawk. Johnson's force was ambushed by a combined French, Canadian, and Caughnawaga (Canadian Iroquois) near LAKE GEORGE on September 7, 1755. Hendrick and his Mohawk, along with the Massachusetts regiment they were guiding, were taken by surprise. Fifty of the Massachusetts soldiers died in the ambush, along with 40 Mohawk—including Hendrick himself. His death marked the end of the personal relationship and support Johnson had enjoyed with the Mohawk and furthered the estrangement between the British and the Iroquois.

Hertel, François (ca. 1643–ca. 1723) *French Canadian soldier, war leader*

François Hertel belonged to one of the highest-born families in French Canada. The formative event of Hertel's life was his capture at the age of 18 by the MOHAWK, who were fighting the French-allied HURON at the time. The Indians raided the settlement of Trois Rivières on the upper St. Lawrence River during the summer of 1661. Unlike many of his fellow prisoners, Hertel was not killed by the Mohawk. He was, however, tortured and mutilated. He wrote to the Jesuit priest Simon Le Moyne, who was negotiating among the ONONDAGA, another member of the IROQUOIS CONFEDERACY, that he had had one of his fingers burned and had lost the thumb off his other hand.

Hertel learned much from his Native American captors. Despite his injuries, he proved his prowess by fighting in KING WILLIAM'S WAR (1689–97), leading Huron and irregular Canadian troops in raids on British targets and their Iroquois allies. In retaliation for the Iroquois raid on Lachine, Canada, Hertel led a mixed force of French Canadians and Indians in an attack on Salmon Falls, New Hampshire. Thirty-four British settlers were killed in the raid, and another 54 were captured. Then a larger force of British militia came up and threatened the French and Indian raiders. Hertel himself covered his men's retreat by holding the bridge over the Wooster River against the British. In 1716, Hertel was ennobled for his services to the French crown. His descendants are counted among the foremost French-Canadian families.

Hidatsa   See MANDAN.

Holston Treaty (1791) *treaty between the U.S. government and the Cherokee Nation*

On July 2, 1791, the U.S. government signed a treaty with the CHEROKEE that set the northern border of Cherokee territory at the town of Holston in Tennessee. The Holston Treaty echoed the terms of the 1785 HOPEWELL TREATY signed with the Cherokee: it banned U.S. citizens from settling on Indian land, placed the Indians under federal protection, guaranteed their right to any land not specifically ceded by treaty to the United States, and arranged for the restoration of PRISONERS. However, it also took some powers away from the Cherokee. The U.S. government demanded the right to build a road through Cherokee territory as well as the right of navigation on the Tennessee River. It also demanded the right to regulate all trade with the Indians. The Holston Treaty remained in force until 1835, when ANDREW JACKSON ordered the Removal of all Cherokee from their native lands west of the Mississippi River (see TRAIL OF TEARS).

Honey Springs (1863) *Civil War battle in Indian Territory (Oklahoma)*

On July 17, 1863, 5,000 Confederate CHEROKEE, CREEK, CHOCTAW, CHICKASAW, and Texans clashed with 3,000 Union Cherokee, Creek, blacks, and whites just south of present-day Muskogee. At midnight on July 16, James G. Blunt, commander of the Northern District of the Frontier, led the Union forces from Fort Gibson (in Cherokee Nation territory), across the Arkansas and Verdigris Rivers into the Creek Nation. Blunt's men marched south to within one-half mile of the Confederate camp, arriving about 8:00 A.M.

Meanwhile, Confederate Brigadier General Douglas H. Cooper prepared his troops for battle in the rain at Elk Creek, two miles north of Honey Springs. At 10:00 A.M., General Blunt positioned his men with six artillery pieces at each end of the line and ordered them to advance toward the Confederates. The Confederate troops, with only four howitzers and inferior, rain-dampened Mexican gunpowder, fought admirably, holding back the Union advance for more than two hours. At the height of the battle, the Second Union Indian Regiment advanced ahead of the First Kansas Colored Infantry and into the line of fire. Union officer John Bowles then ordered the Indians to withdraw.

Thinking that the Union forces were in retreat, Colonel Charles DeMorse, commander of the 20th Texas Regiment, ordered his Confederate forces to charge the First Kansas Colored Infantry. The 1st Kansas and the 2nd Colorado Infantry, however, returned a volley and broke through the Confederate line, forcing DeMorse's Texans to retreat. The battle, the largest in Indian Territory during the CIVIL WAR (1861–65), continued until about 2:00 P.M. But in the end the Confederates were no match for the superior firepower of the smaller Union forces. The Confederates withdrew in an orderly fashion, but were compelled to burn virtually all of their supplies at Honey Springs to prevent confiscation by Union troops.

The Union victory at Honey Springs shook Indian confidence in the Confederacy and prompted desertions among them, as well as among the non-Indian troops. More important, it opened the way for Blunt's occupation of Fort Smith on September 1.

See also FIRST CHEROKEE MOUNTED RIFLES; FIRST CHOCTAW AND CHICKASAW REGIMENT; FIRST CHEROKEE REGIMENT; KEETOOWAH SOCIETY.

Hooker Jim (Hooka) (ca. 1825–1879) *Modoc leader during the Modoc War*

Hooker Jim, a chief of the MODOC tribe, was jointly responsible, along with SCARFACED CHARLEY, Black Jim, Schonchin John, and CAPTAIN JACK, for the death of General EDWARD R. S. CANBY on April 11, 1873, during a peace conference aimed at ending the MODOC WAR. In the years after the California gold rush of 1849, the Modoc had lost much of their homeland on the California/Oregon border to non-Indian settlers. Between 1864 and 1870, the Indians tried repeatedly to return to its traditional land near TULE LAKE. Finally, in 1870, the Modoc, under the leadership of Captain Jack, left the Klamath Lake reservation, where they had been placed by the U.S. government, and fled to Lost Lake in northern California. They resisted all efforts to return them to the reservation.

Hooker Jim did not initially accompany Captain Jack to Lost Lake. Late in 1872, however, he was attacked by a posse of local settlers. In retaliation he and his followers, along with another band under the leadership of Modoc Curly Headed Doctor, killed 12 settlers at a nearby ranch. The combined bands then joined Captain Jack in a rough (but highly defensible) site known as the LAVA BEDS (in present-day Oregon). In mid-January 1873, the U.S. Army, led by Lieutenant Colonel Frank Wheaton, attacked the Modoc in a battle known as the Lava Beds. The army was unable to force the Modoc out of their position, and General Canby, the commanding officer of the district, began to negotiate with the Indians. On April 11, 1873, Captain Jack shot Canby during a parlay.

Although he initially supported the council's resolution to kill Canby and the U.S. negotiators, Hooker Jim came to regret the decision. Canby's death only increased the U.S. Army's determination to force the Modoc back to the Klamath reservation. Within months of Canby's death, Hooker Jim made a separate peace for himself and his family, offering to turn Captain Jack over to the U.S. authorities in exchange for his life and freedom. The new commander, General Jeff Davis, agreed—even though he knew Hooker Jim had killed the Oregon settlers. The surviving Modoc, including Hooker Jim and his family, were taken to Indian Territory (present-day Oklahoma) and confined. Hooker Jim died there in 1879. The 51 remaining members of the tribe were restored to the Klamath Reservation in 1909.

Hopewell Swamp (1675) *skirmish between colonial militia and Nipmuc Indians during King Philip's War*

On August 25, 1675, Massachusetts militia under Captains Thomas Lathrop and Richard Beers pursued a band of Nipmuc Indians from Hatfield north along the Connecticut River valley. The Indians, under suspicion of having assisted in raids on local settlers, had been ordered to surrender their weapons to the Massachusetts forces the previous day. Rather than obey and put themselves at the mercy of the colonials, the band chose to flee during the night. The infantry caught up with the tribespeople at Hopewell Swamp, where the Indians turned and killed or wounded nine of the militiamen. Hopewell Swamp brought the Indians of the Connecticut River valley into the conflict with known as KING PHILIP'S WAR (1675–76).

Hopewell Treaties (1785–1786) *series of three treaties between the United States and southeastern tribes negotiated at Hopewell, South Carolina*

After the AMERICAN REVOLUTION (1775–81), the United States sought peace on its southern frontier by negotiating with Indians who had been British allies. In 1785, U.S. representatives obtained land concessions from the CHEROKEE, the CHOCTAW, and the CHICKASAW in treaties that were intended to end, for good, the problem of Indian-settler conflict on the southern frontier. These treaties called for an end to hostilities on both sides, allowed for mutual exchange of PRISONERS and punishment of offenders, and tried to set limits on American encroachment on Indian territory.

Each of the three treaties had several elements in common. In each case, the treaties tried to define the boundaries of Indian territories and forbade any U.S. citizen to settle on Indian land without the permission of the Indians. The settlers already established on Cherokee lands in the state of Franklin (later eastern Tennessee) were specifically omitted from the treaties. If any terms of the treaties should be broken, the Indians were to seek redress before retaliating. The treaties also allowed any U.S. citizen to trade with the Indians, brought the Indians under the protection of the federal government, and required them to report any antigovernment activity—an attempt to keep the tribes away from the influence of the Spanish in nearby Florida. In addition the Indians swore to maintain peace and perpetual friendship with the government of the United States.

The Chickasaw and the Choctaw remained at peace with the Americans for years after signing the Hopewell Treaties. The Cherokee, however, did not. During the early 1790s the Cherokee were faced with continual encroachment on their lands. They signed away more of their lands in another treaty in 1791 but were still unable to keep white homesteaders from encroaching on their property. Although they had the nominal support of the U.S. government, the Indians were unable to expel these settlers. The squatters, for their part, distrusted the federal government and refused to adhere to the terms of the treaties. In 1795 the Cherokee made a brief peace without resolving the settlement problems.

Hopi *members of the southwestern Pueblo culture group*
The Hopi celebrate their peaceful heritage in their name, *Hopituh,* meaning "the peaceful ones." They are descendants of the ancient Mogollon and Anasazi peoples of the American Southwest, who built multichambered houses, called pueblos, some in cliffs, between about 800 and 1100. Sometime around 1299, the ancestors of the modern Hopi moved south into northern Arizona, where they built new towns and continued to practice their traditional ways until the arrival of the Spanish.

In 1541, Spanish explorer FRANCISCO VÁSQUEZ DE CORONADO led a small band of soldiers into Hopi territory, looking for the fabled Seven Cities of Cíbola—cities reputedly as rich or richer than those of the Aztec Empire. Coronado captured Hopi towns and enslaved the inhabitants, demanding food, women, and housing from them. The Hopi and ZUNI (also a tribe of PUEBLO INDIANS) briefly revolted in 1541, but they were quickly overcome by Niño de Guzmán, then governor of New Spain. Coronado left two missionaries with the Hopi when he departed in 1542. When the Spanish returned in 1581, they learned that the missionaries had been killed. Two more friars left with the Hopi met the same fate later that year.

The Hopi also suffered under Don Juan de Oñate, Spanish governor of New Mexico, who invaded ACOMA PUEBLO (1599) and killed and enslaved the Indians there. Oñate mutilated two Hopi who happened to be at Acoma by cutting off their right hands. Further conflict with the Spanish came with the mass baptisms performed by the Christian friars and priests who came with Oñate. The Hopi religion was central to their way of life. The friars, however, ran an ecclesiastical state, prescribing heavy penances for practices that the Indians considered an integral part of their culture, such as rituals in underground rooms called *kivas.*

Persecution by Spanish friars led to Hopi participation in the PUEBLO REBELLION (1680), joining the medicine man POPÉ in overthrowing the Spanish, killing the resident priests, and destroying the missions. The Hopi also attacked Indians who chose to remain Christian; the village of Awatobi, which remained friendly to the Spanish, was totally destroyed and its residents divided up and taken as hostages into other Hopi villages. When Popé's revolt did not bring about better conditions, many Hopi sought refuge with their Havasupai and Zuni neighbors or relocated their villages to the tops of mesas. Some returned to their own villages after the Spanish reconquest of present-day New Mexico and Arizona.

The Hopi avoided the Indian wars of the 19th century, partly by living on marginal soil that non-Indian settlers did not want and partly because of their acceptance of many aspects of non-Indian culture. They also continued their tradition of civil disagreement among themselves. Many Hopi villages of today were formed through colonization, when political disputes caused a group to leave its old home and create a new one.

The Hopi still live on their ancestral lands in northern Arizona, and much of their culture remains intact. They still practice their traditional activities, including the kachina dances and the famous Snake Dance, and they use one of the most complex Native American religious calendars. They practice farming, stock-raising, weaving, silverwork, and other crafts, and are one of the most prosperous Indian tribes in North America.

Further Reading
Gutiérrez, Ramón. *When Jesus Came, the Corn Mothers Went Away: Marriage, Sexuality, and Power in New Mexico, 1500–1846.* Palo Alto, Calif.: Stanford University Press, 1991.
Loftin, John D. *Religion and Hopi Life.* 2nd ed. Bloomington: Indiana University Press, 2003.
Page, Susanne, and Jake Page. *Hopi.* 1982. Reprint, New York: Harry N. Abrams, 1994.
Waters, Frank, and Oswald White Bear Fredericks. *Book of the Hopi.* 1963. Reprint, New York: Penguin Books, 1977.

Horseshoe Bend (1814) *U.S. victory over the Creek Indians in east-central Alabama*
The battle of Horseshoe Bend marked the climax of the southern CREEK WAR, in which ANDREW JACKSON and the Tennessee militia, along with CHEROKEE and CHOCTAW allies, broke the power of the CREEK Nation. The Creek homeland was relatively untouched by the struggles in the 18th century between British colonists and Native Americans. The Creek had, in fact, gained in power, using their geographic location (in present-day Alabama, Georgia, and South Carolina) to negotiate equally with the Spanish, the French, and the British. As late as the AMERICAN REVOLUTION (1775–81), the Creek could field as many as 6,000 warriors.

After the Revolutionary War, however, the Creek faced increasing American encroachment on their lands. The nation split into two major factions over the question of their response to this contact. One faction, known as the RED STICKS, promoted war. They advocated driving Americans out of Creek territory by force. The faction that supported

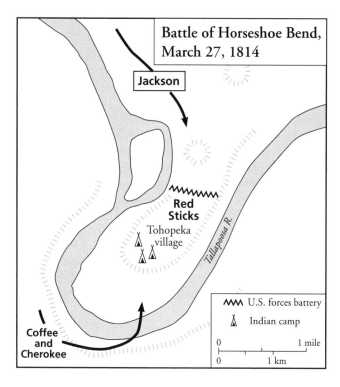

Battle of Horseshoe Bend, March 27, 1814

peace was called the White Sticks. Red Stick leader Little Warrior had served with SHAWNEE leader TECUMSEH in TECUMSEH'S REBELLION (1811) and the WAR OF 1812 (1812–14). He had also been among the Indian allies who destroyed James Winchester's troops at RAISIN RIVER (1813), south of Fort DETROIT. When Little Warrior returned to Creek territory, he was arrested by Big Warrior, leader of the White Sticks, and executed.

The Red Sticks responded by joining the British against the Americans. On August 30, 1813, a band of 1,000 Red Sticks, led by the Creek warrior RED EAGLE (William Weatherford), attacked FORT MIMS (1813) in southern Alabama. Four hundred settlers died in the battle of Fort Mims that followed. Thirty-six settlers and a number of black slaves escaped. In response to the Indian attack, the government of Tennessee appropriated $300,000 to fund an army led by General Andrew Jackson to punish the Red Sticks. Two hundred White Sticks, nine companies of Cherokee and about 5,000 militiamen banded together in November 1813 to seek out and destroy the Red Sticks.

It was not until March 27, 1814, that Jackson, joined by 600 regular U.S. infantrymen, managed to corner the Red Sticks. The warring Creek had set up a barricade at Horseshoe Bend, a peninsula formed by a loop of the Tallapoosa River. Jackson surrounded the Red Sticks, towed their canoes away, and barraged their position with artillery. The barrage set the wooden barricade on fire, upon which Jackson stormed the Creek position. By the end of the day 750 of the 900 Red Sticks were dead. Jackson's losses amounted to 32 dead and 99 wounded. The Cherokee lost 18, and 36 were wounded; the White Sticks lost 5 and suffered 11 wounded.

The battle effectively ended the CREEK WAR (1813–14). Jackson accepted Red Eagle's surrender a few days after the battle at Horseshoe Bend. In the subsequent FORT JACKSON TREATY (1814), the Creek were forced to cede some two-thirds of their lands to the United States.

Treaty of Horseshoe Bend   See FORT JACKSON TREATY.

Howard, Oliver O. (1830–1909) *U.S. Army general known especially for his role in wars against the Nez Perce*
Born in Maine, Oliver O. Howard attended the U.S. military academy at West Point, graduating in 1854. At the start of the CIVIL WAR (1861–65), he received a commission as a colonel in a Maine volunteer regiment. Promoted to general, he saw a great deal of action throughout the war, serving in both eastern and western fronts. After the war Howard was appointed the first head of the Freedman's Bureau, a government agency designed to assist former slaves.

In 1872, President ULYSSES S. GRANT appointed Howard as a special peace commissioner to the Chiricahua APACHE in the Arizona Territory. Through his efforts, Apache leader COCHISE agreed to relocate his tribe to a reservation near the Mexican border.

Howard's most notable duty was soon to follow. In 1874, Howard replaced EDWARD CANBY as head of the Department of the Columbia. At an 1877 conference with Nez Perce leaders CHIEF JOSEPH, OLLIKUT, LOOKING GLASS, and others, he ordered the Nez Perce to leave their lands in the Wallowa Valley and relocate to a reservation. The Indians refused, and the outbreak of the NEZ PERCE WAR (1877) quickly followed. During this war, Howard commanded troops in the Battles of WHITE BIRD CREEK (1877) and CLEARWATER (1877). He also pursued CHIEF JOSEPH'S band in their unsuccessful four-month flight from Idaho to Canada. Soon after, Howard led a military campaign against the BANNOCK in the BANNOCK WAR (1878). The following year, he led troops in the SHEEPEATER WAR (1879) against the Bannock and the SHOSHONE.

Howard left the Northwest in 1881 and returned east. He retired from the military in 1894. Despite his campaigns against the Indians of the Northwest, Howard was known as a friend of the Indians, largely because of his efforts to negotiate peace before resorting to battle.

Hunkpapa   See SIOUX.

Huron (Wyandot) *Iroquoian-speaking people inhabiting the region around the upper St. Lawrence River valley east of present-day Lake Huron*
When French explorer Jacques Cartier explored the St. Lawrence River in the 1530s, he found Huron villages all along

the river. The French gave the Indians the name Huron because of the spikelike hairstyle of the warriors. By the early 1600s the major Huron territory was east of Lake Huron, where the tribe had formed a large confederacy that dominated the Indian-French fur trade in Canada. It is estimated that in 1620 about 20,000 Huron lived in some 18 fortified villages along the lake. Farmers as well as traders, the Huron were especially famous for their tobacco cultivation and were often referred to as the Tobacco Nation.

Through their fur trade the Huron gained iron, cloth, and weapons from the French. But they gained something else from their contact with Europeans. By 1640, about half their population had fallen victim to measles and smallpox. At the same time the Huron came under attack by the powerful IROQUOIS CONFEDERACY, allies of the English, who sought to expand their own fur trade (see BEAVER WARS, 1638–84, 1690–1701).

Well equipped with weapons from the English, the Iroquois raided northward and began pushing into Huron territory, burning villages, killing most of the people, and taking the rest captive. It is estimated that thousands of Huron perished in the Beaver Wars, while others, mostly women and children, were absorbed into the tribes of the Iroquois Confederacy. The few survivors fled into what is now Wisconsin and Michigan, where they joined other tribes.

These Huron fought alongside the OTTAWA in PONTIAC'S REBELLION (1763). They also fought on the side of the British in both the AMERICAN REVOLUTION (1775–81) and the WAR OF 1812 (1812–14).

Later migrations brought some survivors of the Beaver Wars to Indian Territory. Today the tribe has territory in both Oklahoma and the Province of Quebec, where they are more commonly known as the Wyandot.

Indian Appropriations Act (1851) *federal legislation to carry out provisions of Indian treaties and reorganize federal dealings with Indian tribes*

The Indian Appropriations Act codified appropriations for the "current and contingent Expenses of the Indian Department, and for fulfilling Treaty Stipulations with various Indian Tribes, for the year ending June the thirtieth, one thousand eight hundred and fifty-two." The act is considered significant in having legalized and legitimized the reservation system, the idea of concentrating tribes in certain areas, primarily Indian Territory (present-day Oklahoma). When the act was passed, the government had already anticipated white migration west of the Mississippi. Moreover, California was already a state, so there was no place left for the Indians to move. The period of Indian removal, initiated in the early 1800s, was coming to an end, and a new era was beginning. The original intention had been to keep the reservations large enough to allow the Indians to continue to hunt. However, growing non-Indian land hunger led to the idea that if the Indians could be taught agriculture, their land would be more "productive" and they would need less land.

Indian Bureau   See BUREAU OF INDIAN AFFAIRS.

Indian Claims Commission   See GENERAL ALLOTMENT ACT.

Indian Creek (1832) *attack on frontier settlement during the Black Hawk War*

During the brief BLACK HAWK WAR (1832), strife along the frontier in northern Illinois led to several raids by SAUK and FOX (Mesquakie) Indians and their allies on non-Indian settlements. The most devastating encounter occurred in summer 1832 at the settlement of Indian Creek, near present-day Ottawa, Illinois. A war party of POTAWATOMI attacked the village, killed the three families of 15 men, women, and children, and captured two young girls. Non-Indian outrage over the Indian Creek attack led to the strengthening of American forces in the region and the final defeat of the Indians at the battle of BAD AXE (1832) later that summer.

Indian Removal Act (1830) *legislation designed to relocate Indians living in the eastern portion of the United States to lands west of the Mississippi*

During the first half of the 1700s three major powers coexisted in the northeast. The French occupied the area along the St. Lawrence, the IROQUOIS CONFEDERACY controlled an area that now includes New York State, and the British dominated the Atlantic seaboard. In time the balance of power changed. By 1763, the British had defeated the French in the FRENCH AND INDIAN WAR (1754–63). The Americans, in turn, defeated the British in the AMERICAN REVOLUTION (1775–81). By the time of the WAR OF 1812 (1812–14), the Americans were clearly the power to be reckoned with east of the Mississippi.

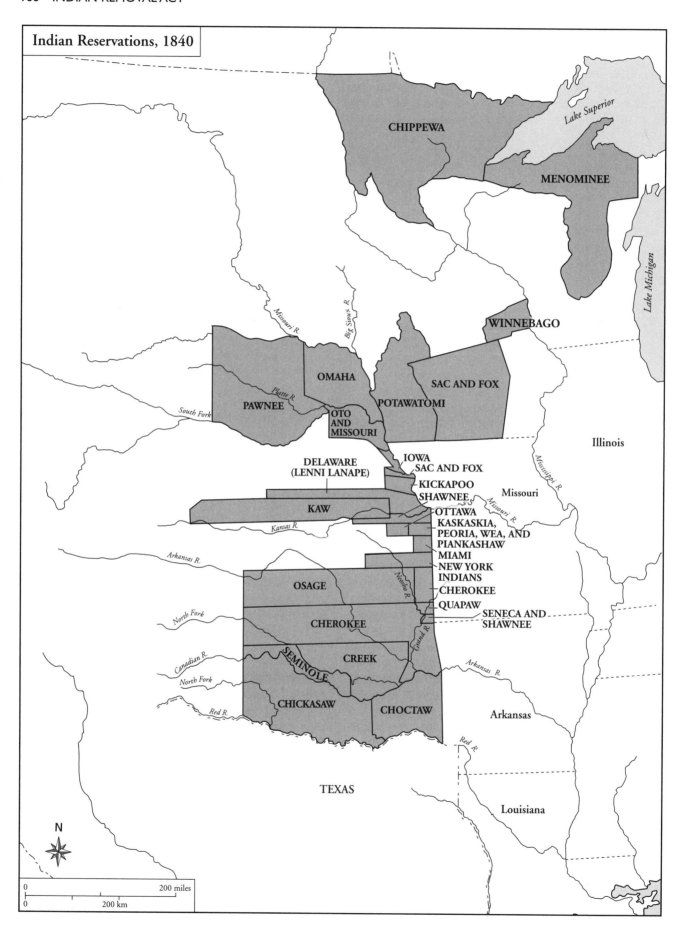

Indian Reservations, 1840

As Americans expanded inland from the East Coast, they began pushing Indian tribes farther and farther west. Tensions mounted, battles raged, and Indians lost an ever increasing amount of land. In August 1794, for example, military forces led by ANTHONY WAYNE decisively defeated Native American forces in the battle of FALLEN TIMBERS (1794). In the resulting TREATY OF GREENVILLE (1795) the Indians ceded large tracts of land to the Americans. Meanwhile, to the south the American government agreed to help Georgians remove local tribes from lands they desired. Thus, great pressure was placed on Southeastern Indian groups such as the CREEK, CHOCTAW, and CHEROKEE to give up their land and move farther west.

Eventually, Americans who wanted to remove the Indians, as well as those who were concerned with the Native American's well-being, supported the notion that the Indians should be removed to the West. According to anthropologist Edward H. Spicer, "The view which was crystallizing was that Indians, for their own well-being …, should be moved into the still dimly conceived lands beyond the Mississippi, perhaps concentrated together somewhere, where they could lead their own lives pretty much as they pleased out of the way of the settlers."

In 1830, this idea was embodied in a law enacted by Congress called the Indian Removal Act. The legislation authorized the president of the United States to remove eastern Indians to the lands west of the Mississippi River with the condition that the Indians gave approval. In reality, the president and Congress used every means possible to coerce the Indians into signing the appropriate treaties. Within the next 10 years, the Creek, Choctaw, Cherokee, CHICKASAW, and SEMINOLE were moved west along the infamous TRAIL OF TEARS. Soon tribes along the Ohio River and the Great Lakes were removed as well, including the OTTAWA, SHAWNEE, KICKAPOO, WINNEBAGO, LENNI LENAPE (Delaware), MIAMI, SAUK, FOX (Mesquakie), and other tribes that were relocated west of the Mississippi.

Further Reading

Satz, Ronald N. *American Indian Policy in the Jacksonian Era.* Lincoln: University of Nebraska Press, 1975.

Inkpaduta ("Scarlet Point") (ca. 1815–ca. 1882)
Dakota leader of an uprising in Iowa and Minnesota
Inkpaduta was born about 1815 into the Wahpekute band of the Dakota (see SIOUX). When he was 13 his father, Wamdesapa, killed the principal chief of the Wahpekute. Consequently, Wamdesapa and his followers were exiled. The outcasts were forced to lead a nomadic life on the prairies of modern-day eastern South Dakota and adjacent parts of Iowa and Minnesota Territory.

Wamdesapa died in 1848, and Inkpaduta became the band's leader. One year later he took revenge on the Wahpekute by killing their principal chief and 17 of their warriors. In 1854, Inkpaduta's wrath was kindled against non-Indians when his brother and his family were murdered by a horse thief named Henry Lott. For a time Inkpaduta concealed his simmering anger and periodically begged food from the newly arrived settlers. During the severe winter of 1856–57, his beleaguered band begged food and raided some non-Indian settlements in order to stay alive. Then a spark ignited all-out aggression. One of Inkpaduta's men was bitten by a settler's dog, which the Indians immediately killed. A posse of settlers disarmed them. The Indians rearmed themselves and began overt hostilities.

On March 8, 1857, Inkpaduta and his warriors attacked a settlement at Lake Okoboji, Iowa. They killed 34 people and took three women PRISONERS. Moving north, they then descended upon another settlement near Spirit Lake, killing another settler and taking his wife prisoner. About two weeks later, they approached a small settlement called Springfield (near modern Jackson, Minnesota). The settlers had been forewarned and many remained safe behind the doors of one house.

Heavy snow prevented troops from nearby FORT RIDGELY from catching up with Inkpaduta's band. In May 1857, military commanders and the Indian Bureau recruited a party of allied Indians to rescue the kidnapped women. Eventually two were returned, but two more were found dead. Meanwhile, terrified settlers in southern Minnesota fled to small towns like St. Peter and Mankato. Unbeknownst to the settlers, Inkpaduta's band was composed of only 12 to 14 men plus some women and children.

By summer, other Dakota Indians were told that they would not receive their annuity payment unless they caught Inkpaduta. On July 18, Mdewakanton chief LITTLE CROW and 100 men went out in pursuit. They returned on August 4, having killed three or four of the renegade band and captured two women and a child. Inkpaduta was seen fleeing to the west, but he was never captured.

Inkpaduta continued his war. He may have participated in the MINNESOTA UPRISING (1862). The next year he fought alongside the Lakota Sioux in the battle of WHITESTONE HILL (1864) in North Dakota. By this time, he reportedly had about 1,000 followers. In 1876, he reportedly fought alongside SITTING BULL and CRAZY HORSE in the battle of the LITTLE BIGHORN (1876). From there he fled to Canada, where he died in either 1878 or 1882.

Iroquois   See IROQUOIS CONFEDERACY.

Iroquois Confederacy (Haudenosaunee) *powerful alliance of several Iroquoian-speaking tribes in northeastern North America*
The Iroquois Confederacy, or Iroquois League, was originally a union of five tribes—SENECA, MOHAWK, CAYUGA, ONEIDA, and ONONDAGA. They occupied what is today upper New York State and the Lake Ontario region of Canada. In the early 1700s, a sixth tribe, the TUSCARORA (who migrated from North Carolina), joined the confederacy.

According to legend, HURON prophet Deganawidah, the supernatural benefactor of the Iroquois, grieved because the Iroquois tribes were fighting among themselves. This left the

Iroquois vulnerable to their enemies. Deganawidah chose Hiawatha, a Mohawk chief, to build a union among five of the Iroquois-speaking tribes. The alliance was in place by the late 1500s, sometime before Europeans arrived in their territory.

The tribes met regularly in a "great council" to discuss and make decisions on issues crucial to all. Women of each tribe chose the sachems, or chiefs, who served on this 50-member council. The council governed the confederacy and dealt with matters of intertribal war, peace, and diplomacy. The confederacy had no voice in the affairs of the individual tribes except to act as a mediator in internal disputes.

In the early 1600s, the Dutch in New Netherland employed the Iroquois in the fur trade, furnishing them with guns and ammunition in exchange for furs. Armed and skillful warriors, the Iroquois soon became one of the most powerful Indian military forces in colonial America and quickly subjugated surrounding tribes. The Iroquois had poor relations with the French, who had established a fur-trading alliance with the Iroquois's traditional enemies, the Huron. The Huron persuaded French explorers Samuel de Champlain to wage war against Iroquois groups in the Saint Lawrence valley region. From that time the Iroquois Confederacy were inveterate ene-

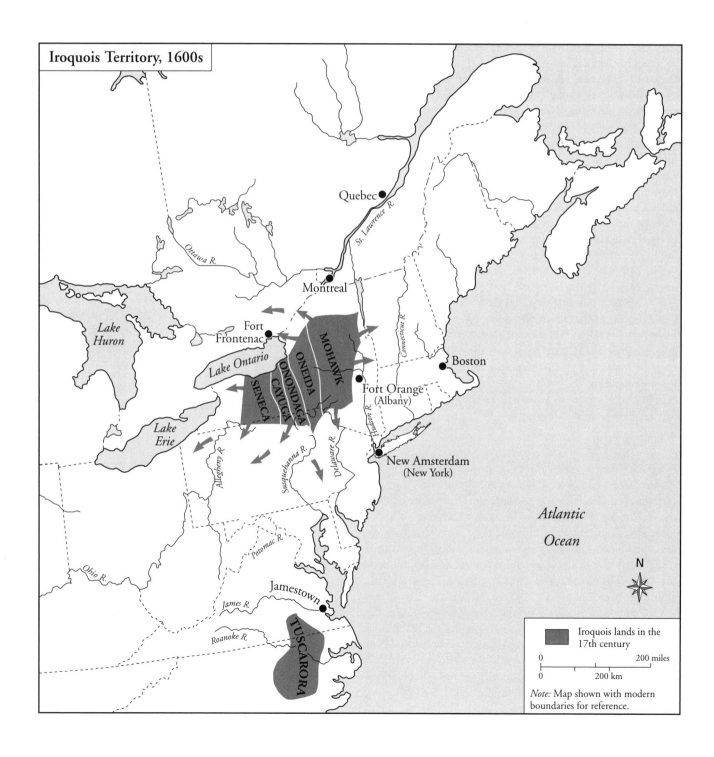

Iroquois Territory, 1600s

Quebec

St. Lawrence R.

Ottawa R.

Lake Huron

Montreal

Fort Frontenac

Lake Ontario

MOHAWK
ONEIDA
ONONDAGA
CAYUGA
SENECA

Connecticut R.

Boston

Fort Orange
(Albany)

Hudson R.

Lake Erie

Allegheny R.

Susquehanna R.

Delaware R.

New Amsterdam
(New York)

Potomac R.

Atlantic Ocean

N

Ohio R.

Jamestown

James R.

TUSCARORA

Roanoke R.

Iroquois lands in the 17th century

0   200 miles

0   200 km

Note: Map shown with modern boundaries for reference.

Drawing of Iroquois being defeated by colonial militia in border warfare, by Felix Darley *(Courtesy New York Public Library)*

mies of the French. The heavily armed Iroquois frequently raided French settlements and attacked the Indian allies of the French, persisting in their efforts until they had wrested control of the Huron fur trade. Moreover, the Iroquois's formidable presence successfully blocked the southward expansion of the French, who were forced to divert their trade westward. In 1664, the English took control of the Dutch colony of New Netherland, renamed it New York, and included the Iroquois Confederacy within their fur-trading networks. Around 1713, the Tuscarora joined their kinsmen in the Confederacy (thereafter known as the Six Nations); they had left their homeland in the Carolinas following devastating attacks on them by colonial and Indian forces from the YAMASEE, CHEROKEE, and other southern tribes (see TUSCARORA WAR, 1711–13).

During the FRENCH AND INDIAN WAR (1754–63), the Iroquois League fought on the side of the British. They maintained this alliance until the Seneca joined with the pro-French OTTAWA Chief PONTIAC during PONTIAC'S REBELLION (1763–64). The British, eager to regain their loyalty, successfully reincorporated the Seneca after Pontiac's defeat.

At the beginning of the AMERICAN REVOLUTION (1775–81), the British advised the Iroquois Confederacy to remain neutral. Before long, however, both the British and Americans were trying to recruit the Indians. Divided loyalties soon split the Confederacy, and the Tuscarora, Oneida, and a small number of Mohawk sided with the colonists, while the Seneca, Onondaga, Cayuga, and most of the Mohawk fought on the side of the British. The Confederacy irreparably broke when brother fought against brother at the battle of ORISKANY CREEK (1877) in Upper New York.

During 1788 and 1789, a combined force of British led by Colonel John Butler and Iroquois forces led by Mohawk Thayendanegea, known by the British as JOSEPH BRANT, attacked outlying New York settlements. General GEORGE WASHINGTON sent General JOHN SULLIVAN to retaliate. He fought a pitched battle with part of the confederacy and their British allies near Elmira, New York. He then marched through the large Seneca towns, destroying houses, orchards, and everything in his path. Many Indians thus went without food and shelter that winter, and hundreds died. The consequent split ultimately broke the confederacy as a formidable military force. (It remained, however, as a focal point of Iroquois culture, and still remains so today.) At the end of the American Revolution, significant numbers of Iroquois moved to Canada. The major portion, however, live today on various reservations in New York State.

Jackson, Andrew (1767–1845) *U.S. president who took part in several Indian wars and initiated removal policies to relocate southeastern Indians*

Born in the Carolinas, Jackson fought in the AMERICAN REVOLUTION (1775–81) while still a teenager. After the war he studied law and settled in Tennessee. He became active in politics and served as a U.S. congressman and senator. He also became an officer in the Tennessee state militia.

Following the CREEK attack on FORT MIMS (1813) in Alabama, Jackson raised a volunteer militia to fight in the CREEK WAR (1813–14). He won a major victory against the Indians at the battle of HORSESHOE BEND (1814), decimating the Red Stick Creek and ending the uprising. The following year, Jackson won a major battle with the British in the battle of New Orleans, the final engagement of the WAR OF 1812 (1812–14). Jackson's role in these events brought him national prominence as a military hero.

In 1818, Jackson led a campaign against the SEMINOLE during the First SEMINOLE WAR (1818–19). He used the conflict with the Indians as an excuse to invade Spanish Florida. After the war the United States obtained Florida from the Spanish, and Jackson was appointed territorial governor. He served only a year, however, before returning to Tennessee for a term as U.S. senator.

Jackson was elected president of the United States in 1828 and again in 1832. As president, he supported the INDIAN REMOVAL ACT of 1830, which enforced removal of most southeastern Indians—including the Creek, CHOCTAW, Seminole, CHICKASAW, and CHEROKEE—west of the Mississippi River. When the U.S. Supreme Court ruled that the state of Georgia could not annul federal treaties with the Cherokee, Jackson refused to support the ruling. In 1835–36 he lobbied Congress to ratify treaties with the Cherokee, leading to their forced removal from the Southeast. This became known as the TRAIL OF TEARS, in which Indians were made to march west to Indian Territory (present-day Oklahoma).

During Jackson's presidency, the U.S. government signed some 90 treaties with Indians of the Southeast and Old Northwest Territory (the area south and west of the Great Lakes). Under these treaties the tribes ceded almost all of their lands east of the Mississippi River, thus expanding U.S. territory and opening vast new lands to non-Indian settlement.

Jesup, Thomas Sidney (1788–1860) *quartermaster general of the U.S. Army and commanding officer in the Second Seminole War*

Born in what is now West Virginia, Thomas Sidney Jesup entered the army at an early age and served in the WAR OF 1812 (1812–14). In 1818, he was appointed quartermaster general of the army; he subsequently rose in rank to major general. By 1836, Jesup was in command of U.S. forces in campaigns against the CREEK in Alabama and Georgia. That same year Jesup was appointed commander of U.S. forces in Florida in the Second SEMINOLE WAR (1835–42). In May 1837 Jesup called a peace conference at Fort Mellon with SEMINOLE leader OSCEOLA and other chiefs. Jesup had gathered a fleet of ships on nearby Lake Monroe, intending to capture the chiefs and transport them to Indian Territory, but Osceola and others escaped.

As Seminole raids on non-Indian settlements and the army continued, Jesup arranged another peace conference with tribe leaders. On October 21, 1837, Osceola and 75 warriors met with Jesup under a flag of truce. Rather than talk peace, however, Jesup ordered the Seminole arrested. Although a party of warriors escaped, Osceola was imprisoned. Jesup continued his campaign against the Seminole, although he was not successful. In January 1838, he was wounded in a skirmish at Jupiter Inlet, and in May 1838, he was relieved of his command. Following his return to Washington, Jesup was criticized by some members of Congress for his conduct in the Florida campaign. He was, however, exonerated and resumed his duties as quartermaster general, a post he held until his death.

Johnson, Guy (1740–1788) *colonial superintendent of Indian affairs in North America for the British*

Born in Ireland, Guy Johnson arrived in America in 1757 and worked for his uncle, Superintendent of Indian Affairs WILLIAM JOHNSON, first as private secretary and then as deputy agent. Like his uncle, he was adopted by the Indians of the IROQUOIS CONFEDERACY and given the name Uraghquadirha, meaning "The Rays of the Sun Enlightening the Earth." Guy became superintendent of Indian affairs upon the death of William in 1774. As the AMERICAN REVOLUTION (1775–81) approached, he continued his uncle's delicate work to keep the Iroquois loyal to British interests. With the help of his secretary, MOHAWK chief JOSEPH BRANT, he was successful in securing the support of all but the ONEIDA and TUSCARORA.

With the outbreak of the American Revolution, Johnson was forced to leave his home in the Mohawk Valley and move to Canada, where he planned joint Native American and Loyalist raids against the colonists, including the destructive campaign that Colonel John Butler carried out at WYOMING VALLEY (1778). Johnson was also responsible for the care of refugees who flocked north from New York after American general JOHN SULLIVAN's campaign in the Mohawk Valley in 1779.

Johnson moved to England after the war, where it is believed that he died in poverty.

Johnson, William (1715–1774) *primary negotiator between the British and the Iroquois Confederacy*

William Johnson played a major role in the British victories in KING GEORGE'S WAR (1744–48) and the FRENCH AND INDIAN WAR (1754–63). For many years he had been active in the fur trade with the MOHAWK Indians in the Mohawk Valley of east-central New York. Johnson, known to the Indians as Warrughiyagey, helped keep the Mohawk and other members of the IROQUOIS CONFEDERACY from allying with the French during King George's War. In 1746, he was named superintendent of Indian affairs for the region. In 1753, he married a Mohawk woman named MOLLY BRANT and adopted her brother JOSEPH BRANT as his protégé. In 1754, Johnson won the support of the Mohawk and their major chief, HENDRICK,

against the French. The following year, he personally led a combined Indian and British force against French-hold Crown Point in the battle of LAKE GEORGE (1755).

Johnson was credited with winning the battle. He subsequently received a baronetcy and the office of superintendent of Indian affairs for the Northern Department in 1756. In that capacity he tried to regulate trading with the tribes of the Ohio valley, ensuring that the Indians not be cheated or mistreated. His reputation for fair dealing was great enough to keep most of the Iroquois out of PONTIAC'S REBELLION (1763–65), and in 1766 he personally accepted SHAWNEE leader PONTIAC's surrender.

During the last years of his life, Johnson tried, with limited success, to enforce the terms of the PROCLAMATION OF 1763, in which British and Indian territories were separated. After his death in 1774, his successors, Guy Johnson and Joseph Brant, led Iroquois and British forces during the AMERICAN REVOLUTION (1775–81).

Juh (Tasnbinbilnojui, "He Brings Many Things With Him") (ca. 1820s–1883) *Apache chief and warrior*

Juh was a member of the Nednhi band of the Southern Chiricahua APACHE, who traditionally lived in southern Arizona, New Mexico, and adjacent Mexico. He married a first cousin of GERONIMO. Tall, heavy, and burdened with a severe speech impediment, Juh became a consummate raider and chief of his band by age 30.

In 1862 Juh participated in the battle of APACHE PASS (1862). Nine years later, he and his followers fled into Mexico rather than accept confinement on a new reservation in Arizona. In 1879 Juh suddenly appeared at Casas Grandes in Mexico and expressed his willingness to accept reservation life. His intentions were short-lived. Within a month he had returned to attacking wagon trains and settlers along the border. By this time, Juh had joined forces with VICTORIO and Geronimo; many of the military accomplishments attributed to the latter two chiefs were most likely his handiwork. In time, Juh and Geronimo split from Victorio, and in 1880 the former chiefs surrendered and settled on the San Carlos Reservation in Arizona.

After the battle of CIBECUE CREEK (1881) there was a significant military build-up in Arizona, and the Juh-Geronimo band fled the reservation. Juh successfully led hundreds of Apache men, women, and children more than 200 miles through heavily patrolled desert to freedom in Mexico. He then vainly attempted to get the other Apache at San Carlos to join him. Although doggedly pursued by ALBERT SIEBER and his scouts, Juh managed to slip back to San Carlos to try and gain a larger following.

Failing to win much support, Juh once again fled to Mexico, where he conducted numerous raids and successfully eluded Mexican and U.S. troops. On September 21, 1883, the great chief suffered a heart attack while riding his horse and fell into the Casas Grande River. His son jumped in and held his father's head above water, but Juh died in his arms.

Julesburg Raids (1865) *response by several groups of Plains Indians to the massacre at Sand Creek*

When the remnants of CHEYENNE leader BLACK KETTLE's people who had survived the SAND CREEK Massacre (1864) reached the Cheyenne camp on Smoky Hill, runners carried ceremonial tobacco pipes signifying war to other Indian tribes on the central Plains. In early December 1864, between 800 and 900 lodges of Southern Cheyenne, Northern ARAPAHO Oglala and Brulé Lakota (see SIOUX) met on Beaver Creek in Colorado. Roused to anger, the tribes set out to avenge the Sand Creek massacre. In late December, war chiefs chose 1,000 warriors to strike the first blow. The targets were Fort Rankin and the stage station of Julesburg, Colorado.

By January 6, 1865, the warriors had reached their destination and concealed themselves in the hills south of Julesburg. The following morning, Big Crow, chief of the Cheyenne Crooked Lance society, selected 10 warriors to serve as decoys. These warriors rushed a few soldiers posted outside Fort Rankin. The ploy worked: Captain Nicolas J. O'Brien, his cavalry, and a few civilians dashed out of the fort. As the cavalry followed the Indians toward the hills, some of the younger warriors waiting there could not be restrained and charged from their concealed positions before the soldiers were fully into the trap. Alerted, O'Brien and his men turned back toward the stockade. Before they could reach safety, however, the entire force of warriors closed in on them. Only between 14 and 16 of O'Brien's 60 men survived this skirmish. Rather than attack the rest of the men in the fort, the warriors withdrew to Julesburg and spent the day plundering the station, its store, and the stage company's warehouse.

After January 14, 1865, large war parties of up to 500 warriors continued to raid the South Platte area. After several weeks of raiding, another council was held, and it was decided to continue fighting. On January 26, 1865, war parties of Lakota took the road east of Julesburg, the Cheyenne took the west road, and the Arapaho concentrated their activities near Julesburg itself. Two days later, the Indians struck. The warriors burned almost every ranch and stage station, ripped up miles of telegraph wire, plundered wagon trains, ran off cattle herds, and blocked routes to Denver from the East. The soldiers, holed up in their stockades, usually did not venture out. Twenty-three miles west of Julesburg, the Indians pitched camp on the north bank of the Platte River; their lodges extended almost four miles along the river's banks. For six days they remained unharassed by the troops.

On February 2, the Indians set out for the North Platte River, but a contingent of about 1,000 warriors went down the South Platte to have one more try at the soldiers of Fort Rankin. As they had done previously, the Indians sent out a small decoy party. This time, however with the lesson of January 7 fresh in their minds, the officers kept their men inside the stockade. Once it was obvious that their ploy would not work a second time, the Indians gave up. They returned to Julesburg, where they looted the buildings for the second time in a month and then burned them.

K

Kamiakin (Kamaiakin) (ca. 1800–1877) *Yakama chieftain who led his people in the Yakama War*
After spending most of his youth among the Palouse and Spokan (in present-day Oregon and Washington), Kamiakin married into one of the leading Yakama families in 1825. Forceful and honest, Kamiakin was influential among the young Yakama members and was admired by many NEZ PERCE, Spokan, Palouse, and Coeur d' Alene.

For almost 15 years, Kamiakin remained friendly toward non-Indians. Then, in 1853, ISAAC I. STEVENS became governor of the newly created Washington Territory and set out to open the territory to non-Indian settlement. This meant that the Plateau Indians would have to be removed. In the summer of 1853, Stevens sent out surveying expeditions. Kamiakin, worried about the Americans' intentions, kept the interior tribes—Nez Perce, Spokan, CAYUSE, and Walla Wallas—informed of the expedition's movements.

In early 1855, the Yakama learned of treaties that Stevens had forced on the Indians of the Puget Sound area (in present-day Washington state). Stevens arrived in Yakama country in April that year. Reticent at first, Kamiakin and other headmen nevertheless finally agreed to participate in the WALLA WALLA COUNCIL (1855). After treaties were signed in May 1855, Stevens assured the Indians that it would be two to three years before the treaties would be ratified by the U.S. Senate. Yet only 12 days after the signing, the *Oregon Weekly Times* newspaper printed an article signed by Stevens announcing that the lands were open for non-Indian settlement. Land-hunters and prospectors immediately headed for the Cascades. Believing that Stevens had lied to them, Kami-

akin led the Yakama and allied Indian tribes in the YAKAMA WAR and the subsequent COEUR D'ALENE WAR (1858). Kamiakin was wounded in this latter conflict in at the battle of SPOKANE PLAINS (1858). He managed to escape to Canada and hid out among the Kootenai Indians. He returned to the United States in 1861 and lived out the remainder of his life on the Spokane Reservation.

Keetoowah Society (Pins) *secret society of approximately 2,000 men within the Cherokee Nation in Indian Territory prior to and during the Civil War*
The greeting of identification among the members of the CHEROKEE Keetoowah Society consisted of turning a lapel downward toward the heart to reveal a pin configured in an "X." Thus, they became known as Pin Indians or simply as Pins. "Keetoowah" came from the name of an ancient Indian people who later became known as "Cherokee." Keetoowah, or Cherokee full-bloods, thus viewed the name as denotive of the true spirit of *Ani-yun-wiya,* or the "real Indian people," and chose it for their patriotic, political organization.

In 1855, the Cherokee government in Indian Territory (now Oklahoma) was controlled by a minority of mixed-blood Cherokee slaveholders, many of whom were members of a proslavery secret society called the Knights of the Golden Circle. The Keetoowah opposed slavery, but their primary goal was to protect the sovereignty of the Cherokee Nation from all outsiders. They therefore began to organize Cherokee full-bloods, who formed a majority of the tribe, to seize control of the Cherokee National Council. Fearing their political activities would be viewed as subversive by powerful mixed-bloods, the Keetoowah originally met in remote lodges at night. Organized under a formal constitution in 1858, by 1861 the Keetoowah held a majority in both houses of the Cherokee government.

Chief JOHN ROSS initially aligned himself with the Keetoowah and endorsed their policy of neutrality in the CIVIL WAR (1861–65). Then, on October 7, 1861, Ross signed a treaty of alliance with the Confederate States of America. The Cherokee Home Guard, a group consisting almost entirely of Keetoowah, was drafted into the Confederate Army as the FIRST CHEROKEE MOUNTED RIFLES. According to the treaty, the duty of this group was solely to protect the Cherokee Nation. On December 8, when ordered to fight against pro-Union CREEK at the battle of Bird Creek, Keetoowah soldiers deserted and fought alongside the Creek. At the end of the battle some Keetoowah escaped into Kansas with the Creek, while others returned to their homes in the Cherokee Nation. Chief Ross, who needed Keetoowah support against his archrival STAND WATIE, pardoned the deserters and allowed them to re-enlist. In March 1862, Keetoowah fought at the battle of PEA RIDGE (1862) in Arkansas, and on June 28, 1862, Union and Confederate forces, both with Keetoowah Cherokee Regiments, met at the battle of LOCUST GROVE (1862). Once again southern Keetoowah deserted to fight with Union Keetoowah.

At the end of the Civil War, the Keetoowah negotiated a treaty with the United States; however, their service to the Union won them no favor with the federal government.

Two Keetoowah organizations presently exist in Oklahoma. The Keetoowah Society is a traditional Cherokee religious organization. The United Keetoowah Band of Cherokees is a federally recognized, governmental body of Cherokee organized under the 1934 Indian Reorganization Act and the 1936 Oklahoma Indian Welfare Act. Both organizations trace their roots to the Keetoowah Society of 1858.

Kelly, Luther Sage ("Yellowstone Kelly")

(1849–1928) *Indian scout and agent*
A native of Geneva, New York, Luther S. Kelly enlisted in the U.S. Army at age 16, just as the CIVIL WAR (1861–65) had drawn to a close. Transferred west, he served out most of his enlistment in the Dakota Territory. Following his discharge, Kelly remained in the region as a trapper, hunter, and army courier and scout, learning a good deal of the Lakota (see SIOUX) language in the process. After Kelly presented Colonel NELSON A. MILES with a large bear paw as a calling card, Miles hired him as his chief scout. From 1876 to 1878, Kelly held that post with distinction, serving in Miles's campaigns against SITTING BULL, CRAZY HORSE, and CHIEF JOSEPH. Later, Kelly served during the UTE WAR (1880).

With Miles's help the old frontiersmen worked as a WAR DEPARTMENT clerk at Chicago; Governors Island, New York; and Washington. From 1898 to 1899. Kelly acted as a guide for several army explorations in Alaska, and he fought in the Philippines insurrection as a captain. He was agent at the San Carlos Reservation in Arizona from 1904 to 1908. Kelly published his reminiscences, *"Yellowstone Kelly": The Memoirs of Luther S. Kelly,* in 1926. He died two years later. One of the army's best post–Civil War scouts, Kelly was buried at Kelly Mountain near Billings, Montana.

Kickapoo ("he moves about, standing now here, now there," Kiikaapua, Kiwegapaw) *Indian tribe that inhabited an area between the Wisconsin and Fox Rivers in Wisconsin*

According to Kickapoo legend, the tribe migrated from the east at some indeterminate time. The Kickapoo belong to the ALGONQUIAN linguistic family and are closely related to the SAC and FOX (Mesquakie). They were primarily farmers and lived in bark-covered houses. When on buffalo-hunting expeditions, which they did part-time, they lived in portable wigwams. The Kickapoo were introduced to horses while hunting on the plains and became excellent horsemen.

In the late 18th century, the Kickapoo, Sac, Fox, POTAWATOMI, OTTAWA, CHIPPEWA, and other tribes defeated the Illinois Indian Confederacy and divided the lands of present-day Illinois among themselves. The Kickapoo moved into southern Illinois and migrated east to the Wabash River.

The Kickapoo were implacable foes of European settlers from first contact with them, and frequently united with other tribes in fighting non-Indians. In agreement with the DELAWARE PROPHET, who advocated a return to traditional ways, the Kickapoo joined the OTTAWA in PONTIAC'S REBELLION (1763). Twenty-seven years later, they joined the MIAMI in LITTLE TURTLE'S WAR (1790–94) for the Old Northwest Territory. The repudiation of European civilization by both TECUMSEH and TENSKWATAWA, SHAWNEE leaders, struck a responsive chord with the Kickapoo, who joined in TECUMSEH'S REBELLION (1809–11). They also fought against the Americans during the WAR OF 1812 (1812–14).

In 1819, after ceding their Illinois land to settlers, most Kickapoo moved west to Missouri. However, two bands, led by Mecina and Kennekuk respectively, refused to leave Illinois for more than a decade. (See KICKAPOO RESISTANCE [1819–1831].) At the onset of the BLACK HAWK WAR (1832), resisting Kickapoo from both bands joined the Sac and Fox in open warfare with non-Indians.

The Missouri lands of the Kickapoo were relinquished in 1832, and the tribe was assigned a reservation in northeast Kansas. In 1862, part of the Kansas reservation was allotted to individual Indians, and the "surplus" land (123,000 acres) was purchased by a railroad company at a fraction of its worth. One band of Kickapoo then went to Texas and joined with CHEROKEE there. In 1839, these Texas Kickapoo were forced into the CHOCTAW Nation in Indian Territory (Oklahoma). They remained there until 1851, when they followed Wild Cat, a SEMINOLE leader, into Mexico. Although they returned to Indian Territory in 1871, they maintained their Mexican Kickapoo identity. Another band of Texas Kickapoo moved into the CREEK Nation in Indian Territory. However, when the CIVIL WAR (1861–65) began, this group also went to Mexico. A series of border skirmishes followed. Finally, induced by the U.S. government to return to Indian Territory in 1873—after their settlement at Naciement, Mexico, was destroyed by Colonel RANALD S. MACKENZIE and the 4th Cavalry—they were assigned a reservation in 1883. In 1893, the reservation was relinquished to the United States, and individual Kickapoo received 80-acre land allotments. The remaining land was then claimed by whites who staked their claims on May 23, 1895. The tribe currently exists as the officially recognized Texas Band of Kickapoo and the Kickapoo Tribe of Oklahoma. There are also several settlements on the Texas-Mexico border.

Further Reading

Gibson, Arrell M. *The Kickapoos: Lords of the Middle Border.* Norman: University of Oklahoma Press, 1963.

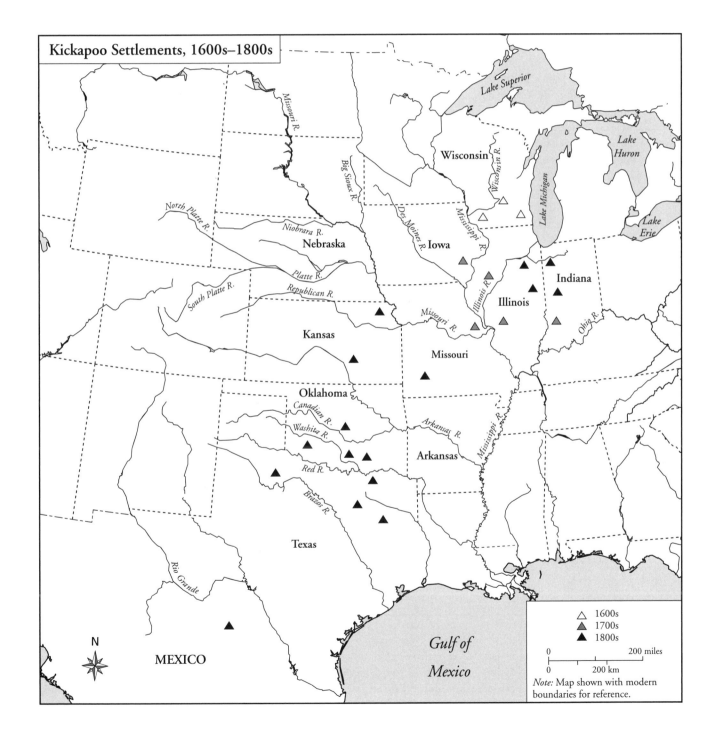

Kickapoo resistance (1819–1831) *refusal by two groups of Kickapoo Indians to surrender Illinois lands to non-Indians*

The KICKAPOO had fought hard against the United States during the WAR OF 1812 (1812–14). They previously had ceded part of their lands in Illinois and Indiana to the U.S. government in 1809. In 1819, under the provisions of the Treaty of Edwardsville and the Treaty of Fort Harrison, most Kickapoo were willing to cede the remainder of their lands. In exchange the U.S. government agreed to move the Kickapoo into Missouri and compensate them with money and goods.

Most Kickapoo moved to Missouri in 1819. However, two bands refused to leave Illinois. One was led by Mecina, chief of a Kickapoo village on Peoria Lake. Guiding the other was Kennekuk, who served as both chief and prophet to his people.

As had SHAWNEE leader TECUMSEH, Mecina maintained that land could be sold to the U.S. government only if all Indians consented to the sale. His followers mounted a determined guerrilla-style campaign against settlers, raiding exposed positions and avoiding open confrontations with larger enemy forces. After several months of military pressure, Mecina's supporters were forced west of the Mississippi River into Missouri, but they returned to Illinois each spring, occupying desirable lands on the Sangamon River and raiding settlers' goods.

A traditionalist, Kennekuk pleaded with his fellow tribespeople to abandon all their European ways. He also managed to repeatedly delay the removal of his people. In several meetings with government officials, he agreed in principle to lead his followers west but always found some excuse, such as an outbreak of illness or recent poor harvest, to delay the trip. Kennekuk's band delayed their removal for 12 years via this passive resistance. In 1831, however, a substantial number of Kickapoo from Kennekuk's band as well as Mecina's joined the SAC and FOX (Mesquakie) Indians under Chief BLACK HAWK, who was waging war on non-Indians. After the BLACK HAWK WAR (1832), which failed to win Indians the right to remain east of the Mississippi River, most of the resisting Kickapoo left Illinois, with the remnants of Mecina's band joining Kennekuk's band and relocating to Kansas. By 1835, the last Kickapoo holdouts had left Illinois and relocated west.

Further Reading

Axelrod, Alan. *A Chronicle of the Indian Wars.* Englewood Cliffs, N.J.: Prentice Hall, 1993.

Gibson, Arrell M. *The Kickapoos: Lords of the Middle Border.* Norman: University of Oklahoma Press, 1963.

Kieft's War (1641–1645) *war between Indians and settlers of the Dutch colony of New Netherland*

The Dutch had an economic imperative in the New World that none of their European competitors had. Their primary objective was to make money through trading furs with local Native Americans in exchange for European goods. As long as the fur stocks held and the Dutch were making a profit, Dutch-Indian relations were quiet. However, when the supply of fur-bearing animals became exhausted in the 1630s, tensions between the Dutch and their Native American neighbors escalated. Faced with shrinking profits, the Dutch began selling guns to the Indians. This policy was prompted by the colony's governor Willem Kieft, who planned to employ armed Indians, especially the MOHAWK, against the southern farming tribes within New Netherland (which included parts of present-day New York and New Jersey.)

Although most of the Dutch colony's profits came from trade, some colonists had arrived to settle land along the Hudson River. Kieft tried to offset the cost of maintaining the forts that protected Dutch farmers by taxing the local Native Americans. The Indians resented both the taxes and the infringements on their lands. This inevitably led to violence. In 1641, the Raritan Indians of Staten Island retaliated against a Dutch farmer whose cattle had destroyed their cornfields. In 1642, a Raritan killed a man named Claes Rademaker because he believed Rademaker had been involved in the death of a relative.

In February 1642, Kieft's Mohawk allies tried to extort money from the Wappinger Indians of what is now New Jersey. The Wappinger sought protection from Kieft at New Amsterdam (present-day New York City). Instead, however, Kieft turned the Mohawk loose on them. Seventy Wappinger died in the fighting and others were captured by the Mohawk. On the night of February 25–26, in an effort to enforce Kieft's policies, Dutch soldiers killed 80 Wappinger women and children refugees at Pavonia (near present-day Jersey City, New Jersey). Thirty others were tortured to death in public. This "Slaughter of the Innocents," as it was called, roused the Indians against the Dutch. By mid-March, Kieft was trying to negotiate with the New York Indians, offering them presents in return for peace. However, on October 1, 1643, a small band of Native Americans captured the town of Pavonia, killed its inhabitants, and burned it to the ground. Panicked settlers from all over New Netherlands fled to New Amsterdam seeking shelter. New Amsterdam itself fell under siege for more than a year.

The siege was not lifted until the Dutch hired British Captain JOHN UNDERHILL, a veteran of the PEQUOT WAR (1636–37), to harass local Indian villages. In March 1644, Underhill surrounded a large Indian village with musketeers in the same way that he had surrounded Mystic Village during the Pequot War. The soldiers killed about 180 Indians in the initial assault; by the time the fighting ended, Native American losses amounted to around 500 killed and wounded. The Europeans lost one man, and a few others were wounded. Shocked by the demonstration of European firepower, the Native Americans raised the siege of New Amsterdam; they made peace with the Dutch the following year. Willem Kieft, whose aggressive policies had provoked the war, was recalled to the Netherlands in 1646.

Further Reading

The American Heritage History of the Thirteen Colonies. New York: American Heritage, 1967.

Killdeer Mountain (1864) *one of a series of attempts to end Lakota resistance to non-Indian settlement west of the Missouri River*

In late June 1864, General ALFRED SULLY led an expedition of some 2,200 officers and troops up the Missouri. He was looking for a site for one of a series of forts to be built along the Missouri River to keep the Lakota (see SIOUX) from raiding along the Minnesota-Iowa border. Near the mouth of the Cannonball River, a detail from his army began construction of Fort Rice. The main body of Sully's force, however, went out to investigate the report of a buildup of about 1,600 Lakota forces near Killdeer Mountain. On June 28, 1864, Sully's troops met and defeated a large group of Lakota warriors in the battle of Killdeer Mountain. Sully then crossed the badlands to the Yellowstone River, where he skirmished with the Lakota and destroyed much of their camp equipment. The army suffered 15 casualties. Sully estimated that his troops killed 150 Indians, but the Lakota admitted to only 31.

See also CIVIL WAR; SIOUX WARS.

King George's War (War of the Austrian Succession) (1744–1748) *war between the French and the English fought mainly in North America*

Like the earlier KING WILLIAM'S WAR (1689–97) and QUEEN ANNE'S WAR (1702–13), King George's War was largely an extension of the war that the British and French were fighting in Europe. The two sides fought only a few European-style battles, including the French assault on Annapolis Royal (Port Royal), Nova Scotia, and the British siege of Louisbourg on Cape Breton Island. Both sides enlisted Indians to fight as irregulars in smaller battles. The French were more successful at this than the British. During 1745 and 1746, they persuaded the ABENAKI Indians to raid New England, as they had in the past. In 1747, WILLIAM JOHNSON, British agent to the IROQUOIS CONFEDERACY, recruited warriors from the MOHAWK for a proposed campaign against Montreal. Poor planning on the part of the New York colonial government defeated Johnson's ambition. Instead, Johnson put his warriors to work raiding French supply lines along the New York frontier.

King George's War began in July 1745, when Indians who were allied with the French came down the Connecticut River valley into Massachusetts and attacked the colonial fort at Great Meadows, taking several captives. In November of that same year they returned to Great Meadows and repeated the attack with similar results. For the next two years the northern frontier of New England suffered from campaigns by French-Canadian and Indian forces. Most of these were concentrated in Maine (then part of Massachusetts), but late in November 1745, a combined force seized Fort Saratoga and burned it to the ground. Charleston, New Hampshire, suffered five separate assaults between April 1746 and April 1747. In each case the colonials drove off the attackers and suffered only light casualties. Other battles of the war were on a similar scale, usually with no more than 200 combatants involved on any one side.

Civilians suffered many of the casualties during the raids in King George's War. Some of the victims survived the attacks and later published the stories of their experiences in so-called captivity narratives, which were so popular that they sparked a literary fashion. (See CAPTIVES, WAR.) One of these authors was Eunice Allen, a Massachusetts woman who was tomahawked at the Barrs Fight near Deerfield on August, 1746. She survived and lived to the age of 80. During the same fight, Samuel Allen, Jr., was captured and taken to live among the Indians in Canada. When he was rescued almost two years later, Samuel had become so attached to his Indian captors that he refused at first to return to his Massachusetts home.

Most of the Indians involved in King George's War were allied with the French. At the war's outbreak only the Mohawk were strictly allied with the British. The Iroquois were technically neutral during the war, but they also leaned toward friendship with the British. As the war progressed, more and more Indians sought friendship and trade with the British. Client tribes of the Iroquois from the Ohio Country, such as the Wyandot and the MIAMI, officially allied themselves with the British colonists in Pennsylvania. In November 1747, the SHAWNEE sent a delegation of warriors to Philadelphia, asking the colonial authorities for arms and ammunition to fight the French on behalf of the British. These alliances would, over the next 50 years, bring the Indians in conflict with the settlers who moved into the Ohio Valley.

Further Reading

Axelrod, Alan. *Chronicle of the Indian Wars.* Englewood Cliffs, N.J.: Prentice Hall, 1993.

Steele, Ian K. *Warpaths: Invasions of North America.* New York: Oxford University Press, 1994.

King Philip See METACOM.

King Philip's War (1675–1676) *colonial war between the British in Massachusetts and the local tribes*

King Philip's War was the first major outbreak of violence in New England after the PEQUOT WAR (1636–37), almost 40 years earlier. The peace that had marked the previous four decades ended for several reasons. For one, a booming colonial population wanted to open new lands to settlement—lands that the WAMPANOAG chief Philip (see METACOM) did not want to sell. In addition, the mutual trade that had enriched both colonists and Indians for years began to disintegrate as trappers depleted southern New England of its fur-bearing animals. The individuals who had negotiated earlier agreements on the basis of mutual respect—the Puritan fathers on the one hand and tribal leaders like MASSASOIT on the other—were dead. Finally, the Puritans were expanding their culture, especially the Christian religion, at the expense of the Native Americans, founding "praying towns" of Indian converts. By 1674, more than 1,100 Native Americans were practicing Calvinist Christianity in their

The battle in Tiverton, Massachusetts, was one of the battles in Kings Philip's War. Because King Philip (Metacom) burned both white and Indian settlements, he almost succeeded in wiping out the English settlements in New England. *(Courtesy Library of Congress, Negative no. 97114)*

isolated villages, no longer a part of traditional tribal society but not welcomed into the settlers' communities either.

The tensions that brought about King Philip's War began as early as 1667, when the General Court at Plymouth granted permission for settlers to found the town of Swansea, only four miles away from Philip's home village. Philip's protests were ignored, and in March 1671, he was summoned to appear in the town of Taunton to answer charges of conspiracy to make war. Philip was coerced into signing a treaty that surrendered all Wampanoag arms to the Plymouth elders. His appeal to the court of the colony of Massachusetts was unsuccessful; the commissioners only confirmed the Plymouth treaty and increased Philip's fine to £100. Philip paid the fine through a land sale, using the extra cash to purchase more arms and ammunition.

The death of one of the Native American converts marked the outbreak of King Philip's War. John Sassamon, a Christianized Indian minister who had studied at Harvard, served during the 1660s as Philip's secretary and adviser. He left that position and settled in the "praying town" of Nemasket, but still kept his ties with Philip's court by carrying messages between the British and the Wampanoag. Late in 1674, Sassamon reported to the elders at Plymouth that Philip was plan-

ning a war. Sassamon was killed on his way home from the meeting and his body was pushed under the ice of Assawompsett Pond. Three Wampanoag were arrested and charged with murder; they were convicted by a jury that included six "Praying" Indians, then hanged on June 8, 1675.

Although the Wampanoag had been convicted on the testimony of another Indian, and one of them later confessed to the murder, many of the tribespeople bitterly resented the imposition of British justice on the tribes. On June 20, some young warriors moved into Swansea and sacked, looted, and burned some of the deserted houses there. By the 23rd the remaining townspeople had begun to fight back; on that day, one of the Indian looters was shot and killed by a young townsman. On the 24th, the Wampanoag retaliated, killing at least nine colonists and fatally wounding two others in four separate incidents.

King Philip's War soon spread to other areas of New England, including the valley of the Connecticut River and the coast of Maine. It was driven in part by Native American hopes, but mostly through the fears of the colonists. In August 1675, colonial forces attempting to disarm natives near Hatfield in western Massachusetts suffered a defeat at the battle of HOPEWELL SWAMP (1675). The following month, while evacuating the town of Deerfield, colonists were caught in an ambush at BLOODY BROOK (1675), which cost them 64 casualties. For the first time, the colonists faced Native Americans possessing modern flintlock FIREARMS. Combining these with their traditional bows and arrows, the Indians posed a formidable enemy indeed. Because of the speed with which the war spread, many settlers subscribed to a "conspiracy theory," believing that all the Indians of New England were involved in an attempt to drive the British entirely out of the New World. Because of this belief, they often behaved callously toward Native Americans, even toward tribes such as the NARRAGANSETT, who were not allied with Philip. In December 1675, the combined forces of the New England colonies launched an assault against the Narragansett, motivated by fear that they would ally themselves with Philip.

Philip's raiding and guerrilla tactics proved very successful, but his quest to find allies was less fortunate. Late in 1675, he traveled to New York to seek help from the Mahican tribes north of Albany. However, the British governor of New York, EDMUND ANDROS, opposed Philip and encouraged the MOHAWK, members of the IROQUOIS CONFEDERACY, to attack him. Philip retreated to Mount Hope in Massachusetts. In August 1676, he was cornered in nearby BRIDGEWATER SWAMP by British forces under Benjamin Church and killed. The British decapitated him and carried his head back to Plymouth, where it was displayed at the end of a pike for many years. Most of the Wampanoag who survived the war itself were either quickly executed by the Plymouth authorities or sold into slavery in Bermuda or the West Indies.

Further Reading

Josephy, Alvin M., Jr. *500 Nations.* New York: Alfred A. Knopf, 1994.
Leach, Douglas E. *Flintlock and Tomahawk: New England in King Philip's War.* New York: Macmillan, 1959.
Starkey, Armstrong. *European and Native American Warfare 1675–1815.* Norman: University of Oklahoma Press, 1998.
Steele, Ian K. *Warpaths: Invasion of North America.* New York: Oxford University Press, 1994.

King William's War (war of the League of Augsburg) (1689–1697) *colonial war between France and England*

King William's War began in the colonies after the settlers learned of the accession of Dutch William of Orange to the throne of England as William III. England joined with the Hapsburg Empire and the Netherlands in the League of Augsburg to defeat the ambitions of Louis XIV, king of France. For England and France the struggles in their New World colonies were simply sideshows to the major power struggle in Europe. To the French and British colonists and the Native Americans, however, the outbreak of war between the mother countries sanctioned their attempts to expand their own power.

The most successful of the forces involved in the war were the Indians and the French, who exploited the tactics of raiding and ambush learned from them. The troops mustered by the French usually consisted of a mixed band of colonists—French Canadians—and Native Americans, who launched quick raids, usually under cover of darkness. The major objective of these raids was terrorism: to kill people, burn their property, and seize as many captives as possible to drive their enemies away or convince them to make peace. For the Five Nations of the IROQUOIS CONFEDERACY, allies of the British, the war allowed them the opportunity to drive the French and their Indian allies out of the fur trade in the Great Lakes and the valleys of the Ohio and the upper Mississippi Rivers.

King William's War opened with a battle that showed the effectiveness of raiding. On August 5, 1689, a force of about 1,500 Iroquois sacked and burned the village of Lachine, killing 24 inhabitants, 40 soldiers, and a few Christianized Indians. Although the French could not respond in kind immediately because of lack of instructions from Europe, they demonstrated the effectiveness of their tactics during the winter of 1689–90 through raids on Schenectady, New York (in which 60 Dutch settlers were killed and 27 captured); Salmon Falls, New Hampshire (34 killed, 54 captured); and Forts Casco and Loyal in Maine. Native Americans, accompanied by a few colonials, responded in kind, burning the Canadian town of La Prairie in August 1690.

The British were for the most part less willing to use French tactics, and were correspondingly less successful. Sir William Phips, a Boston merchant who led the Massachusetts troops, planned a traditional naval European expedition against Port Royal in Acadia in May 1690. The fort, which was undermanned and outgunned, surrendered without a fight. Later that same year, Phips launched an invasion of Canada in conjunction with an overland expedition from Albany, but poor timing, disease, and lack of manpower combined to defeat him even before he landed his forces below Quebec on October 16, 1690.

King William's War did not prove very instructive for all parties involved. The British and the French learned that colonial warfare in America was both expensive and indecisive. Most of the gains the two nations had made against each other were eliminated. According to the terms of the Treaty of Ryswick, signed in September of 1697, Acadia was restored to France, while Newfoundland and Hudson Bay were recognized as English possessions. For the Indians, however, the war represented a net loss. The New England colonies pursued their struggle with the French-influenced Catholic ABENAKI until 1699, while the Iroquois fought the colony of New France in a long, indecisive war that only ended with the GRAND SETTLEMENT OF 1701. The Indians were caught, as they later recognized, between the warring Europeans like cloth between scissors. The blades, they said, fought noisily against each other, but the cloth received all the cuts.

Further Reading

Morrison, Kenneth M. *The Embattled Northeast: The Elusive Ideal of Alliance in Abenaki-Euramerican Relations.* Berkeley: University of California Press, 1984.

Richter, Daniel K. *The Ordeal of the Longhouse: The Peoples of the Iroquois League in the Era of European Colonization.* Chapel Hill: University of North Carolina Press, 1992.

Kiowa Wars   See COMANCHE WARS.

Kiowa   *southern plains tribe allied with the Comanche*
Members of the Tansen linguistic family, pre-contact population of the Kiowa is estimated at 2,000. Originally from the headwaters of the Missouri and Yellowstone Rivers, in the 1700s they migrated to the Black Hills and then again to parts of Kansas, Oklahoma, Colorado, and the Texas Panhandle. After acquiring horses, they became known for their daring raids and violent struggle against non-Indian domination. In the 1790s the Kiowa formed a lasting alliance with the COMANCHE.

In 1834, in order to protect non-Indian wagon freighters, Colonel Henry Dodge negotiated an informal peace agreement with the Kiowa: This agreement lasted more than a decade. The Kiowa, along with the Comanche, eventually resumed their attacks when gold-seeking miners swarmed across the prairies, slaughtering BUFFALO and bringing disease.

The Kiowa later signed the FORT ATKINSON TREATY (1853), but they did not cease their attacks in Texas and Mexico, as they had agreed to do. In November 1864, Colonel CHRISTOPHER "KIT" CARSON launched successful attacks against the Kiowa and Comanche, actions that helped initiate the MEDICINE LODGE TREATY (1867). However, General WILLIAM TECUMSEH SHERMAN's withdrawal of hunting-ground privileges in September 1868 led to more raids and battles. In July 1874, Sherman ordered all Indian men on the southern plains to report for weekly roll calls or be declared hostile and tracked down. This plan helped to bring about the RED RIVER WAR (1874–75). The defeated Kiowa leaders considered most dangerous, including Sky Walker, White Bear, and LONE WOLF, were imprisoned in Fort Marion, Florida, and Huntsville, Texas.

Contemporary Kiowa live mainly on trust lands in Caddo County, Oklahoma. They are still closely associated with the Comanche and Apache.

Kit Fox Society   *warrior society among the Plains Indians*
The Kit Fox Society was one of several warrior societies (see DOG SOLDIERS) created by various tribes of the Plains Indians, including the SIOUX (Dakota, Lakota, Nakota), CROW, BLACKFOOT CONFEDERACY, and Hidatsa. Kit Fox warriors were often charged with police duties in addition their main purpose of fighting battles. Their regalia and equipment varied from tribe to tribe. Officers of the society were distinguished from rank-and-file members by a particular item of regalia. Among the Oglala Lakota, for instance, regular members wore kit fox skin necklaces, forehead bands with kit fox jawbones, and crowns of crow and eagle feathers. Their officers painted their bodies yellow and carried special lances.

knives   *tools used in hunting, households, and warfare*
Native American warriors carried knives into battle for close combat. Before the arrival of Europeans, Indian knives were made of bone or flint. Metal knives arrived with French, English, and Dutch traders in the 1600s and became valued items as traders expanded westward. Whether on foot or horseback, a warrior tried to plunge his knife into an enemy's body with a downward stroke or used the blade in a sideways motion aimed to slash the ribs or stomach. Many warriors were also experts at throwing a knife at a target.

Lake George (1755) *battle in the French and Indian War*
In 1755, colonial Indian agent WILLIAM JOHNSON launched a British-sponsored military expedition against the French Fort St. Frederic on Lake Champlain in what is now upstate New York. With the help of his IROQUOIS CONFEDERACY allies and New England militia, Johnson hoped to drive the French out of New York and back into Canada. In September 1755 Johnson and his allies assembled at Lake George, about 50 miles south of their goal, with a smaller garrison at nearby Fort Edward. About 700 Canadian militia, 200 French regulars, and 600 Indian allies under Baron de Dieskau launched a preemptive strike against Johnson's forces. On September 8, the French/Indian/Canadian attack against Johnson's fortified encampment failed, in part due to the defenders' effective use of artillery. An attack against reinforcements moving up from Fort Edward also failed.

Casualties on either side were nearly equal: 331 British versus 339 French. Many of these casualties came from the considerable variety of battle methods employed by both sides. Dieskau, a regular army officer, effectively used guerrilla tactics and ambush during the early part of the battle, but he also tried a standard European infantry maneuver that resulted in one-third casualties. Johnson and his allies effectively managed to fight off a potentially serious surprise attack that resulted from inadequate scouting. Although the British won the battle, the French succeeded in stopping Johnson's campaign against New France. In addition, the heavy death toll among British Indian allies deprived Johnson of Iroquois troops for about four years (see FRENCH AND INDIAN WAR, 1754–63).

Lake Okeechobee (1837) *largest battle of the Second Seminole War*
After the SEMINOLE Indians eluded early attempts to remove them to reservations, command of American troops was given to Colonel Zachary Taylor. Colonel Taylor abandoned all large-scale operations in favor of guerrilla warfare, a tactic effectively employed by the Seminole. In late 1837, Taylor, who commanded 1,000 men (mostly infantry), marched from Tampa to Lake Okeechobee with 80 wagons, hoping this action would draw his enemy into an open confrontation. On December 25, 1837, Taylor attacked Seminole warriors led by Chief Alligator. The Indians were behind well fortified defensive positions on a mound of dry ground that was wooded with cypress and palmetto trees.

Taylor opened the assault with mounted infantry, but they soon became bogged down in the marshes. He ordered them to dismount, and the troops pressed on until stopped by a deadly volley of fire from the Seminole position. When the U.S. troops began to withdraw, Taylor ordered his regular infantry to attack the Seminole at the high ground. The troops accomplished their objective, and the Seminole disappeared into the woods. Taylor's successful attack at Lake Okeechobee cost the lives of 28 soldiers, and at least 111 were wounded. Seminole casualties were unknown, but it is believed their losses were probably smaller. Thereafter, the Seminole reverted to guerrilla-style tactics, avoiding such pitched confrontations.

Lakota See SIOUX.

lances *weapons for hunting and warfare common among Native Americans, especially tribes in the West*

Indians used lances both for hunting buffalo and in warfare. A hunting lance was a utilitarian tool; its staff was thicker and longer than that of a war lance, and it was generally undecorated. A war lance was about six-and-a-half- to seven-and-a-half-feet long and was often ornately decorated. A lance's ornamentation had significance for its owner. A lance wrapped from its end to its point in mink, beaver, or weasel fur signified the swiftness of these animals and was thought to be especially powerful in driving the lance into an enemy. Lances were sometimes wrapped in strips of blanket and adorned with beads, fringe, and clusters of eagle feathers. In warfare the throwing lance was decorated with feathers twisted around the shaft. Among the PAWNEE, a lance decorated with owl feathers symbolized the North Star, which they believed to be a guardian of their camp. Horsehair tails were often tied to lances, and some were decorated with the scalps of enemies.

Warriors used their lances in several ways, but the most common was its use by mounted men who held the lance so that its shaft was pointed forward and held tight under the armpit between the side and the arm. In this way the warrior got as close as possible to the enemy and stabbed him through with the weapon. Lances could also be gripped by the shaft with both hands, raised overhead, and then thrust downward in a stabbing fashion. A throwing lance was used as a spear; boys were trained early in this use of the weapon. Employed as a defensive weapon, a lance, even a broken one, could defend against a CLUB or ax.

A warrior on horseback sometimes carried his lance with the shaft end held against his thigh or in the crook of his arm, or he might sling it across his back with a shoulder loop. Most war lances were equipped with a wrist thong for the warrior to slip his arm through and a thong at the butt end so that the lance could be tied to a horse's saddle. On the battlefield, warriors who were chosen to assist the war chief were often outfitted with a staff with a top bent into a crook and the shaft wrapped in fur. Although the points were could be sharpened, and they were sometimes used in warfare, these were not true weapons. Lances were not the only weapons carried into battle, but they were one of the most important of the warriors' arsenal.

This image depicts two Indians on horseback fighting, one with a lance and one with a bow and arrow. *(Courtesy of the National Museum of the American Indian, Smithsonian Institution #17112)*

Lava Beds (Battle of the Stronghold) (1873)
skirmish in the Modoc War

In 1864, the MODOC had been moved to a reservation in northern California that they shared with the Klamath Indians. One Modoc leader, Kenitpoos or Kintpuash, called CAPTAIN JACK by non-Indians, led his band back to their home along California's Lost River. In November 1872, U.S. Army troops tried to force the Modoc back to the reservation, an action that led to the MODOC WAR (1872–73). The Modoc took refuge from the army troops in the Lava Beds near TULE LAKE. The twisted rocks and underground passageways of this area, known as "Captain Jack's Stronghold," made it a virtual fortress for the Modoc, who piled up more rocks to strengthen the natural defenses. There was sufficient grass for their cattle to graze, and Tule Lake provided drinking water. Sagebrush and greasewood was used for fuel. About 60 warriors and their families held out for months against more than 1,000 soldiers.

Lieutenant Colonel Frank Wheaton assumed command of the troops on December 21, 1872, and reinforcements were sent from Camps Warner, Harney, Bidwell, and Vancouver. In addition to these troops, there were two groups of militia from Oregon and one from California. On January 16, 1873, under cover of darkness, Wheaton tried to blast the Modoc from their hiding places with cannon and a frontal assault. He moved his men to the fringes of the Lava Beds, while Major John Green went to the west and Captain Reuben F. Bernard moved to the east. Green's and Bernard's columns were to go around the Modoc stronghold and prevent the Indians from moving south. At dawn on January 17, Wheaton's soldiers advanced as howitzers fired in front of them. A dense fog, however, made this maneuver more dangerous for the soldiers than for the Indians. The Modoc kept up a heavy stream of rifle fire and held the soldiers back.

Meanwhile, Green's and Bernard's men came to chasms that they could not cross, so the assault was halted. Green and Bernard then decided to unite forces along the lake's shoreline to the north. By the time their troops had settled among the rocks along the shore, the fog had risen, and Green and Bernard found themselves directly in the Modoc line of fire. The troops were thus pinned down until darkness enabled them to retreat. The battle of the Lava Beds ended with nine soldiers killed and 28 wounded. No Modoc were killed, and the retreat demoralized Wheaton's men. The poor performance of the regular troops in the battle was a great embarrassment to the U.S. Army.

Lawyer (Aleiya, Hallalhotsoot) (ca. 1795–ca. 1876)
head chief of the Nez Perce

Born about 1795, Hallalhotsoot, called Lawyer by Americans because of his abilities in argument, was part NEZ PERCE and part FLATHEAD Indian. Lawyer headed the Christian or "progressive" faction of the Nez Perce tribe that cooperated with the Americans. He persuaded Reverend Asa B. Smith and his wife, Sarah, to start a mission at Kamiah in Northern Idaho in 1839. Hallalhotsoot became their instructor in the Nez Perce language. Because of his relationship with the Smiths and the gifts he received from them, he rose in prestige among his own people.

After the massacre at the WAIILATPU MISSION (1847) and the subsequent CAYUSE WAR (1848), Lawyer, who had been hunting buffalo at the time, returned home. He convinced territorial officials that the Nez Perce were pro-American and gathered the Nez Perce's Christian element together into a peace faction. Lawyer continued the teachings of the missionaries, including religious instruction, farming, and cattle raising. In May 1855 he represented the Nez Perce at the WALLA WALLA PEACE COUNCIL (1855). Throughout the Nez Perce wars of the 1850s, Lawyer remained friendly with the Americans. By this time, his bands of followers numbered about two-thirds of a tribe of about 4,000 people.

Lawyer traveled to Washington, D.C., in 1868 to protest the breaking of treaties with the Nez Perce. Replaced as chief in 1871, he died shortly before the outbreak of the NEZ PERCE WAR (1877).

leaders, war *warriors whose skill and leadership abilities give them positions of power within a tribe*

Most Native American tribes and bands made a distinction between peace leaders and war leaders. Some tribes had both types of leaders during times of either peace or war. Among many tribes, leaders were elected by a council of elders who selected them on the basis of merit. War leaders were usually selected on their abilities, as demonstrated through raids on other tribes and through their own personal bravery. Among Plains tribes such as the CHEYENNE, COMANCHE, ARAPAHO, and KIOWA, young men gained social status through combat. Warriors skilled at COUNTING COUP on an enemy—touching him with a special COUP STICK, a LANCE, or, in the bravest cases, the palm of his hand—won enormous honor and were likely to be chosen as leaders in future fights.

Native American war leaders were respected members of their society. They fulfilled an important role in maintaining relations between neighboring tribes: they were respected for their bravery and their leadership qualities by friend and foe alike. They based their ability to lead on their reputations. APACHE leaders MANGAS COLORADAS, COCHISE, and GERONIMO kept the respect of their warriors throughout their fighting careers. Other leaders had more difficulty in uniting their bands. OTTAWA chief PONTIAC, leader of PONTIAC'S REBELLION (1763–65), saw his revolt against the British fall apart because he was unable to resolve differences between feuding tribal factions. The MODOC warrior known as CAPTAIN JACK, or Kintpuash, was maneuvered by members of his band into shooting General EDWARD R. S. CANBY during peace negotiations. The band then accused him of cowardice and threatened to turn him out of his leadership position.

Because personality and ability were more important than family background, many persons of mixed blood became important Indian war leaders. COMANCHE chief QUANAH

PARKER was the son of Comanche chief Peta Nocona and Cynthia Ann Parker, a settler whom the Comanche had kidnapped and adopted into their tribe when she was only nine. Quanah became the leader of the Kwahadi, a militant band of Comanche, and led attacks against U.S. Army commander RANALD S. MACKENZIE in 1871 and against the settlement of ADOBE WALLS in 1874.

Even persons who had no Indian heritage at all could become leaders of Native American forces. French Canadian soldier FRANÇOIS HERTEL, born into an aristocratic family, was captured by IROQUOIS CONFEDERACY warriors in a 1661 raid. He later led the enemies of the Iroquois, the ALGONKIN of southern Canada, in raids against New England settlements during KING WILLIAM'S WAR (1689–97). SIMON GIRTY had been captured by SENECA during the FRENCH AND INDIAN WAR (1754–63). He was known by settlers during the AMERICAN REVOLUTION (1775–81) as "the Great Renegade," because he led Tory militia and Native American forces in raids on frontier settlements.

Some Indians also became influential leaders of European and American troops. JOSEPH BRANT, a MOHAWK leader, led British irregulars and Iroquois troops during the American Revolution. Seneca ELY PARKER became a member of the clerical staff of General ULYSSES S. GRANT during the CIVIL WAR (1861–65). CHEROKEE chief STAND WATIE led Confederate troops during the same war. Clarence L. Tinker, a member of the OSAGE tribe, became a major general of the U.S. Army Air Corps during WORLD WAR II (1941–45). He was killed in combat in 1942.

Further Reading

Time-Life Books, ed. *The Mighty Chieftains.* Alexandria, Va.: Time-Life Books, 1993.

Utley, Robert M., and Wilcomb E. Washburn. *The American Heritage History of the Indian War.* New York: American Heritage, 1977.

Left Hand (Nawat) (ca. 1823–1864) *chief of Southern Arapaho band*

At about age 10, Left Hand learned to speak English after his sister MaHom (Snake Woman) married white trader John Poisal. Perhaps because of his relationship with Poisal, Left Hand was friendly with non-Indians, even as they pushed onto Indian lands and abused his people. Sometime in the mid-1850s, Left Hand became a chief of the Southern ARAPAHO.

Until his death in 1864, Left Hand strove to mediate relationships between non-Indians and Arapaho around Denver, Colorado, and to forge a peaceful coexistence between the two groups. In fall 1860, Left Hand participated in negotiations that led to the FORT WISE TREATY (1861), but was absent when the treaty was finally signed in February 1861. Along with the signatories of the treaty, Left Hand later repudiated it. Yet even though the Southern Arapaho believed they had been lied to, and the treaty provisions never reached them, Left

Hand and fellow chief Little Raven strove to maintain peace with non-Indians.

During spring and summer 1861, when dissatisfaction over the Fort Wise Treaty drove the CHEYENNE to begin raiding again, Left Hand asked William Byers, editor of the *Rocky Mountain News,* to deliver the message that the Arapaho were friendly. By mid-June of that year, however, non-Indian attacks on Southern Arapaho forced them to leave the Denver area. By late that summer, Governor Gilpin had organized the First Regiment of Colorado, with preacher JOHN M. CHIVINGTON as its major. Three years later, in November 1864, ill and still hoping to create lasting peace, Left Hand waited with his band of 50 to 60 people at SAND CREEK (1864), along with the Cheyenne peace faction. When Chivington attacked the Indians at Sand Creek, Left Hand sustained a mortal wound, from which he died a short time later. Only four other Arapaho left Sand Creek alive.

Legion of the United States *composite force, organized by Congress in 1792 to fight Native Americans*

The defeats of General JOSIAH HARMAR and Governor ARTHUR ST. CLAIR by chiefs LITTLE TURTLE of the MIAMI and BLUE JACKET of the SHAWNEE were in part due to the poor discipline of the American troops. Both Harmar and St. Clair relied on militia, mostly non-Indian frontier fighters from Kentucky, western Pennsylvania, and Virginia. The militiamen, although good hunters and experienced at ambush, broke and ran when the Indians attacked in force. Harmar's expedition ended in the battle called HARMAR'S DEFEAT (1790). A little more than a year later, St. Clair suffered a worse defeat on the Wabash River in what is now Indiana (see ST. CLAIR'S DEFEAT, 1791). In both cases the lack of discipline and training of the U.S. troops was a deciding factor in their routs.

In spring 1792, President George Washington gave General ANTHONY WAYNE the assignment to pacify the Ohio Indians, who had been raiding frontier settlements in Kentucky and Ohio (see LITTLE TURTLE'S WAR, 1786–95). Wayne summoned 1,000 recruits to Pittsburgh the following summer and gave them the title "Legion of the United States." He spent the next two years training and disciplining his men, first at Legionville on the Ohio River, then further downstream at Fort Washington (now Cincinnati, Ohio). In spring 1794, Wayne took the legion on an expedition northward from the Ohio River toward Lake Erie, building Forts Greenville, Wayne, and DEFIANCE on the way. The legion subsequently confronted and defeated a combined Native American force in August at the battle of FALLEN TIMBERS (1794). The legion later became the basis on which the regular U.S. Army was organized.

Lenni Lenape (Delaware) *confederacy of tribes that occupied large areas in southern New York, northern New Jersey, and eastern Pennsylvania*

The Lenni Lenape ("the people," also known as the Delaware) were among the oldest groups of the Eastern Woodland Indians. Other tribes, such as the MOHEGAN, NANTICOKE, and SHAWNEE, claim descent from the Lenni Lenape and referred to them as "grandfather." The Lenni Lenape may have numbered as many as 12,000 before Europeans arrived. The tribe subsequently had many contacts with non-Indians beginning in the early 1600s with the Dutch and the Swedish, with whom they traded and to whom they sold land. The Wappinger, a sub-tribe of the Lenni Lenape, are thought by some scholars to have sold Manhattan Island to the Dutch in 1626.

Although first contacts between the Lenni Lenape and Europeans were generally peaceful, by the mid-1600s incursions of traders and settlers brought conflict in the Hudson Valley and on Long Island. In Pennsylvania the Lenni Lenape lived peacefully with William Penn's Quaker colony, having signed a treaty with Penn in 1682 pledging eternal friendship. The peace lasted until 1737, when Penn's son Thomas tricked Lenni Lenape chiefs into ceding a large area of land through the WALKING PURCHASE TREATY (1737).

During the DELAWARE WARS (1643–45), the Dutch governor of New Amsterdam launched a two-year war against the Lenni Lenape and Wappinger that took some 1,000 Indian lives. The Lenni Lenape later fought on the side of the French in the FRENCH AND INDIAN WARS (1689–1763).

Pressured by advancing white settlement and the powerful IROQUOIS CONFEDERACY, which controlled the fur trade and through conquest claimed Lenni Lenape lands, the Lenni Lenape ceded more of their territory. By the mid-1750s, most had been forced west beyond the Allegheny Mountains into the Ohio Valley. They also continued to take part in battles, siding again with the French in PONTIAC'S REBELLION (1763–64).

Some Lenni Lenape sided with the British during the AMERICAN REVOLUTION (1775–81). In 1778, however, the Americans concluded a treaty with the tribe that would allow soldiers to march through their lands to attack the British along the Great Lakes. It was the first treaty made by the United States with a Native American tribe—but it did not last long. In 1782, a band of frontiersmen attacked a Christian Indian settlement near Sandusky, Ohio, and massacred the inhabitants. Pushed by settlers and forced to cede more land through treaties, the Lenni Lenape were crowded out of the Ohio country, moving into Indiana, Arkansas, Missouri, and as far west as Texas. By 1835, the Lenni Lenape had been forced onto a reservation in Kansas; by 1867, they were living with in the Cherokee Nation in Indian Territory (present-day Oklahoma).

Present-day Lenni Lenape reside near Anadarko, Oklahoma. The Eastern Delaware hold lands in northeastern Oklahoma. Other bands still reside on lands in their historic territories in the Ohio Valley and in the East.

Little Arkansas River Treaties (1865) *post–Civil War treaties between the U.S. government and Plains tribes*
During the CIVIL WAR (1861–65), western frontiersmen militarized but saw no action. Frustrated, they vented their wrath on the Plains Indian tribes. Incidents such as SAND CREEK (1864)—a massacre of CHEYENNE and ARAPAHO by Colonel JOHN M. CHIVINGTON and his troops—incited large war parties of Cheyenne and Arapaho to attack farms, trading posts, wagon trains, and stagecoach stations throughout the Platte River region. Chivington's massacre aroused eastern public indignation. Nevertheless, the U.S. government sought to neutralize the Plains tribes and remove them from the path of westward expansion.

In 1865, a government commission went to conclude postwar settlements of the "Indian problem" with the tribes of the central and southern plains. The commission summoned Indian leaders to a council at the mouth of the Arkansas River, near present Wichita, Kansas. BLACK KETTLE, Little Raven, Seven Bulls, and Little Robe represented the Cheyenne and Arapaho. KIOWA delegates included LONE WOLF, Black Eagle, and Stinking Saddle Blanket. Rising Sun, BUFFALO HUMP, and Ten Bears represented the COMANCHE, and Plains APACHE delegates included Poor Bear, Iron Shirt, and Wolf Sleeve.

By the terms of the Little Arkansas River Treaties, signed in October 1865, the tribes ceded their territories north of the Arkansas River to the U.S. government. The commission then assigned the Cheyenne and Arapaho to a reservation in southwestern Kansas and northwestern Indian Territory (present-day Oklahoma) between the Arkansas and Cimarron Rivers. The commission assigned the Kiowa, Comanche, and Plains Apache to territory bounded east and west by the 90th and 103rd meridians and north and south between the Cimarron and Arkansas Rivers. In return, the government agreed to pay annuities to the tribes for 40 years. Though a temporary peace had been brought about, the Little Arkansas River Treaties did not resolve the controversy, because among other violations of the agreed terms, the reservations were not actually established.

Little Bighorn (Greasy Grass) (1876) *battle fought between the U.S. Army and Native American forces*
Stamped in the pages of U.S. history, the battle between the 7th Cavalry and Lakota (see SIOUX) and Northern CHEYENNE warriors was a powerful example of the struggle between two very different cultures. Although undoubtedly an Indian victory, the celebration was bittersweet, for the scope of the U.S. Army's disaster would focus national attention upon efforts to crush the Plains tribes' resistance to the U.S. government.

Little Bighorn is in many ways the story of two men: SITTING BULL of the Lakota and GEORGE ARMSTRONG CUSTER, commander of the U.S. 7th Cavalry Regiment. Sitting Bull was an important Lakota leader whose influence became widespread among other Plains Indian tribes. The great chief despised non-Indians so much he did not yield or compromise, nor did he ever consider negotiations. Sitting Bull's hatred of U.S. settlers and military was directly related to their constant encroachments onto Indian lands.

George Armstrong Custer was an arrogant, confident, and at times harsh cavalry commander. A veteran of the CIVIL WAR (1861–65) and often acclaimed as the nation's best "Indian fighter" after the battle of the WASHITA (1868),

Custer's flamboyant style made him the object of both criticism and respect. He openly criticized the administration of President ULYSSES S. GRANT, for which he was censured. As the SIOUX WARS (1854–90) reopened in earnest in 1876, Custer's desire for public acclaim, overconfidence in himself and his men, and lack of respect for the Indians would prove to have disastrous consequences.

Fueling the fires of discontent among the Indians was the matter of the Black Hills of Dakota, a region sacred to the Indians and thought by non-Indians to be rich in mineral resources. The FORT LARAMIE TREATY (1868) had conditionally placed the Black Hills within the boundaries of the Great Sioux Reservation. This kept the U.S. Army out of the area, but many surveyors and prospectors ignored the agreement. In response to these trespassers, many Lakota raided unceded territory, terrorizing Indian tribes friendly to non-Indians and contesting any further advancement of the Northern Pacific Railroad into the Dakota Territory. By the mid-1870s, public pressure led the

U.S. government to make an unsuccessful attempt to purchase the Black Hills from the Indians. In early 1876, therefore, the Indians were given an ultimatum by the government: either move within the Great Sioux Reservation or be considered hostile. If the Indians were considered hostile—which they became after failing to meet the government's demands—then military action could be used to force Indian compliance.

After a futile winter campaign against the Indians, General PHILIP HENRY SHERIDAN began planning summer operations, hoping that by organizing converging columns he might force the Lakota and Northern Cheyenne into battle. The plan called for Colonel JOHN GIBBON, commander of the "Montana Column," to proceed from Fort Ellis on March 30, 1876, with a total of 450 men. General ALFRED H. TERRY left Fort Abraham Lincoln on May 17, with Colonel Custer in command of the cavalry. Terry's force numbered about 925 men and included several Gatling guns. General GEORGE CROOK then set out from Fort Fetterman on May 29 with a force of just over a

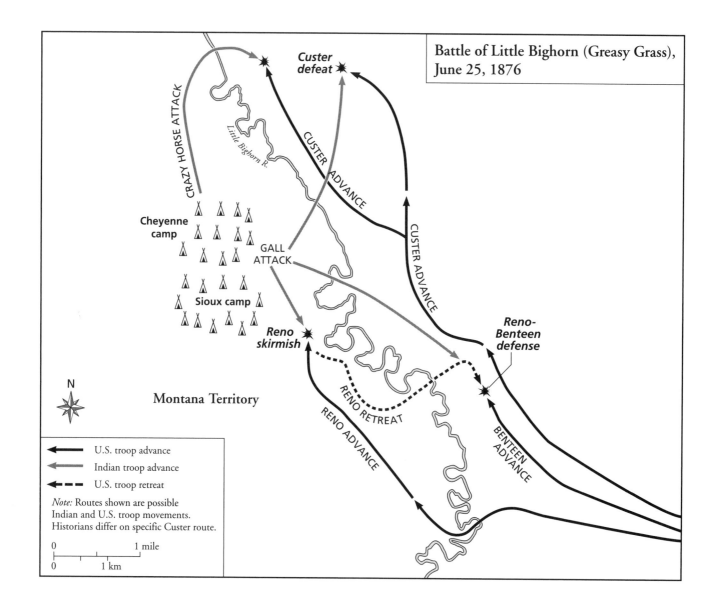

Battle of Little Bighorn (Greasy Grass), June 25, 1876

Crazy Horse Attack

Little Bighorn R.

Custer defeat

Custer Advance

Cheyenne camp

Gall Attack

Sioux camp

Reno skirmish

Reno-Benteen defense

Custer Advance

N

Montana Territory

Reno Retreat

Reno Advance

Benteen Advance

→ U.S. troop advance
→ Indian troop advance
- - → U.S. troop retreat

Note: Routes shown are possible Indian and U.S. troop movements. Historians differ on specific Custer route.

0   1 mile

0   1 km

Drawing of the battle of Little Bighorn, 1876, by a Sioux artist. War chief Crazy Horse is depicted in the foreground. *(Courtesy New York Public Library)*

thousand men. Crook stopped and established a base camp on Goose Creek near the TONGUE RIVER in Montana.

On the evening of June 21, 1876, Terry, Gibbon, and Custer met to discuss the plan of the attack. CROW scouts working for the army had determined that the Lakota were encamped near the Little Bighorn River, in a place the Lakota called Greasy Grass. The plan called for Custer to march his 7th Cavalry up the Rosebud River and drive down the Little Bighorn from the south. Gibbon would ascend the river and enter the Little Bighorn Valley from the north. Custer was to attack the Indian encampment, with Gibbon cooperating as a blocking force to prevent the Indians' escape.

Custer had written orders specifying his role in the plan of attack. These orders, however, allowed Custer a good deal of latitude to change them should the situation warrant. These orders would subsequently cause years of speculation about whether or not Custer had disobeyed his instructions.

At noon on June 22, Custer led the 7th Cavalry to their date with destiny. The regiment numbered about 600 to 700 horsemen, accompanied by six of Gibbon's Crow Indian scouts. The regiment had enough food and ammunition for 15 days, but missing were Gatling guns offered by Terry but rejected by Custer, who feared the guns would slow his progress. Terry had further offered to reinforce Custer with additional man-

power, which was also declined, Custer stating that there was nothing out there the 7th Cavalry could not handle.

On June 24, Custer's troops reached the point where the Indian trail led westward. Terry's plan called for Custer to continue up the Rosebud; instead, he turned his troops west on the trail and led them to the divide between the Rosebud and Little Bighorn. Marching through the night, Custer arrived within a few miles of the divide, but he exhausted his men in the process. Scouts spotted the Lakota-Cheyenne encampment some 15 miles in the distance, and Custer immediately ordered his troops to move forward for an attack. He assumed that the Indians would attempt to escape and determined that he must strike quickly lest they did so.

At noon on June 25, Custer's troops reached the summit of the divide. From there he split his forces, hoping the converging columns would trap the enemy. Custer sent about 115 men, under Captain Frederick W. Benteen, to scout the area to the south, Custer assigned three columns of men to Major Marcus Reno; he kept five with himself. Suddenly, about 40 Lakota warriors appeared, riding toward the Indian village. Custer ordered Reno to attack, promising that his troops would support the assault. Custer was unaware that the Indian encampment lay just ahead across the Little Bighorn River, stretching for about three miles between the Lakota and

CHEYENNE contingents. Historians are unsure of the number of warriors in the huge Indian encampment, but estimates range from 1,500 to as many as 3,000; some believe that the number may even have approached 4,000 to 6,000. Some of these Indian warriors were armed with Winchester repeating rifles; buoyed by their recent success at ROSEBUD CREEK (1876) and determined to protect their women and children, they were not about to retreat.

Meanwhile, Major Reno forded the river and charged the upper end of the village, where Lakota warriors rode out to meet him. He halted the attack, ordered his troops to dismount, and formed a thin skirmish line. The Indian warriors quickly flanked the soldiers, who now remounted their horses and rode back to the river they had forded earlier. During this encounter, Major Reno lost about half of his command. Meanwhile, the flamboyant Custer had turned north and was riding parallel to the river, heading toward the lower end of the Indian encampment. Chief GALL, the leader of the Hunkpapa band of the Lakota, led a group of warriors toward the center of the encampment, forcing Custer and his men to fall back to a high ridge further downstream. The warriors who had fought Reno's troops now joined Gall, while another group led by CRAZY HORSE circled in from the north. Custer and his men were trapped in broken terrain, attempting to fight from both sides of the ridge. The fight probably lasted only about an hour. Not a single soldier survived the so-called Custer's last stand.

The following day, both Reno and Benteen were repeatedly attacked by the warriors who had destroyed Custer and his command. However, upon the arrival of Terry and Gibbon, the Indians quickly retreated. The losses for Custer's famous 7th Cavalry added up to over half the regiment. The battle of Little Bighorn was a disaster for the U.S. Army and a great victory for the Indian war chiefs.

Further Reading

Gray, John S. *Custer's Last Campaign: Mitch Boyer and the Little Bighorn Reconstructed.* Lincoln: University of Nebraska Press, 1991.
Sklenar, Larry. *To Hell with Honor: Custer and the Little Bighorn.* Norman: University of Oklahoma Press, 2000.

Little Crow (Taoyateduta, Cetan Wakan Mani, "the Sacred Pigeon-Hawk which Comes Walking")

(1810–1863) *leader of the Mdewakanton band of the Santee Dakota*

Named Taoyateduta at birth, Little Crow was the son and grandson of Mdewakanton Dakota (see SIOUX) chiefs. He grew up with his parents in the village of Kaposia, at the junction of the St. Croix and Mississippi Rivers near present-day St. Paul, Minnesota.

As a youth, Taoyateduta showed such signs of leadership as self-sacrifice and a sense of direction. When he was 12 years old, a companion slipped through the river ice. Taoyateduta crawled out onto the thin ice and saved his friend.

By the 1830s, an ever growing number of non-Indians were settling in the Mdewakanton's territory. Taoyateduta, by

now given the adult name of Little Crow, believed that his people would be best served by adapting to the new culture. Thus, he attended a mission school, where he learned to read and write in the recently transcribed Dakota language. He also mastered the basics of English, arithmetic, and card playing, particularly poker. Indians and non-Indians alike agreed that he was highly intelligent, a meticulous dresser, a skilled orator, and somewhat charismatic. On the other hand, Little Crow was reportedly also lazy, a heavy drinker, and a womanizer. Perhaps because of these traits, in 1845 his dying father bypassed Little Crow and chose a younger son to be his successor as chief. The next year, Little Crow confronted his brother, who shot Little Crow through both forearms then fled. Little Crow then became chief.

The responsibilities of leadership and marriage to four wives mellowed Little Crow. He promoted peaceful coexistence between the Mdewakanton and the settlers. In 1851, he signed the Treaty of Mendota, in which the Mdewakanton ceded much of their land and agreed to relocate along the Upper Minnesota River. In 1857, at the behest of the Indian Commission, Little Crow led 100 warriors after renegade Wahpekute Santee leader INKPADUTA. The next year the chief visited Washington, D.C.

By 1862, Little Crow was living in a two-story house. He had abandoned his native religion and was attending services

Photograph of Little Crow, a leader of the Sioux uprising in Minnesota in 1862, by Joel E. Whitney of St. Paul *(By permission of the Western History Collections, University of Oklahoma Library)*

at the Episcopal mission. He dressed in European-style clothing and cut his hair to shoulder length. Yet he remained a Dakota chief.

Later that year, friction between the settlers and Dakota along the Upper Minnesota River finally reached a flashpoint when a group of frustrated young warriors killed some settlers. That night, the Dakota chiefs held a council and asked Little Crow to lead them into war. After a series of questions and answers, Little Crow began to speak. Soon he held his audience spellbound. He warned them of the folly of going to war, but in the end he responded, "Ta-o-ya-te-du-ta is not a coward: he will die with you." (Quoted by Gary Clayton Anderson; see Further Reading.) On August 18, 1862, the MINNESOTA UPRISING began, with Little Crow as its leader.

The war between the settlers and warriors raged into September. By early November most of the Indians had surrendered. Little Crow, however, was neither captured nor did he capitulate. Instead, he and about 150 followers fled into present-day North Dakota. By this time the SIOUX WAR (1854–90) had fully erupted across the Plains. Little Crow eluded his pursuers, and in May 1863 he went to Fort Garry (now Winnipeg) for supplies. The next month he led 16 warriors, one woman, and his 16-year-old son Wowinape back to Minnesota on a horse-stealing foray.

On the evening of July 3, 1863, Little Crow and his son were picking raspberries near the town of Hutchinson when they were spotted by two hunters, who opened fire. Little Crow fired back but then fell, mortally wounded with a bullet in his chest. Wowinape stayed with Little Crow until he died, then he put new moccasins on his father's feet, covered the body with a blanket, and fled. The next day, townspeople went to the site, where they found a dead Indian. Unaware that it was Little Crow, they scalped and mutilated the body and buried it in a pile of offal in town. Only weeks later, when Brigadier General HENRY SIBLEY's troops captured Wowinape, did they learn the identity of the Indian. In time, the Minnesota Historical Society obtained Little Crow's skeleton and scalp and put them on exhibit. Eventually the chief's remains were returned to his people for burial.

Further Reading

Anderson, Gary Clayton. *Little Crow: Spokesman for the Sioux.* St. Paul: Minnesota Historical Society Press, 1986.

Little Crow's War   See MINNESOTA UPRISING.

Little Turtle (Michikinikwa, Michikiniqua, Meshikinnoquah, Mishekunnoghwuah) (1752–1812)
war chief of the Miami Indians during the American Revolution and the Indian Wars in the Ohio territory

MIAMI chief Little Turtle was the principal leader of the allied tribes in LITTLE TURTLE'S WAR (1786–95). Together with his primary ally, SHAWNEE warrior BLUE JACKET, Little Turtle developed a program of ambushes and hit-and-run raids that defeated two separate American armies between 1790 and 1795. He lured the undisciplined soldiers far from their bases of supply and only attacked when they were weakened, low on supplies, and tired. Generals JOSIAH T. HARMAR and ARTHUR ST. CLAIR both proved unable to match the Indian leader's strategy. Little Turtle finally lost to General ANTHONY WAYNE at the battle of FALLEN TIMBERS (1795). He signed the TREATY OF GREENVILLE (1795) that year and never took up arms against the Americans again. He spent the remainder of his life touring eastern cities and advocating place

Little Turtle's War (1786–1795) *Indian war fought over the territories of Kentucky and Ohio between U.S. forces and a combined Indian army led in part by Miami chief Little Turtle*

After achieving victory in the AMERICAN REVOLUTION, the newly formed United States regarded the SHAWNEE and other tribes of the Ohio country as a conquered people because of their alliance with the British during the war. In January 1786, representatives of the U.S. government met with Shawnee leaders to negotiate a treaty ceding lands in what are now Kentucky and Ohio. The Shawnee, under chief Kekewepellethe, or Tame Hawk, reluctantly agreed. However, two major war chiefs, LITTLE TURTLE of the MIAMI and BLUE JACKET of the Shawnee, refused to recognize the validity of the treaty and declared war instead. Revolutionary War veteran GEORGE ROGERS CLARK was sent to stop them, but he proved unable to organize or lead the American militia. His force dissolved without ever contacting the Indians.

In October 1790, the allied Indian forces twice ambushed a combined force of regular soldiers and Kentucky militia led by JOSIAH T. HARMAR in what is now northeastern Indiana. The first attack, led by Little Turtle on October 19, routed the American soldiers with few casualties. The second attack, known as HARMAR'S DEFEAT (1790), resulted in more losses on both sides. The U.S. militia suffered 108 casualties before breaking and running away. Seventy-five of the regular soldiers were killed, and the Shawnee lost about 100 warriors. Harmar's force escaped to Fort Washington (modern Cincinnati) without being pursued. The Indians followed up their victory with a series of winter raids against settlements near Fort Washington, even carrying out attacks on boats navigating the Ohio River.

In the wake of Harmar's Defeat, the British—still in possession of forts in the Ohio valley that they did not wish to evacuate—proposed a peace settlement. The Indians angrily rejected it, and President Washington sent a punitive expedition led by ARTHUR ST. CLAIR, governor of the Old Northwest Territories. St. Clair's party, consisting of about 1,400 troops, met with the Indian warriors on a plateau along the upper Wabash River some miles south of the site of Harmar's defeat. At dawn on November 4, 1791, combined Indian forces attacked St. Clair's camp. They achieved a complete surprise; the Americans lost 623 soldiers, and another 271 were wounded. The Indians lost 21 warriors, and 40 were wounded. ST. CLAIR'S DEFEAT (1791) still stands as the U.S. Army's worst loss in its history of wars against Indians.

After St. Clair's defeat, the U.S. government decided to send representatives to the Shawnee, asking for peace. The government hired chief RED JACKET of the IROQUOIS CONFEDERACY to negotiate, but the Shawnee refused to accept the terms offered by the United States. Meanwhile, St. Clair resigned his position, and President Washington found a new general in ANTHONY WAYNE, a Revolutionary War veteran with a reputation as a strict disciplinarian. Unlike Harmar and St. Clair, Wayne took the time and effort to train and drill his troops carefully. In the spring of 1794, Wayne and his forces advanced north to the site of Harmar's defeat and constructed Fort Recovery. He also built other forts deep in Shawnee territory, including Fort Greenville, Fort Adams, and FORT DEFIANCE. In May 1794, Wayne drove off an assault launched on Fort Recovery by the OTTAWA, who were allies of the Shawnee, and began advancing toward Lake Erie in the hope of bringing the Indians to battle.

By this time, the Indian alliance was breaking up, partly because of intertribal rivalries and partly because of the lack of promised support from the British. Little Turtle gave up his overall command of the combined forces in early August 1794, claiming that he no longer believed the Indians could defeat Wayne. Blue Jacket assumed overall command and attempted to ambush Wayne's army at a site on the Maumee River near the British at Fort Miami (modern Toledo, Ohio). A tornado that had recently passed through the area had knocked down trees, providing cover for the fighters. On August 20, 1794, Blue Jacket attacked, launching the battle of FALLEN TIMBERS (1794). Although he achieved an initial surprise, the American soldiers did not break and run; instead, they rallied, counterattacked, and drove the Shawnee and their allies off in a rout.

In January 1795, Blue Jacket and his people came to Fort Greenville to make peace with General Wayne and end the war. The TREATY OF GREENVILLE (1795), which was signed there, required the Shawnee and their allies to give up most of the Ohio Territory, parts of Indiana, and certain strategic sites east of the Mississippi River, including DETROIT, Michigan; Toledo, Ohio; and Chicago and Peoria in Illinois. It also authorized payments to the Indians of $20,000 for their land, plus annual payments of $9,500 in perpetuity.

Further Reading

Axelrod, Alan. *Chronicle of the Indian Wars.* Englewood Cliffs, NJ: Prentice Hall, 1993.

Josephy, Alvin M., Jr. *500 Nations: An Illustrated History of North American Indians.* New York: Alfred A. Knopf, 1994.

Locust Grove (1862) *Civil War battle within the Cherokee Nation (in Indian Territory)*

By spring 1862, there were 8,000 to 10,000 Indian refugees of the CIVIL WAR (1861–65) living in Kansas. Kansas citizens demanded that something be done to stop the influx of Indians from the south and to return the refugees to Indian Territory. Kansans also demanded security from Confederate invasion along their southern border.

With these goals in mind, the BUREAU OF INDIAN AFFAIRS and Kansas officials decided on an Indian expedition into CHEROKEE Nation. Two thousand Indian recruits and 8,000 regular Union soldiers made up the expeditionary force, with Colonel William Weer in command. The units met at Baxter Springs, Kansas, to organize, and then entered Cherokee territory from Missouri at Cowskin Prairie.

In 1862, Major General Thomas Hindman, Commander of the Confederate Department of the Indian Territory, ordered Colonel Douglas Clarkson's regular forces to unite with Cherokee troops at Locust Grove in the northern Cherokee Nation to stop the Union invasion. The FIRST CHEROKEE MOUNTED RIFLES, led by Colonel John Drew, and the FIRST CHEROKEE REGIMENT under General STAND WATIE, rendezvoused with the Confederate regulars at Locust Grove on the morning of July 3.

Weer's Union forces, including two Indian regiments (one consisting of KEETOOWAH SOCIETY Cherokee) surprised the Confederates at Locust Grove later that day. Clarkson and many of his men were captured. Stand Watie's Confederate regiment retreated toward the Neosho River, crossing to safety at Fort Davis in the CREEK Nation. Colonel Drew's regiment, which consisted of antislavery, full-blooded Keetoowah Cherokee, defected a second time to the Union. One week later, they joined other Keetoowah Cherokee to form the Union's Third Indian Regiment. Colonel Drew, deserted by his men, withdrew to Fort Davis. He remained loyal to the Confederacy, although he was never again given a command.

Union forces then drove south across Cherokee Nation without opposition. Chief JOHN ROSS and other Cherokee Nation officials were placed under house arrest at Park Hill. While waiting at Fort Gibson for an overdue supply train from Kansas, Weer began drinking heavily, and on July 18, he was relieved of his command by Colonel Frederick Salomon, the second-in-command. The following day Salomon ordered the Union regulars back to Kansas, leaving the two Cherokee regiments behind to guard the Cherokee Nation. By not following-up on the Locust Grove victory, the Union failed to accomplish its goals of securing the southern Kansas border and stopping the influx of Indian refugees.

The battle of Locust Grove, relatively insignificant in the greater scope of the Civil War, nevertheless served to firmly and finally polarize the Cherokee people. The majority of Cherokee, whose primary goal had been merely to preserve the integrity of their own nation, became firmly planted in the Union camp. Thus, for the first time, a clear distinction was drawn between Union and Confederate Cherokee.

Lodge Trail Ridge (1866) *battle in the War for the Bozeman Trail*

During summer 1866, Colonel HENRY B. CARRINGTON led a battalion of 700 soldiers into what is now Wyoming and southern Montana. Carrington was under orders to build a series of forts intended to subdue the local Oglala Lakota (see SIOUX) and their ARAPAHO and CHEYENNE neighbors. The previous summer, Oglala leader RED CLOUD had rejected a U.S. offer to purchase land and, assisted by warrior CRAZY HORSE, began a series of harassing raids on Carrington's troops. Carrington established his base at Fort Phil Kearny, near the modern Wyoming-Montana border and settled down for the winter, refusing to risk a counterattack against the Native Americans.

On December 6, 1866, the Indians attacked a supply train bringing fuel wood to Fort Phil Kearny at Lodge Trail Ridge, a site about three-and-one-half miles from the fort. In conjunction with Captain WILLIAM J. FETTERMAN, Lieutenant Horatio S. Bingham, and about 55 cavalrymen, Carrington led a counterattack against the Indians. Although the supply train was rescued, Carrington's inexperience allowed the Oglala warriors to escape. His soldiers panicked when the Indians attacked and fled back to the safety of the fort. Lieutenant Bingham was a casualty, riddled with arrows. The engagement encouraged Captain Fetterman to insist that he be allowed to engage the Indians personally when they launched their next raid. That raid occurred on December 21 and resulted in an action that became known as the FETTERMAN FIGHT (1866).

Lone Wolf (Guipago) (ca. 1821–1879) *Kiowa warrior who became principal chief in 1866*

Lone Wolf was one of the signers of the MEDICINE LODGE TREATY (1867), which set the boundaries of the Kiowa and COMANCHE reservations in Indian Territory (Oklahoma). When the Kiowa failed to appear at the reservation as agreed in the treaty, General PHILIP HENRY SHERIDAN took Lone Wolf and fellow chief SATANTA hostage as leverage to force Kiowa compliance.

In 1873, Lone Wolf traveled as a Kiowa representative to Washington, D.C., where he met President Abraham Lincoln and pledged himself and his people to peace. However, when his only son was killed by a detachment of the U.S. 4th Cavalry in January 1874, Lone Wolf became committed to war. During the RED RIVER WAR (1874–75) he participated in the unsuccessful battle of ADOBE WALLS (1874), led by Comanche chief QUANAH PARKER. He also fought Colonel RANALD S. MACKENZIE's forces in defense of the PALO DURO CANYON (1874). The Indian forces were devastated by the loss of most of their vast horse herds during the Palo Duro battle. Shortly after, in February 1875, Lone Wolf surrendered at Fort Sill in Indian Territory. He was sent into exile at Fort Marion, Florida, where he contracted malaria. Lone Wolf was allowed to return to his homeland in 1878, and he died the following year.

Long Walk of the Navajo (1864) *forced removal of the Navajo (Dineh) Indians to the Bosque Redondo camp*

During the first half of the 19th century, the NAVAJO (Dineh) had only sporadic contact with non-Indians. Beginning in 1846, however, this changed. When the NAVAJO WAR (1863–64) began, army posts were built on Navajo land, and misunderstandings led to broken treaties. In 1862, while the U.S. Army was preoccupied with the CIVIL WAR (1861–65), the Navajo seized the opportunity to step up their raids on nearby settlements on the Rio Grande. By summer 1863 Colonel CHRISTOPHER ("KIT") CARSON, under the command of Brigadier General JAMES H. CARLETON, began a relentless pursuit of the Navajo using ruthless scorched-earth tactics. As winter wore on, the homeless, hungry, and fatigued Navajo began surrendering. Only pockets of resistance held out under the leadership of chiefs such as MANUELITO and BARBONCITO.

On March 6, 1864, a total of 2,400 Navajo who had surrendered, along with 30 wagons of supplies, 400 horses, and 3,000 sheep and goats were force-marched southeast from Dinetah, their homeland, toward Fort Sumner and the prison camp of BOSQUE REDONDO. Just weeks earlier 1,445 Navajo had been escorted similarly from their homeland. Soon other caravans of refugee Navajo were sent on their way. Only the very elderly, the sick, and the very young rode in wagons; the rest walked. Boys scarcely 10 years old walked every mile. The Navajo covered about 15 miles a day for 300 miles—a sad and deadly journey that they called the Long Walk. Records show that 126 Navajo died of dysentery at Fort Canby, the point of embarkation, before the trek began. Hundreds more died of natural causes or were shot along the way.

The Long Walk ended at Bosque Redondo where further hunger, disease, and death awaited the Navajo. In all, more than 9,000 Navajo made the journey from Dinetah to Bosque Redondo. Perhaps as few as 1,000 to 2,000 remained in hiding in their homeland. It was the largest tribal surrender in all the Indian wars. Eventually the horrors of the Long Walk and Bosque Redondo were publicized, and the surviving Navajo were allowed to return to Dinetah.

Looking Glass (Allalimya Takanin) (ca. 1823–1877) *chief of the Alpowai (Asotin) Band of Nez Perce*

NEZ PERCE chief Looking Glass initially advocated neutrality in the NEZ PERCE WAR (1877). However, an attack on his camp by General OLIVER O. HOWARD in 1877 caused Looking Glass to turn militant, and he formed an alliance with the Wallam Watkin band's CHIEF JOSEPH.

After the battle of CLEARWATER (1877), in which Looking Glass and Chief Joseph fought together, the Nez Perce chiefs decided to seek refuge with the CROW in Montana. On July 16, the Nez Perce headed northeast over the 150-mile-long Lolo Trail through the Bitterroot Mountains of northern Idaho. Having traveled the trail often, Looking Glass was chosen to lead the march. After 11 days, the Nez Perce descended into Montana's Lolo Canyon, where a barricade had been erected by Captain Charles Rawn from Fort Missoula. Looking Glass masterminded an early-morning escape around the barricade by traveling along a narrow rim of the canyon wall. Shortly after, on August 9, the Nez Perce suffered losses at the battle of BIG HOLE (1877).

When the Nez Perce reached Crow territory, they were denied asylum. The Nez Perce chiefs then sent messengers to request refuge with SITTING BULL in Canada. On October 4, 1877, the Nez Perce were besieged by the forces of General NELSON A. MILES and General Howard near the Bear Paw Mountains. While discussing their options, the chiefs heard horses approaching. Hoping that it was the messengers returning from Sitting Bull, Looking Glass stepped forward from where they had taken refuge, upon which a soldier's bullet pierced his head and killed him. Chief Joseph then surrendered. Credited with masterly leadership on the march to Montana, Looking Glass nevertheless bore some blame for Nez Perce losses at Big Hole and BEAR PAW (1877).

Lord Dunmore's War (1773–1774) *war between Virginia militia and the Shawnee and several allied tribes*

Early in 1773, Lord Dunmore, royal governor of Virginia, declared that he would issue land permits in territory claimed by Virginia beyond the Appalachian Mountains to veterans of the FRENCH AND INDIAN WAR (1754–63). He commissioned two surveyors, Michael Cresap and John Floyd, to survey the territory so that the land could be divided up for sale. Dunmore's declaration was in violation of both the PROCLAMATION OF 1763, which forbade colonists from settling west of the Alleghenies, and the FORT STANWIX TREATY (1768), which reserved lands north and south of the Ohio River valley for the SHAWNEE.

The surveyors crossed the Ohio River on May 29, 1773. A Shawnee warrior named Peshewa confronted them, warning the Virginians to turn back; they shot him. The remaining warriors killed several surveyors but sent one back to Virginia to warn others not to trespass on Indian territory. The Virginia government agent, John Connolly, reacted with an informal declaration of war. The principal Shawnee leader, CORNSTALK, tried to ward off hostilities by meeting with Virginia leaders at Fort Pitt (present-day Pittsburgh, Pennsylvania). However, frontiersmen ambushed his party and killed his brother, Silverheels. Cornstalk therefore abandoned his attempts at peacemaking and returned to the Ohio Country.

Cornstalk soon gained allies from the Mingo, the SENECA, and the CAYUGA, along with a few LENNI LENAPE (Delaware) and Wyandot. The tribes joined with the Shawnee after one of Dunmore's surveying parties attacked and killed the family of a principal chief of the Mingo, a man known as John Logan. The warriors responded with violence, killing 13 Virginians. Finally, on June 10, 1774, Lord Dunmore declared war, gathered a 1,500-man militia, and marched to Fort Pitt to began his campaign in the back country.

Dunmore's original plan called for him to rendezvous at the Ohio River with another 1,000 militia under Andrew Lewis. Cornstalk learned of this plan and resolved to attack

Lewis before he could reach the meeting site. On October 10, 1774, the Shawnee and their allies attacked Lewis's camp at POINT PLEASANT (1778) on the Ohio River. Although casualties were high on both sides, the battle was inconclusive. Point Pleasant proved to be the only major engagement of Lord Dunmore's War. On October 26, 1774, the major parties negotiated a truce that effectively ended hostilities.

Louisiana Purchase (1803) *purchase of land in what is now the south-central United States by the U.S. government from the French government*

When President Thomas Jefferson offered Napoleon Bonaparte $12,000,000 for the French province of Louisiana, which stretched from the Mississippi River to the Rocky Mountains, he believed he was obtaining "an empire for liberty" that would absorb America's land hunger for generations to come. He also believed that the long-standing disputes between colonists and Indians over land rights could be resolved by creating special territories for the Native Americans on the western side of the Mississippi River. By the time Jefferson made the deal, however, thousands of Americans had already moved into those lands, carving farmsteads out of tribal lands and shipping their produce down the Mississippi for sale in New Orleans.

Jefferson's purchase was legally questionable for several reasons. First, he was not certain that his constitutional powers as president allowed him to make the acquisition. Second, no one knew exactly how far west the continent stretched. He planned to resolve this question by sending an expedition, led by Meriwether Lewis and William Clark, to find a route to the Pacific Ocean. He sent with them a large quantity of trading goods to stimulate goodwill among the Native Americans they met and to interest them in trading with the United States.

The third of Jefferson's problems was that French title to the territory was unclear. The French had lost the Louisiana territory to Spain in 1763 under the TREATY OF PARIS (1763), but they had recovered it through secret deals with Spain in 1801 and 1802. Napoleon had planned to create a new colonial empire to replace the lost French Canada, but a revolution in Santo Domingo by African-American Toussaint Louverture and threats from the British Navy ended his dreams. Because the French had recovered the territory so recently, it remained largely unknown to Europeans, with its borders undefined. Borders were later worked out with Spain and Great Britain, but despite their limitations the Louisiana Purchase effectively doubled the land area of the United States.

For Native Americans, the Louisiana Purchase meant two things. First, western tribes would soon encounter U.S. settlers and government forces and be faced with the same pressures to sell their land that the eastern Indians had undergone for the previous 200 years. Second, it gave the U.S. government a reason to compel the tribes still living on their own lands in the east to move west of the Mississippi. Presidents Jefferson and Madison hoped that the Mississippi would be a barrier between the United States and the Native Americans. They believed that most Indians would relocate voluntarily, encouraged by the concept of a world free from non-Indian intrusion. Madison suggested this in a special message to Congress late in 1824.

Many of the Indians at whom this concept was aimed, including the CHEROKEE, CREEK, and CHICKASAW, adamantly resisted the idea of Removal. Between 1789 and 1825, the tribes had surrendered lands in 30 different treaties; they did not want to give up any more of their ancestral territory. However, state and federal pressures eventually forced all of them to be removed to lands in the Louisiana Purchase. The Creek ceded most of their territory to the state of Georgia by 1826. The last of it was seized by Governor George M. Troup, despite threats of federal intervention by President John Quincy Adams. The Cherokee tried to protect their land rights through the U.S. legal system, but the passage of the INDIAN REMOVAL ACT (1830) forced all but a small group to move west of the Mississippi. The Chickasaw left their eastern homeland in 1837.

Jefferson's and Madison's belief that the Mississippi River would place a barrier between Indians and the United States was a gross miscalculation. Within a decade after Jefferson's death in 1826, settlements were being established throughout the new territory. By the end of the century the United States had claimed all the territory Jefferson had wanted to reserve for the Indians, and more. Instead of providing for the peace, the Louisiana Purchase brought the U.S. government into conflict with new tribes and led to the great Indian wars of the 19th century.

Further Reading

Boorstin, Daniel J. *The Americans: The National Experience.* New York: Random House, 1965.

Cerami, Charles A. *Jefferson's Great Gamble: The Remarkable Story of Jefferson, Napoleon and the Men behind the Louisiana Purchase.* Naperville, Ill.: Sourcebooks, 2003.

Kastor, Peter J. *The Louisiana Purchase: Emergence of an American Nation.* Washington, D.C.: CQ Press, 2002.

Kukla, Jon. *A Wilderness So Immense: The Louisiana Purchase and the Destiny of America.* New York: Alfred A. Knopf, 2003.

Tucker, Robert W., and David C. Hendrickson. *Empire of Liberty: The Statecraft of Thomas Jefferson.* New York: Oxford University Press, 1989.

Lovewell's War   See DUMMER'S WAR.

Lozen (ca. 1840–1890) *Chiricahua Apache warrior; sister of the noted chief Victorio*

Lozen deliberately chose to be an APACHE warrior, unlike many other female warriors who took on the role to exact revenge for the death of a relative or out of necessity. As a young woman, Lozen became expert at riding and roping, and she frequently brought home enemy horses from a raid. She was also an excellent shot and a cunning strategist. Because of these skills and her leadership ability, Lozen attended many war councils and rode with her brother, Apache leader VICTORIO, on many raids. By the age of 40, she was reportedly as agile as younger men, and although she no longer competed in races, she had outrun most of the men in her youth. Because her uniqueness was clearly visible, Chiricahua men respected her ability and integrity.

Lozen was also a medicine woman. It was said that during her puberty ceremony she was given the power to determine the location and distance of the enemy by praying. While standing with arms outstretched, her hands reportedly would change colors when pointed toward the enemy. In fact, many Chiricahua believed that had Lozen been with Victorio at TRES CASTILLOS (1880), that ambush would not have occurred. Lozen was one of the two women GERONIMO sent to meet with American troops to arrange his surrender. She was also among the Apache PRISONERS sent to Fort Marion, Florida, in 1886 and then to Mount Vernon Barracks, Alabama, in 1887. Lozen died in Alabama, most likely of tuberculosis.

See also WOMEN WARRIORS.

Mackenzie, Ranald S. (1840–1889) *U.S. Army officer during the Civil War and the wars for the southern plains*
Born in New York City, Ranald Slidell Mackenzie was the son of author and naval officer Alexander Slidell Mackenzie. In 1862, Ranald graduated from West Point at the top of his class. Wounded four times during the CIVIL WAR (1861–65), Mackenzie was a brevet brigadier general by the end of that conflict. In the smaller post–Civil War army, he served as colonel of the 41st and later the 24th Infantry Regiments, both composed of black enlisted personnel and white officers. He received a transfer to the all-white 4th Cavalry Regiment in 1871.

Energetic, ambitious, and aggressive, Mackenzie engaged in a grueling series of campaigns against numerous Indian peoples during the 1870s and early 1880s. An adept tactician, he repeatedly gained the advantage by surprising and attacking unsuspecting Indian villages, destroying possessions, and sometimes slaughtering the Native Americans' horse herds. The KIOWA nicknamed him "Bad Hand" because of two missing fingers on his right hand (the result of Civil War wounds).

Mackenzie's first major Indian engagement came in 1872 along MCCLELLAN CREEK (1872) in Texas. The following year, acting on suggestions from General PHILIP HENRY SHERIDAN, Mackenzie and his troops crossed the Rio Grande and burned KICKAPOO and Lipan and Mescalero APACHE encampments near REMOLINO (1873) during a 32-hour incursion into Mexico that was officially unauthorized. During the RED RIVER WAR (1874–75), Mackenzie won an important victory over combined Kiowa, COMANCHE, and CHEYENNE forces at the battle of PALO DURO CANYON (1874). Following the battle of the LITTLE BIGHORN (1876), Mackenzie and his regiment were ordered north from Texas and assigned to General GEORGE CROOK'S Powder River Expedition, which won a hard-fought battle against DULL KNIFE's Cheyenne warriors. Mackenzie was then shifted back to Texas to lead another expedition into Mexico, this time with the government's permission. The expedition started out in June 1878, but when confronted by Mexican regulars, Mackenzie averted an international incident by pulling his troops back into the United States.

In 1882, following postings in Colorado, Arizona, and Arkansas, Mackenzie finally received his cherished brigadier general's star in the regular army. His health and mental stability had deteriorated, however, and in late 1883, he was transferred from San Antonio, Texas, to a New York asylum. He never returned to active duty and died of "progressive paresis" (attributed in some accounts to syphilis) on January 19, 1889.

Described by ULYSSES S. GRANT as "the most promising young officer in the army," Ranald Mackenzie was an irascible disciplinarian, loyal to his friends but intolerant of fellow officers he deemed incompetent. An ambitious man frustrated by the slow promotion of the postbellum army, his success in the Indian Wars was rivaled among his contemporaries only by Crook and NELSON A. MILES.

Colonel Ranald Mackenzie of the 4th Cavalry *(By permission of the Western History Collection, University of Oklahoma Library)*

Man-Afraid-of-His-Horses (Young-Man-Afraid-of-His-Horses, Tasunkakokipapi) (ca. 1830–1900)
Oglala warrior best known for his action in the Powder River area of Wyoming and Montana

The English translation scarcely does justice to Tasunkakokipapi's name. It really means that he was so powerful in battle that the mere sight of his horse produced fear in the hearts of his enemies.

Man-Afraid-of-His-Horses was an Oglala Lakota (see SIOUX) chief who fought under RED CLOUD in the War for the Bozeman Trail of 1866–68 (see BOZEMAN TRAIL) and RED CLOUD'S WAR (1866–68). In these, conflicts he lived up to his name through skill and acts of bravery. After the FORT LARAMIE TREATY (1868) was signed, he settled at the Oglala agency. In time he became president of the Pine Ridge Indian Council and made several trips to Washington, D.C., to represent his people. He died at Pine Ridge, South Dakota, in 1900.

Mandan *tribe that inhabited the "big bend" region of the upper Missouri in present-day northern Nebraska and southern South Dakota*

During prehistory, the Mandan apparently migrated from the upper Great Lakes area to Minnesota, down the Mississippi, and overland to their location on the Missouri. Because of their comparatively fair skin, the Mandan became known as "white" Indians. They were accomplished farmers, credited with developing a variety of maize adapted to the short growing season of the upper Missouri region. They also produced squash, beans, and tobacco.

Mandan dwellings were permanent circular lodges made of timbers covered with earth. Villages served as busy trading centers where various products were exchanged. The Mandan and the neighboring Hidatsa bartered with the BLACKFOOT CONFEDERACY, the Lakota (see SIOUX), the CHEYENNE, and the ARAPAHO, exchanging a variety of agricultural products for buffalo products, such as robes, and garments ornamented with feathers and porcupine quills. They obtained guns, powder, and axes from the ASSINIBOINE and CREE, who got them from the French in Canada. From American traders they got a variety of manufactured goods, such as woven fabrics, glass beads, kettles, blankets, and rifles. From the Southern Plains COMANCHE and KIOWA they obtained Spanish horses. Mandan traders also traveled west to trade with tribes beyond the Rocky Mountains.

A cycle of alternate trading and fighting developed between the Mandan and some of the tribes they traded with, particularly the Lakota and the Blackfoot Confederacy. The Mandan and their two allied neighboring tribes, the ARIKARA and the Hidatsa, fought together against these more powerful enemies. The Mandan fought no armed conflicts with non-Indians but were virtually exterminated by European diseases, which entered their villages through contact at trading posts or on riverboats.

In 1837, the Mandan were so decimated by smallpox that only 150 of more than 1,600 tribe members survived. The survivors signed the FORT LARAMIE TREATY (1851) and eventually relocated to the Fort Berthold Reservation in North Dakota, where they currently live with the Arikara and Hidatsa as the Three Affiliated Tribes.

Mangas Coloradas (Red Sleeves Dasoda-hae, "he just sits there") (ca. 1797–1863) *Chiricahua Apache war chief*

Mangas Coloradas was born into the Mimbreno band of the Chiricahua APACHE between 1790 and 1795 somewhere in southern New Mexico. During his youth, the Apache carried out continual raids into Mexico. The Mexicans responded by offering pesos for Apache scalps. In 1837 a group of trappers and scalp hunters invited some Mimbreno to a feast and then murdered them for their scalps. The Mimbreno retaliated by killing a group of miners.

By 1838, Mangas Coloradas had become chief of the Mimbreno. He not only united his people, he also married three of his daughters to prominent leaders in other tribes (one of whom was COCHISE), thus forming a great alliance. For the next 10 years, his fighters helped the Chiricahua reassert control in the entire region.

In time, however, Mangas Coloradas decided to pursue a policy of peace. In 1846 he made overtures to General

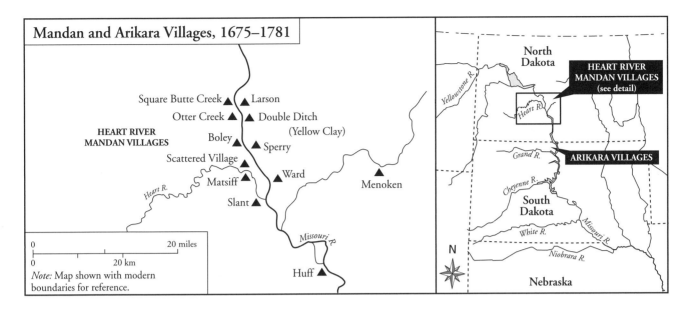

Mandan and Arikara Villages, 1675–1781

Square Butte Creek ▲ ▲ Larson
Otter Creek ▲ ▲ Double Ditch
(Yellow Clay)
Boley ▲ ▲ Sperry
HEART RIVER
MANDAN VILLAGES
Scattered Village ▲ ▲ Ward
Matsiff ▲ ▲ Menoken
Slant ▲
Heart R.
Missouri R.
Huff ▲

0 _____ 20 miles
0 _____ 20 km
Note: Map shown with modern boundaries for reference.

North Dakota
HEART RIVER MANDAN VILLAGES (see detail)
Yellowstone R.
Heart R.
Grand R.
ARIKARA VILLAGES
Cheyenne R.
South Dakota
White R.
Missouri R.
Niobrara R.
N
Nebraska

Stephen Watts Kearny to help the United States fight against the Mexicans. While the gesture was politely declined, a general peace prevailed for a time. Then gold was discovered near modern-day Silver City, New Mexico. Mangas Coloradas tried to lure the miners away by speaking of mineral wealth in distant Sonora. Detecting his ploy, they seized and severely flogged him.

Once released, Mangas unleashed his anger by leading war parties against the settlers and travelers. He soon dominated the area. When the CIVIL WAR (1861–65) broke out, many of the troops in the Southwest were recalled, and some of the forts were abandoned. To protect the transportation routes to the coast, the governor of California sent out two columns of troops. On July 14, 1862, Apache under the direction of Mangas Coloradas and Cochise attacked the advance troops of Colonel JAMES H. CARLETON at APACHE PASS (1862). During the fight, Mangas was shot in the chest. His followers took him to Janos, Mexico, where they forced a doctor, at gunpoint, to tend to his wound. He recovered and resumed his activities.

In January 1863, General Joseph West of Carleton's command offered Mangas Coloradas safe conduct if he would come to the army camp near Pinos Altos to negotiate a peace. The chief agreed. No sooner did he arrive than he was seized and taken to Fort McLane. There, West made it known that he wanted Coloradas dead. On the night of January 18, 1863, two soldiers heated their bayonets in a fire and applied them to the sleeping chief's feet and arms. When Mangas Coloradas jumped up and protested, they shot him dead, ostensibly for "trying to escape." His body was buried but later dug up. Mangas's huge head was severed from his body and boiled in a pot. His skull was then sold to a New York phrenologist-lecturer named Orson Squire Fowler. It remains missing to this day.

Manuelito (Hastin Ch'ilhajinii, Childhajin, "the man of the black weeds"; Hashkeh Naabah, "the angry warrior"; Dahaana Baadaani, "Texan's son-in-law") (ca. 1818–1894) *prominent Navajo war chief*

Manuelito was born in what is now southeastern Utah near Bear Ears Peak. From his youth, the NAVAJO (Dineh) had been at war with the UTE, Mexicans, and eventually with the United States. By the 1850 the Navajo and non-Indians were on a collision course, and Manuelito was in the forefront.

Between 1846 and 1850, Indian raiding parties, many led by Manuelito, stole hundreds of animals in northwestern New Mexico. In 1851, the U.S. government established a post (later called FORT DEFIANCE) in the midst of Navajo land to put an end to the raids. In 1858, the post commander identified a large grazing area near the fort to be used exclusively for military livestock. Manuelito defiantly grazed his horses on the recently commandeered land; the animals were slaughtered. Enraged, some Navajo killed an African-American slave belonging to the post commander. In response, the military carried out three expeditions against the Navajo, which resulted in only a few deaths.

The Navajo continued their raids into New Mexico. Meanwhile, Chiefs Manuelito and BARBONCITO were convinced that they could drive the soldiers out of their land. On April 30, 1860, they led approximately 1,000 Navajo in an attack on Fort Defiance. After a two-hour battle, they were driven back by artillery. Not long thereafter, Fort Defiance was closed, and newly constructed Fort Fauntleroy (later Fort Wingate), some 35 miles to the south, took center stage. There, in January 1861, Manuelito, Barboncito, and other chiefs met with the soldiers to establish peace. It was not to last. In September, a horse race was held at the fort. Someone cut Manuelito's bridle rein, and he was therefore unable to control his mount. The Navajo were incensed, and when the judges refused to re-run the race, the Indians rioted. Ten Navajo were killed as soldiers shot artillery into the crowd.

Manuelito and the Navajo thereupon stepped up their raiding. In response, General JAMES H. CARLETON and Colonel CHRISTOPHER ("KIT") CARSON waged war against the tribe (see NAVAJO WAR, 1863–64). Many Navajo surrendered in 1864 and made the LONG WALK to BOSQUE REDONDO. Manuelito fought for two more years before finally surrendering.

At Bosque Redondo, essentially a prison camp, conditions for the Navajo were terrible. Manuelito and Barboncito traveled to Washington, D.C., to plead the Indians' case. The NAVAJO TREATY OF 1868 resulted, and the Indians went home. In 1872, Manuelito agreed to become the chief of the Navajo police. In 1876 he again traveled to Washington, this time to protest that Navajo lands were being seized by the Atlantic and Pacific Railroad. Thereafter, he lived quietly until his death in 1894 at the age of 76.

Marias River (Marias Massacre) (1870) *massacre that led Congress to outlaw the appointment of military officers as Indian agents*

On January 23, 1870, as the temperature hovered at −20°, Major EUGENE M. BAKER and four cavalry companies attacked a Piegan (see BLACKFOOT CONFEDERACY) village of 37 lodges on the Marias River in Montana. Baker thought he was attacking the village of Mountain Chief, head chief of the Piegan, whose warriors had been raiding Montanans for the past several years. Unfortunately, he was wrong. The village was actually that of Heavy Runner, a lesser headman and ally of the United States, whose people were suffering from a smallpox epidemic. The charging cavalry slaughtered 173 Piegans, 53 of whom were women and children. They also captured 140 women and children and some 300 horses. After burning lodges and camp equipment, the troops turned the PRISONERS loose with no homes or goods for the winter. This action was promptly termed a massacre and roused a temporary storm of protest among easterners against the army's treatment of Indians. News of events along the along the Marias River helped to convince Congress to block the proposed return of the BUREAU OF INDIAN AFFAIRS to the WAR DEPARTMENT.

Maricopa (Pee-Posh) *Indian tribe living along the Gila River in Arizona*

Originally, the Maricopa, who belong to the Yuman language group, lived along the lower Colorado River south of the present town of Parker, Arizona. In the 1700s, because of chronic inter-tribal warfare with the YUMA and MOJAVE Indians, they migrated eastward along the Gila River until they entered the lands of the Pima (now known as AKIMEL O'ODHAM). During the first half of the next century, they were joined by other groups from the Colorado River who also had been displaced by warfare. Together, the displaced tribes became known as the Maricopa, and they allied themselves with the local Pima against common foes.

In 1857, a Yuma and Mojave force moved along the Gila River near Maricopa land. In the battle at MARICOPA WELLS (1857), the Maricopa and their Pima allies defeated these traditional enemies. Approximately 140 Yuma and Mojave allies engaged in the battle. When the fighting was done, only 11 survived. This huge loss of men devastated those tribes and effectively ended their warfare with the Maricopa.

Further Reading
Kroeber, Clifton B., and Bernard L. Fontana. *Massacre on the Gila.* Tucson: University of Arizona Press, 1992.

Maricopa Wells (1857) *last battle in the Southwest fought between opposing Indian tribes*

Early on the morning of September 1, 1857, a band of MOJAVE and YUMA warriors (estimates range at 600 to 700), who had traveled some 160 miles on foot from their settlements along the Colorado River, attacked two MARICOPA Indian villages at a place called Maricopa Wells (along the Gila River north of present-day Tucson, Arizona). Although related, the Yuma and Maricopa were traditional enemies. Over the years, the Maricopa had moved away from the Colorado River region to escape the Yuma and live with the Pima (see AKIMEL O'OD-HAM) tribe along the Gila.

The Maricopa, who may have numbered approximately 200 warriors, fought back with clubs, LANCES, and BOWS AND ARROWS. Some warriors managed to get to their horses and ride east to Pima settlements for help. Considering themselves victorious, the Mojave and Yuma paused, and some Mojave as well as a group of APACHE who had joined them, left the battlefield and headed north. The Mojave and Yuma who remained were taken by surprise, however, when a band of Pima warriors on horseback arrived to aid their Maricopa allies. In the battle that followed, the remaining Mojave were killed. The Yuma warriors were all but decimated, although 11 survivors managed to flee west to the rocks of the Sierra Estrella range, about three miles away.

Isiah Woods, an overseer on the overland mail route from San Antonio, Texas, to San Diego, California, was on his way to Tucson when he and his pack train stopped to camp at Maricopa Wells, a way station on his route. Woods and his men saw the battle that raged about half a mile from their camp, but they refused to help when a Maricopa chief appealed for aid. Reports of the battle are based on Woods's account, in which he estimated that about 140 Mojave and Yuma were overwhelmed by possibly as many as 1,200 Maricopa and Pima in the final stage of the battle.

masks, Pacific Northwest, in warfare *cultural artifacts used by Native Americans in the Pacific Northwest*

Among the Kwaikiutl of the Pacific Northwest coast, masks were regarded as heirlooms and used to make connections with its past and with family ancestors. Masks were important in warfare because they invoked the presence of influential spirits. A dancer who donned a ritual mask was no longer himself; he *became* the spirit the mask represented. For family masks, a dancer became his own ancestors, sharing in the traditions, visions, and power of his family line. This power was extremely important in warfare. The influence of a spirit could help turn the tide of battle in a warrior's favor. The same spirit could help a warrior win fame and renown and increase his rank in society.

The Tlingit of southern Alaska wore animal masks not only to invoke the aid of spirits but also to protect their faces during battle. In the 1790s, when Russian traders first fought Tlingit who objected to their interference in the fur trade, they found the Indian masks were so well constructed that they could repel bullets.

Mason, John (ca. 1600–1672) *colonial Massachusetts soldier in the Pequot War*

John Mason was a native of England who came to the colony of Massachusetts around 1633. By 1635 he had helped found the colony of Windsor on the Connecticut River and held the rank of militia captain. In May 1637, the Connecticut General Court, the governing body of the colony, ordered Captain Mason to take 90 men (including 20 under Captain JOHN UNDERHILL) and 70 MOHEGAN allies under Chief Uncas and move against the PEQUOT leader Sassacus at his village on the Mystic River.

Rather than assault Sassacus's village directly, Mason chose to travel by water further west, where he picked up 500 NARRAGANSETT allies. He then approached Mystic Fort from the west, surprising and surrounding the Pequot. He gave orders to set the village on fire and to kill all Indians in it who tried to escape. Of the approximately 500 Pequot in Mystic Fort, only five survived the assault and escaped. Mason's losses were two colonists killed and 20 wounded. Twenty of his Indian allies were also wounded.

Mason was promoted to major for his role in defeating the Pequot. He later wrote a history of the conflict, which was printed in Increase Mather's *A Relation of the Troubles that Have Hapned in New England* (1677) and in Thomas Price's *A Brief History of the Pequot War* (1736). Mason served in the Connecticut government, managing Indian affairs for the colony and for the New England Confederation until his death in 1672.

Massachuset *Indian tribe that lived in an area of the state that now bears their name, from north of Salem around Boston Bay and south to Brockton*

The Massachuset lived in dome-shaped, birch bark–covered houses common to New England ALGONQUIAN tribes. They hunted, fished, and cultivated a number of crops, such as beans, pumpkins, and tobacco. During the summer months, they harvested seafoods, such as lobster and clams. Their clothing, made of soft, tanned animal skins, was sometimes decorated with porcupine quills, feathers, shells, and paint. It is recorded that they sang, drummed, danced, and performed ceremonies having to do with harvest, peacemaking, and warfare.

The Massachuset's location destined them to be one of the first tribes to have contact with Europeans and European diseases. Between the departure of Captain JOHN SMITH (1616) and the arrival of Plymouth colonists (1620), a smallpox epidemic decimated the Massachuset. Another smallpox epidemic between 1831 and 1833 virtually wiped out the tribe; only 1,000 remained of an estimated population of 10,000 (see SMALLPOX, EFFECTS OF). Many pilgrims viewed the decimation of the Indians by European diseases as demonstrative of their own favored status with God.

In 1640, Pastor John Eliot of Roxbury began working to convert the Massachuset to the Puritan religion. He learned their Algonquian dialect and preached to them in their language. He also helped them build 17 villages, where the converts lived and practiced their new religion. As a result, the Massachuset became known as the "Praying Indians."

The conversion of the Massachuset to Puritanism isolated them from former allies and engendered intertribal animosities. In June 1675, for example, colonists hanged three WAMPANOAG for the murder of a Praying Indian. This incident was the last in a series of events that precipitated KING PHILIP'S WAR (1675–76). The Massachuset were caught in the middle during the war and were attacked by both sides—the Wampanoag, NARRAGANSETT, and Nipmuck on one side and colonists who hated all Indians on the other. As a result, the Massachuset were almost wiped out again. The few survivors chose either to live among the colonists or to seek refuge with other Indian tribes. The result was the disappearance of the Massachuset tribal identity, although some families still live in Massachusetts and in Bermuda, where their ancestors had been sent as slaves.

massacre *any fight that results in the deaths of a number of noncombatants, especially women and children*

The word *massacre* is used loosely to describe any large-scale killing of people, regardless of race and whether soldiers or nonsoldiers. Both Indians and non-Indians have perpetrated such slaughters. In 1660, for example, a band of about 800 ONONDAGA, ONEIDA, and MOHAWK destroyed a raiding party of 61 French, HURON, and ALGONKIN raiders at a camp on the Ottawa River. The survivors were ritually tortured to death. In 1704, a combined force of about 48 French troops and their Indian allies surprised the Massachusetts town of Deerfield (see DEERFIELD RAID). About 48 British colonists died in the assault. Between 400–800 whites were killed in the opening stages of the MINNESOTA UPRISING (1862).

Massacres were also perpetrated against Native Americans. In 1637, for example, the colonists of Connecticut and

Massachusetts with their MOHEGAN and NARRAGANSETT allies surrounded the PEQUOT village of Mystic Fort and killed 500 of the inhabitants, including women and children. Only five Pequot survived the assault. The CIVIL WAR (1861–65) saw two of the most infamous such massacres. One, at BEAR RIVER (1863), left some 250 Shoshone dead and mutilated following an engagement with California volunteers. On November 28, 1864, Colonel JOHN M. CHIVINGTON and 700 U.S. soldiers surrounded CHEYENNE leader BLACK KETTLE's camp at Sand Creek, Colorado. The following morning, Chivington attacked and killed between 150 and 200 Cheyenne and ARAPAHO, the majority of them women and children, in the massacre at SAND CREEK (1864). Many of the dead were mutilated, their skulls crushed and their bellies slit open.

The Sand Creek massacre was followed four years later by another attack on Black Kettle's village, this time carried out by GEORGE ARMSTRONG CUSTER and the 7th Cavalry at the battle of the WASHITA (1868), where 101 Cheyenne died in the fighting.

On April 30, 1871, between 86 and 150 Western APACHE—again, mostly women and children—died at the hands of a mob of settlers in what became known as the CAMP GRANT MASSACRE (1871). But perhaps the most infamous massacre of Indians was the one that occurred on December 29, 1890, when troops from the 7th Cavalry surrounded a band of Minniconjous Lakota (see SIOUX) led by BIG FOOT at Wounded Knee Creek in South Dakota. When an Indian's rifle went off accidentally, soldiers and Indians both opened fire amid the Lakota camp. When the carnage was finally ended, the camp lay in shambles. More than 150 Indians lay dead, with another 50 or so wounded, many of whom died later. Twenty-five soldiers had also been killed and 39 wounded. Some veterans described the bloodshed at WOUNDED KNEE (1890) as worse than that of the Civil War because the casualties included so many women and children.

See also main article on Warfare Terminology.

McClellan Creek (1872) *battle between the Comanche and the U.S. Army during the Comanche Wars*

On September 29, 1872, while on a campaign begun that spring to capture COMANCHE leader QUANAH PARKER, Colonel RANALD S. MACKENZIE and a troop of 20 scouts and 222 soldiers of the 4th U.S. Cavalry came upon a Comanche village at McClellan Creek, a tributary of the Red River in the Texas Panhandle. In the surprise attack that followed, 50 Indians were killed and 124 were taken prisoner, all of them women and children. The troopers also captured a thousand ponies and burned everything—lodges, blankets, hides, and drying meat—as part of Mackenzie's "scorched-earth" strategy. The Comanche recaptured most of their ponies soon afterward. Mackenzie's disappointment at the loss of these horses no doubt influenced his decision two years later to destroy Indian horses at the battle of PALO DURO CANYON (1874).

McCulloch, Benjamin (1811–1862) *soldier known for his leadership of the Texas Rangers in actions against the Comanche*

Born in Tennessee, as an adult Benjamin McCulloch moved to Texas to take part in the Texas revolution against Mexico. In 1837, McCulloch and his brother Henry were among those authorized to raise military companies to intercept raiding Comanche. He subsequently became one of the TEXAS RANGER leaders responsible for the defeat of BUFFALO HUMP and his Comanche warriors at the battle of PLUM CREEK (1840).

Considered one of the best frontier military leaders, McCulloch led a ranger company in the Mexican War (1846–48), serving as a scout for General Zachary Taylor's army. McCulloch later engaged in a variety of other activities, including surveying and gold mining in California. In February 1861, during the CIVIL WAR (1861–65), he commanded the Texas Confederate forces that received the surrender of Union troops in Texas. Three months later, he was appointed a brigadier general in the Confederate army and put in command of the Indian Territory (now Oklahoma). His first major assignment there was to negotiate treaties between the Confederacy and local Indian tribes, including the Comanche, CHOCTAW, CHICKASAW, CREEK, SEMINOLE, WICHITA, OSAGE, SENECA, Quapaw, and SHAWNEE. McCulloch was killed on March 7, 1862, at the battle of PEA RIDGE (1862).

McGillivray, Alexander (Isti-atcagagi-thlucco, "Great Beloved Man," Hobo-hili-miko, Hippo-iki-mico, "Good Child King," Emperor) (1759–1793) *Creek war leader and statesman*

Alexander McGillivray was born in a CREEK village in Alabama to a Scottish trader and his French/Creek wife. He was educated locally until he was 14, at which time he was sent to Charleston, South Carolina, for more formal education. McGillivray's education, abilities, and hereditary status did not go unnoticed by the Creek, who made him a chief.

When the AMERICAN REVOLUTION (1775–81) began, McGillivray accepted a commission as assistant commissary in the British Indian service. His main task was to establish and maintain cordial relations between the British and the Creek Nation. During the war, McGillivray supported the activities of Cherokee chief and British ally DRAGGING CANOE and led attacks on American settlements in Tennessee and Georgia.

When the war ended and Great Britain signed the TREATY OF PARIS (1783), the Creek were in a precarious position, surrounded by former enemies. At first McGillivray tried to establish a separate Creek nation. When this failed, he signed trade agreements and treaties, including the Treaty of New York, with both the Spanish and the Americans.

McGillivray's peacetime diplomacy was very successful, allowing the Creek a crucial decade to withstand pressure from American settlers. Meanwhile, he received annuities from both Spain and the United States and was secretly commissioned a brigadier general in the U.S. Army. In 1791, exhausted from his political efforts and plagued with chronic illnesses, Alexander McGillivray died at age 34 while visiting a friend in Pensacola, Florida.

McIntosh Treaty See FORT GIBSON TREATY.

Means, Russell (1939–) *Oglala Lakota/Yankton Dakota activist and actor*

Russell Means was born in 1939 to a Yankton Dakota mother and an Oglala Lakota father in Greenwood, South Dakota. (Both Dakota and Lakota are branches of the SIOUX.) He divided his childhood between Oakland, California, and South Dakota, where his grandparents lived. Though a bright student, Means had a troubled youth and abused alcohol and drugs, but he completed high school in 1958. He drifted in and out of several jobs and numerous barroom fights. In 1964, he participated in his first activist action, the occupation of Alcatraz Island. Married and a father by then, in 1968 Means moved with his family to Cleveland. There he met Clyde Bellecourt and Dennis Banks and became involved in the AMERICAN INDIAN MOVEMENT (AIM).

Means proved to be a provocative representative for Indian rights. In 1972, Means led activists from Seattle to Washington, D.C., in the Trail of Broken Treaties demonstration, where they occupied the BUREAU OF INDIAN AFFAIRS building. He is perhaps best known as one of the leaders of the 1973 armed Lakota seizure of the approximate site of the WOUNDED KNEE MASSACRE (1890) in South Dakota. The standoff between Lakota activists on one side and federal law enforcement officials on the other side lasted 71 days. The troubles arose after both a territorial dispute with the federal government and a political dispute on the Pine Ridge Reservation between Means and AIM and the tribal government under Dick Wilson, who had defeated Means for Pine Ridge tribal chairman (see WOUNDED KNEE SIEGE [1973]). Means spent much time in the legal system after what some call Wounded Knee II, defending himself from charges related to the siege.

Again in 1981, Means led a group of AIM members in an occupation of federal lands, this time the Black Hills of South Dakota, held sacred by the Sioux. Although Indians lived at the Yellow Thunder Camp for several years, federal authorities did not award the Black Hills to the Sioux as AIM demanded.

Means did not confine his activities to Indians in the United States but traveled to Nicaragua in 1984. There he came to the controversial conclusion that the country's Sandinista rebels, whom AIM had supported, were abusing local Miskito Indians. In 1984, Means again tried to win election as the Pine Ridge Reservation tribal chairman, and in 1986 he pursued the U.S. presidential nomination of the Libertarian Party, both unsuccessfully. Since 1991, he also has worked as an actor, appearing in such films as *Dances with Wolves* and *The Last of the Mohicans*. In 1995, he published an autobiography, *Where White Men Fear to Tread*. He remains involved in pro-Indian causes.

Medal of Honor recipients, Native American

Native Americans who have received the United States's highest military award

The Medal of Honor, established in 1861, is awarded to those military personnel who have displayed exceptional heroism and whose acts have "far exceeded any just demand of duty." Native Americans have fought in all American wars, from the AMERICAN REVOLUTION (1775–83) through the Gulf War (1991–92). Twenty-four have received the Medal of Honor for their service in such conflicts as the Indian Wars of the latter 1800s through the Korean War (1950–53).

The first Indian to be given the award was a PAWNEE scout, Sergeant Co-Rux-Te-Chod-Ish (known as Mad Bear), who served with the U.S. army in a campaign during the COMANCHE WARS (1840–75). On July 8, 1869, at the Republican River, Kansas, Mad Bear broke from the army column in pursuit of an Indian enemy and was badly wounded by a bullet from his own army column. He was awarded the medal on August 24, 1869.

Many APACHE served as scouts with the army during the APACHE WARS (1861–86). Ten earned their medals of honor for gallant conduct during the 1872–73 campaign. Among them were Alchesay, Jim, Kosoha, and Chiquito.

More than 25,000 Native Americans served in World War II. Five received the Medal of Honor: Van T. Barfoot, a CHOCTAW; Ernest Childers, an Oklahoma CREEK; Ernest E. Evana, a Pawnee; Jack Montgomery, an Oklahoma CHEROKEE; and John N. Reese, an Oklahoma Creek. Second Lieutenant Van T. Barfoot risked his life and displayed exceptional gallantry near Carano, Italy, on May 23, 1944. Alone, he destroyed two German machine-gun nests and took 17 prisoners. Barfoot also fired on a German tank, killed its occupants, and advanced into enemy territory to destroy a field gun. He rescued two of his wounded fellow soldiers.

In the war in the Pacific, Private First Class John N. Reese displayed extreme heroism and gave his life near Manila in the Philippine Islands. On February 9, 1945, during an attack on a railroad station held by the Japanese, Reese and another soldier crossed U.S. lines and advanced across an open field toward the station. Under two-and-a-half hours of intense fire, the two killed more than 82 of the enemy, routed the Japanese defenders, and opened the way for other soldiers to take the station. Reese, who drew enemy fire to himself and away from his companion, was killed in the action.

Three Native Americans won the Medal of Honor in the Korean War: Charles George, an Eastern Cherokee; Raymond Harvey (tribe not known); and Mitchell Red Cloud, a WINNEBAGO. On November 5, 1950, near Chonghyon, Korea, Corporal Mitchell Red Cloud spotted a Chinese communist patrol approaching his company's position. Sounding the alarm, Red Cloud began firing into the patrol until his company could rally. Although wounded, he refused help and, supporting himself against a tree, continued firing. Red Cloud was fatally wounded, but his act stopped the enemy from overrunning his company and gave the others time to regroup and evacuate the wounded.

More than 42,000 Native Americans served in the Vietnam War (1957–75), and 3,000 participated in the Persian Gulf War (1991). None have received the Medal of Honor for service in these wars.

Medicine Bottle (unknown–1864) *chief of the Mdewakanton Dakota*

As chief of the Mdewakanton band of the Santee Dakota (see SIOUX), Medicine Bottle took part in the MINNESOTA UPRISING (1862). The Mdewakanton Dakota had been confined to a reservation along the upper Minnesota River in 1851. The people there depended on payments from the U.S. government and on trade goods from non-Indian merchants, who consistently cheated them. After the winter of 1861–62, during which the tribe nearly starved, Chiefs Medicine Bottle, Shakopee, and LITTLE CROW gathered their warriors. In August 1862 war parties spread out along the river, taking settlers by surprise as they attacked towns and settlements. Within a month, war parties had killed more than 450 settlers.

In September 1862, troops under Colonel HENRY H. SIBLEY finally put down the uprising and captured 2,000 Mdewakanton men, women, and children. Medicine Bottle, Shakopee, and Little Crow escaped and fled to Canada. Two years later, in 1864, Medicine Bottle and Shakopee were captured in Canada, drugged, and carried across the border on a dogsled. On November 11, 1864, Medicine Bottle was hanged at Fort Snelling, Minnesota.

medicine bundles, war *objects made and used for sacred or medicinal purposes, primarily by Great Plains groups*

Medicine war bundles were sacred packets owned by individuals, clans, or tribes. Bundles were made of animal skin and contained charms and relics of weasel fur, buffalo horn, rattlesnake rattles, and human scalps. The pouches were symbols of past victories with magical power to protect the owner. The pouch was worn into battle. All bundles were unique, and the contents had special meaning or powers for their owners. Many Indians included tobacco and a pipe in their tribes' medicine war bundles. Among the Ponca, the bundles usually contained birdskins with human scalps attached to them. After a successful battle or expedition, a new item, such as a scalp, was added. Tribal bundles were carried by the leader of the war party. In the winter, bundles were hung at the back of the lodge; in the summer, as long as the weather was good, they were hung outside.

Individuals also owned bundles. A personal bundle might protect an individual from harm, warn of danger, or endow him or her with the qualities of the animal, thing, or person represented by the item or items. Ethnologist John Ewers noted that of 50 Blackfoot medicine war bundles he had seen, the most common contents were single feathers or bunches of feathers. Necklaces, lances, knives, shirts, headdresses, and bandoliers were also considered powerful by some warriors.

Medicine Creek Treaty (1854) *one of a series of treaties negotiated by the U.S. government with tribes of the Oregon and Washington territories*

The influx of miners and settlers into Oregon and Washington following the Gold Rush of 1849 also brought conflicts with the Indians of the Northwest. In 1853, Indians along the Rogue River in southern Oregon attacked miners who were killing and abusing Indians. A military campaign against the Indians resulted in the ROGUE RIVER WAR (1855–56). Before full-scale war broke out, however, the new governor of the Washington Territory, ISAAC I. STEVENS, concluded a series of treaties designed to force small tribes north of the Columbia River and west of the Cascade Mountains onto reservations. Stevens met with representatives of the tribes of Puget Sound in December 1854. On December 26, 62 chiefs and heads of clans signed the Medicine Creek Treaty.

According to the terms of the treaty, the tribes were to move to reservations, receive payment for their land with goods, and be taught to farm. Stevens concluded a later treaty at the WALLA WALLA PEACE COUNCIL (1855) with the more powerful tribes east of the Cascades, including the YAKAMA. Most representatives of the tribes signed the treaty. Stevens, however, broke his promise that the tribes would have two years to relocate to reservations and immediately opened up Indian lands to non-Indian settlement. Some of the tribes resisted removal, and the hostilities resulted in the YAKAMA WAR (1855–57).

Medicine Lodge Treaties (1867) *agreements signed at Medicine Lodge Creek, Kansas, between representatives of the U.S. government and delegates from the major Plains tribes*

The SAND CREEK Massacre (1864) and FETTERMAN FIGHT (1867), along with continued violence on the central Plains and along the BOZEMAN TRAIL, had convinced Congress to attempt to chart a new course in U.S.-Indian relations by creating the United States Indian Peace Commission in July 1867. Chaired by Nathaniel G. Taylor, a deeply religious man recently appointed commissioner of Indian affairs, the committee also included noted reformers Senator John B. Henderson, Samuel F. Tappan, and John B. Sanborn. From the army, WILLIAM TECUMSEH SHERMAN, WILLIAM S. HARNEY, and ALFRED TERRY rounded out the delegation. The Peace Commission was empowered to meet with chiefs of tribes then at war with the government, investigate the causes of conflict, and negotiate peace agreements. Reservations were to be established for those tribes not currently on such designated land. Should the commission fail, the secretary of war was authorized to call up 4,000 volunteers to force the issue.

Delegates from the Peace Commission convened in October with leaders from the KIOWA, COMANCHE, and Kiowa-APACHE at Medicine Lodge Creek, site of a SUN DANCE ground popular among Plains tribes. Following custom, feasting, speeches, and the distribution of gifts initiated the meeting. On October 21, Indian leaders already present fixed their marks to agreements. Reluctant CHEYENNE and ARAPAHO, who had heretofore refused to enter the talks, came and signed similar agreements a week later.

The Medicine Lodge treaties reflected the goals of contemporary Indian affairs reformers. The Kiowa, Comanche, and Kiowa-Apache would be concentrated on one large reservation in western Indian territory (present-day Oklahoma). The Cheyenne and Arapaho would be situated on a second reservation. For the next 30 years, the United States was obligated to distribute clothing, rations, and agricultural supplies. The government would furnish teachers as well as limited amounts of weapons and ammunition to the reservation agencies. Unauthorized non-Indians were to be prevented from trespassing. In return, the Indians agreed to respect the agreed-upon reservation boundaries, except when hunting buffalo south of the Arkansas River. They also promised not to block the expansion of railroads and military posts or to harm settlers or their property.

Reformers clearly expected the Medicine Lodge treaties to transform the nomadic plains peoples into prosperous farmers who shared the values of non-Indian Americans. Congressional approval of the Peace Commission's work was delayed by the impeachment of President Andrew Johnson, but the Senate finally ratified the agreements on July 25, 1868.

Despite the high hopes of reformers, the Medicine Lodge Creek treaties brought only a temporary respite to the violent struggles for military domination of the southern plains. Congress's delay in funding Indian appropriations slowed distribution of the promised government annuities. Discontent on the reservations gradually mounted, especially among the Cheyenne. In mid-August 1868, some 200 Cheyenne, accompanied by a handful of Arapaho and Lakota (see SIOUX), launched a series of attacks against non-Indians along the Saline and Solomon Rivers in Kansas, thus leading to the SOUTHERN PLAINS WAR (1868–69).

See also FORT LARAMIE TREATIES.

Further Reading

Prucha, Francis Paul. *The Great Father: The United States Government and the American Indians.* Lincoln: University of Nebraska Press, 1984.

Utley, Robert M. *Frontier Regulars: The United States Army and the Indian, 1866–1891.* Lincoln: University of Nebraska Press, 1984.

Meeker Agency (Meeker Massacre) (1879) *battle that led to the removal of the Ute from Colorado*

In 1878 Nathan C. Meeker replaced H. E. Danforth as Indian agent for the UTE at the White River Agency in Colorado. An agrarian socialist, Meeker saw the appointment as

In fall 1879, Ute killed Indian agent Nathan Meeker and several employees of the Meeker Agency. *(By permission of the Colorado Historical Society)*

an opportunity to end hostilities by teaching Indians how to farm.

When Meeker arrived on the White River reservation, he began his agricultural pursuits in meadows the Ute used as pasture for their ponies. The Ute, who wanted nothing to do with farming, angrily opposed Meeker's plans. As their antagonism grew, Meeker called for military support. In 1879, Major Thomas T. Thornburgh entered the reservation, where he and 11 of his soldiers were killed (see MILK CREEK, 1879). Simultaneous with this assault was an attack on the White River Agency itself. During the attack, Meeker and eight others were killed, and Meeker's wife and daughters were taken captive.

Although the assault was the work of a small group of Ute and was quickly quieted, Coloradans used the incident as an excuse to begin a war of extermination against the Ute (see UTE WAR, 1879). By March 1880 the Ute had signed an agreement with the federal government in which they agreed move to the Uintah Reservation in Utah. As a result, their reservation land was opened to non-Indian settlement.

Menewa (Manawa, Hothlepoya, "crazy war hunter") (ca. 1765–1865) *chief of the Creek and leader in the Creek War*

Menewa was born around 1765 in CREEK territory along the Tallapoosa River in central Alabama. His mother was a Creek and his father is thought to have been white. In his youth, Menewa was known as Hothlepoya ("Crazy War Hunter") for his horse-stealing raids on non-Indian settlements in Tennessee and Georgia. His courage and daring won him a reputation among the Creek, and he was chosen as a war chief. Defiantly antiwhite, Menewa supported SHAWNEE leader TECUMSEH when he asked the Creek to join in his struggle against settlers who were moving westward into Indian lands.

Menewa became a commander of the Creek faction called the RED STICKS (because they carried red war CLUBS into battle or because they erected tall red poles as declarations of war). Following a Red Stick attack on FORT MIMS (1813), a force of Tennessee militia and allied Indians under ANDREW JACKSON marched into Creek territory in Alabama. On March 27, 1813, Jackson cornered the Red Sticks under Menewa's command at a place called Horseshoe Bend on the Tallapoosa River. When the day-long battle of HORSESHOE BEND (1813) was over, only 70 of 900 Red Stick warriors remained. Menewa himself was hit seven times and left for dead, but he survived and escaped through the swamps. His village of Ofuskee was destroyed, and his home and livestock were taken.

By the time Menewa recovered, settlers were already pouring into Creek territory. In 1825, Menewa negotiated an agreement with the government to allow some Creek to retain their lands, although Menewa was not among them. Ten years later, Menewa and some of his Creek followers fought on the U.S. side in the Second SEMINOLE WAR (1835–42) against the SEMINOLE in Florida. For his service the government promised to return Menewa to his own lands. The promise was not kept,

however, and Menewa, along with his fellow Creek, was forced into exile in Indian Territory (present-day Oklahoma). He died there in 1865.

Metacom (Metacomet, King Philip, Philip, Pometacom, Wagwises) (ca. 1600–1676) *leader, or sachem, of the Wampanoag tribe*

Metacom was the younger of the two sons of WAMPANOAG sachem Massasoit. Despite early friendly relations between the Wampanoag and the Pilgrim fathers, the two groups became estranged after the deaths of the original Plymouth settlers during the 1650s and the death of Massasoit himself in 1661. When Wamsutta, Metacom's brother, became chief of the Wampanoag, he began selling land to colonists who were not part of the Plymouth settlement. The Plymouth colonists saw the proximity of these settlers as a threat to their newly won freedom of religion and their self-government. The Indians, meanwhile, saw the rapid expansion of the European population and the growing number of Christian converts as threats to their way of life. In 1662, the English settlers took Wamsutta hostage and brought him to Plymouth to answer charges of plotting against the colony. Wamsutta fell ill and died while he was in their hands.

Metacom followed Wamsutta as sachem of the Wampanoag. Unlike his brother, Metacom was less willing to sell land to settlers. However, the Plymouth colony continued to authorize new towns inland in Wampanoag territory. In 1671, the English summoned Metacom—or King Philip, as he was known to the settlers—to Plymouth to answer charges of plotting against the colony. The Wampanoag chief was forced to sign a treaty in which he was forced to surrender all of his tribe's muskets. However, he soon purchased new ones by selling more of his lands. The uneasy truce between the Indians and the colonists came to an end in 1675, when three Wampanoag were executed for the murder of a Christian Indian convert.

KING PHILIP'S WAR (1675–76) began with an outbreak of violence at Swansea, near Philip's home village of Mount Hope, in June 1675. Authorities differ on the question of whether Metacom had actually conspired to drive the English out of Massachusetts altogether. Some believe that as early as the 1670s he had contacted the NARRAGANSETT and the Nipmuc in the hope of forming an alliance with them. Others argue that Metacom was woefully unprepared for war, having only 300 warriors and no confirmed allies when the conflict broke out in 1675. In addition, his efforts to gain allies through diplomacy during the war were largely unsuccessful. France remained neutral, and the New York tribes he contacted were unwilling to support him. The allies who did join him were mostly from tribes that had been the victims of colonial assaults and bore grudges against the settlers.

At first, the war went well for Metacom and the Wampanoag. The Nipmuc Indians joined him after they killed several pursuing Massachusetts militiamen at the battle of HOPEWELL SWAMP (1675). The Indians then burned settlements on the Massachusetts frontier and killed many colonists in the ambush at BLOODY BROOK (1675). Fearful that the previously peaceful Narragansett tribe would join Metacom's war, colonial troops surrounded the tribe and killed most of its members in the GREAT SWAMP FIGHT (1675).

The tide turned in the settlers' favor after the winter of 1675–76. Without a chance to plant crops, the Indians suffered severely from hunger. In addition, their gunpowder stocks ran low. Metacom held out for a long time by hiding in the Great Swamp in southern Rhode Island. On August 12, 1676, colonial troops, with a group of Christianized Indians under BENJAMIN CHURCH, surprised Metacom and a small band of Wampanoag near his old home at Mount Hope. The chief was shot by a Christian Indian named Alderman. The settlers cut Metacom's head from its corpse and displayed it at Plymouth for the next 24 years. His death marked the end of King Philip's War. Some surviving Wampanoag found shelter among neighboring tribes and nursed a hatred of British colonists that colored future wars in the region. Others were sold into slavery in the Caribbean.

Further Reading
Bourne, Russell. *The Red King's Rebellion: Racial Politics in New England 1675–1678.* New York: Atheneum, 1990.
Leach, Douglas E. *Flintlock and Tomahawk: New England in King Philip's War.* New York: Macmillan, 1959.
Steele, Ian K. *Warpaths: Invasions of North America.* New York: Oxford University Press, 1994.

Métis *persons of mixed blood, usually of French-Canadian and Cree or Ojibwa ancestry, living in western Canada*
The Métis are mixed-blood descendants of French-Canadian fur traders—known as *coureurs de bois* or *voyageurs*—who had explored the western portion of the country in the 17th and 18th centuries. After the collapse of the fur trade in the 18th century, most of the voyageurs settled in what is now Saskatchewan and Manitoba, intermarried with local Native American women, and settled down as farmers, hunters, and trappers along the river valleys of western Canada. They mixed elements of both their European and Indian heritages, speaking French and Algonquian languages, and following Catholicism as well as native beliefs.

Because of their unique way of life, the Métis came into conflict with the Hudson's Bay Company and the Canadian government. The company maintained a monopoly on trade in furs, and in the 1840s it tried to stop the Métis from taking their pelts to markets in the United States. In 1849 Louis Riel, Sr., interrupted the smuggling trial of a fellow Métis at Fort Garry (Winnipeg), Manitoba, in what became known as the COURTHOUSE REBELLION (1849). Riel had a personal grievance against the Hudson's Bay Company as well: The company wished to maintain restrictions on manufacturing in the west and had stopped Riel's plans for a cloth factory. These incidents indicated to the Métis that the Canadian government had little respect for their interests.

In 1869 the Hudson's Bay Company sold its interests in western lands to the Canadian government. The company had discouraged settlement in the far west to preserve the fur trade. The Canadian government, on the other hand, wanted to open these lands to settlers. The government thus sponsored a survey of land in Manitoba and Saskatchewan, instructing the surveyors to divide the territory into squares of 800 acres each, in line with British practices. The Métis, however, measured their property differently. They followed the French practice of dividing their land into long strips that included riverfront, woodlands, and prairie in a single holding. This disagreement over land measurement led to the First RIEL REBELLION (1869–70).

The Métis, led by Riel's son LOUIS DAVID RIEL, overcame Canadian government forces sent against them and established their own provincial government. Despite negotiations with the Canadians, the Métis found that new settlers did not respect their land rights. As a result, many of them moved westward to Saskatchewan. By the early 1880s the Métis were again being crowded out of their lands by settlers. Louis David Riel led the Second RIEL REBELLION (1884–85) in defense of Métis rights. The Métis were joined by members of the CREE Nation, but 900 Canadian troops confronted and defeated them at Batoche on May 9, 1885. Government casualties were eight dead, 46 wounded, while the Métis suffered 16 dead and 30 wounded. The battle broke Métis power in the Canadian west.

Further Reading
Flanagan, Thomas. *Louis David Riel: Prophet of the New World.* Toronto: University of Toronto Press, 1979.
Friesen, John M. *The Riel/Real Story.* Nepeom, Ontario: Borealis Press, 1994.

Miami *tribe that occupied territory in what is now Indiana, western Ohio, and eastern Illinois*
From their original homeland in northern Wisconsin, the Miami people migrated into present-day Indiana in the early 1700s. Their territory centered on present-day Fort Wayne. Living in villages of lodges covered with bark or hides, the Miami farmed and gathered wild plants. They also hunted, traveling onto the prairies after buffalo when the great herds appeared in their territory.

During the FRENCH AND INDIAN WAR (1754–63), the Miami, along with other tribes of the Ohio valley, rallied to the French side. Following France's final defeat in 1763, all lands, including those of the Miami, fell into British hands. During the AMERICAN REVOLUTION (1775–83), the Miami, fearing the loss of their lands if the Americans won, sided with the British. When the Americans did win, and Great Britain ceded all lands from the Great Lakes south, Miami territory became part of the United States.

Alarmed by the steady advance of Americans into the Ohio valley, the Miami joined with the SHAWNEE, Ojibway (now Anishinabe), OTTAWA, and other tribes in a determined resistance to retain their villages and hunting grounds. Raids by the Miami and other tribes along the Ohio frontier took more than 1,000 settlers' lives between 1783 and 1790. General JOSIAH T. HARMER, commander of the Old Northwest Territory, was dispatched to quell Indian resistance. A tribal coalition under the Miami leader LITTLE TURTLE ambushed and routed the general's forces in a battle known as HARMER'S DEFEAT (1790). Subsequently, in the fall of 1791 during the conflict that was part of what came to be called LITTLE TURTLE'S WAR (1783–95), the tribes crushed a force of some 2,000 men under Major General ARTHUR ST. CLAIR (see ST. CLAIR'S DEFEAT, 1791).

The Miami continued to fight, but Little Turtle, believing that further resistance was futile, withdrew from the alliance. Following the defeat of the tribes at the hands of General ANTHONY WAYNE (see FALLEN TIMBERS, 1794), the Miami and other tribes signed the TREATY OF GREENVILLE (1795), ceding most of their lands to the United States. Miami territory was thereupon reduced piece by piece as non-Indian settlement expanded beyond the Ohio valley. In 1840 the Miami ceded the last of their lands in Indiana, and by 1867 most had moved to Indian Territory in the West.

Most contemporary Miami live in Oklahoma as the Miami Nation. Others have remained on some of their traditional lands as the Miami Nation of Indiana.

Miami War   See LITTLE TURTLE'S WAR.

Miantonomo (Miantonomi) (ca. 1600–1643)
Narragansett sachem (or chief) and ally of the British settlers during the Pequot War in New England

Miantonomo was a friend to the Massachusetts colonists at Plymouth and Massachusetts Bay as well as to Roger Williams, founder of the colony of Rhode Island. When he learned that Captain John Oldham and his crew had been killed by NARRAGANSETT Indians on BLOCK ISLAND (1636), Miantonomo, who was sachem of the tribe, launched a punitive raid, taking 200 warriors to punish the members responsible for the deaths. In March 1637, Williams convinced the Narragansett sachem to ally with the colonists in the PEQUOT WAR (1636–37). Miantonomo joined the assault on the Pequot stronghold at Mystic River in 1637, but protested the massacre of women and children that followed. Nonetheless, he accepted the terms of the Treaty of Hartford (1638), which assigned 80 Pequot survivors as slaves to his tribe.

Miantonomo recognized the impact that the Hartford treaty would have on his tribe. The Connecticut colonial authorities used the terms of the treaty to claim jurisdiction over his people. In addition, they supported MOHEGAN leader Uncas in his efforts to win the support of former Narragansett allies. In 1641 and 1642, Miantonomo traveled among the New England Indians, seeking to create an intertribal union that would drive the British from New England. Early in 1643,

however, he was captured by Uncas, who turned him over to the Connecticut authorities. The colonists held Miantonomo until September, then returned him to Uncas, who executed him. Miantonomo was the first Indian leader to attempt a pan-Indian union to resist European incursions on Native American territory.

Miles, Nelson A. (1839–1925) *U.S. Army officer who rose to prominence during the Civil War and in campaigns against Plains tribes*

Born near Westminister, Massachusetts, Nelson Miles joined the Union army following the attack on Fort Sumter, South Carolina, which marked the beginnings of the CIVIL WAR (1861–65). Despite his youth and lack of formal military education, Miles proved to be an excellent combat commander. During the war, he fought in virtually every major battle in the east except Gettysburg, and he was wounded three times at the hands of the Confederates. He was later awarded a Medal of Honor for his actions during the battle of Chancellorsville in 1863. An inspirational leader and a fine tactician, Miles emerged from the Civil War as a brevet major general, but he was given a rank of colonel in the much-reduced regular army. After the war he briefly oversaw the safekeeping of former Confederate president Jefferson Davis before being assigned to Reconstruction duties in North Carolina. In 1868 he married the niece of General WILLIAM TECUMSEH SHERMAN.

As commander of the 5th Infantry Regiment, Miles saw his first combat with Indians during the RED RIVER WAR (1872–75), during which he fought the COMANCHE, KIOWA, CHEYENNE, and ARAPAHO. Hampered by shortages of supplies and severe drought followed by torrential rains and severe winter blizzards, Miles secured his first victory against the Indians in that war on August 30, 1874, at the battle of Tule Canyon. He remained in the field through most of the winter, distinguishing himself for his determination and stubborn pursuits of the enemy.

When the SIOUX WARS (1854–90) erupted again in 1876, Miles pressed General Sherman for an opportunity to manage the problem. Following the battle of the LITTLE BIGHORN (1876), he and the 5th Infantry were transferred north and given the assignment of holding the Yellowstone River valley. Establishing what eventually became Fort Keogh, Miles won the battle of CEDAR CREEK (1876) against SITTING BULL and his Lakota (see SIOUX) followers. His campaign in pursuit of Sitting Bull covered some 408 miles.

On January 8, 1877, Miles engaged warriors under CRAZY HORSE at Tongue Valley during the battle of WOLF MOUNTAIN (1877). His victory, along with Miles's continued winter operations, helped convince a number of Indians to turn themselves in later that spring. On May 7, Miles led his command against Miniconjou Lakota warriors at the battle of MUDDY CREEK (1877), in which he almost lost his life. During discussions with their chief, Lame Deer, before the engagement, Miles barely dodged a bullet that killed a cavalryman standing behind him. In the ensuing battle, Miles destroyed most of the Miniconjou lodges and captured much of their pony herd.

In September 1877, yet another opportunity for action confronted Miles, this time involving the NEZ PERCE under the leadership of the young CHIEF JOSEPH. Upon receiving calls for assistance from General OLIVER O. HOWARD, Miles caught up with Nez Perce in northern Montana in the Bear Paw Mountains, about 40 miles south of the Canadian border. After an unsuccessful attack on the Indian camp, Miles's command settled in for a siege (see BEAR PAW, 1877). Following a series of meetings, Joseph surrendered on October 5.

Promoted to brigadier general in 1880, Miles was given command of the Department of the Columbia in 1881 and the Department of the Missouri in 1885. When General PHILIP HENRY SHERIDAN became dissatisfied with the efforts of GEORGE CROOK in defeating the APACHE, Miles was transferred in 1886 to command the Department of the Arizona. Following Sheridan's directive that he depend more heavily on his regular troops than had Crook, Miles launched an aggressive campaign against the Apache. He reorganized border defenses, used mirrors to send flash messages, and assigned mobile columns to intercept raiding Apache. Miles assigned Captain Henry W. Lawton to take a force into Mexico and track down GERONIMO, a search that covered 2,000 miles. Only once did Miles's force manage to locate any Apache; when they did, the Indians detected them and fled. His early efforts having done little save wear out his regulars, Miles opted for different measures. He employed additional Indian scouts to help track Geronimo's followers and removed all Chiricahua and Warm Springs Apache from Arizona. Exhausted by the constant pressure and troubled by the removal of their families, Geronimo and most of his followers finally surrendered to Miles on September 4, 1886. Miles was later criticized for having made unauthorized promises to Geronimo in the process of securing his surrender.

In 1890, General Miles was assigned to command the sprawling Division of the Missouri. As the GHOST DANCE spread among the northern plains tribes, he directed army operations that culminated in the controversial massacre at WOUNDED KNEE (1890). There, on December 29, 1890, one of Miles's subordinates, JAMES FORSYTH, mishandled efforts to disarm the Lakota followers of BIG FOOT. Furious at the debacle, Miles brought charges against Forsyth, accusing the latter of having disobeyed his direct order to avoid intermingling his troops with the tribe. Much to Miles's dismay, however, the WAR DEPARTMENT, anxious to put the entire matter behind it, overruled the court martial and restored Forsyth to command.

Miles was promoted to major general in 1890. As commander of the reorganized Department of the Missouri during the Pullman railroad strikes of 1894, he directed the army's efforts to restore rail service in and around Chicago. With the retirement of John M. Schofield a year later, Miles was named commanding general of the army. He commanded the force that occupied Puerto Rico during the Spanish-American War (1898). Promoted to lieutenant general in 1900, his resistance

to army reform and unsubstantiated claims that the War Department had supplied troops with "embalmed beef" during the Spanish-American War rankled President Theodore Roosevelt, who refused to allow Miles to remain in active service past his mandatory retirement in 1903. Miles died while taking his grandchildren to the circus in Washington, D.C.

A controversial figure, Miles had little tolerance for what he perceived to be the incompetence of some of his fellow officers. Inordinately ambitious, he was quick to criticize others and exploited every political and personal influence he possessed in often unseemly efforts to gain promotion and glory. A firm believer in the government's insistence that Indians be moved to reservations, by force if necessary, Miles sometimes proved an outspoken defender of leaders such as Chief Joseph, who demanded that treaty promises be kept. He stands with George Crook and RANALD S. MACKENZIE as among the army's leading figures in the Indian Wars of the late 19th century.

Further Reading
Wooster, Robert A. *Nelson A. Miles and the Twilight of the Frontier Army.* Lincoln: University of Nebraska Press, 1993.

military societies *social and political warrior societies common among the Indian tribes of the Great Plains*
Military societies among Native Americans had both private and public functions. In its private function, a society acted as a fraternal or social organization for the individual members. Each society had a lodge in which man could relax, sleep, eat, dance, sing, and interact with fellow members. The societies also had serious public duties associated with them, such as policing the people at certain times—for example, at the SUN DANCE, while traveling, or when the entire band or tribe left for the hunt.

Native American military societies were mainly restricted to men, and the number of societies varied from tribe to tribe. The MANDAN and Hidatsa, for example had 10 military societies, whereas the KIOWA and the CHEYENNE had six, and members of the BLACKFOOT CONFEDERACY had seven. Some of the names of the societies were the same from tribe to tribe, but they might be found at different levels of the tribal hierarchy. The KIT FOX SOCIETY, for instance, was found among most tribes, and it is thought that there may have been a single prototype for this society. Probably the most famous military society was the DOG SOLDIERS.

Membership in military societies was voluntary and was usually purchased from existing members. The "buyer" took the original members' place, and the "seller" remained fixed in the group because he, in turn, bought the rights and privileges of an older member. Prospective members amassed goods and gifts and picked a sponsor; the older man would then teach new members the songs, dances, correct behavior, dress, and emblems associated with the different ranks within the society. Theoretically, this process was repeated until the original members had reached the highest ranks of the society.

When members sold their top ranks, they retired from the society. If, however, a young man could not gather enough gifts to buy membership in a higher rank, he remained at his current level.

Most military societies fostered a warrior ethic. A man was expected to be brave, but only a few exceptional men were chosen as officers. These men had certain badges of rank, such as distinctive dress, and were expected to flout danger. The officers of the Kit Fox Society of the Oglala Lakota (see SIOUX), for example, wore special dress that distinguished them, and they also painted their bodies yellow. The four bravest men carried LANCES and led the men into battle; they were expected to stand firm in the face of the enemy. Among the Mandan, the Half-Shaved Head Society carried lances. The Kiowa had the Ka-itsenko (or Koitsenko), who were the 10 greatest warriors of a band. These warriors wore a distinctive HEADDRESS, lance, and sash. In battle, they used their lances to pin their sashes to the ground so they could not retreat. Only another Ka-itsenko could release them. Similarly, among the Dog Soldiers of the Northern Cheyenne, one man carried the *Is tu tam tsit,* or "black dog rope," an eight- or 10-foot piece of buffalo hide about 8 inches wide, ornamented with feathers and quillwork. If this man dismounted during a battle, he would pin the dog rope to the ground, pledging not to retreat. The ARAPAHO and Kiowa-APACHE military societies also made use of the dog rope, or sash.

Whatever the tribe, military societies played an important role in Indian society, providing an organization in which men could socialize and inculcate younger men of the tribe to the values of warrior culture.

Milk Creek (1879) *opening battle of the short-lived Ute War*

By the late 1870s, conditions among the UTE Indians at the White River Agency had long been deteriorating under the administration of the local agent, Nathan C. Meeker (see MEEKER AGENCY). In September 1879 Major Thomas T. Thornburgh responded to Meeker's request that soldiers occupy the agency. On September 29 about 120 of Thornburgh's cavalrymen encountered a slightly smaller number of Ute Indians, led by Jack, on the northern boundary of the Ute Reservation at Milk Creek.

In the skirmish that followed, Thornburgh was killed early, and the remainder of the cavalry, led by Captain J. Scott Payne, fell back to the expedition's supply trains under heavy fire from Ute positioned in the surrounding hills. Hoping to rout the cavalry from their positions in the wagons, several Ute set fire to the prairies. By nightfall, 11 troopers had been killed, another 23 wounded, and most of the detachment's horses and mules hit. The Ute admitted to 23 losses. That same afternoon, the Ute struck the White River Agency, killing Meeker and nine others. They took five women and children, including Meeker's wife and daughter, into captivity.

The siege at Milk Creek continued for nearly a week. On October 2 a troop of 9th Cavalry arrived, but they soon found themselves crippled by the loss of all of their horses to Indian fire. Another 20 cavalrymen were wounded. Only with the appearance of Colonel Wesley Merritt and nine companies of reinforcements on the scene did the Ute withdraw. Six days later, Merritt's men found the bodies of Meeker and the others at White River Agency.

News of the Indian victory at Milk Creek, and the accompanying deaths at White River, led the army to send 1,500 men to the area, keeping 2,000 others ready nearby. With the intervention of Ute leader OURAY and Secretary of the Interior CARL SCHURZ, however, further bloodshed was avoided and the CAPTIVES were returned safely.

See also UTE WAR.

Mims, Samuel   See FORT MIMS.

Miniconjou   See SIOUX.

Minnesota Uprising (The Dakota Conflict, Sioux Revolt, Sioux Uprising of 1862) (1862) *Indian uprising that marked the beginning of the Sioux Wars*

The Minnesota Uprising spanned but a few months in late summer and fall 1862. During that time, however, a group of Dakota Indians (see SIOUX), some German farmers, and the U.S. Army engaged in several costly encounters. By the time the battles were over, perhaps as many as 800 non-Indian settlers and soldiers and an unknown number of Indians were dead. The revolt officially ended the day after Christmas, when 38 Dakota were publicly hanged in what became the largest mass execution in American history. The conflict continued a number of bloody battles that together constitute the SIOUX WARS, which lasted from 1854, with the GRATTAN DEFEAT, until 1890, with the massacre at WOUNDED KNEE.

There was no single cause of the 1862 uprising. Rather, it was the end result of a series of unfortunate events experienced by the Dakota. A few years earlier, settlers had begun to encroach on Dakota land. By means of treaties, the U.S. government purchased most of the Dakota's land (almost 24 million acres) for cash and annuities to be doled out over a period of years. The government, however, often diverted the funds to the Indian traders or were late with payments and supplies. In August 1862, the Dakota, living on two small reservations in southern Minnesota, were hungry and angry. They wanted the food and money due them and were incensed when a white trader, Andrew Myrick, made the sarcastic remark, "If they are hungry, let them eat grass."

The conflict began when four hungry Dakota men stole some eggs and, filled with bravado, killed five settlers. That night the Dakota chiefs had a general council, and LITTLE CROW reluctantly agreed to lead the Indians in a war to drive

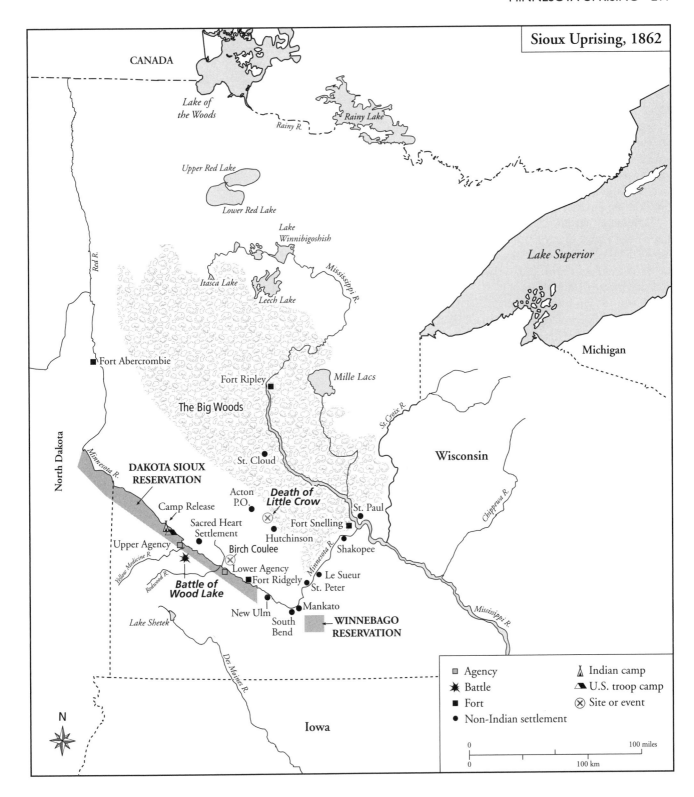

Sioux Uprising, 1862

CANADA

Lake of
the Woods

Rainy R.

Rainy Lake

Upper Red Lake

Lower Red Lake

Lake
Winnibigoshish

Lake Superior

Red R.

Mississippi R.

Itasca Lake

Leech Lake

Michigan

Fort Abercrombie

Fort Ripley

Mille Lacs

The Big Woods

North Dakota

Minnesota R.

DAKOTA SIOUX
RESERVATION

St. Cloud

Wisconsin

St. Croix R.

Chippewa R.

Camp Release

Acton
P.O.

**Death of
Little Crow**

St. Paul

Sacred Heart
Settlement

Fort Snelling

Upper Agency

Birch Coulee

Hutchinson

Yellow Medicine R.

Lower Agency

Shakopee

Redwood R.

**Battle of
Wood Lake**

Fort Ridgely

Le Sueur

Minnesota R.

St. Peter

Lake Shetek

New Ulm

Mankato

South
Bend

**WINNEBAGO
RESERVATION**

Mississippi R.

Des Moines R.

N

Iowa

▪ Agency	⚐ Indian camp
✶ Battle	◣ U.S. troop camp
■ Fort	⊗ Site or event
● Non-Indian settlement	

0   100 miles

0   100 km

the settlers from the Minnesota River valley. The next morning, on August 18, 1862, the uprising began. A large number of Dakota attacked the federal Indian administrative center known as the Lower Sioux Agency, setting fire to the buildings and killing about 20 people. Among them was Andrew Myrick, his mouth stuffed with grass.

Many of the 47 settlers who survived headed for FORT RIDGELY, about 13 miles away. When the fort's commanding officer heard the news, he set out for the burning agency with 46 enlisted men. As the soldiers reached the Minnesota River near the agency, the Indians attacked. Two dozen soldiers and one Indian were killed.

The next day, Indians began a series of raids on the Upper Sioux Agency. Thereafter, raiding parties attacked settlers throughout southern Minnesota. The conflict at this time was almost totally one-sided. Few Indians died, but hundreds of settlers were killed. Of the latter, many were unarmed Germans who huddled together in disbelief, for they had assumed they were on friendly terms with the Dakota. The survivors fled to Fort Ridgely and NEW ULM for safety.

On August 20 and 22, the Dakota attacked Fort Ridgely. Little Crow's army of nearly 800 warriors was repelled by cannons, with which the Indians were unfamiliar. The casualty list for the two attacks on Fort Ridgely included three dead settlers and an estimated 100 Indians.

About the same time, on August 19 and 23, the Dakota attacked nearby New Ulm. After intense fighting the town was burned, but the defenders held their ground. In the battle 34 settlers were killed and 60 wounded. An unknown number of Indians met the same fate.

By August 31, the main body of Indians seemed to have left the area, and a burial party proceeded to the Lower Sioux Agency, where two weeks earlier the fighting had begun. The burial detail bivouacked at a site along Birch Coulee Creek. Just before dawn on September 2, the Indians attacked. When the smoke cleared in the battle of BIRCH COULEE (1862), two Indians had been killed along with 17 soldiers and 90 horses; 47 soldiers were wounded.

As September wore on, raiding parties attacked settlers throughout southern and western Minnesota, and various battles were fought, including actions at Fort Abercrombie and WOOD LAKE (1862) on September 23. But the Dakota were not unified. Soon "friendly Indians" turned over prisoners to General HENRY SIBLEY, the army commander, and gathered at his headquarters. Many of the warriors also surrendered, expecting to be treated as PRISONERS of war.

Between September 28 and November 5, a military commission convened a series of superficial trials. In all, 307 Indian men were sentenced to death. Eventually President Abraham Lincoln pared the list down to slightly less than four dozen.

On the day after Christmas in 1862, the 38 Dakota warriors were marched to the gallows in the public square in Mankato, Minnesota. Shortly after 10:00 A.M. America's largest mass execution took place.

In the months that followed, the Dakota were imprisoned and then taken from Minnesota to Nebraska and the Dakota Territory. Hundreds died in transit. Ironically, some of the payment originally due the Dakota was appropriated to pay the settlers for damages incurred in the uprising. The Minnesota Uprising was over but not forgotten, for it served as the prelude to the nearly three decades of bloody battles that constituted the Sioux Wars.

Further Reading
Carley, Kenneth. *The Sioux Uprising of 1862*. St. Paul: The Minnesota Historical Society, 1976.
Josephy, Alvin M., Jr. *The Civil War in the American West*. New York: Alfred A. Knopf, 1991.
Schultz, Duane. *Over the Earth I Come: The Great Sioux Uprising of 1862*. New York: St. Martin's, 1992.

Modoc *small tribe that traditionally inhabited a 50-mile-radius area around Tule Lake, located astride the present-day Oregon-California border*
The Modoc of northern California remained in virtual isolation from white American contact prior to the Treaty of GUADALUPE HIDALGO (1848) with Mexico and the subsequent discovery of gold in California. During the gold rush years, most of California's 100,000 native inhabitants were quickly subjugated or annihilated by prospectors and settlers who invaded the region. The Modoc, however, often fought back, attacking wagon trains along the South Emigrant Trail, which skirted TULE LAKE's eastern shore.

Miners searching for gold on Modoc land were attacked, but they fought back more effectively than the settlers. Gold was never discovered on Modoc land, however, and a sort of passive tolerance developed between the miners and the Modoc. The same could not be said of non-Indian ranchers, who took possession of the rich, well-watered Modoc lands. By 1864, the Lost River Valley of northern California and southern Oregon was filled with settlers, prompting the federal government to seek a reservation treaty with the Modoc, Klamath, and Yahooskin Band of the Snake Indians. Kintpuash (CAPTAIN JACK), a Modoc chief, initially refused to sign the TREATY OF 1863. The Indian agents then declared Kintpuash's rival, Schonchin John, "legal" chief of the Modoc. Schonchin John readily signed; Kintpuash reluctantly signed later. As a result of the treaty, the Modoc lost all their land and were moved north to a reservation in Klamath territory. The Klamath, with whom the Modoc shared no affection, resented the Modoc presence and refused to allow them to cut timber or hunt on the reservation. After one year of unbearable reservation life, Kintpuash led about 175 people back to Tule Lake. In the meantime, however, settlers had moved on to Modoc land and established residences, even though the treaty remained unratified. The reappearance of the Modoc surprised and frightened the newcomers, who responded in panic. Their appeal for immediate return of the Modoc to the reservation went unheeded, mainly because of military preoccupation with the CIVIL WAR (1861–65).

In 1869, President ULYSSES S. GRANT made Indian affairs a priority of his administration, with the goal of confining all Indians to reservations. He appointed a friend and supporter, Alfred B. Meacham, as Indian superintendent of Oregon. In December 1869 Meacham met with Kintpuash and persuaded him to return to the reservation. The Modoc's relationship with the Klamath, however, grew steadily worse. Kintpuash complained to the Indian agent, who responded by cutting off all Modoc rations. In desperation, Kintpuash once again led his people, and many of Schonchin John's followers, back to Tule Valley. Thereafter, Kintpuash refused to discuss returning to the Klamath reservation, even though settlers were again clamoring for his removal. He pleaded several times for a reservation within Tule Valley, but the federal government never seriously considered that as an option.

In 1872, Meacham's replacement, Thomas B. Odeneal, was ordered to return the Modoc to the Yainax agency (set aside for the Modoc) on the Klamath reservation by any means, peaceful or otherwise. Meacham sent two emissaries to ask Kintpuash to come in to talk. Kintpuash refused; he also had to restrain the faction who wanted to start a war on the spot by killing the emissaries. When Odeneal heard of the talk of war, he immediately went to Fort Klamath and requested that the army act. Thus began the MODOC WAR (1872–73).

Following the Modoc War, leaders Kintpuash, Schonchin John, Black Jim, and Boston Charley were hanged for their parts in the Modoc War and the murder of General EDWARD R. S. CANBY. The remainder of the Modoc (about 155) were exiled to the Quapaw reservation in Indian Territory (Oklahoma), where many died of malaria. Longing for their old home persisted, and in 1909, those who wanted to return to the Klamath Reservation were allowed to go. A small remnant, now known as the Modoc Tribe of Oklahoma, remained behind.

Further Reading

Andrist, Ralph K. *The Long Death: The Last Days of the Plains Indian.* New York: Macmillan, 1993.

Brown, Dee. *The American West.* New York: Scribner's, 1994.

Debo, Angie. *A History of the Indians of the United States.* Norman: University of Oklahoma Press, 1970.

Modoc War (1872–1873) *conflict between the Modoc Indians and the U.S. government*

In 1870, the MODOC tribe of northern California and southwestern Oregon had fewer than 300 people, but they possessed a reputation among local non-Indians for violence, as well as for being plunderers and slave traffickers. Years of war against non-Indians, however, seemed a thing of the past to federal troops, with whom the Modoc developed a friendly trade relationship. Some of the young warriors, in fact, were given American nicknames such as Bogus Charley, HOOKER JIM, Steamboat Frank, and Shacknasty Jim. Among them was one who bitterly opposed friendly relations with the whites—CAPTAIN JACK.

Some years before, Captain Jack had, with great hesitation, signed a treaty providing for his Modoc tribe to settle with and live among the Klamath Indians on a reservation in southwestern Oregon. After a miserable year at the reservation, Captain Jack became fed up with the Klamath and led his followers

away, settling among the lava deposits at the base of the Cascade Mountains where the Lost River meets TULE LAKE.

On November 29, 1872, a troop of cavalry from Fort Klamath approached Captain Jack's camp. After a brief exchange of fire, the Indians scattered southward, attacking all non-Indians in their path. Captain Jack led his people to the south shore of Tule Lake to an area of huge LAVA BEDS that the Indians called Land of Burnt Out Fires. Soldiers who later attempted to dislodge the Modoc referred to this area as Captain Jack's Stronghold.

Army troops under the command of Brigadier General EDWARD R. S. CANBY gathered at Tule Lake. Canby ordered Colonel Frank Wheaton to blast the Modoc out of Captain Jack's Stronghold on January 16, 1873. After an artillery barrage, riflemen assaulted the site, but heavy fog set in, making the artillery fire too dangerous to friendly troops. The Indians, lodged in virtually impregnable defensive positions among the rugged lava outcroppings, laid down deadly fire on the approaching troops. As night fell, the soldiers retreated, having suffered nine dead and 28 wounded. The troops were demoralized by their defeat, and their frustration worsened when they realized that none of them had even seen a Modoc defender.

Stung by this initial failure, the U.S. government opted for diplomacy. General Canby held a meeting with Captain Jack, who demanded a place for his people to live. Canby retorted that only unconditional surrender was acceptable. Temporarily breaking off discussions to consider Canby's terms, Captain Jack was astonished to discover that many of his own people were calling him a coward. Unconditional surrender and removal was not an option for the Modoc people. The militants convinced Captain Jack to murder the peace commissioner as a way of sending a message to the U.S. government.

On April 11, 1873, Captain Jack again met with Canby, who had ignored warnings of Modoc aggression toward his peace party. Reverend Cleeson Thomas and Alfred B. Meacham accompanied Canby during the talks. Shortly after the council began, Captain Jack shot Canby in the face and proceeded to stab the general until he was dead. Jack took the dead soldier's uniform jacket as a prize. Other Modoc killed Thomas and wounded Meacham, while another peace commissioner fled for his life.

U.S. officials were outraged when they received news of Canby's death. Meanwhile, Captain Jack took his Modoc to yet another lava bed farther south. On April 26, the Modoc spotted an army reconnaissance detachment accompanied by Indian scouts. The troops had stopped for lunch in the middle of a small depression, providing a perfect place for an ambush. SCAR-FACED CHARLEY, the real war leader of the Modoc, took several warriors and attacked the army detachment. After a brief one-sided struggle, the army lost all five officers and 20 enlisted men. Sixteen wounded men and the survivors listened as Scarfaced Charley called out to them "all you fellows that ain't dead had better go home. We don't want to kill you all in one day."

However, pressure from the soldiers continued. As their morale deteriorated, many Modoc who had earlier advocated killing General Canby now wanted to settle for peace. By mid-May the Modoc had scattered. The new commander of the U.S. troops, Colonel Jefferson C. Davis (not the Confederate president), was a veteran of the Georgia campaign led by WILLIAM TECUMSEH SHERMAN during the CIVIL WAR (1861–65). Under his leadership, the army gathered up several Modoc parties, and on June 1 one of Davis's patrols persuaded an exhausted Captain Jack to surrender.

Sherman demanded that the Modoc responsible for Canby's death be brought swiftly to justice. One month after his surrender, Captain Jack and five other Modoc were tried for murder. Without the benefit of an attorney and tried by a military commissioner, they were sentenced to death. Although President ULYSSES S. GRANT commuted two of the sentences, Captain Jack, Boston Charley, Black Jim, and Schonelin John were hanged on a scaffold on the Fort Klamath parade grounds.

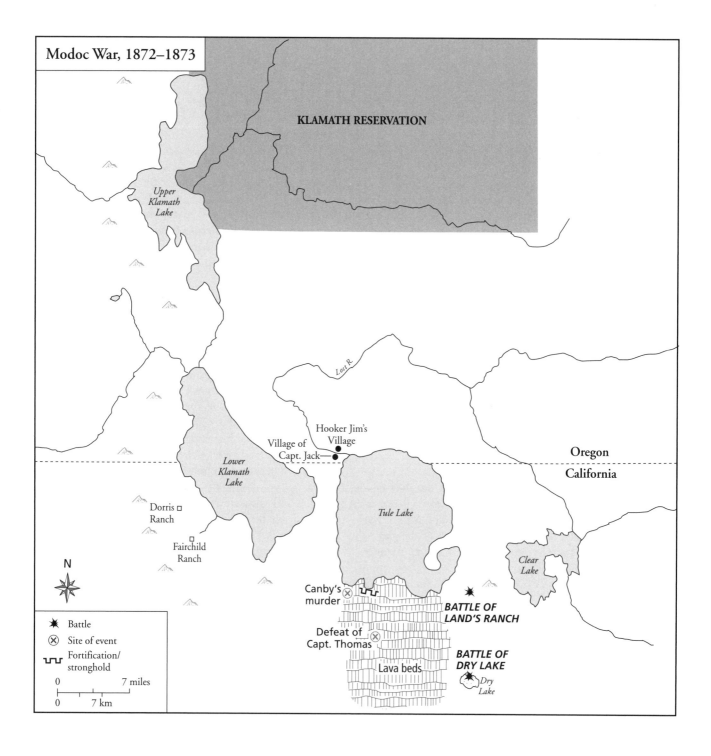

Illustration of the Modoc from *London Times,* 1862. During the Modoc War, Modoc and U.S. troops engaged in several battles among the lava beds near the borders of California and Oregon. *(Courtesy New York Public Library)*

Only 155 Modoc remained to make the journey to their new home in Indian Territory. The Modoc War had ended.

Further Reading

Utley, Robert M. *Frontier Regulars: The United States Army and the Indian, 1866–1891.* New York: Macmillan, 1973.

Mohawk *easternmost tribe of the Iroquois Confederacy*

The Mohawk lived in an area roughly bounded by the Hudson, Susquehanna, Mohawk, and St. Lawrence Rivers in present east-central New York State. Along with fellow tribes of the IRO-QUOIS CONFEDERACY, they lived in bark-covered longhouses by the waterways, which they navigated in elm-bark canoes.

After the arrival of Europeans in North America, many Indian tribes became involved with and ultimately dependent on the fur trade, and this sometimes led to fierce competition among various tribes. Thus, the Mohawk frequently raided the HURON, ALGONKIN, and OTTAWA, taking valuable furs. In 1609 Samuel de Champlain, convinced that French traders were losing fur profits to the Mohawk, led a combined Huron-French force against 200 Mohawk on Lake Champlain. This competition between French trading partners and the Iroquois, who were allies of the English, caused continual conflict. Ultimately, the Iroquois Confederacy sought to establish a fur-trading monopoly by subduing competing tribes in a sustained effort known as the BEAVER WARS (1638–84).

The Mohawk became fast allies of the British, mainly through the influence of chiefs HENDRICK (Theyanoquin) and JOSEPH BRANT, both of whom were friends of WILLIAM JOHN-SON, British superintendent of Indian affairs for the northern districts. The Mohawk fought alongside the British during the

FRENCH AND INDIAN WAR (1754–63) and again during the AMERICAN REVOLUTION (1775–81), when Brant led the Mohawk, SENECA, CAYUGA, and ONONDAGA with the British in battle. Two other members of the Iroquois Confederacy, the TUSCARORA and ONEIDA, allied with the colonists.

During the war the Iroquois were subjected to a devastating campaign by American General JOHN SULLIVAN. At the war's end, the TREATY OF PARIS (1783) ignored the Indians, making no provisions for any Iroquois tribes, even those allied with the Americans. Joseph Brant expressed his belief that Britain had betrayed the Indians by giving away Indian land that was not theirs to give. Nevertheless, deciding once again to entrust the fate of his people to the British, Brant's Mohawk

remained in Canada, where they continue to live on the Six Nations Reserve in Brantford, Ontario. Other Mohawk groups live at various sites in northeastern New York State, Quebec, and Ontario.

Mohawk-Mahican War   See DUTCH-INDIAN WAR.

Mohegan   *inhabitants of the region surrounding the northern Thames (or Pequot) River in Connecticut*
Although the spelling of the tribal name differs, the Mohegan are the apparent subject of James Fenimore Cooper's famous

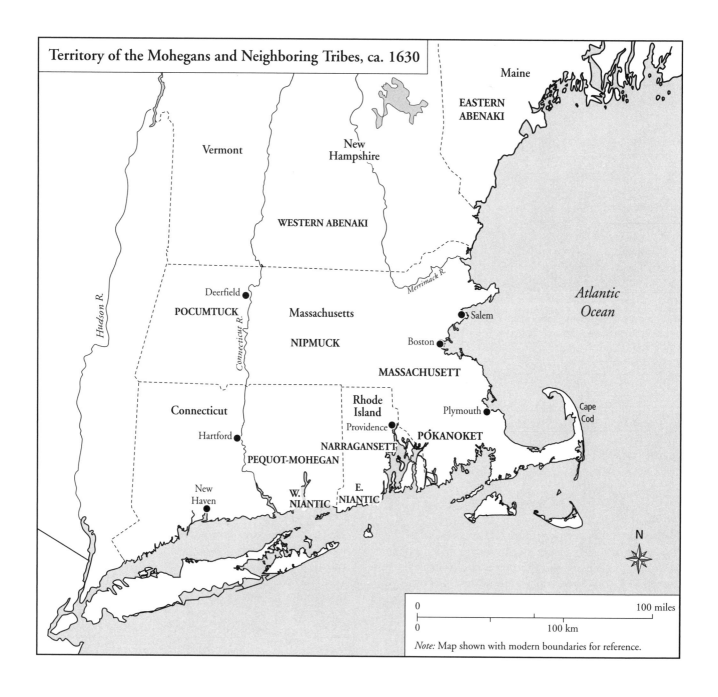

Territory of the Mohegans and Neighboring Tribes, ca. 1630

Note: Map shown with modern boundaries for reference.

novel *The Last of the Mohicans.* The Mohegan, whose name means "wolf" in ALGONQUIAN, hunted, fished, and gathered food from nearby rivers, lakes, bays, and forests. They lived in dome-shaped wigwams or rectangular houses covered with birch bark and built light, streamlined, birch-bark canoes or hollowed out logs for dugout canoes.

The Mohegan and the PEQUOT originally belonged to the same group, sharing the same Algonquian language dialect and a common ancestry. They split after the arrival of Europeans in the 17th century. In 1620, one group of Pequot rebelled (for some unknown reason) against Sassacus, the Pequot chief, and moved to another location on the THAMES. This group established an independent village and became known as Mohegan. The Mohegan and Pequot, though closely related, remained enemies and frequently fought on opposing sides in various colonial wars.

In 1636, Chief Uncas of the Mohegan sent a message to the colonists that the Pequot were planning to initiate hostilities against the Connecticut and Massachusetts Bay colonies. Subsequent Pequot attempts to avert a war with the colonists, however, tend to prove Uncas's message a fabrication. During the PEQUOT WAR (1636–37) that followed, Uncus declared Mohegan loyalty to the colonists. The colonists were nervous about Mohegan intentions, but Uncas soon allayed their fears when he delivered four Pequot heads to them. After the defeat of the Pequot, the Mohegan enlarged their population by a few hundred, including 80 Pequot warriors.

As allies of the colonists, the Mohegan maintained their lands longer than the nonallied tribes. Eventually, however, the Mohegan were driven from their lands, and some were sold into slavery. Many Mohegan also died during epidemics of European diseases. A small number of Mohegan and Pequot presently live on two small reservations in Connecticut.

Mojave (Mohave) *Indian tribe living on the Arizona-California border*

The word *Mojave* comes from the Indian name "Ahamakave," which means "beside the water"—that is, the Colorado River. The Mojave were known for their abilities in war and their willingness to defend their homeland. They maintained friendly relations with the nearby YUMA and Chemehuevi and the more distant Western APACHE and YAVAPAI, but they were chronically at war with the MARICOPA, Pima (see AKIMEL O'ODHAM), and Papago (see TOHONO O'ODHAM). In 1857, the Mojave and the Yuma were soundly defeated by the Maricopa and Pima at the battle of MARICOPA WELLS (1857). This engagement effectively ended the warfare between the two alliances.

The Mojave then turned their attention to a new enemy: non-Indian settlers. During the 1840s, fortune seekers streamed through Mojave territory on their way to California and its gold mines. In 1858 a group of Mojave attacked a wagon train, killing nine and wounding 16. The U.S. government responded by building Fort Mohave to protect the travelers. On August 5, 1859, a detachment of the 6th Infantry fought with a Mojave war party about 10 miles south of the fort. The Indians' weapons were no match for the soldiers' rifles, and many died.

Between 1870 and 1890, the Mojave suffered from disease and poverty. Since the turn of the century, conditions have gradually improved. Contemporary Mojave live on three separate reservations, which they share with several other tribes, in northern Arizona, southwestern California, and southern Nevada.

Montgomerie, Archibald (1726–1796) *commander of British troops during the Cherokee War*

Born in Scotland, Archibald Montgomerie headed a regiment of Scottish Highlanders at the start of the FRENCH AND INDIAN WAR (1754–63). In spring 1760, Colonel Montgomerie was ordered by General Jeffrey Amherst, commander of the British armed forces in North America, to defend the colony of South Carolina against the CHEROKEE. Once allies of the British, the Cherokee had suffered many depredations from settlers, including the loss of their lands and harassment of female tribe members.

By April 1760, Montgomerie and his troops were engaged in the CHEROKEE WAR (1759–61) in South Carolina, where they were joined by 300 rangers, 40 militiamen, and 50 Catawba warriors. Montgomerie led a punitive expedition against the Cherokee towns nearest the British settlements. He burned the town of Estatoe and three others (all of them deserted by their inhabitants), killed between 60 and 80 warriors, and took another 40 Cherokee prisoner. When he reached Fort Prince George, Montgomerie threatened the Cherokee with continued reprisals if they did not agree to negotiate. When Montgomerie's ultimatum expired, he resumed his campaign, heading for the town of Etchoe. On the way, he was ambushed by a Cherokee force, which killed 17 of his soldiers and wounded another 66. Montgomerie rallied his men and drove the Cherokee off. The battle was claimed as a victory by both the British and the Cherokee—the British because they drove the Indians away, the Indians because Montgomerie had to return to the north without subduing them.

Moore, James (unavailable–1706) *English colonial official and military leader*

Probably born in Ireland, James Moore came to South Carolina about 1675 and later helped overthrow the governor. He married into a prominent family and opened a lucrative trade with Indians in goods and slaves.

Moore served as governor of South Carolina from 1700 to 1703. Upon the outbreak of QUEEN ANNE'S WAR (1702–13), which pitted England against France and Spain, he organized an expeditionary force against Spanish-occupied Saint Augustine in present-day Florida. Consisting of about 1,000 Carolina volunteers and Indian auxiliaries, as well as 14 small ships, Moore's force laid siege for two months before being driven off by the arrival of two Spanish frigates.

Determined to regain his reputation, in late 1703 Moore organized another army, this time numbering 50 Carolina volunteers and 1,000 CREEK allies. Moore's column attacked and captured a large Apalachee village early the following year, burning the town, killing some 400 inhabitants, and enslaving the rest. His subsequent victory over a combined Spanish-Apalachee force at Saint Lewis Fort laid the Apalachee homelands open to Moore's continued offensive. After destroying several villages, he returned to South Carolina with more than 1,000 Indian prisoners, who were sold into slavery.

Moore's assaults, in conjunction with later Creek attacks, forced the remnants of the Apalachee people into either Spanish- or French-held areas. They also demonstrated the profitability of slave raids into Indian lands.

Moraviantown   See THAMES.

Muddy Creek   (1877)   *campaign in the Sioux Wars*
On May 7, 1877, NELSON A. MILES, commanding 10 companies of regulars and a squad of CHEYENNE auxiliaries, located about 50 Miniconjou Lakota (see SIOUX) on Muddy Creek, a tributary of the Rosebud River (in present-day Montana). Miles led a dawn charge, capturing most of the Indian pony herd and cutting off a defiant group of warriors, led by Lame Deer, from the rest of the tribe. Miles was nearly killed during an abortive peace parlay, but Indian resistance soon collapsed amid the amy's return fire. Colonel Miles counted 14 Lakota dead on the field, while setting his own losses at four killed and seven wounded.

Mud Springs   (1865)   *battle in continuing retaliation for the massacre at Sand Creek*
On February 2, 1865, after burning Julesburg (see JULESBURG RAIDS), a war party of Lakota (see SIOUX), CHEYENNE, and ARAPAHO raiders decided to move north. Two days later, Indian scouts were sighted near Mud Springs, a stage station with a telegraph office and a small detachment of troops. While the nine soldiers and five civilians at the station held off the warriors, the telegraph operator wired for aid from Fort Laramie and Camp Mitchell. Responding to the call, Lieutenant William Ellsworth and 36 men of the 11th Ohio Cavalry arrived at Mud Springs 12 hours later. The cavalry and the Indians fought for almost a day. Finally, Ellsworth released his troops' horses from the corral, hoping that the Indians would concentrate their attention on them. The ploy worked. The Indians rounded up the stock and returned to their camps on Rush Creek.

Later that evening, Lieutenant Colonel William O. Collins, commander of Fort Laramie, led 120 men out from the fort to aid Ellsworth. The main body of troops arrived at Mud Springs on February 6, and the Indians pressed the attack for two more days. Finally, on February 8, Collins charged the Indians' camp. Although the Indian warriors outnumbered the soldiers 5 to 1, they could not hold their position. By the early afternoon of February 9, the Indians had been routed and forced to retreat to the nearby hills. Only seven soldiers were wounded, while it is believed that about 28 warriors were killed or wounded.

mutilation   *practices by some Native American tribes and some settlers, involving the removal of skin, organs, or body parts*
Both Europeans and Native Americans practiced mutilation, although sometimes for different reasons. Some Indians regarded self-mutilation as a form of worship, a ritual sacrifice that gave the worshipper special powers for defense or in battle. Some European settlers mutilated dead bodies to show contempt for their opponents. Most Indians and Europeans, however, mutilated captives or bodies of warriors killed in battle to send a clear message to survivors that they faced a powerful and angry enemy.

This last message was perhaps the most common reason for mutilation of living captives as well. In spring 1540, Spanish conquistador HERNANDO DE SOTO (1500–42) mutilated Timucua captives who had plotted to kill his expedition. After the Indians surrendered, de Soto had his soldiers surround most of the survivors and cut them to pieces with their swords. The soldiers also tied some of the captives to posts and shot at them with arrows. Later in the expedition, members of the Mobile tribe threatened de Soto with mutilation—they said that the Spanish should be "torn into pieces for their infamy"—before he sacked their town and killed its residents.

The Spanish colonists maintained a strong belief in the deterrent powers of the threat of mutilation. After the siege of ACOMA PUEBLO (in modern New Mexico) in 1599, Don Juan de Oñate set up a chopping block in the main squares of the towns along the Rio Grande. Each of the surviving Acoma men had one foot cut off. In addition, all the survivors—men, women, and children—were sentenced to 20 years of slavery to the Spanish colonists. Two HOPI men who were caught in Acoma Pueblo when the siege began were also mutilated by the Spanish. Their right hands were cut off and they were sent home as a warning to their people not to upset the Spanish.

Some Native Americans also used mutilation to send messages to their enemies. During the first POWHATAN WAR (1622–32), Indians of the POWHATAN CONFEDERACY killed and mutilated George Thorpe, an English colonist who had made a special effort to befriend them. The Powhatan believed that he wanted to take their children away to be educated in the European fashion, and the mutilation of his body was a protest against the idea. In 1661 French-Canadian settler FRANÇOIS HERTEL lost part of one hand to the MOHAWK of the IROQUOIS CONFEDERACY, who considered him an ally of their HURON enemies.

Certain settlers also mutilated their enemies. Soldiers who faced SHAWNEE leader TECUMSEH at the battle of the THAMES (1813) skinned the bodies of dead Native Americans, intending to tan the skins like leather and use them for tobacco pouches and other items.

SCALPING, a specialized form of mutilation, was not primarily used as a way to send messages to survivors. The practice only became common among Native Americans after non-Indian colonists began paying Indians to kill their enemies. The scalplock, a tuft of hair with its attached skin usually taken from the crown of the head, served as a sort of receipt. It offered proof to the payer that the killing had in fact taken place. Scalping was usually performed after a person had been killed, but there are references to people who were scalped and survived the process. It represented the causal attitude toward life and death and the hostile feelings that many Native American and non-Indian groups had toward each other.

Further Reading

Josephy, Alvin M., Jr. *500 Nations: An Illustrated History of North American Indians.* New York: Alfred A. Knopf, 1994.

Thomas, David Hurst, et al. *The Native Americans: An Illustrated History.* Atlanta, Ga.: Turner Publishing, 1993.

Maynard, Jill, ed. *Through Indian Eyes: The Untold Story of Native American Peoples.* New York: Reader's Digest, 1995.

Nana (Nane, Nanay) (ca. 1810–ca. 1895) *Chiricahua Apache warrior*

Born in present-day New Mexico, Nana was a nephew of Delgadito, a prominent Mimbreno Apache chief. He was associated with VICTORIO during hostilities with non-Indians in the 1860s and 1870s and remained with him until Mexican troops killed Victorio at TRES CASTILLO (1880). Nana, who at the time was leading a group in search of ammunition, eluded the Mexicans. Although he was an old man, he led the remaining survivors and 25 to 30 Mescalero Apache on successful raids against settlers across southern New Mexico. The group traveled more than 1,200 miles, fought eight battles, killed 100 settlers, and captured 200 horses.

In 1883, Nana and his followers turned themselves in to General GEORGE CROOK, who settled them on the reservation at Fort Apache. Soon after resettling there, Nana, GERONIMO, and several other Apache leaders left the reservation with 134 men, women, and children. In the resulting war over returning them, the Apache successfully avoided capture for several years. In January 1886, Lieutenant Marion B. Maus attacked their camp in the Sierra Madre Mountains of northern Mexico, but the elusive Apache escaped. In August the Apache agreed to turn themselves in to General NELSON A. MILES, who sent them first to Florida and then to Alabama. In 1894, the military brought Nana, Geronimo, and the others as prisoners to Fort Sill, Oklahoma. Nana died there probably in 1895, still a PRISONER of war.

Nanticoke *tribe that traditionally inhabited the eastern shore of Chesapeake Bay along the Nanticoke River in eastern Maryland and southern Delaware*

According to Nanticoke tradition, they were originally part of the LENNI LENAPE (formerly Delaware) tribe. Their culture was similar to that of the Iroquois tribes of the eastern seacoast (see IROQUOIS CONFEDERACY). Nanticoke villages were usually compact and palisaded. Nanticoke men built birch-bark and dugout canoes and hunted deer, bears, turkeys, and other game. Nanticoke women cultivated tobacco, corn, beans, and pumpkins. They wove baskets, made pottery, and gained a reputation for skillful creation of decorative shell beads.

After the arrival of Europeans, conflicts between the Nanticoke and colonists broke out as the non-Indian population increased and contact became more frequent. In 1675–76, a war with Maryland and Virginia colonists began when some Nanticoke took possession of several hogs in payment of a debt owed them by Virginia planter Thomas Mathew. It ended with the burning of Jamestown in a colonial civil revolt that became known as BACON'S REBELLION (1676). Following the war, in 1678, the Nanticoke signed a treaty with Maryland placing themselves under the protection of the colony. The Nanticoke subsequently signed a number of similar treaties, the last in 1742.

As a tributary of the Iroquois Confederacy, the Nanticoke of Broad Creek (Delaware) received permission from the Confederacy to remove to Pennsylvania. Immigrating in 1743, they

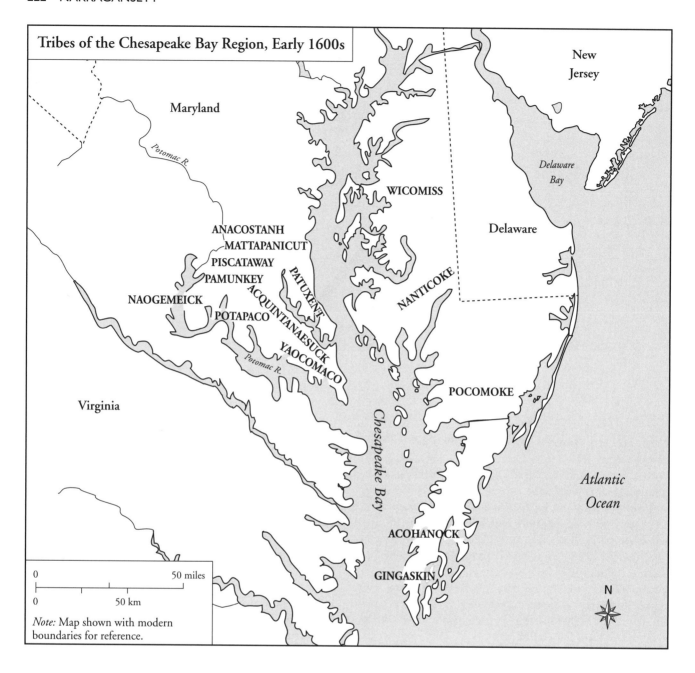

Tribes of the Chesapeake Bay Region, Early 1600s

Maryland

New Jersey

Potomac R.

WICOMISS

Delaware Bay

Delaware

ANACOSTANH
MATTAPANICUT
PISCATAWAY
PAMUNKEY
NAOGEMEICK
POTAPACO
PATUXENT
ACQUINTANAESUCK
YAOCOMACO
NANTICOKE

Potomac R.

POCOMOKE

Virginia

Chesapeake Bay

Atlantic Ocean

ACOHANOCK

GINGASKIN

0   50 miles
0   50 km

N

Note: Map shown with modern boundaries for reference.

established a village at the mouth of the Juniata River in Pennsylvania. Over the next several years, they were joined by other groups of Nanticoke. In 1753, the Nanticoke were admitted as nonvoting members of the Iroquois Confederacy. Under the protection of the CAYUGA, they became known as the "Wolf Clan."

The Nanticoke remained neutral during the FRENCH AND INDIAN WAR (1754–63) but sided with the British during the AMERICAN REVOLUTION (1775–81). After the Revolution, a majority remained with the Cayuga at the Six Nations Reserve in Canada. Nanticoke land reserves in Maryland and Delaware were sold in 1768. A remnant that remained in Maryland working as indentured servants lost their status as Indians and

became classified as "free Negroes." A few remained in Delaware, where they were classified as "free colored." Some joined the Lenni Lenape tribe and migrated with them, eventually settling in Indian Territory (Oklahoma).

Narragansett (Narraganset) *once powerful Indian tribe of New England*

At the beginning of the colonial period, the Narragansett occupied portions of present-day Rhode Island. In the early 1600s Europeans began settling nearby, and by 1633 smallpox had spread through the tribe, killing an estimated 700 Narragansett (see SMALLPOX, EFFECT OF). Relations with English colonists were strained, and in 1636 the Massachusetts Bay Colony launched a large but unsuccessful raid on the Narragansett at BLOCK ISLAND.

In spite of the epidemic and hostilities, the Narragansett became early allies of the English. Together they fought against the PEQUOT in the PEQUOT WAR (1637). As population problems increased, however, the Narragansett shifted their allegiance away from the Europeans and began to resist settlers' encroachment on their territory. They joined the WAMPANOAG and Nipmuc against the colonists in KING PHILIP'S WAR (1675–76), during which a Narragansett named CANONCHET became a principal leader of the tribe. In the GREAT SWAMP FIGHT (1675), which effectively ended the war, about 1,000 colonists defeated Canonchet and the Narragansett. During the battle, some 600 were killed and another 400 captured and sold into slavery. The remnant of the Narragansett eventually merged with ABENAKI, Mahican, and Niantic.

Narragansett Treaty (Hartford Treaty) (1638)
treaty that marked the end of the Pequot War
The NARRAGANSETT were allies of the Massachusetts Puritans in the PEQUOT WAR (1636–37). Their leader, or sachem, MIANTONOMO, was a good friend to Roger Williams, founder of the colony of Rhode Island. Before the war, Miantonomo had agreed with the leaders of the Massachusetts Bay Colony that the Narragansett would receive the Pequot hunting grounds in exchange for their support. After the war, however, Miantonomo found that colonists from Connecticut and their MOHEGAN allies were already occupying the land that had been promised to the Narragansett. In addition, immigrants from England began landing in the Connecticut River valley. These newcomers bartered for territory with Narragansett client tribes rather than the Narragansett themselves. In the treaty signed at Hartford in 1638, the leaders of the Connecticut colony claimed jurisdictional authority over Miantonomo and the Narragansett. In response, Miantonomo urged an uprising among all the tribes of the Northeast—known as the Narragansett War—in which it was planned that all the British colonists would be killed and the Europeans driven from the shores of North America (see NARRAGANSETT TREATY, 1645).

Narragansett Treaty (1645) *treaty ending the brief Narragansett War of 1645*
The NARRAGANSETT sachem, or leader, MIANTONOMO had been an ally of the British colonists during the PEQUOT WAR (1636–37). With the signing of the NARRAGANSETT TREATY (1638) at Hartford, Connecticut, however, Miantonomo came to realize that the colonists meant to destroy him. He began negotiations with the MOHAWK, the Montauk, and other Indian tribes in an effort to create a union that would overthrow colonial power and force the British out of New England.

Miantonomo was captured by MOHEGAN leader Uncas in 1643. Uncas accepted a Narragansett ransom for Miantonomo but then surrendered him to the colonists. The colonies of Plymouth, Connecticut, Massachusetts, and New Haven then ordered Uncas to execute Miantonomo for breaking the Narragansett Treaty of 1638. The Narragansett went to war with the Mohegan in revenge, but they were defeated when the colonists joined the fight in 1645. The treaty signed by the Narragansett that same year forced them to submit to additional fraudulent land purchases. The Narragansett nation nonetheless survived until 1675 by exploiting their friendship with the Mohawk and the colonists of Rhode Island. After the GREAT SWAMP FIGHT (1675), however, their population was nearly decimated.

Natchez (Natchee) *tribe of the Creek Confederacy*
The Natchez originally inhabited the Lower Mississippi region near the present town of Natchez, Mississippi. In 1650 their population was estimated at 4,500. The tribe practiced a complex system of sun worship. Transfer of leadership occurred through succession within a royal family believed to be of divine origin.

The Natchez welcomed early French settlers to their country and helped them to survive, but eventually tensions developed. Ill feelings reached a flashpoint when the governor of Louisiana tried to seize land considered sacred by the Natchez. On November 28, 1729, they attacked Fort Rosalie, killing 250 men and taking 300 women and children prisoner. The French and their CHOCTAW allies recaptured the prisoners and decimated the Natchez people.

The tribe never recovered from the devastation following the NATCHEZ REVOLT (1729). Approximately 200 Natchez sought refuge with the CHICKASAW, who refused Choctaw-French demands to give them up. The French and Choctaw then took vengeance on the Chickasaw. A few hundred Natchez escaped to sanctuary among CREEK and CHEROKEE. More than 400 were shipped to Haiti and Santo Domingo as slaves.

A few Natchez descendants presently live in the hills of southeast Muskogee County, Oklahoma. They are known locally as Natchee Creek or Natchee Cherokee.

Natchez Revolt (1729) *early 18th-century conflict between France and the Natchez Indians*
In 1716, the French established Fort Rosalie directly across the Mississippi River from the main village of the NATCHEZ in the lower Mississippi valley in Louisiana, where French settlers were trying to establish tobacco plantations. Dealings between the French and Natchez had begun smoothly in the 1680s, and the two groups occupied close quarters to facilitate trade and resist outside attack. By the 1720s, relations had become strained, but general warfare had been avoided due to the efforts of Tattooed Serpent, brother of a Natchez chief known as the Great Sun.

After Tattooed Serpent's death, the governor of Louisiana, Sieur Chépart, ordered the removal of the Natchez Indians from their village so the land could be used as a tobacco plantation. Despite the disapproval of the tribal "queen mother," Tattooed Arm, the Natchez rulers decided to attack Fort Rosalie. They did so on November 28, 1729, seizing the post and killing approximately 200 whites. In the successful attack, the Natchez captured approximately 300 women and children as well as the Louisiana governor. They detested the Frenchman so much that no warrior would shame his weapon by killing him. The task of execution was finally given to a Stinkard, a member of the lowest part of Natchez society, who promptly beat the man to death.

The French and their CHOCTAW allies quickly retaliated. In early 1730 the French recovered most of the Fort Rosalie captives, and by 1731 their assault nearly annihilated the Natchez and their Indian allies, the Yazoo. The French sold more than 400 Natchez into slavery in Haiti and Santo Domingo. Surviving remnants of the tribe fled the area to join neighboring peoples, including the CHICKASAW, the CREEK, and the CHEROKEE. (See also CHICKASAW RESISTANCE, 1720–63.)

The Natchez Revolt sharply reminded French settlers of their vulnerability if groups of Native Americans or African slaves joined forces against them. Afterward, to discourage further rebellions, the French increased their efforts to build alliances with tribes along the Mississippi. They likewise encouraged rivalries and suspicion among non-French peoples to keep potential enemies from uniting against them.

Navajo (Dineh) *Indian tribe living in the "Four Corners" region of Arizona, New Mexico, Utah, and Colorado*

The Navajo, who are linguistically and culturally related to the APACHE Indians, arrived in the American Southwest sometime prior to A.D. 1600. From their contact with the PUEBLO INDIANS, the Navajo learned weaving, agriculture, sandpainting, and ceremonial rituals.

They also received their common name, which comes from the Tewa Pueblo "Navahu," meaning "cultivated fields." (Their Native name is Dineh, meaning "the people.")

From the Spanish, the Navajo acquired sheep, goats, and horses. Once equipped with horses, the tribe intensified one of their major economic pursuits—raiding. Raiding parties targeted Spanish and nearby Indian communities looking for livestock, food, and captives. In 1846, the United States assumed control of New Mexico and immediately sought to control the Navajo by establishing military posts in their territory. Federal representatives signed treaties with the Navajo chiefs, but they failed to realize that these chiefs were merely advisers to small bands and that their jurisdiction did not hold sway over the entire tribe. Navajo resistance to government control became inevitable, and the NAVAJO WAR (1863–64) erupted.

In 1863, the U.S. government sent Colonel CHRISTOPHER ("KIT") CARSON to round up the Navajo. Following leaders such as BARBONCITO and MANUELITO, the Navajo defied government demands that they give up their traditional lands. Following a series of devastating attacks on Navajo settlements, the Navajo War finally was close to an end. The infamous LONG WALK in 1864 and incarceration at BOSQUE REDONDO followed. The NAVAJO TREATY OF 1868 allowed the Navajo to return to their homeland, where they turned sheep and cattle herding into the mainstay of their economy. Navajo rug makers and silver workers found a ready market among non-Indian collectors and traders. Meanwhile, the tribe grew from approximately 11,000 in 1868 to more than 35,000 in 1930.

During WORLD WAR II, Navajo soldiers distinguished themselves as Code Talkers. They transmitted combat information from one position to another in a code based on the Navajo language. The Japanese were never able to decipher the code.

Today, the Navajo Nation includes 24,000 square miles (16 million acres) of plateau land in the Four Corners area. The tribe numbers about 200,000 members, making it the largest reservation-based Indian tribe in North America.

Navajo Treaty of 1868 *treaty that allowed the Navajo Indians to return to their home territory, known as Dinetah*

In 1864, toward the end of the NAVAJO WAR (1863–64), the vast majority of the NAVAJO (Dineh) were removed from their homelands in northeastern Arizona and northwestern New Mexico and subjected to the infamous LONG WALK. They were then incarcerated at a prison camp at BOSQUE REDONDO, New Mexico. Conditions there were deplorable: insufficient housing; shortages of food, water, and wood; and constant attacks by COMANCHE all became a way of life. In 1865 smallpox killed 2,321 of the 8,000 Navajo in two months' time (see SMALLPOX, EFFECTS OF).

By May 1868, U.S. government peace commissioners had resolved to move the Navajo. They considered sending them to Texas or to Indian Territory, but, the Navajo desperately wanted to return home. The respected and eloquent chief BARBONCITO insisted on going home, and the government listened. On June 1, 1868, the Navajo Treaty was concluded and signed by 18 leaders, including Barboncito and MANUELITO. On July 25, it was ratified by the U.S. Congress.

The treaty allowed the Navajo to return to a 3.5-million-acre tract of land, a portion of the 23 million acres that they had claimed prior to incarceration. It also specified that the government would set aside $150,000 for tribal assistance. The United States promised a total of 15,000 sheep and goats and 500 head of cattle to help rebuild the Indians' livestock holdings. According to the treaty, the Navajo promised never again to raid or make war against Americans, Mexicans, or other Indian nations. In addition, the Navajo agreed to send their children to U.S. government schools.

On June 18, 1868, the Navajo began the 300-mile Long Walk back home. The treaty with the Navajo was one of the last made by the U.S. government with an Indian tribe before the Indian Appropriation Act of 1871 prevented future treaty making between the United States and Indian nations.

Prior to 1871, the government negotiated agreements with Indian tribes through treaties. Making of treaties with Indians was terminated that year. Thereafter, texts of agreements were submitted to the Congress in the form of bills which when enacted became laws. Future agreements would be ratified by both houses of Congress, rather than the Senate alone.

Navajo War (1863–1864) *series of conflicts between the Navajo Indians and the U.S. military*

During the 1700s and early 1800s, the NAVAJO (Dineh) launched frequent raids into Mexico and against their PUEBLO neighbors in New Mexico. During this time they had limited contact with non-Indian Americans. That was soon to change. In 1846, the United States entered a war with Mexico. That year, Colonel Stephen Kearny led 1,600 men into New Mexico and established a headquarters in Santa Fe. He then announced that the United States would henceforth protect the people from Indian raids (a similar promise was made two years later in the TREATY OF GUADALUPE HIDALGO, 1848). Although most historians record the Navajo War as 1863–64, hostilities between Navajo and U.S. forces began shortly after the arrival of the first U.S. troops in the region.

Kearny sent out officers to establish treaties with the Navajo. The Navajo, however, were not a tribe united under common leadership, a fact that Kearny failed to understand. Thus, leaders such as Zarcilla Largo and Narbona signed treaties, but their promises extended to only a few hundred followers. When other Navajo continued to raid, Kearny maintained that the treaties had been broken. As a result, in the next three years, five punitive expeditions were launched into Navajo territory. For the most part, the battles were indecisive.

In 1851, in an attempt to exert control over the Indians, the military built FORT DEFIANCE in the heart of Navajo territory. It was manned by four companies of cavalry, one of artillery, and two of infantry. In 1858, the post commander annexed a large area of Navajo grazing land near the post and ordered his soldiers to shoot Navajo horses found on that range. Some of the horses belonged to influential chief MANUELITO, who, along with BARBONCITO, became a consummate foe of the military. In April 1860, the two chiefs amassed a force of 2,000 warriors and attacked Fort Defiance. BOWS AND ARROWS were no match for rifles and artillery, however, and after two hours the Navajo retreated, having sustained heavy losses. Thereafter, the Navajo stepped up their raiding. New Mexicans responded by capturing as many as 100 Navajo prisoners, mostly women and children, and enslaving them.

In April 1861, the military abandoned Fort Defiance, and many of the soldiers withdrew from the Southwest. The Navajo war leaders believed their efforts to drive out the army was working, unaware that the soldiers had gone to fight in the CIVIL WAR (1861–65).

Despite the war in the East, the Union was determined to keep the trails and lines of communication open to the far west. To do so the government needed to neutralize the Navajo threat to non-Indian travelers and settlers. Thus, Brigadier General JAMES HENRY CARLETON was put in command of New Mexico Territory. He subsequently assigned Colonel CHRISTOPHER ("KIT") CARSON to prosecute the war against the Indians. Carson's forces first overwhelmed the Mescalero APACHE and confined 400 of them at the BOSQUE REDONDO. In June 1863, the Union declared war against the Navajo. Carson's orders were to force the Navajo to surrender, after which they would be sent to Bosque Redondo.

That fall, Carson launched a campaign designed to destroy Navajo supplies. His troops devastated Navajo crops and slaughtered their livestock. By early winter some Navajo had begun to surrender. In 1863, some 300 Indians were killed, 87 wounded, and 703 captured; the military lost only 17 soldiers. In January 1864, Carson and 375 troops closed in on CANYON DE CHELLY in Arizona, where many of the remaining Navajo had congregated. Freezing and starving, many Indians surrendered. The soldiers gave food to those they captured. This precedent reassured other Navajo, who likewise surrendered. In February and March, those who had surrendered began the notorious LONG WALK. Eventually, as many as 9,000 made the journey to Bosque Redondo. Fewer than 2,000 Indians remained behind. They were led by Manuelito, Barboncito, and others who preferred war and perhaps death to captivity. By fall 1866, however, even Barboncito and Manuelito had surrendered.

After four years in captivity at Bosque Redondo, the Navajo were allowed to return to a large reservation in their former territory. In 1868 the made the Long Walk back home, bringing the Navajo War to an end.

Further Reading

McNitt, Frank. *Navajo Wars: Military Campaigns, Slave Raids and Reprisals.* Albuquerque: University of New Mexico Press, 1972.

Bailey, Lynn R. *The Long Walk: A History of the Navajo Wars, 1846–68.* Pasadena, Calif.: Socio-Technical Books, 1970.

Iverson, Peter. Diné. *A History of the Navajos.* Albuquerque: University of New Mexico Press, 2002.

Moore, William Haas. *Chiefs, Agents & Soldiers: Conflict on the Navajo Frontier, 1868–1882.* Albuquerque: University of New Mexico Press, 1994.

Spicer, Edward H. *Cycles of Conquest.* Tucson: University of Arizona Press, 1962.

Underhill, Ruth M. *The Navajos.* Norman: University of Oklahoma Press, 1971.

Neighbors, Robert S. (1815–1859) *federal Indian agent and veteran of Texas's struggle for independence from Mexico*

As an Indian agent in Texas, Robert Neighbors helped create two large reservation areas along the upper Brazos River in 1854 in an effort to stop intertribal warfare on the Texas frontier. Neighbors later became the supervising agent for all Texas Indians, including the COMANCHE and APACHE, dedicating his life to bringing peace to the area, saving lives, and securing the rights and property of Indians. In 1859, after an attack on Indians by JOHN R. BAYLOR and his vigilantes, Neighbors was convinced that the only way to protect the Indians from further harassment was to move them from the Brazos reserve to Indian Territory (present-day Oklahoma). Largely through his efforts, the Brazos Indians made the move uneventfully.

Disillusioned by the problems in Texas, Neighbors went to San Antonio to close his office. Later that year, in Fort Belknap, Texas, his years of service to Texas and the United States was ended when he was shot in the back by a man who supposedly was angry over Neighbors's defense of the Indians.

New Archangel (1802–1813) *series of sieges in which Tlingit Indians attempted to regain their Alaskan land from the Russians*

Between 1741 and 1867, the Russians controlled territory in North America from the Aleutian Islands of Alaska down to a portion of northern California. Inuit lived in scattered settlements, mainly on the Arctic Coast and near the Bering Sea, and had little contact with the newcomers. As the Russian traders moved eastward, they met the Tlingit, Haida, Kwakiutl, and Tsimshian, who lived along the coast, as well as some tribes of the interior. The Tlingit, called "Kolush" by the Russians, presented the greatest problem to the Russian fur trade.

The Tlingit controlled some of the prime sea otter grounds in Russian North America. They were also a fiercely independent people. By the time the Russians came into their territory, the Tlingit were trading with the British and Americans. Russians rarely traded guns and ammunition, but British and American firearms, including cannons, found their way into Tlingit possession. The Tlingit became quite skillful in the use of these weapons, which would become a major problem for the Russians in their eventual confrontations with the Indians. Warriors would further confound the Russians by wearing armor of wooden rods bound together with leather thongs, large wooden hats, and MASKS representing heads of various animals to protect their faces. Russian bullets could not penetrate this thick covering.

In the 1790s, Alexander Baranov, governor-general of a Russian trading company, established the settlement of New Archangel at Sitka, Alaska. The Russians antagonized the Tlingit of the region by invading their territory to hunt sea otters, whose pelts were the most highly sought. The Indians were concerned about the extermination of the animals that were necessary for British and American trade. The Russians exacerbated the problems by kidnapping Tlingit women to serve as concubines, although some became common-law wives.

In 1802, the Tlingit made the first of several attempts to rid their land of Russians. War parties ambushed Russian-Aleut hunting and trading parties throughout their area. A large group of Tlingit also invaded and captured New Archangel, burning all its buildings, confiscating 4,000 pelts, and killing 20 Russians and 130 Aleuts. Two years later, Baranov returned,

with an armada of war ships and shelled the Tlingit positions at New Archangel. After much bloodshed, Baranov and his men landed and reestablished Russian dominance in the area.

The Tlingit's next attempt to expel the Russians was thwarted by tribal women living at New Archangel. In 1806, 2,000 warriors in 400 boats set sail for another assault on Sitka, but Tlingit women in the fort warned Russian officials of the impending attack. Knowing that they could not withstand such an enormous force, officials invited tribal leaders to a feast at the post. Thus, the Indians' plan to destroy New Archangel was deflected with lavish gifts and entertainment.

The Tlingit did not stop their harassment of the Russians, however. By 1808, when Baranov moved the seat of company government from Kodiak to New Archangel, guerrilla attacks by Tlingit raiders was making life extremely uncertain. A year later, and again in 1813, these attacks became so serious that Baranov appealed to the Russian navy for protection. By 1818, a Russian warship was patrolling the harbor at Sitka.

Interaction between Russians and Tlingit became slightly more stable after a series of councils. Baranov wanted the Indians to stop trading with the British and Americans, but the Tlingit refused because they considered Russian trade goods inferior. Moreover, British and American sea merchants had guns, hatchets, knives, blankets and textiles, which the Russians could not supply. The Russians did, however, agree to an exchange of hostages to ensure better relations. Baranov gave the Tlingit two young men of mixed European and Indian ancestry in exchange for the chief's nephew. Hostilities quieted for a time and some trade occurred.

Nevertheless, Russian officials remained wary of the Tlingit well into the second half of the decade. As late as 1850, there was concern over the 500 well-armed Tlingit who lived close to New Archangel. In 1863, officials went so far as to warn the parent trading company that military provisions at New Archangel needed to be reinforced to repel Tlingit attacks. Then, in 1867, the United States purchased all Russian territory in North America. The fort at New Archangel was formally transferred to the United States on October 18, 1867, and the Russians fur traders left North America.

The influx of American settlers, with their alcohol and diseases, quickly decimated the Tlingit population. Current Tlingit are part of the Alaska Native Brotherhood and are accomplished fisherpeople, artisans, and craftspeople.

New Echota Treaty (1835) *treaty between the Cherokee nation and the United States*

With the INDIAN REMOVAL ACT (1830), the U.S. Congress declared that all the Indian tribes east of the Mississippi River had to give up their lands in exchange for territory in the West. Over the course of several years, the CHOCTAW, CHICKASAW, and CREEK signed treaties surrendering their lands and moved west. Although CHEROKEE under the leadership of chief JOHN ROSS challenged the legality of the act, chiefs STAND WATIE and John Ridge signed a treaty with the United States on December

29, 1835, at the Cherokee capital New Echota in Georgia. In exchange for $5 million and some eight million acres of land in the west, the Cherokee ceded all their lands in the east. They were to relocate to the West within two years after the treaty was ratified, and the government would pay for the Removal and give them aid for one year after their relocation.

The Cherokee Nation was divided, however. While Stand Waitie and John Ridge supported the treaty, the principal chief, John Ross, opposed it. Ross presented a petition to Congress signed by more than 15,000 Cherokee protesting the legality of the treaty. Nevertheless, although the Treaty of New Echota was never approved by the Cherokee Nation, it was ratified by the U.S. Senate in 1836, upon which the government began removing thousands of Cherokee from their lands.

See also CHEROKEE TREATIES.

Newtown (1779) *battle between Indians and colonial troops in Pennsylvania during the American Revolution*
In May 1779, Major General JOHN SULLIVAN led 5,000 men through the Mohawk Valley in a campaign against the IROQUOIS CONFEDERACY. In support of their British allies, Confederacy warriors were increasing their attacks on frontier settlements in New York and Pennsylvania. As Sullivan's column pushed west, MOHAWK leader JOSEPH BRANT and about 1,000 warriors, supported by BUTLER'S RANGERS and other Tory militia units, prepared an ambush for the Americans in a ravine near the village of Newtown in New York, but scouts spotted the trap on August 29 and warned Sullivan. Frustrated at having lost the element of surprise, Brant attacked Sullivan's lead brigade anyway, hoping to lure it into the ambush. The Americans held their ground, however, while Sullivan sent a large detachment to attack the Indians from the flank and rear. But Brant detected the attempted encirclement before it could close and managed to escape with his forces intact.

American casualties at the battle of Newtown included 11 dead and 32 wounded. Brant's losses were somewhat greater—17 dead and an undetermined number wounded, including several chiefs. The greater loss, however, was to Iroquois morale; Brant realized he had lost his best chance to stop Sullivan, who proceeded to devastate the entire Mohawk Valley.

New Ulm (1862) *battle during the Minnesota Uprising*
During what became known as the MINNESOTA UPRISING, the town of New Ulm was twice attacked a war party of the Santee Dakota (see SIOUX). The fighting was intense and in many cases hand to hand. The bloody battle was characterized by acts of individual bravery as well as brilliant military tactics.

New Ulm was the biggest town near the Dakota reservations in what is now southern Minnesota. When the fighting began, the town had a population of about 900, mostly German farmers. For safety many hundreds more crowded into New Ulm. They were rural area residents, farmers, and so on.

From the Indian perspective New Ulm was ripe for the taking: the residents were poorly armed and inexperienced in fighting. In addition, most of the houses were spread out on two terraces on the side of a bluff, making them vulnerable to surprise attacks.

On August 19, 1862, the Dakota launched an assault on New Ulm. Approximately 100 Dakota opened fire from the woods above the town, which by now had swelled with refugees from outlying areas. Militia members returned fire. The two groups fought each other to a standstill until a thunderstorm discouraged the Indians, and they withdrew. Over the next few days, Judge Charles E. Flandrau, a former Indian agent and member of the Minnesota Supreme Court, devised strategies to defend the town and the 1,000 women, children, and unarmed men who huddled within a small barricade near the main street. On August 23, the Indians attacked again, with about 650 warriors under chiefs Mankato, Wabasha, and Big Eagle. The town's defenders numbered about 225 armed men. As the Indians rushed the town, their shouts unnerved the militiamen, who retreated but then rallied. General fighting then broke out as the Indians closed in on the barricade amid burning houses and billowing smoke. About 60 warriors had begun to charge when, in an unexpected move, the defenders suddenly launched a countercharge. This proved to be the turning point of the battle. By the end of the day, 34 villagers were dead and 60 wounded. An unknown number of Indians were killed or wounded. Two days later, the 2,000 survivors of the battle of New Ulm loaded into 153 wagons and made the 30-mile journey to Mankato and safety.

Nez Perce (Chopunnish, Nimiipu) *original inhabitants of a vast territory comprising most of Idaho, southeastern Washington, and northeastern Oregon*
The Nez Perce are of the Sahaptian linguistic family. Situated between the Pacific Coast Indians and the Great Plains Indians, Nez Perce culture evolved as a combination of the two groups. They fished the streams of the Northwest, but also took long buffalo-hunting excursions across the Rockies to the Great Plains. A nonagricultural tribe, their food sources included wild game, fish, and wild vegetable foods, including roots.

The only Indians known to have used selective breeding, the Nez Perce and related Palouse Indians developed the distinctive Appaloosa horse breed. They were noted as fierce, competent warriors, although they did not regularly engage in warfare. Nez Perce social organization allowed for wide latitude in individual freedom, but certain behaviors, such as theft, rape, and lying, were not tolerated. Chiefs governed as counselors or advisers, never as absolute rulers. Important decisions involving the whole community were made by a council of men who used debate and oration to reach consensus.

American explorers Meriwether Lewis and William Clark encountered the Nez Perce in the fall of 1805, when the Indians provided food and shelter for their party. The explorers characterized the Nez Perce as "happy . . . people, somewhat introverted and reserved, with a dignified, proud bearing and high moral standards."

In 1836, Protestant missionaries Eliza and Henry Spalding established a mission near Lapwai in Idaho. In spite of the Spalding's methods, which including beatings and whippings, many Nez Perce converted to Christianity. Tuekakas (Old Joseph), CHIEF JOSEPH's father, was among the converts. However, after the TREATY OF 1863 was forced on him, he tore up his "Book of Heaven" and reverted to his traditional beliefs.

In 1853, the U.S. Congress created the Washington Territory. Two years later ISAAC I. STEVENS, the new territorial governor, persuaded the Nez Perce to give up one-third of their land. By the terms of the WALLA WALLA PEACE COUNCIL Treaty of 1855, the Nez Perce retained 12,000 square miles of their former territory as a reservation. Non-Indians were forbidden on the reservation unless tribal permission was granted. Stevens immediately opened the remaining land for settlement, although congressional approval did not occur until 1859.

In 1860, Elias Pierce, a prospector trespassing on the Nez Perce Reservation, found gold. Five thousand miners quickly converged on the Indian land. The town of Lewiston sprang up

and land speculators began selling lots. By 1862, $3 million in gold had been extracted from Nez Perce land, and 15,000 non-Indians had settled on the reservation. In response to this situation, the Treaty of 1863 was negotiated by Superintendent of Indian Affairs Calvin H. Hale and a few Nez Perce, led by LAWYER. Old Chief Joseph and four other chiefs repudiated the treaty and began 14 years of passive resistance to non-Indian domination. Events were thus set in motion that would lead to the NEZ PERCE WAR (1877) and, eventually, young Chief Joseph's unsuccessful attempt to lead his people to Canada.

Contemporary Nez Perce occupy the Colville Reservation in Washington and the Nez Perce Reservation near Lapwai, Idaho. The tribe operates the Nez Perce National Historic Trail, which traces the flight of Chief Joseph and his followers to Canada.

Nez Perce War (1877) *bloody conflict between the U.S. Army and the Nez Perce Indians*

In 1855, a number of NEZ PERCE Indians agreed to move to a government reservation. Others, however, coalesced around the dynamic young CHIEF JOSEPH and refused to join in the Removal. During the 1870s, pressure from non-Indians anxious to dislocate the recalcitrant Nez Perce led the federal government to renew removal negotiations. In 1877, upon learning that some of his young warriors, emboldened by whiskey, had gone on a killing spree, Chief Joseph began moving his people eastward to the plains in an effort to avoid war. The Indians were overtaken by a small contingent of regulars and volunteers led by Captain David Perry. Chief Joseph led a peace party to speak to Captain Perry, but the volunteers opened fire on the Indians, leading to the battle of WHITE BIRD CREEK (1877). The Indians then turned and attacked the army force, chasing them up a nearby canyon to White Bird Hill, where Captain Perry dug in for a stand. However, he was soon forced to retreat. In the end Perry lost 34 men; the Nez Perce lost none.

General OLIVER O. HOWARD, commander of the overall operation, sent Captain Stephen Whipple and troops to capture Chief LOOKING GLASS, another prominent Nez Perce leader. But after soldiers fired on Looking Glass's village without provocation, he joined forces with Chief Joseph.

Howard's forces attacked the Indians on July 11, 1877, at their encampment on CLEARWATER River. The battle that ensued was a desperate struggle, with the Nez Perce forced to fight on the army's terms. The fighting raged on for close to seven hours. Subjected to howitzer fire and grazing fire from Gatling guns, Joseph broke off the battle and headed northward. He had planned to hunt buffalo in Montana and possibly join the CROW Indians there. Now he considered heading toward Canada to join forces with SITTING BULL. Howard, meanwhile, began to pursue the Nez Perce with a force of 560 cavalry and infantry, 25 BANNOCK scouts, and a 350-mule pack train. Howard also sent word ahead to Fort Shaw, asking for help in cutting off the Nez Perce.

As the Nez Perce continued their arduous journey, Looking Glass demanded that Joseph stop in Montana's Big Hole

The Nez Perce were a powerful Indian tribe that lived in the mountainous regions of northeastern Oregon and western Idaho. During their hunting seasons they often lived in tipis, because they were easy to move. *(By permission of the Colorado Historical Society)*

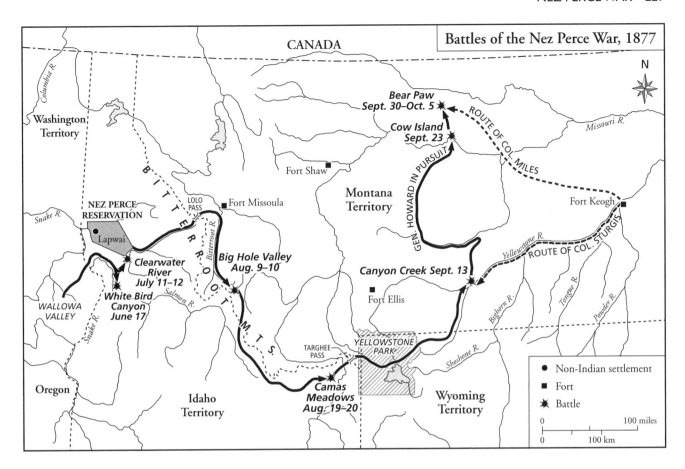

Battles of the Nez Perce War, 1877

Basin to rest. Confident that he had successfully outrun Howard's force, Joseph relaxed, failing to post sentries. This proved to be a major mistake. Colonel JOHN GIBBON, in response to Howard's calls for assistance, had gathered a force of about 200 men and was pushing up the Bitterroot Valley from Fort Shaw. On August 9, Gibbon's troops attacked the Indian village at BIG HOLE (1877). Although taken by surprise, able Nez Perce marksmen soon boxed in the soldiers, forcing Gibbon to appeal for assistance from Howard. As Howard approached the scene, the Nez Perce warriors fell back to rejoin their escaping families.

The fight at Big Hole had cost Gibbon 32 dead and 37 wounded, but the Nez Perce suffered 87 casualties, many of whom were warriors the Indians could ill afford to lose. Joseph now headed across the Continental Divide toward the Lenhi Valley of Idaho. On August 19 and 20, the Nez Perce won another victory at CAMAS CREEK (1877), driving off many of the soldiers' pack mules and cavalry horses. Demoralized and unable to rally his dejected troops, Howard telegraphed General WILLIAM TECUMSEH SHERMAN with a request that he be allowed to call off the pursuit. Sherman, in an angry reply, ordered Howard to purse the Nez Perce to the death as the Indians fled east.

Other army columns joined the pursuit. From Little Bighorn country, Colonel Samuel D. Sturgis led six troops from GEORGE ARMSTRONG CUSTER's 7th Cavalry, followed closely by the 5th Regiment under Colonel Wesley Merritt. Chief Joseph feigned movement toward the Shoshone River, drew Sturgis in closer, and then moved along Clark's Fork, where he was able to reach the open plains. Chief Joseph's scouts then caused the Indian leader to make a grave error when they reported that the route was blocked ahead. The Indians' resulting detour allowed Howard time to join Sturgis. On September 3 the army caught up with the Nez Perce, but the Indians were able to hold off Sturgis's forces. Chief Joseph now led his people to BEAR PAW Mountain, only 30 miles from the safety of the Canadian border. There Looking Glass convinced Joseph to stop and let the exhausted Indians rest.

Unknown to the Nez Perce, Colonel NELSON A. MILES and 400 men were moving quickly to cut off their retreat into Canada. Lakota (see SIOUX) and CHEYENNE scouts employed by Miles located the Nez Perce village on the morning of September 30, 1877, and Miles immediately launched an attack. Joseph managed to get his warriors into the woodline on a nearby ridge, where his marksmen again took a heavy toll on the soldiers. As his casualties mounted, Miles broke off the assault; 31 were dead and 38 wounded. However, he now set in to conduct a siege against the Nez Perce, an operation that would continue for five days. Finally, with his people completely surrounded and his calls for help from Sitting Bull and the Lakota unanswered, Joseph surrendered about 400 of his people to Colonel Miles on October 5, 1877.

Of the 800 Nez Perce who had followed Chief Joseph, 120 had died during the 1,700-mile trek. The Nez Perce had killed about 180 soldiers and wounded about 150 more. Contrary to promises made by Miles, the Nez Perce were exiled to reservations in Kansas and Indian Territory (present-day Oklahoma). Once there, many of the people became sick and died. In 1885 the Nez Perce were allowed to resettle at the Colville Reservation in Washington Territory, near their traditional homeland.

Further Reading
Hampton, Bruce. *Children of Grace: The Nez Perce War of 1877.* New York: Henry Holt, 1994.

Niagara (1763) *siege in Pontiac's Rebellion*
When the uprising known as PONTIAC'S REBELLION (1763–65) broke out in late spring and summer in 1763, many British forts fell to surprise attacks by Indian forces. There were three major exceptions: Forts DETROIT, Pitt, and Niagara each had garrisons large enough and commanders wary enough to resist the Indian attackers. Niagara was attacked by a small band of Chenussio SENECA Indians late in the summer of 1763, but the stone walls of the fort repelled the assault. The road leading from the falls to Lake Erie, however, was much more vulnerable. On September 14, 1763, 300 Seneca ambushed a supply train on its way to the fort at Devil's Hole, near the falls. Seventy-two British soldiers and carters died in the assault.

By the beginning of 1764 the Chenussio Seneca and their allies had retreated from the vicinity of Niagara. This was partly because the rest of the Seneca refused to enter the war against the British. They followed the policy of the rest of the IROQUOIS CONFEDERACY and, in fact, sent warriors on an expedition against Susquehanna Delaware (see LENNI LENAPE), who had been raiding the Pennsylvania frontier. News of the PROCLAMATION OF 1763 also had an effect, encouraging the Indians to believe that they had won separation from the incursions of non-Indian settlers. By the time a relief expedition reached Niagara in 1764, the Chenussio Seneca had made peace with the garrison, guaranteed the return of prisoners, and ceded lands around the fort to the British.

Nohoroca (Neoheroka) (1713) *final battle in the Tuscarora War*
Between 1710 and 1713, the TUSCARORA Indians fought a running war with settlers in North Carolina. The Tuscarora had been the victims of traders who cheated them out of their lands by getting them drunk and then making deals with them. In addition many traders also led slaving raids on the tribe, selling the kidnapped Indians in the West Indies. The matter came to a head in 1710, when Swiss settlers at New Bern forced the Tuscarora to abandon one of their towns with the compliance of the North Carolina government. In September 1711, the Tuscarora retaliated, killing between 120 and 200 of the New

Bern settlers. For the next 18 months raids and counterraids by Indians and settlers troubled the North Carolina frontier.

In March 1713, the combined colonial militias and Indian allies of North and South Carolina—estimated at between 900 and 1,600 troops—led a raid on the Tuscarora camp of Nohoroca. The battle was a complete success for the colonists; 192 Tuscarora died in the conflict. In addition, just under 400 Indians were captured and sold as slaves in the West Indies. Most of the profits from the sale were used to defray the costs of the expedition. The remainder was divided between the colonists and their Indian allies.

Nohoroca almost destroyed the Tuscarora nation in North Carolina. Most of the surviving Indians sought shelter among the IROQUOIS CONFEDERACY in New York, where they were welcomed them as the sixth member of the confederation in 1722. The few who remained in North Carolina signed a treaty with the colonial government on February 11, 1715 (see TUSCARORA TREATY; TUSCARORA WAR).

Norridgewock (1724) *principal battle of Dummer's War*
The village of Norridgewock, near the headwaters of the Kennebec River in what is now Maine, was located in the territory of the Kennebec tribe of the eastern ABENAKI. Because their territory was so near the boundary between New England and New France, it was hotly contested by the two European nations. The Abenaki maintained their existence by playing the two powers against each other.

In August 1724, William Dummer, acting governor of the Massachusetts Bay Colony, sent a band of men to arrest a French Jesuit missionary named SÉBASTIEN RÂLE. Râle had lived with and ministered to the Abenaki in Norridgewock since 1694, and the British believed that he was responsible for inciting the Indians to attack colonists in the area of Brunswick. An earlier expedition had burned the town in 1722. Although the expeditionary force was only supposed to arrest Râle and frighten the Indians into compliance, they surprised the village instead and began shooting. The Indians, Râle among them, fought back. The battle ended only after Râle and many of the Abenaki had been killed. The attackers cemented their victory by burning Norridgewock and taking scalps from the dead Indians.

The battle of Norridgewock and the death of Râle marked the end of DUMMER'S WAR. In 1725 the British negotiated a treaty with the PENOBSCOT tribe, who claimed to represent all the Abenaki (see ABENAKI TREATY). Although the Penobscot had not actually won the war, they were still a force to be respected. The peace they negotiated with the British lasted until the beginning of the FRENCH AND INDIAN WAR (1754–63).

Northwest Confederacy See GREENVILLE, TREATY OF.

Numu See PAIUTE.

Ojibwa See CHIPPEWA.

Ollikut (Ollokot, Frog) (ca. 1842–1877) *younger brother of Nez Perce leader Chief Joseph, and an important military leader during the Nez Perce War*

Ollikut was an imposing figure. He stood 6′4″ and weighed more than 200 pounds, but he was quick and graceful. Just slightly taller than his older brother, Joseph, they were often mistaken for twins. Kindly and popular among his tribesmen, Ollikut was a leader of the young men. By his early 20s, he had distinguished himself as a warrior in skirmishes with enemy tribes, principally the BLACKFOOT CONFEDERACY.

In 1855, the Nez Perce signed a land-cession treaty following the WALLA WALLA PEACE COUNCIL. However, by refusing to sign the land-cession TREATY OF 1863 and by spurning reservation life, Old Joseph and four other chiefs began 14 years of passive resistance.

On May 14, 1877, General OLIVER O. HOWARD ordered the non-treaty bands of Nez Perce to report to the Lapwai Reservation in Idaho within 30 days or face the U.S. army. Ollikut and his brother CHIEF JOSEPH influenced the other leaders to acquiesce. Subsequently the rebellious bands arrived and camped close to Lapwai. When talk of war among the Indians in the camp eventually led to the killing of 18 non-Indians, Ollikut and Joseph recommended an attempt at a peaceful settlement. Fearing indiscriminate retribution, however, the people hastily packed and fled south toward White Bird Creek.

At WHITE BIRD CREEK (1877), Ollikut and others executed their impromptu battle tactics well. Six Nez Perce went out to meet Captain David Perry under a flag of truce. An officer fired two stray shots toward the peace party. Nez Perce sharpshooters answered, knocking a dozen soldiers from their saddles. The buglers were then picked off, making troop coordination impossible. Perry's troops were completely routed.

Ollikut took charge in the battle of CLEARWATER (1877), in which General Howard surprised the Nez Perce with howitzer fire. However, his position was revealed when the gunfire fell short. Accurately anticipating Howard's movements, Nez Perce warrior Toohoolhoolzote and several men crossed the river and climbed the bluff opposite their camp. They began firing at the soldiers, who immediately dug in with only tall grass for cover. Ollikut and several other marksmen took position in a ravine. With amazing accuracy, they pinned the soldiers all day and through the night. The next day Captain Marcus Miller charged the Nez Perce who, tiring of the battle, fled and again escaped.

At CAMAS CREEK (1877), the Nez Perce managed to stay one day ahead of General Howard's troops. Ollikut led 28 warriors back to Howard's camp and stole 200 pack mules, thus creating a three-day delay for Howard and extending the Nez Perce's lead.

At BIG HOLE (1877), the Nez Perce were caught sleeping in a surprise attack at dawn. They nevertheless managed to outmaneuver Colonel JOHN GIBBON's troops and caught them in a crossfire. Ollikut and other sharpshooters held the soldiers pinned for 24 hours while the tribespeople packed their belongings and escaped.

Although Ollikut was an advocate of peace, his skills as a battle tactician helped his people evade capture by U.S. Army troops for nearly three months. He was killed on the first day of the battle of BEAR PAW (1877) in Montana, 30 miles from Canada.

Oneida *one of the six nations of the Iroquois Confederacy*

The Oneida, along with the MOHAWK, ONONDAGA, CAYUGA, TUSCARORA, and SENECA, were members of the IROQUOIS CONFEDERACY. Sandwiched between the Mohawk and Onondaga, the Oneida lived in what is now the Finger Lakes region of New York.

The Oneida and the other members of the confederacy supported the British in the FRENCH AND INDIAN WAR (1754–63). During the AMERICAN REVOLUTION (1775–81), however, the Oneida and Tuscarora, unlike the other tribes, sided with the Americans against the British.

Following the Revolution, the Oneida were forced to sell most of their holdings in New York to the government and non-Indian settlers. Some of the Indians stayed behind in New York, and others relocated to Wisconsin and Ontario. The three groups continue to live on these lands today.

Onondaga *one of the six nations of the Iroquois Confederacy*

The Onondaga were situated geographically in the center of the IROQUOIS CONFEDERACY (new present-day Syracuse, New York), with the MOHAWK and ONEIDA to the east and the CAYUGA and SENECA to the west. As the central tribe of the confederacy, they were Keepers of the Council Fire and hosted the annual Iroquois Great Council Meeting. They were also keepers of the wampum belt that served as a record of the meetings.

The Iroquois sought power and domination over the northeastern Indian tribes to control trade with Europeans. This resulted in a long period of conquests known as the BEAVER WARS (1638–84).

The 200-year-old Iroquois Confederacy was broken during the AMERICAN REVOLUTION (1775–81). The Onondaga preferred neutrality, but they were persuaded by Mohawk Chief Thayendanegea (JOSEPH BRANT) to join with the Mohawk, Cayuga, and Seneca on the side of the British. The TUSCARORA (admitted to the Iroquois Confederacy in 1722) and the Oneida chose to ally with the Americans. In 1777, the Onondaga and other British-allied Iroquois suffered defeat at ORISKANY CREEK (1777), and the Iroquois Confederacy erupted in civil war. The next year, American Generals JOHN SULLIVAN and James Clinton and Colonel Daniel Brodhead wreaked havoc on the British-allied Iroquois. The Sullivan campaign destroyed 40 villages and many acres of crops and orchards. The British-allied Iroquois took vengeance on the Oneida and Tuscarora. Although their villages were in ruins, the British-allied Iroquois warriors continued their resistance until a short time after the British surrender at Yorktown in 1781.

After the Revolutionary War, most Onondaga acknowledged the sovereignty of the United States and were eventually granted a reservation in central New York, where their descen-

dants continue to live. Other Onondaga live on the Six Nations Reserve in Ontario, Canada. The Iroquois Confederacy tribes have again united and the Onondaga Reservation serves as the their capital. The *Tadodaho,* or chief of the combined Iroquois tribes, is chosen from among the Onondaga.

Opechancanough (Opechankino, Apechancanought) (ca. 1556–1646) *war leader, or* werowance, *of the Pamunkey tribe*

Opechancanough was the last Indian war chief who had both the chance and the ability to force the English out of North America altogether. He was half brother to the POWHATAN CONFEDERACY's principal chief POWHATAN, or Wahunsonacock, and became chief of the confederacy on Powhatan's death in 1618. He came into conflict with the English under JOHN SMITH many times during the early days of the settlement at Jamestown.

Opechancanough was the primary mover behind the POWHATAN WARS (1622–32, 1644–46) against the English in Virginia. Although he engineered the deaths of about one-third of the colony's total population in a single day (March 22, 1622), Opechancanough miscalculated the settlers' determination. He expected that the remaining English would retreat to their own country, and therefore he did not press his attack against them. Instead, the English counterattacked, killing Indians indiscriminately. At the end of the last of the wars in 1646, Opechancanough was captured by the English and murdered by an angry soldier while in their custody.

Oriskany Creek (1777) *battle in upstate New York during the American Revolution*

In 1777, the British war effort in the AMERICAN REVOLUTION (1775–81) was focused on General Sir John Burgoyne's strategy for severing the New England colonies from those in the south. Burgoyne proposed to lead a large army from Canada south along Lake Champlain and the Hudson, hoping to join another army moving north from British-held New York City. Meanwhile, Lieutenant Colonel Barry St. Leger would sweep through the Mohawk Valley from the west, leading a mixed force of 1,000 regulars and Tories and 700 IROQUOIS CONFEDERACY warriors from the MOHAWK, CAYUGA, and SENECA tribes, all under Mohawk chief JOSEPH BRANT.

St. Leger's first major obstacle was FORT STANWIX (present-day Rome, New York) and its garrison of 700, to which he laid siege to on August 2, 1777. Two days later, a relief force composed of 800 colonial volunteers and 60 ONEIDA under the command of General Nicholas Herkimer was ambushed in a ravine about a mile and a half west of the Oriskany Creek and six miles from the fort.

At first, the ambush, sprung by Brant at the head of 1,000 Indians and Tories, succeeded brilliantly: Herkimer was shot from his horse, his rear guard was scattered, and his advance was checked in confusion. Severely wounded, Herkimer was carried to a small hill where, propped against a tree in his saddle and smoking a pipe, he rallied his troops into a defensive circle around him. The battle raged on for two hours, both sides fighting from behind the protective cover of trees and boulders.

At midday a torrential downpour and violent thunderstorm brought a lull in the fighting, as men scrambled to keep their powder and muskets dry. Brant's Indians saw the storm as a bad omen, and they began drifting from the field when they heard the sound of gunfire in their rear. They soon discovered that a small party from the fort had raided their base camp, carrying off blankets, clothing, and other supplies, thus leaving the Indians clad only in the breechcloths they had worn in the ambush.

Herkimer, whose wounds from the battle later proved fatal, managed to escape with what was left of his force, having suffered casualties of more than 200 dead and 50 wounded. Even though he'd failed to raise the siege of Fort Stanwix, Herkimer had succeeded in so demoralizing St. Leger's Indian allies—who had lost 35 warriors and five chiefs in addition to all their supplies—that they quickly scattered before the advance of another relief party, this one led by Major General Benedict Arnold. Deprived of Indian warriors, St. Leger himself retreated to Canada and so was sorely missed by Burgoyne, who was defeated two months later at Saratoga in a battle that became the turning point in the Revolutionary War.

In addition to the American victory, the battle of Oriskany Creek was significant because it marked the first time that Indians of the Iroquois Confederacy had fought against each other.

Ortíz Parrilla, Diego (ca. 1715–ca. 1775) *Spanish commander who led campaigns against the Comanche and their allies*
Born in Spain, Ortíz Parrilla joined the royal dragoons and fought the Moors there before being transferred to North America, where he became the Spanish governor of Texas. In 1750 the AKIMEL O'ODHAM (formerly Pima) in what is now Arizona revolted and fled after killing more than 100 Spaniards and Christian Indians. The official report of the affair suggested that Governor Ortíz Parrilla was at fault. As a result, he was demoted to commander of a small fort, or presidio, near the SAN SABA Mission in present-day Menard, Texas, approximately 100 miles from San Antonio.

In 1758 COMANCHE enemies of the Spanish attacked the San Saba mission. Ortíz Parrilla desperately wanted to avenge his honor. When the Spanish viceroy ordered him to crush the attackers, he assembled a force of 480 Spanish soldiers and more than 100 APACHE and their allies. Laboriously dragging a large number of cannon, the military contingent arrived near the Red River at present-day Wichita Falls, Texas. There Ortíz Parrilla found the Comanche and their allies, the WICHITA, in a barricaded log fort over which flew a French flag.

Ortíz Parrilla's military charge and the following battle was a Spanish disaster. The fort's defenders repelled wave after wave of Spanish assaults, while inflicting heavy casualties. They then counterattacked and captured Ortíz Parrilla's artillery. In addition, Apache allies stole many Spanish horses and left the battlefield. After his men begged for a retreat, the defeated Colonel Ortíz Parrilla ordered one and marched south. Despite this disaster, he was later appointed governor of Coahuila, and by 1780 he had been promoted to brigadier general.

Osage *major Indian tribe of the central plains*
According to tradition, the Osage once lived along the Ohio River with related tribes the Kaw, the Omaha, the PONCA, and the QUAPAW. By 1673, however, they had settled on the Osage River in what is now Missouri. From there they also claimed territory as far south as the Arkansas River in portions of Kansas, Arkansas, and Oklahoma.

During the 1700s and into the 1800s, the Osage, who claimed a population of between 5,000 and 6,000 members, were at war with almost all the other Plains tribes, including the Illinois, KIOWA, COMANCHE, and PAWNEE. To many of their opponents their very name became synonymous with the word "enemy." In 1714 the Osage aided the French in defeating the FOX (Mesquakie). During the FRENCH AND INDIAN WAR (1754–63), the tribe sided with the French against the English. Decades later, Osage scouts led the soldiers of WILLIAM TECUMSEH SHERMAN during his campaigns against western plains Indians. On one expedition the scouts guided GEORGE ARMSTRONG CUSTER and his 7th Cavalry to the village of CHEYENNE chief BLACK KETTLE, where the battle of WASHITA (1868) took place.

Between 1808 and 1865, the Osage signed a series of treaties ceding most of their land to the United States. By 1870 the Indians had been assigned to a reservation in Indian Territory (present-day Oklahoma). The discovery of oil on this land in 1896 has brought much wealth to present-day Osage.

Osceola (Talassee Tustenuggee, Billy Powell) (ca. 1803–1838) *leader during the Second Seminole War*
Osceola was born along the Tallapoosa River in Alabama. He moved to Florida as a youth and was just a teenager when he fought in the First SEMINOLE WAR of 1816–18.

In the treaties of PAYNE'S LANDING (1832) and FORT GIBSON (1833), some SEMINOLE leaders mistakenly agreed to relocate their people from Florida to Indian Territory (Oklahoma). Osceola actively urged his people to stay in Florida. When relocation was imminent, he and others hid their families in the Florida swamps. In November 1835, Osceola killed a prorelocation chief and the next month killed the Indian agent who had promoted the treaties. Thus, the Second SEMINOLE WAR (1835–42) erupted. Osceola's warriors won a decisive battle at WITHLACOOCHEE RIVER (1835), and for the next two years the Indians launched numerous guerrilla attacks. In October 1837, General THOMAS SIDNEY JESUP invited Osceola to discuss peace under a flag of truce. Osceola accepted, but upon his arrival at the site near St. Augustine, he was immediately

Osceola, a Seminole war chief, was a tribal leader in the Second Seminole War. *(Courtesy New York Public Library)*

assaulted, bound, and imprisoned. He was transferred to a prison near Charleston, South Carolina, where he died on January 30, 1838.

Ottawa *tribe of the Great Lakes region*

Like other ALGONQUIAN peoples, the Ottawa believed in an omnipotent Great Spirit and lived by hunting, fishing, and occasional farming. With the arrival of the Europeans, the Ottawa began to establish a reputation as traders, functioning as middlemen between the French and other tribes.

Toward the mid-1600s, conflict with the powerful IRO-QUOIS CONFEDERACY sent many Ottawa fleeing across Lake Superior. They returned to their former territories when promised protection by the French, alongside whom they

fought the British for the next 100 years. The tribe's fortunes declined following the French defeat in the SEVEN YEAR'S WAR (1754–63), then revived briefly under the great chief PONTIAC (see PONTIAC'S REBELLION).

The Ottawa were forced west again following the treaties of FORT MCINTOSH (1785) and FORT HARMAR (1789). Today most Ottawa live in Kansas and Oklahoma, though a number have returned to the tribe's traditional homelands in the Great Lakes region, having property in Michigan and Ontario.

Ouray (U-ray, U-re, Willie, The Arrow) (ca. 1820 or 1833–1880) *Ute statesman and spokesman*

The events of Ouray's birth are uncertain. Some sources say he was born among the UTE in Colorado about 1820. Others claim he was a Jicarilla APACHE born in Taos, New Mexico, about 1833. Reasonably well educated, Ouray spoke English and Spanish as well as various Indian languages. As a young man he distinguished himself in battles against the Lakota (see SIOUX) and KIOWA. Later, his only son was taken by the Lakota and never seen again.

By 1860, Ouray had become a chief of his Ute band. Thereafter he became best known for his unwavering alliance

Ouray, a Ute war chief (center), with four members of his tribe, 1868 *(Courtesy New York Public Library)*

After the Ute War, a delegation of Ute chiefs, led by Chief Ouray (front row, second from right), went to Washington, D.C., to negotiate Removal of their tribe from their ancestral territories. *(By permission of the Colorado Historical Society)*

with non-Indians. In 1863, for example, he helped negotiate a treaty with the American government in which the Ute ceded their lands east of the Continental Divide. Four years later, he helped CHRISTOPHER ("KIT") CARSON suppress a Ute uprising. In 1868 he went to Washington, D.C., as a spokesman for various Ute bands.

By the mid-1800s, encroachment onto Ute land had become pronounced. In 1871–72 Ouray attended various councils to try to resolve the matter. Nevertheless, the Ute ended up ceding 4 million acres of land for a paltry annual pay-

ment of $25,000. As a result of this loss of land, Ouray fell from favor among many Ute. In time he killed at least five fellow tribe members who had made attempts on his life.

By 1878–79, tensions between the Ute and their non-Indian neighbors had reached a crisis point, resulting in the UTE WAR (1879). Ouray was called upon to negotiate peace. In 1880 the aging chief traveled to Washington, D.C., for the last time. There he signed a treaty that called for the relocation of the Ute to eastern Utah and southwestern Colorado. Chief Ouray died later that year, on August 24, 1880.

P

paint, war *pigments that Native American warriors applied to their faces and bodies in ritualistic patterns*
Indians decorated their faces and bodies with paint for many reasons: to protect against the elements, to ward off unseen and possibly evil spirits, to designate membership in a particular society, as a mark of achievement, and to mourn the dead. Warriors also painted themselves for war, using their own personal designs to protect them. These personal marks helped war chiefs to identify their warriors in the midst of battle.

Colors had significance. Red paint meant success, power, and war; black paint symbolized death. Among the Plains Indians, a warrior about to go into battle might paint one side of his face red and the other black. Red circles around the eyes were thought to help a warrior see an enemy at a distance. If a warrior wanted paint to remain on his body as a reminder of his prowess after a victory, he would mix the paint with grease. When acting as scouts, PAWNEE men painted their faces all white to symbolize the wolf, whose medicine was especially powerful in scouting and guiding others. Among the CROW, warriors who returned victorious from battle painted their faces black, indicating that they no longer felt the revenge that had prompted their conflict with another tribe.

The painted designs varied among the various tribes. One Omaha war chief painted lines on his face from his eyes to his neck to signify the tears he would shed for the success of his raid. The painted hands of SHOSHONE warriors of the Wind River region symbolized hand-to-hand encounters with the enemy. KIOWA warriors often painted their bodies, horses, and shields with the same design.

Painting the body was not just meant to show the warrior's power and frighten the enemy. The paint was also thought to have magical powers that placed him under the protection of the great spirits, making him invulnerable and often even invisible.

Paiute *tribe of the Great Basin area*
The Paiute lived in an area now designated as the Great Basin Culture. Like other tribes of the Great Basin, they were nomadic, traveling to traditional sites in search of wild game and plant foods. The Northern Paiute (now called the Numu) occupied lands in portions of what is now Nevada, Oregon, northern California, and southern Idaho. The Southern Paiute traditionally lived in parts of Utah, Nevada, Arizona, and California. Their name probably mens "true Ute," indicating a relationship with the UTE.

The Paiute were friendly with the first American settlers in the 1820s, but they became increasingly hostile following the Gold Rush of the late 1840s. The Northern Paiute were considered the more warlike; they took part in the COEUR D'ALENE WAR (1858), the PAIUTE WAR (1860), the SNAKE WAR (1866–68), and the BANNOCK WAR (1878). In the late 1880s a Southern Paiute, named WOVOKA originated the GHOST DANCE religion, which led to the last major outbreak of hostilities on the frontier.

Probably the most famous members of the Northern Paiute are the Winnemuccas. The patriarch, Truckee or Winnemucca, served as an interpreter and scout for explorer John C. Frémont's 1845–46 expeditions in California. Winnemucca's son, who became known as Old Winnemucca, maintained peace among his band during the Paiute War. He also traveled to Washington, D.C., with his daughter, SARAH WINNEMUCCA, to speak on behalf of his tribe. Sarah, who gained fame as a tireless spokesperson for Native American rights, wrote the book *Life among the Paiutes, Their Wrongs and Claims* (1883), and spent many years educating Indian children.

The Paiute of today live on various reservations in the Great Basin area. They are famed for their skill at basket weaving.

Paiute Prophet   See GHOST DANCE.

Paiute War   (1860–68)   *final stand of the Paiute in Nevada*
On May 7, 1860, the Williams Station trading post in the Nevada Territory was burned by Indians attackers and five non-Indians were killed in response to the rape of two PAIUTE girls by traders from the station. Reports of the incident led to the formation of four volunteer detachments, comprising 105 inexperienced and undisciplined men.

On May 12, the volunteers descended into the valley on the east side of the Truckee River. Major William M. Ormsby ordered the men to pursue a band of Paiute up on a plateau. About half of the men charged ahead—and fell directly into a Paiute ambush. The soldiers' horses became unmanageable, riders lost their rifles and gear, and the volunteers began a retreat to lower ground and their slower comrades. Discipline disintegrated entirely when the troops met the Paiute band, led by a warrior named Chiquito, during their retreat. The narrow trail leading out of the meadow hindered the volunteers' ability to maneuver, providing the Paiute with an opportunity to kill them easily. The panicked volunteers consequently abandoned their posts and fled. A total of 42 of Ormsby's men were killed, 30 were reported missing, and 33 later reported back to their towns.

When reports of the incident arrived in Carson Valley, Nevada, Jack Hays, formerly of the TEXAS RANGERS was given command of a new force. On May 24, he led 550 volunteers and 200 regular troops in pursuit of the Paiute. They finally caught up with the Indians on June 2 between the big bend of the Truckee River and Pyramid Lake. After a brief battle, the Paiute were defeated. About 46 Indians were killed, and 11 soldiers were killed or wounded. Hays then pursued the remaining Paiute and harassed them until they broke into small groups and scattered. Hays subsequently built Fort Churchill to defend the valley and the California Trail.

Palo Duro Canyon   (1874)   *surprise attack by U.S. Army forces on Native Americans during the Red River War*
Located in the rugged Staked Plains of the Texas Panhandle, Palo Duro Canyon (formed by the main fork of the Red River) had long offered southern plains tribes a refuge against the U.S. Army. During the RED RIVER WAR of 1874–75, however, cav-

alry commanded by Colonel RANALD S. MACKENZIE discovered the site.

Just after daybreak on September 28, 1874, Mackenzie led a column of cavalry and their horses single file on a perilous, thousand-foot descent down the steep canyon walls. Below, stretched over two miles, they found some 200 lodges belonging to KIOWA followers of Maman-ti, COMANCHE led by O-ha-ma-ti, and Southern CHEYENNE under Iron Skirt. Regrouping at the canyon base, Mackenzie's regulars remounted and rushed into the campsites. A melee followed as the surprised Indians scrambled for safety, leaving virtually all of their possessions and their main pony herds behind. Skirmishing continued for much of the day as the soldiers looted and burned the camps. The next morning, after distributing the best captured ponies among his soldiers and scouts, Mackenzie ordered the remaining 1,000 animals slaughtered.

Human casualties in the battle of Palo Duro Canyon were minimal—army reports listed one soldier wounded and four Indians killed—but the Indians never recovered from the devastating loss of their horses and winter stores. The defeat soon led to their surrender to reservation life.

Pamunkey   *principal tribe of the Powhatan Confederacy in Virginia*
The Pamunkey were one of a number of tribes led by the great chief POWHATAN, whose homeland was in the upper valley of the York River in tidewater Virginia. The Pamunkey participated in Powhatan's campaigns to enlarge his territory, including raids against the Kecoughtan in 1596–97 and the Chesapeake, whom he destroyed entirely. Powhatan respected the Pamunkey so well that he established his half brother OPECHANCANOUGH as their *werowance,* or war leader.

The Pamunkey were among the first members of the POWHATAN CONFEDERACY to have significant contact with the Jamestown settlers. In December 1607, Jamestown leader JOHN SMITH was captured by Opechancanough and held as a prisoner for a few months. In 1609, Smith returned to the Pamunkey, demanding corn to feed the starving colonists. At one point he held Opechancanough at gunpoint until his demands were met. Opechancanough was later captured by the British and executed in 1646.

The Pamunkey fought the English settlers in the POWHATAN WARS (1622–32, 1644–46). Their last significant action was the battle of PAMUNKEY (1656), a raid, assisted by the British militia in Virginia, against an invading group of Indians known as the Richahecrians. The Pamunkey's *werowance,* Opechancanough's successor Necotowance, died in the fighting along with almost 100 of his warriors. The last of his people were driven from their homelands by NATHANIEL BACON near the start of BACON'S REBELLION (1676).

Presently, the Pamunkey and the Mattaponi are the only two members of the Powhatan Confederacy to hold state reservation lands in Virginia.

Pamunkey, battle of (1656) *battle in Virginia between the combined force of British and Pamunkey and invading Native Americans*

By the 1650s, the British had effectively neutralized the powerful POWHATAN CONFEDERACY. However, there were still many other Indians in the Virginia colony who, in the opinion of some settlers, posed a threat to British interests. In 1655, about 700 well-armed Native Americans appeared in PAMUNKEY territory and settled near the falls of the James River—the point marking the edge of Tidewater Virginia. The Virginia Assembly ordered Colonel Edward Hill to lead the militia against the newcomers, who were known as Richahecrians. Hill took a force of 100 men to deal with the situation.

Hill was joined in his fight by Necotowance, OPECHANCANOUGH's successor as head chief of the Powhatan, and about 100 warriors. The militia leader asked the Richahecrians for a meeting, and five chiefs came to negotiate. Using tactics the British had used against the Powhatan in the POWHATAN WARS (1622–32, 1644–46), Hill captured the Richahecrian chiefs and had them killed. In the pitched battle that followed, Necotowance and many of his warriors died; their allied militia survived by running away. The Richahecrians then disappeared from Virginian history as mysteriously as they had come.

Papago   See TOHONO O'ODHAM.

Paris, Treaty of (1763) *peace treaty that ended the French and Indian War*

Although the fall of Quebec on September 8, 1759, marked the end of French resistance to the British in North America, an official peace treaty ending the FRENCH AND INDIAN WAR (1754–63) was still three and a half years in the future. Fighting continued on the high seas and in Europe. Spain entered the war on the side of France on January 2, 1762. The British navy exercised its advantage over its enemies by seizing French and Spanish islands in the Caribbean. Between February and October 1762, the British took the islands of Martinique, Santa Lucia, and Grenada, plus the important ports of Havana, Cuba, and Manila in the Philippines. Although these British victories did not have a direct impact on Native Americans, they were important bargaining chips in the negotiations that led to the Treaty of Paris.

France tried to compensate the Spanish for their Caribbean losses through the secret treaty of San Ildefonso, signed on November 3, 1762, which turned over all French possessions west of the Mississippi River to Spain. However, with the signing of the Treaty of Paris on February 10, 1763, the entire European picture in the Americas changed. The terms of this agreement pushed France out of North America and restricted the Spanish to territories west of the Mississippi River. For Native Americans such as tribes of the IROQUOIS CONFEDERACY, who had maintained their power by playing the British off the French, the Treaty of Paris was an ominous sign of changing times.

The terms of the Treaty of Paris involved much territory that was part of North America. France ceded its Canadian territories to Britain without restriction, except for several small islands near the mouth of the St. Lawrence River where French fishermen could land and dry their nets. In addition, France ceded to Britain its claims to all territory east of the Mississippi River, with the exception of the port of New Orleans. Since the treaty of San Ildefonso had already surrendered French territorial claims west of the Mississippi to Spain, French dominion in North America was effectively ended. In return, Britain restored the Caribbean islands of Guadeloupe and Martinique to French control. For its part, Spain ceded East and West Florida to the British and received in return the islands of Cuba and the Philippines.

The terms of the Treaty of Paris meant that for the first time Britain had complete control over Indian policies throughout virtually all of eastern North America. Without competition from French or Spanish traders, the British could set their own rates of exchange for furs and weapons. In addition, the British considered themselves lawful possessors of the lands that French and Spanish explorers had taken from the Indians. While neither of the other two European powers had pursued their claims to western land, the Native Americans believed that the British would do so. Moreover, Indian allies of the French in the French and Indian War feared persecution for their role. The Indians' fears of the British relationship was a contributing factor in the outbreak of hostilities known as PONTIAC'S REBELLION (1763–64).

Paris, Treaty of (1783) *peace agreement that ended the American Revolution*

The terms of the 1783 Treaty of Paris pushed the border of the United States westward from the Allegheny Mountains to the Mississippi River. The Native Americans whose hunting grounds were within this vast expanse sent no delegates to the peace convention and, except for the provision that a reservation be created in Canada for Iroquois (see IROQUOIS CONFEDERACY) refugees from the devastated Mohawk Valley, British commissioners gave little thought to the interests of their former Indian allies.

There was nothing unusual or chauvinistic in this exclusion. Before the war, when territories were transferred among the colonial powers, responsibility for the Indians whose territories were involved was transferred as well. Although the system was hardly just, the British government and its colonies believed that each tribe had what was called a "right of soil"—control of the land if not actual possession in a European sense—that needed to be purchased through treaties.

Frontier hostilities during the AMERICAN REVOLUTION (1775–81), however, engendered such intense hatreds that this traditional policy was discarded. It was decided that the Native Americans had forfeited all rights to their lands because of their support of the British, and thus the "right of soil" was automatically transferred to the United States. Rather than negotiate treaty terms, it was considered sufficient to merely dictate them, and in the first few treaties signed immediately after the Paris convention—those of FORT STANWIX (1784), FORT MCINTOSH (1785), and FORT FINNEY (1786)—the tribes were simply ordered from their lands.

These treaties had little practical effect, however, because the government lacked the means of enforcing them. Through most of the 1780s the United States was governed under the Articles of Confederation, which reserved most powers to the states. The weakened central government already found it difficult to raise money for such measures as national defense, and a report by the secretary of war in 1787 estimated that the army would need to be tripled to secure the frontier, making it clear that treaty enforcement was not possible.

The situation was further complicated by the fact that several states, particularly in the South, reserved the right to independently negotiate treaties with Native Americans on lands now claimed by the states. The establishment of separate Indian departments north and south of the Ohio River in 1786 was only a minor improvement.

By this time the failure of Indian policy under the Articles of Confederation was becoming obvious. Moreover, a new conscience had begun to appear in the nation's Indian policy. In August 1787 a congressional committee, influenced by the secretary of war's report on the costs of securing the frontier by force, concluded that the Native Americans should be treated "more on a footing of equality." It was decided that it was less expensive to buy the Indians' land, along with their good will, than to wage war on them. The FORT HARMAR TREATIES (1789) were the first concluded under the new policy. These reaffirmed the cessions of land made at the earlier treaties of Fort McIntosh and Fort Stanwix, but now the United States agreed to compensate the Indians for the lands that were taken from them.

Unfortunately, the damage had already been done. To the cruelties of the war years the Native Americans now added resentment of the new nation's presumed right of authority over their lands. And for U.S. citizens the Indian policy begun in 1789, instead of being seen as evidence of the nation's sense of justice, was interpreted instead as a sign of weakness.

Parker, Cynthia Ann (ca. 1827–1864) *non-Indian woman captured as a child by the Comanche during a Texas raid and the mother of Comanche chief Quanah Parker*

In 1836, nine-year-old Cynthia Ann Parker, her brother James, and three others were abducted from the Parker homestead near Groesbeck, in east-central Texas. Young COMANCHE raiders entered the stockaded settlement, known as Parker's Fort, killed five, and left with the captives.

While living with the Indians, Cynthia and James quickly learned the Comanche language and adapted their way of life. At about age 14, Cynthia became the wife of Chief Peta Nocona and gave birth to three children: Quanah, Pecos, and Prairie Flower.

Texans occasionally sighted Cynthia, but she refused all offers of ransom. She apparently was happy with her life among the Comanche. However, in December 1860, TEXAS RANGERS and U.S. cavalrymen under the command of Captain Sul Ross attacked the Comanche camp on the Pease River. Several Indians were killed and some were taken PRISONER—Cynthia and the infant Prairie Flower among them. After her uncle confirmed her identification, he took Cynthia and Prairie Flower back to east Texas. Cynthia's several escape attempts were thwarted by her relatives.

QUANAH PARKER failed in his persistent attempts to find his mother. During the talks for the MEDICINE LODGE TREATY (1868), he learned that Cynthia had starved herself to death following the death of her daughter, Prairie Flower. After the Comanche settled on a reservation in Oklahoma, Quanah Parker had his mother's remains moved and reinterred on Comanche land.

Parker, Ely (ca. 1828–1895) *mixed-blood Seneca Indian commissioner, army officer, aide*

SENECA chief Ely Parker, or Do-ne-ho-ga-wa, was born in about 1828 on the Tonawanda Reservation in New York State. The grandson of RED JACKET, Parker was a close friend and coworker of ethnologist Lewis Henry Morgan, whom he assisted in writing the *League of the Ho-de-no-sau-nee or Iroquois* (1851).

Parker received his degree in civil engineering at Rensselaer Polytechnic Institute. At the outbreak of the CIVIL WAR (1861–65), he was working on the home of his friend ULYSSES S. GRANT. Together, the two men joined the Union army. Parker later distinguished himself at the battle of Vicksburg. As a captain he became an assistant adjutant general. As General Grant's secretary, he drew up the surrender document signed by Robert E. Lee. By the war's end he had become brigadier general of volunteers. He joined the cavalry, and by the time he resigned from the army, he was a brevet brigadier general.

Parker resigned from the army in 1869, when President Grant asked him to become his commissioner of Indian affairs. Parker was placed in charge of GRANT'S PEACE POLICY, but he retired from service in 1871, following a power struggle between the Board of Indian Commissioners and the DEPARTMENT OF THE INTERIOR. From then on, Parker practiced civil engineering until his death in 1895.

Parker, Quanah (Quana, Sweet Odor) (1845–1911) *leader in the Comanche Wars*

During the first half of the 1800s, the COMANCHE roamed the southern plains of Kansas, Oklahoma, and the Texas Panhandle. The Texans and Comanche became bitter enemies, chronically raiding one another. On one such raid in May 1836, a group of Comanche killed a white man and captured five family members, including his nine-year-old daughter CYNTHIA ANN PARKER. In time Cynthia married Peta Nocona, chief of the Nocona band, and bore three children. She named the first Quanah, (sweet odor) after the sweet smell of the prairie flowers that were then in bloom.

In 1860, while Quanah and his father were off hunting buffalo, TEXAS RANGERS raided their camp, carrying off Cynthia Parker and her daughter, Prairie Flower. Not long thereafter, Quanah's father died of an infected wound and his brother, Pecos, succumbed to a disease. Quanah had lost his entire family.

The young warrior left his band and joined the independent Kwahadie Comanche band. When other Comanche signed the MEDICINE LODGE TREATY (1868), the Kwahadie

Quanah Parker and his wife, Tonarcy, 1875. Parker was a Comanche war leader who fought against the Texas Rangers and the U.S. Cavalry. (Courtesy New York Public Library)

refused. They preferred to fight and die rather than live on a reservation.

By age 20, Quanah had begun leading raids throughout the southern plains. At age 26 he led a night charge through the cavalry camp of Colonel RANALD S. MACKENZIE, who had specific orders to subdue Quanah and his band. By this time Quanah was notorious for his guerrilla tactics.

Although many Comanche eluded the army's grasp for a time, the wholesale slaughter of bison by both settlers and soldiers threatened to end to the Comanche way of life. On June 27, 1874, Quanah led 700 warriors in an attack on a buffalo hunters stockade at ADOBE WALLS (1874), but the Indians' weapons were no match for the buffalo rifles. Defeated and angry, the Indians conducted small attacks throughout the territory. The army responded by a massing some 3,000 troops, who relentlessly pursued the Indians during the RED RIVER WAR (1874–75). The battle of PALO DURO CANYON (1874) finally convinced the Comanche of the hopelessness of their situation. On June 2, 1875, Quanah and the Kwahadie surrendered on the promise that they would not be punished.

White hunters were in the process of exterminating the millions of BUFFALO that roamed through Kansas, Oklahoma, and Texas. In doing so, they ended the Comanche traditional way of life. With no recourse, Quanah adopted mainstream American culture. In time he became a very successful rancher, well known by U.S. presidents and congressmen. He served as a tribal judge and as chief of the Comanche.

Quanah died of pneumonia on February 22, 1911. His funeral procession stretched for two miles and included 1,500 people. His body was laid to rest beside his mother, Cynthia Ann, and his sister, Prairie Flower.

party, war *group of warriors who engage in battle with or carry out raids against the enemy*
Although motives differed among tribes, it is generally true that North American Indian tribes went to war for one of two reasons: honor or revenge. Along with the glory of a successful fight came bounty in the form of horses, women and children, or goods. While fighting occurred where areas of occupation or hunting grounds met or overlapped, rarely did native peoples go to war for the acquisition of more territory.

Occasionally a war party involved the entire tribe. If a large number of their war leaders or warriors were killed, the BLACK-FOOT CONFEDERACY warriors sought revenge on the entire enemy tribe. Among the CHEYENNE, if the injury was great the whole tribe sought revenge and carried a sacred hat and medicine arrows into battle.

Leadership of a war party depended on personal influence. Those who joined a war party were volunteers; a leader did not command or control them. No man (or woman) was coerced into joining a war party or made to feel like a coward if he or she did not join. Generally, however, if two or more men were close friends, they accompanied each other. A leader could also reject any person he felt was unreliable and could

To declare war against another tribe, Indians of some tribes stuck locks of hair in arrows and placed them along the main paths. *(Courtesy New York Public Library)*

deny someone inclusion in a war party if he believed it was large enough. Members of the war party generally agreed on a location where they would all meet, usually either late in the evening or in early morning. In many Indian bands the time and location was kept secret to avoid attracting unwanted companions.

The manner in which warriors were summoned to a war party differed among tribes. Among the CHIPPEWA, the leader sent a messenger with tobacco to ask warriors to join him. The messenger traveled to each village, requested the warriors to assemble, filled a pipe, and offered it to each warrior. All who were willing to join signified this fact by smoking the pipe (see PEACE PIPE). If the matter was extremely important, the messenger might carry a symbolic hand made of buckskin, stuffed with moss, and smeared with red paint, which signified blood. This symbol was used to seal all important agreements.

One of the major goals of a leader in any tribe was to bring the war party home alive. If the party was successful, and the entire group survived, the leader could expect praise and glory. But his reputation suffered if any warriors died. Warriors might

be less inclined to follow a leader who lost too many men, and his chance of rising in the tribe's social organization would decrease as well. Among some tribes, such as the Illinois, a war party leader had to pacify the family of any warrior killed on a raid. PONCA leaders were held responsible for the members of their war parties. In some instances, failure of a raid and the death of war party members could be punished with a severe flogging.

War honors were important for all tribes, but what constituted a war honor differed. Among Southeastern Indians, glory was associated with scalps taken from the enemy, not as plunder but as a token of bravery; the more scalps, the more prestige. This practice, however, arrived with Europeans (see SCALPING). With most Plains Indian tribes, touching a live enemy was more highly regarded than killing him (see COUNTING COUP). For the Indians of the Blackfoot Confederacy, the more courage displayed in winning a war honor, the higher the honor. For example, capturing an enemy's gun earned the most prestige, but the capture of a WARBONNET, war shirt, ceremonial pipe, bow, or war shield (see BODY ARMOR) came in a close second. Taking a scalp, however, ranked below these deeds. War honors were also important, particularly among the Plains Indians, for one to rise in rank in social organizations. Cheyenne war honors depended on the type of weapon used. Going into battle with a weapon, such as a rifle, that could kill an opponent at a distance was considered less courageous than carrying a war club (see CLUB, WAR) or hatchet.

Integrity and honesty were integral parts of warfare and the war party. Oaths were sworn to attest to the truth of one's war claims. In many tribes, if a warrior lied about his exploits he could be put to death. Among the Cheyenne, an oath was taken on special ritual arrows, and it was believed that if a warrior made a false statement, he or a member of his family would die.

Pavonia Massacre (1643)   See KIEFT'S WAR.

Pawnee   *tribe originally inhabiting territory on the Great Plains*

The name *Pawnee* means "horn" in their Caddoan dialect and describes the distinctive patch of hair that Pawnee warriors wore on the crowns of their heads. They shaved their heads except for a scalplock that was greased to stand up stiffly, resembling a horn.

It is thought that the Pawnee originally migrated northward from east Texas in the 14th century. By the 1700s their villages stretched along the banks of the Arkansas River. One band, the Skidi, lived along Nebraska's Platte River. The Pawnee farmed and gathered their food, but in the fall they journeyed to the plains to hunt buffalo.

Around 1800 the Pawnee numbered some 10,000, but the population was reduced in the early 1800s when cholera and smallpox ravaged their villages (see SMALLPOX, EFFECTS OF). By 1880 only about 1,300 Pawnee remained.

The Pawnee were traditional enemies of the Lakota (see SIOUX) and OSAGE, and intertribal raids for horses and captives were frequent. Generally, however, the Pawnee were friendly to non-Indians, often serving as guides for settlers and later as SCOUTS for the U.S. Army. Through a series of treaties, the Pawnee gradually ceded their territory to the United States, except for a reservation along the Loup River in Nebraska. Between 1874 and 1876, because of constant raids by the Lakota, the Pawnee voluntarily ceded their remaining land to the United States and moved to Indian Territory (present-day Oklahoma), where their descendants remain today.

Pawnee Killer   (ca. 1860s)   *Oglala Lakota warrior best known for his exploits during the 1860s*

The PAWNEE were traditional enemies of the Lakota (see SIOUX). Pawnee Killer was undoubtedly named because of his exploits against that tribe.

By the 1860s Pawnee Killer had also gained the attention of his non-Indian enemies. In 1867 General WINFIELD SCOTT HANCOCK launched a major campaign against the Indians of the central plains. His field commander was a young cavalry officer named GEORGE ARMSTRONG CUSTER. Custer's 7th Cavalry pursued the CHEYENNE and Pawnee Killer's Lakota through the Plains, but with little success. On September 17, 1868, Tall Bull of the Cheyenne, Pawnee Killer of the Lakota, and a force of about 600 attacked about 50 soldiers under the command of Major GEORGE FORSYTH in the battle of BEECHER'S ISLAND (1868).

Pawnee Killer and his band eventually settled in Nebraska at the Red Cloud Agency. History fails to record what happened to him after that.

Paxton Riots   (1763–1764)   *anti-Indian violence during Pontiac's Rebellion*

The violence that marked the FRENCH AND INDIAN WAR (1754–63) continued on the frontier long after the fall of Quebec in 1759. Native Americans, angry at the increasing numbers of colonists moving onto their lands, launched raids from the Ohio Country against settlements in western Virginia and Pennsylvania. The Pennsylvania legislature, dominated by pacifist Quakers who favored peaceful relations with the Indians, took little action to protect the settlers.

One of the settlements that had suffered from Indian raids during PONTIAC'S REBELLION (1763–65) was the community of Paxton in western Pennsylvania. The town had been raided and burned by Native Americans in 1755, and many of the inhabitants had been killed. The Presbyterian minister of the town, John Elder, and two leading citizens named Matthew Smith and James Gibson, organized community defenses and promoted anti-Indian feeling. In December 1763 news came to Smith that an Indian raider had been seen in the company of some Christianized Conestoga Indians (a surviving remnant of the SUSQUEHANNOK tribe). Calling themselves the Paxton Boys, Smith and Gibson led a group of about 50 colonists to a Conestoga settlement in Lancaster County, Pennsylvania. On December 14, 1763, they surrounded the settlement and shot or hacked to death the six Native Americans found there.

Local magistrates tried to protect the Conestoga by gathering them together in a workhouse. However, on December 27, the Paxton Boys broke in and killed the remaining 14 Conestoga men, women, and children. At the same time another band of angry settlers was threatening the Christianized LENNI LENAPE (formerly Delaware) Indians living in the Delaware River valley of Pennsylvania. State authorities removed a band of about 140 of these Native Americans to Province Island in Philadelphia for their own safety. In January 1764, the Paxton Boys, now numbering about 500 strong, marched on Philadelphia to kill the Indians, but the town's inhabitants rallied to defend them. The Paxtons were finally persuaded to disband, partly through the arguments of Benjamin Franklin and partly because the Philadelphians outnumbered and outgunned them. Fifty-six of the Delaware Christian converts, confined to the cold and barren Province Island, fell ill and died. The remainder returned home to find their houses burned. Some of them removed westward to the Ohio Country. Others died at the hands of still-angry settlers.

With OTTAWA chief PONTIAC's surrender in 1766, anti-Indian feelings died down. Settlers on the frontier, however, never fully lost their fear and resentment of their Native American neighbors. The same anger that brought about the Paxton Riots contributed to other anti-Indian demonstrations during LORD DUNMORE'S WAR (1773–74), the AMERICAN REVOLUTION (1775–83), LITTLE TURTLE'S WAR (1786–95), and many others.

Payne's Landing, Treaty of (1832) *treaty that provided for the removal of the Seminole to Indian Territory (Oklahoma)*

Shortly after the TREATY OF TAMPA (1823) was signed, non-Indian settlers in Florida began demanding the Removal of the SEMINOLE to the west. On May 9, 1832, Indian commissioner James Gadsden pressured a few Seminole chiefs to sign the Treaty of Payne's Landing. For the small sum of $15,400 and a $3,000 annuity, the chiefs relinquished all Florida territory and agreed to unite with their CREEK kinsmen in Indian Territory (Oklahoma). The treaty also promised a blanket to each warrior and a homespun frock to each woman and child. Seminole of mixed African and Indian ancestry were to be treated as runaway slaves. All cattle were to be surrendered in exchange for payment at a value set by a "discreet person" appointed by the U.S. president.

Concurring with the provisions of the Payne's Landing Treaty, the Creek signed the FORT GIBSON TREATY (1833) and agreed to allow the Seminole to settle within their lands in Indian Territory. A delegation of seven Seminole chiefs traveled to the western Creek Nation and accepted the offer. At the end of 1835, the date by which the Seminole were to complete their Removal, no Seminole had left Florida. Georgia Militia General Wiley Thompson, who was the Seminole Indian agent, called the Seminole together to sign another treaty. When OSCEOLA approached the signing table, he said, "This is your heart . . . and this is my work" and stabbed the treaty through with his hunting knife. Osceola then exhorted the Seminole to resist Removal, which led to the Second SEMINOLE WAR (1835–42).

peace pipe (Calumet) *sacred pipe smoked by Native Americans at special ceremonies*

Indians crafted several kinds of smoking pipes, but none had such symbolic power as the peace pipe, or calumet. The name *calumet* comes from the French word *chalumeau,* meaning "tube" or "reed" and describes the stem of the pipe, which was first seen by French missionaries. Later, calumet came to refer to the entire pipe.

Made of light wood, the stem of a calumet was painted and often carved with animal figures or decorated with feathers, quills, fur, and beadwork. The pipe bowl was carved from a soft stone called pipestone, which gradually hardened.

Native American tribes used tobacco in a variety of ways: they smoked it for pleasure, crushed or boiled its leaves to make medicine, chewed it to alleviate hunger, and placed it around homes to ward off ghosts. One of its most important uses, however, was in the calumet ceremony, which began among the ALGONKIN and later spread to the Great Plains tribes.

Because the smoke from burning tobacco rose to the sky and was pleasing to the unseen spirits, the pipe itself was a sacred instrument. Indians smoked the calumet when treaties were ratified, so non-Indians came to call it the "peace pipe." But the calumet was also used in other rituals—for instance, to greet strangers, to decide on war or peace, or to draw power from the spirits. The calumet was such a sacred and powerful object that, according to French explorer Jacques Marquette, a warrior who carried it could walk in safety among his enemies. Displaying the calumet in battle could bring an end to the fighting, and if the warring sides agreed, a peace council was arranged. Enemies who smoked the peace calumet together gave their pledge to settle their differences through treaties rather than war. Smoking the calumet was a solemn oath taken by those who smoked it and signified that the smokers were telling the truth. Used this way, the calumet was an object to swear by and to make a contract binding.

Peach War (1655–1664) *conflict in the Dutch-Indian Wars between the Lenni Lenape Indians and the Dutch in New Amsterdam (present-day New York)*

Following KIEFT'S WAR (1642–45), hostilities ended between the Dutch and the Raritan, Wappinger, and LENNI LENAPE (Delaware) Indians, not because of mutual agreement but because of mutual exhaustion. Traders put pressure on Dutch Governor Willem Kieft to end the killing of Indians in and around New Amsterdam since the violence interfered with trade. However, the differences between the two cultures had not been resolved, and violence needed only an excuse to break out again. In 1655, a Dutch farmer shot and killed a Lenni Lenape woman who was picking green peaches from his orchard. Her family then ambushed and killed the farmer. Other Lenni Lenape bands struck at Dutch settlements, including New Amsterdam itself. The ensuing violence continued off and on for the next nine years (see DUTCH-INDIAN HOSTILITIES), until Governor Peter Stuyvesant seized Lenni Lenape hostages and enlisted the help of the MOHAWK to bring the Peach War to an end.

Pea Ridge (1862) *Civil War battle in which Indians figured heavily*

In January 1862, the newly appointed brigadier general EARL VAN DORN came west from service in Virginia to take over command of Confederate forces in Arkansas. His forces included 7,000 Missouri militia under Sterling Price, 8,000 regular Confederate army troops under Benjamin McCulloch, and more than 1,000 Native Americans of the Five Civilized Tribes who sympathized with the Confederate cause. These tribes were the CREEK, SEMINOLE, CHEROKEE, CHICKASAW, and CHOCTAW living in Indian territory (present-day Oklahoma) under the leadership of Albert Pike, who had recruited them. Among Pike's Native American troops was Cherokee Colonel STAND WATIE, who would be promoted to brigadier general himself before the war was over.

Van Dorn discovered a Union force of 10,500 soldiers under Samuel Curtis in northwest Arkansas by a granite outcrop called Pea Ridge. Rather than assault Curtis's defenses head-on, Van Dorn chose to take the larger portion of his army on a nighttime march around Pea Ridge to attack the federal troops in their rear—from the northeast—at dawn on March 7. He left Pike and his Native American recruits, along with a division of non-Indian troops, behind with orders to assault the Union lines from the west and distract Curtis from the large force coming up behind him. The Native American assault broke Curtis's line, but they stopped after they overran the Union position and captured some cannon.

The fighting at Pea Ridge demonstrated the differences between the Indian and non-Indian and objectives in battle. In most Indian cultures, combat was a matter of one man against another; warriors fought as individuals for personal glory rather than as a unit for larger objectives. The idea of fighting in lines against ARTILLERY was therefore not part of the Native American warrior culture, and thus Pike was unable to get the 1,000 Indians—disorganized after their initial success—to return to the attack. The exception was Colonel Stand Watie, who distinguished himself by holding his regiment steady against a federal counterattack. The following day Curtis launched a decisive counterattack that routed Van Dorn's army.

Pend D'Oreilles   See FLATHEAD.

Penobscot   *Indian tribe of what is now New England*
The Penobscot are generally considered to be a subtribe of the eastern ABENAKI. Historically, they were located along the river and bay in Maine that bears their name. The Penobscot may have been the most populous group in the Abenaki confederacy.

From the time of European contact until 1749, the Penobscot participated in all the wars on the New England frontier. These included the Tarrantine War (1607–15), KING PHILIP'S WAR (1675–78), KING WILLIAM'S WAR (1688–99), QUEEN ANNE'S WAR (1702–13), DUMMER'S WAR (1721–25), and KING GEORGE'S WAR (1744–48). In 1749, after the end of King George's War, the Penobscot signed a peace treaty with the colonial officials of New England. From that point on, the tribe remained at peace with non-Indians.

Present-day Penobscot live in their traditional homeland at Indian Island, Maine.

Pequot   *Algonquian tribe that traditionally lived in what is now Connecticut*
The Pequot Indians were one of the most militaristic of the southern New England tribes and thus dreaded by non-Indians. At one time the Pequot and the MOHEGAN were united, but they divided into two distinct tribes in the early 1600s when Uncas, a subchief, left the main body after a dispute with Sassacus, a principal chief. Uncas and his followers became known as Mohegan, a name of one of their towns, while the body under Sassacus were referred to as Pequot, meaning "destroyers."

The Pequot from the north invaded and split the Niantic Indians of Connecticut. They then took possession the land along the Niantic River and a few miles into present-day Rhode Island. The Pequot dominated the Niantic who had settled on their western border; the eastern group took refuge with the NARRAGANSETT Indians. Before the arrival of the English, the Pequot under Sassacus controlled 26 subordinate chiefs and dominated the tribes of Connecticut east of the Connecticut River, the coast west to New Haven, and all of Long Island in New York.

The English had little trouble in establishing jurisdiction over the coastal Indians, who were weakened by epidemics (see SMALLPOX, EFFECTS OF). The Pequot, however, frequently attacked English traders and even killed nine of them during one raid. In 1634 the Massachusetts Bay Colony attempted to force the Pequot into a treaty wherein the Indians agreed to surrender the killers, pay a large fine in pelts, and relinquish a substantial part of Connecticut for English settlement. The Pequot ignored the treaty except for paying a small number of pelts.

In 1636, Narragansett Indians accused of killing a trader during a raid fled to Pequot country. Ninety Puritans marched into Pequot territory and demanded the Indians relinquish the accused. A battle followed in which a few Indians were killed or wounded and two Puritans were wounded. The Pequot retaliated by attacking traders, killing 30 colonists and taking many women and children captive. A year later, the PEQUOT WAR (1637) erupted when the Massachusetts and settlers in Connecticut Bay Colony had had enough. Tribes who were paying tribute to the Pequot, along with the Mohegan and Narragansett, joined the Puritans in defeating the tribe.

The Pequot defeat opened most of New England to non-Indian settlement. About 3,000 Pequot remained after the 500 or 600 were killed in a battle at Mystic River, and a number were sold into slavery. The rest, who were forbidden by the colonists to use their tribal name, were forced to live with other tribes or submit to the English. Their plight was so desperate that the English gathered the remaining 1,500 Pequot and settled them on their old land in two villages near the Mystic River. Today, members of the Pequot tribe still live in Connecticut.

Pequot War   (1637)   *early conflict that fundamentally altered the balance of power between Native Americans and colonists in New England*
In the 1630s, Dutch and English settlers in the Connecticut valley encroached on Pequot lands. The Pequot tried to oust the

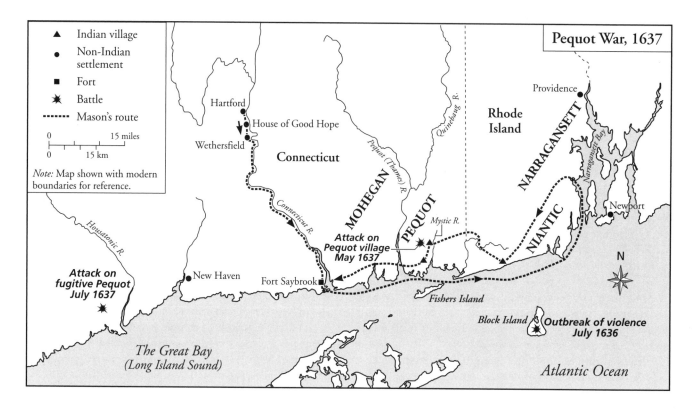

Pequot War, 1637

Dutch and the Dutch retaliated by killing a Pequot sachem, Tatobam. War looked inevitable. The English were out of the picture until a disreputable trader (pirate) arrived. Accounts vary as to what happened to the trader and by whom, but this was the spark.

The murder of an English trader led the Massachusetts Bay Colony, Plymouth, and Connecticut to declare war in the spring of 1637 on the PEQUOT a powerful tribe in the Connecticut Valley. The Pequot proposed that their rivals the NARRAGANSETT, join them in a war of attrition, a strategy that might have proven disastrous to the colonists. Roger Williams, a minister who was greatly respected among the Narragansett, persuaded the tribe to ally themselves with the colonists instead.

The war's decisive engagement took place in May, when 90 Connecticut militia and some 300 Indian allies surrounded the majority of the Pequot tribe in their palisaded village on the Mystic River. In a surprise attack at dawn, the colonists set fire to the village, then killed the Pequot as they emerged from the flames; only seven villagers, including the chief, Sassacus, managed to escape the slaughter. Seven others were taken CAPTIVE. Other Pequot bands fled west toward Dutch New Netherlands, but most were massacred in a swamp near what is now New Haven, Connecticut.

The almost total destruction of the Pequot tribe opened the Connecticut frontier to settlement and acknowledged the colonists as the dominant military power in New England.

Pima   See AKIMEL O'ODHAM.

Pima Butte   See MARICOPA WELLS.

Pine Leaf (Bar-chee-am-pe) (ca. 1820–unknown)
Crow (Absaroka) woman who became a warrior at the age of 12 to avenge the death of her twin brother
Vowing that she would not marry until she had killed 100 enemy warriors, Pine Leaf was always the first to volunteer to accompany a war party. She often rode with JAMES BECKWOURTH, a trapper and trader who lived with the Crow and who described her as always riding the fastest horse so that none of the warriors could outrun her. He also depicted her as having the agility of a cat, killing the enemy while others were preparing to attack. Beckwourth usually invited Pine Leaf to ride with him because he believed his strength and courage was multiplied with her by his side. Although he repeatedly asked her to marry him, she rebuffed these offers because of her vow and because she thought he already had too many wives.

Pine Leaf was known as a brave warrior. In one battle with the CHEYENNE, she counted three coups (see COUNTING COUP). In another encounter with the BLACKFOOT CONFEDERACY, she counted six coups and killed four enemy warriors. During yet another expedition, her arm was broken just below the elbow by an enemy bullet. Only after killing three more warriors with her LANCE did she leave the battle because of the loss of blood.

As her war deeds accumulated, Pine Leaf gained great influence among the Crow. According to Beckwourth, she had

Pine Leaf, an Absaroka (Crow) woman warrior, rode faster and killed more enemies than any of the male warriors of her tribe. *(By permission of the Colorado Historical Society, Negative no. 86.296-5335)*

a gift of oratory that even the bravest warriors envied. Her advice was sound, and she was listened to with admiration.

In 1836, Pine Leaf, having more than fulfilled her vow, finally agreed to marry Beckwourth. Yet he stayed in the Crow Nation for only five weeks after their marriage, leaving her to return to St. Louis, Missouri.

See also WOMAN WARRIORS.

Pins See KEETOOWAH SOCIETY.

pipes, sacred *tribal artifact, used by several tribal groups that represented a widespread relationship between warfare and religion*

For many tribes, the tobacco plant was sacred. As early as A.D. 500, Indians in the East were smoking it in wooden or stone pipes. CHEROKEE medicine men used tobacco juice to treat snakebite and made a tea to treat fevers from its leaves. The CREEK placed tobacco in postholes to keep unfriendly spirits away and used it in their bitter, purgative "black drink." It was thought to drive evil away, make sick people well, and change the weather favorably. Native Americans believed that it relaxed their minds and souls and brought them into closer contact with the spirit world. It was also believed that tobacco smoke carried prayers directly to the Great Spirit.

The communal war pipe was common to many Native American tribes, primarily in the eastern part of what is now the United States. Because of the sacred nature of tobacco, pipes often were used while discussing the issue of waging, making, or ending war (see PEACE PIPE) and while making other important decisions that affected the future of the tribe. It was believed that the holy nature of tobacco ensured that decisions made while smoking a pipe were correct and that the smokers would speak only the truth. The smoke also would bind a community together in the final decision of its leaders.

European settlers quickly learned the importance of tobacco to Native Americans. Specially manufactured war pipes were among the items carried by early traders.

The Plains Wars (mid-to-late 1800s) *series of struggles between Indians and non-Indians on the Great Plains*

The Great Plains culture areas was an enormous expanse of land extending from the Mississippi River Valley to the Rocky Mountains and from portions of Canada to Texas. The grasslands were home to the BUFFALO and to numerous Indian tribes including the SIOUX, CHEYENNE, COMANCHE, PAWNEE, KIOWA, and dozens of others. The Great Plains was also the scene of numerous fights, battles, and wars, such as the SOUTH-

ERN PLAINS WAR (1868–69), RED RIVER WAR (1874–75), and SIOUX WARS (1854–1890). The history of the area includes the names of the famous and infamous such as RED CLOUD, WILLIAM J. FETTERMAN, CRAZY HORSE, G. A. CUSTER, BLACK KETTLE, and SITTING BULL.

During the 1800s, the goal of the U.S. government's Indian policy was to place all western Indians on federal reservations without recourse to military coercion. Most tribes, all too aware that they could no longer successfully resist the demands of the United States, accepted their fate. The nomadic buffalo-hunting societies of the Great Plains and certain other western tribes, however, proved to be a markedly different case for two reasons: They still controlled vast domains by 1865, and they possessed the strength of their convictions in combi-

nation with superb martial skills. The resistance of these tribes to the government's policies, and the military's absolute determination to enforce them, resulted in several decades of deadly confrontations: the Plains Wars.

The wars erupted primarily because the Plains Indians were striving to continue their buffalo-hunting and horse culture, which was absolutely dependent on vast space, abundant game, and freedom of movement. They rejected reservation life because it required abandoning their traditional way of life. Aside from motives such as revenge or retaliation, the Indians fought to prevent American disruption of their heritage and to defend their cultures. Undoubtedly, many material goods of mainstream American society appealed to them as an enhancement of their own lifestyle, but American society as a whole did not have any appeal. The American public regarded those tribes that resisted the government as a dangerous impediment to expansion, enterprise, and settlement. Inevitably, if peaceful measures failed, the United States felt it necessary to pursue implementation of government Indian policy by force of arms.

Yet given the considerable advantages apparently held by the United States, why did it take the army so long to accomplish the military subjugation of the Plains Indians? The population of the United States in 1870 was almost 40 million. By contrast, all Indians from the Great Plains westward to the Pacific numbered fewer than 239,000 in 1872. Moreover, the Americans obviously held the greater technological advantage. The army had railroads and the telegraph as well as modern industrial plants capable of mass-producing vast quantities of items, particularly those needed to prosecute war. The Plains Indians, on the other hand, lacked the technology to make a wheel, much less the weapons of modern warfare.

In light of these factors and others, why did quick victory elude the United States? What factors, for a time, offset the army's seeming overwhelming advantages? The physical conditions of the western prairies and plains were one advantage to the Indians. Summers on the Great Plains are extremely hot and exceedingly dry. Unless Indian scouts accompanied the troopers to direct them to water and other necessary resources, these conditions often took their toll on men and animals. The sheer size of the region made it difficult for the army to locate enemy positions, especially when the Plains Indians' nomadic way of life dictated nearly continuous movement. When soldiers finally located and engaged the Indians, warriors usually fought only a holding action against the army while the main tribal body escaped and dispersed. It often seemed to soldiers that the vastness of the plains simply swallowed them.

The difference in military training and skills between Indians and soldiers played an important role, too. Indian males trained from youth to be warriors. As a result they were usually superior in horsemanship, endurance, tracking, scouting, and most martial skills when compared with their army counterparts. Soldiers first encountered military life and training in early adulthood and simply did not have the time needed to master the skills needed to fight in the Plains environment.

The Plains Indians esteemed courage and placed a high value on martial achievements and honors. Because honors were so important to them, in fact, warfare was endemic to their culture. However, they typically refused to involve themselves in mass engagements because of the inevitability of high casualties. Plains warriors preferred to engage enemies, Indian or not, in a "hit-and-run" style, or by using ambush or guerrilla tactics. The relatively small size of the adult male population also made it necessary to use tactics that preserved the lives of their combatants. Death in battle could bring glory, but living to care for your family and to fight another valorous battle was usually judged wiser. Therefore, unless the chance of success was overwhelmingly in their favor, or when a village with women and children was threatened, Plains warriors usually avoided massed, frontal engagements.

Only when the army combined conventional TACTICS with more innovative ones that took advantage of vulnerable aspects of the Plains Indians' way of life—i.e., winter campaigns against tribes and their horse herds while sedentary—did the military finalize the concentration of western Indians on reservations and successfully conclude the Plains Wars.

— Philip Weeks

Platte Bridge (1865) *first strike of the Powder River valley tribes of Wyoming in the Indian wars of 1865*

In late July 1865, warriors from the Lakota (see SIOUX), CHEYENNE, and ARAPAHO tribes began mounting a massive war expedition against Platte Bridge Station, 130 miles west of Fort Laramie, Wyoming, where Major Martin Anderson and part of the 11th Kansas Cavalry guarded the Oregon-California Trail. Anderson and his 119 men had recently had a brief skirmish with the Indians. Now he learned of a train of five empty wagons approaching from the west. He sent out Lieutenant Casper W. Collins with about 20 cavalrymen to escort the wagons to the fort. Everyone knew Indians were near, but no one suspected that there were between 1,000 and 3,000 warriors lying in ambush in the hills.

The Indians waited until Collins and his men had crossed the Platte Bridge and were about a mile up the road. Then they sprang from their hiding places. Some raced to the bridge to cut off the soldiers' escape route, while the rest bore down on the small cavalry detachment. The resulting fight at Platte Bridge took place in such close quarters that the Indian warriors had to use SPEARS and TOMAHAWKS rather than BOWS AND ARROWS to avoid shooting their own men. Collins was killed while trying to help one of his men. Detachments sent out from the stockade struggled to keep the bridge open. All the soldiers were wounded, eight seriously, in the skirmish, but only Collins and four men died.

The Indians next turned their attention to the wagon train. Hearing the howitzer being fired during the skirmish at the bridge, Sergeant Amos Custard sent four men to investigate. They rode directly into the warriors, and more fighting ensued. Three of the four soldiers made it safely back to the stockade. Meanwhile, Sergeant Custard managed to circle the wagons, making it difficult for the Indians to stage a mounted attack—but not impossible. The warriors gradually surrounded the wagon circle and then, in overpowering numbers, leaped over the wagons and killed and mutilated the defenders. With 60 warriors dead and 130 wounded during this assault on the wagons, the Indians ended their offensive. For them the war was over, and they scattered to hunt BUFFALO. For U.S. troops a renewed struggle against the Lakota and Cheyenne had just begun.

Plum Creek (1840) *battle between Comanche Indians and Texas Rangers*

The engagement at Plum Creek; part of the COMANCHE–REPUBLIC OF TEXAS WARS, was preceded by a massacre of COMANCHE leaders at the Council House in San Antonio, Texas. This incident began when chiefs of the Penateka band of Comanche and their families (75 people in all) met with representatives of the Texas Republic on March 19, 1840. The Texans demanded the release of about 200 white CAPTIVES before the actual council could start. The leading Comanche chief, Mook-war-ruh (Spirit Talker), replied that the captives could be ransomed from the bands that actually held them. In response, the Texans took the Penateka chiefs captive with the intention of holding them until all white prisoners were returned. In the fighting that followed, 33 Comanche were killed (including almost all the Penateka chiefs), and 32 women and children were taken PRISONER.

Such actions demanded revenge. BUFFALO HUMP, the last surviving Penateka war chief (and a nephew of Spirit Talker), led 400 warriors and 600 of their family members on a revenge raid. Several Texas towns, including Victoria and Linnville, were attacked as the Indians made their way to the Gulf of Mexico. Returning north, the Comanche became bogged down with enormous amounts of goods and horses. At that point, in August 1840, they were attacked by Texas forces at Plum Creek, north of San Antonio. The Texas forces were led by Edward Burleson, Felix Huston, and BENJAMIN MCULLOCH. The soldiers' TACTICS consisted of riding around the fringes of the great mass of Comanche and their animals, shooting warriors out of their saddles. The Comanche were routed in the battle, losing most of their horses and supplies and about one quarter of their warriors. The surviving Indians retreated back to Comanche territory.

Pocahontas   See POWHATAN.

Pocasset Swamp (1675) *site of inconclusive engagement during King Philip's War*

In summer 1675, colonial forces thought they had WAMPANOAG chief Philip (see METACOM) trapped on Mount Hope Peninsula in what is now Rhode Island. However, Philip managed to escape to the mainland across Narragansett Bay.

Some 200 colonial militiamen and 50 allied Indians then tracked him to the Pocasset Swamp, south of what is today the city of Providence. The wild undergrowth made the area almost impenetrable, but the English were intent on Philip's capture, and on July 19, they plunged into the swamp in three columns. They were immediately fired upon and lured deeper into the swamp. Despite the difficulties of the terrain and constant fire from Philip's retreating forces, the soldiers pressed on. By the end of the day, eight militiamen had been killed and an undetermined number wounded. Although they destroyed a number of abandoned Wampanoag shelters, the elusive Philip had escaped again (see KING PHILIP'S WAR).

Point Pleasant (1774) *principal battle of Lord Dunmore's War*

On June 10, 1774, Lord Dunmore, royal governor of Virginia, declared war on the SHAWNEE Indians. He raised 1,500 militia and brought them to Fort Pitt (present-day Pittsburgh, Pennsylvania), intending to rendezvous with another 1,000 militia commanded by Andrew Lewis. Their proposed meeting place was Point Pleasant on the Ohio River. Shawnee chief CORNSTALK learned of the expedition and resolved to ambush Lewis's force before it could combine with Dunmore's larger group.

On the morning of October 10, Cornstalk and a combined force of his Mingo, Wyandot, and LENNI LENAPE (formerly Delaware) allies—totaling around 700 warriors—attacked Lewis's troops. Lewis, however, had been alerted to the Indians' presence by a small party of non-Indian hunters, and was therefore prepared for them; he had time enough to construct crude shelters out of fallen trees. The fight was fierce; casualty estimates range between 150 and 220 militia killed or wounded, and between 100 and 300 Native Americans killed. Whatever the exact figure, the Indians retreated at the end of the battle and later negotiated a peace with the Virginians.

See also LORD DUNMORE'S WAR.

Ponca *tribe that originally inhabited the Central Plains*

Occupying territory in northeastern Nebraska, the Ponca were one of the smaller of the Plains groups, numbering around 800 people in 1800. A sedentary village tribe, the Ponca farmed and seasonally hunted BUFFALO. In the early 1800s their numbers were reduced by SMALLPOX and cholera brought by traders and settlers. By the mid-1800s, the Ponca had ceded much of their territory to non-Indians, and in 1865 a treaty guaranteed them a reservation in northeastern Nebraska. Eleven years later, the U.S. Congress passed legislation to remove the Ponca from their reservation and send them to the Indian Territory (present-day Oklahoma). This was to make way for the Brulé Lakota (see SIOUX), to whom Congress had earlier deeded the land. Some 681 Ponca were forcibly moved to Indian Territory despite the pleas of their chief, STANDING BEAR. Many died during the two-month journey, and more perished when they arrived in Indian Territory.

Pontiac, a war leader of the Ottawa, smoking a peace pipe with Major Robert Rogers in a temporary truce with the British *(Courtesy Library of Congress, Negative no. 14142)*

The plight of the Ponca aroused the sympathy of many non-Indians in Nebraska, and the Indians' case was taken to court by sympathetic lawyers. Although federal lawyers argued that Indians were not persons under the U.S. Constitution, the judge ruled for the Ponca, declaring that they were in fact persons under the law. Many non-Indians in Nebraska began to demand that the Ponca be compensated for their land and that those who wished to should be allowed to return to Nebraska, since the Brulé had never moved onto the Ponca reservation. In 1881 the government agreed and also compensated the Ponca for their land. Standing Bear and 170 others chose to return to Nebraska. Most Ponca, however, remained in Indian Territory, where they had made new lives.

Descendants of the Ponca now live in both Nebraska and Oklahoma. The court's ruling in favor of the Ponca established the legal precedent that Indians were indeed persons and retained rights under the law.

Pontiac (Ponteach) (ca. 1720–1769) *Ottawa leader and chief*

Pontiac was born sometime around 1720 in a village near present-day Detroit, Michigan. His father was probably an OTTAWA and his mother a CHIPPEWA or MIAMI. As a youth, he may have participated in the FRENCH AND INDIAN WAR (1754–63), siding with the French, although precise information is lacking. Nevertheless, it is certain that by 1760 Pontiac was highly regarded by his fellow Indians as an able warrior and a persuasive orator.

During the 1600s, the French and local Indians had established a symbiotic relationship in the Great Lakes region. The

French took furs and established trading posts and gave the Indians guns, ammunition, and trade goods in return. In the early 1700s, the British began competing with the French for Indian furs. During the French and Indian War, the Ottawa consistently sided with the French and were dismayed when DETROIT fell to the British in 1760. Pontiac and others chafed under the British, who offered poor trade goods and who failed to provide guns and ammunition that the Ottawa needed for hunting.

By 1762, Pontiac was delivering passionate speeches against the British. He was heard by growing numbers of Indians from various tribes. Meanwhile, the DELAWARE PROPHET was likewise proclaiming an anti-white message that strongly influenced Pontiac's thinking.

The time finally came for Pontiac to act. On April 27, 1763, he held a council attended by more than 400 Ottawa, HURON, and POTAWATOMI. Pontiac masterfully encouraged them to go to war. Four days later, he and 50 warriors staged a ceremonial dance at Detroit for the entertainment of the city's inhabitants. During the dance some of his men slipped away and surveyed the fortifications and gun emplacements.

Pontiac planned to return a few days later with his warriors and hold a council during which the Indians would bare KNIVES, TOMAHAWKS, and sawed-off muskets hidden under their blankets and attack. However, the post commander, Major HENRY GLADWYN, learned of the plan and made preparations. The meeting took place, but once inside the fort, Pontiac realized the soldiers were ready for an attack. Wisely, Pontiac only spoke and soon withdrew. When a second covert attempt to surprise the fort failed, Pontiac besieged Detroit and unleashed his warriors on British settlers scattered throughout the countryside. Meanwhile he sent emissaries to more distant tribes to raise additional warriors.

As spring turned to summer in 1763, Pontiac managed to unify warriors from the Ottawa, Huron, Chippewa, Potawatomi, LENNI LENAPE, Mingoe, Illinois, Miami, KICK-APOO, Mascouten, SAC, SENECA, SHAWNEE, and several other tribes. They soon managed to capture eight of 12 British forts, force the abandonment of another, and engage in prolonged sieges of Fort Detroit and Fort Pitt (see DETROIT, 1763). At the same time Pontiac's warriors killed about 2,000 settlers and 400 soldiers and won decisively at the battles of Point Pelee and Bloody Run (see PONTIAC'S REBELLION).

Despite these early successes, as summer turned to fall it appeared obvious to many of the Indians that they would be unable to take Detroit. One by one the bands and tribes involved began to make peace with the British and return home. Pontiac grudgingly lifted the siege of Detroit.

While Pontiac temporarily ended his military activities, he was unable to bury his hatred for the British. From summer through winter of 1764, he traveled among several tribes in an unsuccessful attempt to gain support for another war. Finally, on April 18, 1765, he met with British officers and promised to no longer fight against them. He kept his word, and in the months ahead he cooperated fully with the British. Soon his own people felt that he had sold out to the British.

On April 20, 1769, in Cahokia, Illinois, a Kaskaskia Indian named Black Dog hit Pontiac over the back of the head with a CLUB and stabbed him to death. Ironically, he was paid to do so by an English trader who felt threatened by Pontiac's presence.

Pontiac's Rebellion (Amerindian War of 1763–1765, Pontiac's War, Pontiac's Conspiracy)
(1763–1765) *major conflict between the British and the Indians of the Great Lakes and the Ohio country*

The conflict known as Pontiac's Rebellion was not exclusively linked to the famous OTTAWA chief PONTIAC. In fact, the war was actually a series of coordinated assaults by members of many different tribes against British outposts in the Great Lakes and the Ohio country. It began as a reaction by Native American allies of the French to the end of the FRENCH AND INDIAN WAR (1754–63). The rebellion also marked the end of one era of colonial-Indian warfare and ushered in another.

Pontiac's Rebellion grew out of the deep misunderstandings and conflicts between Native Americans and the British. With the end of the French and Indian War, a flood of British settlers moved westward into Indian land. Indian protests to British authorities were ignored. Around this time, a religious revival led by reformers such as Neolin (see DELAWARE PROPHET) preached the overthrow of the British and a return to traditional lifestyle. Like the later practitioner of the GHOST DANCE in the 19th century, the Indian prophets of this period preached that Native Americans could win back their strength and drive the Europeans out of their lands if they put aside intertribal rivalries, gave up British goods and habits (especially alcohol), and purged themselves of the evils of European civilization.

Native Americans also protested having to return British prisoners of war without compensation. Indians traditionally seized PRISONERS to replace family members killed in the fighting. The prisoners were often adopted into Native American families. In some cases they settled down among the Indians and raised families of their own. Tribal leaders were unwilling to break up Indian families at the request of British leaders. Indians were also put out by the attitude of British commander Jeffrey Amherst, who refused to continue the French practice of distributing presents to the Native Americans. Amherst regarded the Indians as rebellious subjects of the British king who deserved to be punished for their role in the recent war. He cut costs by eliminating gifts, such as gunpowder and ammunition, traditionally offered to chiefs, but in doing so he alienated many chiefs who regarded these gifts as rent for the British forts maintained on their land.

During 1761 and 1762, Pontiac traveled throughout the country between the Ohio and Mississippi Rivers seeking support for a campaign against the British. Early in 1763, the Indians received news of the terms of the TREATY OF PARIS (1763), which ceded French Canada and French lands east of the Mississippi to the British and turned French forts in the territory over to British control. The former allies of the French distrusted British motives. Pontiac himself behaved as if the French and Indian War had never ended. He displayed the French flag in battle and appointed a French citizen as interim commandant of Detroit.

Pontiac's Rebellion began on April 2, 1763, with a meeting between the Ottawa and the LENNI LENAPE (formerly Delaware) in what is now Lincoln Park, Michigan. Pontiac convinced the tribespeople to take nearby Fort Detroit from the British (see DETROIT, 1763). On May 9 Pontiac and 60 of his warriors gathered at Detroit and requested a council with the commander, Colonel Henry Gladwyn. Once inside, the warriors intended to kill all the British and open the gates to admit the rest of the Indians. However, Gladwyn refused to let the warriors in, allowing only the chiefs to enter the fort. Tradition reports that Gladwyn had been warned of Pontiac's intentions by an Ottawa girl who was in love with him. Pontiac was therefore forced to lay siege to Detroit.

At the same time that Pontiac was negotiating before the gates of Detroit, other tribes were taking British forts in western Pennsylvania and New York all the way to the Mississippi River. Members of the Ottawa, HURON, Lenni Lenape (Delaware), SHAWNEE, FOX (Mesquakie), Mingo, and MIAMI tribes surprised garrisons and killed or took British soldiers prisoner. Within two months, nearly all the British forts on the frontier had fallen to the Indians: Fort Sandusky in Ohio on May 16; Fort St. Joseph (Niles, Michigan) on May 25; Fort Miami (near modern-day Fort Wayne, Indiana) on May 27; Fort Ouiatenon (Lafayette, Indiana) on June 1; Fort Michilimackinac (Michigan) on June 2; Fort Green Bay (Wisconsin) on June 15; and Fort Venango (French Creek, Pennsylvania) on June 16.

Fort Presqu'Isle (Erie, Pennsylvania) was besieged from June 19 to 21 by SENECA warriors, members of the IROQUOIS CONFEDERACY, with assistance from the Ottawa and Huron. The garrison surrendered on June 21 after receiving promises that their lives would be spared. To the British and the colonists it seemed as though the whole frontier were up in arms.

However, three of the largest British strongholds resisted the initial Indian assault. Forts Detroit, Pitt, and Niagara had garrisons too large to be overrun and commanders too wary to be surprised. All three were besieged, but none surrendered. Fort Pitt, commanded by Captain Simeon Ecuyer, was attacked by Lenni Lenape Indians on June 24. Ecuyer refused to surrender and sent provisions (including alcohol) out to the besiegers to impress them with the fort's preparedness. General Amherst ordered Ecuyer (through his commanding officer Colonel Henry Bouquet) to distribute smallpox-infected blankets and handkerchiefs from the fort hospital to the Indians (see SMALLPOX, EFFECTS OF). The besieging Indians soon retreated, too sick to fight any longer.

Fort Pitt was finally relieved by Bouquet in August after the battle of BUSHY RUN (1763). Fort Niagara held out against the Seneca Indians and their western allies. However, the warriors ambushed a supply train headed for the fort at Devil's Hole on September 14, 1763. Seventy-two men were killed and scalped in the battle, and eight others were badly wounded. The battle of NIAGARA (1763) exacted the heaviest British casualties of Pontiac's Rebellion.

Pontiac lifted the siege of Detroit in autumn 1763, when he learned that the French would not come to help him. On October 3, 1763, he negotiated a peace with the British. However, because Pontiac was only one of several important Indian leaders, hostilities continued into 1764.

Colonial reactions to Pontiac's Rebellion were directed mostly against Indians not directly involved in the fighting. For instance, the Lenni Lenape village of Wyoming, Pennsylvania, was burned to the ground on April 19, 1763. Lenni Lenape activist Teedyuscung died in the blaze. During the PAXTON RIOTS (1763–64) in western Pennsylvania, settlers indiscriminately attacked and killed noncombatant Indians—men, women, and children. Some 400 British soldiers died in Pontiac's Rebellion, as well as around 2,000 settlers. Native American losses—including those that died of disease—were never counted.

Many Native Americans did not continue to fight in Pontiac's Rebellion in 1764, for several reasons. Short of gunpowder and ammunition for hunting, the Indians felt their first responsibility lay in feeding their families. Also, news of the PROCLAMATION OF 1763, which drew a line between the settlers' territory and that of the Indians, reached the Native Americans by the late fall of 1763. Many Indians regarded the proclamation as a victory for them and their rights. In 1764, when Indian agent WILLIAM JOHNSON began working for peace, many tribespeople were disposed to listen to him. By May 1765 the British and the Indians were at peace.

Further Reading

Parkman, Francis. *The Conspiracy of Pontiac.* 2 volumes. Boston: Little, Brown, 1870.

Peckham, Howard H. *Pontiac and the Indian Uprising.* Princeton, N.J.: Princeton University Press, 1947.

Steele, Ian K. *Warpaths: Invasions of North America.* New York: Oxford University Press, 1994.

Popé (Po'png, "Pumpkin Mountain") (unknown–1690) *Pueblo medicine man who led the Pueblo Rebellion*

The name Popé was little known outside of San Juan, New Mexico, prior to 1680. In that year, however, it became known to all the PUEBLO INDIANS and to their enemies the Spanish.

Popé was a Tewa medicine man from San Juan Pueblo. In previous decades the Spanish had begun moving north from Mexico along the Rio Grande into New Mexico. They brought with them priests and the Roman Catholic religion and demanded that the Indians convert to Christianity. Popé and others refused. He was beaten by the Spanish for this on three separate occasions, leaving his back badly scarred. In 1675 Popé and 50 other Pueblo medicine men were arrested by the Spanish for refusing to embrace the new religion. They were taken to Santa Fe, whipped publicly, and released.

Popé then fled to Taos Pueblo, where he and other Pueblo leaders planned and organized a rebellion against the Spanish. On August 10, 1680, Pueblo Indians from across New Mexico and Arizona rose up in arms against the Spanish soldiers, priests, and settlers. Within two weeks the surviving Spanish retreated south, deserting Pueblo territory. The death count for the Pueblo rebellion stood at approximately 250 Indians and 400 Spanish, including 21 of the 33 Catholic missionaries at Taos.

Next, Popé traveled to the various pueblos to supervise the eradication of anything Spanish. The Pueblo burned the Catholic churches and, in defiance of the sacrament, washed the heads of those who were baptized Christians. The Indians destroyed Spanish livestock, crops, and farm equipment and forbade the use of Spanish names and words. He culminated this campaign with the siege at SANTA FE (1693), which forced the Spanish to leave that city.

In the decade that followed, Popé became consumed with power. He moved to Santa Fe and surrounded himself with Spanish-style opulence. He also had his political opponents executed. While Popé had united the Pueblo in 1680, he had effectively divided them by the time of his death in 1690. Nevertheless, the PUEBLO REBELLION (1680) succeeded in forcing the Spanish out of the Rio Grande valley from 1680 to 1692 and represented the only time Indians had successfully stopped and decreased European immigration into their homelands.

Pope, John   See BOZEMAN TRAIL.

Popé's Revolt   See SANTA FE.

Portage des Sioux Treaties   (1815) *treaties between the U.S. government and the Shawnee and other Indian tribes of the Old Northwest Territory*

Following the AMERICAN REVOLUTION (1775–81), the British did not abandon their forts in the Old Northwest Territory but instead used them to furnish Indian hunters with arms and ammunition. Non-Indian frontiersmen were aware of this, and they believed that Great Britain was encouraging its Indian allies to attack frontier settlements. This, in part, led the United States to declare war on Great Britain in 1812. During the WAR OF 1812 (1812–14), the alignment of Indian tribes in the Old Northwest with the British was much the same as in the Revolution. The Indian confederation, led by SHAWNEE leader TECUMSEH, was determined to stop the Americans' advance. However, any united plan of resistance disappeared with the Indians' defeat at TIPPECANOE (1811), the death of Tecumseh at the THAMES (1813), and the ultimate defeat of the British.

The U.S. government was determined to establish sovereignty over the tribes of the Old Northwest and remove them to reservations elsewhere. Federal commissioners met with the tribes at Portage des Sioux in Illinois Territory in 1815. There, all parties signed treaties that agreed to "perpetual peace and friendship" and promised to forgive and forget old injuries and hostile acts. The Shawnee and other tribes thus recognized the dominion of the U.S. government over them. The Portage des Sioux Treaties laid the foundation for future Indian land cessions and, ultimately, their removal to reservations.

Potawatomi   *Indian tribe originally living near the present site of Chicago, Illinois, and on the St. Joseph River in southern Michigan*

According to tribal tradition, the Potawatomi, OTTAWA, and CHIPPEWA (Ojibway) were at one time a single tribe. The Potawatomi hunted, fished, and gathered wild rice from the lakes and streams of the Great Lakes region. They also grew crops such as corn, beans, pumpkins, and tobacco. One band, the Mascouten, hunted BUFFALO on the western prairies. By the late 1600s the Potawatomi were living as a distinct tribe.

The Potawatomi were trading partners with the French and enemies of the IROQUOIS CONFEDERACY, who had apparently driven them from their former territory in the east. They fought for the French against the English-Iroquois alliance during the FRENCH AND INDIAN WAR (1754–63). The Potawatomi, Ottawa, and Chippewa, known as the "Far Indians," traveled long distances to attack the English in that war. Following French capitulation and cession of Indian land to the English, the Indians began a general rebellion against the English known as PONTIAC'S REBELLION (1763–64), in which the Potawatomi aligned with CHIEF PONTIAC's Ottawa, Chippewa, and HURON and waged attacks on English forts. In 1769, Pontiac was killed by an Illinois Indian who was apparently hired by the English. In retaliation, the Potawatomi joined the SAC, FOX (Mesquakie), KICKAPOO, Ottawa, and other tribes in decimating the Illinois Indians, reducing their numbers from approximately 1,600 to 150. The conquering tribes then moved into Illinois, dividing the territory among themselves.

Following the AMERICAN REVOLUTION (1775–81), the Potawatomi refused to accept American domination. They fought against Americans in LITTLE TURTLE'S WAR (1786–95) and in TECUMSEH'S REBELLION (1809–11) and allied with the British during the WAR OF 1812 (1812–14).

The Potawatomi signed a total of 53 treaties with the United States. The first was one of the FORT HARMAR TREATIES (1789), but the most famous was the Chicago Treaty (1833), by which the Potawatomi, Chippewa and Ottawa ceded 5,000,000 acres to the United States. As a result of the treaties, the Potawatomi were moved from place to place, their territory becoming smaller with each successive move. By 1840 most Potawatomi were living west of the Mississippi, some in Iowa and others in Kansas.

The U.S. government attempted to reunite the Chippewa and the Ottawa with the Potawatomi in 1846 by designating a

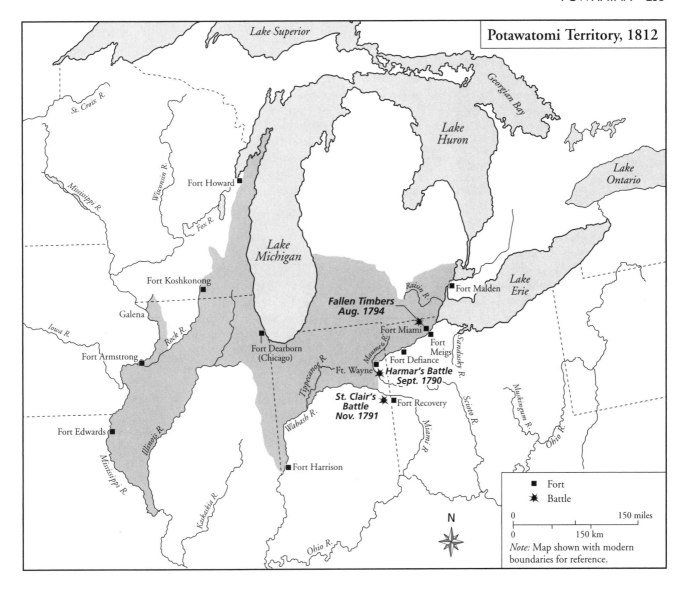

Potawatomi Territory, 1812

576,000-acre reservation for them west of present-day Topeka, Kansas. The PAWNEE, who objected to the settlement of Potawatomi in that region, declared war. A bloody battle resulted in which the Potawatomi were victorious. Subsequent non-Indian settlement in Kansas brought about the Potawatomi Allotment Treaty (1861). The Prairie Band of Potawatomi refused the land allotments and were assigned a reservation in Jackson County, Kansas, where their descendants still live. Those who accepted individual land allotments and took citizenship became known as Citizen Band Potawatomi. In 1867, this group agreed to move to a reservation in Indian Territory (Oklahoma). In 1890–91, this land was likewise allotted to individuals. The "surplus" land became part of Oklahoma Territory and was opened for non-Indian settlement in the land run of September 22, 1891.

Today, there are several Potawatomi bands holding reservation or trust lands in Wisconsin, Oklahoma, Kansas, Michigan, and Ontario.

Powder River   See DULL KNIFE BATTLE OF.

Powhatan (Wahunsonacock, Wahunsenacawk, Ottaniack, Mamanatowick) (ca. 1548–1618) *primary leader of the Powhatan Confederacy*

A proud warrior and a canny politician, Chief Powhatan united a group of Indian tribes, the POWHATAN CONFEDERACY, in what is now Virginia into a single nation at the beginning of the 17th century. British settlers, unable to pronounce his name, are responsible for giving him the name Powhatan, after a village in his territory. He often dealt with the English at their Jamestown settlement and recognized early in his negotiations that the English wanted to take his land away from him. He resisted both this and their attempts to make him a subject of King James I.

During the early years of the Jamestown settlement, Powhatan maintained a muted hostility toward the white settlers, sometimes sharing food with them and sometimes seizing their tools and weapons. At other times, however, he sought alliances with the English, hoping to use them in his wars with other Indian tribes. It was not until 1614, when his daughter Pocahontas married Englishman John Rolfe, that Powhatan fully accepted the English settlers in his land. He maintained a peace with them—the Peace of Pocahontas—until his death in 1618.

Powhatan Confederacy *loose alliance of Virginian tribes*

The Powhatan Confederacy was the dominant force in Tidewater Virginia during the late 16th and early 17th centuries. Encompassing many ALGONQUIAN-speaking tribes, including the Powhatan, Potomac, Appamattuck, PAMUNKEY, Mattaponi, Rappahannock, and Chickahominy Indians, the "tribe" was not a true confederacy. It was ruled by one man, Wahunsonacock, who used the political and military power of the confederacy members to crush rival tribes who opposed him. One of these, the Chesapeake, were entirely exterminated by summer 1608. Wahunsonacock may also have led an expedition against a Spanish mission in the area in 1571.

With the establishment of the British settlement of Jamestown in 1607, the leader, now known as Powhatan to the settlers, faced a new type of challenge. Accustomed to traditional Native American warfare, in which victorious tribes forced those they defeated to move away, Powhatan and his confederacy did not follow up their early victories in the POWHATAN WARS (1622–32, 1644–46). Instead of retreating, the British requested reinforcements from Europe and pursued the Indians. By the 1650s, the confederacy was broken, and Native Americans in Virginia were reduced to a few scattered tribespeople scraping out a marginal existence on a few remnants of their ancestral lands.

Today, there are descendants of numerous bands still in the Tidewater region, but only the Pamunkey and Mattaponi are officially recognized.

Powhatan Wars (1622–1632, 1644–1646) *conflicts between the Powhatan Confederacy and the British colonists in Virginia*

Although there had been fighting between the Indians of the POWHATAN CONFEDERACY and the Jamestown settlers from the time the British landed in 1607, these were mostly isolated incidences. Neither the British nor the Powhatan wanted to destroy the other as long as the great chief POWHATAN lived. When his daughter Pocahontas married British settler John Rolfe in 1614, Powhatan negotiated peace with the British and maintained it until his death in 1618.

Powhatan was succeeded by his half brother OPECHAN-CANOUGH, whose attitude toward the British was much less conciliatory. Opechancanough recognized that the land hunger of the colonists was a major threat to the Indians' traditional lands, and he was determined to strike against them. On March 22, 1622, Powhatan from all members of the confederacy attacked British settlers without warning. Men, women, and children were killed in the initial assault—a total of 347 colonists, or more than a quarter of the colony's population. However, Opechancanough did not follow up his victory. Having no knowledge of European military power, he expected that the British would react like Indians and retreat to their own country. Instead, the colonists counterattacked, concentrating on Powhatan villages and cornfields and confiscating more land.

Most of the battles of the First Powhatan War (1622–32) were ambushes, as in April 1623, when a band of warriors surprised 23 colonists on their way up the Potomac River to buy grain. The following month, the British poisoned 200 PAMUNKEY warriors and scalped another 50 in an ambush. In July 1624, the British fought a two-day pitched battle with the Powhatan in which 60 colonists fought off 800 warriors and escaped with no deaths (16 English were wounded). The Powhatan had the numerical advantage, but the colonists had a distinct technological advantage with their FIREARMS and BODY ARMOR. The warfare dragged on intermittently until 1632, when the two sides finally negotiated a truce.

In 1644, the aged Opechancanough made another attempt to drive the British away in the Second Powhatan War (1644–46). By this time, however, the settlers numbered some 14,000, while the Powhatan population had dropped greatly due to disease, famine, and warfare. Opechancanough's initial attack followed the pattern of 1622. On April 18, 1644, the Indians visited isolated British settlements and struck suddenly, killing 500 colonists. The counterattack, organized by Governor WILLIAM BERKELEY, struck at the Pamunkey, seizing prisoners to sell as slaves in the Caribbean and confiscating land on which Indian villages had stood. In spring 1646, a band of soldiers, including Berkeley, captured Opechancanough and took him to Jamestown. His capture and subsequent death at the hands of an angry soldier marked the end of the Powhatan Wars.

Prairie Du Chien Treaty (1825) *treaty between the Fox and Sac Indians and the Lakota*

During the 17th century, the FOX (Mesquakie) Indians, who were living in the Great Lakes area, had been allies of tribes in the IROQUOIS CONFEDERACY. Because of this alliance, the Fox were often in conflict with tribes allied with the French in the Midwest. Hostility from these tribes and the French drove the Fox further west, culminating in the FOX WAR (1712–42). By the late 18th century, the Fox had settled in what is now Iowa. However, this brought them into conflict with the Santee Dakota (see SIOUX), who shared their hunting grounds. In August 1825, U.S. government officials helped negotiate a treaty between the two tribes at Prairie du Chien. Although the treaty was supposed to bring permanent peace to the region, the Fox and the Dakota continued to fight for some time afterward.

prisoners *Indians and non-Indians held in captivity or restraint by enemies or rivals*

Practices, policies, and treatment of prisoners taken as a result of military action varied greatly according to custom, tradition, and circumstance. Before the arrival of Europeans in North America, Indian groups frequently adopted prisoners into their tribes or ritually killed them. For their part, Europeans had a long tradition of holding prisoners of war as slaves, bartering them for trade or exchange with their enemies, releasing them upon the promise that they would fight no more, or executing them outright.

Both groups tortured their prisoners under certain circumstances. Some Native Americans, for example, believed that the more bravely a prisoner behaved before and during the torture, the more respect he merited from his captors. Members of the IROQUOIS CONFEDERACY considered torturing prisoners the prerogative of women who had lost relatives in battle. Among Europeans, religious and political prisoners could often expect to be tortured, such as during the Spanish Inquisition or the 16th- and 17th-century English witch trials. Torture was also used to extract information.

Generally viewing Native Americans as less than their equals, Europeans felt less obliged to follow generally accepted rules of warfare in dealing with Indian prisoners than they did against other European foes. Thus Spanish slavers routinely raided the Gulf and Atlantic coasts and the Southwest, enslaving the Native peoples found there for work in mines or plantations. A particularly grisly incident followed the revolt against Spanish authority at the ACOMA PUEBLO (1598). After killing 800 Indians, the Spanish cut one foot off of surviving Acoma males over age 25. Men and women over age 12 were sentenced to 20 years of slavery; children were placed on missions. The British sentenced prisoners captured in the PEQUOT WAR (1636–37) and the Second POWHATAN WAR (1644–48) to slavery in the Caribbean or in Spanish America. One of the major causes of the TUSCARORA WAR (1711–13) was the persistent slave-raiding by South Carolina colonists.

While continuing their traditional practices, Native Americans also adopted different means of dealing with prisoners in response to the European invasions. Badly in need of new European weapons and manufactured goods, they often took prisoners for plunder, to be traded later for food, blankets, clothing, FIREARMS, or alcohol. Such exchanges were most common in New England and French Canada during KING WILLIAM'S WAR (1689–97), QUEEN ANNE'S WAR (1702–13), and KING GEORGE'S WAR (1744–48). Indeed, the idea of

Both Indian groups and European groups subjected some prisoners to torture, but surviving depictions, such as this sensational early engraving, tend to emphasize Indian brutality—real and imagined—to their prisoners. *(Courtesy New York Public Library)*

Indian captivity so captured colonial imaginations that "captivity narratives"—stories based on real experiences of people who had been taken prisoner by the Indians—became a popular literary genre through the 19th century. In these works, the narrator was typically seized from his or her home by ferocious savages and witnessed the brutal deaths of friends, spouses, or children. The narrator also typically attributed the sparing of his or her life to the mercy of divine providence, giving the story a moral tone. The stories portrayed Indians as brutal and inhuman, and their popularity helped to spread negative stereotypes and heightened fears of the "bloodthirsty savages." However, there were a few exceptions in which the captive instead comes to admire and respect their Indian captors. One example of this was *A Narrative of the Life of Mrs. Mary Jemison* (1824).

Indian versus Indian warfare continued, but the growing power of the United States accounted for the vast majority of the wars of the 19th century. Although the federal government made some attempt to differentiate between the treatment accorded Native American combatants and non-combatants, the practical effects of being made a prisoner of the United States were quite severe. Tribes defeated in warfare or in treaty negotiations were often removed from their traditional homelands to reservations west of the Mississippi River, with present-day Oklahoma (Indian Territory) serving as the ultimate destination for many. Here one could expect government annuities of uneven quality to supplement whatever resources might be squeezed from the surrounding lands.

Those who defied American expansion or who ventured off reservations without U.S. permission were usually deemed hostile by the U.S. government. Those taken prisoner could expect a variety of punishments, depending on circumstances and their captors. Most were held for a time under close guard before being forced back on reservations or moved even farther away from their ancestral homes, such as the fate suffered by CHIEF JOSEPH and his NEZ PERCE followers. During the MINNESOTA UPRISING (1862), a military commission sentenced more than 300 Dakota Indians to be hanged. Recognizing that the evidence against many had been flimsy, President Abraham Lincoln commuted the sentences to all but 38, who were executed the day after Christmas at Mankato, Minnesota. In 1871, three KIOWA chiefs—Satanta, Satank, and Big Tree—were arrested at Fort Sill, Indian Territory, for various depredations in Texas. While awaiting trial in a Texas state court, Satank was killed during an escape attempt. The other two were found guilty of murder and sentenced to death. Governor Edmund J. Davis commuted their sentence to life imprisonment in the state penitentiary; in 1873, following negotiations in which several Kiowa chiefs promised to end their attacks against Texans, Big Tree and Satanta were set free.

Another notable example came at the end of the APACHE WARS (1860–86). War leader GERONIMO and all the Chiricahua and Warm Springs APACHE were shipped off from Arizona to Florida for confinement. The men were initially held at Fort Marion and their families at Fort Pickens. In 1887, the men were reunited with their families; the following year, the Apache were removed again, this time to a healthier locale at Mount Vernon Barracks, Alabama. In 1894, they were sent to Fort Sill, where Geronimo died in 1909. In 1913, the government finally allowed 187 of the survivors to go to the Mescalero Reservation, New Mexico.

Proclamation of 1763 *attempt to end the violence of Pontiac's Rebellion*

The Proclamation of 1763 was issued on October 7, about six months after the TREATY OF PARIS (1763) ended the FRENCH AND INDIAN WAR (1754–63). The proclamation was a temporary measure, meant to put a stop to the continuing violence that plagued colonial frontiers during PONTIAC'S REBELLION (1763–65). It also served to acknowledge the debts the British government owed its Indian allies for their support in the struggle against the French. British officials wanted to end the frontier fighting—often caused by disputes between settlers and Native Americans over land rights—because it interfered with the fur trade and the profitable shipment of tobacco, a necessary measure since the recent war had been so expensive.

The Proclamation of 1763 had three basic goals. First, it forbade British settlements west of the Appalachian Divide—partly to appease the Indians, and partly to keep the colonists near British-controlled Atlantic ports. Second, it reserved the right to acquire territory from the Indians by treaty to the British government. (Formerly, individual colonies or private citizens had been able to acquire land by treaty on their own.) Third, the proclamation required all traders operating in Native American territory to be licensed. This last provision was intended to address complaints by Indians that traders cheated them of their furs, changing prices for goods at will. Although some of these goals were set out in previously existing treaties negotiated between the colonies and the Indians, their terms were usually not honored by the colonies.

The British found enforcement of the Proclamation of 1763 to be impractical. By the time it was issued, there were already colonial settlements beyond the line of demarcation. Villages and small towns had sprung up in western Virginia, in Pennsylvania near Fort Pitt, and in New York. Europeans could even be found as far west as present-day Kentucky and Ohio. Furthermore, the original charters that had established many of the colonies in the 17th century had given away lands stretching from the Atlantic Ocean to the Pacific. Neither the colonial governments nor the settlers they represented were willing to give up so many of their rights. They resented the interference of the government in faraway London in their affairs, and simply ignored the royal law.

The tribes involved had a different attitude toward the proclamation. They accepted it as a victory for their point of view and withdrew their support for Pontiac's Rebellion. Fighting slackened considerably in 1764, and by the time Pontiac himself made peace in July 1766, raids on British settlements had ceased for more than a year. When they saw that the colonists were not honoring the terms of the proclamation, however, the Indians returned to their raiding. Violence on the frontier continued intermittently for the next 30 years.

Further Reading

The American Heritage History of the Thirteen Colonies. New York: American Heritage, 1967.

Jacobs, Wilbur R. "British Indian Policies to 1783." In *Handbook of North American Indians.* Washington, D.C.: Smithsonian Institution, pp. 5–12. 1988.

Steele, Ian K. *Warpaths: Invasions of North America.* New York: Oxford University Press, 1994.

Pueblo Indians   *group of Native American tribes in New Mexico and Arizona*

The Pueblo Indians were one of the first Indian nations in the present-day United States encountered by Europeans on their explorations of North America. The Pueblo have lived in their current homeland longer than any other people in the United States or Canada. These Indians were named by the Spanish after their word for town (*pueblo*) when they discovered tribespeople living in communities resembling Spanish towns. The Spanish also started the still-current practice of using "Pueblo" to refer to both the villages and to the people. The modern Pueblo live in several communities, belonging to four different groups: the Tewa, Tiwa, Toua, and Keses. Each village has its own government but remains culturally linked to the others.

The Pueblo's first contact with the Spanish was made when the latter established a settlement near an Indian village in 1598. The Spanish forced the Pueblo to work for them and to turn over some of their crops. Missionaries also attempted to force the Pueblo to adopt Roman Catholicism. In 1680, under POPÉ's leadership, the Pueblo revolted and threw out the Spanish (see PUEBLO REBELLION). However, the Spanish reconquered the Indians in 1692. Pueblo territory in Arizona and New Mexico passed to Mexican control in 1820, and then, with the 1848 end of the Mexican War, formally to American control.

Today the Pueblo Indians live at numerous pueblos in the Southwest, many of which have been continuously inhabited by the people since prehistoric times.

Pueblo Indians on horseback. Pueblo, a name given to this group by the Spaniards in 1598, means "town" but has come to refer to certain people. *(By permission of the Colorado Historical Society)*

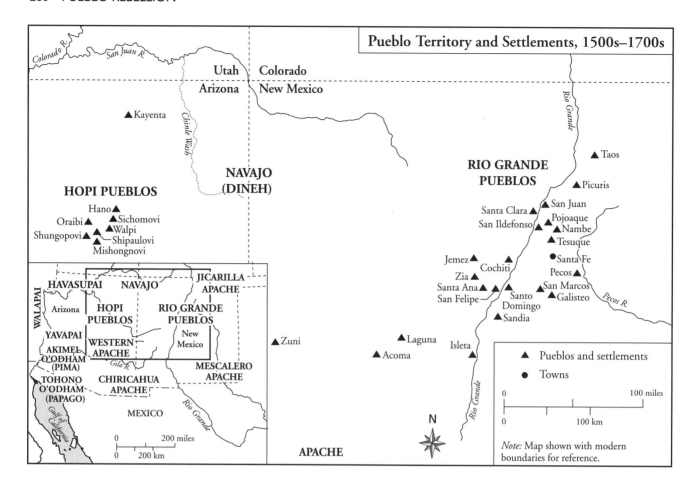

Pueblo Territory and Settlements, 1500s–1700s

Pueblo Rebellion (Pueblo Revolt) (1680–1692)
revolt by the Pueblo, Hopi, and Zuni Indians of New Mexico against the Spanish

Since the late 16th century, Spain had been attempting to convert the Native Americans of New Mexico to Catholicism. Despite Spanish efforts, many Indians had stubbornly continued to practice their traditional religions. When Spanish power weakened as a result of drought, continued APACHE raids, and infighting between religious and military officials, Indian advocates of traditional ways gained more influence. In 1680, PUEBLO INDIAN leader POPÉ, the most militant of the traditionists, organized an elaborately planned insurrection, to begin on August 11. Popé preached that all traces of the Spanish must be obliterated.

Several Spanish outposts fell immediately to Popé's followers. Following a brief siege and some fierce fighting, troops from the Spanish garrison at SANTA FE (1680) fled down the Rio Grande into present-day Texas or Mexico. Some 400 Spanish, including 21 of 33 priests in the affected areas were slain in the initial onslaught.

The Indian rebellion drove the Spanish from New Mexico. Initial attempts to recapture the area were woefully undermanned, because what little resources the Spanish could muster were was directed instead against French intruders in Texas. But Popé's influence soon waned. He refused to allow any of his people to adopt Spanish practices or tools of any sort, and he became a virtual dictator. His death in 1690 completed the rebels' demoralization. The Spanish recaptured Santa Fe in 1692, and the entire province was back under Spanish control by 1696. Though success had been short-lived, the Pueblo Rebellion demonstrated the deep-seated opposition to Spanish authority in much of the New World.

Put-in-Bay, battle of   See THAMES.

Pyramid Lake   See PAIUTE WAR.

Queen Anne's War (War of the Spanish Succession) (1702–1713) *second in the series of colonial wars involving the major European powers*

Like KING WILLIAM'S WAR (1689–97) before it and KING GEORGE'S WAR (1744–48) after, Queen Anne's War was, for Europeans, a minor theater in a larger conflict. The War of the Spanish Succession grew out of a European governmental crisis. King Charles II of Spain was dying and had no heir to follow him on the throne. He nominated as his successor Philip of Anjou, grandson of Louis XIV of France. The British, Dutch, and Austrians objected to Philip's nomination, preferring instead Archduke Charles of Austria, a distant relative of Charles II. For the British in North America, an alliance between France and Spain, which Charles II wanted, would mean that British colonists would be threatened by Canada and Florida along their northern and southern frontiers.

Hostilities opened on the colonial front on September 10, 1702, when the colonial legislature of South Carolina approved a motion to launch an assault against Fort Augustine in Spanish Florida. In December, a mixed force of 500 colonial militia and CHICKASAW warriors assaulted the fort but were driven off. Thus thwarted, they plundered and burned the town of St. Augustine. Minor raids continued on the southern frontier for the next year.

In July 1704, South Carolina governor JAMES MOORE, leading another mixed force of militia and Chickasaw, launched a major campaign into Spanish Florida. The campaign destroyed the Appalachee Indians as an independent nation and opened access to French Louisiana. The French tried to fend off the threatened invasion by wooing support from the CHOCTAW, CHEROKEE, and CREEK. The Cherokee refused to choose sides between the French and the English, maintaining a strict neutrality. A few Creek joined the French, but the greatest numbers of warriors serving with the Europeans came from the Choctaw, who stopped Moore's expedition.

On the northern frontier, the French and their ABENAKI Indian allies raided the New England colonies and were raided in turn. The British struck first. On August 10, 1703, colonials broke into the trading post and home of Jean Vincent de l'Abadie, baron de Saint-Castin, a French-Abenaki nobleman. The Abenaki and their French allies retaliated, raiding and burning settlements all over New England. Local governments were overwhelmed by the ferocity of the raids. On the night of February 29, 1704, a force of 50 French-Canadians and 200 Abenaki and Caughnawaga (French-allied relatives of the MOHAWK) attacked Deerfield, Massachusetts. More than half the population of the village was lost in the DEERFIELD RAID (1704).

Most of the campaigns of Queen Anne's War were merely large-scale raids. There were a few exceptions: an unsuccessful British attempt on Port Royal, Nova Scotia, in 1706; a failed French-Spanish expedition against Charleston, South Carolina; and the French capture of St. Johns, Newfoundland, in 1708. It was not until 1710 that the British began taking a more active interest in the colonial war. In that year British colonists sent a contingent of Mohawk Indians to England, where they staged a theatrical performance to persuade Queen Anne to provide them with military support. Before the end of the year,

British army and navy troops had captured Port Royal, and the following summer they captured French Acadia.

Queen Anne's War ended in 1713, when Archduke Charles, the alternative heir to the Spanish throne, died and Philip became king by default. The Treaty of Utrecht, which marked the end of hostilities, acknowledged the gains the British had made in French Canada. Hudson's Bay and the former province of Acadia (now Nova Scotia) were assigned to the British. The New Englanders for their part acknowledged the right of the Abenaki to their ancestral lands in return for the Indians' recognition of the British Crown's overlordship. The peace on the New England frontier did not last long, however, as colonists began to settle on Abenaki territory.

Further Reading

Axelrod, Alan. *Chronicle of the Indian Wars.* Englewood Cliffs, N.J.: Prentice Hall, 1993.

Josephy, Alvin M., Jr., *500 Nations: An Illustrated History of North American Indians.* New York: Alfred A. Knopf, 1994.

Steele, Ian K. *Warpaths: Invasions of North America.* New York: Oxford University Press, 1994.

raiding versus warfare *different types of military action*
Most American Indians made a distinction between raids and
wars. For the most part, raids were designed to search out and
procure enemy property. Raiding expeditions were generally
directed by an experienced leader and were formed by as few
as five to 15 or more men. Traveling quietly they would locate
an enemy and with as much stealth as possible take enemy possessions and occasionally enemy lives. Wars, on the other hand
involved much more organization and planning. An experienced war chief often led the expedition of many men. The primary purposes of wars were to avenge deaths and kill the
enemy. Both raids and wars also provided opportunities for
novices as well as experienced warriors to gain personal prestige.

When Europeans arrived in North America, they found that
most Native Americans did not engage in defensive and offensive
warfare with large standing armies. Although some tribes had
military societies, such as the DOG SOLDIERS of the CHEYENNE
and the *Kwanamis* of the MOJAVE, every able-bodied warrior
was also a provider for his family and a participant in tribal social
and religious activities. Indians did not subscript or draft their
warriors. They were volunteers, often including those who had
received special spiritual power to carry out such activity.

For warriors, combat was essential to earn honors and dis-
tinguish themselves (see COUNTING COUP). Among the Plains
Indians, the most common cause for raids was stealing horses.
Usually, fewer than a dozen warriors took part in these raids.
The object was to weaken a foe by capturing horses, not to
attack the camp or kill the inhabitants.

In the East, the powerful IROQUOIS CONFEDERACY was
exceptional in its ability to wage war. During the 17th century,
five Iroquois tribes—the MOHAWK, ONEIDA, ONONDAGA,
CAYUGA, and SENECA—united in a political and military league
that dominated much of the Northeast. They were later
strengthened by the addition of the TUSCARORA. This confederacy could mass thousands of warriors, who fought and
defeated surrounding tribes. For more than a half century, the
Iroquois Confederacy carried out large-scale warfare, extending
its control north to the Great Lakes and west to the Mississippi
River (see BEAVER WARS, 1638–84, 1690–1701).

The continual westward expansion of the frontier pushed
eastern Indians onto the lands of western tribes and brought
further rivalry and conflict over hunting and trapping grounds.
Warfare escalated beyond revenge raids or feuds to encounters
on a much larger scale.

The horse had arrived on the Great Plains in the 1500s,
introduced by the Spanish in the Southwest. Through trade
and raids, central and northern Plains tribes acquired horses,
and by the early 18th century, many tribes were already using
horses in warfare. Guns, also introduced by the Spanish and
later acquired from English and French traders, also increased
the Indians' ability to mount large attacks. Pitched battles did
occur among the Plains tribes before they had horses, but there
were few casualties because opposing sides generally lined up
some distance apart and, protected by shields, loosed arrows on
one another. With horses, however, war parties could travel farther to fight, and warriors could charge quickly into enemy
ranks for hand-to-hand combat. A large war party could also
attack and wipe out an enemy camp. This kind of warfare was
more dangerous. Consequently, as intertribal warfare increased
on the Plains, so did Indian casualties.

This oil painting by J. H. Drury depicts a fight between Native Americans of two feuding tribes. *(Courtesy of the National Museum of the American Indian, Smithsonian Institution #10154)*

Rain-in-the-Face (Inomagaia, Amarazhu)

(ca. 1830–1905) *Hunkpapa Lakota warrior*

Born in 1830 in North Dakota, Rain-in-the-Face earned his name at the age of 10, when he became involved in a fight with a CHEYENNE boy. During the fight, his facepaint became streaked as though partially washed off by rain. His playmates thus began calling him Rain-in-the-Face—a name he considered honorable.

A Lakota (see SIOUX) Indian, Rain-in-the-Face was one of the leaders in RED CLOUD'S WAR (1866–68), an attempt to clear the BOZEMAN TRAIL of U.S. military posts. He also participated in the FETTERMAN FIGHT (1866). In 1873 Rain-in-the-Face was caught and imprisoned at Fort Abraham Lincoln in North Dakota after being accused of killing a white doctor. He escaped and joined SITTING BULL in the War for the Black Hills (see SIOUX WARS), including the battle of ROSEBUD CREEK (1876), and the battle of the LITTLE BIGHORN (1876). In recounting war stories to fellow Lakota and Pine Ridge Agency physician Charles A. Eastman, Rain-in-the-Face later

stated, "…in that fight [Little Bighorn] the excitement was so great that we scarcely recognized our nearest friends! Everything was done like lightning!" For a time it was reported that Rain-in-the-Face was the warrior who killed GEORGE ARMSTRONG CUSTER at Little Bighorn. However, in Eastman's book, *Indian Heroes & Great Chieftains,* Eastman states Rain-in-the-Face's conclusion: "So it is that no one knows who killed the Long-Haired Chief [Custer]."

Rain-in-the-Face fought long and honorably to preserve Lakota land and freedom. In 1880 he surrendered to U.S. authorities. Rain-in-the-Face spent his remaining years at Standing Rock Reservation in North Dakota.

Rains Fight (1877) *battle in the Nez Perce War*

In 1877 the U.S. Army was sent to Idaho to drive the NEZ PERCE out of their traditional homelands in Idaho and western Washington and onto reservation lands. The battle of WHITE BIRD CREEK (1877) on June 17, 1877, launched a running battle between the army and the bands of Nez Perce under the leadership of CHIEF JOSEPH. After the battle, in which 34 soldiers but no Indians died, the army lost contact with the Nez Perce. General OLIVER O. HOWARD, the commanding officer in the area, sent scouting parties into western Idaho to locate the Indians. For about a month the Indians escaped the attentions of the army and built their numbers to about 700 people, including 550 women and children. Early in July, however, Lieutenant S. M. Rains and his scouts found the main Nez Perce camp on the banks of the Salmon River. The Indians surrounded the scouts and killed them all. The Rains Fight was the last Indian victory in the Nez Perce war. All the other battles in the war, beginning with CLEARWATER CREEK (1877) on July 11, ended with the Nez Perce fleeing the battlefield. Their flight—and the war—ended on September 30th at the battle of BEAR PAW (1877).

Raisin River (Battle of Frenchtown, Frenchtown Massacre, River Raisin Massacre) (1813) *U.S. defeat in the War of 1812*

During the WAR OF 1812 (1812–14), the settlement of Frenchtown on the Raisin River (present-day Monroe, Michigan) was surrendered to British and Indian forces (including the SHAWNEE chief TECUMSEH) on August 17, 1812, along with Fort Detroit. By January of the following year, Brigadier General WILLIAM HENRY HARRISON had gathered a large force of 3,000 militia in northern Ohio. He sent a vanguard of about 700 men under General James Winchester toward Detroit. They encountered a small British-Indian force at Frenchtown on January 18th and, joined by some local Frenchmen, drove them away. The British called on reinforcements from Brownstown, a community south of DETROIT. Early on the morning of January 22, 1813, 525 British soldiers and 800 Shawnee surprised the American camp. Four hundred of the American soldiers, including General Winchester, fled.

About one-and-a-half miles south of the battlefield, a party of Native Americans who had not taken part in the initial assault were lying in ambush. These included a party of Red Stick CREEK (a warrior faction of the otherwise friendly Creek nation) from the south, allies of Tecumseh led by Little Warrior. They attacked the fleeing Americans and killed and scalped 40 of them before the others surrendered. According to some accounts, another 105 were killed after surrendering. Some of the wounded were killed as well. The remaining Americans surrendered to the commanding British officer, Colonel Henry Proctor. In all, about 495 prisoners were taken.

The Raisin River fight was significant in Native American history for two reasons. First, it seriously crippled Harrison's effort to recapture Detroit by eliminating almost one-third of his army. Second, the killing of soldiers who had surrendered to Tecumseh and his Shawnee warriors, made "Remember the Raisin!" a rallying cry for American fighters in the way that "Remember Pearl Harbor!" was for Americans during World War II.

Râle, Sébastien (Sébastien Rasle) (ca. 1657–1724) *Jesuit missionary best known for his work on Indian languages*

Born in France, in 1689 Sébastien Râle came to Canada, where he became fluent in several Native American dialects. In 1693, he was posted to an ABENAKI mission in Maine, where he soon became embroiled in the Indians' raids on the Massachusetts frontier. The English burned the mission in 1705, but Râle managed to escape.

After Maine was ceded to the English, Râle acted on orders from the governor of New France and continued to incite the Abenaki to violence. Governor Shute of Massachusetts offered to trade an English missionary for Râle, but nothing could persuade the Indians to surrender the popular Jesuit. Râle's mission was burned a second time in 1721, but he again escaped. He was finally tracked down at NORRIDGEWOCK, where he was shot on August 1724. His scalp was taken to Boston amid much rejoicing.

Râle's Abenaki dictionary is still extant, as are several of his prayers, which are recited by Native Americans in Maine to this day.

Râle's War   See DUMMER'S WAR.

Rattlesnake Springs (1880) *skirmish between Warm Springs Apache and U.S. forces*

Between 1877 and 1879, APACHE leader VICTORIO led his band of Warm Springs Apache on raids in both the United States and Mexico. Dissatisfied with his enforced settlement at San Carlos, New Mexico, Victorio led his people in a quest for a satisfactory home. Skilled in the art of warfare, Victorio was an aggressive, charismatic leader whose raids were aimed at keeping his people clothed and fed. He was pursued by soldiers from both countries and successfully avoided capture for many years.

In late summer 1880, Victorio and 150 warriors began a flight from 500 Mexican troops commanded by Colonel Adolph Valle. The Indians crossed the Rio Grande into Texas and headed toward the Mescalero Apache Reservation. Colonel Benjamin H. Grierson, commander of U.S. troops, anticipated that Victorio would enter the United States by way of Texas rather than through New Mexico, as he had done frequently in the past. Grierson therefore established an elaborate system of blocking positions, assigning troops to cover all the vital water holes.

When Grierson learned that Victorio was on the move, he marched two groups of cavalry 65 miles in 21 hours to intercept the Apache leader. On August 6, 1880, Grierson and two additional groups were in position by the water hole at Rattlesnake Springs. When Victorio arrived, he was surprised to see the U.S. troops, and sporadic gunfire was exchanged. Breaking off the fight, Victorio retreated. Later that same day, however, he attacked a supply train, unaware that Grierson had pursued him from Rattlesnake Springs. Once again troops confronted the Apache. Thoroughly frustrated, Victorio turned his warriors and retreated into Mexico, where he was killed by Mexican troops in the battle of TRES CASTILLOS (1880).

Red Bird (Wanig-suchka, Waunigsootshkau, Zitkaduta) (1788–1828) *leader in the Winnebago Uprising*

Red Bird was born where the Mississippi and Wisconsin Rivers converge near modern-day Prairie du Chien, Wisconsin, and grew up near La Crosse. His father was a war chief of the WINNEBAGO (Ho-Chunk) and in time Red Bird, too, became a tribe leader. For some time, he maintained friendly relationships with non-Indians in the area. However, the Indians and non-Indians were on a collision course, and Red Bird was trapped in the middle.

In the 1820s, miners began moving onto Winnebago land near the present Wisconsin and Illinois border in search of galena (lead). Soon the Winnebago began mining galena and selling it to the miners. American officials, however, wanted to take the mineral-bearing lands from the Indians, so they discouraged their mining operations.

In spring 1826, an incident occurred that sparked the so-called WINNEBAGO UPRISING (1826–27). Several Winnebago warriors killed five members of the French-Canadian Methode family on their maple sugar camp across the Mississippi River from Prairie du Chien. Local settlers sought swift justice and made arrests. The Winnebago prisoners were taken to Fort Snelling, Minnesota.

By now the Indians were feeling that U.S. action against them required a response. Non-Indians had entered their lands, miners had abused tribal women, and relatives and friends of the warriors suspected of the Methode murders feared for their safety. In the face of growing pressure, Red Bird finally decided to act.

On June 26, 1827, he and two warriors randomly picked a settler's home where they killed two people and scalped an 11-month-old infant daughter, who miraculously survived. Upon returning to their village, Red Bird and his accomplices urged their kinsman to continue their violent uprising. They next attacked a keelboat returning from Fort Snelling. They killed two non-Indians but lost 12 warriors. According to some sources, the boatsmen had kidnapped and raped some Winnebago women, and the Indians were trying to rescue them.

Red Bird thought that his actions would encourage all the Winnebago to rise up in arms against the Americans. He was mistaken. Through a series of successful negotiations, American officials managed to keep other local tribes and Winnebago from taking up arms, and they successfully isolated Red Bird and his Prairie du Chien followers. Meanwhile, Lewis Cass, the governor of Michigan Territory, and Thomas McKenney, superintendent of Indian affairs, insisted that the Winnebago surrender those Indians responsible for the killings. Their demands were accompanied by a significant military buildup.

Seeing no way out of the predicament, and in order to save his people, Red Bird agreed to surrender. He did so in grand style. On September 3, 1827, Red Bird entered McKenney's camp carrying a white flag and singing his death song. He wore white buckskin with an elaborate fringe, accented by a two-inch beaded collar bordered with wildcat claws. He had painted half of his face red, and the other half white and green. Red Bird was followed by 100 kinsmen, some carrying American flags.

Red Bird and five other Winnebago were held at Fort Crawford near Prairie du Chien. This time American justice was not swift. Weeks turned into months as the prisoners awaited trial. In January 1828 Red Bird died in jail of dysentery.

The encroachment of non-Indian miners on Winnebago lands was the catalyst for the Winnebago actions of 1826–27. In August 1829, at a treaty signed at Prairie du Chien (see PRAIRIE DU CHIEN TREATY), the Winnebago ceded to the American government their territory south of the Wisconsin River, including the galena-rich areas.

Further Reading

Zanger, Martin. "Red Bird." In *American Indian Leaders: Studies in Diversity,* R. David Edmunds, ed. Lincoln: University of Nebraska Press, 1980, pp. 64–87.

Red Cloud (Makhpia-sha, Makhpiya-luta, "Scarlet Cloud") (1822–1909) *Oglala Lakota leader in War for the Bozeman Trail*

One story about Red Cloud's name tells that he was born the night a meteorite sped across the sky, leaving red clouds in its wake. In another explanation, the 19-year-old war leader, then known as Two Arrows, led a Lakota (see SIOUX) war party that wore scarlet blankets over their shoulders, giving them the appearance of red clouds cresting over the hill. From then on Two Arrows was known as Red Cloud.

He was born in 1822 near the present-day town of North Platte, Nebraska. His parents died soon thereafter, and he was raised by a sister and an uncle, Chief Smoke. In 1841, Smoke and Red Cloud feuded with another chief, Bull Bear, whom Red Cloud later killed, creating a division among the Oglala that lasted for 50 years.

In his late 20s, Red Cloud was already considered an excellent warrior, with experience fighting against the PAWNEE, CROW, and other tribes, and he soon also gained a reputation as a medicine man. In 1849, when a cholera epidemic swept through his tribe, Red Cloud devised an extract of cedar leaves that proved helpful to those infected.

In 1862, gold was discovered in what is now Montana. Soon miners and traders began flooding into the area along the BOZEMAN TRAIL, a branch of the Oregon Trail. The Bozeman Trail cut through the heart of the Lakota hunting grounds along the Powder River. By 1865 Indian war parties were attacking anything moving along the trail. That summer DULL KNIFE's Northern CHEYENNE, Black Bear's ARAPAHO, Hump's Miniconjou Lakota, and Red Cloud's Oglala Lakota had amassed a joint army of about 3,000 warriors. They were determined to drive the invaders from their hunting grounds. On July 26, a supply train approached the military stockade called Camp Dodge. Twenty Kansas troopers under the command of Lieutenant Caspar W. Collins left the stockade to warn them that the Indians were massing for an attack. It was too late. After fierce fighting, Indians under the leadership of ROMAN NOSE overpowered the soldiers and wagon train.

The U.S. government then invited the Indian leaders to Fort Laramie, Wyoming, to discuss peace. Red Cloud was furious that Colonel HENRY B. CARRINGTON had been ordered to build a string of forts along the Bozeman Trail, and he and others left the parley. Remaining leaders signed an agreement allowing non-Indian travelers to use the trail but not to disturb the game animals. Meanwhile, Forts Reno, Phil Kearny and FORT C. F. SMITH were equipped and manned. Red Cloud's army, which eventually swelled to about 4,000 Cheyenne, Arapaho, and Lakota warriors, struck at the forts. Several battles, including the FETTERMAN FIGHT (1866), the HAYFIELD FIGHT (1867), and the WAGON BOX FIGHT (1867), demonstrated that Red Cloud's coalition was more than a match for the army regulars.

By 1868, U.S. officials were willing to sue for peace. Red Cloud refused to sign anything until the soldiers were evacuated from the three forts. Grudgingly, the military complied. On November 6, Red Cloud entered the post and signed the FORT LARAMIE TREATY (1868). RED CLOUD'S WAR (1866–68) was over. History would record that Red Cloud led the only western Indian war that was clearly won by the Native Americans.

Red Cloud, an Oglala Lakota chief *(Courtesy New York Public Library)*

Red Cloud promised to never again make war against non-Indians. He was good to his word, but his oath caused him much misery. Two chiefs who refused to sign the Fort Laramie treaty, SITTING BULL of the Hunkpapa Lakota and Two Moons of the Northern Cheyenne, accused him of being duped by the government negotiators. Red Cloud refused to participate in the War for the Black Hills phase of the SIOUX WARS (1854–90). However, when his son Jack fought in the battle of the LITTLE BIGHORN (1876), officials accused him of conspiracy and ousted him as leader at the Red Cloud Agency (named after him). He regained his official government recognition as chief in 1869 after helping convince CRAZY HORSE to surrender. Thereafter, Red Cloud sought to protect the Lakota way of life while at the same time demanding that the government honor its treaty obligations. He died in his house at Pine Ridge on December 10, 1909.

Further Reading

Larson, Robert W. *Red Cloud: Warrior-Statesman of the Lakota Sioux.* Norman: University of Oklahoma Press, 1997.

Red Cloud's War (War for the Bozeman Trail)

(1866–1868) *war between the Lakota and their allies and the U.S. government concerning the right of passage through the Teton mountain range of Wyoming*

RED CLOUD, a rising leader among the Oglala Lakota (see SIOUX), had warily observed non-Indian movements in the West at the end of the CIVIL WAR (1861–65). He and others feared that continued use of the BOZEMAN TRAIL through lands long claimed by the Lakota would pave the way for increased non-Indian movement and settlement toward the North Platte River and on into Montana. In June 1866, Red Cloud and several other prominent chiefs rode into Fort Laramie, Wyoming, to meet with government commissioners. During the meeting a detachment of regular troops under Colonel HENRY B. CARRINGTON arrived. Red Cloud overheard Carrington speaking of his orders to build forts in the Powder River country to protect the Bozeman Trail. While some chiefs signed the agreement, Red Cloud refused and rode off, determined to stop further encroachments by non-Indians.

Carrington set about the task of building Forts Reno and Phil Kearny in north-central Wyoming, and FORT C. F. SMITH near the Bighorn River in southern Montana. During the construction of these forts, U.S. troops were constantly harassed by Indian raids. At this time, Lakota war leader CRAZY HORSE became popular among his people for his great courage in battle and his skillful tactics. By contrast, Colonel Carrington lacked combat experience. As the Indian attacks continued, many of the regular troops, battle-hardened veterans of the Civil War who had not learned to respect the abilities of their new enemies, chafed at Carrington's defensive posture. Among the most discontented was Captain WILLIAM J. FETTERMAN, who boasted that with 80 men he could ride through the entire Lakota nation. Fetterman's naive and reckless attitude would end up getting him and 80 of his men killed in the FETTERMAN FIGHT (1866).

The Lakota had launched most of their attacks against the still-incomplete Fort Phil Kearney, which happened to be Carrington's headquarters. When winter set in, wagon trains often were dispatched to gather wood for fires and construction. These wood-gathering forays were ideal targets for Indian raids. On December 21, 1866, an expedition came under Indian attack. Upon hearing this, Captain Fetterman demanded to be placed in charge of the relief troops. Carrington hesitated, but then allowed the over-confident captain to lead the reinforcements after instructing him not to cross Lodge Trail Ridge. Carrington's reason for not wishing Fetterman to cross the ridge was because if he did, his relief party would disappear from sight of the fort. Across this ridge, Crazy Horse planted his decoy, and Fetterman took the bait. Fetterman, with a total disregard for Carrington's orders, lost sight of the fort after crossing the ridge. Ironically, the relief troops he led numbered 80. In less than an hour, 1,500 to 2,000 warriors annihilated the soldiers in the FETTERMAN FIGHT (1866).

After the Fetterman massacre, the Indians reveled in their victory as they established their winter encampments. The U.S. Army was stunned by the defeat, and the soldiers wanted revenge. Colonel Carrington, deemed partly responsible for the disaster, was relieved of his command and transferred to garrison duty in Colorado. Fresh troops soon took up positions on the Bozeman Trail, but these troops possessed something very new: breech-loading rifles, instead of standard muzzle-loaders, allowing for a quicker rate of fire. The Indians were unaware of this new FIREARM as they planned attacks for summer 1867.

True to their plan, the Indians attacked a small group of hay cutters near Fort C. F. Smith on August 1. They were soundly beaten back by the new weapons in the HAYFIELD FIGHT (1867). The following day the Indians attacked a group of woodcutters near Fort Phil Kearny in the WAGON BOX FIGHT (1867), only to be routed again. Although the success of the new weapons raised army morale, the regulars still found it difficult to regain the initiative.

As the two sides continuing their sparring, interest in the Bozeman Trail waned with the construction of new western railroads. In spring 1868, Red Cloud finally agreed to peace terms. At his insistence, the FORT LARAMIE TREATIES (1868) stipulated that the army abandon its Bozeman Trail positions, that the Powder River country be listed as "unceded Indian territory," and that all the land west of the Missouri River be set aside as the Great Sioux Reservation. Red Cloud—temporarily at least—secured all of his demands.

Further Reading

Larson, Robert W. *Red Cloud: Warrior-Statesman of the Lakota Sioux.* Norman: University of Oklahoma Press, 1997.

Utley, Robert M. *Frontier Regulars: The United States Army and the Indian, 1866–1891.* New York: Macmillan, 1973.

Utley, Robert M., and Wilcomb E. Washburn. *Indian Wars.* Boston: Houghton Mifflin, 1987.

Red Eagle (Lamochatte, Lumha Chati, William Weatherford) (ca. 1780–1824) *Creek leader in the Creek War*

Red Eagle was born among the CREEK along the Alabama River near what is now Montgomery, Alabama. In 1811, he became a follower of SHAWNEE leader TECUMSEH and led the anti-white faction of the Creek known as the RED STICKS. On August 30, 1813, Red Eagle and 1,000 Red Sticks assaulted FORT MIMS on the Tombigbee River in Alabama. Reports indicate that Red Eagle warned the fort of the attack but that the commander ignored it and did not even close the gates. In the battle of Fort Mims some 500 defenders, both soldiers and settlers, were killed. On November 9, Red Eagle was forced to abandon his siege of the pro-white Creek village of Talladega when a force under ANDREW JACKSON appeared on the scene.

Red Eagle was not present at the final battle of HORSESHOE BEND (1814) that ended the CREEK WAR, but he surrendered in person to Jackson a few days later. Red Eagle believed he would be executed. Instead, Jackson pardoned the chief when he agreed to work for peace, perhaps in admiration of Red Eagle's courage and remembering that he had sent a warning before the attack on Fort Mims. In return, Red Eagle asked that the women and children who had taken refuge in the woods during the battle be given protection. Both leaders kept their promises.

Red Eagle lived another 10 years on his farm on the Little River in southern Alabama. He worked for peace between the Creek and non-Indians until his death in 1824.

Red Jacket (Otetiani, Sagoyewatha) (ca. 1758–1830) *Seneca leader allied with the British during the American Revolution*

Red Jacket was born Oti-ti-ani (Always Ready) in present-day New York State. Upon his election as sachem (headman) of the SENECA, he received the title Sagoyewatha, meaning "The Keeper Awake" or "He Keeps Them Awake." To Europeans he was known as Red Jacket because his usual attire was a red jacket that had been presented to him by the British. Red Jacket was distinguished for his agility, intelligence, and eloquence.

Although only 26 years old when the AMERICAN REVOLUTION (1775–81) began, Red Jacket disagreed with the Seneca sachems, or chiefs, who promised to serve the British. He believed it best to stay out of the war, fighting only those who fought them. For his views, which were not the most popular among his people, Red Jacket endured the name of coward. His powers of oratory and his courage in voicing his opinion, however, gained him respect.

As the war progressed, and some tribes of the IROQUOIS CONFEDERACY decided to support the British, Red Jacket acquiesced and lent his support as well. He fought little, however, and participated mainly by carrying dispatches.

By the end of the Revolution, Red Jacket had been elevated to the level of sachem, and he became a spokesman for his people. He first represented the Seneca at the general council with the Americans held at Fort Stanwix in 1784 (see FORT STANWIX TREATY). From this first council until his death, Red Jacket played an important role in the political affairs of his tribe.

Red Jacket also acted as spokesperson for the women of the Seneca nation. Among the Iroquois, leading women, or "clan mothers," had the right to reverse sachems' decision that might jeopardize the safety of their homes. In 1791, for example, at a council meeting at Buffalo Creek, negotiations between U.S. officials and chiefs stalled, and the army colonel in charge of the proceedings announced that he would return to Washington with an unfavorable report on Seneca cooperation. The following morning Red Jacket presented the decision of the women, who had overridden the arguments of the sachems and agreed to the requests of the officials.

Although Red Jacket was committed to forging a lasting peace between Indians and the U.S. government, he nevertheless always acted as a conscience for the Americans, reminding them of past and present depredations committed against Indian peoples and of the broken treaties of the past. A noted orator and defender of Iroquois tradition, he made his last public speech in 1827, seeking to redeem himself in the eyes of his people. Because of his addiction to alcohol, some sachems had renounced Red Jacket as a headman. His eloquence, however, enabled him to regain his title.

Red Jacket's health suffered in his final years. He died in January 1830 at Buffalo Creek, his home on Lake Erie.

Red River War (1874–1875) *decisive conflict in which the U.S. Army broke the military power of the Indians of the southern plains*

The SOUTHERN PLAINS WAR (1868–69) had brought only a brief peace between Native Americans and non-Indians in southern Kansas, Indian Territory (present-day Oklahoma),

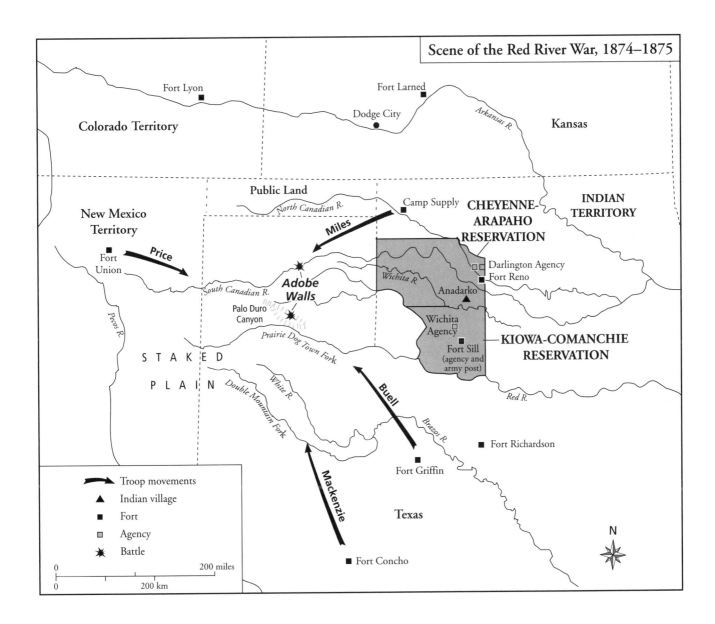

and northern Texas. Army observers were especially critical of what they perceived to be the inability of agents, appointed by Christian religious groups under the new policy of the ULYSSES S. GRANT administration to control the actions of their Indian charges (see GRANT'S PEACE POLICY). For their part, many Native Americans found the supplies provided by the U.S. government under treaty obligation of uneven quality. The Indians were also alarmed about the continuing slaughter of BUFFALO by non-Indian hunters. Furthermore, the reservation boundaries that they were supposed to observe seemed artificial to those who had traditionally hunted much broader areas. Violent incidents became commonplace, and in May 1871, WILLIAM TECUMSEH SHERMAN and a small escort narrowly avoided a KIOWA ambush at SALT CREEK (1871). The arrest of prominent Indian leaders Satank, SATANTA, and BIG TREE failed to bring about a final peace. Army officers, frustrated by the tendency of Native American raiders to use the reservations as temporary safe havens, concluded that only by securing permission to enter the reservations could they defeat the Kiowa, COMANCHE, and Southern CHEYENNE.

On July 16, 1874, growing political pressure and the continuing violence convinced Interior Secretary Columbus Delano to lift the restrictions on the army's movements. Newly empowered to pursue hostile parties onto reservations, PHILIP HENRY SHERIDAN, commanding the military Division of the Missouri, organized a four-pronged offensive. As had been the case in the Southern Plains War, the columns were designed to converge upon suspected Indian haunts. Again using tested procedure, those who opted for peace were to assemble at Fort Sill in Indian Territory; those who did not were declared hostile. This time, however, the attacks would begin in the late summer rather than in the winter, and they would be directed into the Texas Panhandle. Preferring not to delay and thus risk a change of government policy, Sheridan now determined to attack as soon as his columns were ready. As was typical for the army's conduct of the time, field commanders received wide discretion in conducting their individual operations.

The campaign began in August 1874. From Texas, RANALD S. MACKENZIE led 13 companies north from Fort Concho, and Lieutenant Colonel George P. Buell moved eight companies from Fort Griffin. Major William R. Price pushed east with 250 troopers from Fort Union, New Mexico Territory. From Fort Dodge, Kansas, NELSON A. MILES drove south with eight companies of cavalry and four of infantry. Mackenzie struck the most important blow, surprising a large Indian encampment at the battle of PALO DURO CANYON (1874). Miles and detachments from his original command won smaller skirmishes on August 8 at Tule Canyon, on September 7 and 8 along the Salt Fork of the Red River, and on November 8 at McClellan Creek. But as had been the case in the Southern Plains War, the weather—blazing summer heat and drought followed by the onset of an early Plains winter—and the army's relentless pursuit took a greater toll. Even as the exhausted commands of Buell, Mackenzie, and Price returned to winter quarters, small parties of once-defiant Native Americans sur-

rendered. Following a brief respite, Miles launched another month-long sortie in January. He turned up nothing, but the stream of surrendering Indians grew to a torrent that spring, with even the determined Kwahadie Comanche, led by QUANAH PARKER, coming in April and June.

The Red River War broke the organized resistance of the Comanche, Kiowa, and Southern Cheyenne, who would never again challenge the military supremacy of the federal government. Although pitched battles were infrequent, the long chases had worn down morale among the tribes. In the end, life on government reservations seemed preferable to alternatives that apparently promised only the continual hardships of the marches necessary to escape the army.

Red Shoes (Shulush Homa, Shulush Humma)
(ca. 1700–1748) *Choctaw war chief*

Red Shoes's homeland was in what is now Jasper County, Mississippi. In the early 1700s Red Shoes became a ally of the French, who were trading partners of the CHOCTAW Nation. Together, they fought against the CHICKASAW, who were allies of the British. In 1734, after one of his wives was raped by a Frenchman, Red Shoes switched sides and led a band of Choctaw that advocated trade with the British and peace with the Chickasaw. The Choctaw were divided, however, and in 1748, a civil war broke out between the pro-British and pro-French factions. After suffering heavy losses, the two sides agreed to negotiate but refused to include Red Shoes in their council, blaming him for the conflict. He was thus removed from the council. Shortly afterward, while returning from a trading trip with the British, Red Shoes was assassinated by a band of pro-French Choctaw warriors.

Red Sticks *militant faction of the Creek heavily involved in the Creek War (1813–14)*

Following the WAR OF 1812 (1812–14), the CREEK Indians of Georgia, Tennessee, and the Mississippi territory were embroiled in intratribal war. On the one side were the Lower Creek, or White Sticks, who endorsed cooperation with the non-Indian population. The Red Sticks, or Upper Creeks were committed to driving the non-Indians off of their land.

Various Red Stick war leaders led successful attacks against their non-Indian enemies. During the War of 1812, Little Warrior of the Red Sticks participated in the battle known as RAISIN RIVER Massacre (1813). He also raided down the Ohio River on his way home. Later, Red Sticks under the leadership of Peter McQueen attacked a party of settlers at Burnt Corn Creek, Alabama. On August 30, 1813, 1,000 Red Sticks led by William Weatherford (RED EAGLE) attacked FORT MIMS on the lower Alabama River, killing more than 400 settlers.

Retaliation against the Red Sticks was swift and efficient. Major General ANDREW JACKSON, commanding a force of Tennessee militiamen, Cherokee, and White Sticks set out in pursuit. In November 1813, an advanced detachment under

Colonel John Coffee (including Davy Crockett) ambushed and killed 186 Red Sticks. Later that month, another 290 lives were taken. In January of the next year Jackson and General William Claiborne pursued Red Eagle, burning Red Stick towns as they went. On March 27, 1814, Jackson engaged a Red Stick position at HORSESHOE BEND on the Tallapoosa, killing 750 of the 900 defenders. This effectively ended Red Stick resistance. Red Eagle surrendered a few days later.

The Creek were forced to sign the FORT JACKSON TREATY in August of 1814. In this treaty, nearly 23 million acres of land was taken from both the Red Sticks and the peaceful White Sticks. As a consequence of this action, many Creek settled among the Seminole in Florida and participated in the First SEMINOLE WAR (1816–18).

Further Reading

Axelrod, Alan. *Chronicle of the Indian Wars: From Colonial Times to Wounded Knee.* New York: Prentice Hall, 1993.

Waldman, Carl. *Atlas of the North American Indian,* rev. ed. New York: Facts On File, 2000.

Remolino (1873) *attack on Mexican Kickapoo by the U.S. 4th Cavalry*

After a surprise attack by Texans on the KICKAPOO at DOVE CREEK (1865), the Indians initiated retaliatory raids in Texas. Raids by 30 to 50 young warriors on fast mounts lasted from three to four days. The Kickapoo warriors slipped into Texas at night and struck with rapid precision, carrying away horses, cattle, and other transportable booty. Armed with hatchets, KNIVES, guns, and BOWS, they killed many men and took children and women as captives.

The BUREAU OF INDIAN AFFAIRS (BIA) and the WAR DEPARTMENT agreed that the way to halt the Indian raids was to return the Kickapoo to a reservation in Indian Territory. The departments did not agree on the method of accomplishing the task, however. An 1871 attempt by the BIA to negotiate a Kickapoo return to Indian Territory failed. The bureau initiated a second attempt in April 1873. At the same time, General PHILIP HENRY SHERIDAN, Colonel RANALD S. MACKENZIE, and Secretary of War William Belknap were secretly planning a military action against Kickapoo villages in Mexico. Sheridan gave Mackenzie complete control over the action, authorizing "a campaign of annihilation, obliteration and complete destruction…"

The Kickapoo were respected as able fighters. An attack on them required careful preparation. Mackenzie's 4th Cavalry bivouacked near Bracketville, Texas, honed their skills through intense drills and simulated attacks over a period of several weeks. To diminish the chances of detection, army scouts charted a route to the suspected Kickapoo campsites over less-traveled mule and cattle trails. Black SEMINOLE (mixed-blood former slaves) living near the Kickapoo in Mexico were recruited as spies.

On the evening of May 16, word arrived from the Seminole that Kickapoo warriors had ridden west out of their village at dawn. Mackenzie hastened to seize the opportunity of surprise attack on this and nearby Lipan and Mescalero APACHE villages, which were also undefended, which lay near a stream called the Remolino. At dusk on May 17, Mackenzie's six platoons, totaling 360 regulars, 24 Seminole scouts, and 14 civilians, forded the Rio Grande near El Moral and snaked their way over rugged terrain toward the Kickapoo villages. On May 18, the cavalry arrived at the Remolino, dismounted, drank their fill from the stream, and watered their horses. The villages lay visible in the yellow twilight just a mile beyond the stream. Soldiers checked horses, equipment, and weapons, and then mounted up. The high banks of the Remolino provided cover for the 4th Cavalry's steady advance toward the sleeping villages. At the attack order, muffled hoofbeats burst into a thunderous rumble from front to rear of the formation. Each platoon in turn rode the length of the three villages, delivered a barrage of fire, turned sharply right, fell back to the rear, reloaded, and repeated the attack. The women, children, and old men in the villages, taken completely by surprise, fought with whatever crude weapons were at hand. Some sought protection in ravines and thickets or behind rocks. The lead platoon of the cavalry pursued the fleeing Indians. They killed those who resisted and captured others, while some escaped. Soldiers burned 180 lodges, leaving only scorched earth and ashes as evidence of the once prosperous villages. Mackenzie reported 19 Indians killed; one soldier had been killed and two wounded in the unequal melée.

Fearing retaliation, Mackenzie took 40 women and children captive and hastily returned to Texas, covering 140 miles in just over 40 hours. The captives rested briefly at San Antonio before they were escorted to Fort Gibson in northeast Indian Territory. These captives were later used by BIA negotiators to persuade 317 additional Kickapoo to accept reservation life in Indian Territory. Although the victory was substantial, it was only partial. The remaining Mexican Kickapoo warriors continued raids into Texas, on a smaller scale, until about 1885. The battle marked the first time after the Civil War that the U.S. Army had crossed the international border with Mexico—an illegal act—to exact punishment on hostile Indians.

Riel, Louis David (Louis Riel, David Riel, Louis Riel, Jr.) (1844–1885) *Métis leader of Riel's Rebellions*

Louis David Riel was the son of Louis Riel, Sr., a man of mixed Ojibway (see CHIPPEWA), French, and Scottish ancestry. The Riels defended Indians and MÉTIS—persons of mixed ancestry—against the incursions of British-dominated institutions, such as the Hudson's Bay Company, and attempts by the new Canadian confederation to strip them of their traditional land rights in Manitoba and Saskatchewan. In 1849 the senior Riel went to the defense of a fellow Métis, Guillaume Sayer, who was accused by the Hudson's Bay Company of smuggling furs across the border to sell in the United States. Riel and a party of 300 armed Métis entered the courthouse in Fort Garry, Manitoba (present-day Winnipeg) and secured Sayer's release (see

COURTHOUSE REBELLION, 1849). His son continued the tradition of protecting the rights of Métis through his role in RIEL'S REBELLIONS (1869–70, 1884–85).

Louis David Riel was born at St. Boniface along the Red River in Canada in 1844. His parents wanted him to enter the Catholic clergy, so he was educated by nuns at St. Boniface and won a scholarship to a seminary school in Montreal when he was 13. Riel left the seminary without taking vows in 1865 and returned home to the Red River settlement. After his return, he quickly became embroiled in the controversy over the Métis land and status in the new Dominion of Canada. Settlers with little respect for Métis Catholicism and land rights were pouring into the Red River territory. Riel formed the Comité National des Métis to maintain the rights of the original inhabitants of the land. In October 1869, he led a group of 16 Métis to drive Canadian government surveyors out of Métis territory. The resistance, known as the First Riel Rebellion, helped bring the Canadian government to negotiations.

Riel's determination to maintain Métis rights of land, language, and religion led to his being elected president of the new territory of Manitoba. However, trouble broke out when a Protestant settler named Thomas Scott was arrested, accused of plotting against Riel's government, tried by a jury of seven Métis, and executed. Riel, who was a witness for the prosecution, was held responsible by the Canadian public and government for Scott's death. Although the Manitoba Act of 1870 acknowledged the Métis's rights, it did not offer Riel immunity for his role in Scott's death or in the rebellion. In August 1870, the Canadian government sent a constabulary force of 1,200 men, many of whom were angry at Scott's death, after Riel, who sought refuge in the United States. Although his Métis supporters elected him to the Canadian parliament twice, it refused to seat him and denied him the right to return to Canada.

Riel was finally pardoned by the Canadian government in 1875, on the condition that he remain in exile until 1880. Instead, he returned to Canada in 1876 and was confined in mental hospitals in Quebec for two years. Upon his release in 1878, he again sought refuge in the United States, eventually becoming a teacher at a Jesuit mission school in Montana. In June 1884, the Métis contacted Riel there, asking for his assistance. Many of them, driven from their lands in Manitoba by settlers from the east, had settled on the plains of Saskatchewan. They wanted Riel to help them organize their new government. Riel agreed, stipulating that violence was to be avoided.

The Canadian government ignored Riel's Provisional Government of the Saskatchewan; Riel authorized an escalation of hostilities in return. On March 26, 1885, Métis horsemen drove a band of Mounties from their position at Duck Lake, Saskatchewan. The Métis were joined by local CREE Indians, who also stood to lose from governmental inaction. On March 28, Cree Chief Poundmaker struck at Battleford, while Chief Big Bear and his party sacked the town of Frog Lake on April 2. The Métis and their Cree allies were outnumbered and outgunned. After a four-day fight in early May 1885, the main body of Métis surrendered to Canadian government troops. Riel was arrested three days later, and sentenced to death in August 1885 for his role in the death of Thomas Scott and for various crimes against the state. He was hanged at Winnipeg on November 16th.

Further Reading

Charlebois, Peter. *The Life of Louis Riel,* rev. ed. Toronto: New Canada Pubs, 1975.

Flanagan, Thomas. *Louis David Riel: Prophet of the New World.* Toronto: University of Toronto Press, 1979.

Friesen, John M. *The Riel/Real Story.* Nepean, Ontario: Borealis Press, 1994.

Hathorn, Ramon. *Images of Louis Riel in Canadian Culture.* Lewiston, N.Y.: Edwin Mellen Press, 1992.

Riel's Rebellions (First Riel Rebellion, Second Riel Rebellion, Métis Rebellions, Red River Rebellion, North-West Rebellion) (1869–1870, 1884–1885)

violent social protests by Native Americans and persons of mixed blood in Canada, led by Louis Riel, Jr.

By the mid-19th century, the fur trade in Canada and the western United States had dropped considerably from its peak in the 17th and early 18th centuries. The Canadians still engaging in the trade were descendants of the original French traders—*coureurs de bois,* or *voyageurs*—living in what is now Manitoba and Saskatchewan, who had intermarried with women of the local Indian tribes. These people were known by the term *MÉTIS.* Most of them were of French, Scottish, and CREE or other Indian ancestry, and they had evolved an original lifestyle of their own, mixing elements of their European and Indian heritages—for instance, speaking both French and ALGONQUIAN languages and practicing Catholicism as well as Indian beliefs.

While the Canadian government left the Métis to follow their own ways, they lived peaceably, farming for part of the year from European-style frame houses and hunting and trapping for the rest from Native American tipis. During the 1840s, however, the Hudson's Bay Company, which had maintained a monopoly on the fur trade in western Canada for many years, began to pass regulations that threatened the Métis way of life. In particular, they increased restrictions on trade with the United States, eliminating one of the Métis most essential markets. The company also restricted industrial expansion, fearing that it would encourage settlement and reduce profits in the fur trade.

Louis Riel, Sr., was a Métis of French-Ojibway ancestry who was frustrated by the company's restrictions. He had tried to found his own woolen factory, even going so far as to dig a nine-mile ditch to provide water for his mill wheel, but he had been stopped by corporate regulations. In 1849, when the company accused another Métis, Guillaume Sayer, of smuggling his furs across the border to sell in St. Paul, Minnesota, Riel protested. Armed and accompanied by 300 of his fellow Métis, Riel broke into the courtroom in Fort Garry (now Winnipeg) and demanded justice for Sayer. This became known as the

COURTHOUSE REBELLION (1849), and it set a pattern for the Riel rebellions led by Louis's son.

The first of LOUIS DAVID RIEL's rebellions came in the aftermath of the 1867 union of Canada. In 1869 the Hudson's Bay Company sold its interest in western Canada to the new Dominion of Canada. As a result, thousands of settlers began pouring into territory that had been Métis land for many years. Conflicts over land rights arose between the Catholic Métis and the Canada Firsters—mostly Protestants from Northern Ireland who were anti-Catholic, anti-French, and anti-Indian. The Canadian national government sponsored a survey of land in Manitoba and Saskatchewan and instructed the surveyors to divide the territory into squares of 800 acres each, in line with British practices. The Métis, however, measured their property differently. They followed the French practice of dividing their land into long strips that included riverfront, woodlands, and prairie in a single holding. In October 1869 Louis David Riel found the surveyors on Métis property and drove them away.

Despite efforts by the provisional territorial governor, William McDougall, to establish order, Riel's rebellion spread quickly. Riel organized a political action party called the Comité National des Métis, created a border patrol of 40 men,

and captured Fort Garry with a force of 400 without bloodshed. Riel then quickly moved to establish Métis grievances in his "List of Rights," setting forth their desire to keep their lands, their language, and their religion, and their wish to participate in the local, provincial, and federal Canadian governments. By the end of the year, Riel had driven McDougall out of the territory, the Canadian government had sent in a negotiator, and the Comité National des Métis had formed a provincial government. In February 1870 Riel was elected president of the new province.

By this time Riel and his associates felt confident enough in their power to release some of the Canada Firsters they had imprisoned when the rebellion first broke out. One of the former prisoners, a man called Thomas Scott, launched an expedition to relieve Fort Garry, but his conspiracy was discovered and he was arrested again by the Métis. Scott was accused of treason, tried by a jury of Métis, and executed. When the Canadian government passed the Manitoba Act in summer 1870, making the area a province, they addressed the grievances expressed in the "List of Rights," but they also refused to grant clemency for the people directly involved in Scott's death. Riel was forced to flee to exile in the United States.

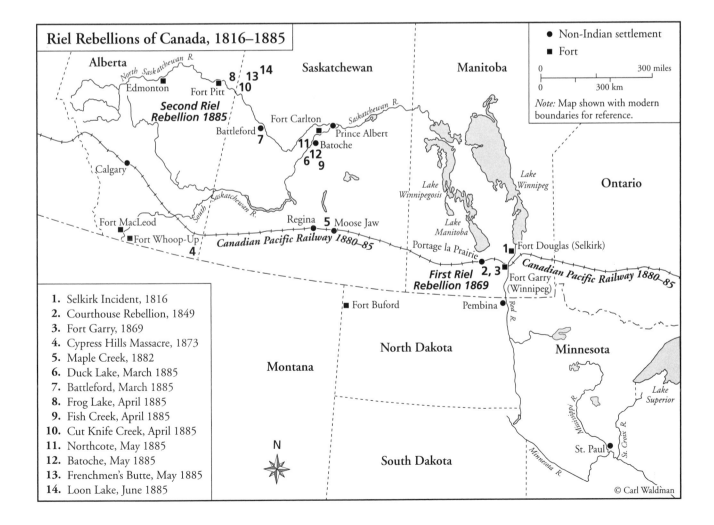

Riel Rebellions of Canada, 1816–1885

● Non-Indian settlement
■ Fort

0 _____ 300 miles
0 _____ 300 km

Note: Map shown with modern boundaries for reference.

Alberta · Saskatchewan · Manitoba · Ontario

North Saskatchewan R.
Edmonton
Fort Pitt
Second Riel Rebellion 1885
Fort Carlton
Saskatchewan R.
Battleford
Prince Albert
Batoche
Calgary

8 13 14
10
7
11 12
6 9

Lake Winnipegosis
Lake Winnipeg
Lake Manitoba

Fort MacLeod
South Saskatchewan R.
Regina 5 Moose Jaw
Fort Whoop-Up
Canadian Pacific Railway 1880–85
Portage la Prairie
Fort Douglas (Selkirk)
1
2, 3
First Riel Rebellion 1869
Fort Garry (Winnipeg)
Canadian Pacific Railway 1880–85

4

Fort Buford
Pembina
Red R.

North Dakota
Minnesota

Montana

N

South Dakota

St. Paul
Mississippi R.
St. Croix R.
Minnesota R.
Lake Superior

1. Selkirk Incident, 1816
2. Courthouse Rebellion, 1849
3. Fort Garry, 1869
4. Cypress Hills Massacre, 1873
5. Maple Creek, 1882
6. Duck Lake, March 1885
7. Battleford, March 1885
8. Frog Lake, April 1885
9. Fish Creek, April 1885
10. Cut Knife Creek, April 1885
11. Northcote, May 1885
12. Batoche, May 1885
13. Frenchmen's Butte, May 1885
14. Loon Lake, June 1885

© Carl Waldman

The province of Manitoba voted Riel into Parliament twice between 1870 and 1875, but the government refused to allow him to take his seat. Riel was eventually pardoned, and he returned to Canada in 1876, upon which he entered a mental institution in Quebec. Later he returned to the United States, became a citizen, and took a position teaching children in a Catholic school in Montana.

Despite the Canadian government's promises, new settlers pouring into Manitoba refused to respect Métis land rights. As a result, many Métis removed westward to the Saskatchewan River. By the early 1880s, the situation was repeating itself: the Canadian government promoted westward expansion through its sponsorship of the Canadian Pacific Railway, and the Métis were crowded out of their lands by settlers who had no respect for their traditions or rights. In summer 1884, Métis leaders located Riel in Montana and asked him to return to Canada to help them in their struggle to maintain their rights. Riel agreed, with the stipulation that the Métis were to avoid violence.

Although the Second Riel Rebellion began peaceably, feelings quickly changed when the Canadian government ignored the Métis demands. By spring 1885 the Métis, with their Cree allies under chiefs Poundmaker and Big Bear, fought the Mounties in battles at Duck Lake, Battleford, and Frog Lake. The government responded by using the new railroad to move 8,000 troops to Saskatchewan. After several indecisive skirmishes, government troops pinned the Métis down at Batoche on May 9th. After four days, the Métis surrendered, having lost 46 fighters. Government losses were 8 dead, and 46 wounded. Riel himself soon surrendered and was sent to Regina for trial.

In summer 1885 Riel was tried on the old charge of murder in the death of Thomas Scott, as well as for crimes against the Canadian government. Despite support from French Catholic Canadians, Riel was found guilty and condemned to death. He was executed on November 16, 1885. His Cree associates were given prison sentences or also executed. Riel's death marked the end of Métis power in the Canadian west and widened the gap between French Canadians, Native Americans, and Canadians of British ancestry.

Further Reading

Flanagan, Thomas. *Louis David Riel: Prophet of the New World.* Toronto: University of Toronto Press, 1979.

McDougal, J. *In the Days of the Red River Rebellion.* Edited by S. Jackel. Edmonton, Canada: University of Alberta Press, 1983.

Walsh, Frederick G. *The Trial of Louis Riel.* Fargo: North Dakota Institute for Regional Studies, 1965.

Rogers, Robert (1731–1795) *British officer and mercenary and the leader of Rogers's Rangers*

A New Hampshire frontiersman, Robert Rogers fought with distinction under WILLIAM JOHNSON at Crown Point, New York, in 1755. In March of the following year, the young captain was appointed to organize and lead what would become one of the most talked-about regiments of the SEVEN YEARS' WAR (1754–63)—Rogers's Rangers. The 600 buckskin-clad frontiersmen of Rogers's Rangers were hardy individualists who fought Indian style, relying on natural cover and fighting from behind trees and bushes. If outnumbered, the Rangers drifted off in different directions to confuse pursuers, then reassembled at a predetermined rendezvous. Mobile and self-sufficient, each man carried a flintlock musket and 60 rounds, a heavy hatchet, and a supply of dried meat and biscuits. Excellent scouts and woodsmen, they were the eyes and ears of British forces in the wilderness of upstate New York and the Canadian border.

Rogers and his men saw action against the French and their Indian allies in New York at Ticonderoga in 1758 and then at Crown Point in 1759. In October 1759 they attacked the town of St. Francis, on the St. Lawrence River, which was home to a group of Christian Indians who had been harassing settlers along the Canadian border. The town was destroyed in a dawn raid that killed some 200; only one Jesuit missionary and a handful of women and children survived. The Rangers took part in the final campaign at Montreal in 1760 and then went as far west as DETROIT to accept the surrender of French posts around Lake Erie. With the French on the verge of total defeat in Canada, Rogers formed an independent company to fight the CHEROKEE in South Carolina.

Promoted to the rank of major after just two years with the regiment, Rogers himself was a colorful character who sometimes took risks that were more spectacular than rational. He was also respected by his Indian foes; his name is immortalized in Rogers's Rock on Lake George, a precipitous promontory down which he escaped from Indian pursuers after the disastrous battle of Snowshoes in March 1758.

After the war, Rogers embarked on an even more checkered career. He went to London, where he enjoyed some success as a memoirist and playwright, but he also piled up enormous debts and was imprisoned. After a brief stint as a mercenary captain for the bey (ruler) of Algiers, he returned to America at the outbreak of the AMERICAN REVOLUTION (1775–81). Offering his services to the highest bidder, he organized a company of Loyalists known as the Queen's American Rangers. Rogers returned to England in 1780, where he died in poverty on May 18, 1795.

Rogue River War (1855–1856) *engagements between the U.S. Army and Indians in southern Oregon*

Non-Indians living along the Rogue River in southern Oregon referred to two local tribes, the Takelma and the Tututni, as Rogue Indians because of their reputation for treacherous acts against travelers. Captain Andrew Jackson Smith, who commanded a troop of dragoons at nearby Fort Lane, had orders to keep the Rogue Indians at bay and to protect peaceful Indians in the area. In October 1855 rumors of war were rampant, and Smith encouraged a group of friendly tribes to move into Fort Lane. Before they did do so, however, members of a local volunteer group fired on them, killing 23 women and children. The following day, young warriors seeking revenge attacked a group of Rogue River settlers, thinking they were responsible for the previous day's massacre. After the fray was over, the attacking warriors realized their mistake, but 27 people had already been killed.

This incident contributed to a public outcry for the complete destruction of all Oregon Indians. Volunteers combed the region, rarely attempting to distinguish between hostile and friendly tribes. General JOHN ELLIS WOOL, commander of the Department of the Pacific, ordered regular reinforcements to be sent into the Rogue River valley in the spring of 1856. In the meantime, the Rogue River Indians attacked Smith's force of 80 soldiers at BIG MEADOW (1856) on the Rogue River. Two Indian women had warned Smith of the coming attack, which was planned by Rogue chiefs Old John, Limpy, and George. Despite the advance warning, when the attack came on May 27, Smith found himself in a desperate situation facing a superior force. When there seemed to be no hope of help, Captain Christopher C. Augur arrived with a company of regulars, and the tide of the battle was reversed. The Indians fled in panic, taking their dead and wounded with them. Army losses totaled 11 killed and 20 wounded.

One month after their defeat at Big Meadow, the dispirited Rogue Indians surrendered. Old John, the most obstinate Rogue chief, was incarcerated at the military prison at Fort Alcatraz in San Francisco Bay. The remainder of the tribe was sent to an area near Fort Hoskins, where they nearly starved during the next several months.

Roman Nose, a Cheyenne chief, played an important role in the Indian wars on the Great Plains in the 1860s. *(By permission of the Colorado Historical Society)*

Roman Nose (Sautie Woquini) (1830–1868)
Cheyenne war leader during the Plains Wars
Roman Nose was a leading figure in the CHEYENNE Himoi-yoqis, or Crooked Lance warrior society. The young warriors of the society had great respect for him. Following the massacre at SAND CREEK (1864), one group of Cheyenne, including Roman Nose, moved to the Powder River area to seek refuge with the Lakota (see SIOUX). He fought with Oglala Lakota chief RED CLOUD in the battle of PLATTE BRIDGE (1865) and also participated in the War for the BOZEMAN TRAIL (see RED CLOUD'S WAR, 1866–68). In 1866 Roman Nose and about 1,000 Cheyenne returned to Kansas, where they soon learned of the LITTLE ARKANSAS RIVER TREATIES (1865). Unlike BLACK KETTLE and the other peace chiefs, Roman Nose and his group would never have agreed to land cessions, nor could they ignore the Sand Creek massacre. Instead, they remained in Kansas and attacked settlers and traders who came into their domain. Despite the pleas of the area's Indian agent, Roman Nose refused to leave.

In hopes of crushing this resistance, General WINFIELD SCOTT HANCOCK and 1,400 soldiers moved into Kansas in 1867 to intimidate the Cheyenne. Before Hancock arrived, the Indians learned of his approach and abandoned the village. Believing that Hancock intended another "Sand Creek," Roman Nose and his followers immediately attacked and stopped all overland traffic in western Kansas (wagon trains and railroad work parties).

President Andrew Johnson sent a peace commission to Medicine Lodge Creek in Kansas to persuade the Plains tribes to voluntarily remove to a reservation in Indian Territory (present-day Oklahoma). The commission also promised those who signed the agreement weapons and ammunition, with which they could hunt buffalo. In October some of the Cheyenne, including Black Kettle, signed the MEDICINE LODGE TREATIES (1867). Roman Nose, however, rejected the proposed treaty and, instead, rode with his followers into central Kansas.

An increasing number of young warriors left the camp and traveled to the area occupied by Roman Nose. Upon receiving large shipments of ammunition and weapons in August 1868, a party of 200 Cheyenne, a few ARAPAHO, and some Lakota attacked settlers on the Saline and Solomon Rivers in Kansas. General WILLIAM TECUMSEH SHERMAN then ordered the soldiers to bring all Indians to their new reservations. The SOUTHERN PLAINS WAR (1868–69) soon erupted. Roman Nose was killed during one of the resulting pitched battles, at BEECHER'S ISLAND (1868).

Rosebud Creek (1876) *battle between U.S. troops and Lakota and Northern Cheyenne during the Sioux Wars*
Following a failed offensive against the Plains Indians during the winter of 1875–76, General PHILIP HENRY SHERIDAN organized another campaign for the late spring. From the east, General ALFRED TERRY led a column that included General

GEORGE ARMSTRONG CUSTER and his 7th Cavalry. Colonel JOHN GIBBON approached from the west, and General GEORGE CROOK marched out of Fort Fetterman. The three groups joined at the Yellowstone River in Montana, close to the very Indians they were seeking.

Unknown to the soldiers, an unusually large number of Lakota (see SIOUX) and Northern CHEYENNE Indians had gathered together for the summer hunt. In early June many participated in a ceremonial SUN DANCE at Montana's Rosebud Creek. There, SITTING BULL told his followers of his vision, in which he saw many soldiers killed as they entered his camp. Upon learning of the approaching regulars, warriors in the huge Indian encampment eagerly sought an encounter.

On the morning of June 17, Crook, with 1,000 men, stopped to rest at the head of the Rosebud. The army's CROW and SHOSHONE scouts provided Crook with just enough warning to organize a defense against the Lakota and Cheyenne attack. His regulars seized the high ground commanding the river valley, giving Crook the confidence to divert Captain Anson Mills and a squadron of the 3rd Cavalry in a strike against the encampment of CRAZY HORSE. This move, however, nearly allowed the Indians to divide Crook's command. Only when Mills broke off his planned mission and threatened the rear of the Lakota and Cheyenne forces did the latter break off the action.

In one of the hardest-fought battles of the government's wars against the Indians, the six-hour battle of Rosebud Creek left Crook's command dazed. Though he held the field, his regulars had seemed confused by the terrain as well as the fighting ability of the enemy. Observers noted that without the tenacity of his Indian scouts, Crook's line might have collapsed. His official reports admitted only 10 killed and 21 wounded, but other accounts suggest the government's losses as three times that number. Lakota and Cheyenne losses totalled about 100.

The battle of Rosebud Creek clearly demonstrated the willingness of the Indians to contest the army's campaigns that summer. Moreover, Crook soon retreated back to his supply camp, thus exposing the other army columns to the full fury of the combined Indian encampment. Nine days later, the Indians would secure one of their most famous triumphs at the Battle of the LITTLE BIGHORN (1876).

Ross, John (Tsan-usdi, Little John; Cooweescoowe, "the egret or swan") (1790–1866) *Cherokee statesman*

John Ross was born in Georgia in 1790 to a Scottish father and mixed Scottish/CHEROKEE mother. He was educated by white tutors at home and later at an academy in Kingston, Tennessee.

During the CREEK WAR (1813–14), Ross served in the pro-American Cherokee Regiment and became known for leading a diversion that helped ANDREW JACKSON win the day at the battle of HORSESHOE BEND (1813). Ross is best remembered, however, as a statesman. He helped found the Cherokee Nation in 1827. When President Jackson signed the INDIAN REMOVAL

John Ross, a Cherokee, was the principal founder of a constitutional government for his tribe. *(Courtesy New York Public Library)*

ACT three years later, Ross vehemently opposed the relocation and refused to sign the NEW ECHOTA TREATY (1835). Eventually, however, settlers in the state of Georgia had their way, and Ross sorrowfully organized the trek known as the TRAIL OF TEARS to Indian Territory (now Oklahoma).

Once there, John Ross helped write the constitution for the United Cherokees and was elected principal chief in 1839. At the outbreak of the CIVIL WAR (1861–65), Ross sought neutrality. Within a year, he encouraged the Cherokee to join the Confederacy, although he eventually led a pro-Union faction. After the war, he tried to convince the government that not all Cherokee had been disloyal to the Union. He died in 1866 while on a trip to Washington to make that point.

Rubí, marqués de (Cayetano María Pignatelli Rubí Corbera y Saint Climent, barón de Llinas) (ca. 1725–unknown) *Spanish official commissioned to inspect military posts in northern New Spain*

As a result of the FRENCH AND INDIAN WAR (1754–63), Spain acquired Louisiana from France and greatly expanded its empire in North America. In 1765 the Spanish government commissioned the marqués de Rubí to tour military posts along the northern border of New Spain, report on the state of frontier defense, and propose any reforms he thought were necessary. Between 1776 and 1778, Rubí traveled 7,000 miles and visited 23 military posts, from Texas to Sonora. Rubí noted that outposts in Texas were continuously attacked by the APACHE and that settlements were too scattered for proper defense. In his final report, issued in 1772, Rubí proposed that Spain abandon all but two outposts in Texas and that the government should establish a line of presidios, or forts, along its northern border for better defense.

Rubí also proposed a new policy toward Native Americans in Texas. He suggested friendly relations with northern tribes, such as the COMANCHE and the WICHITA, but called for all-out war against the eastern Apache, who were living much closer to Spanish settlements, having been pushed farther south when the Comanche came into Texas from the north. Spain accepted Rubí's proposals and set up new regulations for most of their outposts.

Ruddell's Station (Ruddle's Station) (1780) *battle between a force of Indians, British troops, and Canadian frontiersmen and the American militia and army during the American Revolution*

Ruddell's Station was a small settlement in what is now Kentucky, along the South Licking River near present-day Lexington. In June 1780 British Captain Henry Byrd assembled a force of 1,200 LENNI LENAPE (now Delaware), HURON, Wyandot, OTTAWA, Mingo, MIAMI, British regular soldiers, and Canadian frontiersman for a large raid against American settlements in Kentucky. On June 22, after being joined by SHAWNEE warriors as well as SIMON GIRTY and his brothers James and George, Captain Byrd attacked Ruddell's Station. Byrd had brought artillery with him into the wilderness and began a bombardment that soon convinced John Ruddell, founder of the settlement, to surrender along with most of the inhabitants.

Byrd promised Ruddell that the settlers would not be harmed, but he was unable to rein in his allies. When the settlers opened the gates of the stockade, the Indians broke in and massacred the inhabitants. Two hundred men, women, and children died in the assault. Byrd strongly protested the deaths and managed to keep his allies from killing the 100 settlers taken prisoner at Martin's Station a few days later. Shaken by the actions of his Indian allies, Byrd ended his campaign after the capture of Martin's Station.

In response to Byrd's raid, GEORGE ROGERS CLARK assembled about 1,000 militia near the mouth of the Licking River, intending to attack the raiders when they crossed the Ohio River on their way back north. Byrd, the British, and the Canadians avoided Clark, but the Indians were finally forced to make a stand against him at Piqua Town in what is now Ohio. Clark suffered 27 casualties but inflicted three times that many on the Indians. As a result of this success, he was commissioned a brigadier general and sent on a campaign that would eventually bring him to DETROIT.

Running Eagle (ca. 1800s) *the most famous female warrior of the Blackfoot Confederacy*

Running Eagle, a Piegan Indian, sought a way to avenge her husband's death at the hands of the CROW (Absaroka). In her prayers it was revealed to her that as long as she remained celibate, she would have great power as a warrior. From that day forward Running Eagle became a successful and highly respected war leader. During raids and battles, she wore men's leggings, a modified loin cloth, and a woman's dress. Reportedly, her spiritual medicine was so strong that what she dreamed or sang usually came true.

Weasel Tail, a Blood Indian, recalled the stories told to him by White Grass, a band chief among the Piegan, who were members of the BLACKFOOT CONFEDERACY. According to White Grass, on one expedition Running Eagle sent scouts ahead because she had dreamed of meeting NEZ PERCE warriors. A few days later, although the scouts had found no enemy signs, they encountered a Nez Perce camp in the Yellowstone River bottom. Taking her war medicine—two feathers joined to a flat brass disk—from her pouch and tying it in her hair, Running Eagle sang her war song and dug a foxhole a little in advance of the rest of her men. She shot the first Nez Perce warrior who charged and killed many more thereafter. Inspired by her courage, the Piegan repulsed the Nez Perce attack, and Running Eagle led home a successful war party.

Running Eagle was also an excellent raider. During one war expedition, after sighting a FLATHEAD hunting party, she reported a dream in which horses were given to her. She was confident that those horses would be found in the Flathead camp. Claiming that she was not good with a rope, she went into the camp to capture her horses while the men caught as many as they could outside the camp. Once inside, she cut loose five of the best ponies she could find and led them out of the camp. Upon their return home, she gave her horses to relatives.

Running Eagle died in 1860 in an ambush laid by the Flathead. After the Flathead learned that a woman had been the leader of the many raids against them, they began posting night guards with instructions to stop any strange woman in their camp. The next time Running Eagle walked into the camp, she was detained by the guard. Unable to speak the Flathead tongue, she was shot as she backed away.

Rush Spring (1858) *attack by U.S. Army regulars and their Indian auxiliaries from the Brazos River Agency of Texas against Comanche followers of Buffalo Hump*

After years of inconclusive skirmishing in northern Texas and the Indian Territory (present-day Oklahoma), in September 1858, a column of more than 200 cavalrymen and about half as many Indian auxiliaries left Fort Belknap, Texas. Led by Captain EARL VAN DORN, the expedition moved across the Red River into Indian Territory. Along the banks of Rush Spring, they found a large encampment of Comanche, led by BUFFALO HUMP. Just after sunrise on October 1, Van Dorn's force thundered into the sleeping village. The cavalrymen and their allies routed the inhabitants, leaving 58 Indians (including two women) dead on the field. Some 300 horses were captured and 100 tipis burned with the inhabitants' possessions inside. Government losses totalled fewer than 20 but included Van Dorn, who was wounded by arrows in his stomach and wrist.

Only later did the army find that the entire episode had been a tragic mistake. Buffalo Hump had been negotiating with army officers at Fort Arbuckle in Indian Territory and had assumed that he and his followers were safe from army attack. Unfortunately, this information had not been communicated to the Department of Texas, from which Van Dorn's expedition had come. Determined to respond to the unprovoked attack, Buffalo Hump launched a series of raids into Texas during the rest of the year. The following spring, Van Dorn and Texas-based troops launched another offensive, which culminated in the battle of CROOKED CREEK (1859).

Russians, resistance against *Native American resistance against the Russians involving three major groups—the Aleut of the Aleutian Islands; the Tlingit of the present-day Alaska panhandle; and the Pomo of California*
Following Vitus Bering's exploration of 1741, Russian fur traders pushed rapidly east into the Aleutians, the Alaska mainland, and down the Pacific Coast to California. Almost inevitably, the Russians exploited any Indian peoples they encountered. Combining superior FIREARMS with demonstrations of violence and hostage-taking, Russian traders forced the Aleut, Tlingit, and Pomo to do most of the actual work in obtaining furs. Russian treatment of the Indians was often brutal, especially in the early years.

The Aleut frequently offered a spirited resistance. In 1762, for example, the Indians managed to destroy a fleet of five small Russian ships. But in 1766 Russian trader Ivan Solovief organized a powerful expedition, replete with cannon and armed mercenaries. Solovief's fleet soon overwhelmed the organized Aleut opposition. Permanent Russian settlements were subsequently established in the Kodiak Islands, and a monopoly over the Alaskan fur trade was granted in 1799 to the Russian American Company.

To the east the Tlingit, often equipped with British and American firearms, proved much more intractable. In 1802 the Tlingit captured the Russian post at NEW ARCHANGEL on Sitka Island, which would not be recovered for two years. Further concerted Tlingit assaults against Sitka came in 1806, 1809, and 1813. Five years later, Russia even sent a warship to help subdue the Tlingit but they continued their resistance until 1867, when Russia sold Alaska to the United States.

To stake their southernmost claims to the lucrative Pacific fur markets, the Russians established Fort Ross in 1812 in present-California. The Pomo Indians also resisted Russian encroachments, although less effectively than the Aleut and Tlingit. They were subjected to execution, torture, and enslavement, until the Russians abandoned their California outposts in the 1840s.

Ryswick, Treaty of See KINGS WILLIAM'S WAR.

Sac (Sauk Osa' kiwug "people of the yellow earth") *Indian tribe that migrated from the Michigan peninsula to the Fox River area of present-day Wisconsin*

The name "Saginaw" (as in Saginaw, Michigan) is an ALGON-QUIAN word meaning "the place or home of the Sac." The Sac (also known as Sauk) were principally farmers but spent fall and winter hunting BUFFALO on the western tallgrass prairies. Consequently, they are known both as "woodland" and "prairie" Algonquians. Sac bark-covered houses, sometimes 60 feet long, accommodated several families. The Sac entertained themselves with dances, singing, gambling, sleight of hand, and magic tricks.

The Sac are closely related to the KICKAPOO and the FOX (Mesquakie). In 1734, the Sac and Fox formed a permanent alliance. Thereafter, they shared parallel histories while maintaining separate identities. Their geographic location on the Fox River placed them in a position to inhibit French fur trade from Green Bay to the Mississippi. As a result, the French and the CHIPPEWA drove the Sac, Fox, and Kickapoo south into Illinois. In 1769 the Sac displaced the Illinois Confederacy Indians in present-day Illinois.

After the British withdrew from the United States following the AMERICAN REVOLUTION (1775–81), settlers increasingly invaded Sac territory, thus causing an escalation of conflicts between Indians and non-Indians. In 1804, WILLIAM HENRY HAR-RISON, governor of the newly created Indiana Territory, obtained the cession of all Sac and Fox territory on the Mississippi, apparently after supplying copious amounts of alcohol to the chiefs. Sac Chief BLACK HAWK insisted on Harrison's duplicity—which Harrison never refuted. The agreement stood, but the Sac and Fox did not immediately leave their homes. Instead, they launched a long period of resistance. In 1829, Sac Chief Keokuk led a large group of Sac and Fox across the Mississippi to Iowa and remained there.

As a result of Harrison's trickery, the Sac joined with TECUMSEH during TECUMSEH'S REBELLION (1809–11) and with the British during the WAR OF 1812 (1812–14). In 1831 ANDREW JACKSON's administration ordered that ceded Sac land be sold and Black Hawk's band permanently removed west to join Chief Keokuk's Sauk. Angry about the loss of the Sac homeland and the recent murder of several Fox chiefs, Black Hawk began an armed resistance that became known as the BLACK HAWK WAR (1831–32). After Black Hawk's surrender, his band joined the Iowa Sac. In 1867 the Kansas land was relinquished to the United States in exchange for a reservation in Indian Territory (Oklahoma). The Oklahoma reservation later was relinquished to the United States, and in 1890 the Sac accepted 160-acre individual allotments. The surplus land (385,000 acres) was then opened for settlement.

Presently, the tribe members live at three different locations. The combined Sac and Fox tribe has tribal territory in Kansas and Nebraska and in Oklahoma. The group in Iowa are mainly descendants of the Fox and use the name Mesquakie.

St. Clair, Arthur (1726–1810) *U.S. politician and military leader*

Born in Scotland, Arthur St. Clair joined the British army in 1757 and fought in America in the FRENCH AND INDIAN WAR (1754–63). He left the army in 1762 and settled in Pennsylvania, where he played an important role in keeping the colony neutral during LORD DUNMORE'S WAR (1773–74).

Arthur St. Clair was serving as governor of the Old Northwest Territory (the region south and west of the Great Lakes) when, in 1791, he was appointed major general commanding the still very small U.S. Army. St. Clair's immediate task was to pacify the Indian tribes of the Old Northwest Territory. The British, not reconciled to many provisions of the treaty that had ended the AMERICAN REVOLUTION (1775–81), were both arming the tribes and provoking them to attack American settlers.

In November 1791, St. Clair personally led a force from Fort Washington (now Cincinnati) into present-day Indiana. George Washington had warned him to beware of ambush. Nevertheless, on November 4, 1791, St. Clair's forces, encamped along the Wabash river, were attacked and routed by a large Indian force under the MIAMI Chief LITTLE TURTLE and SHAWNEE leader BLUE JACKET (see also LITTLE TURTLE'S WAR, ST. CLAIR'S DEFEAT). St. Clair was replaced as army commander and forced to resign his commission as major general as a result of the defeat, although he stayed on as governor.

St. Clair's Defeat (1791) *battle between U.S. troops and Miami warriors*

Following the AMERICAN REVOLUTION (1775–81), large numbers of settlers began flooding the Old Northwest Territory, an area surrendered to America by the British under the terms of the TREATY OF PARIS (1783). Conflict with Native Americans in the region was inevitable, and although some tribes agreed to negotiate with the new government, others, most notably the MIAMI and the POTAWATOMI, refused, preferring war instead. After 12 settler families were killed at Big Bottom on the Ohio River on January 2, 1791, ARTHUR ST. CLAIR was appointed to bring peace to the region. It was a poor choice. St. Clair, a veteran of the revolution and the current governor of the Old Northwest Territory, was more a politician than a soldier.

The summer months of 1791—the best time to mount a campaign—were wasted as St. Clair mustered his army. Not until late September did 2,300 regulars and a large number of militia set out from Cincinnati, following the track of the Ohio River and heading south. The going was difficult. Despite the months spent in preparation, food supplies ran short, the militiamen deserted 50 or 60 at a time, and many men, including St. Clair himself, became ill. By the time the force reached the Wabash River on November 3, only 1,400 soldiers remained. St. Clair's forces made a camp, with his regulars on one side of the creek and the militia on the other.

Early on the morning of November 4, the soldiers were surprised by 1,000 warriors under Miami chief LITTLE TURTLE and SHAWNEE leader BLUE JACKET. The militia panicked and immediately fled across the creek, where the regulars had formed a square around the artillery. Employing the same TACTICS they had learned from the British during the American Revolution to fight the trained armies of the British, the soldiers remained in close order, delivering volleys on command and even making a few bayonet charges. The Native Americans, meanwhile, fought from behind the cover of trees and bushes, dispersing before the soldiers's bayonets, only to resume their positions once the soldiers had reformed ranks.

The battle continued for four hours, and the American soldiers sustained heavy casualties, especially among the officers, who made good targets in their distinctive uniforms. A desperate St. Clair ordered a final bayonet charge, which drove the Indians back long enough for the soldiers to begin their retreat. The militia gained the trail first, tossing away their muskets, backpacks, even their heavy marching boots to make better time. The regulars followed, leaving behind their artillery, wagons, tents, and many of their wounded. Thus unencumbered, survivors fled back to Fort Jefferson on the Ohio. Their retreat took just 10 hours; the 29-mile trek to the Wabash had taken them 10 days. Little Turtle wanted to pursue the retreating army and destroy it, but the men under his command could not be prevented from taking scalps and plundering the Americans' abandoned supply train.

American losses in St. Clair's defeat were 623 soldiers and more than 200 camp followers; 271 were seriously wounded. The Indians lost only 21 and 40 were wounded—making this the most lopsided defeat in the history of the nation's wars against Native Americans.

Had the Miami been able to follow up their victory at the Wabash they might have driven the bulk of the settlers from the Old Northwest Territory, at least temporarily. But such action was not a priority among the warriors. Nevertheless, George Washington, fearing that St. Clair's defeat might incite other tribes to join the Miami, chose to negotiate a peace settlement, which gave the new nation time to organize a more effective force, this one commanded by ANTHONY WAYNE.

See also FALLEN TIMBERS, 1794.

Salish   See FLATHEAD.

Salt Creek Prairie (Salt Creek Massacre) (1871) *incident that gave renewed impetus to the proponents of Grant's Peace Policy*

By 1871, the KIOWA and COMANCHE had been assigned to the Fort Sill Agency in Indian Territory (present-day Oklahoma). The official in charge was Lawrie Tatum, an Iowa Quaker farmer. Tatum encouraged the Indians at the agency to become farmers, but they resisted. Instead they rode in every two weeks to collect rations due them under the MEDICINE LODGE TREATY (1867). The Indians also refused to send their children to the agency school. Moreover, they continued their tradition of raiding settlements in Texas and offering their CAPTIVES for ransom.

In May 1871, the Kiowa, led by SATANTA, BIG TREE, BIG BOW, Eagle Heart, Old Satank, and medicine man Mamanti, went on a raiding expedition into Texas. They rode to an open area known as Salt Creek Prairie, located between Forts Griffin and Richardson. The warriors readied themselves to attack a small wagon train that had only a small army escort, but Mamanti stopped them. He prophesied that a much larger, richer wagon train would be along soon, and he urged them to be patient. Mamanti proved to be correct. Soon, 10 freight wagons came up the road. The warriors attacked, and in the ensuing fight seven wagoners and three Kiowa warriors were killed. The Kiowa plundered and burned the wagons, mutilated the corpses, and stole 41 mules. Ironically, the smaller wagon train spared by the Kiowa carried WILLIAM TECUMSEH SHERMAN, commanding general of the U.S. Army.

Satanta was captured and arrested soon after the Salt Creek Prairie raid. He proudly admitted to the attack on the wagon train, claiming that the Kiowa had not received items from the government that they needed to survive. He and Big Tree were sentenced to death by hanging. Washington officials, however, convinced the Texas judge to commute the sentence to life impris-

onment; they were later pardoned. Superintendent of Indian Affairs Enoch Hoag blamed the Salt Creek Prairie incident on the actions of the soldiers, thus boosting the confidence of proponents of peace policies advocated by President ULYSSES S. GRANT.

Sand Creek (1864) *massacre of Cheyenne Indians by Colorado volunteers*

On November 29, 1864, Chief BLACK KETTLE and his CHEYENNE band had encamped on Sand Creek in eastern Colorado. Black Kettle was a noted Cheyenne peace chief, having

This painting of the Sand Creek Massacre shows fighting between the U.S. troops and the Cheyenne. *(Courtesy New York Public Library)*

spent the last several years trying to convince his people of the necessity of living peacefully with non-Indian settlers. They had encamped at Sand Creek under army instructions, and thought they had army protection. Very few warriors were in the camp.

Colonel JOHN M. CHIVINGTON, a Denver parson, had helped raise the Third Colorado Cavalry. The unit's 100-day enlistment was almost up, and Chivington decided to use them at least once. In response to some Indian raiding, he had previously urged killing all Cheyenne, wherever they were found.

Just before dawn on November 29th, Chivington's soldiers attacked the Cheyenne camp at Sand Creek. When Black Kettle saw the soldiers coming, he raised a white flag and an American flag. The soldiers ignored these signs of peace, cut off the Indian horses, and began firing. Black Kettle urged his people in the camp to remain calm, assuming the attack was either a show of force to capture some raiders or a mistake. It was neither, and it soon became clear it was not even a battle. Soldiers shot everyone they saw—the few warriors that were there and women and children—and mutilated the bodies. Chivington later declared a great victory and was supported by the Colorado press and the governor. The rest of the country was appalled when reports of what happened emerged. However, no legal action was ever taken against Chivington or his men.

The Cheyenne, however, did take action. Black Kettle survived the massacre, and the peace advocates had their influence severely damaged. In response, Cheyenne, Northern ARAPAHO and southern Lakota (see SIOUX) warriors launched a revenge campaign against settlers or soldiers everywhere in their territories, as evidenced in the JULESBURG RAIDS.

San Ildefonso, Treaty of See TREATY OF PARIS.

San Saba (1758) *Comanche attack on a Spanish mission in Texas*

The APACHE, caught between the Spanish and their enemy the COMANCHE, allied with the Spanish for protection in the mid-1700s. Having failed to Christianize a group of Comanche in New Mexico, the Spanish hoped to expand their frontier by converting the Apache to Christianity, but they too refused to give up their own religious beliefs. Nevertheless, the Spanish built them a small presidio, or fort, and a mission on the San Saba River near present-day Menard, Texas, about 100 miles from San Antonio to continue missionary activities. The post commander was DIEGO ORTÍZ PARRILLA, demoted as a result of his mishandling in Arizona of the Pima (see AKIMEL O'OD-HAM) uprising.

In 1758, the Comanche attacked San Saba and killed several people, including two missionaries. Another deadly strike came the following year. In retaliation, Ortíz Parrilla led a major counterattack north to the twin villages of the WICHITA and CADDO located on the Red River, near present-day Ringgold, Texas. Ortíz Parrilla's subsequent defeat at the battle of TAOVOYA (1759) halted Spanish intrusion into Comanche ter-

ritory. The Spanish later abandoned the San Saba mission in a futile attempt to make peace with the Comanche.

Santa Fe (1680) *battle in the Pueblo Rebellion*

From about 1581, when Franciscan friar Fray Agustin Rodriguez led an expedition into PUEBLO INDIAN country, until 1680, the Spanish colony of New Mexico was nominally under the control of the Catholic Church. The Franciscans did not use force to suppress the Indians in the same way that the Spanish civil authorities did, but they nonetheless alienated many of them. The friars ran an ecclesiastical state, prescribing heavy penances for practices that the Indians considered part of their own culture. This denigration, combined with a series of bad harvests during the 1670s, caused much unrest among the Native Americans. By 1673 the Indians were performing forbidden dances and sacrifices to their ancient gods, and several priests were violently killed by their parishioners.

A San Juan medicine man named POPÉ brought matters to a head during the summer of 1680. Popé had been chastised for practicing traditional rituals, which the Spanish considered a sin. He met with tribal leaders in Taos pueblo and organized the popular dissatisfaction into a broad resistance movement. Popé claimed that the ancient gods had caused the poor harvests. The Indians' gods were angry because the Indians had turned to the god of the Spanish, and they would not be pleased until all the Spanish and their god were dead. The medicine man promised a life of plenty for all when the Indians returned to their traditional ways.

Between August 10 and August 13, 1680, the Pueblo and their APACHE allies had isolated or destroyed all the Spanish outposts in New Mexico except Santa Fe, killing 401 settlers and 21 friars (see PUEBLO REBELLION). The Spanish civil authority, a man named Otermín, refused to surrender to the Indians. Popé's forces besieged Santa Fe for six days. Finally, on August 21 Otermín decided that it would be best to break out in force rather than die of thirst within Santa Fe's walls. A desperate assault scattered the besieging Indians, and the Spanish made their way south to safety. Spanish power in New Mexico, which had been in place for almost a century, was temporarily broken.

Santa Fe (1693) *siege in New Mexico following the Pueblo Rebellion*

After San Juan medicine man POPÉ successfully drove the Spanish from New Mexico during the PUEBLO REBELLION (1680), his efforts to retain power caused disaster. Harvests did not improve, as he had promised. Soon civil war broke out, as PUEBLO INDIAN groups raided each other's grain stores. Popé died in 1690. In 1692, the Spanish returned to New Mexico, spurred by reports that the French were moving into the Mississippi valley. Led by Don Diego de Vargas, the Spanish forces (60 soldiers and 100 Indian auxiliaries) entered Santa Fe unopposed on September 14, 1692. Over the next year, de Vargas's forces visited the Pueblo, winning their support for the reestablishment of Spanish authority.

By December 16, 1693, however, the Pueblo had changed their attitude toward the Spanish once again. The Indians suspected that de Vargas intended to execute those responsible for the 1680 revolt, and they refused to admit him, his soldiers, the friars, and the new Spanish colonists—about 800 people—to the city. On December 28, the Spanish laid siege to the town; two days later, the Indians surrendered. The 70 warriors in the town were executed, and 400 women and children were given as slaves to the colonists. Although there were other revolts throughout the end of the 17th century, European authority had been reestablished in New Mexico for good.

Satanta (Set-tainte, White Bear, The Orator of the Plains) (1820–1878) *Kiowa war chief*

The KIOWA, like their allies the COMANCHE, occupied the southern Great Plains and were renowned for their buffalo hunting skills and huge herds of horses, many of which they secured on raids. Satanta was born into this society in 1820.

At an early age Satanta showed great promise as a warrior. As a result the famous fighter Black Horse gave him his shield, which the Indians believed held supernatural protection for its owner. Satanta carried the buffalo-hide shield into battle with him from then on.

By the 1840s Satanta had conducted successful raids into Texas and Mexico. He had also distinguished himself as an orator and become a leader. In time his people found their unrestricted access to the buffalo herds under threat from non-Indians. In 1845 Texas became a state, and soon non-Indian hunters began invading Kiowa buffalo-hunting grounds in Oklahoma and Kansas. Meanwhile, thousands of immigrants heading for California crossed Kiowa territory on the famous Santa Fe Trail. In response, the Comanche and Kiowa, Satanta included, began ambushing wagon trains and attacking the growing number of settlers.

During the 1860s the area between the Arkansas River and the Rio Grande became a battleground. Satanta distinguished himself in frequent raids in Texas and attacks on supply columns traveling the Santa Fe Trail.

Throughout his life, Satanta had a certain flair in dealing with his enemies. In July 1864 he approached Fort Larned, Kansas, and after an argument he shot two arrows into a sentry. He then absconded with the garrison's horse herd to prevent the troopers from pursuing him. A few days later, he sent a note to the post commander complaining that the stolen horses were of an inferior quality. In November of that year, CHRISTOPHER ("KIT") CARSON led 350 troops in a punitive effort against Satanta. Carson's troops were met by about 1,000 Kiowa and Comanche warriors. As the troopers retreated, they heard the bugle call to advance, which led to much confusion. The bugler was Satanta. Three years later, in April 1867, General WINFIELD SCOTT HANCOCK invited various chiefs to Fort Dodge, Kansas, to discuss peace. Satanta attended and made such an

Satanta, a Kiowa warrior and orator, fought to save the Kiowa territory, 1867. *(Courtesy New York Public Library)*

eloquent speech that General Hancock awarded him a U.S. Army major-general's coat, sash, and hat. A few weeks later, Satanta led a raid against Fort Dodge while wearing his new uniform. During the raid, Satanta turned to the soldiers pursuing him, and doffed his army hat in a mock salute.

In October 1867, the U.S. Congress sent a peace commission to negotiate a lasting treaty. The talks began at Medicine Lodge Creek in southern Kansas. About 5,000 Kiowa, Comanche, ARAPAHO, and CHEYENNE were in attendance. Satanta spoke so eloquently that newspaper reporters dubbed him "The Orator of the Plains." The Orator signed the MEDICINE LODGE TREATY (1868).

The treaty proved disastrous for the Kiowa. According to its terms, they were to live on a reservation in Indian Territory (Oklahoma) but would be free to hunt buffalo in their former haunts in Kansas and the Texas Panhandle. But non-Indian hunters killed the buffalo, and the promised provisions were meager. As a result, many Kiowa began raiding off their reservation. In May 1871 Satanta led a raid against a wagon train in Texas, killing seven teamsters at SALT CREEK PRAIRIE (1871). Within a week he defiantly bragged to the reservation agent about his exploits. Satanta, Satank, and Big Tree were arrested. General WILLIAM TECUMSEH SHERMAN ordered them to Texas to stand trial for murder. Satank, preferring death, drew a knife and attacked a guard; he was immediately shot. Satanta and Big

Tree were tried, found guilty, and given life sentences in the Texas State Prison at Huntsville.

Buckling under pressure from Kiowa and eastern humanitarians, officials released the two leaders in October 1873. By this time hide-hunters had butchered tens of thousands of buffalo. The next year Kiowa, Comanche, Cheyenne, and Arapahoe began attacking non-Indians, especially hunters. Satanta, who claimed he took no part in these raids, was arrested for violating his parole and ordered back to prison for life. Four years later, in August 1878, he plunged head first out a second-story hospital window. He died within hours.

Some years earlier, Lieutenant Colonel GEORGE ARMSTRONG CUSTER had paid fitting tribute to his archrival. In his memoirs he wrote, "Satanta is a remarkable man—remarkable for his powers of oratory, his determined warfare against the advances of civilization, and his opposition to the abandonment of his accustomed mode of life, and its exchange for the quiet, unexciting, uneventful life of a reservation Indian."

Further Reading

Custer, George A. *My Life on the Plains: Or Personal Experiences with Indians.* Norman: University of Oklahoma Press, 1986.
Freedman, Russell. *Indian Chiefs.* New York: Holiday House, 1987.
Robinson, Charles M. *Satanta: The Life and Death of a War Chief.* Austin, Tex.: State House Press, 1997.
Worcester, Donald, "Satanta." *American Indian Leaders: Studies in Diversity.* Edited by R. David Edmunds. Lincoln: University of Nebraska Press, 1980.

Sayenqueraghta (Old Smoke, Old King)

(unknown–1786) *Seneca war chief*

Sayenqueraghta was chief of the SENECA, a tribe in the IROQUOIS CONFEDERACY. His main village was Ganundasaga (present-day Geneva, New York) at the northern tip of Lake Seneca in western New York. In his capacity as chief, Sayenqueraghta participated in treaty negotiations at Philadelphia in 1754; at Easton, Pennsylvania, in 1758 (see EASTON TREATY); at Johnson Hall, New York, in 1757; and at Fort Stanwix in 1768 (see FORT STANWIX TREATY). Sayenqueraghta was also an active ally of the British during the FRENCH AND INDIAN WAR (1754–63), participating with Indian agent WILLIAM JOHNSON in the campaign against the French at Fort Niagara in 1758. After Johnson's death, the chief fought alongside Johnson's adopted MOHAWK nephew JOSEPH BRANT in the AMERICAN REVOLUTION (1775–81), participating in the battle of ORISKANY CREEK (1777), in raids on the Susquehanna valley in New York and Pennsylvania in 1778, and at the battle of NEWTOWN (1779). After the war he retreated with Brant to Canada, where he died in 1786.

scalping *act of removing the skin and hair from the top of an enemy's head with a knife*

There were two basic methods of scalping. By one, a circular pattern about the size of a hand was incised around the back of the head where the hair radiates from the crown. That portion of the victim's hair and scalp was then lifted. By the other method, the incision started at the forehead and continued back along the top of the head, including the crown.

Though neither universal among nor exclusive to North American Indians, scalping became generally associated with Indians during the colonial and frontier periods in America. Scalping was not necessarily fatal. A survivor, however, was disgraced for having lost his scalp to an enemy. The shame was especially acute among those Indian tribes who believed the scalp held the living spirit of the individual. Some southeastern tribes who held this belief left scalps outside their villages at night because of their fear of the spirits. Other tribes celebrated a scalping with a victory or scalp dance, which sometimes lasted for as many as 15 nights. After the victory dance the celebrants used the scalps to decorate war tunics, leggings, war clubs (see CLUB, WAR), horse's bridles, LANCES, SPEARs and shields. Scalps were proof of a warrior's prowess in battle and gained him acclaim within warrior ranks. MANDAN warriors hung scalp locks from poles in front of their dwellings as status symbols and proclamations of valor against the enemy.

The origin of scalping in North America, which cannot be pinpointed to any particular tribe or time period, continues to receive attention and provoke controversy. In 1820, SENECA chief CORNPLANTER accused the British and the French of having invented scalping during the FRENCH AND INDIAN WAR (1754–63) because both the British and the French paid bounties for the scalps of their enemies, whether white or Indian. A similar accusation echoed in 1879, when Susette La Flesche, an Omaha Indian campaigning for Indian rights, protested the killing of UTE Indian men, women, and children. When a reporter accused the Indians of being more barbarous in war than non-Indians and of committing atrocities on CAPTIVES and the bodies of the dead, La Flesche responded by saying that whites had taught Indians how to scalp. Contemporary Indian activist and author Vine Deloria has also blamed the English for the introduction of scalping. He based his opinion on a scalp bounty law enacted in Massachusetts in 1755.

Ethnohistorian James Axtell has countered these accusations by citing archaeological evidence of pre-Columbian Indian skulls whose surfaces were scratched in a manner consistent with scalping. Axtell argues further that scalping terms and words associated with scalping are found in many Indian languages, pointing to a long history or familiarity with the practice. He also cites the writings of Jacques Cartier, HERNANDO DE SOTO, and other early explorers, all of which recount observations of scalping among tribes along the Atlantic Coast of North America. Axtell believes that such evidence proves that scalping was practiced by Indians in the pre-Columbian period.

Although it appears likely that scalping was not of European origin, settlers quickly institutionalized it by practicing it themselves and sanctioning scalp bounties. French fishermen in Newfoundland in the late 1500s encouraged the ABENAKI to kill Beothuk Indians by offering bounties. In 1637, the Connecticut colony paid their MOHEGAN allies for PEQUOT scalps. During the DUTCH-INDIAN WAR (1624–64), the colonists of New Amsterdam paid wampum for the scalps of Raritan Indians. During KING PHILIP'S WAR (1675–76), Rhode Island offered the NARRAGANSETT a bounty of "one coat" for each enemy Indian scalp. In 1688 the French offered Indians a bounty on British scalps, and the British responded in kind.

Scalping took on a certain acceptability when Christian clergy became involved. Chaplain Jonathan Frye was with a Massachusetts militia in 1724 when they killed 10 Indians and returned to Boston to collect bounties on the scalps. Scalping expeditions were profitable and often were financed by businessmen and clergy. In the late 1700s, it was not uncommon to see frontiersmen or Indians walking along the streets of New York, Boston, Albany, or other towns with a bundle of scalps for redemption. One could also view scalps displayed on the walls of the courthouse of Salem, Massachusetts.

Thus, by the end of the 1700s scalping had become a tradition among both Indians and non-Indians. The tradition was carried forward by both sides throughout the Indian wars of the 1800s but finally ended with the close of the PLAINS WARS in 1890.

Further Reading

Axtell, James. *The European and the Indian.* New York: Oxford University Press, 1981.

Catlin, George. *Letters and Notes on the North American Indians.* Edited by Michael M. Mooney. New York: Gramercy Books, 1975.

Utley, Robert M., and Wilcomb E. Washburn. *The Indian Wars.* New York: Barnes & Noble, 1992.

Wright, Ronald. *Stolen Continents.* New York: Houghton Mifflin, 1992.

Scarfaced Charley (Chíkchikam-Lupalkuelátko, "wagon scarface") (ca. 1837–1896) *Modoc chief during Modoc War*

The details of Scarfaced Charley's birth are sketchy. According to one report he was a Rogue River Takelma Indian who joined MODOC leader CAPTAIN JACK when he was 22 years old. Others maintain that he was, in fact, a Modoc and a relative of Captain Jack. What is generally known is that in his childhood Charley was run over or otherwise struck by a wagon, causing the boy to be disfigured. From then on, he was called "wagon scarface" by Indians and Scarfaced Charley by the non-Indians.

Scarfaced Charley had the distinction of firing the first shot in the MODOC WAR of 1872–73. During the war he was the principal military strategist for the Indians, but he also became admired for his compassion. Reportedly, Scarfaced Charley protested the killing of Pastor Thomas and General EDWARD R. S. CANBY by Captain Jack and other Modoc leaders during peace negotiations at the LAVA BEDS.

On April 26, 1873, Scarfaced Charley and 22 warriors ambushed a reconnoitering patrol of 66 soldiers and a dozen Indian scouts who had paused for lunch in a bowl-like depression. After killing 25 and wounding another 16 of Captain Evan Thomas's command, Scarfaced Charley invited his enemies who were still alive to return home before they were all killed. He then allowed them to retreat.

At the close of the Modoc War, Scarfaced Charley surrendered with his people. He and about 150 others were taken to Wyoming, Nebraska, and eventually Oklahoma. By 1874 he was allowed to tour the cities along the East Coast, where he became something of a celebrity.

Schurz, Carl (1829–1906) *U.S. secretary of the interior*

Carl Schurz was born in Prussia in 1829. After participating in the democratic revolutionary movement that swept Europe in 1848, Schurz was forced to flee his homeland. He came to the United States in 1852. Schurz, an ardent antislavery Republican, campaigned strongly for Abraham Lincoln in 1860 and served in the U.S. Army during the CIVIL WAR (1861–65).

In 1876, Schurz became secretary of the interior under President Rutherford B. Hayes, supervising the BUREAU OF INDIAN AFFAIRS (BIA). He opposed many military measures against the Indians, including the plan to transfer the BIA to the Department of War. Schurz favored fairer policies toward the Indians, particularly the need to keep absolute faith with the tribes in treaties and other agreements. He helped arrange a peaceful settlement of the UTE WAR (1879).

Originally in favor of concentrating Indians on reservations, Schurz later defended tribal lands against non-Indian incursions. He eventually supported Allotment, the policy of dividing the land into plots for individual Indian families. Schurz also supported a program of educating Indians to become part of mainstream American society, with the goal of ultimately breaking up the tribes.

Scott, Winfield (Old Fuss and Feathers) (1786–1866) *U.S. Army officer and commanding general of the army from 1841 to 1861*

Winfield Scott saw his first action against Native Americans in the WAR OF 1812 (1812–14), when he faced the British and their allies at Chippewa Creek and Lundy's Lane. Twenty years later, President ANDREW JACKSON gave him command of army troops involved in the BLACK HAWK WAR (1832) in Wisconsin. Scott himself saw no action in the war because of an outbreak of cholera among his troops, but when Black Hawk surrendered he was remanded into General Scott's custody. Scott remained in Wisconsin to negotiate treaties with the SAC and FOX (Mesquakie), in which the tribes agreed to surrender lands in what is now Iowa in return for trade goods. Scott was also given command of army forces moving against the SEMINOLE Indians in Florida during the Second SEMINOLE WAR (1835–42) but left the post without ever fighting a battle because of arguments with his staff.

Two years later, in his role as commander of the Department of the East, Scott supervised one of the most infamous

U.S. actions against any Native American tribe. At the insistence of President Jackson, he directed the expulsion of the CHEROKEE from their own lands in North Carolina, Tennessee, and Georgia. In 1838 and 1839, Scott's soldiers escorted almost the entire Cherokee nation on two separate trips 800 miles westward to the Mississippi and to reservations in Indian Territory. The soldiers drove the Indians at a killing pace, not even allowing them time to stop and bury their dead. Known as the TRAIL OF TEARS, this forced march resulted in the deaths of nearly 4,000 Cherokee, almost a quarter of the entire Cherokee Nation.

Scott also played a significant role in the Mexican War (1846–48), in which he led the amphibious invasion of Veracruz and later captured Mexico City. Quarrelsome and confrontational, Scott became embroiled in petty disputes with many of his superiors during the course of his career. He was nominated for president in 1852 and remained in command of the army until his retirement in 1861.

scouts *Native Americans and non-Indians who acted as guides for the U.S. Army*
Because of their knowledge of the West, former fur trappers and buffalo hunters such as CHRISTOPHER ("KIT") CARSON and WILLIAM F. (BUFFALO BILL) CODY were eagerly sought by the U.S. Army as scouts. Equally valuable were the many Indians from allied tribes who served as scouts and guides in the army's campaigns against Western tribes in the latter part of the 19th century. Their knowledge of the landscape and of other tribes served the army well during the various Indian wars of the West. Not only did Indian scouts guide army forces, they often fought alongside the soldiers (see MARICOPA WELLS, 1857).

Indian scouts were recruited from many different tribes, especially those who earlier had been forced onto reservations and who turned to scouting rather than continue fighting. Members of the PAWNEE, OSAGE, CROW, ARIKARA, SEMINOLE, LENNI LENAPE (Delaware), Western APACHE, and MOJAVE all served as army scouts.

Osage scouts guided GEORGE ARMSTRONG CUSTER to the Washita River in 1868, where Custer's cavalry massacred a CHEYENNE band in the battle of the WASHITA (1868). Two Pawnee Indians, Frank and Luther North, led a band of scouts with Colonel RANALD S. MACKENZIE in his attack on the camp of DULL KNIFE (1869). In 1874–75, Lenni Lenape and Seminole scouts guided Colonel NELSON A. MILES, Mackenzie, and other army officers against the COMANCHE, KIOWA, and Cheyenne in the Indian uprising known as the RED RIVER WAR (1874–75). Arikara, SHOSHONE, and Crow scouts guided and fought under the commands of Custer, Miles, and General GEORGE CROOK in 1876 and 1877 during the SIOUX WARS (1854–90). One Crow scout, CURLY, who was attached to Custer's 7th Cavalry, observed part of the battle of the LITTLE BIGHORN (1876) and was the first to report on the outcome. Cheyenne and Sioux scouts gave valuable guidance to the army

in the GHOST DANCE uprising of their own people. In the Southwest, Apache, Mohave, and Papago (see TOHONO O'ODHAM) Indians served as Scouts and fought against the Eastern Apache in the army's campaigns to rout GERONIMO in 1881–83 and 1885–86.

Second Riel's Rebellion   See RIEL'S REBELLIONS.

Selkirk Treaty (1817) *treaty between a private trading company and Indians of the Great Lakes region*
Thomas Douglas, a majority stockholder of the powerful Hudson's Bay Company, wanted a foothold in the western Great Lakes region of Canada and established a trading colony at Fort Douglas in the Red River Valley. On June 18, 1817, he concluded a treaty with the CREE and CHIPPEWA of the region, awarding them an annuity, payable in tobacco, for their alliance. The treaty allowed Douglas and the Hudson's Bay Company to develop a local monopoly in the fur trade. After Canada was granted dominion status in 1867, the treaty was renegotiated with the Indians.

Seminole *Indian tribe of the Southeast eventually relocated to Indian Territory (present-day Oklahoma)*
When Spanish explorer HERNANDO DE SOTO arrived in North America in the early 1500s, the Indians who became known as the Seminole lived in an area that included the present-day states of Alabama and Georgia. The Seminole were originally part of the CREEK Confederacy, but by the early 1700s they had broken off from the Lower Creek and relocated in what is now Florida and was then occupied by the Spanish.

In 1763, the British laid claim to Florida. While their contact with the Seminole was friendly for the most part, they incited the Indians against the advancing American settlers. Meanwhile, some escaped black slaves sought and found refuge among the Seminole. General ANDREW JACKSON eventually retaliated, leading his troops to victory over the Indians in the First SEMINOLE WAR (1818–19).

In 1819, the United States laid claim to Florida and pressed the Seminole and other Southeastern Indians to relocate to Indian Territory (now Oklahoma; see INDIAN REMOVAL ACT). Some of the Seminole eventually signed treaties and followed the TRAIL OF TEARS to Oklahoma. There the Seminole, Creek, CHOCTAW, CHICKASAW, and CHEROKEE became known as the Five Civilized Tribes.

Some of the Seminole, however, refused to leave Florida. Led by powerful chief OSCEOLA, the Indians hid in the swamps and conducted a guerrilla war in what became known as the Second SEMINOLE WAR (1835–42). The Third SEMINOLE WAR (1855–58) raged between U.S. forces and the Seminole, led by BILLY BOWLEGS, a decade later. Even after all hostilities had ended, some Seminole refused to relocate and remained in Florida.

Historians record that about 3,000 Seminole, either by choice or by coercion, eventually resettled in Oklahoma. Yet, for every two Seminole who moved, one U.S. soldier died in the wars. Today, the Seminole live on reservations in both Oklahoma and Florida.

Seminole War, First (1816–1818) *first war in the campaign by the U.S. government to remove the Seminole Indians from Florida*

Near the end of the WAR OF 1812 (1812–14), the British established a fort at Prospect Bluff, even though this area was still in Spanish hands. In summer 1815 the British withdrew and the fort was occupied by a band of SEMINOLE Indians and fugitive slaves. Eventually known as "Negro Fort," it posed a threat to the free navigation of the Apalachicola, Flint, and Chattahoochee Rivers, which ran into Florida through Georgia and Alabama. The fort was also a defiant symbol to white slave-owners, who believed the garrison served as a haven for runaway slaves.

In response to this perceived threat, Major General ANDREW JACKSON sent EDMUND P. GAINES to build Fort Scott on the Flint River fork of the Apalachicola River in Georgia in 1816. In July Jackson ordered Lt. Colonel DUNCAN L. CLINCH to take 116 regular and 150 allied CREEK under William McIntosh to attack Negro Fort. The assault troops were to be aided by gunboats under Sailing Master Jarvis Loomis.

Clinch launched the attack on July 27, 1816. One of the gunboat skippers, a man named Bassett, decided to heat a cannonball and fire it into the fort with an extra-heavy powder charge. The cannonball landed in Negro Fort's ammunition storage, resulting in a great explosion. In the end, 300 African Americans, including women and children, lay dead among the ruins of the fort. Thirty Seminole also perished.

When the Seminole Indians heard of the Negro Fort debacle, they became furious. Their anger was heightened when Clinch distributed captured muskets, pistols, and swords to his Creek allies. Rather than confront Clinch immediately, the Seminole vented their anger against settlers in Georgia. Tensions grew even more serious when Seminole Chief Neamathla, living in the village of Fowl Town, sent a message to General Gaines demanding that U.S. troops stay out of his village. Angered by this, Gaines sent 250 troops to attack Fowl Town. During the battle, Chief Neamathla escaped, but the troops killed four warriors and a woman and set the village ablaze. One of the Fowl Town villagers who escaped was Peter McQueen, a leader of the RED STICKS, the war faction of the Creek Nation. In retaliation for the Fowl Town attack, McQueen led an attack against 40 soldiers and a small group of their dependents as they sailed down the river toward Fort Scott.

The government responded swiftly. Andrew Jackson returned to Fort Scott and gathered a force of 800 regulars, 900 Georgia volunteers, and a large number of allied Creek warriors. In March 1818, Jackson's troops rebuilt Negro Fort (renaming it Fort Gadsden) as a base from which to mount an attack against the Seminole. Jackson pushed on toward present-day Tallahassee until he reached Saint Marks, a Spanish post where he believed the Indians were hiding. The Indians had in fact previously sought refuge at Saint Marks but had already fled the area in the face of Jackson's march. On April 7, 1818, Jackson took possession of the fort, even though it was under Spanish sovereignty.

A few days later, Jackson proceeded toward Suwannee Town, 107 miles to the east, searching for important Seminole chief BILLY BOWLEGS. Creek scouts located the chief's camp of 150 Seminole and Red Stick warriors and their dependents in a swamp near the Econofina River. On April 12, Jackson attacked the swamp hideout; the battle raged for three hours. In the aftermath of the fight, 37 warriors lay dead. Six were captured, along with 98 women and children. One of the children was the 14-year-old future leader of the Creek and Seminole, OSCEOLA. McQueen and about 100 warriors managed to escape.

General Jackson was in such a great hurry to get to Suwannee Town that he had no time to keep his PRISONERS. He turned them over to Ann Copinger, McQueen's sister, in exchange for her turning traitor against her brother. After Jackson left, however, Copinger betrayed their agreement and led the prisoners to a Seminole camp at the southern boundary of the Okefenokee Swamp.

Pressing on toward Suwannee Town, Jackson's troops fought several skirmishes. Upon reaching the deserted town, they burned it to the ground and captured two British citizens. Jackson returned to Saint Marks, placed the prisoners on trial, and executed one of them and another man on a charge of aiding and abetting the Indians. Jackson then moved on to capture Spanish Pensacola on May 26, 1818. This act embarrassed the U.S. government, but it prompted the Spanish to leave Florida and cede its territory to the United States.

Jackson soon left Florida, and the First Seminole War came to an end, as a great influx of settlers entered Florida. Many Seminole returned to the inland portion of northern Florida, and others fled south. The Red Sticks, including McQueen, moved to the Tampa Bay area. A few years later, the aging and exhausted McQueen died, although the exact date of his death remains unknown.

Seminole War, Second (1835–1842) *second war between the United States and the Seminole Indians*

After enduring the pressure of a growing influx of non-Indian settlers into Florida for several years and the recent effects of a severe drought, several Seminole leaders agreed to the Treaty of PAYNE'S LANDING (1832). The agreement called for the removal of the tribes from Florida within three years in exchange for money and annuities. Although a delegation of Seminole leaders investigated living arrangements in Indian Territory (present-day Oklahoma), as the time of relocation neared, no actual movement occurred.

Many tribal leaders, notably OSCEOLA, claimed the treaty was illegal. Although Osceola was a friend to the RED STICKS, the war faction of the CREEK, he knew the Seminole did not want to live among the Creek, as the treaty provided. Fugitive slaves also became an issue; they remained loyal to their Seminole owners because they enjoyed freedom among the Indians. Long known among the Seminole for his determined opposition to Removal, Osceola was forced to sign a new agreement with Indian Agent Wiley Thompson and General DUNCAN L. CLINCH acknowledging that Seminole immigration would begin in early 1836.

Despite the negotiations, in April 1835, the army suspended sales of guns and ammunition to the Seminole. Osceola took this as a bitter insult and in June he stormed into Thompson's office and denounced the policy. Thompson had him arrested. The following morning, Osceola apologized and Thompson allowed him his freedom, an act he would later regret. Osceola fled to rejoin his warriors, who began raiding non-Indian settlements. Osceola himself engineered the assassination of Seminole chief Charley Emathla, leader of the pro-Removal faction. He also took vengeance on Thompson, ambushing the agent and a small escort at Fort King. This incident ignited the Second Seminole War.

The Seminole united under Osceola, making him their war chief. He would turn out to be a skilled military leader. His assistant commanders were the warriors Alligator and Jumper. Osceola established communications to coordinate his activities with Micanope (King Philip) leader of the Seminole east of the St. Johns River. After raiding a plantation in Philip's territory, Osceola took his people into hiding in the swamplands near the WITHLACOOCHEE RIVER, southwest of Fort King and the Indian agency.

Osceola proved a formidable opponent to the federal government. As his men raided they also burned bridges, slowing down the movement of troops and artillery. The war chief also made excellent use of reconnaissance, so he was always abreast of the army's movements. On December 18, 1835, in an area west of the town of Micanopy (present-day Gainesville), Osceola led 80 warriors in an ambush of a wagon train. The warriors were busy plundering the wagon when a group of 30 mounted militia happened upon the scene. The troops, commanded by Captain John McLemore, were ordered to attack the Indians, but only a handful obeyed. McLemore's tiny force was quickly defeated in the battle of Black Point, with the loss of eight dead and six wounded.

Osceola used King Philip to raid white plantations in his territory, causing the army to funnel off troops, and thus weakening them. On December 28, 1835, Major Francis L. Dade and 110 troops were ambushed while marching to relieve Fort King; the battle of the GREAT WAHOO SWAMP (1835), as it came to be known, was another decisive Seminole victory.

Osceola now directed his attention to the movements of General Clinch, who was on his way with 750 troops to attack Seminole villages along the Withlacoochee River. Assisted by Alligator, the Seminole war chief prepared an ambush. On December 31, 1835, Osceola and Alligator attacked Clinch's force after it had crossed the river. For unknown reasons,

Clinch had allowed his men to stack their guns and rest. They were thus unprepared when the Indian attack came, and the troops were quickly beaten. Clinch lost four soldiers and another 52 were wounded, but more important, as a result of this attack he cancelled his offensive campaign.

During the seven years of the Second Seminole War, a host of U.S. commanders were sent after the Seminole. Taking full advantage of the terrain, the Seminole's hit-and-run tactics completely baffled the U.S. regulars dispatched to Florida. General Zachary Taylor did manage to defeat warriors under Alligator at the battle of LAKE OKEECHOBEE (1837), but that was the extent of the army's success.

THOMAS SIDNEY JESUP finally succeeded in capturing Osceola on October 21, 1837, but only because his rival was under the protection of a flag of truce. General Jesup had the Seminole leader imprisoned at Fort Moultrie, South Carolina, where he fell ill and died on January 3, 1838.

Osceola was buried with honors at Fort Moultrie, while Alligator and Billy Bowlegs continued the Seminole resistance. Gradually, the army's pursuits and scorched earth tactics, wore down Seminole will to resist. By 1842 about 3,000 Seminole, had agreed to be removed, and the war came to a close. The price paid by the United States to remove the Seminole Indians was high, with 1,500 non-Indian deaths from combat and disease and a monetary cost of $30 million.

Further Reading

Harley, William and Ellen. *Osceola: The Unconquered Indian.* New York: Hawthorn Books, 1973.
Josephy, Alvin M., Jr. *The Patriot Chief: A Chronicle of American Indian Resistance,* rev. ed. New York: Penguin Books, 1994.
McReynolds, Edwin C. *The Seminoles.* Norman: University of Oklahoma Press, 1985.
Prucha, Francis Paul. *Sword of the Republic: The United States Army on the Frontier.* Lincoln: University of Nebraska Press, 1969.

Seminole War, Third (Billy Bowlegs War)

(1855–1858) *final war between the Seminole and the U.S. Army*

Despite sporadic assaults by both Seminole and American citizens between 1849 and 1855, the Third Seminole War did not begin in earnest until December 1855. It was the result of American surveying and scouting parties trespassing on Seminole land. Alarmed by this movement and fearing (with good reason) that the Americans were going to take their land, the Seminole decided to attack trespassers.

Between December 7 and 19, 1855, 10 men under Second Lieutenant George Lucas Hartsuff moved through southwestern Florida, then occupied by Holatter Micco (known as BILLY BOWLEGS), the most important Seminole leader, and his bands. Coming upon uninhabited villages, Hartsuff's men amused themselves by hacking down the Seminole banana plants and destroying other vegetation needed by the people. On the morning of December 20, angry Seminole under Bowlegs and war leader Oscen Tustenuggee attacked. Although they outnumbered the Americans, the Seminole withdrew after killing four soldiers and wounding four others, including Hartsuff. The United States immediately declared war against the Seminole, despite the provocation of Hartsuff's men. The Third Seminole War had begun.

By March 1, 1856, Governor James Broome of Florida had assembled 1,460 federal and state troops to combat an Indian force of about 100 warriors. The troops, however, were badly organized, and military commanders relied upon a defensive rather than an offensive strategy. Instead of going directly after Seminole warriors, the American forces, deployed in small units, concentrated on protecting the frontier roads. Seminole leader Oscen Tustenuggee, noting this strategy, took the offensive. With TACTICS used during the SECOND SEMINOLE WAR (1835–42), warriors ambushed the roads and trails traveled by the troops, fired rapidly into their midst, and then quickly retreated. Throughout 1856, small parties of Seminole warriors also attacked scattered settlements. On June 16, 1856, Oscen Tustenuggee was killed in a skirmish along the Peace River after one such attack. His death seriously disrupted the fighting capability of the Seminole.

The following year, the U.S. government took the offensive, sending scouting parties into the Everglades with orders to capture the Seminole and destroy their camps. From then until December 1858, American troops marched into villages, captured women and children, and killed any man who attempted to defend his home. These methods forced only a small number of Seminole to leave their swamps, and those who did were forced to immigrate to New Orleans. The campaign did, however, hurt the remainder of the villagers because the soldiers destroyed houses, crops in the fields, and food-storage facilities.

In January 1858, a group of Seminole from Arkansas was brought to Florida to convince Billy Bowlegs to surrender. Among them was his niece, who persuaded her uncle to give himself up. With his villages and food stores destroyed, and American surveying crews on his lands, Bowlegs apparently decided that his people could not survive any longer on their traditional territory. In return for immigrating west, he accepted $1,000 for each of four subchiefs, $500 for each warrior, $100 for each woman and child in his band, and $6,500 for himself. A total of 164 people left the swamps, 123 voluntarily and 41 who had been captured. Although medicine man and war chief Arpeika (Sam Jones, who was more than 100 years old) and a few families remained, Billy Bowlegs was the last prominent Seminole chief to leave Florida.

Seneca *northeastern tribe that is part of the Iroquois Confederacy*

Prior to 1570, five Iroquoian tribes in present-day New York—the Seneca, CAYUGA, MOHAWK, ONEIDA, and ONONDAGA—had been engaged in chronic warfare with one another. That changed when a HURON prophet named Deganawida and a Mohawk chief named Hiawatha formed the IROQUOIS CON-FEDERACY, which was designed to promote peace. The confederacy grew stronger when the Dutch introduced guns to the Indians. Soon the Iroquois had etched out an empire that stretched to the Great Lakes.

During the first half of the 1600s, the Seneca were the westernmost tribe in the confederacy. They were also the largest, with an estimated population of about 5,000. Because of their location, they often engaged in warfare with the Huron, who lived in the Great Lakes region. Later, during the FRENCH AND INDIAN WAR (1754–63), the Seneca sided with the victorious British, when they supported again during the AMERICAN REVOLUTION (1775–81). During that conflict, two Seneca chiefs rose to prominence: CORNPLANTER and RED JACKET. By 1799 Cornplanter's half brother, Handsome Lake, had established a new practice, the Longhouse Religion, among the Iroquois; it still has adherents among some Iroquois today. Seventy years later, in 1869, a Seneca known as ELY PARKER became the first American Indian commissioner of the BUREAU OF INDIAN AFFAIRS (BIA).

The Seneca today maintain four reservations in New York state: Tonawanda, Cattarangus, Allegany, and Oil Springs. Others live on the Six Nations Reserve in Ontario and with the Cayuga in Oklahoma.

Seven Years' War (1754–1763) *European conflict known in America as the French and Indian War*

As the Seven Years' War got under way in Europe, its American component, which had begun in the backwoods of Pennsylvania quickly spread until it became a conflict among three great colonial powers: France, Great Britain, and Spain. It became known in North America as the FRENCH AND INDIAN WAR.

The war outside North America had only an indirect effect on Native Americans. In general, the British exchanged the territories they captured from the French and the Spanish in Europe, India, and the Caribbean for French and Spanish territories in North America. The British restored sugar-producing Caribbean islands to the French in return for Canada. The Spanish gave up Florida in exchange for French claims to lands west of the Mississippi River. The result for Native Americans, accustomed for decades to maintaining their positions by playing one European power against another, was that there remained only one European partner and opponent in the East: Great Britain.

Sevier, John (Nolichucky Jack) (1745–1815)

Tennessee frontier militia leader, land speculator, politician

Born in Rockingham County, Virginia, of French Huguenot ancestry, John Sevier helped open the territory of present-day Tennessee to non-Indian settlement in 1772. He later served as captain of the Virginia troops that fought the SHAWNEE under CORNSTALK in LORD DUNMORE'S WAR (1773–74). Sevier successfully fought CHEROKEE Chief DRAGGING CANOE and his warriors, who began raiding non-Indian settlements in

Tennessee at the outbreak of the AMERICAN REVOLUTION (1775–81). In 1780 Sevier and other frontiersmen won the battle of King's Mountain against the British and their Indian allies.

Sevier and Colonel Arthur Campbell, with Virginia and North Carolina militias, campaigned against the Cherokee from 1780 to 1782, resulting in the destruction of a number of CHICKAMAUGA towns. Sevier eventually fought more than 30 battles against the Cherokee and was primarily responsible for their expulsion from Tennessee, North Carolina, and Georgia.

Shawnee *tribe inhabiting portions of southern and eastern Ohio*

The name *Shawnee* means "southerners" in ALGONQUIAN. Traditional Shawnee homelands were in present-day Tennessee, south of ALGONKIN territory. However, they were wanderers who split into several groups and migrated into parts of South Carolina, Georgia, Alabama, and Kentucky. Groups also ranged to the north and east into areas in Pennsylvania, Virginia, and New York. During the 1700s major Shawnee homelands were in river valleys in southern and eastern Ohio.

The Shawnee were farmers, hunters, and fur traders who fiercely resisted non-Indian expansion beyond the Appalachian Mountains. As English colonists pushed westward, the tribe sided with the French against the English in the FRENCH AND INDIAN WAR (1754–63). At the end of the war, the Shawnee also joined the OTTAWA Indians in PONTIAC'S REBELLION (1763–64) against the English along the frontier. When the governor of Virginia gave Shawnee lands west of the Appalachians to veterans of the French and Indian War, the Shawnee again rebelled in LORD DUNMORE'S WAR (1773–74). They were defeated and forced to sign a peace treaty that gave up some of their lands.

The AMERICAN REVOLUTION (1775–83) found the Shawnee on the British side, raiding settlements all along the Ohio frontier. Because of their support of the British, the Shawnee received no compensation after the war. Instead, American settlers poured into the Ohio Valley, prompting renewed resistance. Between 1783 and 1790, raids by a coalition of Shawnee and other tribes killed more than 1,000 settlers. In 1794, an army of 3,500 U.S. troops, led by ANTHONY WAYNE, finally defeated the Shawnee and their allies at the battle of FALLEN TIMBERS (1794).

The Shawnee were then forced into Indiana, where resistance flared again in 1811, when their leader TECUMSEH organized a confederacy of the region's tribes. After Tecumseh's death in the battle of the THAMES (1813), the confederacy broke up. Weakened by constant warfare, the Shawnee themselves began to splinter. Some bands settled in Missouri, and others went as far west as Texas. By the 1830s most were settled in northeastern Kansas. In 1870, the Shawnee in Kansas moved and settled near the CHEROKEE Nation in Indian Territory. However, one group remained behind and presently holds land in Ohio.

Shawnee Prophet See TENSKWATAWA.

Sheepeater War (1879) *conflict between the U.S. Army and a small group of Shoshone and Bannock Indians*

The Indians known as the Sheepeater were a small mixed group of BANNOCK and SHOSHONE who eked out a meager existence in the rugged mountains of Idaho. They normally remained neutral in hostilities between non-Indians and local tribes. However, following the close of the BANNOCK WAR (1878), several Bannock who were considered fugitives by the army took refuge among the Sheepeater.

In May 1879, five Chinese miners were killed by Indians at Loon Creek near the Salmon River. In June General OLIVER O. HOWARD dispatched Captain RUBEN F. BERNARD's 1st Cavalry from Boise and Lieutenant Henry Catley's 2nd Infantry from Camp Howard near Grangeville to search for the Indians. This force of about 100 soldiers was later joined by a 20-man Umatilla Indian scouting party led by Lieutenants Edward S. Farrow and William C. Brown. The terrain they searched proved so rugged that the soldiers lost several pack animals, along with rations and other provisions. Then, on July 29, Lieutenant Catley's men were ambushed by the Sheepeater in Big Creek Canyon. The soldiers retreated and tried to exit the canyon the next day, but the Sheepeater surrounded them at Vinegar Hill and set fires around them. The soldiers set back fires, waited until nightfall, and then slipped out of the canyon. Giving up the fight, they headed back to Camp Howard.

For this action, Catley was relieved of his command, court-martialed, and convicted of misconduct. Captain Albert G. Forse assumed Catley's duties on August 13 and joined forces with Bernard, Farrow, Brown, and the scouts. At Big Creek Canyon, near Vinegar Hill, the Umatilla scouts seized a Sheepeater camp, but the Indians escaped and fled in all directions, leaving no trail. The campaign was resumed on September 16 by the Umatilla scouts under Lieutenants Farrow and Brown. Finally, on October 1 the Sheepeater, weary of being chased, surrendered. The Bannock who initiated the conflict escaped and blended in with their relatives on the Lehmi Reservation.

Confined throughout the winter at Fort Vancouver, Washington, the Sheepeater were released to the Fort Hall Reservation in Idaho the following spring. The Sheepeater's most formidable foe ultimately proved to be the Umatilla Indian scouts, without whose skills the army probably would not have captured them so quickly.

See also SCOUTS.

Sheridan, Philip Henry (1831–1888) *U.S. Army officer during the Plains Wars*

Born in New York and raised in Ohio, Sheridan studied at the West Point Military Academy. After leaving West Point, he was assigned to frontier duty in Texas and then in the Pacific Northwest, where he participated in the YAKAMA WAR (1855–57).

Sheridan rose to prominence during the CIVIL WAR (1861–65), gaining the confidence of General ULYSSES S. GRANT in both the eastern and western theaters. Following the war, Sheridan helped organize reconstruction programs in Louisiana and Texas.

In 1868 Sheridan was transferred to the Department of the Missouri, replacing General WINFIELD SCOTT HANCOCK. Among the officers under his command was the brash and arrogant GEORGE ARMSTRONG CUSTER. Soon after his arrival, Sheridan directed operations against the Southern CHEYENNE, Southern ARAPAHO, Lakota (see SIOUX), KIOWA, and COMANCHE in the SOUTHERN PLAINS WAR (1868–69). It was during this war, at the battle of BEECHER'S ISLAND (1868), that he became convinced that large-scale military campaigns were essential to solve the Indian problem.

In 1869, Sheridan took command of a military region known as the Division of the Missouri, a vast area that included most of the Great Plains. After a brief trip to Europe in 1870, Sheridan returned to the Plains. He directed the campaigns of

Painting of Philip Henry Sheridan, U.S. Army commander, who, along with General Sherman, waged "total war" against the Indians, by Thomas Nast *(Courtesy New York Public Library)*

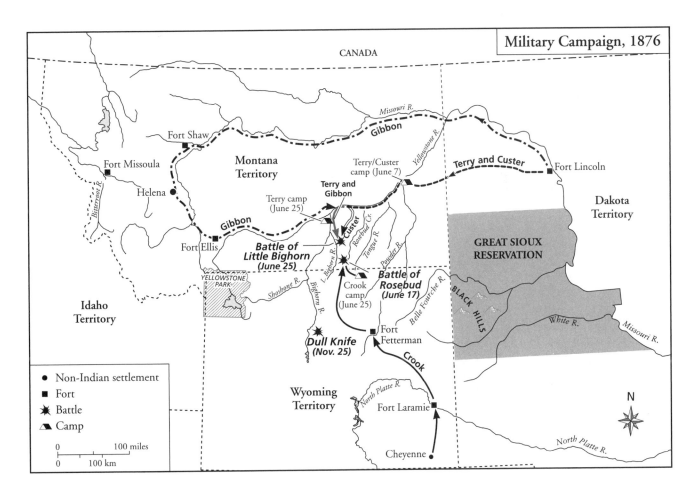

RANALD S. MACKENZIE and NELSON A. MILES against the Comanche, Arapaho, Kiowa, and Cheyenne in the RED RIVER WAR (1874–75). He also directed the campaigns of GEORGE CROOK, ALFRED H. TERRY, and JOHN GIBBON in the War for the Black Hills (see SIOUX WARS, 1854–90).

Sheridan had little sympathy for rebellious Indians. His overall strategy was to wage "all-out" war, attacking not only warriors but entire tribes and destroying Indian villages. He even pursued this strategy in winter, organizing campaigns that trapped Indians in their villages with dwindling food and other supplies.

Sheridan became commanding general of the U.S. Army in 1883, replacing General WILLIAM TECUMSEH SHERMAN. Over the next few years, he directed the last phases of the APACHE WARS (1860–86) against GERONIMO. Sheridan died in 1888 while still in command of the army.

Sherman, William Tecumseh (1820–1894) U.S.
Army general during the Civil War and the Plains Wars
Born in Lancaster, Ohio, and named for the great Shawnee leader TECUMSEH, "Cump" Sherman graduated sixth in his West Point class in 1840. He served as a staff officer during the Mexican War (1846–48), earning a brevet for meritorious service. Sherman resigned from the army in 1853, holding various jobs until he rejoined the miliary at the onset of the CIVIL WAR (1861–65). In 1864, his Union forces captured the key Con-

General William T. Sherman, U.S. Army commander, fought Indians during the second Seminole War and the Plains Indian Wars of the 1860s and 1870s. *(New York Public Library)*

federate city of Atlanta. Proclaiming that "War is hell," Sherman then embarked upon his famous "March to the Sea." His armies cut a wide swath through the heartland of Georgia before turning north into South Carolina. He emerged as one of the Union army's most celebrated leaders.

Appointed lieutenant general in 1866, Sherman took command of the Division of the Missouri. The Civil War hero realized that with a small army and limited supplies, the defeat of hostile Indians would be difficult. The army's greatest ally, as he saw it, was time. He championed the continued expansion of western railroads, concluding that this would not only ease the military's pressing communication and supply problems but also encourage non-Indian settlement. As a member of the Peace Commission, Sherman helped negotiate several treaties—such as the vital MEDICINE LODGE TREATY (1867) and the FORT LARAMIE TREATY (1868)—that had major repercussions for the tribes involved.

After ULYSSES S. GRANT's election as president in 1868, Sherman was appointed commanding general of the U.S. Army. The promotion forced him to leave his beloved St. Louis for the nation's capital, which he detested. His stubborn insistence that the army remain out of politics was admired by some but probably hurt army attempts to secure favorable legislation and additional funding for its activities. Sherman resisted calls from state and local officials and members of Congress for volunteers to fight against the Indians, insisting that such troops were untrained, undisciplined, and unprepared. Instead he maintained that the Indian problem would be dealt with best by the regular army. Similarly, he advocated the transfer of the BUREAU OF INDIAN AFFAIRS from the Department of the Interior to the WAR DEPARTMENT.

Though occasionally expressing some sympathy for the plight of the Native Americans, Sherman believed that the nation's growth was of utmost importance. Thus, he believed that the government should push aside the Indians. "Either the Indians must give way, or we must abandon all west of the Missouri River," he wrote in 1868, "and confess . . . that forty millions of whites are cowed by a few thousand savages." If necessary, he contended, armed force must accompany this process. He thus encouraged subordinates such as PHILIP HENRY SHERIDAN, GEORGE CROOK, GEORGE ARMSTRONG CUSTER, and NELSON A. MILES to help the United States "conquer" the West by defeating any tribes that resisted government demands. Often blunt and sometimes prone to exaggeration, Sherman urged the army to "act with vindictive earnestness against the Sioux, even to their extermination, men, women, and children,"—a statement made after the debacle of the FETTERMAN FIGHT (1866). Though much quoted, such pronouncements suggested a harsher, more ruthless policy than Sherman ever actually sought to implement.

Under Sherman's leadership, Indian military resistance was largely overcome. Following his retirement from the army in 1884, he was besieged by offers to run for political office. His response was typically blunt: "I will not accept if nominated and will not serve if elected." He died in New York City in 1894.

An encampment of Shoshone Indians with war chief's tent in foreground *(By permission of the Colorado Historical Society)*

Further Reading

Marszalek, John F. *Sherman: A Soldier's Passion for Order.* New York: Free Press, 1993.

Shoshone (Newe) *tribe inhabiting the Great Basin west of the Rocky Mountains*

The Shoshone gathered foods, insects, and small game in their traditional mountain homeland. Early in the tribe's history, a split created the two primary divisions: the Western Shoshone and the Northern Shoshone. The Western Shoshone continued to live in the arid region of the Great Basin and remained vir-

tually unaware of European incursion until the 1840s. They never fought a war against the United States.

During the 1840s and 1850s, diminishing game and plant foods resulting from non-Indian migration and settlement brought starvation to the Indians along the western trails. The Shoshone and their neighbors, the PAIUTE, raided settlers' villages in desperate attempts to satisfy their families' hunger and to rid their country of the people they blamed for it. Even after signing the TREATY OF 1863, by which the Shoshone relinquished most of their land and became dependent on the United States, hunger was a daily reality. Yet in spite of the failure of the United States to deliver on its promises, the Western Shoshone lived peacefully with non-Indians who settled on their lands.

The Northern Shoshone, further divided into Northwestern and Eastern Shoshone, established territory from southern Idaho to the Great Salt Lake, across the Rocky Mountains into the Wind River area of Wyoming. Closely allied with BANNOCK and northern PAIUTE, they abandoned food-gathering and sod lodges for buffalo hunting and skin tipis. Nevertheless, by 1857 the once-proud, self-sufficient Northern Shoshone were brought to the verge of starvation, despite promised annuities provided for in the FORT LARAMIE TREATY (1851).

In 1859, WASHAKIE, one of the Shoshone's great chiefs, persistently advocated peace despite the starving condition of his people. In a graphic demonstration of lost confidence, stemming from the government's failure to render payment for relinquished land, Washakie's people "threw him away" as chief and formed an alliance with Chief Pash-e-co, a western Bannock medicine man and prophet.

Regular army troops were engaged in the American CIVIL WAR (1861–65) in March 1862, when Pash-e-co's affiliated warriors began well-orchestrated, simultaneous attacks against travelers and settlers from Bear River in the west to the Platte River in the east (see SHOSHONE WAR). In response, Colonel Patrick E. Connor, leading a California-Nevada militia in an all-out campaign, won a decisive victory several months later at BEAR RIVER (1863). With Indian resistance effectively broken, a series of treaties negotiated on government terms were signed by various tribes and bands over the succeeding eight months.

Restored to chieftainship, Washakie signed a treaty at Fort Bridger in Utah Territory (1868), which facilitated Shoshone settlement on a reservation of their choice in Wind River Valley, Wyoming. Thereafter, the Shoshone contributed to the U.S. campaign against northern Plains tribes—the CHEYENNE, BLACKFOOT CONFEDERACY, and Lakota (see SIOUX)—by acting as military SCOUTS. They fought at the battle of ROSEBUD CREEK (1876) when Brigadier General GEORGE CROOK lost to the Lakota. They also assisted in the defeat of Cheyenne Chief DULL KNIFE at Big Horn Mountain in 1876. Chief Washakie remained on the army payroll until his death in 1900.

The Shoshone currently live on a number of reservations in Nevada, California, Utah, and Idaho.

Shoshone War (1863) conflict between U.S. volunteers and the Shoshone

Between 1860 and 1862, prospectors discovered gold in three locations in Oregon Territory, prompting a gold rush in traditional SHOSHONE lands (in present-day Idaho). Also in 1862, a group of pioneers determined to find a route to the west shorter than the Oregon Trail blazed a new trail through the Shoshone homeland. U.S. authorities did not halt the encroachment of settlers on Indian lands, so the Shoshone, BANNOCK, and PAIUTE took matters into their own hands. That fall they launched a series of attacks along the California and Oregon

Trails, raiding wagon trains, stagecoaches, the overland mails, and telegraph offices and killing prospectors.

Word of the Indian attacks spread, and in response the federal government recruited volunteers to protect the settlers. (The U.S. Army was then focused on winning the CIVIL WAR.) In 1862, Colonel PATRICK E. CONNOR led one such group of 300 men, the 1st California Cavalry, to garrison positions in Utah and Nevada. That year he founded Fort Douglas, near Salt Lake City, from which his troops conducted patrols of Utah, southern Idaho, northern Nevada, and Wyoming.

On January 27, 1863, Connor's volunteers located the camp of Bear Hunter's band, one of the Shoshone bands responsible for raids on Mormon settlers and others. The volunteers flanked the camp, trapping them in a deadly cross fire. When the battle at BEAR RIVER ended, 224 Indians lay dead, including Chief Bear Hunter, while the California Cavalry suffered only 14 dead and 49 wounded. Connor's troops also captured 160 women and children and destroyed a large cache of supplies. Later that spring, Connor established Camp Connor near present-day Soda Springs, Idaho, threatening to inflict similar devastation on other Shoshone groups. By fall, treaties had been made with most of the Utah Indians, although some western Shoshone had fled across the Snake River to join other tribes. With the Shoshone War over, U.S. military forces reopened the telegraph lines and, with minor exceptions, were thereafter successful in protecting settlers in that part of Idaho.

Sibley, Henry (1811–1891) U.S. Army officer during the Minnesota Uprising

Born in Michigan, Henry Hastings Sibley became a manager for the American Fur Company at age 23. In 1849, he was elected a territorial delegate to Congress, but he continued in the fur trade. In treaty negotiations with the Santee Dakota (see SIOUX) in 1851, he represented the traders and succeeded in claiming $145,000 (out of the $475,000 promised the Santee) as overpayments to the Santee for furs. In 1858, Sibley and other traders again entered claims amounting to $266,880 against what the Santee were to receive for selling more land. As a result, the Santee received only $100,000. That same year Sibley became the first governor of Minnesota.

In 1862, Alexander Ramsey, former agent for the Santee, called on Sibley to ride against the Indians, who were now embroiled in the MINNESOTA UPRISING (1862). Sibley, a commissioned colonel in the state militia, led 1,500 men against the Santee in September 1862. In the battle of WOOD LAKE (1862), Sibley succeeded in scattering the Santee and taking some 2,000 captives. Of these, 303 were condemned to death, but President Abraham Lincoln intervened and after consulting the trial records, reduced the number to 38.

The following year, Sibley, now a brigadier general, and General ALFRED SULLY were sent to break up any camps of Santee and Yanktonai found around Devil's Lake. Sibley went up the Minnesota River and across the Dakota prairies to

Devil's Lake. Sibley engaged the Lakota at the battles of DEAD BUFFALO LAKE (1863), Big Mound, and Stony Lake, losing fewer than a dozen men and slaying about 150 warriors. A peace commissioner to the Lakota in 1865 and 1866, he supervised a number of treaty negotiations with the Indians. He retired in 1866 to St. Paul, Minnesota, where he pursued a career in business.

Sieber, Albert (1844–1907) *head scout in the Apache Wars*

Born in Germany in 1844, Albert Sieber moved to Pennsylvania with his family when he was five. During the CIVIL WAR (1861–65), he fought for the Union Army and was twice wounded in the battle of Gettysburg. After the war he moved to Arizona, where he soon became fluent in Spanish and the Athapascan language of the APACHE.

During the APACHE WARS (1860–86), General GEORGE CROOK developed battle TACTICS specific to his foes. He was convinced that to defeat the Apache, the U.S. military had to enlist the help of Apache. Thus, in 1870, Sieber was selected as head of the Apache SCOUTS. They soon distinguished themselves, and in the battle of BIG DRY WASH (1882), Sieber was the hero of the day, for having discovered an enemy ambush. Sieber and the scouts were also credited with repeatedly locating GERONIMO and his followers, who otherwise would have eluded the pursuing armies.

It is reported that Sieber killed more than 50 Indians during his life and that he was wounded 29 times. He died in a rockslide in 1907 while supervising a crew of Apache workers who were building a road.

Sioux (Dakota, Lakota, Nakota) *historic term for related Indian groups ranging from Minnesota to the Black Hills*

The Indians known to history as the Sioux called themselves Lakota, Dakota, and Nakota, meaning allies. Their traditional enemies, the CHIPPEWA, called them Nadoweisiw-eg, meaning "Lesser Adder" (snake). The French shortened the term to Sioux.

During the 1600s and early 1700s, the Sioux occupied the southern two-thirds of Minnesota and adjacent parts of northwestern Wisconsin and northern Iowa. In the 1700s, they began to move out of north-central Minnesota and onto the Plains, eventually reaching the Black Hills of South Dakota. There were two primary reasons for this migration. First, the Chippewa had gained FIREARMS from the French, thus changing the balance of power among Indian tribes in the woodlands of Minnesota. Second, fur hunters had depleted traditional meat supplies.

By the last half of the 1700s, the Sioux had broken into four territorial groups. These, in turn, were subdivided into numerous bands.

The horse appeared in the northern plains about 1750. At the same time, the Teton Lakota began to move into the Black Hills area in what is now western South Dakota, eastern

Branches and Bands	Selected Leaders
Teton Lakota	
Oglala	AMERICAN HORSE, BLACK ELK, CRAZY HORSE, MAN-AFRAID-OF-HIS-HORSES, PAWNEE KILLER, RED CLOUD
Brulé (Sicangu)	Short Bull
Hunkpapa	GALL, SITTING BULL
Miniconjou	BIG FOOT, Hump, Kicking Bear
Oohenonpa	
Itazipco (Sans Arcs)	
Sihasapa	
Santee Dakota	
Sisseton	
Wahpeton	
Wahpekute	INKPADUTA
Mdewakanton	Big Eagle, LITTLE CROW, Mankato, Wabasha
Yankton Nakota	
Yankton	
Yanktonai Nakota	
Yanktonai	
Hunkpatina	
ASSINIBOINE	

Wyoming, and eastern Montana. They soon adapted to a nomadic way of life as they followed the buffalo herds on horseback (see BUFFALO). Consistent with this subsistence strategy, the Indians lived in Portable tipis and produced lightweight yet durable articles for daily living.

The buffalo (*Bison bison*) is the largest North American big game animal. Bulls average 1,400 pounds and stand six feet high at the shoulders. Cows average about half that weight. Experts have conservatively estimated that at one time 60 million buffalo roamed the Plains. With such an abundance of meat, many Indian groups, including the Lakota, became nomadic hunters. Inevitably, different Indian groups collided over territories and hunting grounds, and alliances and conflicts developed. From time to time the Lakota allied themselves with the Northern CHEYENNE and Northern ARAPAHO and were at war with the KIOWA, PAWNEE, CROW, ARIKARA, and others.

Like many of the Plains Indians, the Lakota soon developed MILITARY SOCIETIES, and often personal prestige was based on exploits against the enemy (see COUNTING COUP). The Lakota SUN DANCE was an annual event, and boys went on personal vision quests to find out what spiritual forces would bring them success in war and hunting.

During the last half of the 1800s, non-Indian travelers and miners began traversing Lakota territory in increasing numbers. The Sioux way of life was thus threatened, and the SIOUX WARS (ca. 1850–90) erupted. The Lakota were directly involved in the War for the BOZEMAN TRAIL, which they won under the brilliant leadership of RED CLOUD. In 1874, gold was discovered in the

Black Hills, ushering in the War for the Black Hills and the famous battles at ROSEBUD CREEK (1876) and the LITTLE BIGHORN (1876). Finally, the Indian Wars came to a tragic conclusion for the Lakota at WOUNDED KNEE (1890).

The easternmost Sioux, the Santee or Dakota, adapted to a different way of life. They dwelt along the Minnesota River in the present state of Minnesota. At one time they had lived farther north, near Mille Lacs. In the 1740s, however, they engaged in a series of battles with their enemies, the Chippewa. The Dakota, with their arrows, SPEARS, and CLUBS, were no match for the firearms of their opponents and were driven south. Raiding and warfare between the two Minnesota groups, however, continued for a century.

By the early 1800s, the Dakota had adapted to a different way of life. They gathered nuts, fruits, and berries; fished with spears and hooks; and hunted bear, elk, deer, small game, and buffalo. They were especially fond of *pemmican,* which was dried buffalo meat flavored with cherries or berries. Many of the Dakota spent part of the year in permanent villages, their houses framed with elm wood and covered with elm bark. Throughout the year, families left on gathering or hunting expeditions, during which times they lived in hide-covered tipis.

By the 1830s, more and more non-Indians had pushed into the eastern portion of the Dakota territory. They brought with them corn, plows, and an appetite for the fertile land of the Dakota. In summer 1851, the various bands of the Dakota signed away almost 24,000,000 acres of rich agricultural land in the Treaties of Traverse des Sioux and Mendota. The Indians, numbering about 7,000, relocated to two small reservations about 70 miles long and 20 miles wide, bordering the upper Minnesota River. In 1857, they ceded still more land. Anger,

frustration, and starvation led to Inkpaduta's rampage and eventually to the MINNESOTA UPRISING (1862).

Between the Teton Lakota and the Dakota were the Yankton and Yanktonai. The Yankton Nakota settled along the Missouri River in present-day southeastern South Dakota, southwestern Minnesota, and southwestern Iowa. The Yanktonai Nakota lived along the Missouri River in eastern North and South Dakota. The Nakota are sometimes called the Middle Sioux because of their location. In many ways they drew from the lifestyles of both their western and eastern relatives. In the 1700s they procured horses and hunted buffalo. At the same time, however, they lived in semipermanent villages of grass-covered, domed-shaped houses and raised some crops.

The Nakota were visited by Lewis and Clark in 1804. In 1858, the Yankton ceded much of their land to the United States and moved onto a small reservation. For the most part they refrained from warring with the Euro-Americans until 1862, when some of them joined the Santee in the Minnesota Uprising.

Historians consider the Sioux to have been the consummate hunters and warriors of the Plains. Known for their horsemanship, bravery, and tenacity, they opposed non-Indian encroachment onto their land for nearly four decades (1854–90). The last major engagement between the U.S. government and the Sioux Indians took place near Wounded Knee Creek in what is now South Dakota. With this massacre, the war in the northern plains came to an end.

Many contemporary Sioux live on reservation lands on the northern plains. But many also live in urban areas throughout the United States. In the 1960s, several Sioux men were involved in the creation of the AMERICAN INDIAN MOVEMENT

Indians camped on a reservation. The U.S government established the reservation system as a method of keeping the Indians under the control of the Bureau of Indian Affairs. *(By permission of the Colorado Historical Society)*

This period engraving supposedly represents a Sioux ceremony, billed in the original caption as the "Great Medicine-dance of Endurance." Because little serious Indian ethnography was being done in the 19th century, however, this image—and the ceremony described—may not accurately reflect Sioux practice. *(By permission of the Colorado Historical Society)*

(AIM), a radical organization aimed at protesting the U.S. government's treatment of Native Americans.

Further Reading

Hassrick, Royal B. *The Sioux: Life and Customs of a Warrior Society.* Norman: University of Oklahoma Press, 1988.

Hyde, George E. *Red Cloud's Folk: A History of the Oglala Sioux Indians.* Norman: University of Oklahoma Press, 1975.

Meyer, Roy W. *History of the Santee Sioux: United States Indian Policy on Trial.* Lincoln: University of Nebraska Press, 1993.

Pond, Samuel W. *The Dakota or Sioux in Minnesota as They Were in 1834.* St. Paul: Minnesota Historical Society Press, 1986.

— William B. Kessel

Sioux Uprising   See MINNESOTA UPRISING.

Sioux Wars (1854–1890) *military engagements between the United States and various Dakota, Lakota, and Nakota groups* During the Sioux Wars, which included some of the most celebrated engagements of the entire Plains Indian Wars, strong SIOUX leaders such as RED CLOUD, CRAZY HORSE, and SITTING BULL faced insurmountable odds in attempts to preserve their tra-ditional way of life. Although the MINNESOTA UPRISING (1862) marked the true beginning of the Sioux Wars, other conflicts before that time are also considered part of the overall conflict.

Carl Waldman, in the *Encyclopedia of Native American Tribes,* has chronologically arranged the various phases of the Sioux Wars under five headings: the GRATTAN DEFEAT (1854–55); the Minnesota Uprising and its aftermath (1862–64); the War for the BOZEMAN TRAIL, or RED CLOUD'S WAR (1866–68); the War for the Black Hills (1876–1877); and the tragedy at WOUNDED KNEE (1890).

More than 35 years of war began with a single death, that of a cow. On August 18, 1854, a Brulé Lakota named High Forehead killed a cow. The beast, belonging to a Mormon family that was passing along the North Platte River in Wyoming (see FORT LARAMIE TREATY, 1851), wandered into a Lakota camp. The owner followed but became frightened by the Indians. The next day he falsely reported that the Lakota had stolen his cow. Lieutenant JOHN L. GRATTAN, a recent West Point graduate, led 30 soldiers into the Brulé village. The Indians offered to make restitution, but Grattan wanted to arrest High Forehead. When the officer saw that was not possible, he ordered his men to open fire. The Indians prevailed and killed all but one of the soldiers. In response to the Grattan Defeat, Secretary of War Jefferson Davis ordered General WILLIAM S.

HARNEY to pursue and punish the Brulé. On September 3, Harney led his 600 men in an engagement against the Indian, killing 85, and capturing 70 women and children in the battle of BLUEWATER CREEK (1855). In time the Indians agreed to abide by the terms of the FORT LARAMIE TREATY of 1851, and for a few years there was peace.

Meanwhile, to the east another group of Sioux, known as the Santee or Dakota, were feeling pressure from non-Indian settlers. The latter wanted the rich farmland along the St. Croix, Minnesota, and Mississippi Rivers, where the Indians lived. By means of treaties, the Dakota eventually were removed to two small reservations along the upper Minnesota River. There, beset by hunger and frustration, some warriors attacked and killed five settlers in 1862. Leader LITTLE CROW agreed to lead the Dakota to war, and the Minnesota Uprising began. Within two months, 800 settlers and soldiers and an undetermined number of Indians were dead. On December 26 that year, 38 Dakota warriors were publicly hanged in Mankato for their part in the uprising.

The matter, however, still was not over. Some of the Dakota fled west and settled with the Yanktonai Nakota and Teton Lakota. Generals HENRY SIBLEY and ALFRED SULLY pursued them and engaged them in various battles, including those at WHITESTONE HILL (1863), Big Mound, DEAD BUFFALO LAKE (1863), Stoney Lake, and KILLDEER MOUNTAIN (1863).

The same year the Minnesota Uprising began, an explorer named John Bozeman blazed a trail through Lakota land. It was a direct route for miners to travel as they rushed toward the gold fields in Montana, Colorado, and California. The government sought to establish an agreement with the Lakota whereby travelers would be given free passage along the Bozeman Trail. Knowing that the trail would interrupt herd animals, and fearing that the non-Indians would soon claim their land, Lakota Chiefs Red Cloud, Hump, Sitting Bull, and Spotted Tail and their allies DULL KNIFE of the Northern CHEYENNE and Black Bear of the ARAPAHO refused to sign the agreement and prepared for battle. The result was Red Cloud's War.

The Indians attacked the three forts being garrisoned along the Bozeman Trail by Colonel HENRY B. CARRINGTON. In December 1866, warriors attacked a wood-cutting detail out of Fort Kearny. Captain WILLIAM FETTERMAN and 80 men came to their aid, and they were all killed in the FETTERMAN FIGHT (1866). The next year the Indians went up against the military in the HAYFIELD FIGHT (1867) and WAGON BOX FIGHT (1867). By 1868, U.S. officials were ready to sue for peace. In the Fort Laramie of Treaty 1868, the government agreed to abandon its forts along the Bozeman Trail in exchange for the cessation of hostilities. Red Cloud's war was over. After the soldiers left, the Lakota burned Forts Reno, Phil Kearny, and C. F. SMITH.

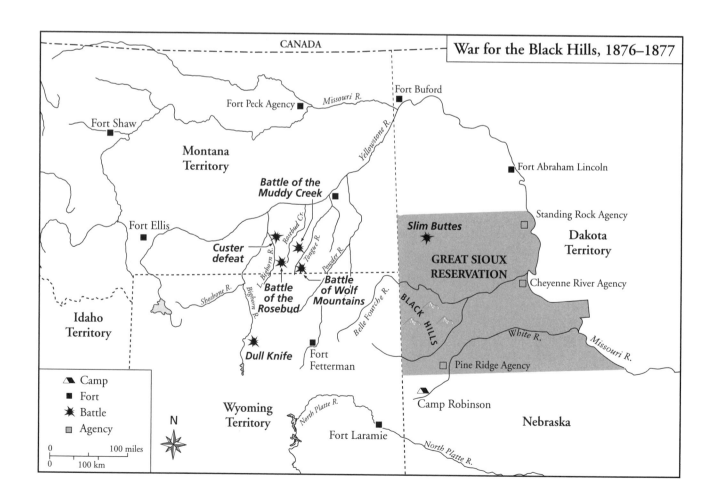

In 1874, gold was discovered in the Black Hills. The Lakota, who had lived there since 1765, were alarmed at the influx of miners. Unable to buy the land from the Indians, the military tried to take possession of the Black Hills by launching preemptive strikes led by General GEORGE CROOK and Lieutenant Colonel GEORGE ARMSTRONG CUSTER. Crook's force was repelled by Crazy Horse at Powder River and in the battle of ROSEBUD CREEK (1876). Scarcely two weeks after the Rosebud fight, on June 25, 1876, Custer's 7th Cavalry met Sitting Bull, Crazy Horse and GALL in the battle of the LITTLE BIGHORN (1876). Custer and his entire command were killed in that battle. Shortly thereafter, the tide of war changed as thousands of army reinforcements poured in. The soldiers soon won the battles of Bonnet Creek, SLIM BUTTES (1876), DULL KNIFE (1876), WOLF MOUNTAINS (1877), and Lame Deer, effectively ending Indian resistance for over a decade.

Finally, on December 29, 1890, Colonel JAMES FORSYTH attacked BIG FOOT's band of Miniconjou Lakota at Wounded Knee in South Dakota. When the attack was over, 150 Lakota men, women, and children lay dead on the frozen ground; 50 were wounded. The remaining Lakota surrendered. Wounded Knee proved to be the last major engagement between government and Indian forces in the northern Plains. The Sioux Wars were over.

Further Reading

Andrist, Ralph K. *The Long Death: The Last Days of the Plains Indian*. New York: Macmillan, 1993.

Axelrod, Alan. *Chronicle of the Indian Wars: From Colonial Times to Wounded Knee*. Englewood Cliffs, N.J.: Prentice Hall, 1993.

Utley, Robert M. *The Last Days of the Sioux Nation*. New Haven, Conn.: Yale University Press, 1972.

Utley, Robert M., and Wilcomb E. Washburn. *Indian Wars*. New York: Houghton Mifflin, 1977.

Sitting Bull (Tatanka Yotanka, Sitting Bull)

(1831–1890) *Lakota war and spiritual leader*

Sitting Bull is, perhaps, one of the most famous American Indians ever. The subject of countless legends, his real life and exploits tell a story of leadership, tenacity, and a determination to maintain a time-honored way of life.

Sitting Bull, a Hunkpapa Lakota (see SIOUX), was born in 1831 near the Grand River, not far from modern Bullhead, South Dakota. As a youth he was called Hunkesni, "Slow," because of his deliberate mannerisms. By age 10, he had killed his first buffalo, and by age 14 he had gained recognition by COUNTING COUP on an enemy CROW Indian. For his bravery his father surrendered his own name to the boy. He was now Tatanka Yotanka, or "Sitting Bull."

By age 22, Sitting Bull had conducted many successful raids against neighboring Indians and became the leader of a warrior society known as the Strong Hearts. In time, he won personal victories over 60 warriors as he led war parties against the ARIKARA, ASSINIBOINE, BLACKFOOT CONFEDERACY, Crow, FLATHEAD, Gros Ventre (Atsina), Hidatsa, MANDAN, Piegan, and SHOSHONE.

By 1862–63, a new enemy had emerged. Following the MINNESOTA UPRISING (1862), General HENRY HASTINGS SIBLEY and ALFRED SULLY pursued the fleeing Dakota into Hunkpapa territory. Sitting Bull retaliated by raiding the soldiers in 1863, orchestrating the battle of KILLDEER MOUNTAIN (1864) and besieging Fort Rice in 1865. When Fort Buford was built in present-day North Dakota in 1866, Sitting Bull stepped up his raids throughout the territory. Meanwhile, Oglala leader RED CLOUD launched attacks along the BOZEMAN TRAIL. In 1868 the government sued for peace.

Sitting Bull refused to sign the Fort Laramie Treaty of 1868, which established the Great Sioux Reservation. He and other nontreaty Indians chose instead to live in the Powder River area off the reservation. Sitting Bull's mistrust of the treaty proved to be well-founded. By 1873, the Northern Pacific Railroad was making plans to lay tracks through the Yellowstone River area. Meanwhile, hundreds of gold miners scattered throughout the Black Hills, which were on the reservation and were sacred to the Lakota. Unable to persuade the Indians to sign a treaty that would hand over the Black Hills, the commissioner of Indian affairs ordered the non-treaty Indians onto the Great Sioux Reservation and out of Powder River country.

Ready to go to war, Sitting Bull summoned Lakota and CHEYENNE warriors from near and far to attend a council at Rosebud Creek, Montana. By June 1876 an estimated 15,000 Indians, including perhaps 4,000 warriors, had massed at the site. Indians recounted that tipis dotted the landscape for three miles along Rosebud Creek and nearly half a mile to the sides. As CRAZY HORSE and the warriors prepared for battle, Sitting Bull, a recognized spiritual leader, participated in the SUN DANCE ceremony. During the three-day event, he had over 50 small pieces of flesh cut from each of his arms, and after collapsing from dancing he had a vision of a great victory over the white soldiers.

On June 17, Sitting Bull's warriors, under the command of Crazy Horse, attacked the advance guard of General GEORGE CROOK's approaching army. The battle of ROSEBUD CREEK (1876) lasted for six hours before both sides withdrew. The Lakota and Cheyenne immediately moved to the Little Bighorn River. There, on June 25, 1876, they attacked Lieutenant Colonel GEORGE ARMSTRONG CUSTER and his 7th Cavalry. Neither Custer nor his men returned from the battle of the LITTLE BIGHORN (1876), in which Sitting Bull did not directly participate. Instead, the chief left the fighting to Crazy Horse and GALL.

"Custer's Last Stand" (as the Little Bighorn battle was known in the popular press) sent shock waves throughout the nation. A virtual flood of soldiers swept onto the Plains, and the Indians found themselves on the defensive. Colonel NELSON A. MILES relentlessly pursued Sitting Bull, but the chief refused to surrender. He fled north into Canada, where he held out for four years. By July 1881, however, Sitting Bull's small band of 187 faced starvation. Reluctantly, he surrendered at Fort Buford, North Dakota. He was held in detention at Fort Randall until 1883. From there he returned to the place of his birth.

Lakota war chief Sitting Bull at age 14 on a horse counting coup is shown in this drawing by his uncle, an artist. *(Courtesy New York Public Library)*

Sitting Bull stood six feet tall; his face was marked with scars from smallpox; he walked with a limp from having been shot by a Crow warrior. He was "The Slayer of Custer," an instant celebrity in mainstream American culture. He eventually joined WILLIAM F. (BUFFALO BILL) CODY'S Wild West Show and toured the East between 1885 and 1886.

However, the aging chief eventually had to attend to pressing matters at home, where miners and settlers had taken possession of the Black Hills and the Powder River area. Meanwhile, the government wanted to buy parts of the shrinking reservation. Sitting Bull was outspoken in his opposition to this purchase but to no avail. Helplessly, he watched the assimilation of Indian children into mainstream culture. Meanwhile, droughts, blizzards, and epidemics swept the Plains Indians during the 1880s. In response, Sitting Bull and others were attracted to the GHOST DANCE religion espoused by northern PAIUTE spiritual leader WOVOKA, which predicted a return of the buffalo and the departure of white people. Fearing that Sitting Bull would once again unite the Indians in a common purpose, the government issued orders for his arrest. On December 15, 1890, 43 Indian policemen surrounded Sitting Bull's cabin and ordered him to surrender. As Sitting Bull came out, some of his followers protested. A shot rang out, hitting a policeman, and Sitting Bull was killed instantly by a bullet to the head. Thus, the great warrior who had tenaciously clung to a traditional Lakota way of life passed into history.

Further Reading

Hoover, Herbert T. "Sitting Bull." In *American Indian Leaders: Studies in Diversity,* edited by R. David Edmunds. Lincoln: University of Nebraska Press, 1980.
Utley, Robert M. *The Lance and the Shield: The Life and Times of Sitting Bull.* New York: Ballantine Books, 1993.

— William B. Kessel

Skeleton Cave (Skull Cave) (1872) *battle in Arizona between the U.S. Army and the Yavapai Indians*

During the 1860s, increasing numbers, of ranchers, miners, and settlers flooded into Arizona. As they encroached onto APACHE and YAVAPAI lands, the Indians responded by raiding the newcomers. In June 1871, General GEORGE CROOK was given the responsibility of pacifying the Indians. He immediately pursued his task with deadly efficiency.

Shortly after Christmas, three companies of the 5th Cavalry and 130 Indian scouts located some Yavapai who were hiding in a shallow cave in Salt River Canyon. About dawn on December 28, the troops, under the direction of Captain William H. Brown, began firing on the cave. The Yavapai, who were safely nestled behind a large sandstone slab, had sufficient food and supplies and were not intimidated by the superior force opposing them. Then Captain Brown changed his TACTICS. He ordered his troops to fire at the ceiling and walls of the cave, knowing that the ricocheting bullets would reach the Indians behind the stone. Shooting commenced. Army records report that 76 Yavapai men, women, and children died under the hail of bullets. Other sources put the figure at 37. Either way, it was a crushing blow for the Indians. The troops took 20 prisoners and slowly headed back to Camp McDowell. They left the bodies unburied.

About the start of the 20th century, the skeletons were found in the cave by a cowboy. Nearly 30 years later the Yavapai took the bones and interred them at the Fort McDowell cemetery.

Skull Cave   See SKELETON CAVE.

Slim Buttes   (1876) *battle between the Oglala and Minniconjou Lakota and the U.S. Cavalry*

In the aftermath of GEORGE ARMSTRONG CUSTER's defeat at the battle of the LITTLE BIGHORN (1876), the U.S. Army continued to try to force the Oglala and Minniconjou Lakota (see SIOUX) back on their reservations in the Black Hills of South Dakota (see SIOUX WARS). On September 9, 1876, Captain Anson Mills and about 150 members of the 3rd Cavalry stumbled over the camp of Oglala chief AMERICAN HORSE. Mills immediately launched an attack on the 37-family outpost. The cavalry did not achieve a complete surprise, and many of the Indians escaped from the camp and found shelter in the surrounding hills. The warriors then began to return Mills's fire from the hills, forcing Mills to stay in the vicinity of the Indian camp. However, Mills was able to pin American Horse himself, four of his warriors, and about 15 women and children in a nearby cave.

Some of the Oglala and Minniconjou took advantage of their position to send for help. Mills's command could have been in serious trouble had it not been for the arrival of his commanding general, GEORGE CROOK, and a supporting force. Chiefs SITTING BULL and GALL arrived with 600 Hunkpapa to help the threatened Indians and found Crook's force blocking their way. Crook's army drove them away and maintained the pressure on American Horse, destroying the village in the process. Eventually, American Horse emerged, having been shot through the stomach. He was the most notable casualty of the battle of Slim Buttes. Crook lost three men, and 12 were wounded.

Slim Buttes was the first American victory after the army's defeat at the Little Bighorn. It was also the first of a series of defeats for the Lakota and CHEYENNE, which culminated in their surrender in August and September 1877.

smallpox, effects of   *infectious disease to which Indians had no immunity at contact*

Among Europeans, smallpox was a common, if potentially serious, childhood disease. For Native Americans, who had no natural resistance, it was deadly. Some scholars suggest that smallpox and other European diseases may have reduced Native American populations by as much as 80 million people between the 15th and the 19th centuries.

Smallpox alone had a decided effect on Native American warfare. Between 1616 and 1618, an epidemic thought to be smallpox killed off a high percentage of the WAMPANOAG, MASSACHUSETT, PAWTUCKET, and Eastern ABENAKI Indians in what would later become New England. In the case of the Wampanoag, the death toll may have been as high as 90 percent. The losses of these tribes brought the Canadian-based Micmac and the NARRAGANSETT in Massachusetts greater influence in far eastern North America. In addition, the many deaths in coastal Massachusetts left cleared fields available for use by the English Pilgrims when they landed at Plymouth in 1620. Other tribes heavily affected by smallpox included the MOHAWK and other tribes of the IROQUOIS CONFEDERACY, the ALGONKIN of New England, and the HURON. In 1633 an epidemic reduced the population of the Mohawk alone from 8,500 to fewer than 2,000. The disease may also have delayed the conflict known as KING PHILIP'S WAR (1675–76) by as much as a generation.

During the 18th century, some European soldiers used smallpox in germ warfare against Native Americans. Angered by reports of atrocities committed by Native Americans on British settlers during the FRENCH AND INDIAN WAR (1754–63), General Jeffrey Amherst ordered that blankets infected with the smallpox virus be distributed to the LENNI LENAPE (Delaware) and Mingo warriors surrounding Fort Pitt. According to some reports, an epidemic broke out among the besieging Indians, allowing the fort to be relieved easily by British troops.

The 19th century brought smallpox to tribes in the Plains, Great Basin, and desert areas of North America. The PAWNEE population was reduced harshly by epidemics of smallpox and cholera. Many other Indians who never even had contact with non-Indians died of disease brought in by Indian traders.

Thus, smallpox and other European diseases probably had the greatest impact on the European conquest of North America.

Smith, John   (ca. 1581–1631) *British explorer and soldier of fortune*

John Smith is best remembered for his role in the establishment of the Jamestown colony in 1607. An experienced soldier who had served in campaigns in the Netherlands against the Spanish and in eastern Europe against the Turks, Smith helped ensure the survival of the Jamestown colony with his hardheaded approach to negotiations with the POWHATAN CONFEDERACY. The Virginia Company, the holders of the colony's charter, were so impressed with Smith's abilities that they made him a member of Jamestown's governing council. He repaid their trust by preserving the colony through the hard winters of 1607 and 1608.

Smith made one of the colony's most important contacts with the paramount chief of the region, POWHATAN (Wahunsonacock). In December 1607, he was captured by OPECHAN-CANOUGH, the *werowance,* or war chief, of the PAMUNKEY; the following month he was presented to Powhatan at his capital of Werowocomoco. Legend has it that Powhatan ordered Smith's execution but was stopped by his daughter, Pocahontas. Whether or not the story is true, Smith was released by the chief.

Smith explored Chesapeake Bay and the Potomac and Rappahannock River valleys throughout 1608. The following winter, when the British colonists were chronically short of food, he used both the respect that the Indians had for him and threats of force to barter for corn, beans, and other foods. One time he held his former captor Opechancanough at gunpoint until his boat was filled with the corn he demanded. He opposed open trade with the Indians, fearing that prices for grain would escalate beyond the power of the British to pay.

Smith was wounded in an accidental gunpowder explosion in October 1609 and subsequently returned to England. In 1614, he made another trip to the New World, trading and exploring the New England coast. In addition to his powers as a negotiator, Smith also set down much valuable information about the Indians of Virginia in his accounts *A True Relation of Occurrences and Accidents in Virginia* (1608) and *The General all Historie of Virginia, New-England, and the Summer Isles* (1624). He died in England in 1631.

Snake Indians   See SHOSHONE.

Snake War (1866–1868) *series of skirmishes between Indians and U.S. forces in the Pacific Northwest*
In 1866, a long period of hostilities between non-Indians and Indians in the Pacific Northwest came to a head. The Yahuskin and Walpapi bands of the Northern PAIUTE Indians, known to settlers as the Snake Indians (and now known as the Numu), occupied southeastern Oregon and southwestern Idaho. In the face of ineffective campaigns by Oregon and Nevada volunteers, the Snake successfully conducted raids against miners pouring into the newly discovered gold regions of southwest Idaho and southeast Oregon. With the end of the CIVIL WAR (1861–65), the U.S. government turned its attention toward hostile Indian groups. The 1st Cavalry and the 14th Infantry were sent to engage the Indians in the Northwest, but they, too, were ineffective. In response to public outcry, the army units were reorganized. The 2nd Battalion of the Fourteenth Infantry was redesignated as the 23rd Infantry and Brevet Major-General GEORGE CROOK was assigned to command it.

A week after Cook's arrival at Fort Boise in Idaho, a Paiute war party struck near the mouth of the Boise River. Crook, accompanied by Captain David Perry's 1st Cavalry, left the fort for a weeklong campaign against the Paiute. Crook would stay in the field for the next two years.

Crook, who despised military formalities, was an avid student of Indian TACTICS and often used them in his campaigns against hostile bands. During the course of the Snake War, he used SHOSHONE auxiliaries and traded his horses and wagons for pack mules. The mule was an animal well suited to negotiate difficult terrain, thus allowing the army better mobility.

The Snake War was not decided by traditional battlefield engagements. Instead, it was a prolonged series of relentless pursuits and skirmishes. Over a two-year period, Crook engaged the Snake Indians no less than 49 times, and kept them constantly on the run. By the middle of 1868, Crook's troops had killed 329 warriors, including the revered Chief Paulina, wounded 20 more, and captured 225. The Snake Indians, who were often attacked by Shoshone SCOUTS as well as army regulars, could no longer withstand Crook's relentless pursuit. Worn down, Snake Chief Old Weawea led 800 of his people into Fort Harney on July 1, 1868, to seek peace with Crook. The general firmly reminded the chief that, while his soldiers were easily replaced, Snake warriors were not. After their surrender, many of the Indians chose to live on the Klamath and Mallewa Indian River Reservations. Others remained free and later joined the BANNOCK in their war against U.S. troops in 1878.

Soldier Spring (1868) *important engagement between U.S. Army regulars and Comanche and Kiowa tribes during the Southern Plains War*
After the battle of WASHITA (1868) during the SOUTHERN PLAINS WAR (1868–69), two army commanders, Colonel EUGENE A. CARR and Major Andrew Evans, marched across the wintery plains with several army columns, searching for hostile Indians. On Christmas Day, Major Evans's New Mexico column attacked a COMANCHE camp on the north fork of the Red River. He ordered howitzers to fire on the camp, and after the Indians fled he seized the encampment. Evans did not realize that there was a KIOWA village a little farther downstream, but he soon learned of it when 200 Comanche and Kiowa warriors launched a counterattack against him and his 300 soldiers.

The battle of Soldier Spring continued for the entire day, with constant skirmishing. Evans's troops burned the village and destroyed stores of supplies, including several tons of dried buffalo meat. The Indians finally became weary and broke off the attack. Hampered by a number of injured horses, Evans decided not to pursue them. He had lost only one man during the battle, but the Indians had suffered the loss of 25 to 30 warriors.

The greatest significance of this daylong battle was not loss of life but rather the Comanche's loss of most of their winter food supply. The Indians were stunned to learn that winter was no longer a guarantee of security from attacks by the army. They fled the area, and many surrendered at various army forts across the Southern Plains. The army thus learned the effectiveness of winter campaigns against the Plains Indians.

Solomon River (1857) *battle between the Cheyenne and the U.S. Army*
As non-Indians moved farther west during the 1850s, violent encounters between the intruders and the Plains Indians grew

more frequent. In spring 1857, Secretary of War Jefferson Davis authorized the army to launch an offensive against the CHEYENNE, who had been among the boldest in resisting non-Indian encroachments. Leading the mixed column of infantry, cavalry, and artillery was Colonel EDWIN VOSE SUMNER, a grizzled veteran of the war against Mexico. After two months scouring the region between the Platte and Arkansas Rivers, on July 29 Sumner's scouts located a large body of Cheyenne near the Solomon River, Kansas. Leaving his infantry and artillery behind, the colonel moved ahead with about 300 hundred cavalry, determined to force an engagement.

Normally, the Cheyenne avoided pitched battles such as this, preferring instead to fight when the odds seemed more in their favor. This time, however, they believed that the conditions were right. Their medicine men had assured them that, having washed their hands in the waters of a magic lake, they would be immune to the soldiers' FIREARMS. A force roughly equal to Sumner's thus arrayed themselves along the Solomon River, ready for battle.

A remarkable scene, perhaps unique in the wars between the U.S. Army and the Native Americans, then unfolded. The lines of both sides surged forward. Sumner, not knowing what his antagonists believed but eager for a fight, then ordered his men to sling their carbines and draw their sabers. Undoubtedly stunned by the order—sabers were usually left behind as too heavy and too noisy—the cavalrymen nonetheless complied.

Unwittingly, Sumner had stunned his foes, whose magic protected them against bullets, not steel. They hesitated, then turned. Savage individual combat between small groups followed in a running battle, which covered nearly seven miles. Two soldiers were killed and 11 were wounded, including Lieutenant J. E. B. Stuart, who would live to become one of the most famous cavalrymen of the CIVIL WAR (1861–65). Sumner reported nine Indians killed.

Two days later, Sumner found the now-abandoned Cheyenne village about 15 miles to the south. In their haste, the villagers had abandoned many of their lodges and possessions, which Sumner ordered destroyed. Although hostilities continued for most of the remainder of the year, 1858 found the Cheyenne much more reluctant to take up arms. The local Indian agent, Robert Miller, attributed this change of heart to the psychological defeat Sumner had inflicted in the battle of Solomon River.

Soto, Hernando De (1500–1542) *Spanish conquistador and explorer*

With the permission of Holy Roman Emperor Charles V, who was also king of Spain, Hernando de Soto launched an invasion of Florida in 1529. His hope was to duplicate the financial successes of HERNÁN CORTÉS in Mexico and Francisco Pizarro in Peru. In May of that year, de Soto and a force of about 600 men, including many veterans of Pizarro's campaign, landed near what is now Tampa, Florida. His equipment included heavy armor for both men and horses and trained war dogs, as well as iron collars and chains for PRISONERS.

During the next three years, de Soto moved through present-day Florida, Georgia, South Carolina, North Carolina,

Tennessee, Alabama, Mississippi, Arkansas, and Texas, searching for the same sort of riches that the Spanish had found in Central and South America. Throughout his campaign he was harassed by Native American warriors. The Spanish fought and won only one major battle, at Mabile (modern Selma, Alabama), where they claimed to have killed 2,500 CHOCTAW defenders while suffering only 20 killed and 150 wounded. In 1542 de Soto fell ill and died while exploring territory west of the Mississippi. His men, pursued by Native Americans, fled down the river and eventually made their way back to Cuba.

Southern Plains War (1868–1869) *conflict between U.S. troops and tribes of the southern plains*

The MEDICINE LODGE TREATIES (1867) had brought only a short-lived truce to the struggle for military supremacy on the Southern Plains. Depredations by the KIOWA, COMANCHE, ARAPAHO, and Southern CHEYENNE had continued despite the treaty agreements, and the federal government had proved slow to provide promised annuity goods. The U.S. Peace Commission—which had, in conjunction with the treaties, placed a temporary moratorium on army offensives—reassembled in 1868. The absence of Senator John Henderson left the military, led by WILLIAM TECUMSEH SHERMAN, in control of a majority of delegates. By October 1868 the Peace Commission had removed most of the restrictions on the army's movements and authority.

Anticipating the new freedom of action, the War Department had in September already set loose a column of troops commanded by Lieutenant Colonel Luther P. Bradley to patrol southern Kansas, thus driving a wedge between the tribes of the northern and southern plains. A smaller army scouting detachment had barely escaped annihilation at the battle of BEECHER'S ISLAND (1868), suggesting stiff Indian resistance to any additional army forays. But the biggest blows were yet to come. PHILIP HENRY SHERIDAN, commander of the Department of the Missouri, vowed to maintain the pressure on the southern plains tribes throughout the winter, when the grasses upon which the Indians' animals depended would be most scarce, thus reducing their mobility. Fort Cobb in Indian Territory was designated a safe haven for those tribes choosing peace; all Southern Plains Indians who did not make arrangements there were declared hostile.

Sherman and Sheridan sought to sweep the area between the Arkansas and Platte Rivers clear of Indians. To force the enemy to fight, Sheridan designed a three-pronged offensive, with each column converging in the southwestern reaches of the Indian Territory. In mid-November Major Andrew W. Evans led 563 men out of Fort Bascom, New Mexico, and headed east down the South Canadian River. From Fort Lyon, Colorado, Major EUGENE A. CARR took a second column, some 650 strong, and began driving south toward the Antelope Hills. Sheridan intended to personally accompany the most powerful force—16 companies of regulars and the 19th Kansas Volunteer Cavalry Regiment organized at Fort Dodge, Kansas, and Camp Supply, Indian Territory.

Logistical difficulties, however, prevented Sheridan's grand column from taking the field immediately. Anxious to strike quickly, Sheridan ordered GEORGE ARMSTRONG CUSTER to proceed ahead from Camp Supply in late November. Although heavy snowfall nearly obliterated any Indian trails, Custer soon located and destroyed BLACK KETTLE'S CHEYENNE village in the battle of the WASHITA (1868). Sheridan finally joined Custer and continued the campaign, only to find that many of the Indians he was pursuing had already been promised safety by officers at Fort Cobb, Indian territory. Meanwhile, Evans had pushed across the Texas Panhandle and moved into present-day southwestern Oklahoma. After several weeks in the field, in the battle of SOLDIER SPRING (1868), Evans's command tracked down and burned a Nokoni Comanche village on December 25 before retiring to winter quarters.

Demoralized by the army's relentless pursuits and the onset of winter, most of the Kiowa and Comanche had either turned themselves in by the end of the year or would do so shortly. Large groups of Southern Cheyenne, Arapaho and Kwahadi Comanche, however, still refused to accept government terms.

The army's effectiveness was increasingly diminished by the winter's exertion. Custer broke up his command in late March 1869 following the surrender of several additional Cheyenne resistance groups. With their animal stocks severely depleted, most of the protagonists on both sides were now content to recover from their ordeal. By early summer, however, Tall Bull's Cheyenne and Arapaho followers had once again made their way north to their old Republican River hunting grounds in defiance of the army. Carr, stung by his failure to defeat the Indians, was assigned to track down Tall Bull. He finally did so, and at the battle of SUMMIT SPRINGS (1869), he overcame the Indians and destroyed the military cohesion of the vaunted DOG SOLDIER society in the process.

Sheridan deemed the operations a tremendous success. "The Indians," he reported, "for the first time begin to realize that winter will not compel us to make a truce with them." Indeed, although Indian resistance on the southern plains would not be finally crushed until the RED RIVER WAR (1874–75), the winter campaigns of the Southern Plains War had forced the tribes south to reservations in Indian Territory. As historian Robert M. Utley has concluded, the Southern Plains Indians had not "lost their spirit of independence, but a large step had been taken toward their ultimate conquest."

Further Reading

Utley, Robert M. *Frontier Regulars: The United States Army and the Indian, 1866–1891.* Lincoln: University of Nebraska Press, 1984.

Wooster, Robert. *The Military and United States Indian Policy, 1865–1903.* New Haven, Conn.: Yale University Press, 1988.

—Robert Wooster

spear *weapon used by both Native Americans and Europeans during the early contact period*

The spear was a common weapon in Native American warfare only in the early years of contact between Indians and Europeans. It might be as simple as a long stick, sharpened to a point, with the pointed end hardened in a fire. The spear could also be very complex, with a beautifully chipped flint point attached to a shaft with animal sinews and held in place with a glue made from blood. After contact, metal spear heads became common on Native American weapons; they were generally trade items or were taken from Europeans in battle.

Eastern tribes, such as the POWHATAN CONFEDERACY and the ABENAKI, used modified spears to fish. Plains Indians, including the tribes of the BLACKFOOT CONFEDERACY, Gros Ventres, ASSINIBOINE, CROW, Northern and Southern CHEYENNE, Dakota (see SIOUX), and COMANCHE, used large spears or LANCES where they hunted buffalo on horseback, but by the time they came into conflict with Europeans they had acquired FIREARMS. In intertribal wars, which were mainly raids fought for status and horses, spears were largely replaced by COUP STICKS–unpointed weapons used to touch an enemy in order to gain prestige. The exceptions to this were certain tribes in California and Pacific Canada, which fought wars to win territory and gain status by demonstrating their disdain for material possessions. These tribes, including the Nootka, the Tlingit, and the Chinook, often fought with traditional weapons such as spears and used BODY ARMOR for protection.

For the most part, spears were largely used by Europeans in their early battles with Native Americans. Thanks to their advanced metallurgy, Europeans had a variety of spear shapes and designs available, including short pikes with round tips, spears with shafts measuring up to nine feet in length, and bills such as the English BROWN BILL, which combined a spear head with an axe blade. In warfare, Europeans used spears in conjunction with muskets to keep cavalry from disrupting their infantry. They brought this style of war making with them to the New World. HERNÁN CORTÉS and his army carried large metal-tipped spears in their invasion of Mexico. After the beginning of the POWHATAN WARS (1622–32, 1644–46), the Jamestown government requested almost 1,000 brown bills to defend the colony from the Virginia Indians. As gunpowder technology improved, spears were gradually abandoned. They were rarely used in battle after the end of the 17th century.

Spokane Plain (1858) *battle between U.S. troops and the Yakama Indians and other Indians in the eastern Washington Territory*

After the YAKAMA WAR (1855–57), the Indians of eastern Washington Territory were still aroused against non-Indians. YAKAMA chief KAMIAKIN pushed for a general uprising to prevent non-Indians from seizing Indian land. Violence between Indians and non-Indians escalated and led to a number of significant battles.

In summer 1858, General Newman Clarke instructed Colonel GEORGE WRIGHT to launch vigorous attacks against hostile Indians. Wright and his forces began marching throughout eastern Washington in pursuit of the Yakama and other resisting tribes. Late in August, some 600 Indian warriors gathered on the Great Spokane Plain, southwest of present-day Spokane, Washington, to stop Wright's advance. The two sides met on September 1, 1858. Armed with new long-range infantry rifles and backed by heavy artillery, the soldiers easily outgunned the muskets and bows and arrows of the Indians in the battle of Spokane Plain. Chief Kamiakin was severely injured in the battle, and the Indians soon fled back to their homes.

The battle of Spokane Plain showed the Indians the dangers of trying to confront the better-armed soldiers in open battle. It also revealed the superiority of the soldiers' military organization. After the battle, Colonel Wright continued his campaign against the Indians, and his harsh measures soon sapped their spirit of resistance.

Spotted Tail (Sinte Galeshka) (ca. 1830–1881) *chief of the Brulé Lakota*

Born on the White River in southern South Dakota, Spotted Tail ascended to chieftaincy through his prowess in intertribal warfare, principally against the PAWNEE. He attracted military notice following the GRATTAN DEFEAT (1854) by killing some Salt Lake City mail wagoneers to avenge the death of Brulé chief Conquering Bear. A battle with General WILLIAM S. HARNEY ensued, during which Spotted Tail received two bullet wounds and two sabre lacerations. He and two other Brulé willingly submitted to trial and were convicted. They arrived at Fort Leavenworth prison in Kansas on December 11, 1855, but received a pardon on January 16. Nevertheless, Spotted Tail remained at Fort Leavenworth during that winter and spring, observing the military personnel. He apparently decided that peace was the path to pursue, and was later instrumental in the surrender of CRAZY HORSE's band.

Spotted Tail was one of the first Lakota chiefs to sign the FORT LARAMIE TREATY of 1868. Because of Spotted Tail's outspoken advocacy of peace, General GEORGE CROOK later appointed him head Brulé chief, thereby conferring upon him exclusive power to deal with Washington. This caused jealousy and animosity among other Indians. Spotted Tail's ego also apparently became somewhat inflated after his appointment, spurring suspicion and mistrust among his people. He was shot by fellow Brulé Crow Dog on the eve of a planned trip to Washington, D.C.

Spring Wells Treaty (1815) *one of a series of treaties between the U.S. government and tribes in the Old Northwest Territory*

Article IX of the TREATY OF GHENT (1814), which ended the WAR OF 1812 (1812–14), provided that Native American tribes allied with the British during the war would receive all lands and whatever privileges they had enjoyed in 1811, before the outbreak of hostilities. Between July and October 1815, the United States negotiated 14 separate treaties intended to satisfy this provision. Most were concluded with tribes of the Great Lakes and Ohio valley, which had been most affected by the war. The one group most notably excluded from consideration in these agreements was the war faction of the CREEK, the RED STICKS, who had surrendered to General ANDREW JACK-

Spotted Tail, a Brulé Lakota chief who supported peace with the United States, signed the Fort Laramie Treaty in 1868. *(By permission of the Colorado Historical Society)*

SON in 1814 and been forced to sign the humiliating Treaty of Horseshoe Bend (1814).

One of the important treaties in the series was the Spring Wells Treaty. Negotiated by war hero WILLIAM HENRY HARRISON, it was signed near DETROIT on September 8 with seven tribes of the Northwest Territory. The treaty restored prewar relations with the CHIPPEWA, OTTAWA, and POTAWATOMI tribes. For the SENECA, LENNI LENAPE (Delaware), MIAMI, and SHAWNEE, the Spring Wells Treaty confirmed the terms of an agreement made the previous year at Greenville, Ohio, that granted a blanket amnesty for all Indian crimes committed since that time.

Like the other 13 treaties intended to satisfy the terms of Article IX of the Treaty of Ghent, the Spring Wells treaties guaranteed a return to the status quo without returning a single acre of land to the tribes.

Standing Bear (ca. 1829–1908) *Ponca chief*

In 1877 the federal government forcibly removed Standing Bear and the PONCA from their lands in Nebraska to Indian

Territory (present-day Oklahoma), where many died from the hard journey and the inhospitable new climate. By 1879 Standing Bear's son had also died, and the chief became determined to bury his son's bones in the Ponca homeland. Carrying the body in a wagon, he set out with an escort of 30 warriors. Before reaching Nebraska, however, Standing Bear and his warriors stopped briefly with their allies, the OMAHA Indians. Soldiers soon arrived with orders to arrest Standing Bear and his party and return them to Indian Territory. Prominent Omaha lawyers appealed to U.S. District Court Judge Elmer S. Dundy, who ordered the release of the Ponca.

Standing Bear's case attracted a good deal of attention and brought about some changes. Journalist and reformer Thomas Henry Tibbles took the chief to several eastern states to appeal for support. President Rutherford B. Hayes ordered a commission, headed by General GEORGE CROOK and NELSON A. MILES, to recommend action. Congress responded by appropriating money to purchase a permanent home for the Ponca in Nebraska and gave the Ponca who remained in Indian Territory better land. They also paid the Ponca for losses sustained during their Removal.

Standing Bear's use of the legal system to seek justice set a precedent for Indians defending their rights. He was approximately 80 years old when he died and was buried in his ancestral homeland in Nebraska.

Standish, Miles (Myles Standish) (ca. 1584–1656)
professional soldier and one of the founders of Plymouth Colony
Miles Standish played the same role for Plymouth Colony that JOHN SMITH had for the Jamestown settlement in Virginia. Like Smith, Standish was a professional soldier who served in the Dutch wars of independence against the Spanish. In 1620 he was approached by English Puritans who had left England to find religious freedom in Holland. Standish joined the Puritans as their military attaché and sailed on the *Mayflower* that fall. In December 1620 he arrived in Massachusetts and helped found Plymouth colony.

Standish's primary function in the colony was to negotiate with the local Native Americans and to defend the Puritans from attack. Like Smith, Standish learned the language of the local Indians and won their confidence. He promoted a close relationship with Massasoit, the WAMPANOAG *sachem,* or leader, who provided Standish with a military adviser named Hobomok. Together, the two men also engineered an assault on a coalition led by Wampanoag Indian separatists Aspinet and Iyanough in 1623. Standish also led a raid against a Massachuset *sachem* who was rumored to be planning an attack on the neighboring British settlement of Wessagusett (present-day Weymouth). After killing the defeated chief, he mounted the chief's severed head on a pole in front of Plymouth colony as a warning.

Standish represented the interests of the Plymouth colony in England from 1625 to 1627, but he returned to the New World in 1628 to attack Thomas Morton of the neighboring settlement of Merrymount after learning that Morton had been trading guns with the Indians. In 1631 Standish cofounded with John Alden the settlement of Duxbury, Massachusetts, where he lived until his death in 1656.

Stand Watie, Cherokee tribal leader and confederate general during the Civil War *(By permission of the Western History Collections, University of Oklahoma Library)*

Stand Watie (Degataga) (1806–1871) *Cherokee leader and Confederate general*
Stand Watie was born near Rome, Georgia, in 1806, in what was then the CHEROKEE Nation. He became a planter and slave owner and assisted in the publication of the *Phoenix,* the Cherokee newspaper. Watie was one of the Cherokee leaders to sign an 1835 treaty by which the remaining Cherokee in Georgia agreed to their Removal to Indian Territory (now Oklahoma). The treaty caused a split among the Cherokee, and Watie become leader of the minority treaty party.

At the start of the Civil War, Watie joined with the minority of Cherokee supporting the Confederacy and mustered several Cherokee regiments. They did not, however, perform well at their major engagement, the battle of PEA RIDGE (1862). In 1864 Watie was commissioned a brigadier general, a year after becoming principal chief of the prosouthern faction of the Cherokee Nation. In June 1865 Watie became one of the last Confederate commanders to surrender to Union forces.

After the war, Watie helped rebuild the Cherokee nation and ran a successful tobacco business.

Steptoe, Edward (1816–1865) *U.S. Army officer involved in the Indian wars of the Pacific Northwest*
Virginia-born Edward Steptoe graduated from West Point in 1837, serving thereafter in the Second SEMINOLE WAR (1835–42) and the Mexican War. In March 1856 Lieutenant-Colonel Steptoe assumed command of a relief force organized by Colonel GEORGE WRIGHT during the YAKAMA WAR (1855–57). By November of that year, Steptoe had been placed in command of Fort Walla Walla.

On May 6, 1858, a small settlement of non-Indians living at Colville, Washington, asked for military assistance from Steptoe. Ignoring warnings that the Spokan and other Indians were assuming his presence to mean war, Steptoe took a column of 164 troops out of Fort Walla Walla and across the Snake River. On May 16, 1858, he found himself surrounded by several hundred (some reports indicate as many as 1,000) Palouse, Spokan, Coeur d'Alene, and a few NEZ PERCE. His inadequate force and antiquated equipment, forced Steptoe to retreat the following morning. In the battle that followed, an early encounter in the COEUR D'ALENE WAR (1858), Steptoe lost two officers and six men, with 11 wounded; the Indian forces lost nine, and between 40 and 50 were wounded, but they captured Steptoe's artillery and camp equipment.

Steptoe's defeat revived the Indians' determination to fight. It also increased the military's opinion that the power of the Northwest Indian peoples had to be destroyed once and for all. Steptoe resigned from the army in 1861 and suffered a paralytic stroke that same year. He died in Lynchburg, Virginia, in 1865, at the age of 49.

Stevens, Isaac I. (1818–1862) *governor of the Washington Territory and treaty negotiator*
Born in Massachusetts, Isaac I. Stevens graduated from West Point and served with General WINFIELD SCOTT in the Mexican War as an engineering officer. In 1853 Stevens resigned from the Army Engineer Corps to become the territorial governor of the Washington Territory, a position that also included the duty of superintendent of Indian affairs.

A champion of the transcontinental railroad, Stevens's major concern was to clear his territory of its Indian residents and settle them on reservations. In late 1854 he engineered treaties with the Squazon, Nisqually, and Puyallup of the Puget Sound area. He then negotiated three treaties in spring 1855 with the YAKAMA, Salishan, Walla Walla, Palouse, CAYUSE, Umatilla, and NEZ PERCE at the WALLA WALLA PEACE COUNCIL (1855). Stevens had been successful primarily through fast talk and intimidation, and many groups signed simply to pacify him. During years of the YAKAMA WAR (1855–57), most of the reluctant signatories fought the settlers who moved onto land given up in the treaties. Stevens ruthlessly tried to suppress the uprisings with the territorial militia. He even persecuted and arrested non-Indians who sympathized with the Indians and who spoke out on their behalf.

Stevens served as Washington's territorial delegate to Congress in 1857. He returned to active duty in the army during the CIVIL WAR (1861–65) and was killed in battle in Virginia.

Stillman's Run (1832) *encounter between U.S. troops and Sac warriors led by Black Hawk*
In the early 1800s SAC chief BLACK HAWK, defiantly violating a treaty signed in 1804, refused to move to the western side of the Mississippi River. A number of years later, on May 14, 1832, the chief was intercepted by Major Isaiah Stillman and a force of 270 volunteers. Black Hawk dispatched three messengers to meet with Stillman under a flag of truce. When the messengers failed to return quickly, he sent five emissaries to locate them. Stillman's men attacked the emissaries, killing two of them and infuriating Black Hawk. With 40 warriors, he prepared an ambush for Stillman's men. When the troops were close enough, the Indians opened fire; to their surprise, the soldiers fled in panic to their base camp some 25 miles distant. By morning it was believed that Stillman's entire command had been wiped out, but some troops slowly began returning to the camp. Several soldiers under General Samuel Whiteside proceeded to the battle area, where they buried 11 soldiers who had been severely mutilated. The hasty retreat by the soldiers during the ambush became known as Stillman's Run or Stillman's Rout.

See also BLACK HAWK WAR, 1831.

Stokes Commission See FORT GIBSON TREATY.

Stoney Lake See DEAD BUFFALO LAKE.

Stronghold See LAVA BEDS.

Stumbling Bear (Setimkia) (ca. 1832–1903) *Kiowa war chief and peace negotiator*
KIOWA chief Stumbling Bear originally resisted U.S. incursions onto his tribe's territory. At age 32 he faced CHRISTOPHER ("KIT") CARSON at the battle of ADOBE WALLS (1864). He was a member of the Kiowa negotiating team at the MEDICINE LODGE TREATY (1867) on the Texas frontier, along with his relative Kicking Bird and warrior chiefs LONE WOLF, SATANTA, and Satank. At one point during the negotiation, Stumbling Bear tried to shoot commanding general WILLIAM TECUMSEH SHERMAN with an arrow. However, sometime before the beginning of the RED RIVER WAR (1874–75), his attitude changed from a pro-war stance to that of peacemaker.

In 1872 Stumbling Bear traveled to Washington, D.C. as part of a negotiating team to bring peace to the Texas frontier. When Lone Wolf and Satanta began new raids into Kansas and Texas in spring 1874, Stumbling Bear pursued peace efforts instead. He was rewarded by the U.S. government for his efforts in 1878, when the government established a permanent home for him in Indian Territory (present-day Oklahoma). He died there in 1903.

Sullivan, John (1740–1795) *colonial army officer*
The son of a New Hampshire schoolteacher, John Sullivan ran a successful law practice until the outbreak of the AMERICAN REVOLUTION (1775–81). He was a committed patriot and

served as a delegate to the First Continental Congress. In 1774, in the first overt military action against the British during the war, Sullivan led a surprise attack against Fort William and Mary, which netted the colonists large stores of arms and munitions. He served with Generals Richard Montgomery and Benedict Arnold during the invasion of Canada in 1775 and kept the army intact during its retreat.

Sullivan's glories were unfortunately overshadowed by two notable failures in 1777. In August of that year, he led an unsuccessful raid on Staten Island. Then he was unfairly chosen as the scapegoat for the American defeat at the battle of Brandywine in September. Sullivan pressed his case with George Washington, who relented and gave him another chance. In 1779, he was chosen to lead a campaign in New York's Mohawk Valley. Washington planned the campaign as retaliation for Indian raids in Pennsylvania, including the encounter at WYOMING VALLEY (1778), the year before.

In summer 1779, Sullivan took command of 5,000 men and moved up the Susquehanna River. He encountered resistance only at NEWTOWN (1779), where MOHAWK Chief JOSEPH BRANT and BUTLER'S RANGERS had prepared an ambush. He defeated this force and effectively eliminated all resistance in the region. He proceeded unopposed to the Genesee River, laying waste to the country of the SENECA and CAYUGA, both members of the IROQUOIS CONFEDERACY. Some 40 Indian villages were burned and thousands of bushels of corn destroyed. As a result, that winter 5,000 Iroquois had to be fed by the British at Niagara in Canada.

After the war, Sullivan reentered political life. He became attorney general of New Hampshire and served two terms as governor. As president of the New Hampshire Constitutional convention in 1778, he played an important role in ratifying the U.S. Constitution. In 1789 Washington appointed Sullivan to serve as district court judge, a position he held until his death on January 23, 1795.

Sully, Alfred (1821–1879) *U.S. Army officer and Indian superintendent*

A native of Philadelphia, Alfred Sully began his military career in 1841. Soon after, he participated in the last phases of the Second SEMINOLE WAR (1835–42). During the CIVIL WAR (1861–65) he was given command of the Department of Dakota, where he became involved in the conflicts with the Santee Dakota (see SIOUX).

To deal with the Indian unrest following the MINNESOTA UPRISING, the WAR DEPARTMENT created several military "districts." Sully was placed in command of the District of Iowa, within the Department of the Northwest. Sully's forces were supposed to link up with those of HENRY SIBLEY, but delays caused him to miss the rendezvous. Sully's failure to meet Sibley at the appointed time allowed the majority of Indians to escape west of the Missouri River. Sully did, however, engage a Santee Dakota band led by INKPADUTA at the battle of WHITE-STONE HILL (1863), resulting in the largest victory of his expedition. The campaign temporarily drove the Santee Dakota west of the Missouri River.

Sully also participated in Major General John Pope's summer campaign of 1864. He was to erect two forts upstream from Fort Sully in the vicinity of Heart River and near the mouth of Powder River (on the Yellowstone River). In addition, Sully had orders to hunt down and fight any large camps of Lakota. In early July 1864, Sully assembled a 3,400-man expedition to make war on the Lakota, who were subsequently engaged and defeated at KILLDEER MOUNTAIN (1864).

The following summer, Sully and 840 cavalrymen traveled to Devil's Lake, South Dakota, to talk with the Teton Lakota. However, his departure was delayed, and the Indians had left by the time he got there. As a result, the three-week march to Devil's Lake and back was a failure.

In fall 1868, Sully fought in PHILIP HENRY SHERIDAN's campaign against the CHEYENNE, ARAPAHO, KIOWA, and COMANCHE. The next year he became superintendent of Indian affairs for Montana. His involvement in the massacre of 170 Piegan Indians at MARIAS RIVER (1870) brought heavy criticism of the War Department from eastern reformers.

Summit Springs (1869) *battle between Cheyenne Dog Soldiers and U.S. troops*

On June 9, 1869, Major EUGENE A. CARR led the "Republican River Expedition" of nearly 500 men, eight companies of the 5th Cavalry, and 150 PAWNEE scouts under Major Frank J. North to the Republican River valley in Kansas to punish the CHEYENNE's DOG SOLDIERS for their campaigns against non-Indians. WILLIAM (BUFFALO BILL) CODY went along as chief scout and guide. Early in July, Carr found the main camp of Dog Soldier leader Tall Bull, which included some Lakota (see SIOUX) and ARAPAHO, at Summit Springs, Colorado. The Indians, who had been waiting for the Platte River to subside, were caught by surprise when Carr's entire column charged. Army scouts Frank and Luther North and Pawnee scouts reached the village first, riding directly through it. Some of the cavalry encircled the camp, cutting off the Cheyenne from their ponies.

The Dog Soldiers could only flee or die. The few ponies in the camp were given to women and children; families with no horses were sent to the ravines while the men defended them. The battle continued all afternoon. When the fighting ended, the troops found that they had killed 52 people, including Tall Bull, and captured 17 women and children. The cavalry then burned the Indians' lodges. The surviving Dog Soldiers and their families were harassed out of the region, stopping only when they finally reached the Lakota camps on the White River.

Sumner, Edwin Vose (1797–1863) *U.S. Army officer*

Born in Massachusetts, Edwin Sumner entered the army in 1819 and eventually became a dragoon (mounted infantry) officer. After service in the Mexican War (where he earned the nickname "Bull" after a Mexican musket ball bounced off his skull at the battle of Cerro Gordo), Lieutenant Colonel Sumner was put in charge of U.S. military forces in the New Mexico Territory. His job was to protect travelers on the Santa Fe

Trail from attacks by the APACHE, NAVAJO and UTE. Sumner moved his troops out of Santa Fe to new forts around the territory, including Fort Mann near the Cimaron Crossing on the Arkansas River, Fort Larned on Pawnee Fork, and Fort Union on the Mora River at the western edge of the New Mexico settlement. In August 1851, he led a campaign that failed to dislodge the Navajo from their stronghold at Canyon de Chelly. Continually at odds with the New Mexico territorial government, Sumner once even advised the federal government to abandon the territory.

In 1857, Sumner was placed in command of the 1st Dragoons, based at Fort Leavenworth, Kansas. That summer, in his last campaign against Indians, he began an offensive designed to stop CHEYENNE attacks in the area between the Arkansas and Platte Rivers. On July 29, Sumner won a battle at the SOLOMON RIVER, in western Kansas. The Indians taking part in the battle had believed that if they bathed in the waters of a "magic" lake they would be immune from soldier's bullets. Sumner won the battle by using a cavalry saber charge, a tactic that was rare by that time. He later became a Union general during the CIVIL WAR (1861–65), serving until his death in 1863.

Sun Dance *annual ceremony of spiritual and tribal renewal among the Plains Indians*

The Sun Dance (a name given by the Lakota [see SIOUX] to emphasize the fixed gaze of the dancers on the sun) usually occurred in summer, when the tribes left their winter camps and embarked on the summer buffalo hunt. The dance was a tribal affair, one in which all the bands participated. It could not take place without a large gathering, because the priests who led it and the people who vowed to participate in it were scattered. During the period of the Sun Dance, other ceremonies for individuals and for the whole tribe also took place. Social dances were held so young men and women could meet. Warriors renewed their medicine. Trading, gambling, visiting friends and relatives in other bands, and sports competitions also took place.

The duration of the Sun Dance ceremonies varied among tribes, lasting anywhere from four to 12 days. Among the Lakota, it lasted for 12 days that were divided into three stages. The first four days consisted of ceremonies that reinforced Lakota ideals and customs. The second four were used to instruct the dance participants. During the final four days, the dance area was readied and the dance took place.

The CHEYENNE ceremony, known among the tribe as the Medicine Lodge, lasted anywhere from five to eight days, depending on the chief priest who ran the ritual. The Sun Dance was sponsored by an individual, male or female, who had asked for supernatural aid in a time of crisis. Among the BLACKFOOT CONFEDERACY, however, the dance was sponsored by one or more women, who saw to preparations and incurred expenses associated, and who then played a leading role in the ceremonies.

A central feature in the Sun Dance for most tribes was the dance itself. Again, individuals determined how long they

Several Plains tribes practiced the Sun Dance, a religious ritual of renewal that often lasted three or four days. *(By permission of Colorado Historical Society)*

would dance. Some vowed to dance throughout the ceremony, fasting the entire time; others might dance for shorter periods of time. Among most Plains tribes the dance also included self-torture. The giving of flesh and blood was the highest honor one could pay to the supernatural powers. In the MANDAN Okipa ceremony, shamans cut slits in the back, breast, and legs of certain young warriors. Wooden slivers or skewers were passed through each slit and a thong was attached to each sliver. Buffalo skulls were tied to the leg thongs. The supplicants were then suspended from the ceiling of the ceremonial lodge by the breast and back thongs. Through the warriors' endurance of torture, the world was revitalized and the society strengthened. Among the Lakota, Cheyenne, and Blackfoot Confederacy the participants were not suspended but were instead attached through breast or back skewers to the central pole of the dance lodge. They then had to pull against the ropes attached to the pole to break free. Sometimes the breast skewers were attached to the pole and buffalo skulls were attached to the back skewers. During the time the participants danced, they blew eagle-bone whistles and gazed toward the top of the Sun Dance pole and therefore toward the sun.

Susquehannok *Indian tribe of the northeastern United States*

In 1550, the Susquehannok were living in what are now the states of New York and Pennsylvania. By 1600, they were centered mostly in the latter state and by the mid-1600s they had migrated to Maryland and as far south as Virginia.

Although the Susquehannok's appearance in the historical record was brief, it was not uneventful. During the 1600s, the Indians were at war with the LENNI LENAPE (formerly Delaware) and the tribes that comprised the IROQUOIS CONFEDERACY. Hostilities between the Susquehannok and Lenni Lenape ended in about 1641, but frequent raids and full-scale warfare continued with the Iroquois. In 1652, for example, one Susquehannok village lost about 2,000 members to the Iroquois. For a time thereafter, the Susquehannok held their own against their traditional enemies. Then a new enemy—SMALLPOX—made a tragic appearance, and the Susquehannok, who survived quickly lost their advantages against the Iroquois.

About this time, the British governor of Maryland, in order to calm tensions between the Susquehannock and Iroquois, invited the former to relocate to an area just below present-day Washington, D.C. The move proved disastrous for the Susquehannok. They quickly became embroiled in the events surrounding BACON'S REBELLION (1676). In the years following, many Susquehannock settled among their former enemies, the Iroquois and Lenni Lenape. By 1690, however, some of the Susquehannok had returned to their homeland and settled in a village at the confluence of Conestoga Creek and the Susquehanna River.

In the decades that followed, various Indian groups migrated to the area and intermarried with the Susquehannok.

In 1763, the tribe fell victim to PONTIAC'S REBELLION (1763–64) and the infamous PAXTON RIOTS (1763–64). Demoralized and reduced in number by wars and disease, the Susquehannok survivors ceased to exist as a tribe and the individual families merged with other tribes. Some descendants now live among the SENECA and CAYUGA in Oklahoma.

Suwanee River (1818) *military encounter during the First Seminole War*

In spring 1818, during the final stages of the First SEMINOLE WAR (1816–18), General ANDREW JACKSON led 1,500 soldiers and 1,800 allied CREEK in a two-pronged campaign to end SEMINOLE resistance in north-central Florida. On April 12, the Creek, led by mixed-blood William McIntosh, discovered a much smaller force of 200 Seminole under Peter McQueen in a swamp between the Econfina and Suwanee Rivers. The Creek forced the Seminole into the open and virtually destroyed them. When the fighting was over, 37 men were killed and some 100 taken prisoner.

A few days later, on April 16, Jackson reached the town of Seminole chief BILLY BOWLEGS on the Suwanee River. The Indians had fled upon learning of the Americans' approach, but the town had become a haven for escaped slaves. Those who remained in the town made a brief stand before fleeing across the river. After razing the town, Jackson and his men marched on Pensacola. Encountering no resistance along the way, the troops continued their advance, and the campaign ended shortly thereafter.

Swaanendael (1632) See DUTCH-INDIAN HOSTILITIES.

sweat lodge *ritual space used in cleansing ceremonies by many Indian tribes*

Several Indian groups, mainly on the Great Plains, considered sweating an essential purification process preparatory to any major ceremony or to a battle. When a war party set out, a sweat might be undertaken beforehand. Sacrifices of small pieces of skin sometimes accompanied the sweat.

The typical sweat lodge was a low, dome-shaped structure composed of willow saplings. The number of willows used for the frame depended upon the tribe and occasion. The CHEYENNE seldom used fewer than 12, with 16 being the most common. Fourteen were usual among the CROW and BLACKFOOT CONFEDERACY, but the CROW used as many as 100. The lodge was completely covered with mats or skins, and rocks that had been heated red-hot were placed in the center of the lodge. The Indians then sprinkled water onto the rocks, creating dense steam and heat and causing the participants to sweat profusely. Someone outside would periodically remove the covering for short periods to allow participants to cool off. After the final sweating (usually fourth in a series of sweats), the participants dashed into the nearest creek.

tactics, Native American *procedures used in battles fought by Native Americans*

In precontact times, Native Americans warfare was undertaken by warriors on foot armed with handmade weapons, such as SPEARS, LANCES, and BOWS AND ARROWS, and carrying large rawhide shields. Both pitched battle and guerrilla tactics were used. After the introduction of guns and horses, however, the needs of battle changed, and guerrilla tactics came to predominate in American Indian warfare.

An eyewitness named Saukamappee recorded a 1720 battle that suggests how Indians may have engaged in pitched battles in precontact times. The combatants were 350 CREE and Piegan against roughly the same number of similarly armed SHOSHONE, none of whom used horses or guns. Staging an open battle, these warriors crouched behind their shields and each side shot volleys of arrows at the enemy. The archery exchange inflicted no serious wounds in the battle Saukamappee described, a result he said was not uncommon. At that point, the fighting might move into a second stage: a charge into the enemy, initiated by a startling war cry. Brief but bloody hand-to-hand fighting would then ensue, with warriors wielding stone-headed war clubs (see CLUB, WAR).

Pedestrian warfare, that is warfare on foot, such as that described by Saukamappee prevailed in the Great Lakes region, and petroglyphs suggest that such weapons and methods of warfare were in use throughout the Plateau and Plains regions. Accounts of early Spanish explorers on the southern plains also describe Indians using large buffalo-hide shields that covered the entire body. Likewise, early painted hides show pedestrian warriors (probably Plains APACHE),

their torsos entirely hidden behind their ornate circular shields.

Guns caused these ancient tactics to fall into disuse in the early 17th century. BODY ARMOR was likewise abandoned at this time (except in the Pacific Northwest, where Tlingit warriors continued using it quite successfully). Made of hardened leather or boards woven together with leather strips, Native American armor was effective against arrows and spears but did not protect the wearer against bullets. Instead, Indians relied on guerrilla tactics, using light weapons and divided forces.

American Indians were skilled practitioners of guerrilla warfare. Besides being intimately acquainted with the land, as hunters they were experienced in the techniques of ambush and stalking the enemy. Indians also used raids to great effect. A war party might stalk an isolated enemy camp with no more than a few dozen people, such as a hunting camp, and make a surprise attack at dawn, destroying the entire camp and gaining territory and goods. Unlike their European counterparts in North America, Indians routinely sent SCOUTS to gather information on both the lay of the land and the enemy. Members of a war party would keep close enough together to support one another. When overcome, they would retreat to the nearest stand of trees. By contrast, the European armies marched in close columns into unknown territory and fought in formation, making their location and their troop strength obvious.

At first disdaining the "disorganized" methods of their Native American opponents, Europeans eventually saw their value but faced a steep learning curve. The English colonizers of New England, for example, encountered fierce resistance from METACOM, a WAMPANOAG chief whom they called King

Philip. His warriors carried out many successful raids and ambushes by hiding in the Rhode Island wilderness. In 1675, the Rhode Island militia tried this promising tactic themselves but clumsily gave away their position. A few days later, they killed seven to 15 of their own troops in the confusion of guerrilla warfare at the battle of POCASSET SWAMP. The English finally defeated Metacom only after enlisting the services of 140 Indians, who with 60 English soldiers pursued the war chief in 1676. Over time, more French and British commanders sought the aid of Indians, who played a central role in the French and Indian Wars (1689–1763).

By the early 1700s, numerous Indian groups had acquired horses. Equestrian travel demanded freer use of arms and legs, so horse-riding warriors wore shorter protective garments and carried smaller shields than their pedestrian forebears had done. Because Indians directed their horses with their knees, their hands remained free for fighting. Modern military historians often rate the horsemanship of Plains Indian warriors as superior to that of the U.S. Army cavalry. The military tactics of mounted Indians included psychological warfare: Several tribes on the central and northern plains used the COUP STICK to strike an enemy without harming him. Doing so suggested that the person who had counted coup could have easily defeated the person who had been struck. Among many tribes it was considered braver to touch an enemy but not harm him than to kill him.

Throughout the 19th century, non-Indian settlers continued their westward advance. After the CIVIL WAR (1861–65), the U.S. Army attempted to confine the populations of American Indians living on the Great Plains to reservations in order to open more land for non-Indian settlement. Once again they faced guerrilla warfare. Besides being fine horsemen, American Indian warriors on the Plains as were excellent military tacticians, according to modern scholars. One of the finest of these was CHIEF JOSEPH of the NEZ PERCE. Some of the strategies and battle plans that Chief Joseph devised as part of his 1,600-mile retreat from the U.S. Army in 1877 are still taught today at West Point, a U.S. military academy. Historians today tend to ascribe the Indians' loss of the protracted Plains Wars not to lack of military skill, but to leadership structure: American Indian war chiefs led coalitions of fighters, all of whom were volunteers, whereas U.S. Army generals commanded their soldiers and were in turn commanded by a chain of superior officers up to the president of the United States.

According to modern military historians, American Indians lost the fight to keep their lands *despite,* not because of, their military tactics. Instead, they lost because the non-Indian settlers arrived with both guns and germs. Never as well armed as the new settlers, North American Indians were reduced by warfare and disease until too few remained to effectively to defend their homelands.

Further Reading

Keoke, Emory Dean, and Kay Marie Porterfield. *Encyclopedia of American Indian Contributions to the World.* New York: Facts On File, 2002.

Taylor, Colin F. *Native American Weapons.* Norman: University of Oklahoma Press, 2001.

tactics, non-Native American *procedures used by non-Indians in battles fought with Indians*

Tactics used against Native Americans in North America varied according to time, place, and technology. In their earliest encounters with the tribes of the Southwest, Spanish conquistadores enjoyed three enormous advantages: BODY ARMOR, FIREARMS, and horses. With the proliferation of horses among Indian groups in North America during the 18th and 19th centuries, many of the Plains peoples became much more formidable opponents. Indians generally avoided open confrontations, except when the odds were in their favor. Experience also demonstrated that early muskets were wildly inaccurate and difficult to reload. Thus, BOWS AND ARROWS often proved much more effective in the long-range skirmishing that characterized battles on the Plains. As muskets became more accurate, many tribes secured similar weapons through trade with other Europeans, especially the French. Of course, the increasingly widespread use of firearms would render body armor obsolete.

In the Eastern Woodlands, French, English, Dutch, and Spanish invaders engaged in a much different type of warfare. Traditional European tactics—which called for two or three lines of soldiers to stand shoulder-to-shoulder in the face of the enemy—were often ineffective in the woodland terrain. In battles such as BRADDOCK'S DEFEAT (1755), European regulars often met their match in the Native Americans. In addition, mounted troops were too expensive to be deployed in the woodlands, swamps, and mountains. With less room to maneuver, warfare with groups such as the IROQUOIS CONFEDERACY, CHEROKEE, CREEK, MIAMI, MOHAWK, PAMUNKEY, and NATCHEZ often took a much more violent turn. Indians and non-Indians frequently launched raids or direct assaults against enemy homes and villages, such as POWHATAN CONFEDERACY leader OPECHANCANOUGH's widespread attacks in Virginia (1622). Both sides relied on FORTIFICATIONS to protect strategic positions. In a few cases, Europeans deployed heavy cannon against their Indian foes, but the difficulty of moving these enormous guns on land limited their effectiveness. (See also ARTILLERY, USE OF.)

With the TREATY OF PARIS (1783) and the ratification of the U.S. Constitution, the United States replaced Britain as the chief military threat to the tribes. The small American regular army, often reinforced by state militia or volunteers, continued to use European-style tactics against the Native Americans, with mixed results. Without proper training or leadership, American forces suffered disastrous losses in HARMAR'S DEFEAT (1787) and ST. CLAIR'S DEFEAT (1791). But when they were well trained and competently led, as in the battle of FALLEN TIMBERS (1794), disciplined American forces proved quite effective.

Tactics generally evolved as the nation expanded onto the prairies and plains of the Midwest. Here the sieges and pitched battles of the east became less common. During the 1820s and 1830s, mounted Plains warriors, such as the COMANCHE, CHEYENNE, and Lakota (see SIOUX), initially enjoyed enormous advantages over U.S. infantry regulars. By virtue of their mobility, these tribes could pick the time and place of battle. Only in 1832 did Congress authorize a mounted regiment; other cavalry units would be added in the coming years. By the 1850s the development of a mass-produced rifled musket had swung the pendulum in the other direction. Foot soldiers who carried these new weapons, which were easier to load, longer-ranged, and more accurate than earlier firearms, became deadly enemies. Mounted troops gradually added repeating pistols.

By trial and error, successful military figures such as RANALD S. MACKENZIE, GEORGE CROOK, and NELSON A. MILES came to develop several common tactics after the CIVIL WAR (1861–65). Successful officers recognized the importance of surprising the enemy. When fighting became intense, U.S. troops usually dismounted to retain unit discipline and to fire more accurately. To reduce Indian mobility, some campaigns, such as the SOUTHERN PLAINS WAR (1868–69) and the RED RIVER WAR (1874–75) were conducted in the winter, when forage for Indian horses was less available. Typically, they employed large numbers of Indian auxiliaries to help them locate their foes. To force their enemies to fight, commanders often deployed several columns that would converge on a village or encampment from different directions. Having captured the site, army units routinely destroyed the tribe's food, clothing, and shelter. In the Pacific Northwest and Far Southwest, successful U.S. commanders often replaced their traditional wagons with large numbers of mules, gaining additional mobility while maintaining their logistical advantage.

When successful, attacks such as the one conducted by GEORGE ARMSTRONG CUSTER during the battle of the WASHITA (1868) could be devastatingly effective. But in the melees that usually followed, order and discipline could be lost, and large numbers of women and children killed. Converging columns also meant that friendly forces had to be divided in the face of the enemy. If several tribes formed a coalition, as did many Lakota and Northern Cheyenne in 1876, the leader of one column could be at a tremendous disadvantage. Such was Custer's fate at the battle of the LITTLE BIGHORN (1876), when he faced an enemy ready to fight and enjoying overwhelming numerical superiority.

Surprisingly, the U.S. Army spent little time developing tactics against such foes. Many believed, as noted historian Robert M. Utley has concluded, that the Indian wars were "a fleeting bother," not worth their intellectual attention. This attitude undoubtedly reflected the more general racism within American society as a whole and proved costly to many soldiers unprepared to deal with the challenges they would meet during the nation's long campaigns against the Native Americans.

Further Reading
Starkey, Armstrong. *European and Native American Warfare 1675–1815.* Norman: University of Oklahoma Press, 1998.
Steele, Ian K. *Warpaths: Invasions of North America.* New York: Oxford University Press, 1994.
Utley, Robert M. "The Frontier and the American Military Tradition." In *The American Military on the Frontier: Proceedings of the 7th Military History Symposium,* edited by James P. Tate. Colorado Springs, Colo.: Office of Air Force History, 1978.
Wooster, Robert. *The Military and U.S. Indian Policy, 1865–1903.* New Haven, Conn.: Yale University Press, 1988.

— Robert Wooster

Talladega (1813) *siege of a Creek Indian village during the Creek War*

With the defeat of the RED STICKS at TALLASAHATCHEE fresh in their minds, the CREEK in the village of Talladega thought it prudent to place themselves in good favor with the Americans. In response, Chief RED EAGLE, leader of the pro-war Red Sticks, vowed to take vengeance on all Creek who aligned themselves with the invading forces of the United States. Intent on making an example of the Talladegans, Red Eagle ordered his 1,000 Red Sticks to seal off the village.

One quick-thinking Talladegan chief disguised himself and slipped through Red Stick lines at night. He traveled the 30 miles to Fort Strother, where General ANDREW JACKSON's troops were headquartered. The news of the action presented Jackson with a dilemma, for his troops had not eaten in some time and were not physically ready for battle. On the other hand, he could not afford to allow the Red Sticks to execute judgement on Talladega, thereby risking the prestige Americans had won at Tallasahatchee. Jackson opted to strike quickly. At midnight on November 7, 1813, 1,200 infantrymen moved out from Fort Strother, leaving their supplies and the injured virtually unguarded. They arrived within six miles of Talladega by evening of November 8. At dawn on November 9, the men marched toward Talladega according to Jackson's plan, with infantrymen in the center, backed and flanked by cavalry. When the soldiers were within 80 yards, the Red Sticks sprang forward and began firing both guns and arrows. The infantrymen fell back as the Red Sticks rushed toward them, upon which the cavalry encircled the Indians, catching them in a deadly cross fire. One section of inexperienced militia dropped back, either through fear or confusion, allowing 700 Red Sticks to escape.

Jackson reported 299 Red Sticks killed, a number vigorously denied by the Indians. It was not determined how many Red Sticks were injured. Seventeen soldiers were killed and 80 were wounded. Jackson had high praise for his troops, even though they were not able to pursue the escaping Red Sticks.

Although Red Eagle and his Red Sticks lost the battle, they nevertheless enjoyed some success by destroying livestock and crops, making it impossible for troops to live off local provisions. The army's civilian contractors unwittingly abetted this situation by their slow and unpredictable delivery of food and other battlefield essentials. Consequently, Jackson's ranks became plagued with desertion and mutiny.

Tallasahatchee (1813) *first battle of the Creek War*

In 1813, Tennessee officials were handed a long-sought excuse to invade CREEK territory when the RED STICKS (traditional-minded Creek warriors influenced by SHAWNEE leader TECUMSEH) destroyed the garrison and killed refugees in the battle of FORT MIMS (1813), an incident in the Creek Civil War. The *Nashville Clarion* declared that the Creek, "have supplied us with a pretext for a dismemberment of their country." The Tennessee legislature immediately appropriated $300,000 and authorized a 3,500-man militia for service against the RED STICKS Creek warriors (traditional-minded Creeks influenced by SHAWNEE leader TECUMSEH). ANDREW JACKSON was appointed to head the operation. Although pale and weak from a recent dueling injury, Jackson pushed his men south at the rate of 20 miles per day. When they reached Ten Islands on the Coosa River in present-day Alabama, Jackson received a report of 200 Red Sticks at nearby Tallasahatchee. Jackson dispatched 1,000 men to Tallasahatchee under the command of General John Coffee.

Coffee divided his men into two groups and sent them to encircle the village. When they became aware of the militia, the Red Sticks began beating drums and yelling to warn of danger and unify their counter efforts. As the militia's forward guard advanced into the village, the Red Sticks stood their ground and, with violent effort, fought through to Coffee's main line. The militia then caught the Red Sticks in a deadly cross fire. Forty-six Indians bolted for a nearby house and were trapped by pursuing militiamen, among whom was a young Davy Crockett.

A total of 186 Creek were killed in the battle of Tallasahatchee, including some women and children. Eighty-four women and children were taken prisoner. Coffee's casualties included 41 wounded and five dead. General Jackson considered the victory just payment for the defeat at Fort Mims. He later wrote to Tennessee Governor Willie Blount: "We have retaliated for the destruction of Fort Mims . . . . Not one of the warriors escaped to carry the news."

Tall Bull (Hotoa-qa-ihoois) (ca. 1830–1869) *leader of the Cheyenne Dog Soldiers*

Taking a hereditary name often borne by respected CHEYENNE leaders (another man called Tall Bull, for example, fought at the battle of the LITTLE BIGHORN), Tall Bull came to prominence as a leader of the Cheyenne DOG SOLDIER society, a group of particularly accomplished fighters. It is believed that overly aggressive actions against peaceful Cheyenne camps by Colorado volunteer units during the CIVIL WAR (1861–65) convinced Tall Bull to take up arms against the United States. He refused to promise peace in negotiations with General WINFIELD S. HANCOCK in 1867 but later that year agreed to more favorable terms under the MEDICINE LODGE TREATY (1867).

Peace on the Southern Plains, however, proved elusive. Tall Bull participated in the unsuccessful assault upon non-Indian buffalo hunters at BEECHER'S ISLAND (1868). For most of the SOUTHERN PLAINS WAR (1868–69), his hit-and-run tactics were an effective counter to the army's attempts to force as battle on unfavorable terms, and he attracted additional supporters from the SIOUX and ARAPAHO. On July 11, 1869, however, his camp of 84 lodges was surprised by an army column commanded by Major EUGENE A. CARR at SUMMIT SPRINGS. Tall Bull was killed in the fighting, with both WILLIAM CODY and Frank North later claiming to have slain the leader of the Dog Soldiers.

Tampa, Treaty of (Fort Moultrie Treaty) (1823) *treaty between the U.S. government and the Creek Indians*

General ANDREW JACKSON's victory over the SEMINOLE in the First SEMINOLE WAR (1816–22) resulted in the U.S. acquisition of Florida from Spain. On December 15, 1823, the Treaty of Tampa was signed by a few nonrepresentative Seminole chiefs and warriors who were Jackson's recent allies against their own people. The treaty required the Seminole to remove themselves from the coastal areas desired by American settlers to the swampy interior of Florida. The United States, meanwhile, pledged to protect the Seminole from depredations by non-Indians. Farm implements, livestock, a school, a blacksmith, and a gunsmith were to be provided, along with farm land and rations for one year. In return the Seminole agreed to allow the free passage of U.S. citizens through their territory and to refrain from war against foreign nations unless permitted by the United States, which also promised a bounty for the return of runaway slaves and other fugitives.

The difficulties of removal to the specified territory and the failure of the United States to keep its treaty obligations brought hardships and starvation to the Seminole, who began raiding settlers' farms for food. Settlers soon began to demand the removal of the Seminole, which eventually resulted in the Indians' forced signing of the PAYNE'S LANDING TREATY (1832). Many Seminole preferred armed conflict to migration to Indian Territory (Oklahoma), as required by the treaty. This led to the Second SEMINOLE WAR (1835–42) with the United States.

Taovoya (1759) *Spanish attack on Indian villages in what is now Texas*

The Caddoan-speaking WICHITA and CADDO, called the Taovoya by the French, were the middlemen between the French and the powerful COMANCHE and KIOWA during the early 1700s. The Taovoya provided the Comanche with French guns and ammunition in exchange for buffalo robes and plunder from the Red River settlements in Texas. Although primarily merchants, they sometimes accompanied the Comanche on raids into Texas. The Taovoya were also agriculturists and supplied Plains Indian hunters with beans, corn, melons, pumpkins, and salt.

Following their attack on the Spanish SAN SABA (1758) Mission in Texas, the Comanche went to the Taovoya's fortified twin villages on the Red River near Ringgold, Texas. Spanish commander DIEGO ORTÍZ PARRILLA, with a Spanish military contingent that also included APACHE and some of their allies, pursued the Comanche and began a futile and costly assault. The Spanish launched wave after wave of attacks, only to be repelled by the defenders each time. The Taovoya and Comanche counterattacked, capturing many cannons that the Spanish had laboriously dragged with them. In the midst of battle, many Spanish horses were also stolen by Apache allies.

Completely demoralized, the Spanish soldiers begged their officers to allow them to retreat. Parrilla gathered the remnant of his forces and retreated south. The battle of Taovoya ended any further Spanish intrusion into Comanche territory in the late 18th century.

Tavibo   See GHOST DANCE.

Tecumseh (Tekamthi, Tecumtha, "panther lying in wait") (1768–1813) *Shawnee leader and organizer of pan-Indian rebellion*

Tecumseh was a SHAWNEE, born in the sprawling village of Old Piqua northeast of modern-day Dayton, Ohio. Following OTTAWA leader PONTIAC'S REBELLION (1763–64), non-Indian settlers flooded into the Ohio valley and claimed Indian land. Wars erupted, and Tecumseh experienced personal tragedy: His father was killed by frontiersmen during LORD DUNMORE'S WAR (1773–74). Young Tecumseh was then raised by an elder brother, who was killed in the AMERICAN REVOLUTION (1775–81). About the same time, Tecumseh's hero, Shawnee Chief CORNSTALK, was murdered by settlers in 1777. He later lost another brother in LITTLE TURTLE'S WAR (1786–95).

As a young man, Tecumseh distinguished himself as a warrior, fighting against Kentucky settlers in the southern Ohio valley and later with MIAMI leader LITTLE TURTLE. He also participated in battles against Generals JOSIAH HARMAR and ARTHUR ST. CLAIR, and against ANTHONY WAYNE in the battle of FALLEN TIMBERS (1794).

As much as Tecumseh disliked non-Indians, he had a strong sense of humanity. He learned to speak and read English and poured over history books and the Bible. He had also seen Indians burn a white man at the stake. Perhaps because of these things he advocated compassion in war. He treated prisoners well, refrained from torturing his enemies, and abhorred mutilation of the dead.

Between 1795 and 1805, Tecumseh, known for his oratory skills, began to proclaim that Indian land belonged to the Indians. His pronouncements came at a time when the governor of Indiana territory, WILLIAM HENRY HARRISON, was amassing huge tracks of Indian land through treaties with various tribes.

A contemporary artist's depiction of the death of Shawnee chief Tecumseh in the battle of the Thames, October 1813 *(Courtesy Library of Congress, Negative no. LC-USZ62-8)*

Tecumseh soon realized that if the various Indian tribes united they might be able to resist the loss of their territory. Tecumseh's dream of an Indian confederacy was soon furthered by his brother TENSKWATAWA, the Shawnee Prophet. In 1805 the latter had a dream and began proclaiming a message that advocated returning to the traditional Indian way of life, unencumbered by European culture, religious beliefs, and liquor.

In 1808, Tecumseh and the Shawnee Prophet established Prophetstown, or Tippecanoe, in Indiana Territory. Soon LENNI LENAPE (Delaware), MIAMI, POTAWATOMI, OTTAWA, WINNEBAGO, CHIPPEWA, Wyandot, Shawnee, and other Indians began to gather at the thriving community. Their numbers swelled into the thousands, as Tecumseh traveled hundreds of miles speaking to large groups of Indians.

Tecumseh's vision of an Indian Confederacy was shattered in 1811. In late fall that year, Harrison sent about 1,000 infantry soldiers toward Prophetstown, ostensibly to reclaim stolen army horses. Tecumseh wanted to avoid conflict with the army until his alliance was solidified. On November 7, however, the Shawnee Prophet, driven by religious confidence and Winnebago encouragement, ordered warriors to attack the enemy force. The warriors managed to kill 61 and wound 127

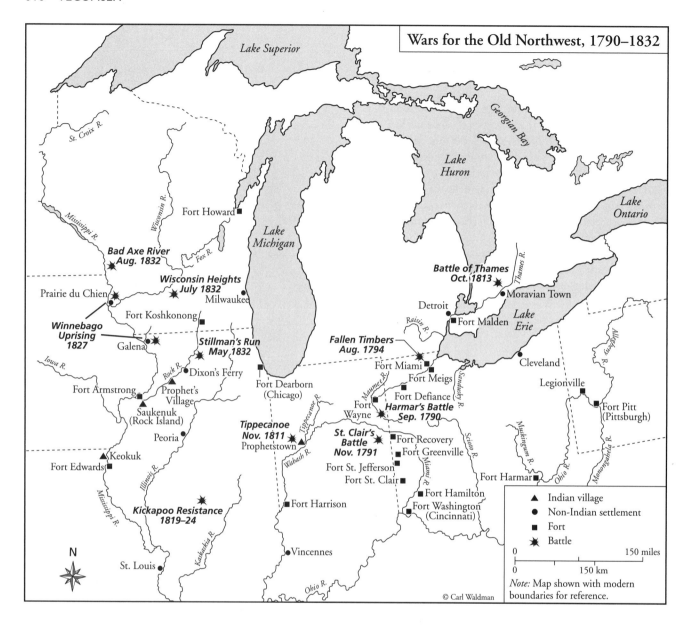

Wars for the Old Northwest, 1790–1832

Lake Superior

Georgian Bay

Lake Huron

Lake Ontario

St. Croix R.

Wisconsin R.

Fort Howard ■

Lake Michigan

Mississippi R.

Bad Axe River Aug. 1832 ✳

Fox R.

Wisconsin Heights July 1832 ✳

Prairie du Chien ●

Milwaukee ●

Fort Koshkonong ■

Battle of Thames Oct. 1813 ✳

Thames R.

Moravian Town ●

Detroit ●

Winnebago Uprising 1827

Galena ●✳

Stillman's Run May 1832 ✳

Raisin R.

■ Fort Malden

Lake Erie

Iowa R.

Rock R.

Dixon's Ferry ●

Fallen Timbers Aug. 1794

Sandusky R.

Cleveland ●

Fort Armstrong ■

▲ Prophet's Village

Fort Dearborn (Chicago) ■

Fort Miami ■

Fort Meigs ■

Legionville ■

Saukenuk (Rock Island)

Tippecanoe R.

Maumee R.

Fort Defiance ■

Harmar's Battle Sep. 1790 ✳

Fort Pitt (Pittsburgh) ■

Peoria ●

Tippecanoe Nov. 1811 ✳
Prophetstown

Fort Wayne ■

St. Clair's Battle Nov. 1791 ✳

■ Fort Recovery

Scioto R.

Muskingum R.

Monongahela R.

Wabash R.

▲ Keokuk

Fort Edwards ■

Illinois R.

Fort St. Jefferson ■
Fort St. Clair ■

■ Fort Greenville

Miami R.

Fort Harmar ■

Ohio R.

Allegheny R.

Kickapoo Resistance 1819–24 ✳

■ Fort Harrison

Fort Hamilton ■

Fort Washington (Cincinnati) ■

Kaskaskia R.

Mississippi R.

N

St. Louis ●

● Vincennes

Ohio R.

▲	Indian village
●	Non-Indian settlement
■	Fort
✳	Battle

0 ————————— 150 miles
0 ————————— 150 km

© Carl Waldman

Note: Map shown with modern boundaries for reference.

---

as the soldiers repelled the attack. The Indians lost between 25 and 40 and then fled. The next day Governor Harrison moved his army into abandoned Prophetstown and burned it to the ground, destroying the Indians' possessions and food stores. "Tippecanoe and Tyler Too" later became Harrison's presidential campaign slogan. (See TIPPECANOE, 1811.)

Tecumseh's confederacy began to crumble as members of the various tribes returned home to fight by themselves. Then the WAR OF 1812 (1812–14) erupted. Tecumseh sided with the British, who made him a brigadier general.

Tecumseh was successful in recruiting and leading thousands of Indians in the British cause against the Americans. He and his warriors participated in the capture of DETROIT (1763), the siege of Fort Meigs, and other encounters. On October 4,

1813, as the British and Indians prepared for yet another battle against the Americans, Tecumseh had a premonition that he would die. The next morning he dressed in his buckskins rather than his general's uniform. He was killed that day in the battle of the THAMES (1813).

In the decades following his death, Tecumseh has been recognized by non-Indians and Indians alike as one of the greatest of all Indian leaders. He mixed determination with compassion. Above all he had a broad and clear vision of pan-Indian unity.

Further Reading

Josephy, Alvin M., Jr. *The Patriot Chiefs: A Chronicle of American Indian Resistance.* New York: Penguin Books, 1989.

Sugden, John. "Early Pan-Indianism: Tecumseh's Tour of the Indian Country, 1811–1812." In *The American Indian: Past and Present*, edited by Roger L. Nichols. New York: McGraw-Hill, 1992.
                                              — William B. Kessel

Tecumseh's Rebellion (1809–1811) *war between united Indian tribes and the U.S. military*

The struggle known as Tecumseh's Rebellion began a little over a decade after the signing of the TREATY OF GREENVILLE (1795) had brought peace to the Ohio country. Early in 1805, a SHAWNEE named Lalawethika had a religious experience. Like the earlier DELAWARE PROPHET Neolin, Lalawethika believed that he had been given a mission from the Great Spirit of the Indians: He was to lead a return to Native American values and traditions that would, in turn, result in a restoration of the Shawnee world. Lalawethika changed his name to TENKSWATAWA and began recruiting followers of his new creed.

One of Tenkswatawa's earliest recruits was his older brother TECUMSEH. Tecumseh had been raised and trained as a warrior and had participated in the battle of FALLEN TIMBERS (1794). He saw in Tenkswatawa's revival an opportunity to reestablish Native American power in the Ohio country. Tecumseh began traveling among tribes from the Great Lakes to the Mississippi River, spreading the message of Indian revitalization and a call for unification against the United States. At the same time, the governor of Indiana Territory, WILLIAM HENRY HARRISON, recognizing the demand by incoming settlers for more land, began a series of negotiations with local chiefs of the LENNI LENAPE (formerly Delaware), MIAMI, SAC, FOX (Mesquakie), Wyandot, and OTTAWA tribes to buy their land, in violation of the Greenville treaty. In September 1809 Harrison summoned some of these chiefs to Fort Wayne and bribed them into signing a treaty ceding about 3 million acres of land in what is now central Indiana.

One of the primary points of Tecumseh's plan of unification was that all Indian land should be held in common, with no one having the right to sell or give it away. Infuriated by the Fort Wayne treaty, he began to prepare for war. Hundreds of young warriors, seeking a chance at battle, began trips to Prophetstown on the Tippecanoe River in northeastern Indiana. By the spring of 1810 Tecumseh commanded a sizable force. Harrison became worried by the presence of so many warriors. Tecumseh made two trips, in 1810 and 1811, to the capital at Vincennes to reassure him.

Harrison was not comforted by Tecumseh's reassurances, however, and in October 1811 he moved 1,000 men to the vicinity of Prophetstown while Tecumseh was away gaining more support. Tenkswatawa, disregarding Tecumseh's orders, attacked Harrison with 600 warriors on the morning of November 7, 1811. Harrison drove the Indians away and burned Prophetstown. Tecumseh's Rebellion died on the battlefield of TIPPECANOE (1811). Tecumseh later became an ally of the British during the WAR OF 1812 (1812–14).

Tenskwatawa (Shawnee Prophet) (ca. 1775–1836) *Shawnee visionary and prophet*

Originally called Lalawethika, meaning "Loud Voice" or "Rattle," Tenskwatawa was a younger brother of SHAWNEE chief TECUMSEH. One of a set of triplets, he was born around 1775 near Springfield, Ohio. In 1805 Tenskwatawa had a vision that told him to proclaim to the Shawnee the rejection of all European culture and a return to the traditional Indian ways. Tenskwatawa also called upon all Indians to unite in a confederacy to maintain their heritage and thwart non-Indian advancement—a cause his brother Tecumseh took up as well. His message and his correct prediction of an eclipse of the sun in 1806 won him fame as a prophet. Consequently, he took the name Tenskwatawa, "The Open Door."

In 1808, at Tippecanoe Creek in the Indiana Territory, Tenskwatawa and Tecumseh established the village of Prophetstown, where followers flocked to their cause. Tenskwatawa's vision was shattered, however, in 1811. While Tecumseh was away, Prophetstown was attacked and burned to the ground by a force of 1,000 men under WILLIAM HENRY HARRISON at the battle of TIPPECANOE (1811).

The Prophet was not a military leader, and his prediction that Harrison would be defeated destroyed his prestige. Tenskwatawa took refuge in Canada, eventually returning to Ohio in 1826, and finally moving west to Indian Territory (present-day Oklahoma) with the remainder of the Shawnee. He is thought to have died in Kansas in 1836.

Terry, Alfred H. (1827–1890) *U.S. general*

Alfred H. Terry was born in Connecticut in 1827. When the CIVIL WAR (1861–65) began, Terry entered on the side of the Union as a volunteer militia colonel. He was one of the ablest non-West Point-trained officers, and he ended the war a brigadier general in the regular army.

Terry remained in the army after the Civil War, becoming commander of the Department of Dakota. In 1867 he served on the Peace Commission charged with negotiating peaceful removal of the Plains Indian tribes. The same commission settled RED CLOUD'S WAR (1866–68) and evacuated the BOZEMAN TRAIL. In 1875 Terry was one of the U.S. officials who tried, unsuccessfully, to negotiate the purchase of the Black Hills from Lakota (see SIOUX) leaders RED CLOUD and SPOTTED TAIL. During the War for the Black Hills (see SIOUX WARS), Terry personally commanded all columns of troops, including that of GEORGE ARMSTRONG CUSTER. After the battle of the LITTLE BIGHORN (1876), extensive controversy arose over whether Custer was obeying or exceeding Terry's orders when he attacked the Lakota and CHEYENNE camps and provoked the battle. Terry never commented publicly on this controversy.

After follow-up campaigning in the Dakotas, Montana, and Nebraska—which dispersed the Lakota to Canada and to reservations in the United States—most of the Lakota surrendered by the spring of 1877. Terry became a major general in 1886, retiring two years later. He died in 1890.

Tewa See PUEBLO INDIANS.

Texas Rangers *Texan paramilitary organization whose 19th-century responsibilities included frontier and border protection*
Although the first "rangers" in Texas were organized as early as 1823, the first force known specifically as Texas Rangers was created in November 1835, on the eve of that area's war for independence against Mexico. The Republic of Texas commonly employed rangers, inevitably mounted men and usually numbering between 50 and 150, in its border fights against COMANCHE and CHEROKEE, most notably at PLUM CREEK (1840). Notable ranger captains included BEN and Henry McCULLOCH, W. A. A. "Big Foot" Wallace, and JOHN C. ("Jack") HAYS.

With the annexation of Texas by the United States in 1845, the federal government assumed official responsibility for defense of the state's frontiers. But the state legislature often criticized what it believed to be the regular army's ineffectiveness, and periodically raised ranger units. During the war against Mexico, Texas Rangers were noted for their ruthless effectiveness; hostile and fearful Mexican citizens dubbed them "Los Diablos Tejanos." Ranger units were also present in several engagements against Native Americans during the 1850s. Most notable was the May 11, 1858, attack of about 100 Rangers and 110 Tonkawa volunteers, led by Captain John S. "Rip" Ford, against Iron Jacket's Comanche village at the Canadian River, Indian Territory. The Ranger-Tonkawa force destroyed the village, claiming to have killed 76 Comanche, including Iron Jacket, and capturing 18 women and children. Ford calculated his own losses at two killed and two wounded.

During the CIVIL WAR (1861–65), several Texas Confederate units referred to themselves as Rangers, but the next officially sanctioned force was authorized in 1874. The Texas Rangers were now divided into two groups—the "Frontier Battalion," led by Major John B. Jones; and the "Special Force," under Captain Leander H. McNelly. Jones's command, consisting of six companies of 75 men each, fought in several Indian battles as well as acting as a de facto state police force against criminals. McNelly's "Special Force" operated along the Mexican border, attempting to intercept Indian as well as Mexican marauders. As had been the case before the Civil War, the Texas Rangers established a reputation as being lethally effective in carrying out their operations against those deemed enemies of the state.

The 20th century saw substantial reductions in the size of the Texas Rangers and significant changes in their mission. In bloody conflicts in South Texas between 1914 and 1919, they were estimated to have killed 5,000 Hispanics. Scandals resulting from these government-sanctioned outrages and the changing nature of Texas led to wholesale changes. The modern-day force of just over 100 Texas Rangers serves as the state's elite law enforcement agency.

Thames (1813) *battle in the War of 1812 between Americans and a British-Indian alliance*
The battle of the Thames put an effective end to Native American resistance east of the Mississippi and north of the Ohio River. With the death of its most notable participant, SHAWNEE war leader TECUMSEH, the battle also destroyed the pan-Indian movement. It marked an end of the eastern tribes' resistance to British and American territorial aggression that had begun in 1607 with the establishment of Jamestown.

The battle of the Thames was in some ways a counterpart to the battle of TIPPECANOE (1811), which ended TECUMSEH'S REBELLION (1809–11). The major players were the same: Tecumseh, who had been commissioned a British officer and placed in charge of the Indian auxiliaries, and WILLIAM HENRY HARRISON, who led the American forces. At the beginning of the WAR OF 1812 (1812–14), Tecumseh and the British seized Fort Detroit from its American commander, William Hull. They held the fort and its counterpart across the Detroit River, Fort Malden, until September 13, 1813, when Commander Oliver Hazard Perry drove the British fleet off Lake Erie in the battle of Put-in-Bay. Without a secure supply line to his bases, the British commander, Colonel Henry Proctor, ordered Forts Detroit and Malden abandoned and began a retreat eastward across present-day Ontario.

Tecumseh was outraged by the abandonment of the forts. Confronted by Harrison's army of 3,000 men, he retreated to the banks of the Thames River, but there he stopped and refused to go farther. On the morning of October 5, 1813, Tecumseh placed his troops in a low-lying, swampy area and awaited Harrison's attack. The American commander obliged in the mid-afternoon, when he charged and broke through the British line. Proctor and his men fled the battlefield. Tecumseh, however, remained on the battlefield and died during the fighting. His body was never located, and no one was able to say who had killed him.

The-Other-Magpie (unknown–unknown) *Crow woman who became a warrior when her brother was killed*
In 1876, eager to avenge the death of her brother, who was killed by the Lakota (see SIOUX), The-Other-Magpie joined some 175 Crow warriors who rode with troops commanded by General GEORGE CROOK in the battle of ROSEBUD CREEK (1876) against the Lakota and CHEYENNE. As part of her medicine, this woman warrior wore a stuffed woodpecker on her head and painted her forehead yellow. Pretty Crow, a Crow medicine woman, remembered The-Other-Magpie as being wild, brave, and pretty, with no husband.

In the battle at Rosebud Creek, the Crow SCOUTS bore the brunt of the attack. While many scouts were armed with .50 caliber breech-loading rifles, The-Other-Magpie carried only her belt knife and a willow COUP STICK. At one point in the battle, riding her black horse straight at the Lakota, she rode against a Lakota warrior and struck him with her coup stick, counting coup on him. She later took his scalp (see SCALPING), which was one of only 11 scalps taken by the Crow that day.

Tidewater Wars   See POWHATAN WARS.

Tiloukaikt (d. 1849) *Cayuse leader*
In 1836, CAYUSE Chief Tiloukaikt welcomed American Methodist missionaries Dr. Marcus Whitman and his wife, Narcissa, to Cayuse territory. They built a mission on Indian land at Waiilatpu in the Walla Walla Valley of present-day Oregon. The Whitmans did not understand that Tiloukaikt had not relinquished ownership and that he believed that they should pay him for staying on the land. (With no concept of individual ownership of land, the Indians believed it was their natural right to live on the land and use its resources.) Further, the Whitmans offended Tilaukaikt's sense of hospitality by barring any Cayuse from entrance into their house, whereas they were welcome to enter Indian homes. They also refused to allow Cayuse horses to graze on land adjacent to the mission's buildings, and they expected the Cayuse men to engage in farming, a task considered by the Indians to be women's work.

Before the Whitmans came to Oregon, non-Indian immigrants going west had brought diseases and death to the Plateau Indians. Soon after their arrival, a new wave of immigration introduced measles to the Cayuse, killing more than 200. Tiloukaikt watched his people die as non-Indians generally recovered because of their greater immunity to the disease. In retaliation, he and a number of Cayuse warriors killed the Whitmans and approximately 12 of their workers, taking the rest as slaves (see WAIILATPU MISSION). This marked the beginning of the CAYUSE WAR (1848–50). In retribution, the U.S. government convicted and hanged Tiloukaikt and four others in 1849.

Tinaja de las Palmas (Quitman Canyon) (1880)
site of U.S. victory in the campaigns against Apache leader Victorio
Apache fighters led by VICTORIO had since 1877 largely eluded the U.S. government's efforts to force them into a pitched battle, instead preferring the hit-and-run TACTICS that had made them a potent military force in the Southwest. Traditionally, army pursuits of the skillful Victorio had come up empty-handed amid the rugged mountains of southern New Mexico, western Texas, and northern Mexico. In summer 1880, Benjamin Grierson, colonel of the 10th Cavalry Regiment, determined that he would try a new tactic. Rather than engage in the trailing efforts that had failed so frequently in the past, Grierson garrisoned the waterholes of the arid trans-Pecos region. He personally commanded the 24 men holding that at Tinaja de las Palmas in Quitman Canyon, Texas.

On the morning of July 30, Grierson's scouts learned that Victorio was approaching with about 150 men. Long-range skirmishing ensued, with Grierson's position secure in the rocky fortifications, but his men unable to sally forth and bring about a more decisive engagement. The arrival of U.S. reinforcements finally ended the confused four-hour fight as most of Victorio's force got away. Grierson claimed that seven Indians had been killed, admitting one dead and one wounded among his own command. Critics would later charge that Grierson should have mounted a more determined pursuit, but the colonel had clearly won the day's fighting.

After Tinaja de las Palmas, Victorio encountered other army detachments at the waterholes at Alamo Springs and RATTLESNAKE SPRINGS. Stung by these sharp little engagements and unable to operate freely without more dependable water sources, Victorio fled into Mexico, where he was killed at TRES CASTILLOS (1880).

Tippecanoe (1811) *battle between U.S. troops and a multitribal force in the war for the Old Northwest Territory*
On the eve of the WAR OF 1812 (1812–14), the United States was not only confronted with hostilities from Great Britain but also from the SHAWNEE Indians led by TECUMSEH. The great leader's brother, TENSKWATAWA, known as the Shawnee Prophet, preached that the great spirit had told him to encourage all Indians to abandon the white man's ways and return to traditional Indian ways. Tecumseh listened to his brother but did not share many of the Shawnee Prophet's beliefs. Tecumseh favored the use of European-style farm tools, but he believed his people should live as hunters in the traditional way. He consequently sought to build a confederation among nearby tribes, including the Wyandot, LENNI LENAPE (Delaware), KICKAPOO, CHIPPEWA, and OTTAWA. Tecumseh carried out his campaign for confederation throughout the territory with some success, until he was challenged by WILLIAM HENRY HARRISON, governor of the Indiana Territory.

During Tecumseh's absence, Harrison summoned chiefs from some of the other tribes to Fort Wayne, where he bestowed a great amount of liquor on them. He also gave them $7,000 for the cession of 3 million acres of Indian land. When word got back to Tecumseh, he became furious and began threatening hostile action against the U.S. troops. Harrison skillfully allowed the chief, accompanied by 400 of his warriors, to air his grievances.

Four days later, Tecumseh went on an expedition to gather support for his confederacy. Once again, Harrison took advantage of his absence. Armed with the excuse that an Indian had stolen an army horse, Harrison marched a force of 1,000 men to Tippecanoe, an area a short distance from Tecumseh's village Prophetstown, which served as the main meeting place for various tribes. The Prophet requested a meeting with Harrison on November 7, 1811. Although Tecumseh had ordered that no hostile action take place in his absence, Tenskwatawa had already planned a sneak attack against Harrison's force. In order to gain support from his warriors, the Prophet told them that several of the soldiers were already dead, having been killed by

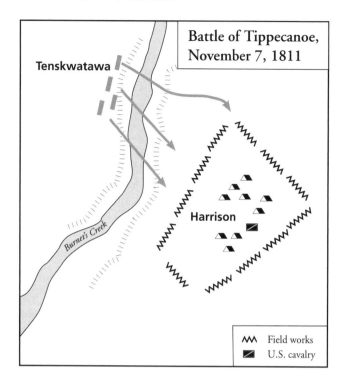

Battle of Tippecanoe, November 7, 1811

Tenskwatawa

Burnet's Creek

Harrison

∧∧∧ Field works
◪ U.S. cavalry

his magic. He ordered some warriors to infiltrate the army camp and kill Harrison. The Indians killed the sentinels, but one fired a warning shot before he died. The shot woke Harrison, who, finding warriors in his camp, calmly rallied his inexperienced troops and encouraged them to fire on the attackers.

The warriors pressed the attack three times before coming face-to-face with a bayonet charge. Fearing the weapons, they broke off the battle. Harrison entered Prophetstown unopposed, secured as many supplies as his men could carry, and set fire to the town. Although Harrison claimed victory at Tippecanoe (and would later use the battle to help secure the presidency), it was closer to a draw. Harrison had lost 61 men and 127 men were wounded, with Indian losses being unknown. The battle of Tippecanoe may not have been a military victory for Harrison, but there is no doubt it was a psychological defeat for Tecumseh in his efforts to form a confederacy.

Tohono O'odham (Papago) *Indian tribe of southern Arizona*

In 1687, the Spanish priest and explorer, Father Eusebio Kino, began work among the Tohono O'odham (historically known as the Papago). He introduced not only Christianity to the Indians but also wheat, chick peas, onions, and melon seeds. More important, he brought horses, cattle, and sheep with him. The relationship between the Spanish and the Tohono O'odham was for the most part friendly, although some of the latter participated in the AKIMEL O'ODHAM (formerly Pima) resistance against the Spanish in 1751.

In 1853, the United States negotiated the GADSDEN PURCHASE with Mexico. With it, the American government took control of about 30,000 acres of real estate on which lived about 5,000 Tohono O'odham. By this time Apache Indians were raiding the Tohono O'odham and absconding with horses, cattle, and anything easily transportable. In response, the Tohono O'odham loosely allied themselves with non-Indian settlers to fend off the Apache. The two groups combined to deal the Apache a crushing blow at the CAMP GRANT MASSACRE (1871).

The present-day Tohono O'odham own four reservations in Arizona, one of which they share with the Akimel O'odham.

tomahawk *Native American weapon and tool*

The tomahawk, a small hand ax, was perhaps the best-known Native American weapon of war. The word *tomahawk* comes from the ALGONQUIAN word *otomahuk,* which means "to knock down." Tomahawks came in different sizes and shapes, but most measured less than 18 inches long and were light enough to be used with one hand. The shape of some tomahawks was virtually identical to the modern hatchet. Early tomahawks had a head of stone or bone mounted on a wooden handle. After Europeans arrived in North America, the Indians traded with them for iron tomahawk heads. The tomahawk of the Lakota (see SIOUX), had an iron ball and spike at one end instead of a flat iron blade.

In battle, warriors used their tomahawks as clubs or threw them at their enemies. The tomahawk was also used like a modern hatchet or a hammer, for purposes such as chopping wood, driving stakes into the ground, and processing game. Another kind of tomahawk was used for ceremonial purposes. These *pipe tomahawks* had a pipe bowl on the head and a hollow handle. Some, such as those used by the Lakota, were decorated with feathers or dyed porcupine quills.

Tongue River (1865) *battle between U.S. troops and Arapaho Indians under Chief Black Bear*

Under the leadership of Brigadier General PATRICK E. CONNOR, three U.S. Army columns moved toward the Powder River in Wyoming Territory. They were to join together on September 1 at Rosebud Creek, a tributary between the Tongue and Bighorn Rivers. General Conner accompanied the "left column," marching from Fort Laramie on July 30, 1865. Conner's force was made up of cavalry supplemented by PAWNEE and OMAHA Indian SCOUTS. The three columns represented a large and comprehensive operation against the Plains Indians, including the ARAPAHO.

On August 11, Conner's column reached the upper Powder River, where it stopped to build Fort Conner. Patrols sent out through the area had no problem finding evidence of Indians nearby, and three separate skirmishes occurred, one of which had unfortunate results. A group of Pawnee scouts pursued a group of CHEYENNE over a 12-mile area, finally catching up with them. The scouts returned to Fort Conner waving 27 scalps (see SCALPING), which led to two days of celebration and much dismay for the commanding general.

Leaving a detachment to complete the work on Fort Conner, the general led his troops northwest along the BOZEMAN TRAIL. On August 28, Pawnee scouts reported to General Conner the presence of an Indian village 40 miles upstream at the head of the Tongue River. Conner led 125 cavalrymen and 90 scouts on a night march to overtake the Indians. Early on August 29, Chief Black Bear and his Arapaho were dismantling their lodges when Conner ordered his men to attack. The Indians, caught by surprise, fled south with their families. The Pawnee scouts rounded up the Arapaho pony herd while some of Conner's soldiers burned the village. Other soldiers chased the fleeing villagers. The ensuing 10-mile chase completely scattered Conner's command; realizing what had happened, the Arapaho then counterattacked. Only Conner's howitzers saved the outnumbered soldiers from potential disaster.

At the end of the battle of Tongue River, Conner reported killing 35 warriors, while claiming his own losses to be only seven wounded. The following month found Conner and his troops slogging up and down the Tongue River enduring horrific rain and snow storms. On September 11, he was informed that the other two converging columns had met with serious setbacks along the way and their troops had almost starved to death.

See also CHEYENNE-ARAPAHO WAR.

Tonto Basin Campaign   See APACHE WARS.

torture of prisoners *ritual injury or maiming of enemies taken in warfare*

Native American groups differed in their treatment of PRISONERS taken in war. Some tribes adopted prisoners of war, giving them equal status with warriors born into the tribe. Others subjected prisoners to torture. Through ritual torture an enemy warrior was stripped of his power and rendered weak and unable to endanger the tribe again. Prisoners were also tortured to instill fear in the enemy.

Whereas the process of torture often had personal and political motives, for some Native Americans it was an expression of religious faith. The more bravely the prisoner behaved both before and during the torture, the more respect he won from his captors. If a warrior behaved particularly bravely in battle, he stood a better chance of being adopted by the victorious tribe. On the other hand, if he had been maimed or disfigured in some way, he was more likely to be subjected to torture. His reaction to the torture could also affect his future.

During the 18th century, the PAWNEE of the western plains celebrated a ritual called the "Morning Star" ceremony. It was meant to cement a relationship between the tribe and the power represented by the morning star. The Pawnee chose for the ceremony a young woman taken captive in a raid on another tribe. They prepared her for her role by treating her

with great reverence for three days. At the end of that time, she was taken to the top of a platform, where a warrior killed her by piercing her heart with an arrow. The practice came to an end after a Pawnee warrior seized a girl in protest and rode away with her before she could be killed.

Although European settlers were quite familiar with torture, few of them understood the Indians' motivation. The Spanish, who arrived in Mexico in 1519 with HERNÁN CORTÉS, were horrified by the Aztec practice of human sacrifice on a massive scale. When the HURON tortured their MOHAWK opponents before the French explorer Samuel de Champlain in 1609, Champlain was shocked and angry. He finally persuaded his Huron hosts to let him kill their prisoner. For the Mohawk themselves and other members of the IROQUOIS CONFEDERACY, the torturing of prisoners was considered the prerogative of women who had lost relatives in battle. It served as a way for them to relieve their grief. In much the same way, the TUSCARORA of North Carolina burned to death John Lawson, a resident of New Bern, at the start of the TUSCARORA WAR (1711–13) as a way to vent their anger at having been defrauded of their lands.

For some tribes, such as the SHAWNEE, the torture process was more of a social occasion: everyone participated in the mistreatment of the prisoner. When frontiersman Simon Kenton was captured by the Shawnee in 1778, he had to undergo many tortures. The most famous of these was the gauntlet—the captive had to run between two rows of men, women and children who beat him with CLUBS. If he showed any hesitation or if he stumbled and fell, he had to start again from the beginning. The process ended when the prisoner died from the blows or successfully made his way from one end of the line to the other.

European colonists also tortured Indians captives at times. In the early years, few Indians were tortured in the English colonies because they were worth money as slaves in the Caribbean; torturing would damage their potential. Settlers living on the frontier during the 18th century employed torture as a way of expressing anger or frustration. During the TUSCARORA WAR (1711–13), a settler named William Brice tortured and killed a principal chief of the Coree. Generally, however, the Europeans preferred to kill the Indians than torture them.

Further Reading
LaFarge, Oliver. *A Pictorial History of the American Indian.* Revised by Alvin M. Josephy, Jr. New York: Crown, 1974.

Trade and Intercourse Acts   See BUREAU OF INDIAN AFFAIRS.

Trail of Tears *early 19th-century forced emigration of Native American tribes from their homelands in the Southeastern United States*
In 1830, the INDIAN REMOVAL ACT mandated that Native American tribes living in the Southeast be relocated to new

lands west of the Mississippi River. The CHOCTAW were the first tribe to be removed under the act. Between 500 and 1,000 of them were forced to march to Indian Territory (present-day Oklahoma); the emigration lasted from winter 1831 to 1834. The first winter was particularly severe, and the Choctaw traveled without blankets, shoes, or winter clothes. About a quarter of them died along the way. Many more perished from disease and starvation after their arrival in Indian Territory.

The CHICKASAW, most of whom left the Southeast after 1837, fared somewhat better on their march west, although they too suffered grievously on their new lands. The CREEK resisted relocation at first (see CREEK WAR), but beginning in 1836 they were forced west in chains; an estimated one-fifth of the tribe died. The CHEROKEE followed in spring 1838, and their ranks were eventually reduced by one-third. Some 3,000 SEMINOLE were also forced westward, although many stayed in Florida and waged a guerrilla campaign that led to the Second SEMINOLE WAR (1835–42).

The "Trail of Tears" is often used collectively to encompass the Removal of all five tribes, but the expression is a Cherokee one, and it referred originally and more specifically to their ordeal. The Cherokee fought the efforts of Georgia to obtain their lands and even took their case to the Supreme Court, which ruled in their favor in 1832. President ANDREW JACKSON, however, a staunch foe of all Native Americans, refused to enforce the decision. Instead, in 1835 his administration negotiated with the tiny minority of Cherokee that favored Removal and gave this faction authority to speak for the entire nation. The NEW ECHOTA TREATY (1835) that resulted required the Cherokee to give up their lands in return for $5 million.

A deadline for Removal was set for May 23, 1838, but when the day came only 2,000 Cherokee had emigrated. The U.S. Army, led by Generals WINFIELD SCOTT and JOHN WOOL, moved in and rounded up the 15,000 Indians who remained on their lands. These Indians were herded into stockades, where they passed the sweltering summer months. In the fall and early winter the first groups of Cherokee set out with army escorts on the 1,200-mile journey to Indian Territory and lands they had never seen before. Many died along the way; some 4,000 shallow graves marked their passage. One Georgia soldier who helped in the roundup and removal—and who later fought in the CIVIL WAR (1861–65), where he saw "men shot to pieces and slaughtered by thousands"—remembered the Trail of Tears experience as "the cruelest work I ever knew."

Treaty of . . .   See under specific name of treaty.

Treaty of 1863 *revision of the Walla Walla Council treaty between the Nez Perce and the U.S. government*
The discovery of gold on Clearwater River in 1863 brought a rush of immigration to the Nez Perce Reservation, a 10,000-square-mile tract located in the area of the present-day borders of Washington, Oregon, and Idaho. The U.S. government moved quickly to obtain possession of the land by calling for a council with the NEZ PERCE in the Lapwai Valley on June 9, 1863.

The treaty signed at this council reduced the size of the reservation to 1,000 square miles. Land belonging to the five Lower Nez Perce bands was relinquished, forcing the Indians to move north. LAWYER, a chief of the Upper Nez Perce, whose land was unaffected, willingly signed the treaty. But the Lower bands, led by Old Chief Joseph, White Bird, LOOKING GLASS, Toohoolhoolzote, and Red Echo, strenuously objected and refused to sign the treaty. Thereupon, the tribe split into opposing factions—the treaty and the nontreaty bands. Many Nez Perce of both factions had already converted to Christianity. The treaty men cut their hair in the style of non-Indians, while the nontreaty men tore up their Bibles and wore long hair as a symbol of resistance and adherence to the old ways.

In addition to annuities provided in the 1863 treaty, the Nez Perce received $262,500 to be expended as designated by the U.S. government for the development and promotion of European-style agriculture, education, and religion. Non-Indians with the appropriate skills and education were employed to bring about this cultural transformation. Consequently, merchants, teachers, and craftsmen ultimately received the most monetary benefit from the treaty.

The treaty also provided for the Allotment of land to individuals. Adult males and heads of households received 20 acres of tillable ground. The remainder of the land was held in common. Persons who refused to accept the treaty conditions of ownership could, at the discretion of the president, be disinherited.

The nontreaty bands left the council, ignored the territorial restrictions placed upon them, repudiated the actions of the treaty bands, and refused to be bound by a treaty they had not signed. Over the next several years, settlers and politicians became more demanding and vociferous in their opposition to the nontreaty bands' noncompliance. In May 1877, General OLIVER O. HOWARD ordered the nontreaty bands to resettle within the 1863 treaty reservation boundaries. They reluctantly agreed and arrived at the Lapwai Reservation before the deadline. Upon their arrival, an unfortunate unraveling of events brought about the NEZ PERCE WAR (1877), the only war between the Nez Perce and the U.S. army.

Tres Castillos (1880) *battle in which Apache leader Victorio was killed*
Between 1877 and 1879, Mimbreno APACHE leader VICTORIO attempted to cope with the problems associated with the American government's reservation policy. He tried to live on the desolate San Carlos Reservation in Arizona and his old reservation at Ojo Caliente, which the government had closed down, and also to settle with the Mescalero Apache, but none of these solutions worked for him. Finally, in frustration, Victorio and 60 warriors attacked a contingent of BUFFALO SOLDIERS Ojo

Caliente in September 1879, thus beginning VICTORIO'S RESISTANCE (1879–80).

By October 1880, Victorio and between 125 and 150 warriors had been forced into Mexico and were camped among three low peaks, called Tres Castillos by the Mexicans. On October 15, the Apache awoke at dawn to find themselves under attack by Mexican soldiers and Tarahumara Indian allies, led by Colonel Joaquim Terrazas. With their horse herd driven off, Victorio and his men had no choice but to fight. Scrambling up one of the Tres Castillos hills, they made their stand. The two sides exchanged fire for a day and a night. After the Apache tried but failed to slip away in the night, they hurriedly built rock fortifications, sang their death chant, and prepared to fight to the death. At daybreak on October 16, the Mexicans began picking their way through the boulders. When the final, hand-to-hand combat was over, the Apache had lost the battle, with 78 dead and 68 taken captive by the Mexican. Victorio was among the dead. The battle of Tres Castillos was one of the last Apache rebellions against the reservation system.

trophies, war *physical evidence of a warrior's prowess in battle*

Warfare was a major social force in the lives of some Native Americans. Young men—and occasionally young women—gained social status through their behavior on the battlefield. For these people warfare was a highly individual search for personal glory. Particularly brave deeds were recognized by the presentation of war trophies. These could be items taken from an enemy in battle or awards given to commemorate acts of courage. European American fighters also took war trophies in battle, although their culture did not share the Native American emphasis on individual personal glory as much as on the glory of the armies as a whole.

Among the most common war trophies were items taken from an enemy. These could include KNIVES and guns or other weapons, personal belongings, and horses. In cases where the enemy was killed, parts of his or her body could be taken as trophies. The most common of these were scalps—locks of hair taken from the crown of the head. SCALPING became common among Native Americans only after non-Indians began paying bounties for killing their enemies; proof of the death had to be presented to collect the bounty. A few Native American tribes, such as the HURON and some Caribbean tribes, practiced ritual cannibalism, cooking and eating an enemy to absorb his spirit and abilities in much the same way that parts of animals killed in the hunt were ritually eaten to honor them and absorb their qualities.

Trophies could also be awarded for acts of courage. The closer a warrior came to an enemy in combat, the greater was the honor given. The greatest honor was reserved for those who actually touched an enemy with their hands or with a special COUP STICK, an act known as COUNTING COUP. Among the Lakota (see SIOUX) tribes, feathers were awarded to warriors who performed brave deeds in battle. The Lakota chief Iron Tail, for example, owned a WARBONNET that, with its long trailer, held more than 50 separate eagle feathers—each one of which honored a brave act in war.

Native Americans displayed their trophies in many ways. Tribes of the Lakota nation and some APACHE braided scalp locks and wore them as fringe on headdresses, shields, and battle shirts. Among the CROW, feathers were displayed on shields. The tribes of the BLACKFOOT CONFEDERACY trimmed their coup sticks with prized feathers. Knives or guns seized in hand-to-hand combat were thought to provide protection in battle. Warriors also commemorated brave deeds in pictures on war shirts and in war dances. After a successful battle, warriors gathered for special celebration dances that could last for several days. They recounted their own deeds and reenacted the coup they had counted in the fight.

Sometimes the honor awarded to successful warriors was less tangible. In 1876, Buffalo Calf Woman, a CHEYENNE, won great honor in a battle in which her brother, Chief Comes in Sight, was wounded. Buffalo Calf Woman rode into the battle and rescued her brother from his enemies. The Cheyenne commemorated Buffalo Calf Woman by naming the fight after her, calling it "The Fight Where the Girl Saved Her Brother." Island Woman, wife of Cheyenne chief White Frog, also won a lasting reputation for her fighting prowess. In a fight with the PAWNEE. Island Woman counted coup on a Pawnee warrior who attacked her with a hatchet. She took the hatchet away from him and knocked him off his horse. Yellow-Haired Woman (Ehyophsta) was another Cheyenne warrior who fought in the battle of BEECHER'S ISLAND. (1867) and counted coup in fights with the SHOSHONE the following year.

European Americans were known to take scalps from Indians. While these were usually turned over to government or military agencies in exchange for cash bounties, settlers were known to skin dead Native American enemies for war trophies (see MUTILATION).

Further Reading
Josephy, Alvin M., Jr. *500 Nations: An Illustrated History of North American Indians.* New York: Alfred A. Knopf, 1994.
Utley, Robert M., and Wilcomb E. Washburn. *The American Heritage History of the Indian Wars.* New York: American Heritage, 1977.

Tule Lake (1872) *initial skirmish of the Modoc War*
On November 28, 1872, a company of the U.S. Army's 1st Cavalry under the command of Captain James Jackson rode into the MODOC village of leader CAPTAIN JACK along Tule Lake in northern California. Jackson's orders were to return Captain Jack and his warriors and their families to the Klamath Reservation in southern Oregon, which the Modoc had left to go back to their traditional lands in California.

As initial negotiations began, the Modoc chief, SCARFACED CHARLEY grabbed a gun and pointed it at a soldier, who immediately fired his pistol. Both sides opened fire with rifles and arrows. Casualties were minimal, however, with one Modoc and one trooper killed and about the same number wounded. Jackson gave limited pursuit to the warriors who fled, but he burned the Modoc village, forcing the inhabitants to leave the camp. This incident marked the beginning of the MODOC WAR (1872–73).

Captain Jack and the warriors later met up with their families and took refuge in the lava beds south of Tule Lake, where they held out against U.S. forces for several months.

See also LAVA BEDS, 1873.

Tuscarora *tribe originally inhabiting territory in North Carolina that joined the Iroquois Confederacy in the 18th century*
The Tuscarora were coastal Indians who fished and gathered crustaceans and mollusks from the bays of North Carolina. They also cultivated beans, corn, pumpkins, and tobacco and gathered roots, nuts, berries, and greens from the forests.

The Tuscarora generally did not engage in conflicts with settlers. Even though colonists squatted on their property, stole from them, and supplied them with liquor to cheat them, the Tuscarora remained neutral. Many suffered at the hands of slave traders, who kidnapped them and sold them to West Indian plantations. In 1710 Tuscarora land was sold by North Carolina to a Swiss entrepreneur, Baron Cristoph von Graffenried. Graffenried's attempt to drive the Indians away finally brought them to the breaking point and initiated the TUSCARORA WAR (1711–13). After the war, the Tuscarora, ragged and destitute, were driven from North Carolina. They migrated to New York and found acceptance among their distant relatives, the Iroquois. They became the sixth member nation of the IROQUOIS CONFEDERACY in 1722.

During the AMERICAN REVOLUTION (1775–81), Iroquois Confederacy tribes attempted to maintain a neutral position. However, the SENECA, MOHAWK, ONONDAGA, and CAYUGA were persuaded by Mohawk chief JOSEPH BRANT (Thayendanegea) to support the British. Their alliance was formalized at a great council in July 1777. During the battle of ORISKANY CREEK (1777), most of the Tuscarora and the Oneida fought for the Americans, and the Iroquois Confederacy erupted in civil war. Following Oriskany, the Tuscarora and Oneida joined General Horatio Gates in defeating British General John Burgoyne's campaign down the Hudson River from Canada. After Generals JOHN SULLIVAN and James Clinton invaded Iroquois country, burned 40 villages, and destroyed many acres of crops and orchards, the Oneida and Tuscarora suffered the vengeance of their fellow Iroquois.

After the Revolutionary War, the American-allied Tuscarora were settled on a reservation in northwestern New York near present-day Lewiston, where their descendants continue to live. British-allied Tuscarora settled on the Six Nations Reserve on Grand River in Ontario, Canada.

Tuscarora Treaty (1713) *treaty ending the Tuscarora War*
In the aftermath of the TUSCARORA WAR (1711–13), the remnants of a once-powerful North Carolina tribe, the TUSCARORA

were given a choice: They could migrate north and seek shelter with allied tribes, or they could negotiate a peace with the settlers. In the settlement that followed, most of the Tuscarora chose to leave their homes in North Carolina. Many moved to New York, where they found acceptance as the sixth nation of the IROQUOIS CONFEDERACY. Those few Tuscarora that remained, led by a chief called Tom Blount by the British, signed a separate treaty with the colonists on February 11, 1715, in which they surrendered most of their lands to the colonial government. Tuscarora of villages that had not taken part in the uprising (war) were allowed to stay in North Carolina unmolested. In the years that followed, they too joined the other Tuscarora, especially when in 1722 the Iroquois made the Tuscarora official members of the League of the Iroquois, becoming the sixth nation.

Tuscarora War (1711–1713) *war between the Tuscarora and the colonists of North and South Carolina*
In the early years of the 18th century, about 7,000 Tuscarora lived along the rivers and streams of southern Virginia and North Carolina. Their relationship with their neighbors, both European and Native American, was uneasy. They were regularly cheated of their lands by developers from North Carolina and captured in slave raids by the SUSQUEHANNOK and SENECA as well as the South Carolinians. In 1707 the Tuscarora fell victim to a smallpox epidemic (see SMALLPOX, EFFECTS OF). Two years later, they petitioned the leaders of Pennsylvania for permission to resettle in that colony.

The Pennsylvania government refused the Tuscarora petition because the southern colonies would not vouch for the Indians' good behavior (since doing so deprive themselves of a lucrative source of slaves). In September 1711 Tuscarora warriors struck back at colonists who were infringing on their lands. A Swiss nobleman, Baron Cristoph von Graffenried, was surveying a site for a colony of immigrants, which he planned to call New Bern. Von Graffenried chose as the site of his colony a spot already occupied by a Tuscarora village. Rather than bargain with the Indians, von Graffenried petitioned for and received the rights to the land from the government of North Carolina.

The Tuscarora attacked von Graffenried's surveying party on September 22, 1711, then turned on other nearby frontier settlements. About 120 colonists died in the raids. In retaliation, one of von Graffenried's settlers, William Brice, launched a punitive counterattack. Brice captured one of the principal chiefs of the Coree, allies of the Tuscarora, and tortured him to death (see TORTURE OF PRISONERS). Brice's action, however, only increased tensions between the two groups and brought the Indians back into open conflict with the colonists.

The colonists responded to Indian attacks by using the TACTICS they had perfected in slave raids against the Tuscarora and other local tribes. They advertised for Native American allies, promising them guns, cloth, and a share in the profits made from the sale of Tuscarora as slaves. Early in 1712, a band of 500 warriors, mostly YAMASEE, joined with 30 South Carolina settlers under Colonel JOHN BARNWELL in an attack on the Tuscarora village called Hancock's Town. After an indecisive siege, Barnwell negotiated a peace with the Tuscarora chief Hancock, but the colonial governments refused to accept Barnwell's terms. In March of the following year, 800 CREEK, CHEROKEE, and Catawba joined 100 South Carolina militia in an assault on the Tuscarora town of NOHOROCA (1713). The colonists and their allies killed 192 Tuscarora in this assault and took another 392 PRISONER, later selling them as slaves. Tuscarora casualties for the whole war are placed at around 1,400, or about one-fifth of the tribe's total prewar population.

The Tuscarora War destroyed the Tuscarora as a powerful and independent nation. About half of the survivors—between 1,500 and 2,000 members—fled north and sought shelter among the members of the IROQUOIS CONFEDERACY. In 1722, the Iroquois admitted the Tuscarora as the sixth nation of their confederacy. The Tuscarora who stayed in North Carolina signed a treaty on February 11, 1715, in which they surrendered most of their lands to the colonial government (see TUSCARORA TREATY).

Uncas See MOHEGAN.

Underhill, John (ca. 1597–1672) *colonial militia officer and mercenary*
Born in Warwickshire, England, John Underhill fought in the Netherlands as a soldier of fortune, serving under the Prince William of Orange, from whom he received excellent military training. His association with English refugees at this time led him to become a Puritan—although his later conduct suggests that this outward conversion was not accompanied by inner faith. He sailed to Boston in 1630 and soon became the Massachusetts Bay Colony's foremost military authority. In due course he organized a militia and became captain of the force. In 1636 he was second in command of JOHN ENDECOTT's Block Island expedition against the PEQUOT.

At the outbreak of the PEQUOT WAR in 1637, Underhill, in charge of small force of Massachusetts militia and Native American volunteers, joined up with an army from Connecticut under JOHN MASON. Together they surrounded a large Pequot camp on the Mystic River and set it ablaze in a dawn raid. Men, women, and children either died in the flames or were "received and entertained with the point of the sword" as they straggled out, reported Underhill, who was wounded in the hip during the engagement. Several hundred Pequot were killed in the raid. The colonists' Indian allies were appalled at the slaughter, but Underhill justified the action, saying that he had been merely doing God's work in destroying unbelievers—a common Puritan argument.

Underhill might have returned to Boston a hero, but the colony was enmeshed in a serious theological dispute. He supported Anne Hutchinson, who believed that Christians were saved by grace alone and thus under no real obligation to follow the strict moral laws of the Puritans. For this heresy, Underhill was stripped of his commission, then banished from the colony in 1638 for "gross and palpable dissimulation and equivocation." He was finally excommunicated for adultery two years later.

After drifting around New England for several years, Underhill was hired by the Dutch to fight against the Indians of the lower Hudson Valley (see KIEFT'S WAR, 1642–45). In February 1644, he led an attack on a Westchester Indian village near Pound Ridge that killed more than 500 Native Americans.

Underhill later changed employers, fighting with the English against the Dutch in the Anglo-Dutch wars of the 1650s and helping the English take over New Amsterdam in 1664. Toward the end of his life, Underhill became a Quaker. He died on Long Island, where he had served as a sheriff.

Ute *tribe occupying lands in western Colorado and eastern Utah*
In the years prior to European contact, the Ute were nomadic hunter-gatherers living in small bands throughout their territory in what is now Utah. After acquiring horses from the PUEBLO INDIANS in the 17th century, the Ute hunted buffalo on the Great Plains and often raided Spanish settlements in the Southwest, as well as those of the HOPI, PAIUTE, NAVAJO, APACHE, and the Plains tribes, to capture horses, women, and

Ute discover a gold prospector digging on their land in violation of a treaty with the government. *Harper's Weekly,* October 25, 1879. *(Courtesy New York Public Library)*

children. The Ute sold their CAPTIVES as slaves to the Spanish and Mexicans. When the Mormons settled in Utah in the mid-1800s, they banned the Indian slave trade and established friendly relations with Ute. In 1853, however, when several Ute of the Timpanogos band were killed by settlers, Timpanogos chief Walkara began raiding Mormon farms and towns. Walkara agreed to peace, however, when the Mormons mounted a successful defense.

In 1868, the Ute were forced to move from Utah to reservations in Colorado, but other Indian leaders on those reservations began a campaign to drive the tribe out. Ute leader OURAY tried to negotiate peace but he was unable to manage tribal unrest. In 1879, convinced they would have to fight for their reservations, two White River Ute bands attacked the Indian agency and ambushed a U.S. Army force (see UTE WAR, 1879). The uprising was quelled when more troops were called in. Not all the Ute had taken part in the conflict, but between 1880 and 1882, most of the bands were moved back onto two

reservations in Utah. The exception were the Southern Ute, who remained on a reservation in southern Colorado.

See also MEEKER AGENCY.

Ute War (1879) *confrontation between Ute Indians and white soldiers in Colorado in 1879*
Some 4,000 UTE Indians were located on a reservation in western Colorado and eastern Utah in the latter half of the 19th century. During the Colorado silver strikes of the 1870s, the Ute were forced to relinquish 4 million acres of their land to the miners. In 1876, Colorado joined the Union and began agitating for the Removal of all Ute to Indian Territory. This would open reservation land to white settlement and mining.

The situation for the Indians grew worse in 1878, when an unqualified and inept Indian agent, Nathan Meeker, tried to force the Ute to give up their hunting-gathering way of life in order to pursue conventional farming. In September of the next year the situation went from bad to critical when Meeker proposed that the Ute plow under their traditional horse-grazing meadows. Following a dispute with a medicine man known as Johnson, Meeker called for soldiers to protect him, the agency employees, and their families (see MEEKER AGENCY). In response, Major Thomas T. Thornburgh proceeded with 175 infantry and cavalry from Fort Fred Steele in Wyoming to the White River Agency in Ute territory. On September 29, horsemen from Thornburgh's detachment entered the reservation. There they were met by Chief Jack and 100 warriors who blocked the trail. Both sides tried to defuse the situation, but a shot was fired and the battle of MILK CREEK was ignited. Major Thornburgh was soon struck by a bullet and died. For almost a week the Ute and besieged soldiers exchanged fire. On October 2, black troops of the 9th Cavalry arrived to assist the soldiers. Three days later, when a strong relief force arrived, the Ute withdrew. Military casualties from the skirmish numbered 13 dead and 48 wounded. Furthermore, the Ute killed Meeker and nine other agency employees and took his wife, her daughter, and another woman captive.

Thousands of federal soldiers arrived on the scene and were prepared for all-out war with the Ute. The secretary of the interior, CARL SCHURZ, insisted that peace negotiations first be attempted. Eventually Charles Adams, a former agent to the Ute, together with a highly respected Ute chief named OURAY, met with the other Ute chiefs. The latter agreed to give up the hostages, and no Ute were punished for the skirmish.

The Milk Creek and Meeker killings accelerated the new Coloradans attempt to open the Ute Reservation for white settlement. The Indians soon lost most of the White River territory and were confined on smaller reservations in eastern Utah and southwestern Colorado.

Further Reading

Axelrod, Alan. *Chronicle of the Indian Wars: From Colonial Times to Wounded Knee.* New York: Prentice Hall, 1993.

Utley, Robert M., and Wilcomb E. Washburn. *Indian Wars.* Boston: Houghton Mifflin, 1987.

Waldman, Carl. *Atlas of the North American Indian,* rev. ed. New York: Facts On File, 2000.

Van Dorn, Earl (1820–1863) *U.S. and Confederate military officer*

Born in Mississippi, Van Dorn graduated from West Point in 1842 and was wounded and cited for gallantry during the Mexican War. Following brief stints in Florida during the Third SEMINOLE WAR and in administering military asylums for disabled veterans, in 1855 he secured a captaincy in the 2nd Cavalry Regiment. In 1858, General David Twiggs, commander in Texas, ordered Van Dorn to take a battalion of the 2nd Cavalry and establish a base inside Indian Territory (now Oklahoma) for campaigns against the COMANCHE. Van Dorn and his men subsequently won several engagements. He was wounded at the battle of RUSH SPRINGS (1858) and won a conclusive victory at the battle of CROOKED CREEK (1859).

Van Dorn was promoted to major in 1860, but in January 1861, he resigned his commission to join the Confederacy. Named a major general, he commanded Confederate and Indian troops in the battle of PEA RIDGE (1862). He later led an important raid against the Union supply depot at Holly Springs, Mississippi, dealing a fatal blow to ULYSSES S. GRANT'S initial attempts to move against the Confederate stronghold of Vicksburg. In May 1863, he was murdered at his Tennessee headquarters by a jealous husband, suspicious of Van Dorn's relationship with the man's wife.

Vargas Zapata y Lujan Ponce de León, Diego de (ca. 1643–1704) *Spanish colonial governor best remembered for his pacification of the Pueblo Indians*

Born into an illustrious Spanish family, Vargas was a veteran of imperial campaigns in Italy when he sailed to the West Indies in 1672 at the age of 29. Appointed governor of New Mexico in 1690, his most urgent task was to restore peace to the frontier in the aftermath of the PUEBLO REBELLION (1680). He began by putting together an army that eventually totaled 100 soldiers and an equal number of Indian allies. The force left El Paso in August 1692 and headed north toward Santa Fe. He arrived there in September and settled in for a siege. Vargas eventually induced the PUEBLO INDIANS to surrender "without wasting an ounce of powder [or] unsheathing a sword," in the words of one chronicler. He returned to El Paso at the end of the year, acclaimed as "the new Cid."

In October 1693, Vargas set out from El Paso again with 70 families following behind his army, intent on recolonizing the region around Santa Fe. The town had been reoccupied by Native Americans in his absence; this time Vargas captured it after a brief skirmish. Over the course of the next three years, Vargas quelled Indian resistance through a combination of forceful persuasion and promises of complete amnesty should the Indians reaffirm their allegiance to the Spanish Crown.

Despite his success in New Mexico, Vargas was replaced by a new governor in July 1697 and jailed on charges of embezzlement, mismanagement, and having provoked hostilities in 1695–96. After his case was reviewed in both Mexico and Madrid, he was restored as governor in November 1703. The following year, while campaigning against the APACHE, who had supported the Pueblo in their revolt, Vargas contracted pneumonia. He died on April 8, 1704.

Victorio (Bidu-ya, Beduiat) (ca. 1825–1880) *chief and military leader of the Warm Springs Apache*

Legends abound suggesting that Victorio was a Mexican, stolen at an early age by the APACHE and raised as one of their own. Most scholars, however, contend that he was Indian, born in southern New Mexico between 1820 and 1825.

As a youth, Victorio was no stranger to warfare. He lived through raids, killings, and retaliations between the Apache and the Mexicans. Then came skirmishes with U.S. citizens, especially miners, who wanted Apache land. During the 1850s and early 1860s, Victorio fought alongside respected Mimbreno Apache chief MANGAS COLORADAS and participated in the battle of APACHE PASS (1862). When Mangas Coloradas was killed in 1863, the mantle of leadership was passed to Delgadito, who was killed in 1864, upon which Victorio became leader. During

Victorio, an Apache war chief, led an Indian resistance force in 1880. *(By permission of the Western History Collections, University of Oklahoma Library)*

the 1860s and 1870s, Victorio's band alternated between raids in New Mexico and Texas and confinement on reservations.

By the mid 1870s, government officials had committed themselves to a "Removal policy," whereby all the Apache in Arizona and New Mexico were to be confined on a single reservation in San Carlos, Arizona. Victorio's group had been content to live at Ojo Caliente (Warm Springs), New Mexico, but in 1877 they were ordered to San Carlos. They arrived there on May 20.

Victorio and his Warm Springs Apache were unhappy at San Carlos. There was mistrust among the various Indian groups now living closely together there. The Indian Bureau and military officials were constantly bickering. Finally, on September 2, 1877, Victorio and Loco bolted from the reservation along with 310 men, women, and children. They headed east, taking with them livestock belonging to the White Mountain Apache. Within weeks most of the renegades surrendered at Fort Wingate (near present-day Gallup, New Mexico). Victorio, however, fled to Mexico. In February 1878 he surrendered at Ojo Caliente.

For months government officials debated the fate of Victorio and his band. They thought of moving them back to San Carlos, to Fort Sill, Oklahoma, or to the Mescalero Apache reservation. The Indians, however, wanted to stay at Ojo Caliente. In July 1879 Victorio was indicted for murder and horse theft. On September 4, he fled, thus beginning VICTORIO'S RESISTANCE (1879–80). Aided by some Mescalero Apache, Victorio's warriors carried out attacks in Mexico, Texas, New Mexico, and Arizona. For a year he eluded his pursuers, skirmishing with the U.S. Army at the battles of RATTLESNAKE SPRINGS (1880) and TINAJA DE LAS PALMAS (1880). On October 15, 1880, Victorio's band was met by an army of 350 Mexicans and Tarahumara Indians in the battle of TRES CASTILLOS (1880). The Apache were soundly defeated. Victorio was found among the dead.

Even as the details of his birth were surrounded by uncertainty, so were those of his death. Historians debate whether he was killed in the fighting or whether he took his own life before his enemies could touch him.

Amid the warfare and bloodshed, Victorio married and had five children. A medical officer in 1873 described him as a "virtuous" man. Historians have now placed Victorio with GERONIMO and COCHISE as one of the greatest of all Apache leaders.

Victorio's Resistance (1879–1880) *war with U.S. troops and Apache led by Chief Victorio*

In May 1877, the Warm Springs APACHE under the leadership of VICTORIO were forced to relocate from southern New Mexico to the San Carlos Reservation in Arizona. In September, the chief escaped along with 310 followers. Most of this group soon surrendered, but Victorio fled south into Mexico. In February 1878 he too surrendered at Ojo Caliente, New Mexico.

For a year, Victorio consistently refused to return to San Carlos, but by the summer of 1879, he had agreed to live on the Mescalero Apache reservation there. Before the relocation occurred, however, he was indicted for murder and horse stealing. Fearing for his life, Victorio fled and went to war on September 4, 1879. Within days, his raiders killed two shepherds and stole their horses and then attacked a cavalry horse camp, killing eight and taking 46 horses. On September 18, Captain Byron Dawson, with the 9th Cavalry and 46 NAVAJO scouts, advanced on Victorio's stronghold in the Black Range of New Mexico. There they were ambushed and 10 were killed. Victorio captured more horses and booty in the process. By late October, local newspapers were reporting that southwestern New Mexico was in the hands of the Apache.

By the time Victorio led his band into Mexico, they had killed between 75 and 100 people. In Mexico, they were joined by an additional 350 Chiricahua and Mescalero Apache warriors and perhaps some COMANCHE. There they won various skirmishes against Major A. P. Morrow's pursuing force. Early in the new year Victorio again entered New Mexico, cutting telegraph wires, killing prospectors, and fighting skirmishes against the army. Meanwhile, Morrow was in hot pursuit with five companies of cavalry but failed to capture Victorio.

By May, Victorio's Apache were spotted in Arizona, apparently headed for San Carlos. One paper reported that the Apache had killed 78 that month alone. Later that month, H. K. Parker, chief of SCOUTS under General Edward Hatch, caught up with Victorio in New Mexico and won a decisive battle near the headwaters of the Palomas River. Again, Victorio headed south into Mexico, killing settlers as he went. By now newspapers had attributed more than 500 deaths to the chief.

Eluding a 500-man Mexican force, Victorio crossed the Rio Grande into the trans-Pecos region of Texas in July 1880. There, he encountered small U.S. Army detachments at strategic waterholes and skirmished with the troops at TINAJA DE LAS PALMAS (1880) and RATTLESNAKE SPRINGS (1880). Returning to Mexico by October 1880, the Apache were located north of Chihuahua City, Mexico. There, at TRES CASTILLOS (1880), Mexican General Joaquin Terrazas ended Victorio's Resistance by killing about 78 Apache, including Victorio, and taking 78 women and children as prisoners.

Vikings *Norse seamen and explorers*

At the beginning of the second millennium of the Christian era—around A.D. 1,000—a Norse explorer named Leif Eriksson led an expedition to North America. Archaeologists have uncovered a Norse community at L'Anse aux Meadows in Newfoundland that may be Eriksson's settlement in the land he called Vinland. Although Eriksson did not meet any Indians on his journey, the two Icelandic poems that tell of the discovery, *Graenlendinga Saga* and *Eirik's Saga,* record later contacts between the Norse and Native Americans.

According to the *Graenlendinga Saga,* Leif's brother Thorvald Eriksson made a trip to Vinland several years after Leif and stayed for two years in the houses Leif had built. In his second summer in Vinland, Thorvald and his crew surprised a small band of Indians resting under their hide canoes. The Indians, whom the Norse called Skraelings, were probably either Dorset, a paleo-Eskimo tribe, or Tuli Inuit. Thorvald and the other Norsemen killed eight of the Skraelings, but one escaped. The Skraelings then returned in great numbers, and Thorvald was killed in battle by an arrow. He was buried in the New World, the first European casualty in warfare with the Native Americans.

Some years later—around A.D. 1010—an Icelandic merchant named Thorfinn Karlsefni led a larger group of settlers to Vinland. Both *Eirik's Saga* and *Graenlending Saga* record contacts between Karlsefni and the Skraelings. Some of these contacts were friendly; the Skraelings swapped furs and skins for milk from the Norse cattle. At other times they were hostile. On one occasion, the Skraelings were frightened off by a settler's bull, who came charging out of the woods at them. On another they fled when a woman named Freydis confronted them, slapping her naked breasts with a sword. Eventually, the hostility of the Skraelings became so great that Karlsefni abandoned his settlement and returned to Iceland.

The relations between the Karlsefni's group and the Skraelings foreshadowed the same conflicts that would arise some 600 years later between Native Americans and Europeans. *Graenlendinga Saga* states that Karlsefni's friendly relations with the natives ended when one of his men killed a Skraeling for trying to steal some weapons. *Eirik's Saga* tells how, when the Skraelings came to Karlsefni's camp to trade, the Norse traded small strips of red cloth in exchange for furs and skins. When the cloth supply began to run short, the Norse divided it into smaller and smaller strips "no more than a finger's breadth wide," declares the saga, "but the Skraelings paid just as much or more for it."

Vizcarro, Jose Antonio (fl. 1820s) *Mexican army officer and colonial governor*

Appointed governor of New Mexico in 1822, Colonel Jose Antonio Vizcarro was determined to subjugate the NAVAJO (Dineh), who had increased their raiding activities against Spanish colonies. In June 1823, he set out with 1,500 soldiers on a four-month campaign in the Chuska Mountains during which soldiers killed 33 Native Americans and captured some 30 others, most of whom were sold into slavery. They also took a thousand animals. Although the Navajo signed a treaty the following January, and Vizcarro became celebrated in legend as the man who brought peace to the frontier, the Indian raids resumed. Vizcarro was replaced as governor in 1825.

Wagon Box Fight (1867) *battle between U.S. troops and Lakota during Red Cloud's War*

On August 7, outside Fort Phil Kearny in northern Montana, Captain James Powell's company of the 27th Infantry was guarding a wood-cutting party when a group of Lakota (see SIOUX) Indians attacked. With 26 soldiers and four civilians, Powell built a miniature fort by corralling 14 wagon beds, using logs and sandbags to buttress his position. He also used extra arms and ammunition to shore up his defense. Powell then gave his best sharpshooters three repeating rifles each and charged other soldiers with reloading them. Waiting until the charging Lakota were 50 years away, Powell gave the order to fire. The attacking Indians ran headlong into a hail of rifle-balls and immediately retreated. Five hours later, a relief force from Fort Phil Kearny arrived to break the siege. Of his 32-man force, Powell was left with six men dead and two wounded; Lakota losses were estimated at approximately 60 dead and 120 wounded.

Waiilatpu Mission (Waiilatpu Massacre) (1847) *massacre at the Oregon mission of Marcus and Narcissa Whitman*

Marcus and his wife, Narcissa, established a mission in Oregon in 1836. While the CAYUSE and NEZ PERCE saw the initial benefits of his medicine and farming and irrigation techniques, they grew more and more disenchanted by his arrogant insensitivity to the Native religions. His presence also attracted other white people.

Between 1841 and 1847, Cayuse and missionary relations deteriorated. The mission farm was thriving, but the Cayuse were not. Then, as non-Indian settlement in the region increased, Marcus Whitman's manner of dealing with the tribe linked him more strongly with the settlers than with missionary work. This proved to the Cayuse that his loyalties lay with non-Indians, not with them. Furthermore, the Whitmans gave supplies to needy white families, but ordered the Cayuse to plow their land and to have their grain milled.

The final blow came during summer 1847, when measles and dysentery, which Native Americans blamed on the emigrants, struck the Cayuse. Marcus treated the Cayuse with medicine but many died, leading some Cayuse to charge that he was killing them. Indians friendly to the missionaries urged them to leave, but Whitman overestimated his influence and power among the Cayuse and refused. In fall 1847 angry Cayuse met in council and decided that Marcus Whitman must die for having killed (in their view), 200 of their people.

On November 29, 1847, Cayuse headmen Tomahas and TILOKAIKT arrived at the mission with some of their warriors. As Whitman spoke with them, he was shot and tomahawked; Narcissa Whitman also was wounded. Other Cayuse attacked non-Indians working around the mission. By evening the women and children at the mission had retreated upstairs. A Cayuse warrior persuaded them to leave the house, claiming that the house was going to be burned and that he wished to save the women. As the group left the house, however, some Cayuse fired on them, killing Narcissa Whitman and two men. A proud and haughty woman who treated the Indians with disdain, Narcissa was the only non-Indian woman killed; the mutilation of her body suggests the Cayuse's deep anger toward her.

Forty-seven survivors of the Waiilatpu massacre were finally ransomed a month after the attack by Peter Ogden of the Hudson's Bay Fur Company. In January 1848, American volunteer troops reached the area and skirmished with the Cayuse, stealing Indian cattle and horses and burning lodges. They failed, however, to capture those responsible for the attack. Two years later, some of the Cayuse, realizing that they could not continue to oppose the Americans, turned over five men, including Tilokaikt, to the U.S. Army. These men were tried, found guilty, and put to death in less than a month.

Walking Purchase Treaty (1737) *agreement between Lenni Lenape Indians and colonist Thomas Penn*

In 1737, Thomas Penn, son of William Penn, and James Logan, an employee of the Penn family, devised a plan to gain control of lands owned by LENNI LENAPE (formerly Delaware) Indians. In the 1720s, the Penn family was in debt and began selling lands to families even before they had purchased them from the Indians. To demonstrate Pennsylvania's right to govern the new settlements, the Penns needed clear title to the land in the upper Delaware Valley. At Logan's urging, Thomas Penn came to the colony in 1732 to purchase the land from the Indians. He was able to buy some of the desired Indian lands, but not Lehigh Valley. Nutimus, the Lenni Lenape chief, refused Penn's offer in 1733 and 1734. The family then looked for means by which the land could be obtained without seizing it outright. Penn and Logan soon found a 1686 grant for land to William Penn near the Lehigh Valley. The document stipulated that the grant would be bounded by how far a man could walk in a day and a half, starting form a point to be decided upon by the parties. Penn had supposedly paid for the land, but the boundaries had never been measured off.

Secretly, Thomas Penn hired a party of men to make a trial walk to determine the most advantageous route that could be read into the language of the document. His runners blazed a trail through Nutimus's lands, the entire Forks of the Delaware, and into the lands of the Minisink (Munsee) Indians. Once this was determined, he set up a meeting with Lenni Lenape leaders in May 1735. Although Nutimus and other leaders denounced the document, it laid the legal foundation for the Penn family's claim. Two years later, on August 25, 1737, Nutimas and three other Lenni Lenape leaders signed a deed confirming the sale of 1686.

The walk itself took place on September 19, 1737. Thomas Penn hired three of the fastest runners in the region and offered a prize to whoever could cover the greatest distance. The Lenni Lenape observers who set out with the "walkers" bitterly objected that they did not "walk fair" and dropped out. The hardiest hired man covered some 65 miles before collapsing of exhaustion. Even after the deception continued, as names of rivers were apparently switched on the map. To suggest that the Penns had acquired much more land than even the walk had given them. The total claim amounted to 1,200 square miles.

In 1758, Penn gave the northern half of this allotment to the IROQUOIS CONFEDERACY. It was not until 1762 that Sir WILLIAM JOHNSON, the British commissioner of Indian Affairs, ordered that the Indians be paid £400 for land taken deceptively in the land deal.

Walla Walla Council (1855) *treaty designed to end resistance of Indians of Washington State*

In May 1855, more than 5,000 representatives from the NEZ PERCE, Walla Walla, Umatilla, Palouse, YAKAMA, and CAYUSE tribes met with ISAAC I. STEVENS, territorial governor of Washington Territory and ex officio superintendent of Indian affairs to discuss peace. Most of the Indian headmen were offended by the proposed terms of the treaties discussed and by the anticipated effects on their people. However, after nearly two weeks of intense negotiations—which included intimidation by Stevens—the tribes agreed to a series of treaties. The terms of the treaties forced the Indians to give up large portions of their lands and move to reservations. In addition, there were the usual provisions of annuity payments, tools for and instruction in agricultural development, educational instruction, and the Christianization of the Indian peoples. Stevens promised that the Indians would have two to three years to relocate.

Soon after treaty negotiations ended, gold was discovered at Colville in eastern Washington and miners entered Yakama land. At the same time, Stevens announced that Indian lands were now open to settlement. Believing that government officials had lied to them, the Yakama killed six miners and Indian Agent A. J. Bolon. Simultaneous non-Indian settlement of Indian lands in Oregon resulted in similar consequences. These incidents touched off the ROGUE RIVER WAR (1855–56) and YAKAMA WAR (1855–57). Peace did not return to the area until 1858, when Colonel GEORGE WRIGHT and 600 regulars won victories against the Snake, Coeur d'Alene (Skitswish), Spokan, Yakama, and Palouse tribes in the battles of SPOKANE PLAIN (1858) and FOUR LAKES (1858). After defeating the Indians, Wright had most of the leaders put to death as insurgents. As the result of their losses, the tribes had no choice but to resettle on reservation lands under military surveillance. In March 1859 the U.S. Senate finally ratified the Walla Walla treaties.

Walnut Creek (1864) *raid by Cheyenne Dog Soldiers against settlements in western Kansas*

In April 1864, a settler from the Platte River reported to the authorities in Denver, Colorado, that Indians had stolen some of his animals. Colorado Governor JOHN EVANS saw political advantages in an Indian war—he felt that a strong Indian policy would win votes from frontier settlers—and ordered soldiers into the field. Within days, Major Jacob Downing had launched a punitive raid against a CHEYENNE camp of about 56 men, women, and children, who were unconnected with the settlers' loss of livestock. Twenty-six Indians were killed and another 30 were wounded. The Indians' livestock was distributed among Downing's volunteers.

The following month, Colonel JOHN M. CHIVINGTON ordered Lieutenant John S. Eayre to pursue a Cheyenne band accused of stealing cattle from a government contractor. Eayre killed Chief Lean Bear, a noted advocate of conciliation, and his son. Members of the Cheyenne warrior society known as the DOG SOLDIERS quickly launched a retaliatory raid against settlements on Walnut Creek, near the place of Eayre's fight. The Walnut Creek raid was one of the factors that led to the massacre at SAND CREEK (1864).

Wampanoag *Algonquian-speaking tribe of Rhode Island and Massachusetts*

The Wampanoag were traditionally an agricultural tribe. In 1621 the British Pilgrims encountered the Wampanoag when they established Plymouth Colony in present-day Massachusetts. They made peace with the tribal leader, Chief Massasoit, who gave the settlers food and thus helped keep the Pilgrims from starving the first grim year after their arrival. It was with this tribe that the Pilgrims held the first "Thanksgiving" feast.

In 1662, after the Puritans of the Massachusetts Bay Colony absorbed Plymouth colony and following the death of Massasoit, the chief's son METACOM (called King Philip by the colonists) became chief of the Wampanoag. By this time the English settlers in Massachusetts outnumbered the Indians two to one. Philip became increasingly angered by the settlers' encroachment on Indian land and the destructive effects of English liquor. His anger eventually turned to rebellion.

In 1675, Philip united most of the Indian tribes between the Kennebec and Hudson Rivers, including the Nipmuc and the NARRAGANSETT. This alliance attacked English settlements from Connecticut to Boston in an outbreak of violence known as KING PHILIP'S WAR (1675–76). By summer 1676, the tide of battle favored the English, who systematically pursued and defeated parties of Indians. Finally, the Puritans surrounded Philip, who was killed by an embittered relative of one of his warriors.

The colonists placed Philip's head and those of his relatives on the Plymouth blockhouse as a warning to rebellious Indians. They sold Philip's wife and son as well as hundreds of Indian captives into slavery. The Puritans then attempted to erase all traces of the Wampanoag by selling their remaining homeland to settlers. Some Wampanoag remained, however, and their descendants still live in Massachusetts.

Warbonnet Creek (1876) *battle between the Miniconjou Lakota and the U.S. Cavalry*

On July 17, 1876, less than a month after Colonel GEORGE ARMSTRONG CUSTER's defeat at the battle of the LITTLE BIGHORN (1876), the U.S. troops of the 5th Cavalry, commanded by Colonel Wesley Merritt, had encamped on Warbonnet Creek in South Dakota in search of CHEYENNE Indians leaving the Red Cloud Agency. That morning they prepared for the day's operations with the southernmost Black Hills in the distance, determined to prevent the 800-odd warriors from linking up with SITTING BULL. WILLIAM F. CODY (Buffalo Bill) accompanied Merritt's force as a scout. A lookout for the U.S. force spotted a group of Cheyenne warriors, three of whom were identified as Beaver Heart, Buffalo Road, and Yellow Hair (Yellow Hand), all followers of Cheyenne Chief Little Wolf. The Indians were heading northwest.

Cody realized that the U.S. riders would need help, so he set an ambush for the hard-riding Cheyenne warriors. Sporadic fire broke out and reports indicate that Cody himself placed a carefully aimed shot into the chest of Yellow Hair, who fell dead. According to witnesses, Cody scalped (see SCALPING) the fallen warrior, held the hair high in the air, and said, "First scalp for Custer." Other reports indicate Custer and the warrior fought hand to hand armed with knives, and Cody emerged the victor. Whether Cody killed Yellow Hair or not, the skirmish convinced the Cheyenne to return to the Red Cloud Indian Agency.

warbonnets *supernaturally protective head gear characteristic of Plains Indians*

The warbonnet, most commonly associated with the Plains Indians, was composed of eagle feathers (usually the bald eagle) encircling the head and a "tail" trailing down the back. Since the

A Cheyenne warrior in a traditional Plains warbonnet *(Courtesy of the National Museum of the American Indian, Smithsonian Institution #458)*

bald eagle was considered by many Plains tribes to be the strongest bird, it lent considerable protective power to those who wore a bonnet made of its feathers. Other feathers, such as those belonging to sparrow hawks (known for their swiftness), were often used as well. The construction of the head gear and the materials used depended on the visions of the individual who would wear it or the advice of the maker of such head gear. One CHEYENNE warrior, for example, believed that when he wore his warbonnet of grey-eagle feathers, he would not be hit by either bullets or arrows. Whirlwind, another Cheyenne, wore a warbonnet composed of hawk feathers and a preserved hawk perched on the top. He later reported that in an 1854 battle with the SAC (Sauk) and FOX, every feather of his warbonnet had been shot away, but neither he nor the hawk was touched.

Taboos, or restrictions, often accompanied the use of warbonnets. Again, this depended on the individual. Restrictions might include who was allowed to handle the warbonnet, how it was stored, specific rituals that must accompany its use, and even the avoidance of certain foods. ROMAN NOSE, another Cheyenne, was killed in 1866 after breaking one of the taboos associated with his warbonnet.

War Department *former U.S. government department at one time responsible for Native American affairs*
The War Department was established by an act of Congress in 1789. In the early years of the 19th century, it was the War Department's responsibility to protect Native American rights as granted by treaty and guard against non-Indian encroachments on Indian land, as well as, to regulate the transport of liquor into Indian country and to punish crimes committed by members of one group against another.

The BUREAU OF INDIAN AFFAIRS (BIA) was a part of the War Department from its inception in 1824 until 1849, when it was transferred to the newly created DEPARTMENT OF THE INTERIOR. For the next 30 years, the army attempted to regain authority over Indian affairs, spurred in part by the gross corruption exhibited throughout the Interior Department, especially among its Indian agents. The army's efforts were redoubled during and after the CIVIL WAR (1861–65), when it was argued that force would be most effective in restoring order on the frontier and getting the Plains Indians back onto reservations. In addition, according to army officials, would be cheaper in the long run than negotiations, and, as warriors, soldiers would command more respect than agents from Native Americans. Congress, however, rejected several bills that would have transferred the BIA back to the War Department.

With the gradual closing of the frontier toward the end of the 19th century, the War Department's attention began to shift overseas. In 1947 it was renamed the Department of Defense.

War for the Black Hills See SIOUX WARS.

War of 1812 (1812–1814) *war between the United States and Great Britain involving Native American forces*
The War of 1812 was in many respects as much of a land-grab as earlier wars involving Indians had been. In the North the war united the SHAWNEE warrior TECUMSEH and his Indian confederacy with the British; in the South it merged with the CREEK WAR (1813–14) and united CHEROKEE and the peace faction of the CREEK, the White Sticks, with the Americans. In both the North and South, hostilities were driven by men who wanted easy access to land—land that, in many cases, still belonged to Indians and that the United States had promised to protect.

It can also be said that the War of 1812 extended TECUMSEH'S REBELLION (1811), which was brought to a head in the battle of TIPPECANOE on November 7, 1811. After WILLIAM HENRY HARRISON burned the Indian settlement of Prophetstown following the battle, Tecumseh offered his services to British General Isaac Brock at Fort Malden in Ontario. He was commissioned in the British Army and given command of Indian forces.

Tecumseh used his fighting experience to bewilder William Hull, the American commander at DETROIT. In July 1812, he ambushed a 120-man American patrol near Amherstburg, Ontario. On July 16, British captain Charles Roberts, with 400 Indian allies, captured the American garrison at Fort Michilimackinac in northern Michigan. On August 2 Tecumseh brought a war party across the Detroit River and attacked an American supply train, convincing Hull to pull his forces back. On August 16, Hull surrendered Detroit and 1,500 soldiers to Brock and Tecumseh without offering any resistance.

Hull's surrender marked the beginning of a number of losses for the Americans. Fort Dearborn (at present-day Chicago) surrendered on August 15, and local POTAWATOMI Indians killed 35 of the defenders as they emerged from the fort. Tecumseh's allies also attacked Fort Wayne, Indiana, on September 5, but they were driven off by future president Zachary Taylor. Fort Madison (near present-day St. Louis), Fort Harrison, and the town of Pigeon Roost in Indiana all fell to Indian attackers. The heaviest British casualty was the loss of General Isaac Brock on October 13. He was replaced by a less competent man, Colonel Henry Proctor.

Proctor's debut did not immediately spell disaster for the Indians. In January 1813, Harrison began to move his force across the Lake Erie ice to assault Fort Malden. The leader of his vanguard, James Winchester, ran into an ambush by 500 British regulars and 600 Indians at RAISIN RIVER (1813) in present-day Monroe, Michigan. Only 33 of the 960 Americans engaged in the battle managed to escape. About 400 were killed and 500 captured—one of the worst American defeats of the war. Harrison was forced to fall back and regroup. In late April and early May 1813, Proctor besieged Harrison at Fort Meigs, near Toledo, Ohio. He retreated after many of his Canadian and Indian allies grew tired and began to trickle away. In late July, after he was joined by western Indians, Proctor launched an unsuccessful assault on Harrison's supply base in Sandusky, Ohio.

In fall 1813, events began turning against Tecumseh and Proctor. On September 13, 1813, Commander Oliver Hazard Perry sunk or drove off the British fleet that guaranteed Proctor's supply line. As a result, Proctor abandoned Fort Malden and retreated across Ontario. Tecumseh finally stopped him at the battle of the THAMES (1813) and insisted on making a stand. The Indian leader died there on October 5, 1813.

In the South, General ANDREW JACKSON made progress against the RED STICKS, the war faction of the Creek. The Red Sticks had been inspired by Tecumseh's example and oratory; a band of them had participated in the Raisin River battle. With the help of his Cherokee and White Stick Creek allies, Jackson defeated the Red Sticks at the battle of HORSESHOE BEND (1814) on March 27, 1814. He later moved on to capture Pensacola, Florida, from the Spanish and to defeat the British at the battle of New Orleans on January 8, 1815—after the TREATY OF GHENT (1814) ending the war had been signed.

At the conclusion of the War of 1812, the Americans had effectively secured power over all lands east of the Mississippi. Although there would be further outbreaks of violence—such as BLACK HAWK'S WAR (1832)—Native Americans would never again be able to threaten American power in the east.

Further Reading

Gilbert, Bill. *God Gave Us This Country: Tekamthi and the First American Civil War.* New York: Doubleday, 1989.

Hickey, Donald R. *The War of 1812: A Forgotten Conflict.* Champaign: University of Illinois Press, 1990.

warrior societies   See MILITARY SOCIETIES.

Washakie (Pina Quanah, Smell of Sugar; Gourd Rattle) (ca. 1804–1900) *Shoshone chief known for his assistance to the U.S. Army*

Washakie was born in the Bitterroot Valley of Montana. While Washakie was still a youth, his father, a FLATHEAD Indian, was killed by BLACKFOOT CONFEDERACY warriors. Washakie's mother consequently took her children to live with her people, the SHOSHONE, in the Rocky Mountains in what is now western Wyoming.

By his own admission, Washakie killed many Blackfoot and CROW enemies when he was young. At the same time he also cultivated friendships with some non-Indians, notably CHRISTOPHER ("KIT") CARSON and Jim Bridger. By the 1840s Washakie had become principal chief of the Eastern Shoshone and was renowned for his bravery, oratory, and songs.

The Shoshone were a small tribe who were constantly at war with their neighbors the Crow, Blackfoot, Lakota (see SIOUX), CHEYENNE, and ARAPAHO. As non-Indian emigrants passed through Shoshone territory along the Oregon Trail, the Shoshone rendered assistance whenever possible. In return, the emigrants provided them with trade goods, guns, and protection from their enemies. Chief Washakie went so far as to forbid his warriors from harming non-Indians.

In 1859, the Lander Road was opened. It branched off the Oregon Trail and cut through the best hunting grounds of the Shoshone and BANNOCK. Soon some members of both tribes joined forces and began raiding non-Indian settlements. The U.S. government took action, and by 1863 the uprising was over. Washakie had refused to participate in the Shoshone War, advocating peace instead.

With the BUFFALO gone, Washakie encouraged his people to take up farming and cattle herding in the fertile Wind River Valley near present-day Riverton, Wyoming. His wish was consummated in the Treaty of Fort Bridger, signed in 1868. The move north was not easy, however, and Lakota, Cheyenne, and Arapaho hunters and raiders harassed the Shoshone at the Wind River Reservation.

In 1876, General GEORGE CROOK was ordered to subdue SITTING BULL, CRAZY HORSE and others to the east. Washakie saw his opportunity. The Shoshone and Crow were on friendly terms by this time, and groups from each tribe joined Crook's army as SCOUTS against their common foe. Washakie's scouts fought Crazy Horse's warriors at the battle of ROSEBUD CREEK (1876), helped defeat DULL KNIFE two years later, and tracked Sitting Bull.

For agreeing to an alliance with the United States, President ULYSSES S. GRANT sent a silver-embossed saddle to the aging Washakie. During the formal presentation at Fort Washakie (formerly Camp Brown), the chief was choked with emotion. Finally he uttered, "Do a kindness to a white man, he feels it in his head and his tongue speaks. Do a kindness to an Indian, he feels it in his heart. The heart has no tongue." (Freeman)

Later, against Washakie's vehement opposition, the Arapaho were eventually settled on the Wind River Reservation alongside the Shoshone. In his old age, Washakie saw non-Indian encroachment onto his land and experienced broken promises. He died in 1900.

Further Reading

Freeman, Russell. *Indian Chiefs.* New York: Holiday House, 1987.

Wright, Peter M. "Washakie." In *American Indian Leaders: Studies in Diversity.* Lincoln: University of Nebraska Press, 1980.

Washington Covenant Wampum Belt *belt commemorating a peace agreement between the Iroquois Confederacy and the United States*

In 1784, chiefs of the IROQUOIS CONFEDERACY that had sided with the British during the AMERICAN REVOLUTION (1775–81) agreed to the FORT STANWIX TREATY (1784), which ended hostilities between the Iroquois and the former colonies. To record the covenant, the Indians fashioned a wampum belt more than six feet long. The background beads in the belt are white, signifying peace. Along the belt are 13 figures done in purple beads. Representing the 13 new states, the figures are clasping hands in friendship. A Dutch-style house is in the middle of the belt, and on either side of the house are two figures said to be the guardians of the east and west doors of the symbolic Iroquois longhouse. The belt is named for George Washington, who in 1779 had ordered the destruction of Iroquois homelands in New York.

See also AMERICAN REVOLUTION, 1775–84.

Washington, John (1797–1853) *U.S. Army officer*

A relative of George Washington, John Washington graduated from West Point and was posted in South Carolina and Florida as an artillery officer. In the mid-1830s, he fought against the CREEK Indians in Alabama and the SEMINOLE in Florida, most notably at the battle of Lochahatchee during the Second SEMINOLE WAR (1835–42). In 1838–39, he served under General WINFIELD SCOTT and assisted in the Removal of the CHEROKEE to Indian Territory (present-day Oklahoma) (see TRAIL OF TEARS). He later fought in the Mexican War (1846–48) with distinction and assumed executive authority for the territory of New Mexico in October 1848.

In winter 1848 and spring 1849, Washington campaigned against the NAVAJO (Dineh), who had been raiding settlements in the New Mexico territory. During this campaign, he hung one chief and signed a treaty with two others. His success against the Indians of the Southwest was limited, however, and he was replaced in 1849. Washington was lost at sea in 1853 while on a troopship bound for the West Coast.

Washita (1868) *controversial victory of Colonel George Armstrong Custer during the Southern Plains War*

A rivalry existed between CHEYENNE leaders BLACK KETTLE and Tall Bull. Black Kettle advocated peace with the U.S. government, realizing the Indian world as he knew it was changing. Tall Bull, along with Bull Bear and White Horse, wanted to resist encroachment by non-Indians. The three were leaders of a group of warriors known as the DOG SOLDIERS, who had earned a reputation for being superlative warriors, capable of performing great deeds in combat.

Although the Southern Cheyenne had signed a treaty with the United States assigning them a reservation in Indian Territory (now Oklahoma), Tall Bull and his allies ignored the agreement and sought to remain on their former lands. In accordance with the treaty, the Indians were to receive guns and ammunition from the U.S. government for hunting. Because Tall Bull had led a raid on a rival Indian village, the guns and ammunition were withheld. On August 9, 1868, the Indians finally received the weapons. Before this occurred however, a party of 200 angry warriors who had set out to raid a PAWNEE village decided instead to raid non-Indian settlements on the Saline and Solomon Rivers. The Cheyenne killed 15 men, raped several women, burned ranches, and ran off livestock.

Angry and defiant, the Dog Soldiers were joined by some ARAPAHO Indians in their attacks against non-Indians. Those Cheyenne under Chief Black Kettle who sought peace headed toward a new reservation, while the hostile bands proceeded into western Kansas and eastern Colorado.

General PHILIP HENRY SHERIDAN, commander of all U.S. military forces in the area, decided to mount an aggressive winter campaign to locate and destroy the Indians. His plan was to have three columns converge on the valleys of the Canadian and Washita Rivers, near where the Indians had settled into their winter camps on their reservations. One column proceeded from Fort Lyon, Colorado, one from Fort Bascom, New Mexico territory, and the third from Fort Dodge, Kansas, under the command of Colonel GEORGE ARMSTRONG CUSTER.

In a display of aggressiveness, Custer pushed south from his base at Camp Supply across frozen land and located Black Kettle's village in the Washita Valley. With little advance reconnaissance, the colonel deployed his 7th Cavalry on all four sides of the Indian village and attacked. The village's inhabitants were taken by surprise, and the assault ended quickly, but the soldiers soon found themselves in trouble. Unknown to Custer, there were several other Indian encampments nearby; his troopers had to hold off a number of counterattacks as the day wore on. During the fight his men set fire to the village and slaughtered approximately 900 Indian ponies. At dusk Custer mounted his cavalry and left Black Kettle's village, breaking Indian resistance.

Major Joel H. Elliot and 15 of his men had become lost during the battle, but Custer refused to search for them. They were later found dead where they had fallen. In the battle's aftermath, Custer reported five troopers killed (including the grandson of Alexander Hamilton) and 14 wounded. The number of Indian dead was not recorded, but among those killed were Black Kettle and his wife, who were shot down as they attempted to escape. In some army circles, Custer was severely criticized for his actions at Washita because Black Kettle had long sought peace. Custer's defenders countered by claiming that the village had revealed evidence of raids conducted against settlements in Kansas. In addition, they pointed out that the Indians had held four prisoners in the village, two of whom had been executed during the attack. Within the army, many never forgave Custer for his failure to locate Major Elliot and his troopers. Whatever the case, Custer's actions had severely shaken the Southern Plains tribes and clearly illustrated the effectiveness of Sheridan's policy of winter campaigning.

Wayne, Anthony ("Mad" Anthony Wayne) (1745–1796) *U.S. general*

Born in Pennsylvania on January 1, 1745, as an adult Anthony Wayne became a surveyor for settlements on the frontier. He joined the army at the outbreak of the AMERICAN REVOLUTION (1786–95), and commanded light infantry during the war. General Wayne earned his unusual nickname, "Mad" Anthony Wayne, during the war when an old friend and neighbor was arrested for deserting. Learning that Wayne denied ever having heard of him, the neighbor declared, "He must be mad."

Wayne's greatest victory in the Revolutionary War came in 1779, when he led a small band of irregulars (mostly frontiersmen experienced in Indian tactics) in a surprise raid on the British fort at Stony Point, New York. The general did not have enough men to hold the fort, but its capture established his reputation as a cool-headed fighter and strict disciplinarian.

In April 1792, President George Washington appointed Wayne commander of the U.S. Army forces—known then as the LEGION OF THE UNITED STATES—in the Ohio Country and gave him the task of crushing Indian resistance to U.S. expansion. The job had already claimed the military careers of two other leaders, JOSIAH T. HARMAR and Governor ARTHUR ST. CLAIR. Wayne took control of his forces at a camp on the Ohio River he named Legionville. He spent nearly two years training and disciplining his troops while also learning Indian TACTICS and frontier ways.

Unlike St. Clair and Harmar, Wayne concluded that the best way to defeat the Indians was to fight a war of attrition, concentrating on destroying their villages and supplies. On September 11, 1793, an agent of the IROQUOIS CONFEDERACY informed Wayne at his Fort Washington camp (present-day Cincinnati, Ohio) that peace talks between the U.S. government and the SHAWNEE had broken off. In spring 1794, Wayne advanced north to the Maumee River, building Forts Greenville, Wayne, and DEFIANCE.

On August 17, 1794, Indian forces under MIAMI leader LITTLE TURTLE and the Shawnee chief BLUE JACKET tried to ambush Wayne along the Maumee River valley (see LITTLE TURTLE'S WAR). Warned by his own Indian scouts, Wayne let the hostile Indians wait for three days before beginning the battle of FALLEN TIMBERS (1794). His militia panicked under the Indians assault, but Wayne reestablished discipline—in part by shooting the fleeing men—and his highly trained regular troops soon drove the Indian forces off in defeat. In January 1795, Blue Jacket, his people driven from their homes, sought Wayne out at Fort Greenville and asked for peace. Later in August, Wayne and the Shawnee signed the TREATY OF GREENVILLE (1795), which brought peace to the Ohio Country. Wayne died on December 15, 1796.

Wetamoo (Weetamou, Wetamou, Namumpam, Tatatanum) (ca. 1635 or ca. 1650–1676) *sachem, or leader, of the Rhode Island village of Pocasset*

When her father died, Wetamoo, as the eldest child, succeeded him as leader of her village, which was part of the WAMPANOAG Confederacy. She became known as the Squaw Sachem of Pocasset. After the mysterious death of her husband following a visit to Plymouth, Wetamoo joined METACOM (King Philip), her brother-in-law and sachem of the Wampanoag, in his war against the English (see KING PHILIP'S WAR, 1675–76). She personally led 300 warriors and supplied provisions to help the Wampanoag struggle. After enjoying initial success, treachery within Philip's confederation led to its downfall, and by late summer 1676, Wetamoo's 26 remaining warriors were sur-

rounded and imprisoned. Wetamoo escaped but drowned later while trying to cross the Fall River (in present-day Massachusetts). When the English found Wetamoo's body, they cut off her head and set it on a pole as a lesson regarding the fate of any rebellious Indian leader.

See also WOMEN WARRIORS.

whistles, war *devices used by Plains tribes to send signals in combat*

During their battles, Plains Indian war chiefs sent prearranged signals to their warriors, often by blowing whistles, the shrill sounds of which could be heard above the noise of fighting. Depending on the signal given, warrior groups would wheel and turn, attack, or retreat. Whistles were fashioned from eagle-wing bones or the bones of turkey legs and were often decorated with eagle feathers or beads.

White Bird Creek (1877) *first battle of the Nez Perce War*

In 1863, Upper NEZ PERCE chiefs, including LAWYER, signed the TREATY OF 1863 with the U.S. government, relinquishing the lands of the Lower Nez Perce bands. The Lower Bands, however, refused to sign the treaty. In 1877 the U.S. government, impatient with the Lower Bands' obstinacy, ordered them to report to the Lapwai Reservation within 30 days. CHIEF JOSEPH, who had succeeded his father as chief, persuaded the other bands to acquiesce. The Indians arrived early and camped outside the reservation. Meanwhile, Joseph and other Nez Perce men returned to Wallowa Valley to butcher stray cattle left behind in their haste to make the deadline. While the older men were gone, some young men began to advocate war and killed four settlers. Fearing indiscriminate retribution, the Nez Perce broke camp and fled. The caravan of 700 Nez Perce, including only 150 fighting men, proceeded south to White Bird Creek. Chief Joseph, now reluctantly committed to resistance, joined them there.

At this same time, General OLIVER O. HOWARD sent Captain David Perry, with 103 cavalry and 11 volunteers, to protect non-Indian refugees who had fled to a small town called Grangeville, located 50 miles south of the Lapwai Reservation. When Captain Perry arrived at Grangeville, he learned that the Nez Perce were camped only 15 miles away. Unable to resist the strong possibility of an easy military victory, Perry ordered his men to pursue the fugitives. Perry and his troops arrived on a hill overlooking the Nez Perce camp at midnight. Before dawn on June 17, the troops' position was discovered by adolescent Nez Perce pony herders, who reported back to their camp. The Indians, many of whom had drunk excessively the night before, decided to attempt a peaceful surrender. When Perry and his soldiers arrived, the Nez Perce sent out a party of six men under a flag of truce. However, an officer fired two inaccurate shots—a foreshadowing of the soldiers' marksmanship throughout the battle.

Nez Perce marksmen responded by shooting 12 of Perry's men. The next shot felled an army bugler from his horse, and soon the second bugler was targeted, leaving Perry with no means of coordinating his troops. When Perry's left flank folded, OLLIKUT led a charge against the right, and it began to collapse. Perry frantically ordered the center to retreat. The Nez Perce then stampeded a herd of apparently riderless horses into the fray. When they reached the soldiers' rear, riders clinging to the horses' sides emerged. Shouldering their rifles, they commenced firing.

Perry and the remaining two-thirds of his men scrambled to retreat, with the Nez Perce in pursuit. The Indians kept up a sustained attack on the fleeing troops, forcing them to fight a rear-guard action during the remainder of the morning. This allowed time for the Nez Perce to pack, pillage the fallen soldiers for valuables, and escape.

The soldiers sustained 38 casualties—34 killed and four wounded. Only two Nez Perce were wounded. After the crushing defeat at White Bird Creek, General Howard was convinced the Nez Perce could be defeated only by military might. Meanwhile, Chief Joseph and the Nez Perce, realizing that all hope of a peaceful surrender had vanished, resolved to evade capture, and fled toward the Canadian border.

White, James (1747–1821) *U.S. soldier and legislator*

James White was a native of North Carolina who served as a militia captain during the AMERICAN REVOLUTION (1775–81). After the war, he left North Carolina and moved to lands farther west. He was elected speaker of the senate of Franklin, an area consisting of bits of modern East Tennessee and northern Georgia that never achieved statehood. He served in the North Carolina legislature in 1789 and was one of the representatives to the state convention to ratify the U.S. Constitution. White also helped devise Tennessee's constitution in 1796 and, with his friend JOHN SEVIER, played an important role in the establishment of the new state.

White's involvement with Native Americans began in 1786, when he settled at White's Fort (now Knoxville, Tennessee), later made the territorial capital. This settlement was on land that, according to the HOPEWELL TREATY (1785), belonged to the CHEROKEE and should have been kept free of settlers. Intermittent violence continued in the area for many years. One particularly severe outbreak occurred in 1793, when Sevier and White attacked CREEK and Cherokee warriors at Etowah, an Indian village, in retaliation for a raid on the settlement of Cavet's Station. On October 2, 1798, White and a team of negotiators obtained the area around Knoxville from the Indians in the first Treaty of Tellico. He subsequently helped negotiate treaties with CHICKASAW leaders. Late in his life, he served under General John Cocke in the CREEK WAR (1813–14). During this campaign, White's rash attack on the Creek Hillabbec towns, which had already agreed to surrender, turned those Indian into foes of the Americans.

Whitestone Hill (1863) *battle between the Dakota and U.S. troops*

In summer 1863, General JOHN POPE sent two columns of troops, commanded by Generals HENRY SIBLEY and ALFRED SULLY, against the Lakota (see SIOUX). The plan was to have Sully's column march north up the Missouri River from Fort Randall and link up with Sibley, who was to go up the Minnesota River into Dakota Territory and then swing west to the Missouri River. The Lakota would thus be caught between the two columns and unable to escape across the Missouri River.

Sibley's brigade of nearly 1,900 men moved west as planned, skirmishing with the Lakota at Big Mound in Dakota Territory on July 24, 1863, and again two days later at DEAD BUFFALO LAKE (1863). The troops were then attacked by the Lakota on July 28 at Stony Lake. However, the Indians were no match for Sibley's artillery and were forced to flee, abandoning large quantities of meat, hide, and utensils, which the troops destroyed. About 150 warriors were killed.

General Sully's 1,200 horsemen and 4 howitzers, arrived a month late at the rendezvous point where he was supposed to meet Sibley. On September 3 four companies from Sully's contingent, under Major Albert E. House, stumbled on a band of Wahpekute Dakota led by INKPADUTA, who had crossed the river again after Sibley left. House was immediately surrounded by approximately 1,000 warriors at a site called Whitestone Hill. With the soldiers outnumbered, Inkpaduta was confident of victory. He therefore delayed the slaughter so that his warriors could paint themselves and the women could prepare a feast. But Major House had managed to get word to Sully. At dusk, just as the Wahpekute were to begin the assault, the main body of Sully's column arrived. The Indians were startled by the brigade's charge but fought hard to escape. By the time they were able to get away under the cover of the night, 300 warriors had been killed and 250 women and children taken PRISONER. Twenty-two soldiers had died and 50 more were wounded in the battle. The army then destroyed the Indians's lodges, as well as large supplies of their dried buffalo meat.

See also SIOUX WARS.

Wichita *Plains Indian tribe*

In 1541, Spanish explorer Francisco Coronado became the first European to encounter the Wichita Indians, who were living in present-day northeastern Kansas and northern Oklahoma. The Wichita had close kinship ties to another tribe, the CADDO. The two tribes were collectively known by the French as TAOVOYA.

The Taovoya came into the European trading sphere in the 1700s and served as middlemen between the French and the powerful COMANCHE. A traditional enemy of the Taovoya, the OSAGE, forced the Caddoans and their French allies to relocate on the Red River in Texas in the mid-1700s. There they built a stronghold—the twin villages of San Bernardo and San Teodoro, from which they were able to control the regional fur trade. In 1759, they and the

Comanche successfully defended the villages against a sustained but unsuccessful attack spearheaded by Spanish commander DIEGO ORTÍZ PARRILLA.

In 1858, Captain EARL VAN DORN led four companies of U.S. troops in an attack on Comanche who were camped at a new Wichita village at RUSH SPRINGS (1858), in present Grady County, Oklahoma. For many years afterward the Comanche suspected the Wichita of conspiring with U.S. troops in this attack.

The Wichita fled back to Kansas during the CIVIL WAR (1861–65). Most lived as refugees, but some fought on the side of the Union. After the war the Wichita were relocated to Indian Territory (present-day Oklahoma). In 1901, the government drastically reduced their Oklahoma reservation through the GENERAL ALLOTMENT ACT. The contemporary Wichita hold a small reservation themselves and also share a reservation with the Caddo and the LENNI LENAPE (formerly Delaware).

Winnebago (Ho-Chunk) *Indian tribe from Wisconsin*

The Winnebago called themselves Ho-Chunk, which means "People of the Big Speech." The nearby FOX (Mesquakie) and SAC, however, called them Winnebago, "People of the Filthy Water." When French explorer Jean Nicollet encountered the Winnebago in 1634, the tribe was located along the peninsula separating Green Bay from Lake Michigan down to Lake Winnebago in what is now Wisconsin. There they hunted, fished, and grew a variety of crops.

Within 50 years of European contact, the Winnebago were at war. They sided with the British in the FRENCH AND INDIAN WAR (1754–63), in the AMERICAN REVOLUTION (1775–81), and in TECUMSEH'S REBELLION (1811).

By the 1820s the Winnebago were living along the rivers in southern Wisconsin and northern Illinois. The encroachment of non-Indian miners led to the WINNEBAGO UPRISING (1826–27), in which their leader RED BIRD played a major role. Not long thereafter the Winnebago joined the Sac and Fox in the BLACK HAWK WAR (1831). As a result of this last action, many Winnebago were forced to relocate west of the Mississippi River—first to Iowa, then to Minnesota, then to South Dakota, and finally to Nebraska, where many still live today. Others, live on reservation lands in Wisconsin and still others live in Minnesota.

Winnebago Uprising (1826–1827) *encounters leading to the end of the Winnebago threat to the Old Northwest Territory*

During the 1820s, miners and farmers raced into the territory along the western border of Illinois and Wisconsin after lead deposits were discovered there. The settlers camped and farmed on lands belonging to the WINNEBAGO (Ho-Chunk) SAC, and FOX (Mesquakie) Indians. In spring 1826 several Winnebago warriors killed five members of the Methode family, French-Canadian settlers who worked a maple sugar camp near the Mis-

sissippi River. Early the following year, some Winnebago were arrested and presumably sent to Fort Snelling. RED BIRD, a Winnebago leader, thereupon instigated an uprising to avenge the arrests. On June 26, 1827, and two warriors killed a local farmer and his hired hand and also scalped the farmer's infant daughter.

In June 1827, two Mississippi keelboats made a stop at the Winnebago village War Prairie du Chien. The Indians were induced to drink with the boatmen, who then kidnapped some Winnebago women. A few nights later, Red Bird and his warriors attacked the boats, and the women escaped. Four boatmen and about 12 Indians were killed in the encounter. Red Bird then led several unsuccessful raids against the led mining camp, but regular army forces joined local militia to destroy the Indian threat to this border area. Retreating to the interior, Red Bird and his warriors were eventually trapped between two army columns on the upper Wisconsin River. Red Bird's defeat ended the Winnebago Uprising and Indian resistance to settlement of Winnebago territory.

Winnemucca, Sarah (ca. 1844–1891) *Paiute interpreter, educator, peacemaker, writer*

Born in present-day Nevada, Sarah Winnemucca was the daughter of prominent PAIUTE chief Old Winnemucca. While still a young girl, she went with her mother, brothers, and sisters to live with her grandfather in California, where she encountered her first non-Indians. She subsequently learned English while living in the home of a stagecoach agent. After attending a Catholic school, she returned to Nevada and worked as a domestic servant.

At the time of the SNAKE WAR (1866–68), Sarah served as an interpreter in discussions about Paiute-settler relations. Thereafter, she continued working as an interpreter. She also became a peacemaker, meeting with both government officials to discuss their treatment of the Indians and with Indian leaders to persuade them to pursue peaceful policies toward non-Indians. Her efforts during the BANNOCK WAR (1878), however, were unsuccessful.

In 1879, Sarah gave a lecture in San Francisco, California, in which she criticized the policies of the BUREAU OF INDIAN AFFAIRS. Soon after, she went to Washington, D.C., where she met with federal officials and argued for the return of Paiute land and their right to manage their own affairs. Her criticisms of government policy drew a harsh reaction among some officials, but she had friends and defenders among the U.S. military because of her actions as an interpreter.

Sarah toured various eastern cities from 1883 to 1884, giving lectures about Indian rights. Dressing as an Indian princess to draw crowds, she met many important people, including Senator Henry Dawes, whose plan to give land to individual Indians she supported (see GENERAL ALLOTMENT ACT).

After touring the East, Sarah returned to Nevada and founded an Indian school. She operated the school until declining health forced her to retire to her sister's home in Idaho. She died there of tuberculosis in 1891.

Wisconsin Heights (1832) *battle in the Black Hawk War*

The BLACK HAWK WAR began in April 1832, when SAC chief BLACK HAWK led about 2,000 Sac (Sauk) and FOX (Mesquakie) tribe members east over the Mississippi River to their ancestral villages near present-day Rock Island, Illinois. U.S. agents claimed that Black Hawk had surrendered title to these lands 28 years earlier—an agreement that Black Hawk himself believed applied only to hunting rights. On April 28, 1832, General HENRY ATKINSON took command of 1,700 Illinois militia and drove Black Hawk from Illinois. The Indian leader retreated northward into the Wisconsin Territory. The Sac and Fox lived for the next few months in the wilderness, trying to make their way back to the Mississippi, where they would be safe. However, they were pursued by Colonel Henry Dodge and about 600 soldiers, who caught up with the Indians at a point some miles northwest of present-day Madison, Wisconsin.

Early on July 21, 1832, several men of Colonel Henry Dodge's militia found and killed an Indian who was sitting by the grave of his wife; she had died of starvation, which was taking its toll on Black Hawk's band. Dodge then led his militia in pursuit of the rest of the group and trapped the Indians on the banks of the Wisconsin River (near present-day Sauk City, Wisconsin). The warriors moved their families over the river, and then put up a resistance that left 70 of them dead by nightfall. Only one U.S. soldier died in the conflict. The following day the remaining warriors joined their families while Black Hawk's second in command, Neapope, visited Dodge with an offer of surrender. However, the army interpreters had left the camp, and Neapope was unable to make himself understood. The two sides thus separated without coming to an agreement.

The fight at Wisconsin Heights was one of the last Indian battles east of the Mississippi River and north of Florida. By emerging relatively unscathed from the battle, Black Hawk was able to continue his flight across central Wisconsin. The route he chose would eventually lead on August 3 to the massacre at BAD AXE (1832), his own captivity, and the deaths of an additional 300 Sac Indians.

Witawamet (ca. 1500s–1623) *chief of the Massachuset Indians*

In 1623, the Pilgrims at Plymouth colony learned of the presence of a new band of settlers at Wessagusett, north of Plymouth along the coast. The Wessagusett colonists had been surviving by stealing food from the local MASSACHUSET Indians, and the tribe's chief, Witawamet, was reportedly planning to attack them. The elders at Plymouth colony sent MILES STANDISH to warn and aid the Wessagusett settlers. Standish pretended to open negotiations with Witawamet and persuaded him and his followers to come out of the woods. When the Native Americans were clear of the trees, Standish and his fellow Englishmen opened fire.

Witawamet and his tribespeople died in the opening volleys. The chief's 18-year-old son was taken prisoner and later hung by the settlers. Standish removed Witawamet's head and took it back to Plymouth, where it was mounted on the wall of the fort as a warning to Indians in the area. The fate of Witawamet and the Massachuset Indians foreshadowed engagements between the English colonists and Native Americans in New England and Virginia during the PEQUOT WAR (1636–37), KING PHILIP'S WAR (1675–76) and the POWHATAN WARS (1622–32, 1644–46).

Withlacoochee River (1835) *battle in the Second Seminole War*

On December 28, 1835, Duncan Lamont Clinch, a planter and general in the U.S. Army, readied preparations for a march against SEMINOLE chief OSCEOLA and his warriors, who were encamped near the Withlacoochee River in Florida. Clinch planned a quick attack to break the Seminole defense. The next morning 250 regular army troops and 700 militia left Fort Drane, and began the 40-mile march to the Withlacoochee.

Clinch's progress was slow and noisy, as wagons bogged down in the mud and soldiers hacked their way through thick growth. They arrived at the river on the morning of December 31, but they found no ford. A single dugout canoe was spotted across the river. It was retrieved and used to ferry men, six at a time, across the river. As the troops reached the opposite shore, Colonel Alexander Fanning stationed them about 100 yards from the river in an open field, surrounded on three sides by swamp. Sentries fanned out through the marsh grasses to give alarm.

Clinch had been lucky. The ford he had expected to find was two and a half miles upstream, but it was guarded by Osceola and about 250 warriors. Apparently the army's approach had been followed and an ambush planned. When Osceola discovered Clinch's presence downstream, he quietly moved his men toward them. Caught by surprise, the sentries barely had time to sound an alarm. The army troops charged, but instead of falling back as the soldiers expected the Seminole to do, the Indians stood their ground. The closer the soldiers came, the more effective was the Seminole fire. The troops soon faltered and began moving back toward the river. Realizing that the panic of the retreating troops would lead to their deaths, Clinch shouted for them to extend their ranks and hold fast.

Clinch then ordered the militia to advance, but they never appeared. With the Seminole pushing forward and no help from the rear, the army troops continued their retreat. Determined to win the battle, Clinch dismounted and moved to the front of the lines, shouting that he would shoot any man who fell back. At this point several militia volunteers crossed the Withlacoochee to aid Clinch, and they helped stop a Seminole attack from the side.

The battle ended in a standoff. As Osceola's warriors pushed forward, Clinch was barely able to keep his men from retreating. Finally, Osceola gave the order for his warriors to fall back, and they slowly and silently slipped away. The army lost five men and suffered 51 injured, but claimed they had killed

30 Seminole. The Seminole claims were 5 warriors dead and 5 wounded.

Wolf Mountains (1877) *battle between U.S. troops and a loose coalition of Oglala Lakota and Cheyenne*

Following the battles of ROSEBUD CREEK (1876) and the the LITTLE BIGHORN (1876), the army transferred several additional regiments, including NELSON A. MILES's 5th Infantry, into the northern plains region. The troops spent much of the fall of 1876 constructing the Tongue River Cantonment (later Fort Keogh) along the Yellowstone River and campaigning against nonreservation Indians.

Despite the bitter cold, Miles refused to settle into permanent winter quarters. In late December he departed the Tongue River Cantonment with 436 soldiers and two pieces of artillery. On January 7, 1877, Miles's column captured several Indians and fended off a rescue effort. With knee-deep snows covering the rugged terrain of the Wolf Mountains, a major engagement broke out early the next morning. Initial efforts to decoy the soldiers into a trap having failed, 500 to 600 dismounted Oglala (see SIOUX) and CHEYENNE closed to within five yards of the army's lines. But late-morning blizzards, the steady volleys and counterattacks of Miles's veteran infantrymen, the unnerving fire of the army fieldpieces, and the death of influential medicine man Big Crow convinced the Indians to withdraw shortly after noon. Miles broke off the engagement after a three-mile pursuit, concluding that his foot soldiers could not catch the remounted Plains warriors.

Cheyenne and Oglala accounts set Indian casualties at two or three killed and a similar number wounded. Miles estimated that his enemies lost a dozen or so killed and suffered 25 to 30 wounded, admitting but one killed and nine wounded among his own command. Though only a partial victory, the battle of Wolf Mountains helped restore army confidence after the setbacks of the previous year and further split the deteriorating Northern Plains Indians' coalition.

Woman Chief (ca. 1805–1854) *Gros Ventre (Atsina) woman warrior*

A Gros Ventre (Atsina) by birth, Woman Chief was approximately 10 years old when she was taken prisoner by the CROW (Absaroka). Adopted into the Crow tribe, she showed little interest in helping women with their tasks. Instead she preferred to practice her skills with the BOW AND ARROW, guard the family horses, and ride horseback. Her adoptive family encouraged her. Woman Chief grew stronger and taller than most women. As a young woman she was the equal of, if not the superior to, any of the young men at hunting. It was said that she could carry a deer or bighorn sheep home from the hunt on her back. She could also kill four or five BUFFALO in a single chase, butcher them, and load them on pack horses without help. When her adopted father died, she assumed charge of the family.

During the 1820s, Woman Chief organized her own war parties against the BLACKFOOT CONFEDERACY. On her first raid, she captured 70 horses, killed and scalped a Blackfoot warrior, and captured the gun of another. With the accumulation of more and greater war honors, her importance as a warrior grew. As a result, Woman Chief gained a seat in the council of chiefs of the Crow, where she ranked third in a band of 160 lodges. She never married but was unable to carry out the roles expected of both men and women, so she was forced to ceremonially "take" four wives to assume the required tasks. This plurality of wives may have added to her standing and dignity as a chief, since only the more important leaders had many wives.

In 1854, Woman Chief attempted to make peace between the Gros Ventre and Crow. While journeying to the Gros Ventre for this purpose, she and her four companions met a large party from that tribe. Boldly approaching them, she spoke their language and smoked with them. However, as they traveled to the main Gros Ventre camp, she and her companions were shot and killed by some of the party who did not want peace.

women warriors *women who assumed traditional male roles in warfare*

The role of warrior was not prohibited to Indian women. If a woman excelled in the skills associated with raiding, hunting, and war, she was generally accepted as a warrior after having proven herself. Reasons for taking this role varied, but many women—like the men—did it for revenge or defense. Women warriors such as THE-OTHER-MAGPIE (CROW), PINE LEAF (Crow), and RUNNING EAGLE (BLACKFOOT CONFEDERACY) first went into battle after a relative was killed by the enemy. Old Woman Grieves The Enemy (PAWNEE) and Strikes Two (Absaroke) took action when their homes and family were attacked. Although the figure Strikes-Two may be anecdotal, her story suggests how a woman might have been initiated into warfare and accepted as a warrior. When the Lakota (see SIOUX) attacked her village, 60-year-old Strikes-Two bravely picked up her root digger and rode around the camp, singing her medicine song. Her bravery, based on the belief that her song made her totally immune to Lakota bullets and arrow, frightened the Lakota and encouraged the men of her village to drive the enemy from their camp.

Although they were not trained as warriors, the actions of some women—and the inspiration they provided their people—qualified them for the prestige associated with war. For example, Comes Together, a CHEYENNE woman, gained prominence when the Pawnee attacked her camp. She ran away but was caught by a Pawnee warrior. After making signs that signified that she would go peacefully with him, she instead grabbed her hatchet and killed him by splitting his head open. When her tribe later assembled in camp, Comes Together was proclaimed a brave woman and was honored in the same way as other warriors.

The-Other-Magpie and Buffalo Calf Road Woman, a Cheyenne, both fought in the battle of ROSEBUD CREEK

(1876). Buffalo Calf Road Woman also fought in the battle of the LITTLE BIGHORN (1876).

Plains Indian culture was not the only one in which women became warriors. The CHEROKEE also had stories of female warriors. For example, Cuhtahlatah (Wild Hemp) the wife of a headman, snatched up her fallen husband's TOMA-HAWK during an attack and charged the enemy. Because of her bravery the Cherokee turned a retreat into a victory. Another report tells of a Cherokee woman who fought against colonial troops in 1776. After losing 19 men to Indian warriors, the colonists drove back the defenders, but one warrior remained hidden behind a tree and was killed as soon as he was sighted. When the soldiers examined the body, however, they discovered the lone warrior was a woman—painted and armed like a man.

Among the Cherokee were women known as Chighau, or Beloved Woman (translated occasionally as Pretty Woman or War Woman). A woman was elected to this honor by the tribal council after performing a feat of bravery. She sat with the tribal council when decisions regarding war were made, and one of her most important functions was to decide the fate of PRIS-ONERS of war. If she decided that prisoners were to live, they became her slaves or were given up for adoption to families that had lost members.

One of the more well-known Cherokee Beloved Women was Nancy Ward, or Nanyehi (One Who goes About). Born ca. 1738, Nanyehi was given the title of Beloved Woman when she was about 17 years old. In that year (1755), she and her husband, Kingfisher, were on a raid against a CREEK town. When her husband was killed, Nanyehi picked up his musket and continued to fight with the other warriors. Upon her return to the principal Cherokee villages, the tribal council elected her to the position of Beloved Woman. For the next 60 years, Nanyehi used her influence to save the lives of both Cherokee and non-Indians and to promote peace to save her people.

The HOPI have a kachina (kacina), or spirit, that is the per-sonification of He-e-e, the Warrior Girl. According to Hopi legend, He-e-e's mother was in the process of fixing her hair when an enemy was seen outside their village. He-e-e jumped up, grabbed a BOW AND ARROWS, and ran to warn the villagers, then led the defense of the village until the men returned from the fields. She has been personified as a kachina ever since.

Other women, such as WOMAN CHIEF (Crow) and LOZEN (Apache), actually chose the military and raiding life, preferring it to the domestic life of women. Still others, such as Eagle, remained hunter/warriors because of their skill in those roles. Ehyophsta (Yellow-Haired Woman), a Cheyenne, was also con-sidered a warrior. In 1868, a year after her husband, Walking Bear, had been killed in an accident, Ehyophsta proved herself in an important battle between the Cheyenne and the SHOSHONE. During the first day of fighting, when a Shoshone and Cheyenne warrior were engaged in hand-to-hand combat, Ehyophsta rode up to them, jumped off her horse, drew her butcher knife, and stabbed the Shoshone twice. As the battle drew to a close, some Shoshone were found hiding in the rocks. Most were killed immediately, but one was kept for question-

ing. Ehyophsta asked the others to step aside so she could ques-tion the young warrior. As she stepped up to him, however, she lifted his arm, stabbed him in the armpit, and then scalped him (see SCALPING). By this deed Ehyophsta became eligible to join the small society of Cheyenne of women who had been to war with their husbands.

According to one scholar, Priscilla Buffalohead, scattered references to women warriors among the Ojibway indicate that there may have been some accepted way for a female to become a warrior. For example, certain patterns emerge in stories of women warriors: vision quests, or dreams, that point toward a warrior career; superior athletic skills recognized by family and community; and delayed marriages. Favorite sons and daugh-ters were usually given special privileges and allowed to do as they pleased. Hanging Cloud Woman was one such favorite. In the mid-1800s she joined her father and brother on a hunting expedition. A party of Lakota (see SIOUX) attacked them, and her father was killed. Hanging Cloud Woman pretended to be dead. After the enemy left, she snatched up her father's gun and pursued them. Her exploits were honored throughout Ojibway territory.

Another Ojibway, Chief Earth Woman, had a strong desire for glory. She joined a war party by convincing the tribal leader that she had had a dream that gave her special supernatural powers. Through these powers she was able to predict the movement of the Lakota and thus help her group overtake the enemy. When the first Lakota was killed, Chief Earth Woman ran up to him as he fell and scalped him. Upon their return to camp, she joined in the celebrations as a warrior.

Examples such as these and others show that gender roles among Indians were often quite flexible. The role of warrior, usually associated with men, could also be fulfilled by women whose skills or extraordinary feats brought them great honor and prestige.

Further Reading

Neithamer, Carolyn. *Daughters of the Earth: The Lives and Legends of American Indian Women.* New York: Macmillan, 1977.

Wood Lake (1862) *pivotal battle in the Minnesota Uprising*
On August 18, 1862, the MINNESOTA UPRISING began in southern Minnesota. During the next month, the Dakota (see SIOUX), under the leadership of LITTLE CROW, fought a series of battles against settlers and soldiers at FORT RIDGELY (1862), NEW ULM (1862), BIRCH COULEE (1862), Acton, and Fort Abercrombie. On September 19 Colonel HENRY H. SIBLEY set out from Fort Ridgely with 1,619 soldiers, including members of the 3rd Minnesota. For four days they leisurely marched northeast up the Minnesota River Valley until, on September 22, they stopped near Lone Tree Lake. Sibley's guide mistook the water for Wood Lake; thus, the battle that followed was misnamed therefore.

That night, Sibley positioned his units near the lake. Con-vinced that Little Crow's warriors were still far off, however, he failed to station his pickets at a reasonable distance from the camp. Meanwhile, only a few miles away, Little Crow and possibly as many as 1,200 warriors were camped. After deciding against a night attack, they prepared for the dawn.

About 7:00 A.M. on September 23, men of the 3rd Minnesota commandeered some wagons and, unknown to him, set out for the agency three miles to the north. They hoped to get some potatoes to supplement their rations. As the wagons headed toward some Dakota warriors hidden in the tall grass, the Indians had no recourse but to open fire. When word of the encounter reached the soldiers' camp, some men of the 3rd Minnesota, without waiting for orders, advanced to help their comrades. The Indians backed away, trying to lure the small column of soldiers into a trap. Wisely, Sibley recalled the troops. As the Indians advanced on the main body, the soldiers opened up with artillery and gunfire. After two hours of fighting, the Indians withdrew. Sibley had lost seven soldiers, with 33 wounded. Little Crow had lost 15 warriors. One of the deceased was chief Mankato, the only prominent Indian leader to lose his life during the Minnesota Uprising. Allegedly, Mankato was too proud to dodge a cannon ball and was thus killed.

The battle of Wood Lake was the turning point in the uprising. The Indians thereafter assumed the defensive and soon surrendered.

Wool, John Ellis (1784–1869) *army officer in the Civil War and Indian wars of the Northwest*

John Wool was born in upstate New York in 1784. Originally a storekeeper, Wool joined the army at the start of the WAR OF 1812 (1812–14) and remained in the military when the war ended. In the 1830s he assisted General WINFIELD SCOTT in forcing the CHEROKEE to relocate to Indian Territory (present-day Oklahoma). After his promotion to brigadier general and service in the Mexican War, Wool commanded the Department of the Pacific. He was in overall control of campaigns against Indians in the YAKAMA WAR (1855–57) and the ROGUE RIVER WAR (1855–56), both of which he considered to be unjust conflicts. After service in the early years of the CIVIL WAR (1861–65), Wool retired in 1863 at the age of 77. He was the oldest officer to exercise command in that war.

Worcester v. Georgia (1832) *U.S. Supreme Court case that established Native Americans' legal right to own land*

In 1832, a man named Samuel Worcester brought a case before the U.S. Supreme Court. Worcester had settled on CHEROKEE land that was also claimed by the state of Georgia. The state ordered him to vacate, claiming that he had not received a license from the Georgia government. In *Worcester v. Georgia*, Chief Justice John Marshall held that the Cherokee Nation was a distinct political body unto itself, not bound by any state laws but only by treaties negotiated with the federal government. Marshall's opinion upheld the rights of the Cherokee—and, by extension, other Indian tribes—to admit people to their land as they saw fit.

The case came as the climax to a series of acrimonious quarrels between the state of Georgia and the Cherokee Nation. The U.S. government had promised Georgia that, in return for turning over its claims to western lands to the federal government, it would receive national assistance in buying Indian lands within its own boundaries. The Cherokee, however, proved reluctant to vacate, and in 1827, they adopted a written constitution and organized as a separate state government. The governor of Georgia, upset by this arrangement, ordered the seizure of Cherokee lands. The Cherokee brought suit, and the case came before the court as *Cherokee Nation v. Georgia* in 1831.

Worcester v. Georgia proved important for Indian-government relations in several ways. President ANDREW JACKSON refused to enforce the Court's decision. He instead chose to pressure the Cherokee into signing new treaties to cede their lands in Georgia and other southern states for new territory across the Mississippi. This led to the infamous TRAIL OF TEARS. The case also convinced the Indians that the U.S. government was unable or unwilling to honor the promises it made or the treaties it signed.

World War I (1914–1917) *conflict fought in Europe between various countries, including the United States*

When World War I started, active warfare between Indian and Non-Indian Americans had long since ended. The government, however, was still making efforts to eliminate Native American culture and turn the Indians into "true Americans." Enthusiastic Indian participation and support for the Allied cause in World War I thus came as a surprise. Before the United States entered the war, hundreds of young Native Americans went to Canada to fight in the British Commonwealth forces. Later, some 10,000 Indians fought in the U.S. Army, and 2,000 in the U.S. Navy. Many Indians were concentrated in National Guard units from states with large Indian populations. There were no specialized Indian units on a federal level, but many National Guard commanders thought Indians had special skills, such as tracking or marksmanship, and grouped them into unofficial special units.

One noteworthy event affected the 36th Infantry Division, commanded by Major General William R. Smith. In late October 1918, the 36th, composed of troops from Texas and Oklahoma, was preparing an attack in the Aisne River near Forest Farm, France. For a few days before the assault, Germany artillery fire increased in intensity and accuracy. And whereas the enemy seemed to be hitting American targets with near-pinpoint accuracy, Allied artillery fire seemed to be doing almost no damage to suspected German targets. Fearing that the enemy had been intercepting and decoding its messages, one of the 36th's front-line artillery units decided to try a different mode of communication: American Indians from the 142nd Infantry Regiment, who spoke Choctaw, would serve as telephone operators and speak to one another in their own language. The tactic worked so well that the Indians were pressed into permanent service in this capacity, and it served as a blueprint for the Navajo Indian Code Talkers of WORLD WAR II (1939–45). Indeed, successful Native American participation in the World War I helped to spur interest in what became the Citizenship Act of 1924, which granted all Indians citizenship.

World War II (1939–1945) *war in Europe and the Pacific involving numerous countries, including the United States*

Despite frequent conflicts between many tribes and the United States, Native Americans generally supported the federal government's involvement in World War II. In a symbolic gesture designed to demonstrate its sovereignty, the IROQUOIS CONFEDERACY even declared war on Germany and Japan, as did the PONCA and the Chippewa of Michigan.

Because all Native Americans had been declared U.S. citizens in 1924, they were subject to the provisions of the Selective Service Act. More than 25,000 Indians were served in the armed forces during the war. They saw action on all the war's major fronts. Perhaps the most noted Native American partic-

Navajo Code Talkers: During World War II, in a Pacific jungle, these soldiers transmitted messages in a code based on their native language, which was never deciphered by the Japanese. *(Courtesy New York Public Library)*

ipants were the Navajo Code Talkers, a group of 450 specially trained Marines who used a code based on their native language—indecipherable to the Japanese—to establish relay messages on the Pacific front. Since many Native Americans were classified as "white" upon their induction, the full range of their military activities will probably never be known. Official records do indicate, however, that 550 Indians were killed in action, with more than 700 others wounded. The nation awarded 47 Bronze Stars, 51 Silver Stars, 71 Air Medals, 34 Distinguished Flying Crosses, and two MEDALS OF HONOR to American Indians.

As occurred in other segments of society, some Native Americans opposed the war. Many of these believed that tribal sovereignty excluded them from the provisions of the selective service. Others attributed this opposition to their traditional religious values, which did not allow for offensive warfare. A few HOPI, Iroquois, Papago (see TOHONO O'ODHAM) SEMINOLE, and UTE, for example, were jailed for their resistance.

World War II had important domestic effects on Native Americans. To free up more room for war activities in the capital, the BUREAU OF INDIAN AFFAIRS (BIA) was temporarily moved from Washington to Chicago. Congress also cut direct appropriations to the tribes. Some 40,000 Native Americans found work in war industries, encouraging an exodus from the reservations to urban areas, where average pay was estimated to be three times higher. They emerged from the war much more determined to seek out and insist upon equal opportunity. As historian Kenneth William Townsend has concluded, "the clearest evidence of the Indians' exercise of self-determination that emerged from their World War II experiences was a conscious and spirited reassertion of their ethnic identity in White America."

Further Reading

Townsend, Kenneth William. *World War II and the American Indian.* Albuquerque: University of New Mexico Press, 2000.

Worth, William Jenkins (1794–1849) *U.S. Army officer*

William Worth was born in the town of Hudson in upstate New York. He became an infantry lieutenant in 1813, eventually serving as an aide to WINFIELD SCOTT during the WAR OF 1812 (1812–14). He remained in the military as a major after the war ended.

In 1838, Worth, now a colonel, was sent to Florida to take part in the Second SEMINOLE WAR (1835–42). In 1841 he became commander of all U.S. forces in Florida. His campaign against Seminole resistance culminated in his victory at the battle of Platka on April 19, 1842.

Worth was noted not just for pursuing Seminole warriors but also for destroying their villages and crops. He forced the surrender of some 3,000 Seminole—many of whom were eventually relocated to the Indian Territory (present-day Okla-

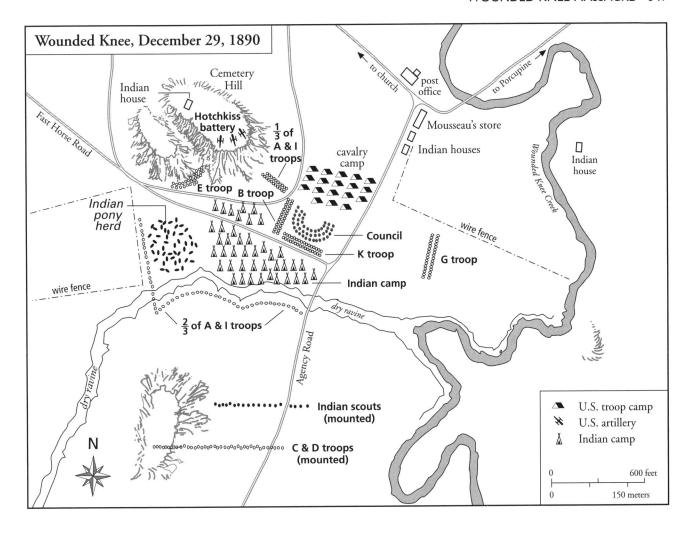

Wounded Knee, December 29, 1890

homa)—by threatening to hang captives. Even so, sporadic Seminole uprisings continued into the 1850s.

After service in the Mexican War, General Worth died in May 1849 while commanding the Department of Texas.

Wounded Knee Massacre (1890) *massacre of Lakota by U.S. Cavalry*

The massacre at Wounded Knee on December 29, 1890, is one of the most controversial incidents between U.S. troops and Indians in the entire period of the Indian Wars. The incident partially inspired the WOUNDED KNEE SIEGE (1973), an Indian takeover of the battle site.

The events leading up to the 1890 Wounded Knee Massacre largely involved the GHOST DANCE religion and rising tension in the area. The decade of the 1880s was a time of despair and near starvation for the Lakota Indians in South Dakota. When the situation seemed almost hopeless a new religion found its way across the Plains. In Nevada a Northern Paiute (Numu) prophet named WOVOKA espoused a doctrine of hope. The white people would disappear, deceased Indians

would be resurrected, and there would be plenty to eat. To prepare for the dawn of the new age the Indians were to perform the Ghost Dance and live sober and honest lives. Members from many western tribes accepted the new religion. Some members of the Teton, Brulé, and Oglala Lakota (see SIOUX) likewise adopted some Ghost Dance tenets.

As the Ghost Dance spread, the U.S. Army planned for the possibility of a new war, especially after Indian agents tried to ban the dance on reservations. In November the BUREAU OF INDIAN AFFAIRS in Washington asked for army help. As part of the efforts to counter the Indian factions who wished confrontation with non-Indians, General NELSON A. MILES ordered the arrest of several Lakota leaders, including SITTING BULL, a supporter of the movement. Indian police were to make the arrest, but as they began to do so, gunfire broke out. Several Indian policemen and Ghost Dancers were killed, including Sitting Bull. This further angered the Lakota and raised the level of anxiety. Nervously, several groups left the vicinity of their government-approved agencies.

By December 23, 1890, many of the Ghost Dancers still had not surrendered to the army. Miniconjou chief BIG FOOT, a former advocate of the Ghost Dance who now sought peace, had led approximately 350 followers to the Pine Ridge Reservation in South Dakota. They were stopped by the 7th Cavalry and forced to encamp at Wounded Knee Creek. On the night of December 23, Colonel JAMES FORSYTH arrived with the rest of the regiment and ordered his troops to set up four Hotchkiss cannon on the low hills around the Indian camp.

The next day 500 soldiers surrounded the Indians—120 men and 230 women and children. However, Yellow Bird, a Lakota medicine man, called on the warriors to resist after a small group of soldiers moved in to disarm the Indians. During a scuffle between an Indian and a soldier, a rifle went off. The few warriors who had rifles opened return fire. A fierce melee ensued as the panicked soldiers involved in the attempts to disarm Big Foot's followers broke out of the encampment. The ARTILLERY opened fire, with its exploding shells destroying the camp. Men, women, and children were killed indiscriminately as they scrambled for safety.

When the fighting ended, more than 160—possibly close to 300—Indians lay dead, including 44 women and 16 children and the peacemaking leader Big Foot. Another 50 or so were wounded. The army pursued those who tried to flee down the dry creek bed, and many more Indians died later. Military casualties numbered 25 dead and 39 wounded.

On New Year's Day, the dead Lakota were buried by the army in a mass grave near the site of the tragedy. Army rein-forcements poured into the Pine Ridge region and surrounded the frightened Indians, some 4,000 of whom had gathered in a huge camp along White Clay Creek. As the pressure tightened, more and more Lakota turned themselves in, with the final surrender coming on January 15.

For his part, Miles blamed the incident on Colonel Forsyth and he removed him from command. Commanding general John Schofield and Secretary of War Redfield Proctor, however, sought to divert public attention away from Wounded Knee, and they restored Forsyth to duty. Army investigations of Wounded Knee revealed no evidence of a deliberate slaughter and even suggested that many of the troops had tried to avoid harming noncombatants. In their view, the episode was a tragedy. Others, however, had not been so careful, as the use of artillery against Big Foot's camp clearly indicated. Given the high proportion of noncombatant deaths and the obvious predisposition of the camp for peace, the conclusion by many observers that this represented a massacre is not at all unreasonable.

Further Reading

American Indians. Pasadena, Calif.: Salem Press, 1995.
Chant, Christopher. The Military History of the United States: The Indian Wars. Tarrytown, N.Y.: Marshall Cavandesh, 1992.
Streissguth, Tom. Wounded Knee 1890. New York: Facts On File, 1998.

U.S. Army personnel gather the frozen bodies after the Wounded Knee Massacre. (By permission of the Western History Collections, University of Oklahoma Library)

Utley, Robert M. *The Last Days of the Sioux Nation,* 2nd ed. New Haven, Conn.: Yale University Press, 2004.

———. *Frontier Regulars.* New York: Macmillan, 1973.

Wounded Knee siege (siege of Wounded Knee)

(1973) *demonstration, standoff, and conflict between federal law enforcement agents and members of the American Indian Movement*

Wounded Knee siege, or the siege of Wounded Knee, was the name given to a 71-day siege and standoff between activist members of the AMERICAN INDIAN MOVEMENT (AIM) and federal law enforcement officials. The standoff arose from what had been intended as a peaceful demonstration for Lakota rights, specifically against the then-current Indian administration of the Pine Ridge SIOUX Reservation.

Within a national context, the siege of Wounded Knee was a dispute over the northwestern eighth of the Pine Ridge Reservation, given to the Lakota in the Fort Laramie Treaty of 1868. The Sheep Mountain Gunnery Range, as this area was known, had been borrowed by the military in 1941 for use as a training area. Despite government promises, it was not returned at the end of WORLD WAR II (1939–45). Indian efforts to recover this territory had become increasingly vociferous by 1971. The issue was complicated by two other factors. First, in 1970, rich uranium deposits were discovered near Sheep Mountain. As a result, federal planners intended to keep the land, regardless of any treaty obligations. Second, Lakota tribal politics also complicated the situation. In 1972, Richard Wilson won the Pine Ridge tribal presidency. Wilson soon received a BUREAU OF INDIAN AFFAIRS (BIA) grant to form what was called a Tribal Ranger Group. The group, reporting directly to Wilson, soon adopted the acronym "GOON," allegedly standing for "Guardians of the Oglala Nation." The members of GOON soon were accused of terrorizing Wilson's opposition, particularly leaders of the land-claims struggle with the U.S. government. GOON opponents formed the Oglala Sioux Civil Rights Organization. This group sought, unsuccessfully, to get the Justice Department to intervene in the Pine Ridge political violence. They also sought to impeach Wilson, gathering more signatures on the impeachment petition than had voted for him originally. The BIA scheduled formal hearings for February 1973, but put Wilson himself in charge of the proceedings. Sixty armed U.S. marshals supervised the hearings. Not surprisingly, Wilson was acquitted.

Wilson then banned opponents from meeting on the reservation. In defiance of this ban, the recently formed Lakota Civil Rights Organization and the Lakota Council of Elders held an emergency meeting. On February 27, 1972, a caravan of cars from these organizations and from AIM, set out for a symbolic press conference at Wounded Knee. The next day, the group at Wounded Knee discovered that it had been sealed into the hamlet by roadblocks erected by GOON members and BIA police. FBI agents and federal marshals added their own roadblocks later that day. That same day, AIM members, who were generally unarmed, broke into a trading post and seized weapons and ammunition, taking the non-Indian owner and some others hostage. They also began to fortify their positions.

The siege at Wounded Knee lasted for 71 days. The federal government offered amnesty to non-AIM members soon after the siege started. No one left the area; instead, other supporters entered. At times it looked as if a major assault, including military personnel, was developing. Shooting incidents occurred almost daily, but casualties on both sides were relatively light. During the course of the siege, two Indians were killed, and 15 were seriously wounded. Federal forces suffered one seriously wounded.

The formal siege ended on May 3, 1973. A major dispute later arose as to the precise sequence of events and whether AIM or the reservation and federal authorities had acted first.

The occupiers of Wounded Knee did not achieve their demands. The federal government refused to discuss demands based on the 1868 Fort Laramie Treaty, citing 1871 legislation that ended treaty negotiations with the Indians. Occupation leaders, including Lakota RUSSELL MEANS, were arrested after the siege. However, the government obtained convictions on only 15 minor charges.

In 1974, Wilson won reelection as the Pine Ridge tribal president, barely defeating Russell Means. The Pine Ridge Lakota eventually gained the right to hold a referendum and reclaim surface rights to the Sheep Mountain Gunnery Range. However, the federal government maintained mining rights.

Wovoka (The Cutter, Wanekia "One Who Makes Life," Jack Wilson) (1856–1932) *Northern Paiute medicine man and prominent leader of the Ghost Dance religion*

Wovoka was the son of Northern PAIUTE (Numa) leader Tavibo, a respected medicine man who reportedly could control the weather. In his early teens, Wovoka worked as a ranch hand for a devout Christian non-Indian named David Wilson. By age 20, Wovoka, who was then known as "Jack Wilson," was married and living in the Mason Valley of Nevada.

Like his father before him, Wovoka became a weather medicine man. His public ceremonies included a circle dance in which the participants received supernatural blessings. The dance itself consisted of men, women, and children joining hands and dancing in a clockwise direction. Symbolically, the community of believers traveled the path of the Sun through the circle of the days. Wovoka's accompanying songs emphasized the Almighty and nature. His sermons stressed universal love.

On January 1, 1889, Wovoka lay very ill with a fever as the Sun was going into eclipse, which terrified the Paiute. Slipping into unconsciousness, the medicine man felt himself taken to the Supreme Being, where he received a divine message. Soon both Wovoka and the Sun recovered from near death. Wovoka immediately gained a reputation as a messiah. Paiute, Mormons, and other Indians flooded into the Mason Valley to learn his teachings and dance.

Wovoka emphasized love and right living; taught peaceful coexistence with non-Indians and hard work; condemned quarreling, lying, and stealing; and promised that those who followed his teachings would one day be united with those who had died in a heavenlike place where game would abound, white people would vanish, and Indian people would live forever young, healthy, and happy. By performing the dance, Wovoka prescribed, people appropriated happiness on earth and hastened the hereafter.

The new religion, called the GHOST DANCE, spread to nearly two dozen Indian groups, including the ARAPAHO, CHEYENNE, SHOSHONE, and Lakota (see SIOUX). However, the Lakota, like other groups, modified Wovoka's teachings. Their Ghost Dance taught that non-Indians would vanish and featured specially decorated shirts through which no bullets could pass. The Ghost Dance made government and military officials increasingly fearful of tribal uprisings, which, in turn led to the death of SITTING BULL and the tragedy at WOUNDED KNEE (1890).

Saddened by Wounded Knee, Wovoka reaffirmed peaceful coexistence with non-Indians. The aging prophet remained the head of his new faith until his death in 1932.

Wright, George (1801–1865) U.S. Army officer

George Wright was an army veteran with more than 30 years' experience when he led troops under the direction of General JOHN E. WOOL at the outbreak of the YAKAMA WAR (1855–57). In spring 1856, while on an unsuccessful hunt for rebel YAKAMA chief KAMIAKIN, Wright put down a Chinook attack on settlements in the Cascade mountains of Oregon and hanged eight of the Indian leaders. He then proceeded to subdue the entire Walla Walla Valley by more peaceful measures.

The uneasy truce that followed the Yakama War was broken by the COEUR D'ALENE WAR (1858). In this conflict Wright was determined to subjugate the rebellious Indians and "make their punishment severe." In September 1858 he won decisive victories over a combined force of Coeur d'Alene, Spokan, and Palouse at FOUR LAKES and SPOKANE PLAIN. Afterward, he went from tribe to tribe in search of rebel ringleaders, hanging 15 warriors and putting many other in chains.

In October 1861, several months after the outbreak of the CIVIL WAR (1861–65), Wright was promoted to brigadier general and named commander of the Department of the Pacific, an office that he managed with firmness and efficiency until he was replaced in July 1864. He drowned in the Pacific Ocean on July 29, 1865, while en route to a new posting in the Washington Territory as commander of the Department of the Columbia.

Wyandot See HURON.

Wyoming Valley (1778) battle during the American Revolution

At the height of the AMERICAN REVOLUTION (1775–81), on June 30, 1778, British officers John Butler and Sir John Johnson led 400 Tories and 600 Indian troops—mainly SENECA and CAYUGA under famous war chiefs CORNPLANTER and Sayenqueraghta—into the Wyoming Valley in Pennsylvania to engage the Americans. That afternoon Butler's army attacked a group of American colonists, capturing three and killing four; American colonist John Harding escaped and sounded the alarm. Butler's troops moved on to Fort Wintermoot, which surrendered without a fight on July 1, and to Fort Jenkins, where a seven-man garrison fell after an unsuccessful defense. The next objective was Forty Fort, which housed 400 untrained and inexperienced colonial militia under Colonel Zebulon Butler.

Although it was improbable that the British and their Indian allies could breach the fort, the threat of destruction to surrounding homes and property brought the colonial militia out. On July 3 the 400-man militia left the fort to drive the British and their Indian allies from the valley. This foolhardy decision cost the militia 300 lives; the remainder of the Americans surrendered the following day. Zebulon Butler escaped and was secreted out of the valley.

After the battle of Wyoming Valley, John Butler tried unsuccessfully to keep the Tories and Indians from pillaging. No civilians were killed, but nearly all the settlers' property and livestock were destroyed. The survivors left the valley, many perishing along the way.

The tales of those fleeing the valley forced Congress to take action. In March 1779 Major General JOHN SULLIVAN took command of a colonial American expedition to eradicate Iroquois villages in central New York in retaliation for their actions against colonists. Sullivan's expedition resulted in a permanent division among the nations of the IROQUOIS CONFEDERACY: Seneca and Cayuga had been pro-British; ONEIDA and TUSCARORA were pro-American; and ONONDAGA and MOHAWK were divided between the two forces. No longer would the Iroquois unite around the Great Council Fire. After 1783, Americans overran the Wyoming Valley, driving out Indian allies and enemies alike.

See also BUTLER'S RANGERS.

Y

Yakama (Yakima) *tribe of the Yakima River Valley in southern Washington State*

Primarily fishers and gatherers, the Yakama were divided into small bands and groups. In 1806 explorers Meriwether Lewis and William Clark visited the territory of the Yakama and estimated the population of the entire tribe to be about 1,200.

The Yakama were relatively undisturbed by outsiders until the mid-1800s, when Oregon was reorganized into the Washington and Oregon territories. Settlers and miners soon began migrating to this region, and military posts were built to protect them. Settlers' demands for land led the U.S. government to pressure the Yakama and other tribes to give up their lands.

In 1855, the governor of Washington Territory, ISAAC I. STEVENS, convened the WALLA WALLA COUNCIL (1855) at Walla Walla, Washington. Representatives of the Yakama, Walla Walla, Umatilla, CAYUSE, and NEZ PERCE tribes signed a treaty ceding about 60,000 acres of land in eastern Oregon and central Washington. In return, the Indians were to be paid up to $200,000 per tribe for the land. The Walla Walla Treaty also required the tribes to live on a single reservation alongside some of their traditional enemies.

Many among the tribes did not accept the Walla Walla treaty or were suspicious of it and urged resistance. Under the leadership of Yakama Chief KAMIAKAN, many warriors of the Umatilla, Cayuse, and Walla Walla tribes rebelled, resulting in the outbreak of the YAKAMA WAR (1855–58). Raids, skirmishes, and battles followed, and for three years the Indians successfully repulsed U.S. troops. Finally, however, the Yakama and their Indian allies were defeated at the battle of FOUR LAKES (1858). Following this defeat the Yakama agreed to settle on a reservation with other tribes. Chief Kamiakan fled to Canada, but 24 other chiefs were captured and executed.

Today the Yakama live on a reservation located south of the city of Yakima, Washington.

Yakama War (Yakima War) (1855–1856) *hostilities between U.S. troops and Yakama Indians in the Washington and Oregon territories*

In September 1855, a group of YAKAMA Indians murdered prospectors traveling to the goldfields of British Columbia. They also murdered A. J. Bloom, a well-liked Indian agent, because they feared he was calling in the army to fight against them. Later, during a parlay, volunteers led by Colonel James Kelly seized Chief Peo-peo-mox-mox (leader of the Walla Walla Indians), killed him, and sent his scalp and ears to the Oregon settlement for display (see SCALPING). Meanwhile, settlers began killing Indians on sight, and angry warriors retaliated by killing innocent settlers. Soon army troops charged with guarding settlers from attacks found themselves protecting noncombatant Indians from vengeful militiamen. Most settlers, who had no trust for the U.S. regular army, chose to have their own militia deal harshly with the Indian problem.

General JOHN E. WOOL, who commanded the Department of the Pacific, thoroughly detested both Governor George Curry of Oregon and Governor ISAAC I. STEVENS of Washington Territory. Wool sympathized with the Indians in the situation and condemning settlers for their acts of violence. At one point he went so far as to order his troops not to fight the Indians unless it became absolutely necessary.

These actions infuriated both governors, who demanded the removal of Wool from command. In response, Wool claimed that the governors were attempting to make money off the government by buying supplies for the militia. With Oregon volunteers combing the region and threatening to expand the war by attacking other tribes, Wool was forced to send 500 troops under the command of Colonel GEORGE WRIGHT to put down the Indian problem once and for all. The campaign was relatively bloodless, and formal hostilities ended by mid-June 1856. (See also ROGUE RIVER WAR, 1855–56.)

There still were some isolated incidents of violence, but by November 1856 forts Simcoe and Walla Walla had been established to keep the peace. Governor Stevens won his fight in the end, as Wool was reassigned in May 1857. However, open conflict soon erupted again in the form of the COEUR D' ALENE WAR (1858).

Yamasee *Southeast Indian tribe originally located in South Carolina*
The Yamasee were a Muskogean-speaking people that occupied the coastal region of South Carolina and the Georgia islands. By 1570, the Spanish had established missions among the Yamasee. The tribe revolted in 1687 when the Spanish attempted to send a number of Indians to the West Indies as slave laborers. The Yamasee attacked several Spanish missions and then crossed the Savannah River into the English colony of South Carolina. There they established several towns within present-day Beaufort County.

English traders in the Carolinas furnished arms and ammunition to the Yamasee in return for their services as hunters and slave catchers. In 1704 combined forces of English and Yamasee destroyed 13 Spanish missions along the coast and captured 328 Indians as slaves. Later, the tribe aided the British during QUEEN ANNE'S WAR (1702–13). The Yamasee also aided the English in their war against the TUSCARORA and were largely responsible for that tribe's defeat.

Despite their alliance, Carolina traders and settlers viciously exploited the Yamasee, selling women and children into slavery. In 1715, the Yamasee, joined by the Catawba, revolted in the YAMASEE WAR (1715–28) and nearly destroyed the English colony. In retaliation, colonial officials nearly exterminated the tribe. Many fled south, where they were welcomed by the Spanish and settled in Florida. The Yamasee are believed to have no descendants today.

Yamasee War (1715–1728) *war between South Carolina colonists and the Yamasee Indians*
Although the YAMASEE Indians were allies of the British during QUEEN ANNE'S WAR (1702–13) and fought with them against the Spanish, hostilities soon broke out between South Carolina traders and the Yamasee. This was partly because

southern colonial fur traders were not stopped by the Allegheny Mountains, as their northern counterparts were. Consequently, they began trading directly with tribes as far west as the Mississippi River and beyond, thus cutting the Yamasee out of the trading circuit. The war also resulted in part from poor colonial treatment of Indian debtors. In addition, the Spanish in Florida and the French in Louisiana may have played indirect roles in the conflict.

The Yamasee had been driven from their villages in north Florida by the Spanish during Queen Anne's War. The British encouraged the displaced Indians to occupy lands in colonial South Carolina, near the Savannah River. Once there, however, the Yamasee quickly fell victim to traders, who encouraged them to go into debt. By spring 1715, according to some sources, the tribe's debt had risen to some £50,000, which they had no hope of repaying. Their creditors seized the debtors' wives and children and sold them into slavery to clear their debts.

On April 15, 1715, the Yamasee seized all South Carolina traders in their territory as hostages and raided and burned frontier settlements. They may have expected assistance from other Europeans against the British. The Spanish governor at St. Augustine had tried, in the period immediately following Queen Anne's War, to establish diplomatic ties with the CREEK, relatives of the Yamasee. Meanwhile, French Governor Bienville of the colony in Louisiana wanted to break British attempts to trade with the CHOCTAW, who might later be induced to turn against the French. Neither country, however, expressed support directly for the warring Indians by offering supplies, ammunition, or troops. Instead, the Yamasee had to rely on other Native Americans to augment their warrior bands. Creek, Catawba, SHAWNEE, CHEROKEE, and several other smaller groups soon began raiding in conjunction with the Yamasee. At one point the attacks came within 12 miles of Charleston, South Carolina.

South Carolina at this time was very vulnerable to assault. There were only 5,500 European settlers in the whole colony. They were outnumbered by their African slaves, of whom there were 8,650 in the colony, and they were nearly equalled in number by the 5,100 Native Americans. The South Carolina militia, trained for putting down slave revolts, refused to launch independent campaigns against the Indians, and appeals for help to Great Britain, Virginia, New England, and North Carolina went unanswered. In desperation the colonial government authorized the formation of an army composed of slaves, Indian allies, and militia to fight the Yamasee. It met with little success and was soon disbanded.

Diplomacy proved more effective than force against the Yamasee. The war slowed down after it became clear to the Indians that Virginia traders, whom they had counted on to replace the trade lost with the South Carolinians, refused to supply them with ammunition. The tribe's original Indian allies withdrew after the first two years of the war, realizing that without European ammunition their efforts were doomed. The Catawba reached an accommodation with the colonists after they were defeated at the Santee River by a small force of militia under Captain George Chicken. Attempts to bring the Cherokee deeper into the war failed, and the tribe began actively assisting the British against the Yamasee during the winter of 1715–16.

The Yamasee and their Creek relatives retreated to Spanish Florida and sought Spanish help. They found shelter in northern Florida and continued to raid into South Carolina intermittently for another 11 years. At the same time they waged a bitter war with the Cherokee, the Creek-Cherokee War, which dragged on until 1728.

The last battle of the Yamasee War occurred in Florida. Great Britain and Spain were again at war, and the South Carolina militia, led by Colonel John Palmer, made an attack on St. Augustine and the fort of San Marcos. They burned the Yamasee village of Nombre de Dios, seized about 15 Indians, and killed another 30. Although the Spanish allowed the Indians to seek shelter inside the fort, they made no move to protect the property of their allies or to challenge the colonial force.

The Yamasee War had a profound effect on both Native Americans and South Carolinians. For the Indians it showed that none of the European powers were interested in helping them achieve their objectives. This may have led the Creek to declare and try to maintain a neutral position in future European wars. Many tribes suffered displacement and carried a lasting grudge against the British and their Indian allies to their new home. The Shawnee moved first to western Pennsylvania, and then to Ohio, while some Creek settled in northern Florida and became the SEMINOLE. The South Carolinians, for their part, suffered huge losses. A greater percentage of the colony's population died in the conflict than did those in New England during KING PHILIP'S WAR (1675–76). Frontier settlements were abandoned, and the profitable Indian trade was interrupted. In addition, the proprietors of South Carolina were forced out of office, and the British government took over its administration in 1719.

Further Reading

Leach, Edward Douglas. *Arms for Empire: A Military History of the British Colonies in North America.* New York: Macmillan, 1973.
Robinson, Stitt W. *The Southern Colonial Frontier, 1607–1763.* Albuquerque: University of New Mexico Press, 1979.
Steele, Ian K. *Warpaths: Invasions of North America.* New York: Oxford University Press, 1994.

Yavapai   *Indian tribe in central Arizona*
The Yavapai traditionally occupied the rugged area of central and west-central Arizona. There the three small bands of Indians led a seminomadic life of hunting and gathering wild food.

During the 1700s and 1800s, the Yavapai regarded the neighboring Walapai, Havasupai, MARICOPA, and Pima (see AKIMEL O'ODHAM) Indians as their enemies. However, they felt a close affiliation to the Tonto band of the Western APACHE, with whom they traded and frequently intermarried.

The American government assumed responsibility for Yavapai Indians with the signing of the TREATY OF GUADALUPE HIDALGO (1848). At that time, prospectors were advancing into Yavapai territory in search of gold. Consequently, tensions and hostilities increased. In 1872, General GEORGE CROOK launched a campaign against the Yavapai and their allies, the Northern Tonto Apache, whom he thought were the same people. This culminated in the massacre at SKELETON CAVE (1872), in which about 75 Yavapai men, women, and children were shot to death.

In 1875, the Yavapai were placed on a reservation at San Carlos, Arizona; they remained there for 25 years. After that they began drifting back to their homeland, where today they live on small reservations.

Yuma   *Indian tribe in southwest Arizona and southeastern California*
The Yuma call themselves the Quechan, a reference to a trail spoken of in their origin story. For hundreds of years they have lived along the southern reaches of the Colorado River, near the modern town of Yuma, Arizona.

The Spanish made contact with the Yuma as early as 1540. For the most part the early relations between the two groups were friendly. However, the Yuma resisted efforts to convert them to Roman Catholicism, and in 1781 they destroyed a mission, killing priests and soldiers.

For many decades the Yuma and their allies, the MOJAVE, warred with the MARICOPA and later the Pima (see AKIMEL O'ODHAM). While they often held the upper hand, they were soundly defeated in the battle of MARICOPA WELLS (1857).

After gold was discovered in California, wagon trains began traversing the Yuma's desert territory. As hostility between Indians and non-Indians increased, the miners began demanding that the U.S. Army provide protection from the Indians. Camp Yuma was established as a result. During the latter half of the 19th century, the Yuma watched as the majority of their land was "appropriated" by miners and settlers. Today, the Yuma live on several shared reservations in California and Arizona.

Yuma/Mojave/Maricopa Wars   See MARICOPA WELLS.

Z

Zuni (A'shiwi, "the flesh") *Indian tribe in New Mexico*
At the beginning of the 16th century, the Zuni lived in six villages in a broad valley south of Gallup, New Mexico. Hawikuh was the largest village settlement.

In 1539, Spaniard Fray Marcos de Niza journeyed north from Mexico in search of the fabled Seven Cities of Cíbola and Montezuma's gold. African explorer Estevánico led Niza's advance party. When Estevánico, who had been to the area in an earlier expedition, arrived at Hawikuh, he was found to be in possession of a sacred object previously stolen from the tribe. Because of this and his arrogance, the Zuni killed him. Meanwhile, Niza continued north until he could see Hawikuh in the distance, its adobe dwellings glistening in the sun. He then returned to Mexico and announced that he had found Cíbola. In 1540 Francisco Coronado led an expedition to Zuni territory. He attacked and captured Hawikuh but found no gold or jewels.

During the next century, the Zuni were often visited by the Spanish, and Franciscans built at mission at Hawikuh in 1629. Three years later, the Indians killed two friars. During the decades that followed, the residents of Hawikuh faced another threat as the APACHE raided the village with ever-increasing frequency. In 1672, the Zunis were forced to abandon Hawikuh, but the Spanish threat had not subsided. As a result, the Zuni supported the PUEBLO REBELLION (1680).

Present-day Zuni live at Zuni Pueblo, near the Arizona-Mexico border, where they raise livestock and engage in a number of craft occupations.

Appendix

INDIAN TRIBES OF NORTH AMERICA ORGANIZED BY CULTURE AREA

ARCTIC CULTURE AREA

Aleut
Inuit

CALIFORNIA CULTURE AREA

Achomawi (Pit River)
Akwaala
Alliklik (Tataviam)
Atsugewi (Pit River)
Bear River
Cahto (Kato)
Cahuilla
Chilula
Chimariko
Chumash
Costanoan (Ohlone)
Cupeño
Diegueño (Ipai)
Esselen
Fernandeño
Gabrieliño
Huchnom
Hupa
Ipai (Diegueño)
Juaneño
Kamia (Tipai)
Karok
Kitanemuk
Konomihu
Lassik
Luiseño

Maidu
Mattole
Miwok
Nicoleño
Nomlaki
Nongatl
Okwanuchu
Patwin (subgroup of Wintun)
Pomo
Salinas
Serrano
Shasta
Sinkyone
Tolowa (Smith River)
Tubatulabal (Kern River)
Vanyume
Wailaki
Wappo
Whilkut
Wintu (subgroup of Wintun)
Wintun
Wiyot
Yahi
Yana
Yokuts
Yuki
Yurok

GREAT BASIN CULTURE AREA

Bannock
Chemehuevi

Kawaiisu
Mono
Paiute
Panamint
Sheepeater (subgroup of Bannock
    and Shoshone)
Shoshone
Snake (subgroup of Paiute)
Ute
Washoe

GREAT PLAINS CULTURE AREA

Arapaho
Arikara
Assiniboine
Atsina (Gros Ventre)
Blackfeet
Blood (subgroup of Blackfeet)
Cheyenne
Comanche
Crow
Hidatsa
Ioway
Kaw
Kichai
Kiowa
Kiowa-Apache
Mandan
Missouria
Omaha
Osage

Otoe
Pawnee
Piegan (subgroup of Blackfeet)
Plains Cree
Plains Ojibway
Ponca
Quapaw
Sarcee
Sioux (Dakota, Lakota, Nakota)
Tawakoni
Tawehash
Tonkawa
Waco
Wichita
Yscani

Northeast Culture Area

Abenaki
Algonkin
Amikwa (Otter)
Cayuga
Chippewa (Ojibway, Anishinabe)
Chowanoc
Conoy
Coree (Coranine)
Erie
Fox (Mesquaki)
Hatteras
Honniasont
Huron (Wyandot)
Illinois
Iroquois (Haudenosaunee)
Kickapoo
Kitchigami
Lenni Lenape (Delaware)
Machapunga
Mahican
Maliseet
Manhattan (subgroup of Lenni
    Lenape or Wappinger)
Massachuset
Mattabesac
Meherrin
Menominee
Miami
Micmac
Mingo (subgroup of Iroquois)
Mohawk
Mohegan
Montauk
Moratok
Nanticoke
Narragansett
Nauset

Neusiok
Neutral (Attiwandaronk)
Niantic
Nipmuc
Noquet
Nottaway
Oneida
Onondaga
Ottawa
Otter (Amikwa)
Pamlico (Pomeiok)
Passamaquoddy
Paugussett
Penacook
Penobscot
Pequot
Pocomtuc
Poospatuck (subgroup of Montauk)
Potawatomi
Powhatan
Raritan (subgroup of
    Lenni Lenape)
Roanoke
Sac
Sakonnet
Secotan
Seneca
Shawnee
Shinnecock (subgroup of Montauk)
Susquehannock
Tobacco (Petun)
Tuscarora
Wampanoag
Wappinger
Weapemeoc
Wenro
Winnebago (Ho-Chunk)

Northwest Coast Culture Area

Ahantchuyuk
Alsea
Atfalati
Bella Coola
Cathlamet
Cathlapotle
Chastacosta
Chehalis
Chelamela
Chepenafa (Mary's River)
Chetco
Chilluckittequaw
Chimakum
Chinook

Clackamas
Clallam
Clatskanie
Clatsop
Clowwewalla
Comox
Coos
Coquille (Mishikhwutmetunne)
Cowichan
Cowlitz
Dakubetede
Duwamish
Gitskan
Haida
Haisla
Heiltsuk
Kalapuya
Kuitsh
Kwakiutl
Kwalhioqua
Latgawa
Luckiamute
Lumni
Makah
Miluk
Muckleshoot
Multomah (Wappato)
Nanaimo
Nisga
Nisqually
Nooksack
Nootka
Puntlatch
Puyallup
Quaitso (Queets)
Quileute
Quinault
Rogue
Sahehwamish
Samish
Santiam
Seechelt
Semiahmoo
Siletz
Siuslaw
Skagit
Skilloot
Skykomish
Snohomish
Snoqualmie
Songish
Squamish
Squaxon (Squaxin)
Stalo
Swallah

Swinomish
Takelma (Rogue)
Taltushtuntude
Tillamook
Tlingit
Tsimshian
Tututni (Rogue)
Twana
Umpqua
Wappato (Multomah)
Wasco
Watlala (Cascade)
Yamel
Yaquina
Yoncalla

PLATEAU CULTURE AREA

Cayuse
Chelan
Coeur d'Alene
Columbia (Sinkiuse)
Colville
Entiat
Flathead (Salish)
Kalispel
Klamath
Klickitat
Kootenai (Flathead)
Lake (Senijextee)
Lillooet
Methow
Modoc
Molalla
Nez Perce
Ntlakyapamuk (Thompson)
Okanagan
Palouse
Pshwanwapam
Sanpoil
Shuswap
Sinkaietk
Sinkakaius
Skin (Tapanash)
Spokan
Stuwihamuk
Taidnapam
Tenino
Tyigh
Umatilla
Walla Walla
Wanapam
Wauyukma
Wenatchee
Wishram
Yakama

SOUTHEAST CULTURE AREA

Acolapissa
Adai
Ais
Akokisa
Alabama
Amacano
Apalachee
Apalachicola
Atakapa
Avoyel
Bayogoula
Bidai
Biloxi
Caddo
Calusa
Caparaz
Cape Fear
Catawba
Chakchiuma
Chatot
Chawasha (subgrop of Chitimacha)
Cheraw (Sara)
Cherokee
Chiaha
Chickasaw
Chine
Chitimacha
Choctaw
Congaree
Coushatta
Creek
Cusabo
Deadose
Eno
Eyeish (Ayish)
Griga
Guacata
Guale
Hitchiti
Houma
Ibitoupa
Jeaga
Kaskinampo
Keyauwee
Koroa
Lumbee
Manahoac
Miccosukee (subgroup of Seminole)
Mobile
Monacan
Moneton
Muklasa
Nahyssan
Napochi

Natchez
Occaneechi
Oconee
Ofo
Okelousa
Okmulgee
Opelousa
Osochi
Pasacagoula
Patiri
Pawokti
Pee Dee
Pensacola
Quinipissa
Santee (Issati)
Saponi
Sawokli
Seminole
Sewee
Shakori
Sissipahaw
Sugeree
Taensa
Tamathli
Tangipahoa
Taposa
Tawasa
Tekesta
Timucua
Tiou
Tohome
Tunica
Tuskegee
Tutelo
Waccamaw
Washa (subgroup of Chitimacha)
Wateree
Waxhaw
Winyaw
Woccon
Yadkin
Yamasee
Yazoo
Yuchi

SOUTHWEST CULTURE AREA

Akimel O'odham (Pima)
Apache
Coahuiltec
Cocopah
Halchidhoma
Halyikwamai
Havasupai
Hopi

Hualapai
Jumano (Shuman)
Karankawa
Keres (Pueblo Indians)
Kohuana
Maricopa
Mojave
Navajo (Dineh)
Piro (Pueblo Indians)
Pueblo
Quenchan (Yuma)
Shuman (Jumano)
Sobaipuri
Tewa (Pueblo Indians)
Tiwa (Pueblo Indians)
Tohono O'odham (Papago)
Towa (Jemez, Pueblo Indians)

Yaqui
Yavapai
Yuma (Quechan)
Zuni

SUBARCTIC CULTURE AREA

Ahtena (Copper)
Beaver (Tsattine)
Beothuk
Carrier
Chilcotin
Chipewyan
Cree
Dogrib
Eyak
Han

Hare (Kawchottine)
Ingalik
Kolchan
Koyukon
Kutchin
Montagnais
Nabesna
Nahane
Naskapi
Sekani
Slave (Slavery, Etchaottine)
Tahltan
Tanaina
Tanana
Tatsanottine (Yellowknife)
Tsetsaut
Tutchone (Mountain)

Chronology

1599
- *January 22:* Acoma Pueblo battle

1622
- *March 22:* Start of Powhatan Wars (1622–1632, 1644–1646)

1632
- Swaanendael attack

1635
- Start of Beaver Wars (1635–1684)

1636
- Block Island raid

1637
- *spring:* Pequot War

1638
- Narragansett Treaty formally ends Pequot War

1641
- *summer:* Start of Kieft's War (1641–1645), the first of the Delaware Wars (1641–1868)

1643
- *February 24–26:* Pavonia massacre

1645
- Narragansett War

1655
- *September 6:* Start of Peach War (1655–1664)

1656
- Pamunkey battle

1675
- *June:* Start of King Philip's War (1675–1676)
- *July 19:* Pocasset Swamp battle
- *August 25:* Hopewell Swamp battle
- *September 18:* Bloody Brook battle
- *December 19:* Great Swamp Fight

1676
- *May–October:* Bacon's Rebellion
- *August 12:* Bridgewater Swamp battle ends King Philip's War

1680
- *August 11:* Start of Pueblo Rebellion (1680–1692)
- *August 15–21:* Santa Fe battle

1689
- *August 5:* Start of King William's War (1689–1697)

1693
- *December 28–30:* Siege of Santa Fe

1701
- *July:* Grand Settlement of 1701 formally ends King William's War

1702

- *September 10:* Start of Queen Anne's War (1702–1713)

1704

- *February 28:* Deerfield Raid

1711

- *September 22:* Start of Tuscarora War (1711–1713)

1712

- Start of Fox War (1712–1742)

1713

- *March:* Nohoroca battle
- *spring:* Tuscarora Treaty ends Tuscarora War

1715

- *April 15:* Start of Yamasee War (1715–1728)

1720

- Start of Chickasaw Resisistance (1720–1763)

1722

- Start of Dummer's War (1722–1727)

1724

- *August:* Norridgewock battle

1725

- Abenaki Treaty fails to end Dummer's War

1729

- *November 28:* Natchez Revolt

1737

- *August 25:* Walking Purchase Treaty

1744

- Start of King George's War (1744–1748)

1754

- *April:* Start of French and Indian War (1754–1763)

1755

- *July 9:* Braddock's Defeat
- *September:* Lake George battle

1758

- *March 16:* San Saba battle
- *October:* Easton Treaty

1759

- Taovoya battle
- *December 26:* Start of Cherokee War (1759–1761)

1761

- *December:* Cherokee Treaties

1763

- *February 10:* Treaty of Paris ends French and Indian War
- *April 2:* Start of Pontiac's Rebellion (1763–1764)
- *May–October:* Detroit siege
- *summer–fall:* Fort Niagara siege
- *August 5–6:* Bushy Run battle
- *December 14:* Start of Paxton Riots (1763–1764)

1768

- *November 5:* Fort Stanwix Treaty between Britain and Iroquois Confederacy

1773

- *May 29:* Start of Lord Dunmore's War (1773–1774)

1774

- *October 10:* Point Pleasant battle

1775

- Start of American Revolution (1775–1781)

1777

- *August 3–23:* Fort Stanwix battle
- *August 6:* Oriskany Creek battle

1778

- *July 3–4:* Wyoming Valley battle
- *November 11:* Cherry Valley massacre

1779

- *August 29:* Newtown battle

1780

- *June 22:* Ruddell's Station battle

1782

- *March 7:* Gnadenhutten Massacre
- *August 19:* Blue Licks battle

1783

- Augusta Treaty
- *September 3:* Treaty of Paris

1784

- *October 22:* Fort Stanwix Treaty between U.S. government and Iroquois Confederacy

1785

- *November:* First of the Hopewell Treaties (1785–1786)

1786

- Start of Little Turtle's War (1786–1795)
- Fort Finney Treaty

1789

- *January:* Flint Creek battle
- *January:* Fort Harmar Treaties

1790

- *July 2:* Holsston Treaty
- *October 18 and 22:* Harmar's Defeat

1791

- *November 4:* St. Clair's Defeat

1794

- *August 20:* Fallen Timbers battle

1795

- *August 3:* Treaty of Greenville formally ends Little Turtle's War

1802

- Start of New Archangel sieges (1802–1813)

1803

- Louisiana Purchase

1809

- Start of Tecumseh's Rebellion (1809–1811)

1811

- *November 7:* Tippecanoe battle

1812

- Start of War of 1812 (1812–1814)

1813

- *January 22:* Raisin River battle
- *July:* Start of Creek War (1813–1814)
- *August 30:* Fort Mims battle
- *October 5:* Thames battle
- *November 3:* Tallasahatchee battle
- *November 9:* Talladega battle
- *November 29:* Autossee battle
- *March 27:* Horseshoe Bend battle
- *August 9:* Fort Jackson Treaty formally ends Creek War
- *December 24:* Treaty of Ghent formally ends War of 1812

1815

- Portage des Sioux Treaties
- *September 8:* Spring Wells Treaty

1816

- Start of First Seminole War (1816–1818)

1817

- *June 18:* Selkirk Treaty

1818

- *spring:* Suwanee River battle

1819

- Start of Kickapoo resistance (1819–1831)

1820

- *October 10–18:* Doak's Stand Treaty

1823

- *December 15:* Treaty of Tampa

1825

- *August:* Prairie du Chien Treaty

1826

- Start of Winnebago Uprising (1826–1827)

1830

- *May 28:* Indian Removal Act
- *September 18:* Dancing Rabbit Creek Treaty

1832

- Black Hawk War
- *May 9:* Treaty of Payne's Landing
- *May 14:* Stillman's Run battle
- *July 21:* Wisconsin Heights battle

- *August 2:* Bad Axe battle
- *summer:* Indian Creek battle

1833

- Fort Gibson Treaty

1835

- *December 28:* Great Wahoo Swamp battle, which Starts Second Seminole War (1835–1842)
- *December 31:* Withlacoochee River battle
- *December 29:* New Echota Treaty

1837

- *December 25:* Lake Okeechobee battle

1840

- *March 19:* Start of Comanche Wars (1840–1875)
- *August:* Plum Creek battle

1846

- *April 25:* Start of U.S.-Mexican War (1846–1848)

1847

- *February:* Start of Cayuse War (1847–1850)
- *late August:* Bent's Fort Council
- *November 29:* Waiilatpu Mission massacre

1848

- *February 2:* Treaty of Guadalupe Hidalgo

1849

- Courthouse Rebellion

1851

- *February:* Indian Appropriations Act
- *September:* First Fort Laramie Treaty

1853

- Fort Atkinson Treaty
- *December 30:* Gadsden Treaty

1854

- *August 19:* Grattan Defeat Starts Sioux Wars (1854–1890)
- *December 26:* Medicine Creek Treaty

1855

- *May:* Walla Walla Peace Council
- *September:* Start of Yakama War (1855–1856)
- *September 3:* Bluewater Creek battle

- *October:* Start of Rogue River War (1855–1856)
- *October 17:* Blackfeet Treaty with U.S. government
- *December:* Start of Third Seminole War (1855–1858)
- *December:* Big Cypress Swamp battle

1856

- *May 27:* Big Meadows battle
- *July 17:* Grande Ronde Valley battle

1857

- *July 29:* Solomon River battle
- *September 1:* Maricopa Wells battle

1858

- *May–September:* Coeur d'Alene War
- *May 11:* Antelope Hills battle
- *September 1:* Four Lakes battle
- *September 1:* Spokane Plains battle
- *October 1:* Rush Springs battle

1859

- *spring:* Crooked Creek battle

1860

- *April:* Fort Defiance battle
- *May–June:* Paiute War

1861

- Fort Wise Treaty
- Start of U.S. Civil War (1861–1865)
- *February:* Start of Apache Wars (1861–1886)

1862

- *March 7:* Pea Ridge battle
- *July 14:* Apache Pass battle
- *July 23:* Locust Grove battle
- *August 18:* Minnesota Uprising
- *August 20:* Fort Ridgely battle
- *August 23:* New Ulm battle
- *September 2–4:* Birch Coulee battle
- *September 23:* Wood Lake battle

1863

- Shoshone War
- *January 27:* Bear River battle
- *June:* Start of Navajo War (1863–1864)
- *June 9:* Treaty of 1863
- *July 17:* Honey Springs battle
- *July 26:* Dead Buffalo Lake battle
- *September 3:* Whitestone Hill battle

1864

- *January 12–14:* Canyon de Chelly battle ends Navajo War
- *spring:* Walnut Creek raid
- *April 12:* Fremont Orchard battle
- *July 28:* Killdeer Mountain battle
- *November 29:* Sand Creek massacre starts Cheyenne-Arapaho War (1864–1865)

1865

- *January 1:* Dove Creek battle
- *January 7 and February 2:* Julesburg Raids
- *February 4–9:* Mud Springs battle
- *late July:* Platte Bridge battle
- *August 29:* Tongue River battle
- *October:* Little Arkansas River Treaties

1866

- Start of Snake War (1866–1868)
- *June:* Start of Red Cloud's War (1866–1868)
- *late July:* Crazy Woman Fight
- *December 6:* Lodge Trail Ridge battle
- *December 21:* Fetterman Fight

1867

- *July:* Medicine Lodge Treaties
- *August 1:* Hayfield Fight
- *August 2:* Wagon Box Fight

1868

- *June:* Navajo Treaty
- *September 17–25:* Beecher's Island battle
- *October:* Second Fort Laramie Treaty
- *November 27:* Washita battle
- *mid-November:* Start of Southern Plains War (1868–1869)
- *December 25:* Soldier Spring battle

1869

- *June 9:* Summit Springs
- *November:* Start of Riel's Rebellions (1869–1870, 1884–1885)

1870

- *January 23:* Marias River massacre
- *February 17:* Council Grove Treaty

1871

- *April 30:* Camp Grant Massacre
- *May:* Salt Creek Prairie battle

1872

- *September 29:* McClellan Creek battle
- *November 29:* Tule Lake battle starts Modoc War (1872–1873)
- *December 28:* Skeleton Cave massacre

1873

- *January 16–17:* Lava Beds battle
- *May:* Dry Lake battle
- *May 18:* Remolino battle

1874

- *June 27:* Adobe Walls battle
- *fall:* Start of Red River War (1874–1875)
- *September 28:* Palo Duro Canyon battle

1876

- *February 1:* Start of War for the Black Hills (1876–1877)
- *June 17:* Rosebud Creek battle
- *June 25:* Little Bighorn
- *July 7:* Warbonnet Creek battle
- *September 9:* Slim Buttes battle
- *November 25:* Powder River battle

1877

- *January 7–8:* Wolf Mountain battle
- *May 7:* Muddy Creek battle
- *June–October:* Nez Perce War
- *June 17:* Rains Fight
- *June 17:* White Bird Creek battle
- *July 11:* Clearwater battle
- *August 8–11:* Big Hole battle
- *August 19–20:* Camas Creek battle
- *September 13:* Canyon Creek battle
- *September 22:* Blackfeet Treaty with Canadian government
- *September 30–October 5:* Bear Paw battle

1878

- *June–August:* Bannock War

1879

- *May–October:* Sheepeater War
- *September 4:* Start of Victorio's Resistance (1879–1880)
- *September 29–October 5:* Milk Creek battle and simultaneous Meeker Agency battle start Ute War (September–October 1879)

1880

- *July 30:* Tinaja de las Palmas battle
- *August 6:* Rattlesnake Springs battle
- *October 15–16:* Tres Castillos battle

1881

- *August 30:* Cibecue Creek battle
- *September 30:* Start of Geronimo's Resistance (1881–1886)

1882

- *August 30:* Big Dry Wash battle

1890

- *December 29:* Wounded Knee Massacre, last major conflict of Sioux Wars
- *December 30:* Drexel Mission battle

Selected Bibliography

Adams, Alexander B. *Geronimo: A Biography.* New York: Da Capo, 1971.

Alderman, Pat. *Nancy Ward – Dragging Canoe: Cherokee-Chickamauga War Chief.* Johnson City, Tenn.: Overmountain Press, 1978.

Ambrose, Stephen E. *Crazy Horse and Custer: The Parallel Lives of Two American Warriors.* Garden City, N.Y.: Doubleday, 1975.

Anderson, Gary Clayton. *Little Crow: Spokesman for the Sioux.* St. Paul: Minnesota Historical Society Press, 1986.

Andrist, Ralph K. *The Long Death: The Last Days of the Plains Indians.* 1964. Reprint, New York: Macmillan, 1993.

Au, Dennis M. *War on the Raisin: A Narrative Account of the War of 1812 in the River Raisin Settlement, Michigan Territory.* Monroe, Mich.: Monroe County Historical Society, 1981.

Axelrod, Alan. *Chronicle of the Indian Wars: From Colonial Times to Wounded Knee.* New York: Prentice Hall, 1993.

Bahti, Tom. *Southwestern Indian Tribes.* Flagstaff, Ariz.: KC Publications, 1968.

Bailey, John W. *Pacifying the Plains.* Westport, Conn.: Greenwood, 1979.

Bailey, Lynn R. *The Long Walk: A History of the Navajo Wars, 1846–68.* 1964. Reprint, Pasadena, Calif.: Socio-Technical Books 1970.

Baldwin, Louis. *Intruders Within: Pueblo Resistance to Spanish Rule and the Revolt of 1680.* New York: Franklin Watts, 1995.

Ball, Eve. *In the Days of Victorio: Recollections of a Warm Springs Apache.* Tucson: University of Arizona Press, 1972.

Bancroft-Hunt, Norman. *Warriors: Warfare and the Native American Indian.* London: Salamander Books, 1995.

Banks, Leo W. "The Buffalo Soldiers." *Arizona Highways* 71, no. 1 (January 1995): 34–37.

Bannon, John Francis. *The Spanish Borderlands Frontier, 1513–1821.* New York: Holt, Rinehart and Winston, 1970.

Barbour, Philip L. *The Three Worlds of Captain John Smith.* Boston: Houghton Mifflin, 1964.

Bataille, Gretchen, ed. *Native American Women: A Biographical Dictionary.* New York: Garland, 1993.

Baydo, Jerry R. *A History of the American Indian.* Wheaton, Ill.: Gregory, 1992.

Beal, Merrill D. *"I Will Fight No More Forever": Chief Joseph and the Nez Perce War.* Seattle: University of Washington, 1963.

Berthrong, Donald J. *The Southern Cheyennes.* Norman: University of Oklahoma Press, 1963.

Betzinez, Jason, with Wilbur Sturtevant Nye. *I Fought with Geronimo.* 1959. Reprint, Lincoln: University of Nebraska Press, 1987.

Billard, Jules B., ed. *The World of the American Indian.* Washington, D.C.: National Geographic Society, 1993.

Billias, George Athan, ed. *George Washington's Generals.* 1964. Reprint, Westport, Conn.: Greenwood, 1980.

Black Hawk. *Black Hawk: An Autobiography.* Edited by Donald Jackson. 1833. Reprint, Urbana: University of Illinois, 1955, 1964.

Blow, Michael, et al., eds. *American Heritage History of the Thirteen Colonies.* New York: American Heritage, 1967.

Boorstin, Daniel J. *The Americans: The National Experience.* New York: Random House, 1965.

Bourke, John Gregory. *On the Border with Crook.* Chicago: Rio Grande Press, 1962.

Brandes, Ray. *Frontier Military Posts of Arizona.* Globe, Ariz.: Dale Stuart King, 1960.

Brown, Dee. *The American West.* New York: Scribner's, 1994.

———. *Bury My Heart at Wounded Knee.* New York: Holt, Rinehart and Winston, 1970.

———. *The Fetterman Massacre* [formerly *Fort Phil. Kearny Massacre*]. Reprint. Lincoln: University of Nebraska Press, 1971.

Brown, John A., and Robert H. Ruby. *The Cayuse Indians: Imperial Tribesmen of Old Oregon.* Norman: University of Oklahoma Press, 1972.

Brown, John P. *Old Frontiers.* Salem, Mass.: Ayer Company, 1986.

Buchanan, Kimberly Moore. *Apache Women Warriors.* El Paso: University of Texas at El Paso Press, 1986.

Bucko, Raymond A. *The Lakota Ritual of the Sweat Lodge: History and Contemporary Practice.* Lincoln: University of Nebraska Press, 1998.

Burnette, Robert, with John Koster. *The Road to Wounded Knee.* New York: Bantam Books, 1974.

Calloway, Colin G. *The American Revolution in Indian Country.* New York: Cambridge University Press, 1995.

———. *Crown and Calumet: British-Indian Relations, 1783–1815.* Norman: University of Oklahoma Press, 1987.

Capps, Benjamin. *The Great Chiefs.* New York: Time-Life Books, 1975.

———. *The Indians.* Time-Life Series. "The Old West." New York: Time-Life Books, 1973.

Carley, Kenneth. *The Sioux Uprising of 1862,* 2nd ed. St. Paul: Minnesota Historical Society, 1976.

Carrington, Frances. *My Army Life and the Fort Phil Kearney Massacre.* 1911. Reprint, Freeport, N.Y.: Books for Libraries, 1971.

Catlin, George, *Letters and Notes on the North American Indian.* Edited by Michael MacDonald Mooney. New York: Clarkson N. Potter, 1975.

Cerami, Charles A. *Jefferson's Great Gamble: The Remarkable Story of Jefferson, Napoleon and the Men behind the Louisiana Purchase.* Naperville, Ill.: Sourcebooks, 2003.

Chalfant, William Y. *Without Quarter: The Wichita Expedition and the Fight on Crooked Creek.* Norman: University of Oklahoma 1991.

Champagne, Duane, ed. *Native North American Almanac: A Reference Work.* Detroit: Gale Research, 1994.

Chant, Christopher. *The Military History of the United States.* 16 vols. *The Indian Wars.* Tarrytown, N.Y.: Marshall Cavendish, 1992.

Charlebois, Peter. *The Life of Louis Riel.* Rev. ed. Toronto: New Canada Publications, 1975.

Chase, Harold W., ed. *Dictionary of American History.* 7 vols. New York: Scribner's, 1976.

Clark, Robert A., ed. *The Killing of Chief Crazy Horse.* Lincoln: University of Nebraska Press, 1988.

Clarke, T[homas] Wood. *The Bloody Mohawk.* 1941. Reprint, Port Washington, N.Y.: I. J. Friedman, 1968.

Clift, G. Glenn, *Remember the Raisin! Kentucky and Kentuckians in the Battles and Massacre at Frenchtown, Michigan Territory, in the War of 1812.* Frankfort: Kentucky Historical Society, 1961.

Cobb, Hubbard. *American Battlefields.* New York: Macmillan, 1995.

Cole, D. C. *The Chiricahua Apache, 1846–1876: From War to Reservation.* Albuquerque: University of New Mexico Press, 1988.

Collier, Peter. *When Shall They Rest? The Cherokees' Long Struggle with America.* New York: Holt, Rinehart and Winston, 1973.

Cordell, Linda S. *Prehistory of the Southwest.* San Diego: Academic Press, 1984.

Corlew, Robert E. *Tennessee: A Short History.* 2d ed. Knoxville: University of Tennessee Press, 1981.

Covington, James W. *The Seminoles of Florida.* Gainesville: University Press of Florida, 1993.

Crum, Steven J. *The Road on Which We Came.* Salt Lake City: University of Utah Press, 1994.

Cruse, Thomas. *Apache Days and After.* Caldwell, Idaho: Caxton Printers, 1941.

Cushman, H. B. *History of the Choctaw, Chickasaw and Natchez Indians.* Edited by Angie Debo. New York: Russell & Russell, 1962. (Reprint. Greenville, Tex.: Headlight Printing House, 1899).

Custer, George A. *My Life on the Plains: or, Personal Experience with Indians.* Norman: University of Oklahoma Press, 1986.

Cutrer, Thomas W. *Ben McCulloch and the Frontier Military Tradition.* Chapel Hill: University of North Carolina Press, 1993.

Darling, Roger. *A Sad and Terrible Blunder.* Vienna, Va.: Potomac Western Press, 1990.

Davis, John L. *The Texas Rangers: Images and Incidents.* San Antonio: University of Texas, Institute of Texas Cultures, 1991.

Davis, Mary, ed. *Native America in the Twentieth Century: An Encyclopedia.* New York: Garland, 1994.

Dawnland Encounters: Indians and Europeans in Northern New England. Edited by Colin Calloway. Hanover, N.H.: University Press of New England, 1991.

Debo, Angie. *Geronimo: The Man, His Time, His Place.* Reprint. Norman: University of Oklahoma Press, 1989.

———. *A History of the Indians of the United States.* Norman: University of Oklahoma Press, 1970.

———. *The Road to Disappearance: A History of the Creek Indians.* Norman: University of Oklahoma Press, 1941.

———. *The Rise and Fall of the Choctaw Republic.* Norman: University of Oklahoma Press, 1961.

Deloria, Vine, Jr., and Clifford M. Lytle. *American Indians, American Justice.* Austin: University of Texas Press, 1983.

———. "This Country Was a Lot Better Off When the Indians Were Running It." *New York Times Magazine,* March 8, 1970.

DeMallie, Raymond J., ed. *The Sixth Grandfather: Black Elk's Teachings Given to John G. Neihardt.* Lincoln: University of Nebraska Press, 1984.

Demos, John. *The Unredeemed Captive: A Family Story from Early America.* New York: Alfred A. Knopf, 1994.

Denig, Edwin Thompson. *Five Indian Tribes of the Upper Missouri.* Edited by John C. Ewers. Norman: University of Oklahoma Press, 1961.

Dillon, Richard H. *Burnt-Out Fires: California's Modoc Indian War.* Englewood Cliffs, N.J.: Prentice Hall, 1973.

———. *North American Indian Wars.* Secaucus, N.J.: Chartwell Books, 1993.

Dippie, Brian W. *The Vanishing American: White Attitudes and U.S. Indian Policy.* Lawrence: University Press of Kansas, 1982.

Dixon, David. *Hero of Beecher Island: The Life and Military Career of George A. Forsyth.* Lincoln: University of Nebraska Press, 1994.

———. *North American Indian Wars.* New York: Facts On File, 1983.

Dockstader, Frederick J. *Great North American Indians: Profiles in Life and Leadership.* New York: Van Nostrand Reinhold, 1977.

Dorson, Richard M., ed. *America Begins: Early American Writing.* New York: Pantheon, 1950.

Driver, Harold E. *Indians of North America.* Chicago: University of Chicago Press, 1961.

Dunlay, Thomas. *Kit Carson and the Indians.* Lincoln: University of Nebraska Press, 2000.

Eastman, Charles A. (Ohiyesa). *Indian Heroes & Great Chieftains.* Lincoln: University of Nebraska Press, 1991.

Eckert, Allan W. *The Wilderness Empire: A Narrative.* Boston: Little, Brown, 1969.

———. *The Wilderness War: A Narrative.* Boston: Little, Brown, 1978.

Edmonds, Walter D. *The Musket and the Cross: The Struggle of France and England for North America.* Boston: Little, Brown, 1968.

Edmunds, R. David, ed. *American Indian Leaders: Studies in Diversity.* Lincoln: University of Nebraska Press, 1980.

Edmunds, R. David, and Joseph L. Peyser. *The Fox Wars: The Mesquakie Challenge to New France.* Norman: University of Oklahoma Press, 1993.

Eisenhower, John S. D. *So Far from God: The U.S. War with Mexico, 1846–1848.* New York: Random House, 1989.

Estergreen, M. Morgan. *Kit Carson: A Portrait in Courage.* Norman: University of Oklahoma Press, 1962.

Ewers, John C. *The Blackfeet: Raiders of the Northwestern Plains.* Norman: University of Oklahoma, 1958.

Fagan, Brian M. *Ancient North America: The Archaeology of a Continent.* New York: Thames and Hudson, 1991.

Fahey, John. *The Flathead Indians.* Norman: University of Oklahoma Press, 1974.

Farr, William E. *The Reservation Blackfeet, 1885–1945: A Photographic History of Cultural Survival.* Seattle: University of Washington Press, 1986.

Faulk, Odie B. *The Geronimo Campaign.* New York: Oxford University Press, 1969.

Faulk, Odie B., and Joseph A. Stout, Jr. *A Short History of the American West.* New York: Harper & Row, 1974.

Fehrenbach, T. R. *Comanches: The Destruction of a People.* New York: Alfred A. Knopf, 1974.

Fiedel, Stuart J. *Prehistory of the Americas.* New York: Cambridge University Press, 1992.

Flanagan, Thomas. *Louis David Riel: Prophet of the New World.* Toronto: University of Toronto Press, 1979.

Flexner, James Thomas. *Washington: The Indispensable Man.* Boston: Little, Brown, 1969.

Foote, Shelby. *The Civil War: A Narrative.* Vol. 1. New York: Random House, 1958.

Forsyth, George A. *Thrilling Days in Army Life.* 1900. Reprint, Lincoln: University of Nebraska, 1994.

Franks, Kenny A. *Stand Watie and the Agony of the Cherokee Nation.* Memphis, Tenn.: Memphis State University Press, 1979.

Freedman, Russell. *Indian Chiefs.* New York: Holiday House, 1987.

Freedman, Russell, and Alvin M. Josephy, Jr. *The Patriot Chiefs: A Chronicle of American Indian Resistance.* 1961. Reprint, New York: Penguin Books, 1989.

Friesen, John W. *The Riel/Real Story.* Ottawa, Canada: Borealis Press, 1994.

Fuess, Claude Moore. *Carl Schurz, Reformer.* 1960. Reprint, Port Washington, N.Y.: Kennikat Press, 1973.

Garbarino, Merwyn S., and Robert F. Sasso. *Native American Heritage,* 3rd ed. Prospect Heights, Ill.: Waveland Press, 1994.

Gibson, Arrell Morgan. *The American Indian: Prehistory to the Present.* Lexington, Mass.: D. C. Heath, 1980.

———. *The Kickapoos: Lords of the Middle Border.* Norman: University of Oklahoma Press, 1963.

———. *The Chickasaws.* Norman: University of Oklahoma, 1971.

Gilbert, Bil. *God Gave Us This Country: Tekamthi and the First American Civil War.* New York: Atheneum, 1989.

Goble, Paul. *Brave Eagle's Account of the Fetterman Fight, 21 December 1866.* Lincoln: University of Nebraska Press, 1992.

Goodwin, Grenville, and Basso, Keith H. *Western Apache Raiding and Warfare: From the Notes of Grenville Goodwin.* Tucson: University of Arizona Press, 1971.

Greene, Jerome A. *Yellowstone Command: Colonel Nelson A. Miles and the Great Sioux War, 1876–1877.* Lincoln: University of Nebraska Press, 1991.

———. *Battles and Skirmishes of the Great Sioux War, 1876–1877: The Military View.* Norman: University of Oklahoma Press, 1993.

Griess, Thomas E. *Definitions and Doctrine of the Military Art Past and Present. The West Point Military History Series.* Wayne: Avery Publishing Group, 1985.

Griffith, Benjamin W., Jr. *McIntosh and Weatherford, Creek Indian Leaders.* Tuscaloosa: University of Alabama Press, 1988.

Grinnell, George Bird. *The Fighting Cheyennes.* 1915. Reprint, Norman: University of Oklahoma Press, 1956.

Gutiérrez, Ramón A. *When Jesus Came, the Corn Mothers Went Away: Marriage, Sexuality, and Power in New Mexico, 1500–1846.* Palo Alto, Calif.: Stanford University Press, 1991.

Haefeli, Evan, and Kevin Sweeney. *Captors and Captives: The 1704 French and Indian Raid on Deerfield.* Amherst: University of Massachusetts Press, 2003.

Hagan, William T. *American Indians.* Chicago: University of Chicago Press, 1968.

———. *Longhouse Diplomacy and Frontier Warfare.* Albany: New York State American Revolution Bicentennial Commission, 1976.

———. *The Sac and Fox Indians*. Norman: University of Oklahoma Press, 1958.

Haley, James L. *The Buffalo War: The History of the Red River Indian Uprising of 1874*. Garden City, N.Y.: Doubleday, 1976.

Hall-Quest, Olga (Wilbourne). *Conquistador and Pueblos: The Story of the American Southwest, 1540–1848*. New York: E.P. Dutton, 1969.

Hampton, Bruce. *The Children of Grace: The Nez Perce War of 1877*. New York: Henry Holt, 1994.

Hartley, William B., and Ellen Hartley. *Osceola: The Unconquered Indian*. New York: Hawthorn Books, 1973.

Hassrick, Royal B. *The Sioux: Life and Customs of a Warrior Society*. Norman: University of Oklahoma Press, 1988.

Hastings, James R. "The Tragedy at Camp Grant in 1871." *Arizona and the West* 1, no. 2 (1959):

Hatch, Thom. *The Custer Companion: Life of George Armstrong Custer and the Plains Indians Wars*. Harrisburg, Pa.: Stackpole Books, 2002.

Hathorn, Ramon, and Patrick Holland, eds. *Images of Louis Riel in Canadian Culture*. Lewiston, N.Y.: Edwin Mellen Press, 1992.

Hauptman, Laurence M. *Between Two Fires: American Indians in the Civil War*. New York: The Free Press, 1995.

Hedren, Paul L. *First Scalp for Custer: The Skirmish at Warbonnet Creek, Nebraska, July 17, 1876*. Glendale, Calif.: A. H. Clark, 1980.

Hodge, Frederick W., ed. *Handbook of American Indians North of Mexico*. Bulletin 30, Part I. Washington, D.C.: U.S. Government Printing Office, 1907–1910; reprinted in 2 vols., Lanham, Md.: Rowman and Littlefield, 1965.

Hoebel, E. Adamson, and Ernest Wallace. *The Comanches: Lords of the South Plains*. 1952. Reprint, Norman: University of Oklahoma Press, 1976.

Hoig, Stan. *Tribal Wars of the Southern Plains*. Norman: University of Oklahoma Press, 1993.

Hook, Jason. *The American Plains Indian*. London: Osprey Publishing, 1985.

———. *The Apaches*. London: Osprey Publishing, 1987.

Horgan, Paul. *Conquistadors in North American History*. New York: Farrar, Straus, 1963.

Horowitz, David. *The First Frontier: The Indian Wars and America's Origins, 1607–1776*. New York: Simon and Schuster, 1978.

Hyde, George E. *Red Cloud's Folk: A History of the Oglala Sioux Indians*. 1937. Reprint, Norman: University of Oklahoma Press, 1979.

———. *A Sioux Chronicle*. 1956. Reprint, Norman: University of Oklahoma Press, 1956, 1993.

Iverson, Peter. *Dine: A History of the Navajos*. Albuquerque: University of New Mexico Press, 2002.

Jackson, Clyde L., and Grace Jackson. *Quanah Parker: Last Chief of the Comanches*. New York: Exposition Press, 1963.

Jackson, Curtis E., and Marcia J. Galli. *A History of the Bureau of Indian Affairs and Its Activities among Indians*. San Francisco: R & E Research Associates, 1977.

Jeffrey, Julia Roy. *Converting the West: A Biography of Narcissa Whitman*. Norman: University of Oklahoma Press, 1991.

Jennings, Francis. *The Ambiguous Iroquois Empire: The Covenant Chain Confederation of Indian Tribes with English Colonies from Its Beginnings to the Lancaster Treaty of 1744*. New York: W. W. Norton, 1984.

Johnson, Allen, and Dumas Malone, eds. 1928. Reprint, *Dictionary of American Biography*. New York: Scribner's, 1988.

Johnson, W. Fletcher. *The Red Record of the Sioux, Life of Sitting Bull and the History of the Indian War of 1890–91*. New York: AMS Press, 1982.

Josephy, Alvin M., Jr. *The Civil War in the American West*. New York: Alfred A. Knopf, 1991.

———. *500 Nations: An Illustrated History of North American Indians*. New York: Alfred A. Knopf, 1994.

———. *The Indian Heritage of America*. 1968. Revised, Boston: Houghton Mifflin, 1991.

———. *The Nez Perce Indians and the Opening of the Northwest*. New Haven, Conn.: Yale University Press, 1965.

———. *Now That the Buffalo's Gone: A Study of Today's American Indians*. New York: Alfred A. Knopf, 1982.

———. *The Patriot Chiefs: A Chronicle of American Indian Resistance*. New York: Penguin Books, 1989, 1993.

Josephy, Alvin M. Jr., et al., eds. *American Heritage Book of Indians*. New York: American Heritage Publishing, 1961.

Kappler, Charles J., ed. *Indian Affairs, Laws & Treaties*. Vol. II. 1904. Reprint, New York: AMS Press, 1996.

———. *Indian Treaties 1778–1883*. 1904. Reprint, New York: Interland Publishing Co., 1973.

Kastor, Peter J. *The Louisiana Purchase: Emergence of an American Nation*. Washington, D.C.: CQ Press, 2002.

Kaywaykla, James [narrator]. *In the Days of Victorio*. Edited by Eve Ball. Tucson: University of Arizona Press, 1970.

Kehoe, Alice Beck. *The Ghost Dance: Ethnohistory and Revitalization*. New York: Holt, Rinehart and Winston, 1989.

Kelley, Joseph J., Jr. *Pennsylvania: The Colonial Years, 1681–1776*. Garden City, N.Y.: Doubleday, 1980.

Keoke, Emory Dean, and Kay Marie Porterfield. *Encyclopedia of American Indian Contributions to the World*. New York: Facts On File, 2002.

Kessel, William B. "The Battle of Cibecue and Its Aftermath: A White Mountain Apache's Account." *Ethnohistory* 21, no. 2 (1994): 123–134.

King, James T. *War Eagle: A Life of General Eugene A. Carr*. Lincoln: University of Nebraska Press, 1963.

Kluckhohn, Clyde, and Dorothea Leighton. *The Navajo*. Cambridge, Mass.: Harvard University Press, 1980.

Knaut, Andrew L. *The Pueblo Revolt of 1680: Conquest and Resistance in Seventeenth-Century New Mexico*. Norman: University of Oklahoma Press, 1995.

Knight, Wilfred. *Red Fox: Stand Watie and the Confederate Indian Nations*. Glendale, Calif.: Arthur H. Clark, 1987.

Kohn, George C. *Dictionary of Wars*. Garden City, N.Y.: Doubleday, 1987.

Kopper, Philip. *The Smithsonian Book of North American Indians before the Coming of the Europeans.* Washington, D.C.: Smithsonian Books, 1986.

Kraft, Herbert C. *The Lenape: Archaeology, History, and Ethnography.* Newark: New Jersey Historical Society, 1986.

Kroeber, Clifton B., and Bernard L. Fontana. *Massacre on the Gila: An Account of the Last Major Battle between American Indians, with Reflections on the Origin of War.* Tucson: University of Arizona Press, 1992.

KTCA/Video. *The Dakota Conflict.* Twin Cities Public Television, St. Paul, Minn.

Kukla, Jon. *A Wilderness So Immense: The Louisiana Purchase and the Destiny of America.* New York: Alfred A. Knopf, 2003.

La Barre, Weston. *The Ghost Dance: Origins of Religion.* Garden City, N.Y.: Doubleday, 1970.

Lacey, Theresa Jenson. *The Blackfeet.* New York: Chelsea House, 1995.

LaFarge, Oliver. *A Pictorial History of the American Indian.* Revised by Alvin M. Josephy, Jr. New York: Crown, 1974.

Lamar, Howard. *The Reader's Encyclopedia of the American West.* New York: Thomas Crowell, 1977.

Lazarus, Edward. *Black Hills, White Justice: The Sioux Nation versus the United States, 1775 to the Present.* New York: HarperCollins, 1991.

Leach, Douglas E. *Arms for Empire: A Military History of the British Colonies in North America, 1607–1763.* New York: Macmillan, 1973.

———. *Flintlock and Tomahawk: New England in King Philip's War.* New York: W.W. Norton, 1958.

Leeds, Georgia Rae. *The United Keetoowah Band of Cherokee Indians in Oklahoma.* New York: Peter Lang, 1996.

Legleu, Stephanie. "Indians and Africans in Slave Society," Department of History, Loyola University. Available online. URL: http://www.loyno.edu/history/ journal/Legleu. html. Downloaded on March 29, 2004.

Loftin, John D. *Religion and Hopi Life.* 2d ed. Bloomington: Indiana University Press, 2003.

Loomis, Noel M. "The Battle of Wood Lake." *In Great Western Indian Fights,* Members of the Potomac Corral of the Westerners. Lincoln: University of Nebraska Press, 1966.

Lowie, Robert H. *Indians of the Plains.* 1954. Reprint, New York: Doubleday, 1982.

Maynard, Jill, ed. *Through Indian Eyes: The Untold Story of Native American Peoples.* Pleasantville, N.Y.: Reader's Digest Association, 1995.

Mails, Thomas E. *Mystic Warriors of the Plains.* 1972. Reprint, New York: Mallard Press, 1991.

Malone, James H. *The Chickasaw Nation: A Short Sketch of a Noble People.* Louisville, Ky.: John P. Morton, 1922.

Marshall, S.L.A. *Crimsoned Prairie: The Wars between the United States and the Plains Indians.* New York: Scribner's, 1972.

Martin, Joel W. *Sacred Revolt: The Muskogees' Struggle for a New World.* Boston: Beacon Press, 1991.

Massacre of Troops near Fort Phil Kearny. Fairfield, Wash.: Ye Galleon Press, 1987.

McDougall, John. *In the Days of the Red River Rebellion.* Toronto, Canada: William Briggs, 1911.

McKee, Jesse O., and Jon A. Schlenker. *The Choctaws: Cultural Evolution of a Native American Tribe.* Jackson: University Press of Mississippi, 1980.

McLoughlin, William G. *After the Trail of Tears: The Cherokees' Struggle for Sovereignty, 1839–1880.* Chapel Hill: University of North Carolina Press, 1993.

———. *Cherokee Renascence in the New Republic.* Princeton, N.J.: Princeton University Press, 1986.

McNitt, Frank. *Navaho Wars: Military Campaigns, Slave Raids, and Reprisals.* Albuquerque: University of New Mexico Press, 1972.

McPherson, Robert S. *The Northern Navajo Frontier, 1860–1900: Expansion through Adversity.* Albuquerque: University of New Mexico Press, 1988.

McReynolds, Edwin C. *The Seminoles.* Norman: University of Oklahoma Press, 1957.

Meyer, Roy W. *The Village Indians of the Upper Missouri: The Mandan, Hidatsas, and Arikaras.* Lincoln: University of Nebraska Press, 1977.

———. *History of the Santee Sioux: United States Indian Policy on Trial.* Lincoln: University of Nebraska Press, 1993.

Milner, Clyde A., II, et al., eds. *Oxford History of the American West.* New York: Oxford University Press, 1994.

Monnett, John H. *The Battle of Beecher Island and the Indian War of 1867–1869.* Niwot: University Press of Colorado, 1992.

Mooney, James. *Calendar History of the Kiowa Indians.* 1898. Reprint, Washington, D.C.: Smithsonian Institution Press, 1979.

———. *The Ghost-Dance Religion and the Sioux Outbreak of 1890.* 1965. Reprint, Chicago: University of Chicago Press, 1989.

———. *Myths of the Cherokee and The Sacred Formulas of the Cherokees.* 1900. Reprint, Asheville, N.C.: New Images, 1992.

Morgan, Ted. *Wilderness at Dawn: The Settling of the North American Continent.* New York: Simon and Schuster, 1993.

Morison, Samuel Eliot, Henry Steele Commager, and William E. Leuchtenburg. *The Growth of the American Republic.* 6th ed., rev. and enlarged. 2 vols. New York: Oxford University Press, 1969.

Morrison, Kenneth M. *The Embattled Northeast: The Elusive Ideal of Alliance in Abenaki-Euroamerican Relations.* Berkeley: University of California, 1984.

Nabokov, Peter, ed. *Native American Testimony: A Chronicle of Indian-White Relations from Prophecy to the Present, 1492–1992.* New York: Viking, 1991.

Neihardt, John G. *Black Elk Speaks: Being the Life Story of a Holy Man of the Oglala Sioux.* Lincoln: University of Nebraska Press, 1979.

———. *When the Tree Flowered: An Authentic Tale of the Old Sioux World.* New York: Macmillan, 1951.

New Handbook of Texas. 6 vols. Austin: Texas State Historical Association, 1996.

Nichols, Roger L., ed. *The American Indian Past and Present.* New York: McGraw-Hill, 1992.

Nielsen, George R. *The Kickapoo People.* Phoenix, Ariz.: Indian Tribal Series, 1975.

Noel Hume, Ivor. *Martin's Hundred,* rev. ed. New York: Alfred A. Knopf, 1988.

Nye, Wilbur Sturtevant. *Bad Medicine & Good: Tales of the Kiowas.* Norman: University of Oklahoma Press, 1962.

———. *Carbine and Lance.* Norman: University of Oklahoma Press, 1969.

O'Connor, Richard. "'Black Jack' of the 10th." *American Heritage* XVIII, no. 2 (1967).

Ogle, Ralph Hendrick. *Federal Control of the Western Apaches 1848–1886.* Albuquerque: University of New Mexico Press, 1970.

Parkman, Francis. *The Oregon Trail: The Conspiracy of Pontiac.* New York: Library Classics Press, 1961.

———. *The Conspiracy of Pontiac.* 1870. Reprint, New York: Literary Classics of the United States, 1991.

Peckham, Howard H. *Pontiac and the Indian Uprising.* 1961. Reprint, Russell & Russell, 1970.

Perry, Richard J. *Apache Reservation: Indigenous Peoples and the American State.* Austin: University of Texas, 1993.

Peterson, John Alton. *Utah's Black Hawk War.* Salt Lake City: University of Utah Press, 1998.

Pierce, Michael D. *The Most Promising Young Officer: A Life of Ranald Slidell Mackenzie.* Norman: University of Oklahoma Press, 1993.

Pond, Samuel W. *The Dakota or Sioux in Minnesota as They Were in 1834.* St. Paul: Minnesota Historical Society Press, 1986.

Prucha, Francis Paul, ed. *Documents of United States Indian Policy.* Lincoln: University of Nebraska Press, 1990.

———. *The Great Father: The United States Government and the American Indian.* Vol. 1 and 2. Lincoln: University of Nebraska Press, 1984.

———. *The Sword of the Republic: The United States Army on the Frontier, 1783–1846.* New York: Macmillan, 1969.

Publications Committee of the Potomac Corral of the Westerners, eds. *Great Western Indian Fights.* Lincoln: University of Nebraska Press, 1960.

Reddy, Marlita A., ed. *Statistical Record of Native North America.* New York: Gale Research, 1995.

Reedstrom, E. Lisle. *Apache Wars: An Illustrated Battle History.* New York: Sterling Publishing, 1990.

Richter, Daniel K. *The Ordeal of the Longhouse: The Peoples of the Iroquois League in the Era of European Colonization.* Chapel Hill: University of North Carolina Press, 1992.

Ritzenthatler, Robert E., and Pat Ritzenthaler. *The Woodland Indians of the Western Great Lakes.* Prospect Heights, Ill.: Waveland Press, 1983.

Roberts, Robert B. *New York's Forts in the Revolution.* Cranbury, N.J.: Associated University Presses, 1980.

Robinson, Charles M., et al. *Bad Hand: A Biography of General Ranald S. Mackenzie.* Austin, Tex.: State House Press, 1993.

Robinson, W. Stitt. *The Southern Colonial Frontier, 1607–1763.* Albuquerque: University of New Mexico Press, 1979.

Roseboom, Eugene H., and Francis P. Weisenburger. *A History of Ohio.* 2nd ed. Edited by James H. Rodabaugh. Columbus: Ohio Historical Society, 1984.

Rothschild, Nan A. *Colonial Encounters in a Native American Landscape: The Spanish and Dutch in North America.* Washington, D.C.: Smithsonian Books, 2003.

Rountree, Helen. *Pocahontas's People: The Powhatan Indians of Virginia through Four Centuries.* Norman: University of Oklahoma Press, 1990.

Rountree, Helen C., and E. Randolph Turner III. *Before and after Jamestown: Virginia's Powhatans and Their Predecessors.* Gainesville: University Press of Florida, 2002.

Salem Press, eds. *American Indians.* 3 vols. Pasadena, Calif.: Salem Press, 1995.

Sandoz, Mari. *Cheyenne Autumn.* 1953. Reprint, Lincoln: University of Nebraska Press, 1992.

———. *Crazy Horse: The Strange Man of the Oglalas.* Lincoln: University of Nebraska Press, 1961.

Schmeckebier, Laurence F. *The Office of Indian Affairs: Its History, Activities and Organization.* 1927. Reprint, New York: AMS Press, 1972.

Schreier, Jim. "The Skeleton Cave Incident." *Arizona Highways* 67, no. 5 (May 1991): 4–9.

Schultz, Duane. *Over the Earth I Come: The Great Sioux Uprising of 1862.* New York: St. Martin's, 1992.

Seaver, James Everett. *A Narrative of the Life of Mary Jemison.* 1824. Reprint, New York: Corinth Books, 1961.

Shaffer, Lynda Norene. *Native Americans before 1492: The Moundbuilding Centers of the Eastern Woodlands.* Armonk, N.Y.: M.E. Sharpe, 1992.

Sheridan, P. H. *Personal Memoirs of P. H. Sheridan, General, United States Army.* New York: Charles L. Webster, 1888.

Simmons, Marc. *The Last Conquistador: Juan de Onate and the Settling of the Far Southwest.* Norman: University of Oklahoma Press, 1991.

Smith, Page. *The Shaping of America: A People's History of the New Republic.* New York: Penguin Books, 1989.

Smith, Sherry L. *Sagebrush Soldier: Private William Earl Smith's View of the Sioux War of 1876.* Norman: University of Oklahoma Press, 1989.

Snipp, C. Matthew. *American Indians: The First of This Land.* New York: Russell Sage Foundation, 1989.

Soldier and Brave: Historical Places Associated with Indian Affairs and Indian Wars. New ed. Washington, D.C.: U.S. Department of the Interior, National Park Service, 1971.

Spicer, Edward H. *Cycles of Conquest: The Impact of Spain, Mexico, and the United States on the Indians of the Southwest, 1533–1960.* 1962. Reprint, Tucson: University of Arizona Press, 1986.

———. *A Short History of the Indians of the United States.* New York: Van Nostrand Reinhold, 1969.

Spier, Leslie. *Yuman Tribes of the Gila River.* Chicago: University of Chicago Press, 1933.

Stands In Timber, John, and Margot Liberty. *Cheyenne Memories*. New Haven, Conn.: Yale University Press, 1967.

Starita, Joe. *The Dull Knifes of Pine Ridge: A Lakota Odyssey*. New York: Putnam, 1995.

Steele, Ian K. *Warpaths: Invasions of North America*. New York: Oxford University Press, 1994.

Sturtevant, William C. *Native Americans: The Indigenous People of North America*. New York: Smithmark, 1995.

Sturtevant, William C., ed. *Handbook of North American Indians*. 1978. Reprint, Washington, D.C.: Smithsonian Institution Press, 1988.

Swanton, John R. *Indian Tribes of North America*. 1952. Reprint, Scholarly Press, 1969.

Sweeney, Edwin R. 1991. Reprint, *Cochise: Chiricahua Apache Chief*. Norman: University of Oklahoma Press, 1996.

Tanner, Helen Hornbeck, ed. *Atlas of Great Lakes Indian History*. Norman: University of Oklahoma Press, 1987.

Taylor, Colin F. *Native American Weapons*. Norman: University of Oklahoma Press, 2001.

Taylor, Theodore W. *The Bureau of Indian Affairs*. Boulder, Colo.: Westview Press, 1984.

Terrell, John Upton. *American Indian Almanac*. 1971. Reprint, New York: Barnes & Noble Books, 1994.

———. *The Navajos: The Past and Present of a Great People*. New York: Weybright and Talley, 1970.

Terzian, James P. *Defender of Human Rights: Carl Schurz*. New York: J. Messner, 1965.

Thomas, David Hurst, et al. *The Native Americans: An Illustrated History*. Atlanta, Ga.: Turner Publishing, 1993.

Thrapp, Dan L. *Al Sieber: Chief of Scouts*. Norman: University of Oklahoma Press, 1964.

———. *The Conquest of Apacheria*. Norman: University of Oklahoma Press, 1967.

———. *General Crook and the Sierra Madre Adventure*. Norman: University of Oklahoma Press, 1972.

———. *Encyclopedia of Frontier Biography*. Glendale, Calif.: Arthur H. Clark, 1988.

———. *Juh, An Incredible Indian*. 2nd ed. El Paso: Texas Western Press, 1992.

———. *Victorio and the Mimbres Apaches*. Norman: University of Oklahoma Press, 1974.

Time-Life Books, eds. *Alogonquians of the East Coast*. Alexandria, Va.: Time-Life Books, 1995.

———. *Tribes of the Southern Plains*. Alexandria, Va.: Time-Life Books, 1995.

———. *The Indians*. New York: Time-Life Books, 1973.

Trafzer, Clifford E. *The Kit Carson Campaign: The Last Great Navajo War*. Norman: University of Oklahoma Press, 1982.

———. *The Nez Perce*. New York: Chelsea House, 1992.

Trafzer, Clifford E., and Richard D. Scheuerman. *Chief Joseph's Allies: The Palouse Indians*. New Castle, Calif.: Sierra Oaks, 1992.

Trefousse, Hans Louis. *Carl Schurz, A Biography*. Knoxville: University of Tennessee Press, 1982.

Trenholm, Virginia Cole. *The Arapahoes, Our People*. Norman: University of Oklahoma Press, 1970.

Trenholm, Virginia Cole, and Maurine Carley. *The Shoshonis: Sentinels of the Rockies*. Norman: University of Oklahoma Press, 1964.

Tucker, Glenn. *Hancock the Superb*. Indianapolis: Bobbs-Merrill, 1960.

———. *Tecumseh: Vision of Glory*. Indianapolis: Bobbs-Merrill, 1956.

Underhill, Ruth M. *The Navajos*. 1956. Reprint, Norman: University of Oklahoma Press, 1971.

Utley, Robert M. *Frontier Regulars: The United States Army and the Indian, 1866–1891*. New York: Macmillan, 1973.

———. *Frontiersmen in Blue: The United States Army and the Indian, 1848–1865*. New York: Macmillan, 1967.

———. *The Indian Frontier of the American West, 1846–1890*. Albuquerque: University of New Mexico, 1984.

———. *The Lance and the Shield: The Life and Times of Sitting Bull*. New York: Henry Holt, 1993.

———. *The Last Days of the Sioux Nation*. New Haven, Conn.: Yale University Press, 1963, 1972.

Utley, Robert M., and Wilcomb E. Washburn. 1977. Reprint, *The American Heritage History of the Indian Wars*. New York: Barnes & Noble Books, 1992.

Utley, Robert M., and Wilcomb E. Washburn. *Indian Wars*. Boston: Houghton Mifflin, 1987.

Van Doren, Charles, ed. *Webster's American Biographies*. Springfield, Mass.: G. & C. Merriam Company, 1974.

Vestal, Stanley. *Warpath and Council Fire: The Plains Struggle for Survival in War and in Diplomacy*. New York: Random House, 1948.

Vetromile, Eugene. *The Abenakis and Their History; or, Historical Notices on the Aborigines of Acadia*. 1866. Reprint, New York: J. B. Kirker, 1977.

Vogel, Virgil J. *This Country Was Ours: A Documentary History of the American Indian*. New York: Harper & Row, 1972.

Waldman, Carl. *Atlas of the North American Indian*. New York: Facts On File, 1985.

———. *Biographical Dictionary of American Indian History to 1900*, rev. ed. New York: Facts On File, 2001.

———. *Encyclopedia of Native American Tribes*. New York: Facts On File, 1988.

———. *Who Was Who in Native American History: Indians and Non-Indians from Early Contacts through 1900*. New York: Facts On File, 1990.

Walsh, Frederick G. *The Trial of Louis Riel* [a play]. Fargo: North Dakota Institute for Regional Studies, 1965.

Warner, Ezra J. *Generals in Blue, The Lives of the Union Commanders*. Baton Rouge: Louisiana State University Press, 1964.

———. *Generals in Gray: Lives of the Confederate Commanders*. Baton Rouge: Louisiana State University Press, 1959.

Washburn, Wilcomb E., ed. *Handbook of North American Indians*. Vol. 4, *History of Indian-White Relations*. Washington, D.C.: Smithsonian Institution Press, 1988.

Wellman, Paul I. *Gold, Glory and God: A Narrative History*. Garden City, N.Y.: Doubleday, 1954.

Weslager, C. A. *The Delaware Indians: A History*. New Brunswick, N.J.: Rutgers University Press, 1972.

Who Was Who in America: A Companion Biographical Reference Work 1607–1896. Chicago: Marquis Who's Who, 1963.

Williams, John Hoyt. *Sam Houston: A Biography of the Father of Texas*. New York: Simon and Schuster, 1993.

Wise, Jennings C. *The Red Man in the New World Drama: A Politico-Legal Study with a Pageantry of American Indian History*. Edited and revised by Vine Deloria, Jr. New York: Macmillan, 1971.

Woodhead, Henry, et al., eds. *People of the Western Range*. Alexandria, Va.: Time-Life Books, 1995.

Wooster, Robert Allen. *The Military and United States Indian Policy 1865–1903*. New Haven, Conn.: Yale University Press, 1988.

———. *Nelson A. Miles and the Twilight of the Frontier Army*. Lincoln: University of Nebraska Press, 1993.

Wormser, Richard. *The Yellowlegs: The Story of the United States Cavalry*. Garden City, N.Y.: Doubleday, 1966.

Wright, Muriel H. *A Guide to the Indian Tribes of Oklahoma*. Norman: University of Oklahoma Press, 1951.

Wright, Peter M. "Washakie." *American Indian Leaders: Studies in Diversity*. Lincoln: University of Nebraska Press, 1980.

Wright, Ronald. *Stolen Continents*. New York: Houghton Mifflin, 1992.

Zuni People. *The Zunis, Self-Portrayals*. New York: Mentor Books, 1973.

Index

Page numbers in **boldface** indicate main entries. Page numbers in *italics* indicate photographs. Page numbers followed by *m* indicate maps. Page numbers followed by *c* indicate chronology entries.